ASIAN POLITICAL, ECONOMIC AND SECURITY ISSUES

# ASIAN ECONOMIC AND POLITICAL DEVELOPMENTS

# ASIAN POLITICAL, ECONOMIC AND SECURITY ISSUES

Additional books in this series can be found on Nova's website
under the Series tab.

Additional E-books in this series can be found on Nova's website
under the E-books tab.

ASIAN POLITICAL, ECONOMIC AND SECURITY ISSUES

# ASIAN ECONOMIC AND POLITICAL DEVELOPMENTS

### FELIX CHIN
### EDITOR

**Nova Science Publishers, Inc.**
*New York*

**NOTICE TO THE READER**

The Publisher has taken reasonable care in the preparation of this book, but makes no expressed or implied warranty of any kind and assumes no responsibility for any errors or omissions. No liability is assumed for incidental or consequential damages in connection with or arising out of information contained in this book. The Publisher shall not be liable for any special, consequential, or exemplary damages resulting, in whole or in part, from the readers' use of, or reliance upon, this material. Any parts of this book based on government reports are so indicated and copyright is claimed for those parts to the extent applicable to compilations of such works.

Independent verification should be sought for any data, advice or recommendations contained in this book. In addition, no responsibility is assumed by the publisher for any injury and/or damage to persons or property arising from any methods, products, instructions, ideas or otherwise contained in this publication.

This publication is designed to provide accurate and authoritative information with regard to the subject matter covered herein. It is sold with the clear understanding that the Publisher is not engaged in rendering legal or any other professional services. If legal or any other expert assistance is required, the services of a competent person should be sought. FROM A DECLARATION OF PARTICIPANTS JOINTLY ADOPTED BY A COMMITTEE OF THE AMERICAN BAR ASSOCIATION AND A COMMITTEE OF PUBLISHERS.

Additional color graphics may be available in the e-book version of this book.

LIBRARY OF CONGRESS CATALOGING-IN-PUBLICATION DATA

*Asian economic and political developments / editor, Felix Chin.*
   *p. cm.*
 *Includes index.*
 *ISBN 978-1-61122-470-2 (hardcover)*
 *1. Asia--Economic policy--21st century. 2. Asia--Politics and*
*government--21st century. 3. Asia--Foreign relations--21st century. I.*
*Chin, Felix, 1962-*
  *HC412.A743 2010*
  *337.5--dc22*
                                                    *2010038625*


*Published by Nova Science Publishers, Inc. † New York*

# CONTENTS

# PREFACE

This book presents and discusses information on the contemporary politics and economics of Asia. The coverage is intended to deal with Asia, its political dynamics, economic policies, institutions, and its future. Topics discussed herein include the European Union and Asia; identity change and the emergence of regionalism; trading security in alliances; China's naval modernization; education in China; the Australia-China economic relationship; and the capability for economic growth in Asia.

Chapter 1 – Fifty years after the signing of the Treaties of Rome, the European Union (EU) stands at a crossroads. It has all but completed its single market, has enlarged to twenty-seven member states, has introduced a single currency, is making progress on a common foreign and defence policy, has flirted with the adoption of a constitution and more. The European Community of six member states that at first merely collaborated on coal and steel, atomic energy and that created a customs union in the 1950s and 1960s, has progressed beyond belief so as to achieve these remarkable successes.

The origins of the EU can be traced back to belligerent parties that decided it was best to leave their militaristic past behind and concentrate on creating something more positive and constructive. France and Germany had gone to war three times in a hundred years and felt the need to leave the past behind. It was clear that it was not only the decisions of the governments of France and Germany that made this new pacifism in Western Europe possible. Other countries played an important role as well.

Chapter 2 – This article analyzes the main themes and initiatives that have characterized the development of the Asia policy of the European Union (EU) in the post-Cold War period. It argues that the current role and presence of the EU in Asia goes well beyond trade relations to include a security dimension which has political and strategic implications for the region's major powers. Particular attention is devoted to two issues that have attracted the attention – and concern – of the United States (US) and its Asian allies: China's participation in the EU-led Galileo satellite system and the proposal to lift the EU arms embargo on China. These initiatives have contributed to making the EU an additional factor in East Asia's strategic balance and are an indication that the EU's China policy needs to be increasingly accommodated with the broader EU Asia strategy as well as with the traditional transatlantic alliance and the EU-Japan partnership.

Chapter 3 – In this article, author try to develop an approach that explains why transnational regional organizations emerge and how they eventually form transnational regional polities. Author specifically compare Europe and Northeast Asia with the prospects for an eventual transnational regional organization/polity across two regions of differing national cultures, social structures, patterns of state-building, political regimes and geo-strategic locations. Author first sketch out twelve 'lessons' drawn from the experience of European integration and then present a number of Northeast Asian reflections on the European 'lessons,' with a view to developing and offering specific proposals that might promote successful regional integration in Northeast Asia in the future. After discussing differing degrees of applicability of various theories of regional integration (i.e., federalism, regulation-ism, intergovernmentalism and neo-functionalism), author conclude the paper by prescribing a neo-functionalist strategy for promoting Northeast Asian regionalism.

Chapter 4 – This article argues against the received view of European Union-China relations as hostage to historical rivalries and competing national interests between EU member states. It analyzes the trends in the EU's economic, political and human rights policies towards China since the 1985 European Community-China Trade and Cooperation Agreement was signed. By focusing on the interactions between three major member states with significant interests in China - Germany, France and the UK - and the Europeanization pressures which undercut national leaders' powers, and shape their preferences and options, it argues that there has in fact been significant convergence in the policies of the major EU states and the European Commission towards China.

Chapter 5 – The article departs from some theoretical hypotheses of deliberative democracy to explore the relationship between deliberation, identity construction and democratic legitimacy in the process of regional integration. The ongoing constitutional process in Europe is employed as a case to provide some empirical evidence for the study. Current literature suggests that certain elements of deliberative politics can be found in the constitution-making process in Europe. However, the constitutional crisis following the negative referendums in France and the Netherlands in spring 2005, demonstrates that this deliberative or quasi-deliberative process is a limited, even flawed process given the power-political constraints. Furthermore, it confirms that the European project, designed by its elites, has to find ways to accommodate the diverse interests of various social groups and to construct a more inclusive European identity. Moreover, this article offers a study of the emerging regionalism in East Asia so as to provide a comparative perspective that explores inspiration and wisdom, indeed lessons, from the European experience. In spite of some empirical and methodological imperfections in the study, the author argues that Europe's constitutional experience is relevant for East Asia in several ways. First, the deliberative spirit in the European experience can provide some philosophical or moral inspiration for East Asia. Second, deliberation may play some complementary role in enhancing the construction of regional identity in East Asia although it may be a very limited, incremental one in a foreseeable future. Third, the constitutional debate in Europe may help East Asian people understand the limits of the deliberative approach. In the current global and regional systems, the wisdom of the postmodernists cannot go beyond the boundaries of power-political constraints.

Chapter 6 – Federations and human rights have a long, ambivalent and contested relationship. The paper addresses one of these concerns: whether human rights-respecting federal arrangements are sufficiently robust against claims to secession. Some fear that federal elements and human rights combine to fuel destabilizing forces. Comparative research suggests that some of these risks are real, though difficult to estimate. I argue that several elements of democratic and human rights can limit these dangers, and rather enhance the long-terms stability of federal arrangements. In particular, the contributions of human rights and political parties to the governance of sub-units and the centre merit close attention. The article has seven parts. It first presents some features of federalism and the challenge of stability. Sections 3 and 4 sketch conceptions of democracy and human rights. Sections 5 and 6 discuss how human rights may both fuel and defuse calls for secession. The concluding section brings these results to bear on attempts at alleviating the 'democratic deficit' of the European Union, and to the People's Republic of China.

Chapter 7 – Despite considerable research on how regional cooperation forms and how a regional integration process starts, the origin of regionalism, with particular reference to identity change and a formative regional identity, has not been fully explained. Meanwhile, although mainstream studies have acknowledged that a crisis may become the crucial catalyst for the emergence of regionalism, they have not generally analyzed how regionalism emerges in a crisis related context. This article examines the effects of international crises on one key element of the emerging regionalism – the development of collective identity. It links the question of identity change under the condition of international crisis with the emergence of regionalism, a perspective distinct from the explanations purely based on rational choice and adaptation. It further addresses the issue of identity change by referring to European and East Asian experiences, thus contributing to the author understanding as to how regionalism emerged in a particular historical context.

Chapter 8 – This article examines the China-European Union (EU) relationship after the end of the Cold War. It argues that the EU uses a 'benign Wilsonian' foreign policy style and is committed to a Wilsonian worldview that is couched in promoting normative values and principles of democracy, the rule of law, freedom of people, free markets and open access to international economic markets. Brussels tries to 'entice' and engage Beijing to follow and adopt European values and principles. However, despite Europe's normative posture, the EU is not hesitant to pursue its own interests.

In this article, the theoretical 'benign Wilsonian' construct will be applied in order to examine particular components of the China-EU relationship: the push for political and social reforms, the human rights issue, economic relations, and geopolitical visions of the nature of the international system.

Chapter 9 – It is often argued in the study of European Foreign Policy (EFP) that there is a 'capability-expectations gap' in European Union (EU) foreign relations, which normally means the gap between excessive expectations toward the EU from abroad and the insufficient capability of the EU that cannot match the expectations. But in EU-Japan relations, a reverse gap that this article calls 'expectations deficit' can often be observed. It is a result of Japan's low expectations of Europe, which remain largely unchanged despite the growing weight and influence of the EU as an international actor. Simply put, Tokyo has yet to regard the EU to be an international (political) actor. This article analyzes the structure that generates the expectations deficit--underestimation of Europe in Japan. It argues that the existence of the 'expectations deficit' prevents EU-Japan relations from flourishing.

Chapter 10 – The extent to which the experience of Franco-German reconciliation is relevant in East Asia is an intriguing question to integration scholars as well as diplomatic practitioners. This article examines scholarly works on the Franco-German experience published in China and Japan during the past fifteen years. The aim is twofold. First, the analysis highlights the factual details upon which the Chinese and Japanese understandings of Franco-German reconciliation are based. Second, author identify the rhetorical patterns adopted by Chinese and Japanese scholars when they argue for the (ir-) relevance of Franco-

German experience in East Asia. Based on the theory of communicative action in world politics, the article contends that, while it is unlikely that China and Japan will follow the exact path of Franco-German reconciliation, the common reference to Europe provides a useful communicative platform to reconsider the relationship between the two Asian countries.

Chapter 11 – Throughout the Cold War period and after, German and Japanese security and alliance policies have been frequently compared. Almost all analysts have stressed and continue to stress the basic similarities, rooted in similar histories, geopolitical circumstances, major alliance partners, constitutional limits, etc. This article claims that Germany and Japan have actually parted ways in their security and alliance policies since the early 1990s. Whereas the core function of German security policy is the 'export' of security, facilitated by the fact that there is no realistic threat to its territorial integrity, the core function of Japan's security policy is to 'import' security (from the US). These different functions explain differing attitudes regarding the necessity of nurturing the alliance with the United States, Germany's and Japan's most important military ally. Whereas norms of multilateral and peaceful conflict resolution and the search for more autonomy are strong forces in both countries, exerting a powerful pressure towards a more independent stance, structural factors, but also the self-constructed role of Japan as security importer, prevent these forces from dominating the country's security and alliance policies. The article makes a functional argument that cuts across the established dichotomy of realist and constructivist approaches.

Chapter 12 – In coming decades, China will become the world's largest source of pollutants causing global warming and resulting in climate change. Given China's rapidly increasing emissions of pollutants, understanding the country's policies on climate change is extraordinarily important. China faces the crucial need to protect its national interests and promote development while joining in global environmental cooperation efforts. According to the fragmented-authoritarianism model of bureaucratic politics, one would expect the making of China's climate change policies to be disjointed, protracted and incremental. However, China's policy making in this area is actually highly coordinated. What variables explain this coordination of environmental – and particularly climate change – policy in China? Why have Chinese bureaucrats paid so much attention to climatic change when the regimr has given economic development prime priority? This essay addresses these questions and related concerns by focusing on domestic policy-making institutions and by linking regime theory with the behavior of Chinese bureaucracy. Both the role of China's National Coordination Committee on Climate and the influence of the United Nations Framework Convention on Climate Change (UNFCCC) on the committees' creation, development and operations will be discussed. It is concluded that China's highly coordinated policy making on climate change was in large part stimulated by the UNFCCC process.

Chapter 13 – Concern has grown in Congress and elsewhere about China's military modernization. The topic is an increasing factor in discussions over future required U.S. Navy capabilities. The issue for Congress addressed in this report is: How should China's military modernization be factored into decisions about U.S. Navy programs?

Several elements of China's military modernization have potential implications for future required U.S. Navy capabilities. These include theater-range ballistic missiles (TBMs), land-attack cruise missiles (LACMs), anti-ship cruise missiles (ASCMs), surface-to-air missiles (SAMs), land-based aircraft, submarines, surface combatants, amphibious ships, naval mines, nuclear weapons, and possibly high-power microwave (HPM) devices. China's naval limitations or weaknesses include capabilities for operating in waters more distant from China, joint operations, C4ISR (command, control, communications, computers, intelligence, surveillance, and reconnaissance), long-range surveillance and targeting systems, anti-air warfare (AAW), antisubmarine warfare (ASW), mine countermeasures (MCM), and logistics.

Observers believe a near-term focus of China's military modernization is to field a force that can succeed in a short-duration conflict with Taiwan and act as an anti-access force to deter U.S. intervention or delay the arrival of U.S. forces, particularly naval and air forces, in such a conflict. Some analysts speculate that China may attain (or believe that it has attained) a capable maritime anti-access force, or elements of it, by about 2010. Other observers believe this will happen later. Potential broader or longer-term goals of China's naval modernization include asserting China's regional military leadership and protecting China's maritime territorial, economic, and energy interests.

China's naval modernization has potential implications for required U.S. Navy capabilities in terms of preparing for a conflict in the Taiwan Strait area, maintaining U.S. Navy presence and military influence in the Western Pacific, and countering Chinese ballistic missile submarines. Preparing for a conflict in the Taiwan Strait area could place a premium on the following: on-station or early-arriving Navy forces, capabilities for defeating China's maritime anti-access forces, and capabilities for operating in an environment that could be characterized by information warfare and possibly electromagnetic pulse (EMP) and the use of nuclear weapons.

Certain options are available for improving U.S. Navy capabilities by 2010; additional options, particularly in shipbuilding, can improve U.S. Navy capabilities in subsequent years. China's naval modernization raises potential issues for Congress concerning the role of China in Department of Defense (DOD) and Navy planning; the size of the Navy; the Pacific Fleet's share of the Navy; forward homeporting of Navy ships in the Western Pacific; the number of aircraft carriers, submarines, and ASW-capable platforms; Navy missile defense, air-warfare, AAW, ASW, and mine warfare programs; Navy computer network security; and EMP hardening of Navy systems.

Chapter 14 – In the last three decades, mainland China has transformed itself from a poor, equal country to a rich, unequal country with weaker family ties and more hierarchical, individualistic cultural values. These massive changes have improved many students' learning but threaten to leave behind disadvantaged students.

China's rapid economic growth increased her children's learning both directly (educational spending on schools, books, teacher training, etc.) and indirectly (e.g., better health care). Students with more educational resources have more learning opportunities on which they can capitalize to learn more, while healthier students are more likely to capitalize on available resources to learn more.

On the other hand, economic reforms that facilitated corruption, favored coastal areas, and open markets reduced equality and reduced student learning through several inequality mechanisms: (a) less sharing among students and teachers, (b) less overall educational investment, (c) greater corruption, (d) poorer student discipline, and (e) diminishing marginal returns.

China's unequal economic growth, concentrated in its coastal cities (e.g., Shanghai), encourages large-scale urban migration. Through internal labor migration, parents earn more to give their children more physical educational resources (e.g., books) and more learning opportunities. However, internal migration worsens schooling for migrant children, increases divorces, and disrupts family ties, all of which can reduce student learning.

Meanwhile, family planning policies and programs (culminating in the one-child policy) have sharply reduced births. Smaller family size enhances learning by reducing sibling competitors for family resources. On the other hand, smaller families reduce the size of extended families and their available resources to aid children's learning.

China's greater inequality, greater internal migration, and weaker family ties have also shifted China's cultural values to become more hierarchical and individualistic. As a result, government, school, and family practices yield less sharing of resources with poorer children. Although China's economic growth and family planning improved student learning overall, her rising inequality, weaker social ties and changing cultural values threaten her poorer students' educational opportunities. Possible strategies for addressing these inequalities while maintaining economic growth include: (a) giving parents a flat, refundable tax credit for each dependent child, (b) improving relationships among students and teachers, and (c) ending urban housing subsidies.

Chapter 15 – There is a new expression in vogue on Chinese university campuses. "We must create an English speaking environment." This statement is usually uttered by a Chinese administrator using Putonghua. Chinese administrators are under the false impression that the creation of an English speaking environment simply requires providing an opportunity for oral English output.

Chapter 16 – As imports from the People's Republic of China (PRC) have surged in recent years, posing a threat to some U.S. industries and manufacturing employment, Congress has begun to focus on not only access to the Chinese market and intellectual property rights (IPO) protection, but also the mounting U.S. trade deficit with China as well as allegations that China is selling its products on the international market at below cost (dumping), engaging in "currency manipulation," and exploiting its workers for economic gain. Members of the 109th Congress have introduced several bills that would impose trade sanctions on China for intervening in the currency market or for engaging in other acts of unfair trade, while the Bush Administration has imposed anti-dumping duties and safeguards against some PRC products and pressured China to further revalue its currency and remove non-tariff trade barriers.

China runs a trade surplus with the world's three major economic centers — the United States, the European Union, and Japan. Since 2000, the United States has incurred its largest bilateral trade deficit with China ($201 billion in 2005, a 25% rise over 2004). In 2003, China replaced Mexico as the second largest source of imports for the United States. China's share of U.S. imports was 14.6% in 2005, although this proportion still falls short of Japan's 18% of the early 1990s. The United States is China's largest overseas market and second largest source of foreign direct investment on a cumulative basis. U.S. exports to China have been growing rapidly as well, although from a low base. In 2004, China replaced Germany and the United Kingdom to become the fourth largest market for U.S. goods. China is purchasing heavily from its Asian trading partners — particularly precision machinery, electronic components, and raw materials for manufacturing. China is running trade deficits with Taiwan and South Korea and has become a major buyer of goods from Japan and Southeast Asia.

In the past decade, the most dramatic increases in U.S. imports from China have been not in labor-intensive sectors but in some advanced technology sectors, such as office and data processing machines, telecommunications and sound equipment, and electrical machinery and appliances. China's exports to the United States are taking market share from other Pacific Rim countries, particularly the East Asian newly industrialized countries (NICS), which have moved most of their low-end production facilities to China.

This report provides a quantitative framework for policy considerations dealing with U.S. trade with China. It provides basic data and analysis of China's international trade with the United States and other countries. Since Chinese data differ considerably from those of its trading partners (because of how entrepot trade through Hong Kong is counted), data from both PRC sources and those of its trading partners are presented. Charts showing import trends by sector for the United States highlight China's growing market shares in many industries and also show import shares for Japan, Canada, Mexico, the European Union, and the Association for Southeast Asian Nations (ASEAN).

Chapter 17 – The Australia-China Free Trade Agreement (ACFTA) is already in the process of being negotiated by the two governments. This paper applies the Computable General Equilibrium (CGE) model using Global Trade Analysis Project (GTAP) database version 6 for a quantitative analysis of the economic effects of proposed ACFTA. Four scenarios are examined in this paper focusing on flexible and fixed current account positions within short run and long run. Equivalent variation (EV) and real consumption are used to measure the welfare effects resulting from the formation of the ACFTA. The results from the GTAP simulations show positive welfare effects for both Australia and China in all cases. The different magnitudes of changes in the two countries represent the relative significance and size of bilateral trade to each country. The modeling results also indicate that the ACFTA has a negligible impact on rest of the world's real GDP and welfare, and would generate trade creation greater than trade diversion for the world as a whole. Specifically, the two economies will obtain gains according to their comparative advantages. In the case of Australia, primary commodities such as grains, sugar and mining products dominate exports to China whereas in the case of China, manufactures such as wearing apparels, textiles and miscellaneous manufacturing benefit most. Labour force is estimated to move from declining sectors to growing sectors in most cases in the two economies. The sectoral adjustments of trade balance, output and demand for primary factors exhibit similar directions of changes. It is evident that an Australia-China FTA would have not only bilateral but global benefits. (JEL F13, F17).

Chapter 18 – This paper examines and compares the patterns of agricultural trade of China and Niger between 2000 and 2006. Author find that both china and Niger agricultural imports were more than doubled in this period. Chinese imports exceed exports two years after china's accession to WTO in 2001 which opened Chinese market to world economy. There was slight decrease in the exports of Niger agricultural trade while imports increased sharply due to high population growth and deficit of food supply in the country.

Both Niger and China mainly export their farm produces to their neighboring countries. China's imports have geographically diversified sources. The study also found that there is little agricultural trading between china and Niger, which was mainly Chinese exports to Niger.

Chapter 19 – This chapter aims to demonstrate that a green measure of GDP, or what might be better termed as a measure of Hicksian national income, should be included in the formal system of national accounts primarily as an alternative or satellite indicator to GDP. The reason for this is that GDP overstates the national product available for consumption yet is increasingly deployed as a guide to the prudent conduct of national governments (Daly 1989). Since, as author aim to show, Hicksian national income constitutes a more appropriate measure of the sustainable national product available for consumption, it can be used as an indispensable tool for both policy-makers and international donor organisations to design the policies required to achieve sustainable development (SD). Although specific policies to achieve SD is not the main aim of this chapter, the results to be later revealed make it possible to: (a) shed some useful light on the nature of Cambodia's recent economic development — a country still recovering from past wars and the devastating impact of the Pol Pot dictatorship; (b) identify what factors have contributed most to the fall or the lack of increase in Cambodia's Hicksian national income; and (c) outline the nature of the policies that are necessary to increase Cambodia's sustainable national product without having to involve the depletion of its income-generating capital.

To achieve its aims, this chapter is organised as follows. Section 2 provides a brief historical overview of Cambodia's social and economic development. In Section 3, a theoretical and empirical overview of green GDP is outlined. In this section, the inadequacies of GDP as a measure of national income are exposed as is the theoretical basis behind the use of green GDP as an alternative measure of sustainable national income. Section 4 presents the methodology employed to calculate the environmental costs and defensive and rehabilitative expenditures associated with the growth of Cambodia's national product. In Section 5, the various costs are deducted from GDP to reveal the Hicksian national income of Cambodia for the period 1988 to 2004. Some general conclusions are outlined in Sections 6 and 7.

Chapter 20 – Opium poppy cultivation and drug trafficking have become significant factors in Afghanistan's fragile political and economic order over the last 25 years. In 2005, Afghanistan remained the source of 87% of the world's illicit opium, in spite of ongoing efforts by the Afghan government, the United States, and their international partners to combat poppy cultivation and drug trafficking. U.N. officials estimate that in-country illicit profits from the 2005 opium poppy crop were equivalent in value to 50% of the country's legitimate GDP, sustaining fears that Afghanistan's economic recovery continues to be underwritten by drug profits.

Across Afghanistan, regional militia commanders, criminal organizations, and corrupt government officials have exploited opium production and drug trafficking as reliable sources of revenue and patronage, which has perpetuated the threat these groups pose to the country's fragile internal security and the legitimacy of its embryonic democratic government. The trafficking of Afghan drugs also appears to provide financial and logistical support to a range of extremist groups that continue to operate in and around Afghanistan, including remnants of the Taliban regime and some Al Qaeda operatives. Although coalition forces may be less frequently relying on figures involved with narcotics for intelligence and security support, many observers have warned that drug related corruption among appointed and newly elected Afghan officials may create new political obstacles to further progress.

The initial failure of U.S. and international counternarcotics efforts to disrupt the Afghan opium trade or sever its links to warlordism and corruption after the fall of the Taliban led some observers to warn that without redoubled multilateral action, Afghanistan would succumb to a state of lawlessness and reemerge as a sanctuary for terrorists. Following his election in late 2004, Afghan president Hamid Karzai identified counternarcotics as the top priority for his administration and since has stated his belief that "the fight against drugs is the fight for Afghanistan." In 2005, U.S. and Afghan officials implemented a new strategy to provide viable economic alternatives to poppy cultivation and to disrupt corruption and narco-terrorist linkages. According to a U.N. survey, these new initiatives contributed to a 21% decrease in the amount of opium poppy cultivation across Afghanistan in the 2004-2005 growing season. However, better weather and higher crop yields ensured that overall opium output remained nearly static at 4,100 metric tons. Survey results and official opinions suggest output may rise again in 2006.

In addition to describing the structure and development of the Afghan narcotics trade, this report provides current statistical information, profiles the trade's various participants, explores alleged narco-terrorist linkages, and reviews U.S. and international policy responses since late 2001. The report also considers current policy debates regarding the role of the U.S. military in counternarcotics operations, opium poppy eradication, alternative livelihood development, and funding issues for Congress. For more information on Afghanistan, see CRS Report RL30588, *Afghanistan: Post-War Governance, Security, and U.S. Policy.* and CRS Report RS21922, *Afghanistan: Presidential and Parliamentary Elections.*

Chapter 21 – Transformation of East Asian countries from imitation to reaching the frontier areas of innovations in a short span of time is a question that has been explored in this paper. Asian continent has emerged as the hub of innovative activities in the fast pace of globalization. Within Asian continent, there are wide differentials in the stage of economic development and transformation as well as in the national innovation systems. Two distinct patterns of economic transformation and systems of innovations which have evolved over time are-one, based on building strong industrial sector as an engine of innovations and growth; two, the engine of growth is the service sector and innovation system is heavily dependent on foreign capital and technology. Public innovation policies played active role in the process of evolving distinct national innovation systems of Asian type. This paper, while drawing lessons from public innovation policy of the successful innovators of East Asian countries, brings out the need for public innovation policies to develop industrial sector rather than prematurely move towards service sector oriented economic growth.

Versions of these chapters were also published in *Current Politics and Economics of Asia and China,* Volume 17, Numbers 1-4, published by Nova Science Publishers, Inc. They were submitted for appropriate modifications in an effort to encourage wider dissemination of research.

In: Asian Economic and Political Development
Editor: Felix Chin
ISBN: 978-1-61122-470-2
© 2011 Nova Science Publishers, Inc.

# 'THE EUROPEAN UNION AND ASIA: WHAT IS THERE TO LEARN?'

*Amy Verdun*
University of Victoria, Canada

Fifty years after the signing of the Treaties of Rome, the European Union (EU) stands at a crossroads. It has all but completed its single market, has enlarged to twenty-seven member states, has introduced a single currency, is making progress on a common foreign and defence policy, has flirted with the adoption of a constitution and more. The European Community of six member states that at first merely collaborated on coal and steel, atomic energy and that created a customs union in the 1950s and 1960s, has progressed beyond belief so as to achieve these remarkable successes.

The origins of the EU can be traced back to belligerent parties that decided it was best to leave their militaristic past behind and concentrate on creating something more positive and constructive. France and Germany had gone to war three times in a hundred years and felt the need to leave the past behind. It was clear that it was not only the decisions of the governments of France and Germany that made this new pacifism in Western Europe possible. Other countries played an important role as well.

The United States encouraged the collaboration of Western European states through its conditionality within the context of offering financial aid through the Marshall Plan. Other Western European states were more than pleased to participate in the creation of a European Community which would include France and Germany. In fact, the Benelux countries had already made progress on regional collaboration prior to the process that led to the signing of the Rome Treaties (Maes and Verdun 2005).

It probably does not come as a complete surprise that the focus of collaboration in the original European Communities was on coal and steel, atomic energy and economic collaboration – sectors that were removed from the eye-catching political ambitions of more federalist-inclined thinkers who may have selected military collaboration or political union. In fact, there had been plans for such goals, such as building a European Defence Community and moving towards further political collaboration. But those grand objectives were met with opposition, in particular from the French, who were not ready to transfer sovereignty to new supranational institutions in these areas of 'high politics' (Hoffmann 1966). The idea to make small steps in functionally desirable areas that were not so politically salient, i.e. 'low politics', was seen to be less threatening to the governments of the day (Haas 1968).

In other words, the formula behind the process of European integration contains the following elements: two larger powers continuously at war with one another deciding to settle their differences (France and Germany); a superpower promoting economic collaboration among these countries (United States); a few neighbours (Benelux countries and Italy) willing to participate in a community with France and Germany; and the availability of some 'functional' areas of policy-making in which easy progress could be made in terms of integration (coal and steel, atomic energy and common market).

Let us now turn to the case of Asia and reflect a moment on what might be the parallel with the EU case. In the case of Asia, there are two larger powers that have continuously been at war: Japan and China. However, there has not been the same interest from a third party outside the region to settle these differences. The European countries were strategically more important in the post Second World War period (with the Soviet Union spreading its influence throughout the region). In the case of Asia there is no clear superpower to promote economic collaboration between these countries. If anything such a 'superpower' could be either the US, or even the EU, perhaps even or Russia. However, there is no immediate interest by any of these powers to promote collaboration amongst the Asian partners in a way similar to what the US did to Western European countries in the postwar period. The EU's interest might be in part about trying to finds ways to seek to promote the EU model to another region. The US has not been that keen to get involved but has still been favourable to building bridges with these countries, albeit that it has not invested in these countries in quite the way as it had done in Western Europe. Russia is keeping a close eye on the developments but is neither willing nor able to sacrifice its affluence.

As for the other countries in the region, the smaller countries that might be pleased to see their collaboration extended so as to include Japan and China are for example the countries who are member of the Association of Southeast Asian Nations (or ASEAN), but we could also look at a number of other countries, for instance those in the North East. It seems that these countries are keen to learn from the European experience and see to what extent lessons could be learnt from that experience for their day to day matters.

How one might want to make steps to progress to further collaboration is subject to debate. Should one go the European route and target 'low politics' areas (areas of policy-making that do not attract major political attention), or should one focus on the issues in which one wants to build bridges? The latter areas might end up being quite contentious, but could possibly bring the greatest satisfaction, should the collaboration prove to be successful.

This comparison between Europe and Asia lies at the heart of this special issue. As guest editor of this special issue I have sought to include contributions that can make a step towards making the comparison in this manner. In addition to looking at Asia and reflecting on how our insights from Europe might inform us about developments in Asia, I have sought, furthermore, to include some articles that deal explicitly with these matters. For instance, this special issue includes chapters that looks at bilateral relations between the EU (and/or its countries) and selected Asian countries. The result is a collection of manuscripts that very nicely examines these questions from a comparative perspective. Let me provide a brief overview of the most important findings of the contributions to this special issue.

In their article 'Comparing Processes of Regional Integration: European "Lessons" and Northeast Asian Reflections', Schmitter and Kim develop an approach that explains why transnational regional organizations emerge and how they eventually form transnational regional polities. They offer a comparison between Europe and Northeast Asia and analyze the likelihood of there being a prospect for an eventual transnational regional organization in Northeast Asia. They offer twelve 'lessons' learnt from European integration experience and subsequently present a number of Northeast Asian reflections on these 'lessons,' in order to offer specific proposals that might promote successful regional integration in Northeast Asia in the future. They prescribe a neo-functionalist strategy for promoting Northeast Asian regionalism.

In the article by Min Shu 'Franco-German Reconciliation and its Impact on China and Japan: Scholarly Debate' we find a more detailed analysis, specifically of the two dominant powers in the region: China and Japan. He starts off by stating that the extent to which the experience of Franco-German reconciliation is relevant in East Asia is an intriguing question to integration scholars as well as diplomatic practitioners. This article examines scholarly works on the Franco-German experience published in China and Japan during the past fifteen years. The aim is twofold. First, the analysis highlights the factual details upon which the Chinese and Japanese understandings of Franco-German reconciliation are based. Second, we identify the rhetorical patterns adopted by Chinese and Japanese scholars when they argue for the (ir-)relevance of Franco-German experience in East Asia. Based on the theory of communicative action in world politics, the article contends that, while it is unlikely that China and Japan will follow the exact path of Franco-German reconciliation, the common reference to Europe provides a useful communicative platform to reconsider the relationship between the two Asian countries.

In the next contribution we turn to the first of four articles that look at the interaction between the EU and the region, and include analyses of the bilateral relations between the EU and each of the two larger countries and also a comparison between an EU and an Asian state.

'What Role for the European Union in Asia? An Analysis of the EU's Asia Strategy and the Growing Significance of EU-China Relations' by Nicola Casarini analyzes the development of the Asia policy of the European Union (EU) in the post-Cold War period, focusing in particular on China. He argues that the current role and presence of the EU in Asia goes well beyond trade relations and includes a security dimension. Particular attention is devoted to two issues: China's participation in the EU-led Galileo satellite system and the proposal to lift the EU arms embargo on China. These initiatives have contributed to making the EU an additional factor in East Asia's strategic balance and are an indication that the EU's China policy needs to be increasingly accommodated with the broader EU Asia strategy as well as with the traditional transatlantic alliance and the EU-Japan partnership.

In his article 'Riding the Asian Tiger? How the EU engaged China since the End of the Cold War', Ben Zyla examines more closely the bilateral relationship between China-European Union (EU) as it has developed over the past few decades. He argues that the EU uses a 'benign Wilsonian' foreign policy style and is committed to a Wilsonian worldview that is couched in promoting normative values and principles of democracy, the rule of law, freedom of people, free markets and open access to international economic markets. According to this author, Brussels tries to 'entice' and engage Beijing to follow and adopt European values and principles. He argues, however, that despite Europe's normative posture, the EU is not hesitant to pursue its own interests. He applies the theoretical term 'benign Wilsonian' construct so as to examine particular components of the China-EU relationship, in particular the push for political and social reforms, the human rights issue, economic relations, and geopolitical visions of the nature of the international system.

The next contribution turns our focus to EU-Japan relations. In his article, Michito Tsuruoka, entitled 'Expectations Deficit' in EU-Japan Relations: Why the Relationship Cannot Flourish' he argues that the literature on European Foreign Policy (EFP) suggests that there is a 'capability-expectations gap' in European Union (EU) foreign relations, i.e. that the EU cannot live up to the excessive expectations that are being place on it. Yet, Tsuruoka argues, in EU-Japan relations, a reverse gap can be found which he calls an 'expectations deficit'. It is a result of Japan's low expectations of Europe, which remain largely unchanged despite the growing weight and influence of the EU as an international actor. He demonstrates that Tokyo has yet to regard the EU as an international (political) actor. The article argues that it is the existence of this very 'expectations deficit' that prevents EU-Japan relations from flourishing.

Hubert Zimmermann offers another comparison, namely German and Japanese security and alliance policies. Throughout the Cold War period and thereafter, these policies have often been compared for similarities. In his article, entitled 'Trading Security in Alliances: Japanese and German Security Policy in the New Millennium' he goes through the opposite exercise. Rather than stressing the basic similarities, rooted in similar histories, geopolitical circumstances, major alliance partners, constitutional limits, etc. as most analysts do, his article claims that Germany and Japan have actually parted ways in their security and alliance policies since the early 1990s. Whereas the core function of German security policy is the 'export' of security, facilitated by the fact that there is no realistic threat to its territorial integrity, the core function of Japan's security policy is to 'import' security (from the US). These different functions explain differing attitudes regarding the necessity of nurturing the alliance with the United States, Germany's and Japan's most important military ally. Whereas norms of multilateral and peaceful conflict resolution and the search for more autonomy are strong forces in both countries, exerting a powerful pressure towards a more independent stance, structural factors, but also the self-constructed role of Japan as security importer, prevent these forces from dominating the country's security and alliance policies. Zimmermann makes a functional argument that cuts across the established dichotomy of realist and constructivist approaches.

The final four articles of this special issue turn the attention to another important aspect of drawing the comparison between the EU and Asia, by focusing issues such as human rights, deliberation and identity formation.

Reuben Wong's article 'Towards a Common European Policy on China? Economic, Diplomatic and Human Rights Trends since 1985' takes time to look at how the EU has sought to deal with the human rights record of China. It argues against the reading of European Union-China relations often provided as though these relations are being held hostage by historical rivalries and competing national interests between EU member states. Wong analyzes the trends in the EU's economic, political and human rights policies towards China since the 1985 European Community-China Trade and Cooperation Agreement was signed. Focusing on the interactions between three major member states with significant interests in China - Germany, France and the UK - and the Europeanization pressures which undercut national leaders' powers, and shape their preferences and options, he argues that there has in fact been significant convergence in the policies of the major EU states and the European Commission towards China.

Wang Zhanpeng's article 'Public Participation, Deliberation, and Regional Identification: European Constitutional Process in Comparative Perspectives' examines what we can learn from the importance of deliberation, identity construction and democratic legitimacy in the process of regional integration. The literature often suggests that deliberative politics can be found in the constitution-making process in Europe. Yet, he finds that the constitutional crisis, following the negative referendums in France and the Netherlands, demonstrates that this deliberative process is limited. It confirms that the European project still needs to find ways to accommodate the diverse interests of various social groups and to construct a more inclusive European identity. Zhanpeng finds three ways in which Europe's constitutional experience is relevant for the emerging regionalism in East Asia. First, the deliberative spirit in the European experience can provide some philosophical or moral inspiration for East Asia. Second, deliberation may play some complementary role in enhancing the construction of regional identity in East Asia. Third, the constitutional debate may help East Asian people understand the limits of the deliberative approach.

Andreas Follesdal's article 'Human Rights, Democracy and Federalism - Part of the Problem or Part of the Solution? Securing Stability in the European Union and the People's Republic of China' offers another perspective on these matters. Departing from the premise that federations and human rights have a long, ambivalent and contested relationship, Follesdal asks the question of whether human rights-respecting federal arrangements are sufficiently robust against claims to secession. There are fears that federal elements and human rights may fuel destabilizing forces. Comparative research suggests that some of these risks are real, though difficult to estimate. In this article Follesdal argues that several elements of democratic and human rights can limit these dangers, and rather enhance the long-terms stability of federal arrangements. In particular, the contributions of human rights and political parties to the governance of sub-units and the centre merit close attention. By presenting some features of federalism and the challenge of stability, and by sketching conceptions of democracy and human rights, Follesdal discusses how human rights may both fuel and defuse calls for secession. He concludes his analysis with how these factors affect attempts at alleviating the 'democratic deficit' of the European Union, and how they affect the People's Republic of China.

The final article, by Chunyao Yi entitled 'Identity Change and the Emergence of Regionalism' provides a broader overview of identity issues. She takes the issues to a higher level of abstraction and examines how we can understand how regional cooperation forms and how a regional integration process starts. In particular, she seeks to understand the role of identity change and a formative regional identity in this process. She argues that, although mainstream studies have acknowledged that a crisis may become the crucial catalyst for the emergence of regionalism, they have not generally analyzed how regionalism emerges in a crisis related context. Her article examines the effects of international crises on one key element of the emerging regionalism – the development of collective identity. It links the question of identity change under the condition of international crisis with the emergence of regionalism, a perspective distinct from the explanations purely based on rational choice and adaptation. It further addresses the issue of identity change by referring to European and East Asian experiences, thus contributing to our understanding as to how regionalism emerged in a particular historical context.

Taken together these articles seek to show lessons from the EU for Asia and to examine more closely EU-Asia relations. From it we learn that some lessons can be more easily drawn than others. We find that there are good reasons for taking a functionalist path to regional integration in Asia. We learn about the importance of good relations between China and Japan. The special issue also sheds light on the specific position the European Union has in Asia. Perhaps the role that was played by the US in Western Europe during the Marshall Plan times, post Second World War, can now be played by the EU in Asia in the first decades of the 21st century? We also gain insights into the role of deliberation, identity formation and human rights in contributing or obstructing integration. But we need to be fair and also acknowledge the limits of the comparison: many circumstances are different on both continents. Nevertheless, the articles in this special issue shed light on developments of regional integration in Asia from a comparative perspective – a rare comparison in the contemporary literature (a noteworthy exception being Plummer and Jones (2006)). This project has shown the benefits of making the comparison and seeking to find ways to learn across cases of regional integration. It offers a snapshot in time that, given the speed of change in contemporary Asia, would be worth repeating in a decade's time.

Finally, before closing the editor of this special issue wishes to thank a number of institutions that have been instrumental in making this research project possible. First, thanks go to the European Commission in particular its Jean Monnet Project programme (grants 2004-2260/001-001 CEN CENRE and 2005-1989/001-001 CEN CENRE) for supporting two international events organized by the International Political Science Association Research Committee (IPSA RC) on European Unification (known as IPSA RC-3), of which the editor of this special issue was President (2000-2006). These events were the main activities of this IPSA RC during these years. The first event was a major international stand-alone conference in Beijing, China on 3-5 May 2005. The second consisted of four panels and related activities held at the International Political Science Association Congress held in July 2006 in Fukuoka. Thanks is also due to the IPSA RC-3 that took these endeavours on board and facilitated getting the best scholars lined up for the events in 2005 and 2006. Furthermore, thanks are due to all the referees that took their time to read the papers. All papers of this special issue went out to two referees in a double-blind refereeing process. Local hosts are also gratefully acknowledged for their contributions to bringing the scholars of this special issue together: the Chinese Academy of Social Sciences (CASS) (in particular Professor Zhou Hong) who provided the venue of the May 2005 conference, and financial support and Fudan University (in particular Professor Dai Bingran). Of great importance were three assistants in particular, two from the University of Victoria – Christina Hamer and Melissa Padfield – and Sophie Cao (and her team) from CASS all of whom assisted importantly in making the Beijing conference unforgettable. Additional financial support for the Japan conference came in part from the IPSA RC-3 as well as those who were able to make a financial contribution to attending the IPSA Congress with a special word of thanks to Hokkaido University. Finally, administrative and editorial support for this special issue has been provided by Benjamin F. Gonzalez, MA student at the University of Victoria (2005-2007), who has recently moved on and now is a PhD student at the University of Washington at Seattle.

## REFERENCES

Haas, Ernst B. (1968) *The Uniting of Europe: Political, Social, and Economic Forces, 1950-1957,* second edition, Stanford University Press, Stanford, California.

Hoffmann, Stanley (1966) 'Obstinate or Obsolete: The fate of the nation-state and the case of Western Europe?' *Daedalus* 95(3): 862-916.

Maes, Ivo and Amy Verdun (2005) 'The Role of Medium-sized Countries in the Creation of EMU: The Cases of Belgium and the Netherlands' *Journal of Common Market Studies* 43(2), June: 27-48.

Plummer, Michael G. and Erik Jones (eds) (2006) *International Economic Integration and Asia,* New Jersey : World Scientific.

In: Asian Economic and Political Development     ISBN: 978-1-61122-470-2
Editor: Felix Chin     © 2011 Nova Science Publishers, Inc.

# WHAT ROLE FOR THE EUROPEAN UNION IN ASIA? AN ANALYSIS OF THE EU'S ASIA STRATEGY AND THE GROWING SIGNIFICANCE OF EU-CHINA RELATIONS

*Nicola Casarini*

European University Institute, Italy

## ABSTRACT

This article analyzes the main themes and initiatives that have characterized the development of the Asia policy of the European Union (EU) in the post-Cold War period. It argues that the current role and presence of the EU in Asia goes well beyond trade relations to include a security dimension which has political and strategic implications for the region's major powers. Particular attention is devoted to two issues that have attracted the attention – and concern – of the United States (US) and its Asian allies: China's participation in the EU-led Galileo satellite system and the proposal to lift the EU arms embargo on China. These initiatives have contributed to making the EU an additional factor in East Asia's strategic balance and are an indication that the EU's China policy needs to be increasingly accommodated with the broader EU Asia strategy as well as with the traditional transatlantic alliance and the EU-Japan partnership.

## INTRODUCTION

This article[1] analyzes the main themes and initiatives that have characterized the development of the Asia policy of the European Union (EU) in the post-Cold War period. The aim is to provide the reader with a better understanding of the current role and presence of the EU in Asia. It begins with an examination of the economic dimension which has always been considered the backbone of EU-Asia relations. Subsequently, the article analyzes the involvement of the EU and its member states in Asian security affairs. The EU's contribution to regional peace and stability has traditionally focused on participating to the region's multilateral security activities and on supporting peace-keeping operations and monitoring missions in the area. The EU continues to provide humanitarian assistance to war-torn societies in the area and support for the protection of human rights and the spreading of democracy, good governance and the rule of law. Moreover, the EU increasingly cooperates with Asian countries to address non-traditional security issues such as climate change,

---

[1] Material for this article comes in part from interviews conducted in Europe (Brussels, London, Paris, Berlin, Rome), China (Beijing, Shanghai), Japan (Tokyo), and the United States (Washington) in 2005, 2006 and 2007.

migration and terrorism. In recent times, however, the EU and its member states have upgraded the level of their engagement in Asian security affairs both in quantity and quality. The establishment of partnership agreements for the development of Galileo (the EU-led global navigation satellite system alternative to the American GPS – Global Positioning System) with some of Asia's major powers, growing advanced technology transfers and arms sales in the region all reflect the EU and its member states' increasing interest in acquiring market shares of the region's aerospace and defence markets and in countering a perceived United States (US) dominant position in these sectors. This also indicates that the EU's current role and presence in Asia goes well beyond trade relations to include a security dimension which has wider political and strategic implications for the region's major powers.

The second part of the article analyzes the recently established EU-People's Republic of China (PRC, or simply China) strategic partnership. In particular, it focuses on two issues that have attracted the attention – and concern – of the United States and its Asian allies: China's participation in the Galileo satellite system and the proposal to lift the EU arms embargo on China. It is argued here that with these initiatives the EU and its member states seek to establish a security-strategic linkage with the PRC in order to take advantage of China's market and, at the same time, help maintain Europe's global competitiveness and political autonomy from Washington. However, the security-related elements of the EU's China policy have the potential to affect the evolving security perceptions of the region's major powers. The Chinese arms embargo issue, in particular, has contributed to making the EU an additional, and for some irresponsible, actor in East Asia's strategic balance, raising the question as to whether the EU is capable, and willing, to assume a security role in the region. In sum, by piecing together the analysis of the EU's Asia policy and the EU's China policy of the last few years this article aims to provide the reader with a better understanding of the EU's current role and presence in Asia.

## THE DEVELOPMENT OF THE EU'S ASIA STRATEGY IN THE POST-COLD WAR PERIOD: THE SIGNIFICANCE OF THE ECONOMIC DIMENSION

The rise of Asian economies over the past decades, the end of the Cold War, and the stated desire of the EU to emerge as a global actor have created the conditions for EU policy-makers' adoption of a distinctive European strategy towards the Far East. In 1993, Germany became the first EU member state to elaborate a strategy towards Asia. In the *Asien Konzept der Bundesregierung*, the German government outlined the new significance of the Asian markets for Europe. This new importance had become evident since 1992, when the EU trade with Asia overtook EU-US trade for the first time. The German concept paper stated that Germany, and Europe as a whole, had to face the challenge of an economically thriving Asia and 'strengthen economic relations with the largest growth region in the world' (Government of the Federal Republic of Germany 1994: 2). Following up on Germany, French Foreign Minister, Hervé de la Charette, announced in 1995 that Asia would receive special attention as the *nouvelle frontière* of French diplomacy. In the same period, also the UK, Italy, and the Netherlands started to devote more energy and resources to the development of relations with Asian countries.

Concurrent with initiatives by individual EU member states, in 1994 the European Commission released its Communication *Towards a New Asia Strategy*, with the aim to strengthen the Union's economic presence in Asia, contribute to the stability of the region, promote economic development, and the consolidation of democracy and respect for human rights in Asia (European Commission 1994: 2). The 1994 Commission's paper covers 26 countries grouped according to three geographic regions: the eight countries and economies of East Asia (China, Japan, North and South Korea, Mongolia, Taiwan, Hong Kong and Macao); the ten countries of South-East Asia (Brunei, Indonesia, Malaysia, Philippines, Singapore, Thailand, Cambodia, Laos, Vietnam, and Burma/Myanmar); and the eight countries of South Asia (India, Pakistan, Bangladesh, Sri Lanka, Nepal, Bhutan, Maldives and Afghanistan). The rationale that the Commission gives for the EU's new engagement towards this vast and complex region is very clear: 'To keep Europe in its major role on the world stage it is imperative to take account of the emergence of these new Asian powers…It is therefore essential that the Union develops the capacity to play its proper role in the region' (European Commission 1994: 6). The New Asia Strategy (NAS) also urged the Union to adopt more pro-active strategies towards Asia.

The further upgrading of EU-Asia relations came into being in 1996, with the establishment of an institutional mechanism: the Asia-Europe Meeting (ASEM). The first ASEM summit took place in Bangkok in 1996 with the participation of 25 countries: on the European side, the 15 EU member states (plus the Presidency of the European Commission). On the East Asian side, ten countries. The 7 countries of ASEAN (Association of Southeast Asian Nations): Thailand, Malaysia, Singapore, Philippines, Indonesia, Brunei, and Vietnam plus China, Japan and South Korea (the so-called ASEAN+3). As a result of the enlargement of the EU in May 2004, the ASEM 5 summit in Hanoi in October 2004 decided to enlarge ASEM to include the ten new EU member states, as well as three new ASEAN countries (Cambodia, Laos and Burma/Myanmar) that were not yet part of the process.

Over the years, ASEM has become the most important inter-regional forum for discussion and cooperation between the EU and East Asia. Although the ASEM process includes three main pillars (political, economic-financial, and cultural-intellectual), ASEM's paramount objective has always been the enhancement of economic exchanges between the two regions. In 2005, the ASEM countries accounted for 43 per cent of global trade and produced 52 per cent of global output (*Il Sole 24 Ore* 2006: 1). From a European perspective, ASEM is used to strengthen Europe's economic presence in Asia in order to take advantage of the region's markets with the overall aim to protect the Union's global competitiveness and its economic security (Casarini 2001: 7).

The Asian region as a whole currently accounts for 56 per cent of the world's population, 25 per cent of world Gross National Product (GNP), and 22 per cent of the world's international trade (European Commission 2007: 1). Along with inter-regional initiatives, the EU has also deepened and widened bilateral relations with Asia's major regional grouping (ASEAN) and powers (China, Japan, and India). The EU considers ASEAN a key economic and political partner for overall EU-Asia relations. In July 2003 the European Commission released *A New Partnership with South East Asia*, reaffirming the growing importance of the relationship and recognizing that the EU-ASEAN partnership is a 'dialogue between equals' (European Commission 2003a: 2). As part of the new South-East Asia strategy, in 2003 the EU launched the *Trans Regional EU-ASEAN Trade Initiative* (TREATI) and agreed, at the ASEM 6 summit in Helsinki in September 2006, to push forward negotiations for comprehensive bilateral partnership and cooperation agreements with Thailand and Singapore, which could pave the way for a wider EU-ASEAN free trade agreement (ASEM 2006: 2).

With regard to Japan, the 16th EU-Japan summit held in Berlin in June 2007 underlined the good shape of the relationship, in particular on economic matters. Japan is currently the EU's fifth largest export market and the EU is Japan's second largest export market. Japan is a major investor in the EU: in 2004, 5 per cent of the stock of EU inward Foreign Direct Investment (FDI) came from Japan, while almost 2 per cent of the stock of EU outward FDI went to Japan. Since 2001, the EU and Japan have decided to develop and enhance their relationship by adopting an Action Plan which has resulted, so far, in the agreement on the Investment Framework in 2004 aimed at fostering growth in two-way direct investment, in the joint participation in the scientific ITER (International Thermonuclear Experimental Reactor) project in 2005 and in the signing of a Japan-Euratom agreement in 2006.

The EU and its member states have also become increasingly interested in further exploiting opportunities arising from strengthening the ties with India, the second most populous country in the world. Since November 2004, the EU and India have established a strategic partnership, launched an Action Plan with the aim to boost economic and trade links and agreed on the terms and conditions for India's participation in the Galileo satellite network. At the 6th EU-India summit in October 2006 the two sides have also converged on a set of concrete areas to enlarge the scope of their economic and political cooperation.

It is with regard to the People's Republic of China, however, that EU policy-makers have been increasingly attracted over the past years. According to interviews conducted by this author, since the late 1990s China has been the Asian country which has received most of the attention (and resources), both from the European Commission and the EU member states. China is currently the EU's second largest trading partner (after the US) and, according to China customs, the EU has become China's largest trading partner – ahead of the US and Japan. If current trends continue, Beijing is poised to become the Union's most important commercial partner. In October 2003, the two sides established a strategic partnership and signed an agreement for the joint development of Galileo and other space technologies. At the 9th EU-China Summit held in Helsinki in September 2006, the two sides agreed to launch negotiations on a new Partnership and Cooperation Agreement (PCA) which will encompass the full scope of their growing bilateral relationship.

Asia as a whole accounts for around 21 per cent of the EU's external exports and has become a major destination for European investments. A growing number of European companies have been relocating activities to Asia (especially China and India) in order to profit from its cost advantage. In the 2004 *European Competitiveness Report*, the European Commission argues that success in the Asian markets – particularly in China – does not only generate growth, but economies of scale which are even more important for large enterprises to protect their strategic position against their international competitors (European Commission 2004: 353-354). Since it is generally assumed that an increase in European exports, as well as the success of European companies abroad would be translated into the creation of more jobs within the EU, it follows that securing market outlets and fair competition for European industries in Asia has become an important element for protecting Europe's economic security. Given the growing significance of Asia for Europe's socio-economic welfare, EU policy-makers have over the past years started to pay attention not only to economic matters but also, and increasingly so, to political and security issues that could affect regional stability.

## THE EVOLUTION OF THE EU'S ASIA STRATEGY: THE EMERGENCE OF A SECURITY DIMENSION

In September 2001, the European Commission released its paper *Europe and Asia: A Strategic Framework for Enhanced Partnership*, with the aim to provide EU member states with a more updated, coherent and comprehensive approach to EU-Asia relations (European Commission 2001). The area covered as Asia is broadened: it includes all the countries in South Asia, South-East Asia and North-East Asia that were covered in the 1994 NAS (bearing in mind the change of status of Hong Kong and Macau after their return to China in 1997 and 1999 respectively) plus Australia and New Zealand. In the document the European Commission argues that the economic prosperity of Europe may be jeopardized not only by economic turbulences in the Asian region – as during the financial crisis of 1997/98 – but also by political instability. Among the occurrences in Asia that could have a bearing on Europe's interests there are disturbances in the economic and political climates of Japan and China (which are currently the world's second and fourth largest economy respectively), tensions in the area that may destabilize the sea lines on which Europe's trade with the region depend, and any instability in Kashmir, the Korean Peninsula or in Cross-Strait relations (i.e. between China and Taiwan) – which would likely involve the United States and other Asian powers. Growing European concerns for Asia's stability have also been included in the *European Security Strategy* (ESS) paper adopted by the European Council in Brussels on 12 December 2003. The ESS states that 'problems such as those in Kashmir [...] and the Korean Peninsula impact on European interests directly and indirectly [...] nuclear activities in North Korea, nuclear risks in South Asia...are all of concern to Europe' (European Council 2003a: 11). In the same vein, in a speech in July 2005, the EU Commissioner for External Relations, Benita Ferrero-Waldner, stated that 'security in the Far East is a topic of direct concern to European interests. It is part of the overall global responsibility for security and stability that lies at the heart of the EU's role in foreign policy' (Ferrero-Waldner 2005: 1). But what have the EU and its member states done, in practice, in order to promote peace and security in Asia?

Europe's involvement in Asian security affairs dates back to the early 1990s and has intensified in recent times. For instance, the EU is a member of the multilateral security activities of the ASEAN Regional Forum (ARF) and the Council for Security Cooperation in Asia Pacific (CSCAP). The ARF as 'track-one' represents the governmental level (in particular, diplomats from the foreign ministries), CSCAP as 'track-two' involves regional experts of think tanks and universities, as well as government officials in private capacity. With the establishment of ASEM in 1996, a 'track-two' has been initiated which also includes a multilateral security dialogue on various levels between Europe and Asia. In September 1997, the EU through the European Commission has also become a member of the Korean Energy Development Organization (KEDO), created to implement denuclearization of the Korean peninsula. Since their establishment all the above inter-regional security cooperation activities have been widened and deepened. Moreover, a number of bilateral security and military cooperation agreements between EU members and Asian countries have been initiated.

The EU and its member states have also contributed to peace and security in the region by assisting the establishment of democratic governments in Cambodia, East Timor and Afghanistan. Moreover, the EU has been instrumental in ensuring the implementation of the peace agreement between the Government of Indonesia and the Free Aceh Movement (GAM), which fights for the independence of the Indonesian province of Aceh. Although Europe has no permanent military forces deployed in Asia after the return of Hong Kong to China, Great Britain is still a member of the Five-Power Defence Arrangements (FPDA), a military consultation agreement with Australia, Malaysia, New Zealand and Singapore. In addition, France has an operational military presence in the Indian Ocean and the South Pacific, with thousand of troops which can be deployed in Asia in a relatively short time.

The EU contributes to regional peace and stability by supporting the protection of human rights and the spreading of democracy, good governance and the rule of law in the region. The European Commission has been instrumental in building global partnerships and alliances with Asian countries in international fora to help address the challenges of the globalization process. In particular, the EU cooperates with Asian countries to address non-traditional security issues like climate change, migration and terrorism. The EU and its member states also provide substantial humanitarian assistance to Asia, in particular in Afghanistan, Timor, North Korea and Indonesia, and in 2005 a major effort was made for the victims of the Tsunami in South-East Asia.

The EU and its member states have also engaged Asian countries in the more traditional security and military spheres. Europeans continue to sell arms and weapons systems in the region. In recent years, Asia has become an increasingly important market for the European defence and aerospace sectors, which depend more and more on exports for the bulk of their revenues. The Asian region, driven mostly by China, India and South-East Asian countries, has emerged as the largest developing world market for arms sales, accounting for almost half of all global purchases made in the period 2001-2004 (Tellis 2005: 27). In addition, the demand for aerospace products (both civilian and military) over the next 20 years is projected to arise outside the US or Europe's markets and come mainly from Asia and, in particular, China and India. In this context, the EU has invited China, India and South Korea to collaborate on the development of the EU-led Galileo satellite system. This entails important European advanced technology transfers (including dual-use technology) in the region. These initiatives represent huge commercial opportunities for Europe's defence and aerospace sectors and reflect an upgrading of Europe's presence in the region. With Galileo, the EU's strategy in Asia is moving beyond trade relations to include a security-strategic dimension with wider implications for the region's major powers. However, the EU has not yet elaborated a clear and comprehensive political vision of Asia and the role that the EU could play in it.

According to Benita Ferrero-Waldner: 'over the medium-term future, three major policy issues will dominate the political agenda in East Asia: (i) how to respond to the rise of China; (ii) ensuring stability on the Korean peninsula; and (iii) a peaceful resolution of tensions between China and Taiwan. The proper handling of all these issues will have major implications both for regional and wider security' (Ferrero-Waldner 2005: 2). With regard to the Korean issue, though the European Commission is a member of KEDO, the absence of the EU from the '6-Party Talks' is a serious hindrance to Europe's capacity to play its proper role. As to the third, although Taiwan does feature in the EU-China Strategic Dialogue meetings, the EU has tended to shy away from the Taiwan issue, maintaining un-official economic links with the island. The EU and its member states abide by the official 'one China' policy and have preferred to ignore the question of the cross-Strait strategic balance. The latter is the responsibility of the US, who is committed to assisting the island under the Taiwan Relations Act which also specifies the quality and quantity of weapons that the US can export to the island. Any strain in cross-Strait relations could presage tensions between Washington and Beijing, as well as between Beijing and Japan (since American troops will come from Okinawa). To complicate matters, political relations between China and Japan continue to be a matter of concern, notwithstanding the buoyant commercial relations and the 'friendly' visit of Wen Jiabao, the Chinese Prime Minister, to Japan in April 2007. The EU cannot but recommend intensification of dialogues between the two Asian powers and serve as a model for reconciliation between two regional foes (France and Germany). The European model of economic and political integration is increasingly studied with interest by Asian scholars. China's rise is often compared to Germany's threatening rise and challenge to the international system at the end of the 19th century and with it the extent to which Beijing may or may not be of similar nature. In this vein, Ferrero-Waldner's first issue – i.e. China's rise – remains the most important issue and the one which has attracted EU policy makers' attention since the mid-1990s.

## THE EU'S RESPONSE TO CHINA'S RISE: FROM CONSTRUCTIVE ENGAGEMENT TO STRATEGIC PARTNERSHIP

The EU's China policy has evolved considerably since the mid-1990s, both in economic and political dimensions. In the context of the New Asia Strategy, in July 1995 the European Commission adopted its new China policy by declaring that 'relations with China are bound to be a cornerstone in Europe's external relations, both with Asia and globally' (European Commission 1995: 1). The point of departure of the Commission's document is the 'rise of China', seen as an unprecedented event since World War II. While the analysis concentrates on China's economic upsurge and the potentialities of its market for European business, the paper lays down a strategy of 'constructive engagement' for integrating China into the world community. Over the years, Europe's policy of engagement with China has consistently aimed at promoting the fullest possible Chinese involvement in the international arena, whether in the economic, social, political, security or military dimensions, with the underlying belief that this approach would lead, over time, to greater opening up of the country, political liberalization and promotion of human rights.

Behind a firm engagement policy, there is Europe's enthusiasm for the Chinese market and its seemingly limitless opportunities. With annual average growth rates around 10 per cent since the open-door policy began, China has become the fourth largest economy and the second largest exporter of goods. For the Chinese leadership, enhancing relations with European countries is viewed as a highly strategic goal, in particular for obtaining advanced technology needed for China's modernization. Since 2004, China has become the EU's second biggest trading partner (after the US) and, according to China customs, the EU has become China's biggest trading partner – ahead of the US as well as Japan. In 2006, two-way trade totalled €254.8 billion. Imports form China rose by 21 per cent to €191.5 billion and EU exports to China rose by 23 per cent to reach €63.3 billion (Eurostat 2007; Atkins 2007: 4). As a result of these increases, China has displaced the US as the largest source of EU imports.

If current trends continue, Beijing is poised to become the European Union's most important commercial partner.

At the political level, since October 2003 the EU and China have acknowledged each other as 'strategic partners'. This strategic partnership is based on the idea that relations between the EU and the PRC have gained momentum and acquired a new strategic significance (European Commission 2003b: 1; Solana 2005: 1). The declaration of strategic partnership has been accompanied by two substantial moves: the signing of the agreement allowing China to participate in the Galileo global navigation satellite system and the promise by EU policy-makers to their Chinese counterparts to initiate discussions on the lifting of the EU arms embargo on China. In the context of increasing EU-China cooperation on security and defence matters, since 2004 France and Britain have also undertaken military exchanges and joint manoeuvres with the People's Liberation Army (PLA). More precisely, France and China held joint military exercises in the South China Sea in March 2004 (just before the presidential elections in Taiwan and during the debate on the proposed lifting of the arms embargo), the first ever naval manoeuvres to take place between China and a Western country.[2] Following France, in June 2004 the UK held joint maritime search-and-rescue exercises with the PLA (Stumbaum 2007: 68).[3] While this form of cooperation is part of European efforts aimed at engaging China at all levels and in all dimensions in order to help the country's insertion in international society, China's participation in the Galileo project and the proposal to lift the arms embargo have raised concerns in Washington and Tokyo on the grounds that these initiatives may contribute to China's military modernization and potentially tilt East Asia's strategic balance in Beijing's favour in a situation where there could be future tensions in US-China and Japan-China relations over Taiwan (but not exclusively).

## EU-CHINA SPACE AND SATELLITE NAVIGATION COOPERATION

Galileo is a Global Navigation Satellite System (GNSS), alternative to the dominant US Global Positioning System (GPS) that will offer both civilian and potential military applications once it becomes operational in 2010-12 (Lindström and Gasparini 2003; Bounds 2007: 13). On 30 October 2003, an agreement was reached for China's cooperation and commitment to finance 200 million euros (out of an estimated total cost at that time of 3.2-3.4 billion euros) of Galileo, making China the most important non-EU member country in the project. According to this agreement, the main focus of Chinese participation will be on developing applications, as well as research and development, manufacturing and technical aspects of the Galileo project (European Community 2003: 1; Casarini 2006: 26-27). EU-China cooperation in Galileo and, more generally, aerospace, must be seen as an answer to the perceived US primacy in the sector. In Europe, since the early 1990s, an independent aerospace capability has been perceived as having a key role for European industrial and technological development and it has begun to be closely associated with concepts of European security and political autonomy.

---

[2] France and China have established a strategic dialogue and held annual consultations on defence and security matters since 1997, complemented by the training of Chinese military officers.

[3] The UK has, since 2003, started an annual strategic security dialogue with the PRC and has also been training PLA officers.

Sino-European space cooperation will boost the two sides' business interests. European industries are eager to collaborate with Chinese companies in space technologies and, more generally, aerospace. Galileo will facilitate European firms' entry into the promising Chinese market while it will allow Chinese companies to acquire know-how and advanced space technology from Europe. In this context, building a strategic partnership with China is perceived as being important for acquiring shares of this market and, as such, maintain Europe's global competitiveness. Analysts estimate that Beijing has now become the second largest market for aerospace, behind the US. This makes China the most important battleground between Boeing and Airbus and, more generally, between American and European aerospace companies. For instance, in November 2005, during the state visit of Wen Jiabao to France, the Chinese Prime Minister started its four days tour in Toulouse, at the headquarters of Airbus. On that occasion, the Chinese Premier committed his government to buy 150 aircraft of the type Airbus A320 (worth US$ 9.3 billion), the biggest ever order for the Airbus conglomerate. Thanks to this order, Airbus regained a large share of China's market and by the end of 2005 the European constructor had surpassed Boeing in terms of 'contracted orders' from China: 804 for Airbus, against 801 for Boeing (Fouquet 2005: 6). In the same vein, the visit of Hu Jintao, the Chinese President, to the US in April 2006 started in Seattle at the headquarters of Boeing, demonstrating the extent to which China has become the most contentious battlefield between the two constructors. In this context of global competition, Airbus sales to China and the EU's offer to Beijing to participate in the Galileo project must be seen as part of increasing EU efforts to acquire market shares of the global aerospace sector in order to counter a perceived American dominance in the market and, at the same time, increase political autonomy from Washington.

China's participation in the Galileo project entails a significant political and strategic dimension. The decision to allow China play a prominent role in the development of the Galileo satellite system must be seen as the logical extension in the security-strategic dimension of the policy of constructive engagement which has characterized Europe's approach towards China since the mid-1990s. Furthermore, EU-China cooperation over Galileo reflects the different conception between the EU and the US regarding the use of space. In essence, Washington places an emphasis on space power and control, while Europe stresses that the space should be used peacefully (Giegerich 2005: 5). Thus, while the US concentrates on leveraging the space to provide America and its allies an asymmetric military advantage, the EU is more concerned in creating useful – i.e. commercial – space applications for European peoples and industries. For EU policy-makers, Sino-European cooperation is meant to boost commercial activities while the US looks at space from a different angle, i.e. the protection of its global interests and primacy in world affairs. The current Bush administration has curtailed cooperation in space activities with Beijing that was initiated by the Clinton administration. The US appears to believe that space technology should not be disseminated (The President of the United States of America 2006: 2). The Europeans, on the other hand, seem to view space-related activites (technology included) as a medium for international cooperation. It is important to stress that according to EU policy-makers, EU-China cooperation in Galileo and other space applications is not meant to isolate the US, or balance against it. Nor it is meant to increase the proliferation of space technologies that would be used for anything other than peaceful aims. For EU policy-makers, Galileo is intended to build trust with China. Unlike the Bush administration, EU policy-makers do not view China as a possible military threat or as a future peer competitor. In addition, it is widely perceived in some European capitals that the EU-China cooperation in Galileo is a reaction of the isolationist space policies of the US in the last years. The US has committed itself to the control and militarization of space, adversely impacting international space cooperation through draconian export regulations. As a result, other space-faring nations such as China and Europe have been pushed to cooperate among themselves.

Beijing views co-operation with the EU over Galileo as an additional initiative aimed at promoting China's space programme. The *White Paper on China's Space Activities* released in November 2000 states that Beijing is intent to industrialize and commercialize space to advance 'comprehensive national strength' in the areas of economics, state security and technology (The Information Office of the State Council of the People's Republic of China 2000: 3). In recent times, China's space programme has become a major political symbol of Chinese nationalism, contributing to fostering both the economic and military sectors. Since November 1999, with the launch of the *Shenzhou 1* (China's unmanned spacecraft), Beijing has made important technological progress, carefully monitored by the US (Meteyer 2005). China's space aspirations pose significant security and strategic concerns for Washington. Although most of China's space programs have mainly commercial and scientific purposes, improved space technology has the potential to significantly improve Chinese military capabilities (Murray and Antonellis 2003: 645).

Washington increasingly views Beijing as a space competitor and it is concerned that through Galileo and related space technology cooperation, the EU is contributing to the modernization of China's space program. Furthermore, the Bush administration seems to be worried that China's participation in the Galileo project will boost the PLA's ability to acquire the expertise that allows armed forces to be integrated for today's increasingly digital warfare, in particular the most advanced early-warning systems and recognition satellites that would put China in a position to counter Taiwanese arms systems imported from the US. In the 2004 *White Paper on Defense*, Chinese military planners make it clear that the use of advanced information technology is a top priority in efforts to make the army a modern force. According to American critics of Galileo, China's participation in the European satellite system is a major setback to US efforts to limit China's access to advanced space technology with potential military uses.

EU officials have rejected suggestions that China could gain a military advantage from Galileo. The European Commission argues that the Public Regulated Service (PRS) will be withheld from China and any other non-EU participants in the system. The PRS is an encrypted signal, meant to guarantee continuous signal access in the event of threats or crisis. Unlike other Galileo signals, the PRS will be accessible even when the other services are not available, making it suitable for security and military-related uses. The European Commission and Chinese officials recognize that EU-China cooperation over Galileo and other space applications will go through 're-adjustments'. Galileo is part of the development of a strategic partnership with China and as such the final content and mechanism of China's participation in Galileo will eventually be determined by the evolution of EU-China political relations. Hence, there is still a fair amount of unpredictability as to what China will be able to use – or not to use – in the end. However, research work on Galileo will assist China – in any case – in fostering the development of its own, independent satellite navigation system (the *Beidou*).

Galileo is also linked to the arms embargo issue. Since high-precision satellite guidance equipment is considered dual-use, it is subject to special licenses before export to China is permitted. It is precisely because of the dual-nature of space technology that the existence of an arms embargo has become a serious hindrance for the further development of EU-China relations in security and defence matters.

# THE PROPOSAL TO LIFT

A few months after the signature of the agreement on the terms and conditions of China's participation in the development of the Galileo satellite system (October 2003), France and Germany officially proposed to start discussions on the lifting of the EU arms embargo on China. At the time, all EU member states agreed, in principle, to initiate discussions on the issue (European Council 2003b: 1). At the European Council in Brussels in June 2005, however, the decision was taken to postpone the issue. This was mainly due to a series of factors that had occurred in the meantime: (i) strong opposition from the US; (ii) increasing uneasiness in many national parliaments and within the European Parliament; (iii) China's failure to provide clear and specific evidence on the improvement of its human rights record; (iv) the passing of China's anti-secession law; (v) the new German government of Angela Merkel (that reversed the previous policy of Gerhard Schröder); and (vi) the accession of 10 new, and more Atlanticist, members to the EU. In a final move, at the 8th EU-China Summit in September 2005, the two sides agreed to set up a Strategic Dialogue to exchange views on North-East Asia's security. Initiated in December 2005, it is meant to complement the EU-US and EU-Japan Strategic Dialogues on North-East Asia (the first initiated in May 2005 and the latter in September 2005). These newly established consultative mechanisms serve the purpose to move forwards EU-China relations after the impasse over the arms embargo and, at the same time, take into account American and Japanese concerns vis-à-vis a rising China (Casarini 2006: 37).

The question of the lifting of the embargo remains, however, on the agenda of the EU-27 (General Affairs and External Relations Council 2006: 6; European Commission 2006: 11). It reflects the distinctive approach of the EU to a rising China. The EU and its member states do not view China in the same way as the US or its Asian allies such as Japan and Taiwan. Contrary to the US, the EU does not regard China as a possible military threat or strategic peer competitor. This largely explains Europe's invitation to Beijing to join in the development of Galileo, the proposal to lift the arms embargo and the continuation of European arms and defence technologies sales to China. The US, instead, increasingly considers China as a possible future peer competitor. In this context, the proposal to lift has become a contentious issue in transatlantic relations and raises the question as to whether the US and its Asian allies' legitimate concerns regarding China's growing military capabilities can be reconciled with the legitimate interests of the EU in furthering security and strategic links with China.

The European advocates of an end to the arms embargo claim that China has changed since the 1989 Tiananmen Square crackdown on students and that, as such, a reward should be made. Moreover, they argue that the EU Code of Conduct on arms sales and normal national arms export policies and controls will still apply, thereby preventing abuses when it comes to exporting arms to China. The lifting would principally serve to show that the EU does not discriminate against Beijing but treats it on a par with nations such as Russia. However, the Nordic countries, the European Parliament and some national parliaments voiced their criticism with regard to the lifting. For instance, in the 2005 *Annual Report on the CFSP*, with 431 votes in favour and 85 against, the European Parliament urged the Council of the EU not to lift the arms embargo until greater progress is made in the field of human rights and arms exports controls in China and on Cross-Strait relations (European Parliament 2006).

The opponents to the lifting argue that, once the embargo is lifted, China may be able to acquire weapons systems from Europe, especially advanced early warning capabilities as well as surface-to-air and air-to-air missile systems, that could significantly affect the military balance across the Taiwan Strait in Beijing's favour and thus affect American and Japanese interests in the area. Washington, in particular, has voiced its opposition, threatening retaliation in EU-US industrial and defence cooperation in case the arms embargo is lifted. The US maintains that the human rights situation in China has not improved to the point where it merits lifting the ban. Moreover, the US has concerns about EU export controls and the ability to protect sensitive technology from being transferred to China since Washington has obligations and interests in maintaining a balance between Taiwan and China and ensuring that Taiwan can defend itself. In response to US criticism, EU officials have asserted that the lifting of the arms embargo would be mainly a 'symbolic gesture'. In other words, the lifting would be a political act that does not suggest that the EU member states seek to sell arms or defence technologies (which the embargo also covers) to China. EU members have clarified that the lifting is neither meant to change the current strategic balance in East Asia, nor to increase arms exports to China 'neither in quantitative nor qualitative terms'. In December 2004, the EU member states stressed that a revised, and stricter, Code of Conduct will be put in place. This new Code of Conduct will amend the one adopted in 1998 and establish criteria for EU arms sales worldwide. According to EU officials, the provisions contained in the EU Code of Conduct are aimed at ensuring mutual political control among member states as well as transparency and accountability.

Notwithstanding official declarations and the commitment to a revised Code of Conduct, some European governments continue to sell arms and weapons systems to China. The Council of the EU in its *Eight Annual Report of the EU Code of Conduct on Arms Exports* published in October 2006 declares that a number of EU member states have partially sidestepped the embargo by supplying China with components for military equipment. Among the EU-25, France accounted for the largest share of exports, followed by the UK and Germany (Council of the European Union 2006: 265-266; Casarini 2007: 377-378). Thus, despite the embargo, some EU governments, and their arms manufacturers, have been able to circumvent it by selling components for arms or dual-use goods (with both military and civilian applications) to China. EU arms producers are very keen on entering into the promising Chinese market. Once the embargo is lifted EU companies might be able to sell to China components or subsystems that could greatly contribute to the modernization of the PLA and fill critical technology gaps, particularly in such areas as command and control, communications and sensors. This includes communications gear, hardened computer networks and night-vision cameras, as well as the most advanced early-warning systems and recognition satellites that could contribute to China's military modernization and put Beijing in a position to counter Taiwanese arms systems imported from the US. In sum, EU arms producers will profit from the lifting of the arms embargo, since it would open the way to arms sales from China's procurement budget, the second fastest growing in the world after the US.

The problem facing industrialists wanting to enter the lucrative Chinese market is that European defence companies are still largely dependent on US cooperation on defence technology, not to mention the importance of the US market for some of them. American retaliation could take the form of target sanctions at specific defence contractors that sell sensitive military-use technology or weapons systems to China. Based on national security concerns, EU companies could be restricted from participating in defence-related cooperative research, development, and production programs with the US in specific technology areas or in general.[4] Washington is adamant in preventing its advanced defence technology, currently shared with the EU allies, from ending up in Chinese hands. The hope in Brussels is that informal consultations with the US on what the EU member states sell to China would prevent sensitive technology transfers and defuse a serious transatlantic dispute. However, this underestimates US opposition to the lifting. Washington complains that the EU is acting irresponsibly towards Asia, an area where the Union has few real strategic interests, but where the US is robustly committed to its security.

Both the Republicans and the Democrats have argued that the proposal to lift the arms embargo is a cynical ploy to open doors for the European defence industry and that, even if arms sales remain limited, the EU is tossing aside more than a decade of human rights concerns for economic gains (Bork 2005: 2). American criticism gathered pace at the beginning of 2005, when all commentators were expecting that the EU would lift the 16-year old arms embargo to coincide with the 30th anniversary of the establishment of diplomatic relations between the EC and the PRC in 1975. On 2 February 2005, the US House of Representatives voted unanimously (411-3) to pass a resolution condemning the EU's moves toward lifting its arms embargo on China. The resolution alleged that lifting the embargo could destabilize the Taiwan Strait and put the US Seventh Fleet at risk. 'It is in this context that the EU's current deliberations on lifting its arms embargo on China are so outrageous' declared Tom Lantos, at that time the senior Democrat on the House of Representatives' International Relations Committee (United States Congress 2005). In sum, what compels US opposition is, firstly, that the EU code of conduct is not legally binding and, secondly, that the embargo is interpreted differently by the 27 member states of the EU. What worries the US more is the possible transfer from the EU to China of advanced technology and weaponry that would put China in a position to counter Taiwanese arms systems imported from the US (Fisher 2004). The US is therefore concerned about Europe's enmeshing – largely unplanned and lacking any clear political vision – in East Asia's strategic balance.

## ENMESHING INTO EAST ASIA'S STRATEGIC BALANCE

East Asia is a region in flux. China's ascendancy is reshaping Asia's economic and political power relations in a context where the US remains the security linchpin for Asia while the US-Japan alliance serves as the cornerstone of the US security strategy in the region (Cossa 2005). According to Wang Jisi, Dean of the School of International Studies at Peking University and Director of the Institute of International Strategic Studies at the Central Party School of the Communist Party of China, 'the general trend in Asia is conductive to China's aspiration to integrate itself more extensively into the region and the world, and it would be

---

[4] US Code, Title 41, Chapter 1, Section 50.

difficult for the United States to reverse this direction' (Wang 2005: 43). The US-China relationship is crucial for the maintenance of regional stability. At the economic level there seems to be an implicit bargain with Beijing: Washington tolerates China's surging exports to the US and the resulting bilateral trade surplus for China, but China recycles its new wealth by helping to finance the US budget deficit. Economically, therefore, China and the US are more and more interlocked. At the political level, though, things are different. In the last years, the debate has resurfaced in the US as to whether China has the potential to challenge Washington's dominant position in Asia (Christensen 2006).

In the 2002 *National Security Strategy*, the Bush administration stated that the US 'welcome[s] the emergence of a strong, peaceful, and prosperous China' (The President of the United States of America 2002: 27) However, the US also believes that China's declared 'peaceful rise' cannot be taken for granted and that the lack of democratisation and political liberalisation in China could presage tensions in future US-China relations. The Taiwan issue continues to loom large on US-China relations. At the beginning of his first mandate in 2000, President Bush dubbed China a 'strategic competitor'. Bush himself has declared his firm commitment to the defence of Taiwan. The Bush administration is worried that China's fast-growing economy and the country's rapid industrialization are giving Beijing previously unimaginable financial and technical resources to modernize its armed forces (Perkins 2005). Blocked by the EU arms embargo and Washington's refusal to authorize arms sales to the mainland, Beijing has depended largely on Moscow as a supplier in recent years (Makienko 2003).

Estimates of the real China's military budget are, however, difficult to assess. During the annual session of the National People's Congress in March 2007, Beijing announced a 17.8 per cent increase in its official defence budget, to about US\$ 45 billion (The Economist Special Report 2007: 5). In 2005, the RAND Corporation concluded that China's total defence expenditures (based on 2003 data) were between 1.4 and 1.7 times the official number (Crane, Cliff, Medeiros, Mulvenon and Overholt 2005: 133). The US and its Asian allies are concerned that China's military spending is growing both rapidly and in a sustained fashion precisely at a time when there is no pressing external threat to China.

The US Department of Defence *Report on the Military Power of the People's Republic of China* (MPPRC) concludes that the modernization of the PLA has gone beyond preparing for a Taiwan scenario and is likely to threaten third parties operating in the area, including the US (United States Department of Defence 2005). While Chinese leaders insist that their country is engaged in a 'peaceful rise' and 'harmonious development', the US says that China is focusing on procuring and developing weapons that would counter US naval and air power, especially in the Taiwan Strait. The US is committed to assisting the island under the Taiwan Relations Act, the 1979 law that accompanied the US switch of diplomatic recognition from Taipei to Beijing.[5] Chinese leaders have always maintained that they reserve the right to use violence at home to keep China intact – and they stress that Taiwan is part of the Chinese territory. China's National People's Congress passed the anti-secession law in March 2005 reiterating the 'sacred duty' for the PLA to take military action if Taiwan takes a decisive step toward declaring independence.

Taiwan is a thorny issue in US-China relations and, more recently, also in Japan-China relations. Tokyo has recently identified China as a potential threat. In February 2005, the US

---

[5] Section 2(b)(6), The Taiwan Relations Act, P.L. 96-8, approved April 10, 1979.

and Japan held top-level security talks at which they agreed to set new common security objectives to deal with what they called 'unpredictability and uncertainty' in East Asia. Following up on the February talks, in October 2005 Tokyo and Washington jointly assented to long-pending changes in bilateral security collaboration. The renewal of the US-Japan security alliance reflects a growing anxiety about the increasing capability of China's armed forces and it clearly signals that Japan has decided to adopt a more assertive stance toward Beijing. In the last few years, the Japanese governments have reiterated worries of an escalation in Cross-Strait relations, since should a war between the US and China break out, American troops will come from Okinawa, thus bringing Tokyo in the conflict.

For the EU and its member states, Taiwan is not an issue of immediate concern. However, any confrontation between the US and China, with the likely involvement of Japan, over the island will inevitably disrupt regional stability and thus jeopardize Europe's interests in the area. In this context, recent European initiatives aimed at establishing a security-strategic linkage with Beijing impact on Sino-US relations and Sino-Japanese relations. This explains the strong opposition of the US and Japan against the lifting of the arms embargo and the need to obtain reassurances that China will not be allowed to access the encrypted features of the Galileo satellite system. In sum, EU-China cooperation in security and defence matters is perceived in Washington and Tokyo as an unwelcome (and disturbing) factor for East Asia's strategic balance.

## CONCLUSION:
## WHAT ROLE FOR THE EU IN ASIA?

The security elements of the EU's China policy indicate that Europe's presence in Asia is changing. It goes, in fact, beyond the traditional trade relations to include security and strategic factors. As discussed earlier, the EU's involvement in Asian security affairs has traditionally focused on contributing to the region's multilateral security activities (ARF, CSCAP, KEDO) and on supporting peace-keeping operations and monitoring missions in the area (Cambodia, East Timor, Aceh, Afghanistan). Moreover, the EU continues to contribute to regional peace and stability by providing humanitarian assistance to war-torn societies and support for the protection of human rights and the spreading of democracy, good governance and the rule of law. Alongside the above initiatives, the establishment of partnership agreements for the development of Galileo with some of Asia's major powers (China, India, South Korea), growing advanced technology transfers, and arms sales in the region indicate that the EU and its member states are increasingly becoming enmeshed in the region's strategic balance. Recent initiatives aimed at establishing a security-strategic linkage with China – in particular, the proposal to lift the arms embargo – have made the EU an Asian power and raised concerns in Washington and Tokyo.

A more robust EU presence in Asia in the security and defence spheres provides EU policy-makers with a crucial – and double – challenge. One the one hand, EU policy makers need to find ways to combine the different strands of the EU's Asia strategy into an integrated and coherent whole underpinned by a clear political and strategic vision of the EU's interests in Asia. On the other hand, EU policy makers should seek to find ways to reconcile the US and its Asian allies' legitimate concerns regarding China's growing military capabilities with the legitimate interests of the EU in furthering security and strategic links with China. In sum, the EU and its member states should seriously work on a common strategic vision that will accommodate the EU's China policy with the broader EU Asia strategy as well as with the more traditional transatlantic alliance and the EU-Japan partnership. The EU's presence in Asia is changing and this raises the question as to whether the EU is willing, and capable, to acquire a security role in the area and whether this will be welcomed – and to what extent – by the region's major powers.

# REFERENCES

ASEM (2006) *Chairman's Statement*, Helsinki: The Sixth Asia-Europe Meeting Summit, 9 September.

Atkins, Ralph (2007) 'China Exports More to the EU Than the US for the First Time' *Financial Times*, Friday 23 March.

Bork, Ellen (2005) *Human Rights and the EU Arms Embargo*, Memorandum to Opinion Leaders, Washington: Project for the New American Century (PNAC), 22 March.

Bounds, Andrew (2007) 'Lost in space: How Europe's Galileo project drifted off course' *The Financial Times*, Thursday 10 May.

Casarini, Nicola (2001) *Asia-Europe Relations within the Evolving Global Economy: The Interplay between Business and Politics*, Milan: ISPI-Bocconi, Working Paper n. 15, October.

Casarini, Nicola (2006) *The Evolution of the EU-China Relationship: From Constructive Engagement to Strategic Partnership*, Paris: European Union Institute for Security Studies, Occasional Paper n. 64, October.

Casarini, Nicola (2007) 'The International Politics of the Chinese Arms Embargo Issue' *The International Spectator* 42(3), July-September: 371-389.

Casarini Nicola and Musu Costanza (eds) (2007) *European Foreign Policy in an Evolving International System: The Road Towards Convergence,* Basingstoke: Palgrave Macmillan.

Christensen, Thomas J. (2006) 'Fostering Stability or Creating a Monster? The Rise of China and U.S. Policy toward East Asia' *International Security* 31(1), Summer: 81-126.

Cossa, Ralph (2005) 'US Security Strategy in Asia and the Prospects for an Asian Regional Security Regime' *Asia-Pacific Review* 12(1): 64-86.

Council of the European Union (2006), *Eight Annual Report of the EU Code of Conduct on Arms Exports*, Brussels: Official Journal of the European Union, 2006/C 250/01, 16 October.

Crane Keith, Cliff Roger, Medeiros Evan, Mulvenon James and Overholt William (2005) *Modernizing China's Military: Opportunities and Constraints*, Santa Monica: RAND.

European Commission (1994) *Towards a New Asia Strategy*, Brussels: COM(94) 314 final.

European Commission (1995) *A Long-Term Policy for China-Europe Relations*, Brussels: COM (95), 279 final, 5 July.

European Commission (2001) *Europe and Asia: A Strategic Framework for Enhanced Partnership*, Brussels: COM (01) 469 final, 4 September.

European Commission (2003a) *A New Partnership with South East Asia*, Brussels: COM (2003) 399 final, 9 July.

European Commission (2003b) *A Maturing Partnership - Shared Interests and Challenges in EU-China Relations*, Brussels: COM (2003), 533 final.

European Commission (2004) *European Competitiveness Report*, Brussels: SEC (2004) 1397, November.

European Commission (2006) *EU-China: Closer Partners, Growing Responsibilities*, Brussels: COM (2006), 632 final, 24 October.

European Commission (2007) *The EU's relations with Asia*. Available from: <http://ec.europa.eu/external_relations/asia/index.htm>. [4 May 2007].

European Community (2003) *Cooperation Agreement on a Civil Global Navigation Satellite System (GNSS) – Galileo – between the European Community and its Member States and the People's Republic of China*, Beijing, 30 October.

European Council (2003a) *A Secure Europe in a Better World: European Security Strategy*, Brussels 12 December.

European Council (2003b) *Presidency Conclusions,* Brussels 12 December.

European Parliament (2006) *Report on the Common Foreign and Security Policy* (Brok's Report, 28 November 2005) discussed and adopted by the European Parliament on 2 February. Eurostat (2007), March.

Ferrero-Waldner, Benita (2005) 'Security in the Far East', Speech of the EU Commissioner for External Relations at the European Parliament in Strasbourg, 6 July, SPEECH/05/421.

Fisher, Richard D. (2004) *The Impact of Foreign Weapons and Technology on the Modernization of China's People's Liberation Army*, draft report for the US-China Economic and Security Review Commission, January.

Fouquet, Claude (2005) 'La France engrange 9 milliard d'euros de contracts avec la Chine' *Les Echos,* Tuesday 6 December.

General Affairs and External Relations Council (2006) *Presidency Conclusions*, Brussels, 11-12 December.

Giegerich, Bastian (2005) *Satellite States – Transatlantic Conflict and the Galileo System*, paper presented at the 46th ISA Annual Convention, Honolulu: Hawaii, 1-5 March.

Government of the Federal Republic of Germany (1994), 'Asien Konzept der Bundesregierung' *Europa Archiv* 6(189): 142-157.*Il Sole 24 Ore* (2006), Tuesday 5 September.

Hughes, Christopher R. (2006) *Chinese Nationalism in the Global Era*, London: Routledge.

Lindström, Gustav and Gasparini, Giovanni (2003) *The Galileo Satellite System and its Security Implications*, Paris: European Union Institute for Security Studies, Occasional Paper n. 44, April.

Makienko, Konstantin (2003) 'Les ventes d'armes de la Russie à la Chine. Aspects strategiques et economiques' *Le courier des pays de l'Est* n. 1032, February : 29-38.

Meteyer, David O. (2005) *The Art of Peace: Dissuading China from Developing Counter-Space Weapons*, Colorado: Institute for National Security Studies, US Air Force Academy, INSS Occasional Paper n. 60, August.

Murray William S. and Antonellis, Robert (2003) 'China's Space Program: The Dragon Eyes the Moon (and Us)' *Orbis*, Fall: 645-652.

Perkins, Dwight (2005) 'China's Economic Growth: Implications for the Defense Budget', in: Ashley J. Tellis and Michael Wills (eds) *Strategic Asia 2005-06: Military Modernization in an Era of Uncertainty*, Seattle: The National Bureau of Asian Research, pp. 363-386.

Solana, Javier (2005) 'Driving Forward the China-EU Strategic Partnership', Speech by the EU High Representative for the Common Foreign and Security Policy at the China-Europe International Business School, Shanghai, 6 September.

Stumbaum, May-Britt (2007) 'Engaging China - Uniting Europe? EU Foreign Policy towards China', in Nicola Casarini and Costanza Musu (eds) *European Foreign Policy in an Evolving International System: The Road Towards Convergence,* Basingstoke: Palgrave Macmillan, pp. 57-75.

Tellis, Ashley J. (2005) 'Military Modernization in Asia', in Ashley J. Tellis and Michael Wills (eds) *Strategic Asia 2005-06: Military Modernization in an Era of Uncertainty,* Seattle: The National Bureau of Asian Research, pp. 3-40.

The Economist (2007) *Reaching for a Renaissance: A Special Report on China and its Region,* 31 March.

The Information Office of the State Council of the People's Republic of China (2000) *White Paper on China's Space Activities,* Beijing, 22 November.

The International Spectator (2007) Special issue on *China's Rise and Implications for Europe,* London: Routledge, Vol. 42, No. 3, September.

The President of the United States of America (2002) *The National Security Strategy of the United States of America,* Washington, September.

The President of the United States of America (2006) *The United States National Space Policy,* Washington, 31 August.

United States Congress (2005) 109th Congress, 1st Session H.Res.57, *Urging the European Union to maintain its arms embargo on China,* February.

United States Department of Defence (2005), *Report on the Military Power of the People's Republic of China* (MPPRC), October.

Wang, Jisi (2005) 'China's Search for Stability with America' *Foreign Affairs* 84(5), September/October: 39-48.

Yahuda, Michael B. (2005) *The International Politics of the Asia-Pacific,* London: Routledge.

In: Asian Economic and Political Development
Editor: Felix Chin
ISBN: 978-1-61122-470-2
© 2011 Nova Science Publishers, Inc.

# COMPARING PROCESSES OF REGIONAL INTEGRATION: EUROPEAN 'LESSONS' AND NORTHEAST ASIAN REFLECTIONS

*Philippe C. Schmitter* [*] *and Sunhyuk Kim* [**]
[*]European University Institute, Italy
[**]Korea University, Korea

## ABSTRACT

In this article, we try to develop an approach that explains why transnational regional organizations emerge and how they eventually form transnational regional polities. We specifically compare Europe and Northeast Asia with the prospects for an eventual transnational regional organization/polity across two regions of differing national cultures, social structures, patterns of state-building, political regimes and geo-strategic locations. We first sketch out twelve 'lessons' drawn from the experience of European integration and then present a number of Northeast Asian reflections on the European 'lessons,' with a view to developing and offering specific proposals that might promote successful regional integration in Northeast Asia in the future. After discussing differing degrees of applicability of various theories of regional integration (i.e., federalism, regulation-ism, intergovernmentalism and neo-functionalism), we conclude the paper by prescribing a neo-functionalist strategy for promoting Northeast Asian regionalism.

## INTRODUCTION

Political life gradually became dominated by one type of unit: the sovereign national state. From its heartland in Europe in the 15th and 16th centuries, this *genus* of political organization in which a monopoly of authority over all coercive functions came to coincide with a distinctive territory and population spread to other continents – usually by violent means. The doctrine of '*Nulle Terre Sans Seigneur*' (no land without a sovereign ruler) also helped in this process of extension. Outside of Europe, only those societies that possessed a singular identity and managed early to acquire rudiments of stateness, e.g., Japan, Thailand and China, were able to escape being subordinated to or colonized by European sovereign national states.

Not surprisingly, the academic discipline of political science has been deeply impregnated with prior assumptions of stateness. All of its proven laws or working hypotheses should be prefaced with the *caveat emptor*: 'Assume the existence of a state or set of states and, only then, will the following assumptions, concepts and relations be true...' We simply do not have a convincing vocabulary or an operational logic for analyzing or even speculating about other forms of political organization.

All of which makes it difficult to discuss the properties of and prospects for integrating 'world' or 'transnational regions.' It is virtually impossible to compare them – unless we are willing to make one of two assumptions: 1) these units are merely sovereign national states at various early stages in their formation and will therefore follow already established developmental trajectories or 2) these units are merely specialized instances of another political organizational type, namely, the 'Intergovernmental Organization' formed voluntarily by consenting sovereign national states and explained exclusively by their powers and purposes. Only if both of these assumptions seem contestable do we have the burden of inventing a distinctive theory of the practice of regional integration. If one suspects that world regions composed of previous sovereign national states are not going to repeat the state-building experience of their members, *and* if one suspects that they might nevertheless develop some capacity to become actors in their own right, then does one have to give serious thought to developing a specialized vocabulary and a distinctive theory of transnational or interstate integration.

In this article we try to develop an approach that explains why (and where) transnational regional organizations might emerge and how they might eventually form semi-sovereign, non-national, semi-states or transnational regional polities. It should be stressed that we focus on the process of regional integration, not regional cooperation.[1] The latter may or may not be rooted in distinctive organizations, but it always remains contingent on the voluntary, unanimous and continuous decisions of sovereign national states. 'Entry' into and 'exit' from regional arrangements is relatively costless; 'loyalty' to the region as such is (and remains) minimal. Hence, their collective efforts are likely to be erratic and confined to pre-specified issues. It is only when a transnational regional organization starts to become a transnational regional polity – i.e., only when it acquires some capacity (however limited) to act on its own by initiating proposals, making decisions, and/or implementing policies – that the process switches from regional cooperation to regional integration. And, in so doing, both 'entry' into the region and 'exit' from it become much more costly – and the latter may eventually become prohibitive.

We are under no illusions about the prospects for semi-sovereign, non-national, semi-states or transnational regional polities. Some will never be more than mere façades; many have already failed; those that persist may not succeed in doing very much. But the potential exists for their eventually providing the building blocks for an alternative, more rule-bound and less violent world order than the present one built on sovereign national states. 'Peace in Parts' was the provocative title of one of the first attempts at comparing transnational regional organizations (Nye 1987). With their recent proliferation in numbers and extension in area, this prospect may have become less remote.

---

[1] In Europe, cooperation at the regional level began as early as 1815 with the creation of the Concert of Europe. It was not until the treaty forming the European Coal and Steel Community (ECSC) in 1952 was signed and ratified that the region acquired its first formal instrument of integration.

# I. 'REGIONS' IN THE POLITICAL SCIENCE

## LITERATURE

Political science has long recognized the descriptive status of 'regions,' but denied the need for any special analytical treatment of them. Considered as sub-units within an existing sovereign national state, regions are merely the remnants of territories that might have gained sovereignty but did not. Their past unique identities may be persistent enough so that their inhabitants continue to contest – sometimes, violently – the domination of the winning sovereign national state, but regions only acquire the status of actors if they actually manage to secede or are granted some recognized (but subordinate) role within a federal or decentralized polity. In the latter case, they are considered especially useful for comparative purposes – precisely because they have already been integrated, i.e., share a common political culture, legal system, constitutional status and, often, party system, and therefore can be expected to vary in performance only due to exogenous shocks and diverse socio-economic conditions.

Considered as supra-units composed of multiple sovereign national states, regions have also been declared useful for comparative purposes. Under the label of 'Area Studies,' political scientists have conducted considerable research based on the presumption of cultural, historical or geo-strategic properties shared by all of the sovereign national states within the same region. Political scientists have virtually never (except in the case of Western Europe) considered the region as such a relevant actor worthy of explanation. If the 'area' happened to have some regional organizations in common, their behaviour was regarded as 'intergovernmental,' i.e., as a mere by-product of the relative power and distinctive interests of its sovereign national state members.

Transnational regional organizations are not a new phenomenon. Functionally speaking, the first to appear was the Central Commission for Navigation on the Rhine in 1868. Territorially speaking, the first was the Organization of American States in 1890. Both still exist and have experienced some expansion in their collective tasks, although neither is remotely similar to a transnational regional polity. Descriptively speaking, transnational regional organizations have increased rapidly in number over the past decades and extended their reach to cover most of the earth – much as national states did several centuries earlier. Today, there are very few sovereign national states that do not 'belong' to some transnational regional organizations, and there are many that belong to many more than one. The reasons for this remarkable proliferation are somewhat obscure, but seem to resemble those that previously promoted national stateness: unconscious diffusion of fashionable practices, deliberate imitation of the success of other regions, self-defense against external predators, calculated imposition by imperial hegemons, and some 'cloning' from one transnational regional organization to another. Their spread and the resulting cacophony of acronyms have produced considerable confusion and some timid attempts at comparison.

The experience of Europe since the early 1950s with integrating – peacefully and voluntarily – previously sovereign national states is by far the most significant and far-reaching among all such efforts. As such, it has attracted far more scholarly attention than any other transnational regional organization. It stands to reason, therefore, that the European Economic Community (EEC), the European Community (EC) and, most recently, the

European Union (EU), are collectively the most likely organizations to provide some lessons for those transnational regions that are just beginning this complex and historically unprecedented process. But such a 'historico-inductive' strategy for theory-building and case comparison is by no means uncontested.[2] Partly, this is because many students of European integration have quite self-consciously defined it as a unique case and described it as such, or they denied its status as a potential transnational regional polity and filed it away as merely an extreme example of regional cooperation among sovereign national states, along with hundreds of other intergovernmental organizations. Moreover, as we shall see shortly, those who did try to identify its more generic 'integrative properties' tended to disagree about what these were and how far they would carry the process. Scholars and practitioners from other regions have not found it easy to exploit their work. In those rare cases where such comparisons were made, the conclusion was invariably negative, i.e., the 'other' region could not possibly expect to replicate the relative success of the EEC/EC/EU.[3]

This article, in addition to being a manifest case of European 'theoretical imperialism' – at least initially – will also attempt to compare a long existing transnational regional organization and embryonic transnational regional polity with the prospects for an eventual transnational regional organization/polity across two regions of differing national cultures, social structures, patterns of state-building, political regimes and geo-strategic locations. In the case of Northeast Asia,[4] the creation of a transnational regional organization – much less an eventual transnational regional polity – is still a very hypothetical notion.

## II. 'LESSONS' TO BE LEARNED AND (CAUTIOUSLY) TRANSFERRED FROM EUROPE[5]

We have only one instrument that can help us to transfer knowledge and lessons from one region to the other: theory. Only by applying supposedly generic concepts, confirmed hypotheses and empirical observations that have already been applied to explaining one existing transnational regional organization can we expect to make a contribution to understanding the conditions under which Northeast Asian 'regional integration' might succeed. And, even then, given the substantial differences between the two cases, there are abundant reasons to be cautious when transferring such lessons.

Unfortunately, there exists no dominant theory of why and how European regional integration works. It is surprising that a process that has been studied in such concrete detail continues to generate such abstract controversy. There is relatively little disagreement over the facts or even over the motives of actors, but there is still no single theory that can adequately explain the dynamics of such a complex process of change in the relationship between previously sovereign national states and persistently more interdependent national economies.

---

[2] A literature has recently emerged that intentionally seeks to liberate the study of regional integration from its European roots and biases. For a representative collection of essays on the 'new' regionalism, see Soderbaum and Shaw (2004); Laursen (2004).

[3] For an early example of this, see Haas and Schmitter (1964).

[4] Northeast Asia in this article includes six sovereign national states, i.e., Russia, China, Mongolia, North Korea, South Korea, and Japan.

[5] Drawn from pp.6-15 of Kim and Schmitter (2005).

The twelve 'lessons' sketched out below have been drawn from several prominent approaches to European integration, but predominantly from the neo-functionalist one. They constitute, we believe, a sort of common denominator of generalizations that can be drawn from interpreting the sinuous course followed by ECSC, EEC, EC and, most recently, EU. With one exception (to be noted), most contemporary analysts of this process of regional integration would agree with them – although they would almost certainly disagree about their causes and consequences. Its initiation clearly requires an explicit agreement among governments and no one would deny that the institutions and *compétences* that they endow it with initially will have a continuous impact on its subsequent trajectory. Moreover, there is a high likelihood that the national states that agree to such a founding treaty will do so with the expectation that it will protect and even strengthen their sovereignty, not transform it. What happens subsequently, once the process of integration has kicked in and begun to generate its intended and unintended consequences, can be quite another matter.

(1) *Regional integration is a process, not a product.* Once it has begun, the peaceful and voluntary integration of previously sovereign national states can proceed in a multitude of directions and produce secondary and tertiary effects not imagined by those who initiated it. Precisely because it has been such an infrequent occurrence, no one can predict how far it will go and what its eventual result will be. Moreover, once national states have made a serious commitment to forming a 'region,' they are very likely to change their motives for doing so. They may begin with security and geo-strategic reasons (Western Europe did so) and then find other applications for their 'joint venture,' e.g., economic prosperity and, more recently and more conflictually, unity of political action. There is no assurance that the initial effort will succeed (indeed, most attempts at regional integration have failed). Depending on conditions prevailing within and between member states, it can just as well 'spill-back' as 'spill-over' – to use the jargon of neo-functionalism. However, under certain conditions (and Western Europe seems to have fulfilled them), actors are more likely to resolve the inevitable conflicts of interest that emerge from the integration process by enlarging the tasks and expanding the authority of their common, supranational institutions. This, in essence, is the core of the neo-functionalist approach.

(2) *Regional integration has to begin somewhere, and the best place to do so under contemporary conditions is with a functional area that is of relatively low political visibility, that can apparently be dealt with separately and that can generate significant benefits for all participants.*[6] After experimenting unsuccessfully with the 'direct' route to integration via common political or military institutions, the Europeans tried a second-best, indirect one – and it has (more or less) worked. The contemporary point of departure is likely to be different (the Europeans started with coal and steel; no one today would even consider this combination), but the strategy is well captured by Jean Monnet's phrase: 'Petits Pas, Grands Effets' (Take small steps that will lead to large effects). One wants a concrete task that can be jointly managed with little initial controversy, but which is sufficiently linked to others (engrenage is the inside term for this) so that it generates secondary effects upon other areas

---

[6] 'Intergovernmentalists' and 'Federalists' are unlikely to accept this lesson. For the former, it presumably does not matter where the process starts – provided that the prospective sovereign national states agree unanimously on its collective purpose and the limits to such a purpose. For example, a Free Trade Agreement (FTA) should be just as promising a place to begin. Whichever, the subsequent trajectory will be determined exclusively by the power and interests of its sovereign national state members. Federalists are very concerned with the specific point of departure which should be a comprehensive founding document – preferably, a constitution – that defines a set of common regional institutions and their respective *compétences*.

of potential joint cooperation. The gamble is that the conflicts generated by trying to fulfil this initial task will be resolved positively. In the case of the EU, sectoral integration was followed by trade liberalization and the Common Agricultural Program and, only belatedly, by monetary integration. Elsewhere, the sequence may be different, but the important point is the need to start out with something that involves cooperation to solve concrete problems in a positive fashion. Trade liberalization alone, e.g., free trade areas, is very unlikely to produce such 'spill-over' effects.[7]

*(3) Regional integration is driven by the convergence of interests, not by the formation of an identity.* International regions are artificial constructs. They are produced, not found. Some of the clusters of national states that share the most in terms of language, religion, culture and historical experience have been the least successful in creating and developing organizations for regional integration, e.g., the Middle East and North Africa, West and East Africa, Central and South America. Ironically, it has been Europe with its multiple languages, firmly entrenched national cultures and dreadful experience with armed conflict that has proceeded the furthest. If nothing else, the EU demonstrates that it has been possible 'to make Europe without Europeans.' Those who anticipated that concerted effort at solving concrete problems, increased economic interdependence or facilitated social communication across national borders would produce a decline in national identities and an upward shift in loyalties have been frustrated. Those who foresaw a shift in loyalty to the supranational level are bound to be disappointed – at least within the fifty year timeframe of the EU. Those such as ourselves who only expected a shift in attention to the supranational level are satisfied when integration inserts an enduring and significant focus of interest. The important thing is that Europeans know, understand and accept that many of their interests can only be satisfied by processes that transcend national borders.

*(4) Regional integration may be peaceful and voluntary, but it is neither linear nor exempt from conflict.* The neo-functionalist strategy (also known in Euro-speak as 'the Monnet Method') involves focusing as much as possible on low visibility and less controversial issues that can be separated from normal – i.e., party – politics. As interest conflicts arise, they are decomposed and then recomposed into so-called 'package deals' that promise benefits for all and compensate the prospective losers with side-payments in other domains. Regardless of the formal rules – and even now that qualified majority voting applies to a wider and wider range of issues – every effort is made to reach a consensus. When such a solution cannot be found, the decision-making aspect of the integration process simply goes into hibernation for an indeterminate length of time. Meanwhile, the processes of expanded exchange continue to produce their intended and unintended effects and, eventually, the participants return to the table. The most visible aspect of the process has been the periodic negotiation of new treaties. Important as these may be, they are but the surface manifestation of a much more extensive process that has facilitated exchanges between individuals, firms and associations in virtually all domains of social, economic and political life and resulted in the creation of a large number of public and private organizations at the European level. Whether this strategy can persist is highly problematic. The EU has run out of low visibility

---

[7] Elsewhere, one of the co-authors of this article has defined this 'spill-over hypothesis' in the following way: 'Tensions from the global environment and/or contradictions generated by past performance (within the organization) give rise to unexpected performance in pursuit of agreed-upon objectives. These frustrations and/or dissatisfactions are likely to result in the search for alternative means for reaching the same goals, i.e., to induce actions to revise their respective strategies vis-à-vis the scope and level of regional decisionmaking.' See Schmitter (1971: 243).

arenas for policy coordination and the issues that it is currently facing, e.g., fiscal harmonization, visa and asylum requirements, police cooperation, common foreign and security policy, can be quite controversial. The increasing difficulty with the ratification of treaties that have been approved by all member governments is a clear sign of 'politicization' and its penetration of domestic partisan politics.

*(5) Regional integration should begin with a small number of member states, but should from the beginning announce that it is open to future adherents.* Moreover, it is desirable that this initial group forms a 'core area' to use Karl Deutsch's term; that is, they should be spatially contiguous and have a higher initial rate of mutual exchange amongst themselves. If the functional area and members are well chosen, this should result in a differentially greater increase in exchanges among themselves and discriminatory treatment of those who have been left outside. Provided they agree on the internal distribution of benefits and do not generate permanent factions (not an easy task), their relative 'success' will attract those neighbouring states that chose initially not to join the region. The process of incorporating new members places a heavy burden on institutions, but becomes a manifest symbol that the 'region' is worth joining. Especially crucial is the ability to protect the acquis when enlarging and not to dilute the accumulated set of mutual obligations as a way of satisfying specific interests in the new member states. It is important to remember that 'regions' do not pre-exist in some cultural, social or economic sense. They have to be created politically out of existing 'raw material.'

*(6) Regional integration inevitably involves national states of quite different size and power capability.* Since it is a voluntary process, the largest and most powerful members cannot simply impose their will – as they would do in an imperial system. They have to respect the rights and presence of the smaller and weaker units. At a minimum, this implies firm guarantees for their continued existence, i.e., that the integration process will not involve their being 'amalgamated' into larger ones, and this seems to require that smaller units be systematically over-represented in regional institutions. Moreover, there is a distinctive and positive role for smaller states to play in the integration process, especially when they can act as 'buffer states' between larger ones. Not coincidentally, the citizens of those states that were smaller and less developed when they entered the EU tend to be among the stronger supporters of the EU.

*(7) Regional integration, however, requires leadership, i.e., actors who are capable of taking initiatives and willing to pay a disproportionate share of the cost for them.* The European experience suggests that this role is better played by a duopoly (France and Germany) rather than either a single hegemonic power (Germany) or a triopoly (Germany, France, and Great Britain). Moreover, it is crucial that these leading regional actors agree to under-utilize their immediate power capability (pace neo-realism and intergovernmentalism) in order to invest it in a long run strategy of legitimating the enterprise as a whole. Fortunately for the integration of Europe, the potential hegemon (Germany) had just suffered a disastrous defeat in war and pre-inclined to downplay its role. France, the ex-great power, has found this more difficult, and its tendency to self-maximize has repeatedly threatened the process of consensus formation.

*(8) Regional integration requires a secretariat with limited but potentially supranational powers.* Not only must this organization not be perceived as the instrument of one of its (hegemonic) members, but it also must possess some degree of control over the agenda of the process as a whole. The EU Commission is composed of members selected by an obscure

process, firmly rooted in nomination by national governments. But it is presumed, once approved, to owe their allegiance to the supranational integration process and, therefore, not to take instructions from the body that chose them. There is evidence that, however flawed the nomination procedure, the Commissioners do tend to acquire a 'collegial' perspective and to act as supranational agents. Moreover, the President of the Commission can under admittedly unusual circumstances not only assert his monopoly over the introduction of new measures, but also play a proactive role in determining what these measures should be.

*(9) Regional integration requires that member states be democratic.* This is a factor that virtually all theories of European integration have taken for granted – as did the earlier practitioners until in the early 1960s when the application of Franco Spain for EEC membership made them explicitly stipulate that 'domestic democracy' was a prerequisite to joining. In the Treaty of Amsterdam (1997) this was extended to cover respect for human rights and the rule of law. There are (at least) three reasons why democracy is necessary: 1)Only governments that have strong legitimacy within their respective national societies can make the sort of 'credible commitments' that are necessary for them to enter into agreements, to ratify them conclusively, and to monitor their eventual implementation. In the present context, 'the only game in town' with respect to domestic legitimacy in Europe is liberal parliamentary democracy; 2)The presence of a democratically accountable government within all members is a supplementary assurance that none of them will resort to force in resolving disputes. Whatever temptation more powerful governments might have to extract concessions by threatening weaker recalcitrant members, it seems unlikely that this would be supported by their own citizens; and 3)If the neo-functionalists are right, a key element driving the integration process forward will be the formation of transnational interest associations and social movements and their intervention in supranational policymaking. Only in national democracies will citizens have the freedoms needed to organize such forms of collective action and to create links with others across national borders.

*(10) Regional integration seems possible with members that are at different levels of development and per capita wealth.* At the beginning, in the EEC only Italy was markedly poorer and less developed. The subsequent incorporation of Ireland, Greece, Portugal and Spain re-confirmed the EU's capacity not just to accommodate this obvious source of tension, but also to react to it. Through a combination of policies – selective derogations at entry, regional and structural funds, agricultural subsidies and the sheer dynamics of wider competitive markets – it promoted a pattern that could be called 'upward convergence.' Those member states (and even their less developed and poorer subnational regions) that entered under less favourable conditions tended to do better subsequently and their standards of living have converged toward the EU norm (and, in one case – Ireland – even exceeded it) – without, however, noticeably depressing the performance of the more favoured member states. The recent addition of ten members is going to test this fortunate pattern severely. The initial differences in poverty and underdevelopment are greater than in past enlargements and, in some cases, this is compounded by structural differences in managerial and property relations rooted in the transition from 'real-existing' socialism to 'real-existing' capitalism. Nevertheless, contrary to the doctrinal assumption that integration into an enlarged market would inevitably widen the gap between wealthy and poor units – vide the national histories of Italy and Spain – so far, the EU has proved the contrary. Regional integration can not only cope with national economic differences at the point of departure, but also diminish them over time.

*(11) Regional integration is basically an endogenous process, but it can be critically vulnerable to exogenous forces, especially in its initial stages.* Once a subset of national states have agreed to create a 'region' by accepting certain mutual obligations and endowing a common organization with specified powers, its subsequent success or failure is primarily a matter of exchanges between these member states, plus the influence of non-state actors within and increasingly across their borders. Obviously, the more the initial powers delegated to the regional organization, the more important will be the role of its leadership and administration. The European experience, however, suggests that in its early stages regional integration can be very dependent on external powers. More precisely, it is doubtful that the process would have even begun with the European Coal and Steel Community in 1952 and the Economic Community in 1958 without the benevolent intervention of the US. Here is where the 'realist' perspective and its 'intergovernmental' cousin should be especially relevant. Presumably, there exists a configuration of power and interest in the broader world system that determines if and when an exogenous hegemonic actor will conclude that it would prefer that its rivals be integrated rather than disintegrated. On the face of it, this seems contrary to the classical doctrine of 'divide et imperum,' i.e., the stronger you are, the more you wish that your opponents are divided – lest they gang up to countermand your dominance. Obviously, the overriding imperative in the case of Western Europe in the 1950s was fear of the Soviet Union. But now that this imperative no longer exists, the implication seems clear: the US will be much less likely to view favourably movements toward regional integration – at least, those in which it does not participate or cannot control.

*(12) Regional integration, at least until it is well established, is a consumer not a producer of international security.* To make sense of this affirmation one has to make a distinction between regional defence pacts and regional integration organizations. The former, usually the product of a hegemonic power that spreads its defence capability over that of subordinate others, e.g., the US and North Atlantic Treaty Organisation (NATO), the Soviet Union and the Warsaw Pact, is exclusively oriented towards protecting the external sovereignty of its participants by military means; the latter's purpose is to supplant or, at least, to pool the internal sovereignty of its participants by removing barriers to economic, social and political exchange. In Western Europe, membership in the two was not coincident and definitely not obligatory. The EEC/EC/EU was no doubt fortunate in its early decades to have existed 'in the shadow of NATO' and, therefore, not to have had to add external security to its already controversial agenda. With the collapse of the barrier between Western and Eastern Europe and the end of the Cold War, NATO's role has become increasingly ambiguous and EU member states have begun – against US resistance – to elaborate their own capability for collective security. Given the enormous difficulty of such a task, it has certainly been fortunate that their 'civilian' regional institutions are already well established and recognized – if not always beloved. What is much more crucial for the success of regional integration is the existence among member states of what Karl Deutsch called a 'pluralistic security community' (Deutsch et al. 1957).[8] This does not require common formal institutions, as would a viable military alliance (indeed, it can exist with allied and neutral members), but involves a firm and reliable, albeit informal, understanding that under no foreseeable circumstances will its members either use or threaten to use military force in the resolution of disputes among them. 'Domestic democracy' in all member states is part of this

---

[8] Also see Van Wagenen (1952).

mutual assurance (along with respect for the rule of law), but it is the daily practice of making deals and reaching consensus within regional organizations that makes this understanding credible.

## III. NORTHEAST ASIAN REFLECTIONS ON EUROPEAN 'LESSONS'[9]

In the previous sections, our analysis was resolutely Euro-centric. Our (disputable) presumption has been that, if Northeast Asia is to become integrated, it should learn from and follow the European pattern. Moreover, we have (surreptitiously) defined integration in European terms, i.e., the process of '...how and why they (national states) voluntarily mingle, merge and mix with their neighbours so as to lose the factual attributes of sovereignty while acquiring new techniques for resolving conflicts among themselves' (Haas 1971: 6). To this classical definition by Ernst Haas, we would only add that they do so by creating common and permanent institutions capable of making decisions binding on all members. Anything less than this – increasing trade flows, encouraging contacts among elites, making it easier for persons to communicate or meet with each other across national borders, promoting symbols of common identity – may make it more likely that integration will occur, but none of them is 'the real thing.'

Under these presumptions, both Asia and Northeast Asia have made very little or no progress toward integration. There have been moments of regional cooperation, solidarity and identification, but they have not created an institutional legacy of much significance, nor have they succeeded in diminishing those 'factual attributes of sovereignty' that Haas mentioned.

Several authors have claimed that there is a distinctive 'Asian' pattern of integration that may not resemble the European 'institutional' one, but nevertheless is capable of resolving regional problems, asserting regional cohesion and building regional identity (Katzenstein 1996; Pempel 2002). We disagree. We think this is a misleading overextension of the definition of 'regional integration.' Regional integration should be conceptually differentiated from simple, i.e., un-institutionalized and usually erratic, regional cooperation or collaboration.

Assuming that regional integration is desirable in Northeast Asia but has made minimal progress so far, here we present a number of reflections on European 'lessons,' with a view to developing and offering specific proposals that might promote successful regional integration in Northeast Asia in the future.

*(1) Regional integration is a process, not a product.* In pursuing regional integration in Northeast Asia, as was the case with European integration, one should never assume that one knows where the process is heading. Not just *la finalité politique* but also *les finalités économiques ou sociales* are unknowable. The process of regional integration is intrinsically uncertain and unpredictable. However, it must be peaceful, voluntary, and, most importantly, transformative. The process must change national states' motives and calculations, enlarge the functional tasks they accomplish collectively, expand the authority and capacity of supranational institutions, and stimulate interest associations and social movements across member states. In this regard, one of the major problems with free trade areas, which are currently popular in Northeast Asia, is that they 'seem' to be and may indeed be 'self-

---

[9] Drawn from pp.26-36 of Kim and Schmitter (2005).

contained.' Free trade areas are very unlikely to generate any of the above effects that a process of integration is expected to produce. Moreover, most of the goals that free trade areas are intended to achieve are already being accomplished through the General Agreement on Trade and Tariffs (GATT) and World Trade Organization (WTO). In short, 'regional' free trade areas are not so regional any more. So-called 'open' regionalism based on a series of free trade agreements does little or nothing to promote integration.

*(2) Regional Integration has to begin somewhere, and the best place to do so under contemporary conditions is with a functional area that is of relatively low political visibility, that can apparently be dealt with separately and that can generate significant benefits for all participants.* For regional integration to proceed, it is essential to promote collective resolution of concrete problems in a positive fashion. That is the main lesson proffered by the original functionalist theorist of integration, David Mitrany (1946). From the very beginning, the integration should be not just about removing barriers ('negative' integration), but also about creating common policies to regulate and distribute benefits ('positive' integration) (Scharpf 1996). It is extremely critical to select a functional area that is initially uncontroversially 'separable,' and 'interconnected.' 'Separable' means that the area must be capable of being dealt with apart and of generating sufficient benefits on its own. 'Interconnected' means that the area must be capable of generating secondary effects that require attention and engendering positive supportive coalitions across borders. Trade liberalization, including the free trade agreements discussed and pursued actively in Northeast Asia, is a form of 'negative' integration and is unlikely to produce 'spill-over' effects and to contribute to regional integration. Furthermore, free trade agreements generate too much resistance and opportunity for cheating and weaseling.

In Northeast Asia, it will be critical to find the contemporary equivalent of 'coal and steel' which is where the EU began in the early 1950s. This could be transport (one functional area) or, better, transport and energy (two highly interrelated functional areas). In the abstract, transport and energy seem to satisfy all the above-mentioned conditions, i.e., relatively low controversiality, separability, and interconnectedness, although given the 'sensitive' nature of the North Korean regime no functional area may be without controversiality. It is in this respect very encouraging that some of the previous projects and current plans for regional integration in Northeast Asia, such as transcontinental railroad and energy development projects, are focused on these two functional areas.

*(3) Regional integration is driven by the convergence of interests, not by the formation of an identity.* International regions do not exist, even where created and administered as such by a colonial power. Common language and religion do not seem to be of much help. Rather, they may even be a hindrance where they hide different 'sects' of the same religion or dialects of the same language. We should be equally careful about the economists' notion of natural complementarity between producers. Regional integration is an intrinsically dynamic process and generates unforeseen and emergent specializations and new divisions of labour among its participants. Hence, pre-existing trade patterns may not be a good indicator of the potential for generating new forms and levels of interdependence.

It is also important that nation states join with convergent – but not identical – motives. They should 'hit on' integration for different reasons and with different expectations. This provides the future potential for making 'package deals' that will include a variety of pay-offs across participants. Also, there seems to be no automatic effect (à la Karl Deutsch) on integration of substantial increases in social communication across national borders.

Decreases in communication may lead to separate identities, but increases do not produce integration. Contrary to the common notion, previously intense national antagonisms can be useful for integration – provided there is a strong motive for overcoming them (usually due to the existence of a common enemy). Something approaching an East Asian identity has certainly emerged after the 1997-98 Asian economic crisis, largely in protest against the hegemony of the US and the dominance of the American developmental model (Kim and Lee 2004; Lee 2006). However, there is little evidence that this new identity is pushing forward regional integration. Identity or loyalty to the region as a whole is the eventual product of, not the pre-requisite for, integration. A lot, in other words, can be accomplished before a common identity or loyalty emerges.

*(4) Regional integration may be peaceful and voluntary, but it is neither linear nor exempt from conflict.* All the participants from the beginning must acknowledge the existence of conflicts. But this is not enough. They must also expect those conflicts to be resolved peacefully. Indeed, the existence of conflicts is inevitable and exploitable. Without conflicts, regional integration would not advance. Of much greater importance is the answer to the question: What is the method for resolving these conflicts? Who 'cooks up' the winning formula? One of the tricks transferable from the European experience is to use the conflicts (usually over inequality in the distribution of benefits) to expand – not to contract – the scope and level of common (supranational) regional authority. Many (but not all) conflicts can only be resolved by increasing the powers of regional secretariat or expanding the scope of common activities (or both) with side-payments to losers. The unanimity rule is crucial at the early stage to reassure potential losers but tends to be transformed as the integration process advances. In Northeast Asia, where there are both democracies and non-democracies, it is especially pivotal to build and develop relations of mutual trust among member national states so that a firm confidence in the peaceful resolution of conflicts can be fostered and nurtured. Cultural and Track II exchanges aimed at enhancing mutual understanding may help to build such trust.

*(5) Regional integration should begin with a small number of member states, but should from the beginning announce that it is open to future adherents.* The EEC originally started with six members, but was open to others. It should not be presumed that initial exclusion is definitive, although it is useful to have small number in the beginning for decision-making and distributive purposes. Demonstration of 'success' through subsequent enlargement is crucial. In choosing member states, there are two factors to consider: spatial contiguity ('core area') and relatively high initial exchange ('relative acceptance ratio'). The latter is important because it increases the 'envy' of outsiders. The unanimity rule, along with tolerance, should be enforced when admitting new entrants. As well, deliberate ambiguity about 'regional' boundaries is sometimes useful. The Northeast Asian region has only six members in total (Russia's Far East, China, Mongolia, North Korea, South Korea, and Japan). If there is a functional area that can involve all six, integration could begin with all six national states as members. Otherwise, a subset of two or three geographically contiguous and relatively accepting countries (e.g., North and South Korea) can initiate a project and then expand it to involve the other countries as the process advances. As regional integration deepens, the Northeast Asian region might even be extended to include countries in the Southeast Asian Region too.

*(6) Regional integration inevitably involves national states of quite different size and power capability.* The key interest cleavages in the process of integration tend to be based on

relative size and level of development. These should be accommodated in institutional rules, e.g., by over-representing small countries and inserting special programs for less developed members. There should be an implicit or explicit guarantee that regional integration does not mean assimilation of small members into large members, or less developed ones into the more developed. Quite the contrary is true: integration is often the best guarantee for the survival of small/less developed states. The best imaginable outcome is 'convergence' whereby the weakest members in economic and political performance find themselves growing fast and becoming more secure relative to those that are strong and stable.

In Northeast Asia, the smallest (in terms of population) and poorest participant would be North Korea. North Korea's inability or unwillingness to cooperate has been and will continue to be the greatest hindrance to further progress in regional integration. Therefore, special measures must be taken to guarantee the survival of North Korea and to ensure that no attempts will be made to assimilate it to South Korea. A symbolic compensation, such as locating major supranational regional institutions in North Korea, would be both necessary and desirable.

*(7) Regional integration, however, requires leadership, i.e., actors who are capable of taking initiatives and willing to pay a disproportionate share of the cost for them.* This is obviously related to the preceding issue of size and development. In the fortunate European pattern, the two cleavages (size and development) do not coincide, but cut across each other. Some small countries are rich and some large ones are (relatively) poor. In Northeast Asia, the situation would be more complicated. Russia and Mongolia are large but (relatively) poor. China is large and rapidly developing. Japan and South Korea are small but rich. North Korea is both small and poor. The important questions to be answered are: 1)Why should a hegemon (or pair or trio of hegemons) be willing to pay the higher price for membership? and 2)What can induce them to under-utilize their intrinsic power advantage? In the case of a hegemonic duo, stability is important but sometimes causes awkwardness among late arrivers. A single 'imperial' hegemon, even if 'generous,' can sometimes have an inhibiting effect – e.g., US in North American Free Trade Agreement (NAFTA) or Brazil in Mercosur. In Northeast Asia, a duopoly of China and Japan is unlikely for various historical and political reasons. South Korea can play a leadership role in regional integration, mediating between China and Japan. The current South Korean government is unprecedentedly enthusiastic about facilitating regional integration in Northeast Asia and has empowered a Presidential Committee on Northeast Asia Initiative. Obviously, South Korea cannot itself be the regional 'hegemon.' Hence, an important practical question is whether a middle power such as South Korea could nevertheless play the required leadership role in Northeast Asia. Or is facilitator-ship (in contrast to leadership) sufficient for regional integration under these circumstances?

*(8) Regional integration requires a secretariat with limited but potentially supranational powers.* Key powers of the secretariat, in the case of EU, include: 1) control over initiation of new proposals; 2) control over distribution of positions within its quasi-cabinet (the European Commission); 3) budgetary discretion; 4) potential to take member states to the European Court of Justice; 5) network position and possible information monopolies, especially with regard to subnational actors (functional and territorial); 6) alliances with the European Parliament; and 7) package-dealing and log-rolling potential. In Northeast Asia, so far all attempts at building a secretariat with supranational powers have failed. No regional institution anywhere in Asia has any of the powers listed above. Building and funding a

supranational secretariat must be the first priority in any future project of regional integration in Northeast Asia.

*(9) Regional integration requires that member states be democratic.* That member states are democratic provides insurance that members will not use force against each other, especially once integration has progressed and their respective civil societies have become intertwined. Some guarantees of government legitimacy and of a 'centripetal/centrist' tendency in partisan competition are also essential so that commitments remain not only constant across parties, but also deeply rooted in citizen expectations. In Northeast Asia, there are two non-democracies (China and North Korea) and four democracies or quasi-democracies (Japan and South Korea, Mongolia and Russia). Moreover, the democracies are at different levels of regime consolidation. Hence, we cannot expect all the positive effects of 'a union of democracies,' as was the case in the EU. It should be noted, however, that the central paradox of regional integration is that it may require democracy, but in the initial stages these national democracies must not be too attentive or interested in the process. This suggests that – at least at the beginning stages – the existence of non-democracies might not necessarily be such a deplorable thing. Rather, regional integration could be initially promoted by cooperation between stable and predictable autocracies, as well as democracies, and as long as they trusted each other sufficiently to keep their commitments and not to resort to force or even the threat of force in resolving disputes. Subsequently, the spreading of integration to new areas and its deepening to include more powers for its secretariat may promote democratization across all member states.

*(10) Regional integration seems possible with members that are at different levels of development and per capita wealth.* The European experience not only shows that regional integration is possible for member national states with different levels of development but also clearly demonstrates that upward convergence is possible for poorer and less developed countries. In other words, integration not only can cope with national disparities at the point of departure, but also diminish them over time. The Northeast Asian region consists of six countries at quite different levels of development and per capita wealth. The poorer and less developed members of the Northeast Asian region must be persuaded that their participation in regional integration initiatives is the best and surest strategy to catch up and compete with advanced economies in the region.

*(11) Regional integration is basically an endogenous process, but it can be critically vulnerable to exogenous forces, especially in its initial stages.* The European experience strongly suggests that in its early stages regional integration can be highly dependent on external powers. In particular, it is extremely doubtful whether the process would have even begun without the benevolent intervention of the US. In Northeast Asia, where the influence of the US has been far greater due to the Cold War generated, 'hub-and-spoke' structure of bilateral alliances, the tolerance, understanding, agreement, and cooperation of the US would be essential for the success of any movement toward regional integration. So far, the US has been relatively inattentive or indifferent to various integration projects in Northeast Asia, including even those attempts in the aftermath of the Asian economic crisis that intentionally excluded the US. But it is rather unlikely that the US will continue such inattention and indifference to various regional integration initiatives in the region. In these circumstances, it is advisable to actively seek the comprehension and cooperation of the US – especially at the beginning stages of regional integration in Northeast Asia.

*(12) Regional integration, at least until it is well established, is a consumer not a producer of international security.* For Northeast Asia, this is the most valuable lesson from Europe. The European integration was from the beginning predicated on the existence of a 'security community' composed of democratic countries. Northeast Asia is starkly different from Europe in this regard: it includes non-democracies, and potentially violent conflicts abound among member national states. Animosities, both historical and present, clearly exist between North and South Korea, between Russia and China, between China and Japan, between Mongolia and China, between North Korea and Japan, between Russia and Japan, etc. Among these multiple conflicts, the most acute and urgent one involves the confrontation between the two Koreas. Without substantial decrease in the military tension between the two Koreas and the subsequent opening and reform of the North Korean economy, it is virtually impossible to pursue any fruitful regional integration projects in Northeast Asia, because North Korea, one of the key members in regional integration in Northeast Asia, will be either unable or unwilling to participate. Upsetting of regional international security by North Korea or any other country would be more than sufficient to suspend the integration process as a whole. International security within the region, in this sense, is not merely a facilitating condition but a strong precondition for the success of Northeast Asia. Regional security, in turn, is impossible without resolving the North Korean nuclear issue, which inevitably assumes improved relations and eventual diplomatic normalization between North Korea and the US and the resultant establishment of a peace system on the Korean peninsula. In this regard, peace-building in the Korean peninsula is an integral building block for any form of integration in Northeast Asia.

## IV. THEORETICAL CONSIDERATIONS AND POLICY PRESCRIPTIONS

It is fairly easy to eliminate two strategies of regional integration that have little or no chance of succeeding in Northeast Asia.

*Federalism* is out of the question because: 1) All potential member states are not democracies; 2)All potential member states are not effectively 'constitutionalized,' nor is the rule of law evenly observed; 3)All federations require a 'core' of stateness, and none of the prospective members is prepared (yet) to concede such powers to the transnational regional organization. The threshold for a Northeast Asian Federation is simply too high. Only after fifty years of intensive cooperation and very extensive interdependence have the EU member states agreed to even begin to discuss the 'F-word' and they are still far from agreeing on its concrete institutions.

*'Regulation-ism'* will not be an option for Northeast Asia either for the following reasons: 1)It only becomes relevant once the level and extent of economic and social interdependence is very high – and Northeast Asia is still very far from either; 2)Given their greater dependence upon 'extra-regional' powers, its potential sovereign national states are more likely to be compelled to conform to standards and norms elaborated and imposed by these 'hegemons,' i.e., by the US and the EU, or to become members of global 'regimes' such as WTO and International Monetary Fund (IMF); 3)Regulatory politics across national borders depends heavily on three factors, none of which are consistently present across Northeast Asia: (a) the observance of the Rule of Law; (b) the relative autonomy and professionalism of state bureaucracies; and (c) 'Epistemic communities' of specialized

experts who share initial premises and operative procedures. The existence and efficacy of regulatory transnational regional organizations depends crucially upon their being embedded in a broader context of political stability and legitimacy that allows these non-democratic groups of experts to take decisions binding on everyone because they can be held accountable by independent parliaments, commissions of inquiry, a free press and partisan competition. None of these properties is evenly distributed throughout Northeast Asia.

This leaves us with two potentially viable strategies-*cum*-theories: intergovernmentalism and neo-functionalism. Both have their problems and using either strategy will certainly be problematic in Northeast Asia, although our tentative assessment is that the former is less promising for the following reasons.

The 'classic' (and apparently easiest) starting point for *intergovernmentalism* would be a 'Free Trade Area' or, more ambitiously, a 'Customs Union (CU).' However, free trade areas and CUs are notoriously difficult to negotiate sector by sector. They usually incorporate many derogations and exemptions, and the disputes they raise tend to drain away most of the enthusiasm and integrative momentum. Moreover, in the present global context where trade liberalization is on the broader agenda of organizations such as the WTO, there are only very limited benefits to be gained and these are conditioned by the 'most-favoured-nation clauses' inserted in most bilateral trade treaties. Unfortunately, the 'victims' of regional trade displacement are concentrated and often well-connected politically; whereas, the 'beneficiaries' are quite dispersed and much less well-organized. This means that the emerging conflicts are likely to be dominated by the interests of the former rather than the latter, making it difficult to meet standing obligations and virtually impossible to generate new ones. The 'logic' of free trade areas (but less so CUs) is to include as many 'regional' partners as possible – e.g., Association of Southeast Asian Nations (ASEAN) + 3 – while the logic of effective regional integration is to concentrate on a small number of initial participants and to share the benefits among them first – and only to expand subsequently once these have been internalized.

In light of the above, it should not be surprising that there is no convincing historical evidence that free trade areas will tend to evolve into CUs and then to turn into Monetary Unions and eventually into Common Markets. Regional experiments with free trade areas in Central America, South America and North America suggest that – if they survive at all – they do so by encapsulating themselves and not by spilling-over into wider arenas of policy-making. They may be easy to adopt (if sufficiently riddled with exemptions), but they are very unlikely to expand into monetary coordination or greater labour mobility. They even have trouble in transferring their 'lessons of successful cooperation' into closely related policy arenas. Free trade areas also seem to be particularly susceptible to problems involving the size distribution of member sovereign national states. The larger ones with greater internal markets are almost always accused of exploiting the small ones – especially in the 'uneven' exchange between manufactured goods and raw materials. When size distribution lines up with level of development, i.e., when the largest member states are also the richest, the conflicts generated become virtually impossible to manage and the free trade area collapses.

Intergovernmentally based regional arrangements are intended to remain intergovernmental. They are not supposed to have a transformative effect on their sovereign national state members, nor should they generate spill-overs that might enhance the authority of regional institutions. If governments only enter into such arrangements voluntarily and rationally, i.e., when they are fully conscious of all costs-and-benefits and have excluded all possible unintended consequences, they are highly unlikely to react to unsatisfactory performance or unequal distributions of benefits by agreeing to upgrade their commitments by drafting and ratifying a new and more expansive treaty. Their response will probably be either to freeze their existing level of commitment or to withdraw from the arrangement altogether – which, of course, as sovereign national states they are by definition capable of doing.

So, this is our tentative assessment: the strategy of intergovernmentalism is not so much impossible to imagine in Northeast Asia as much less consequential with regard to eventual regional integration. It would be relatively easy to accomplish in formal terms – treaties/agreements supposedly establishing free trade areas have been signed relatively frequently within and across world regions – but it would not make that much difference. Many of those free trade agreements were never implemented and, when they were, they did not lead to regional integration – only a relative improvement in regional cooperation.

This leaves us – *faute de mieux* – with *neo-functionalism* as the most promising, if not the most feasible, strategy for promoting Northeast Asian regionalism. The formula is relatively simple. It begins with the selection of a functional task that is manifestly difficult to realize within the confines of a single national state and capable of generating concrete benefits for all participants with a relatively short period of time. Two functional tasks would be better so that trade-offs can be negotiated across them. Moreover, this function must be sufficiently consequential so that, in satisfying it collectively, the actors involved will generate new difficulties in interrelated areas. This 'spill-over' potential will be much easier to exploit if, in the original agreement, the participating national states will have agreed to establish a relatively autonomous and internationally staffed secretariat for a regional organization that has some minimal supranational authority, i.e. can take decisions without a constant need for the unanimous support of its member states. It will be even more favourable if these 'functions' involve a variety of relatively autonomous and discrete agencies of member sovereign national states—and especially not just foreign ministries who will normally try to monopolize intergovernmental transactions—and if these agencies are staffed by technical and not politically appointed personnel. In Northeast Asia, the task of managing the joint energy and transportation infrastructure of the region would seem to provide an appropriate and apparently separable set of 'initial functions,' although ironically these are two transnational policy areas that have been among the last for which the EU was able to generate consensus.

Ideally, the initial participants should form a core area of contiguous sovereign national states with internal lines of communication and more intensive rates of exchange and, if possible, convergent motives for cooperation. In Northeast Asia, considering the importance of North Korea's ability and willingness to cooperate, it might be a good idea to begin with only the two Koreas, but at the same time inviting the participation of China, Russia, Mongolia and Japan. However, going ahead should not be conditional on their initially joining and one should be prepared for one or another of them to 'opt out,' as did Great Britain in the ECSC and the EEC. This 2 + 4 strategy seems to be worth pursuing, even against the initial opposition of the other potential members. Whoever the original participants would be in Northeast Asia, they should insist on their equal status and national sovereignty and discount any pretension to use transnational functional cooperation as a surreptitious mechanism for national unification.

The agencies of the transnational regional organization should be distributed so that a disproportionate number will be located in North Korea (although any financial agency should be in the South for obvious reasons of communicative efficiency), but with jointly staffed secretariat. In all instances of regional administration and decision-making, the smallest and most vulnerable members must be over-represented – as they have been in the EEC/EC/EU. Integration will also be enhanced if the initial task(s) and the initial delegation(s) of authority are sufficient to attract the attention of non-state actors, i.e., business firms, interest associations and social movements, and to provide incentives for them to form transnational alliances that are capable of demanding access to the deliberations of the regional secretariat. Given the present condition of associations and movements in North Korea, this may be impossible to realize for some time.

The external context of Northeast Asia is much less favourable than it was at the founding of the ECSC and the EEC. Regional actors would have to start with very low-visibility and low-sensitivity projects in order not to attract the wrath of the US, which will not in all probability be as 'benevolently inclined' as it was in the case of European integration. The objective should be to convince the US that, eventually, such modest functional tasks will contribute positively to its over-riding goal of security within the region, even if they do not conform to its immediate national objectives. Most significantly, the 'founding fathers' of the Northeast Asian region – no matter how modest their initial tasks – will have to take into account the serious 'security dilemma' existing within the region. If Europe provides any lesson, it is that a functionally-based transnational regional organization – even a transnational regional polity – cannot alone be expected to ensure that its members will not resort to war or the threat to use force. The regional 'Security Community' *à la* Karl Deutsch was initially provided by another institution, the North American Treaty Organisation (NATO). In the case of Northeast Asia where the threats are more numerous within the region and among multiple pairs of potential member sovereign national states, the continued dependence upon external 'hegemonic' power will be even greater. Hence, the need for an especially 'innocuous' task or set of tasks at the beginning with the expectation that if their completion generates greater trust, enhanced status, learning by doing and material rewards among participants, eventually, the prospects for a self-enabling security community in Northeast Asia will be improved.

## REFERENCES

Deutsch, Karl et al. (1957) *Political Community and the North Atlantic Area*, Princeton: Princeton University Press.

Haas, Ernst B. (1971) 'The Study of Regional Integration: Reflections on the Joy and Anguish of Pretheorizing', in: Leon N. Lindberg and Stuart A. Scheingold (eds) *Regional Integration: Theory and Research*, Cambridge: Harvard University Press.

Haas, Ernst B. and Philippe C. Schmitter (1964) 'Economics and Differential Patterns of Political Integration: Projections about Unity in Latin America' *International Organization* 18(4): 705-737.

Katzenstein, Peter J. (1996) 'Regionalism in Comparative Perspective', ARENA Working Paper.

Kim, Sunhyuk and Philippe C. Schmitter (2005) 'The Experience of European Integration and Potential for Northeast Asian Integration' *Asian Perspective* 29(2): 5-39.

Kim, Sunhyuk and Yong Wook Lee (2004) 'New Asian Regionalism and the United States: Constructing Regional Identity and Interest in the Politics of Inclusion and Exclusion' *Pacific Focus* 19(2):185-231.

Laursen, Finn (ed.) (2004) *Comparative Regional Integration: Theoretical Perspectives,* Aldershot: Ashgate.

Lee, Yong Wook (2006) 'Japan and the Asian Monetary Fund: An Identity-Intention Approach', *International Studies Quarterly* 50(2): 339-366.

Mitrany, David (1946) *A Working Peace System*, Chicago: Quadrangle Books (Originally published in 1943).

Nye, Joseph S. (1987) *Peace in Parts*, Washington: University Press of America (Originally published in 1970 by Little, Brown and Company).

Pempel, TJ. (2002) 'The Soft Ties of Asian Regionalism', Paper presented at the conference on 'Building an East Asian Community: Visions and Strategies', 11 December, Seoul, Korea.

Scharpf, Fritz W. (1996) 'Negative and Positive Integration in the Political Economy of European Welfare States', in: Gary Marks, Fritz W. Scharpf, Philippe C. Schmitter, and Wolfgang Streeck (eds) *Governance in the European Union*, Thousand Oaks: Sage.

Schmitter, Philippe C. (1971) 'A Revised Theory of Regional Integration', in: Leon N. Lindberg and Stuart A. Scheingold (eds) *Regional Integration: Theory and Research*, Cambridge: Harvard University Press.

Soderbaum, Fredrik and Timothy M. Shaw (eds) (2004) *Theories of New Regionalism: A Palgrave Reader*, Basingstoke: Palgrave.

Van Wagenen, Richard W. (1952) 'Research in the International Organization Field: Some Notes on a Possible Focus', Center for Research on World Political Institutions, *Publication No. 1*, Princeton University, Princeton, NJ.

In: Asian Economic and Political Development
Editor: Felix Chin

ISBN: 978-1-61122-470-2
© 2011 Nova Science Publishers, Inc.

# TOWARDS A COMMON EUROPEAN POLICY ON CHINA?[1] ECONOMIC, DIPLOMATIC AND HUMAN RIGHTS TRENDS SINCE 1985

*Reuben Wong*
Political Science Department,
National University of Singapore

## ABSTRACT

This article argues against the received view of European Union-China relations as hostage to historical rivalries and competing national interests between EU member states. It analyzes the trends in the EU's economic, political and human rights policies towards China since the 1985 European Community-China Trade and Cooperation Agreement was signed. By focusing on the interactions between three major member states with significant interests in China - Germany, France and the UK - and the Europeanization pressures which undercut national leaders' powers, and shape their preferences and options, it argues that there has in fact been significant convergence in the policies of the major EU states and the European Commission towards China.

## INTRODUCTION

This article examines the Europeanization processes in European Union (EU) foreign policy vis-à-vis a major Asian country (China). The received view of EU policy towards China is that it is hostage to historical rivalries and EU member states' competing national interests (Grant 1995; Neves and Bridges 2000; Barysch et al. 2005: 10-20). The influence of third parties (especially the USA) also looms large in the EU-China relationship. Indeed, EU-China ties have notoriously been characterized as 'secondary' and 'derivative' of relationships with the USA or USSR (Yahuda 1994; Shambaugh 1996). Three episodes since the 1985 European Community (EC)-China Trade and Cooperation Agreement (TCA) are often highlighted as symptomatic of EU incoherence with regards to China. First, the

---

[1] This article is based on an earlier conference paper presented at 'The European Union and the World: Asia, Enlargement and Constitutional Change', organized by IPSA Research Committee 3 on European Unification, in Beijing, 5-6 May 2005. The author is grateful to Amy Verdun, Hans Maull and two anonymous reviewers for their helpful comments, criticisms and suggestions on earlier drafts.

breakdown of European solidarity in the EC's sanctions policy following the Tiananmen massacre in July 1989. One by one, the member states from 1990 broke ranks with the common sanctions in order to gain political and economic favour with Beijing (Wellons 1994; Wong 2006: 88-95). Sectarian (chiefly economic) national interests are often presented as paramount in the calculations of EU foreign policy makers, to the detriment of collective goals such as the promotion of human rights. Second, the April 1997 breakdown of the common General Affairs Council (GAC) position on sponsoring an annual EU resolution criticizing China at the United Nations Commission on Human Rights, leading to a climbdown in the EU's confrontational human rights policy (Clapham 1999; Human Rights in China 1998; Foot 2000). Finally, EU member states barely held together in 2004-5 over German and French attempts to lift the arms embargo on China (in place since 1989); with the EU-25 backtracking in the face of internal divisions and energetic warnings from Washington (Gompert et al. 2005; Godement 2004, 2005).

In contrast to this mainstream view of EU incoherence, a minority view perceives harmonization of the EU's China policies. Some analysts note that the EU is connected to China through extensive channels of cooperation, and that its China policy is 'in progress' (Wiessala 2002: 104; Bâtie 2002). Others argue that increasing Franco-German cooperation would form the nexus of common EU approaches towards China (Nesshöver 1999). This article contends that there has in fact been convergence of EU member states' policies towards China. An analysis of trends in three key areas of EU-China interactions (economics and trade; political-strategic ties; and human rights) and the Europeanization pressures which shape member states' preferences and options, reveals significant convergence in the policies of the major EU states and the European Commission over 20 years.

## Europeanization

The novelty of 'Europeanization' in foreign policy studies is a function of the debate on the existence of a common European foreign policy (Wong 2005, 2007). Yet analyzing the EU's foreign policy is problematic because it is not a unified state actor, neither does it have clear and consistent external objectives. Instead of a coherent and authoritative decision-making centre, national foreign policies persist and operate alongside – and sometimes at variance with – 'EU' policies defined by the European Commission, the European Parliament and/or the General Affairs Council. As the EU is not a unitary actor, 'EU foreign policy' (EFP) is usually understood and analyzed as the sum and interaction of the 'three strands' of Europe's 'external relations system', comprising: (a) the national foreign policies of the member states; (b) EC external trade relations and development policy; and (c) the Common Foreign and Security Policy (CFSP) of the EU (Hill 1993; Ginsberg 1999; Tonra and Christiansen 2004).

The concept of foreign policy Europeanization is often employed to explain the top-down ('downloading') adaptation of national structures and processes in response to the demands of the EU, or what some call 'EU-ization' (Tsardanidis and Stavridis 2005; Miskimmon and Paterson 2003). Under the CFSP, 'Europeanization' can be understood as a process of foreign policy convergence. It is a dependent variable contingent on the ideas and directives emanating from EU institutions in Brussels, as well as policy ideas and actions from member states. Europeanization is thus a process of change manifested as policy convergence (both top-down and sideways) as well as national policies amplified as EU policy (uploading). In this article, Europeanization is understood as three distinct but inter-related processes according to the agents, targets and directions of change. As a downloading process, Europeanization is the process of change in national foreign policies caused by participation over time in foreign policy-making at the European level. As an uploading process, it is the projection of national preferences, ideas and policy models to the EU level. Europeanization is thus a bi-directional process that leads to a negotiated convergence of policy goals, preferences and even identity between the national and the supranational levels (Hill and Wallace 1996; Aggestam 2004; Wong 2007).

## China as a Case Study

China is an interesting case study of EU foreign policy, as it ranks among the most important countries in the EU's external relations. Not only is it the most populous country on earth, China has the fastest growing major economy, is the EU's second largest trading partner after the US, and is the centrepiece of EU policy in Asia. It is increasingly viewed as economically, politically, militarily and even culturally strategic to European interests (Commission of the European Communities [henceforth "Commission"] 1995, 1998, 2001a, 2003; Shambaugh 1996; Neves and Bridges 2000; Edmonds 2002). The EU is China's largest trade partner, and Europe is useful to China as a counterweight to US influence in China's economic and political development, and even as an alternative source of strategic technology (Bâtie 2002; *FEER* 2004; *IHT* 2005). Diplomatic relations were first established in 1975, the first bilateral trade agreement, signed in 1978, and a Trade and Cooperation Agreement, in 1985 (still in force). An EC Delegation was opened in Beijing in 1988, but common political and economic sanctions were imposed by the 1989 Madrid summit following the Tiananmen massacre in Beijing on 4 June 1989.

A common policy on China was officially defined only in July 1995, when then-Trade Commissioner Sir Leon Brittan unveiled the EU's 'A Long-term policy for China' (Commission 1995; Shambaugh 1996). This trade-centred China policy was enlarged in 1998, 2001 and 2003 by EU policy documents to clarify EU political and human rights interests in China after intramural disagreements in 1996-97 (Commission 2003). Political and human rights policies towards China have witnessed a significant convergence of policies between Paris, Berlin, London and Brussels. French-inspired characterizations of the US as an '*hyper-puissance*' that needs to be balanced by other powers – in particular the EU, China and Russia – have updated the Gaullist perspective in which China is the most promising, if not sole rising power capable of challenging continued US hegemony in the 21$^{st}$ century (Védrine 1998; Brzezinski 2000). The rise of China fascinates many Europeans, recalling the Napoleonic prediction that 'when China awakes, the world will tremble' (Peyrefitte 1973, 1996; *Economist* 2000).

Some writers have scoffed at the idea of a credible EU policy in international politics, or even the existence of an EU policy at all (Bull 1983; Clapham 1999). Indeed it has been argued that the EU has so far failed to surmount the national reflexes of member states (especially Britain and France) with significant colonial histories in Asia in order to pursue a common and coherent strategy in China (Neves 1995). While some see the consolidation of Franco-German coordination as the foundation for a common EU policy in China, others argue that member states must surrender more authority and coordination power to a central authority, in particular the Commission (Nesshöver 1999: 95; Ferdinand 1995; Neves 1995).

## I. ECONOMIC RELATIONS

Trade is arguably the backbone of the EU-China relationship (Dent 1999). EU member states adopt a continuum of economic strategies to promote both their national and collective economic interests in China. They range from aggressively championing *national* industries, to partnerships with other EU states, to cooperating on a pan-*European* platform in the pursuit of economic goals.

On one end of the scale is the mercantilist strategy of pushing politically motivated *national* initiatives and large-scale *grands contrats* signed by governments. This has been the typical French approach – with varying degrees of success and often erratic results hostage to fluctuating political relations – since at least 1964 when Paris established full diplomatic relations with Beijing (Taube 2002). Politically motivated deals were the most effective means to 'get back into the game' in a command economy, and for a few years in the 1960s, this strategy worked. In 1981-83 under Mitterrand, French agricultural exports – primarily wheat – increased dramatically to constitute one-third of all French exports to China, but then collapsed to less than 2 per cent in 1984 (Taube 2002: 83). In 1996, President Chirac announced the ambitious goal of tripling the 2 per cent French share of China's trade to 6 per cent within ten years.[2] During a state visit to China in May 1997, Chirac brought with him some 200 French industrialists and CEOs. Beijing agreed to buy 30 new Airbuses worth $1.5 billion, and together with contracts on power stations and car production, the visit yielded $2 billion worth of contracts.

However, French government-led economic initiatives tend to be launched in fits and starts, and have failed to coax small and medium sized French enterprises to invest in China. Many smaller French businesses that ventured in soon after China's opening in 1978 discovered that China would first become a great exporting nation before being a market for luxury products such as cars, perfumes and wines, the products in which France is competitive By some estimates, only 5 per cent of the Chinese population is able to buy goods that are imported or produced by Sino-foreign joint-venture companies (Hubler and Meschi 2001: 158, 168; Chol 2002). Unlike British and German businesses which in the 1980s and 1990s made China a priority country in their international or at least regional (ie. Asian) strategies, French companies still prefer to locate and invest in Indochina. China is a second-tier recipient of French Foreign Direct Investment (FDI), receiving far less from France than from other EU member states, the US and even tiny Singapore (Dorient 2002: 188).

The German strategy is to adopt pragmatic policies that emphasize good political relations and ignore political or human rights differences. West Germany during the Cold War had concentrated its energies on building good economic relations with the People's Republic. This pragmatism can be traced to at least 1955 when despite the 'Hallstein doctrine' which refused diplomatic recognition to all states which recognized the German

---

[2] *Le Monde* (1996). The author's interviews with French Foreign Ministry officials in March 1996 and the Chinese Embassy in Paris in September 2000, confirmed the French determination to match the German presence in the China market.

Democratic Republic, the Federal Republic of Germany (FRG) established a trade office in China. This pragmatic economic policy soon paid good dividends. By 1966, the Federal Republic had become China's top European trading partner (Möller 1996: 708,712). In the 1980s, it was estimated that almost 50 per cent of the foreign technology imported into China came from the FRG (Kapur 1990: 185). In contrast to the state-led initiatives emanating from France, German business dealings in China have tended to be led by the private sector. The government plays the role of trade and investment facilitator rather than initiator.

Compared to France, the German state's support for German firms in China has been more sustained and less disrupted by bilateral political issues. The largest bilateral project in recent years has been the commercial use of the German-built Transrapid magnetic levitation train, a project which met stiff competition from Japanese and French rivals. The strong commitment of Chancellor Schröder and Premier Zhu Rongji was instrumental in this contract being awarded to Germany.[3]

Since the mid-1990s, Germany alone has accounted for nearly 40 per cent of total EU trade with China, over twice as much as Britain, China's second largest EU trading partner (Shambaugh 1996: 21). In 2004, Germany accounted for 41 per cent of the EU 25's total exports to China (Table 1). Germany's policy towards China since 1992 had been founded on three principles: silent diplomacy (hence no human rights confrontation); change through trade (encouraging political liberalization in China via economic development); and a strict 'one-China' policy (Nesshöver 1999: 95). The success of the 'German model' was evident in its enhanced trade position. German exports to China practically doubled between 1992 and 1994, from DM5.7 billion to DM10.2 billion. The UK (+71 per cent), Italy (+71 per cent), Netherlands (+146 per cent), Spain (+226 per cent) also witnessed significant export growth to China. In contrast, French exports only grew 22 per cent in the same period as a consequence of a diplomatic freeze between Paris and Beijing. Meanwhile, Germany systematically depoliticized economic relations with China. Germany recognized the significance of Asian new markets when EC trade with East Asia overtook EC-US trade for the first time in 1992, and took the lead in formulating its 'Asian policy' in October 1993. The central ideas of Germany's Asian policy were 'to strengthen economic relations with the largest growth region in the world', restore high level visits to Beijing and stop applying pressure on human rights (Nesshöver 1999: 9; Maull 1998: 194). In December 1993, Chancellor Kohl returned from a visit to China with a pile of contracts and letters of intent. A few months later, Bonn was the first Western capital to host a visit by Chinese Premier Li Peng, despite Li's close association with the Tiananmen crackdown.

Germany's economic success in China made an unmistakable impact on other EU member states' policies. The British Secretary for Trade and Industry Michael Heseltine visited China in 1994 accompanied by 130 businessmen (Cabestan 1995: 42). A joint Franco-Chinese communiqué was issued in January 1994 during Prime Minister Balladur's visit, which committed France to recognize one China and to refrain from selling new arms to Taiwan. The French Industry Minister Gérard Longuet followed this up by visiting Beijing and Hong Kong in mid-1994 to launch 'Ten initiatives for Asia'. China in the late 1990s became the developing world's top recipient of Foreign Direct Investment (FDI), and even

---

[3] Auswärtiges Amt (2004) claims that, 'as this example shows, strong state support continues to be an important factor in the success of German companies in China'. Available from: <http://www.auswärtiges-amt.de/www/en> [22 June 2004].

edged ahead of the United States as the world's top FDI recipient in 2002 ($53 billion; *Economist* 2003).

**Table 1. EU Trade with China (Percentage shares of largest EU Traders)**

|         | 1978 | 1988 | 1989 | 1992 | 1993 | 2004 |         |
|---------|------|------|------|------|------|------|---------|
| Germany | 52.1 | 41.1 | 35.6 | 42.7 | 43.0 | 40.9 |         |
| Italy   | 9.8  | 19.2 | 17.9 | 17.1 | 18.3 | 8.9  | Exports |
| UK      | 9.2  | 10.8 | 9.9  | 8.6  | 8.3  | 7.9  |         |
| France  | 10.4 | 13.7 | 22.5 | 16.1 | 11.9 | 12.5 |         |

|         | 1978 | 1988 | 1989 | 1992 | 1993 | 2004 |         |
|---------|------|------|------|------|------|------|---------|
| Germany | 30.2 | 31.9 | 33.7 | 38.5 | 40.1 | 22.0 |         |
| Italy   | 16.4 | 18.5 | 18.4 | 14.3 | 12.5 | 8.9  | Imports |
| UK      | 17.6 | 10.2 | 9.5  | 8.6  | 9.6  | 15.6 |         |
| France  | 18.6 | 18.7 | 18.8 | 18.0 | 17.7 | 9.2  |         |

Sources: Eurostat; Richard Grant 1995: 93; and Andreosso-O'Callaghan and Nicolas 2007: 37. NB: Figures for the UK above are artificially low as they exclude trans-shipment trade through Hong Kong.

Among EU member states, Britain and Germany have been the most bullish on China. Since 1999, Germany has been competing with the UK as Europe's largest investor, although both lie far behind Hong Kong, the US, Taiwan and even Singapore. German companies are strong in several sectors – notably in the chemicals industry and in luxury cars. In 2002, China overtook Germany's long-time partner Japan as Germany's most important export market in Asia (Auswärtiges Amt 2004).[4]

French governments have pushed to 'catch up with the Germans' and have tried copying the 'German Model' of strong economic and political relations with China. In 1995, Foreign Minister Hervé de Charette announced that Asia would receive special attention as the *'nouvelle frontière'* of French diplomacy. French leaders' visits to China began to take on a pattern of political dialogue on international developments, accompanied by announcements of contract signatures (Wong 2006: 65-76). The Department of External Economic Relations (DREE) in the French Finance Ministry increased the number of officials working in its East Asian departments; the Ministry also increased its activities promoting trade and spent much time consulting with Chinese and other Asian colleagues during the 1997-8 Asian crisis (Dorient 2002: 180-81).

## Playing the European Card

A third (and increasingly favoured) strategy is to use the 'European card' in economic dealings with China. Since 1985, the Commission has been the engine in developing various forms of economic cooperation between Western Europe and China. The EC-China Joint committee created by the 1978 bilateral agreement and affirmed in the 1985 EC-China Trade

---

[4] If trade with Hong Kong is included, this has been the case since 2000.

and Cooperation Agreement quickly became the most institutionalized component of the EC's interactions with China, with the Commission playing the role of intermediary.[5] The European Community as a whole witnessed a rapid expansion of relations with China in the 1980s.

Against the backdrop of China's phenomenal growth rates, the EC has emphasized commerce with China. This allowed for the EU's economic exchanges with China to continue growing despite the frequent political tensions between individual European actors (the Parliament, Britain and France in particular) through the 1990s (section II of this paper). The 1995 China strategy paper recognized the 'rise of China as unmatched amongst national experiences since the Second World War'. It followed on the Commission's 1994 'Towards a New Asia Strategy' initiative but placed even more attention on China as a 'cornerstone in the EU's external relations, both with Asia and globally' (Commission 1994, 1995). The 1994 and 1995 papers took very similar positions to those of Germany and Britain. All emphasized economic relations and looked upon China as a 'cornerstone' of the EU's 'New Asia Strategy'.

Negotiations following China's 1986 application to join the General Agreement on Trade and Tariffs (GATT)/World Trade Organization (WTO) (achieved in December 2001), further consolidated the Commission's role as the central actor in economic relations between Europe and China. Unlike the US, the EU was receptive to Chinese arguments to be treated as a developing economy and thus brokered China's agreement to accept commitments to an open market economy over a phased schedule. Based on objectives spelt out in the Commission's 1998 'Comprehensive Partnership' country strategy paper, then-External Trade Commissioner Pascal Lamy reached an agreement with China on its WTO accession on 19 May 2000. After years of intense negotiations, the member states succeeded in coordinating their efforts under Lamy to pry open protected sectors such as insurance, telecommunications, banking, aviation and infrastructure building - sectors in which European companies are strong (Le Monde 2000a). Despite the absence of a new TCA (stalled over China's objections to the inclusion of human rights conditionalities) to replace the 1985 Agreement, EU-China trade continued to expand at a spectacular pace, from €17 billion in 1990 and €70 billion in 1999, to over €174 billion in 2004 - total trade increased over forty-fold between 1978 and 2004 (Commission 2006). In 1999, the EU overtook Japan to become China's second largest export market. European companies invested US$4.5 billion in China in 1999, making the EU the largest foreign direct investor in China that year, and the second in 2000.

Overall EU economic policies in China are a blend of national and joint European policies. On one hand, member state governments promote their 'national champions' in Beijing. Yet since the 1985 EC-China TCA, they have uploaded their distinct policy preferences and used the Trade Commissioner as a cover to confront China over trade disputes ranging from textiles to car parts (Mandelson 2005; Straits Times April 10, 2006; Economist 2006; Andreosso-O'Callaghan and Nicolas 2007). Since the 1994 'New Asia Strategy' and slew of China policy papers (Commission 1995, 1998, 2001 and 2003), the member states have entrusted the External Trade Commissioner to conduct economic negotiations with China as a collective unit. They have uploaded to the Commission their individual preferences to tackle an ever-growing trade deficit with China. The convergence of member state and Commission economic policies was achieved only after a series of political

---

[5] A good account of this period is found in Kapur (1990: chapter 9 and 10).

frictions between China and individual EU states. These problems rallied them to an unanticipated level of cooperation in throwing their support behind the Commission so as to maximize their economic leverage as a trading superpower.

## II. POLITICAL AND STRATEGIC RELATIONS

Political relations between the EU as a unit and China are relatively new compared to the ties some member states enjoy with Beijing. This has often resulted in China adeptly 'dividing and ruling' between EU member states competing for political favour with Beijing.

Of all the EU member states Britain probably has the most developed and extensive ties with China. It fundamentally disagreed with the US policy of isolating the People's Republic between 1949 and 1971, and in 1950 was the first major Western country to recognize the People's Republic of China (PRC) (Shambaugh 1996). Hong Kong remains the most important political issue between London and Beijing. From 1979 to 1997, London-Beijing relations were dominated by negotiations and debates about the return of Hong Kong to Chinese sovereignty. Although both sides signed in December 1984 a Joint Declaration on the terms for the handover on 1 July 1997, the fallout from the Tiananmen incident in 1989 raised anxieties about the future of Hong Kong and the protection of its residents' freedoms and human rights. Diplomatic tensions concerning British policies in Hong Kong following the 1992 appointment of an activist Governor, Chris Patten, tended to disrupt otherwise good bilateral ties (Foreign and Commonwealth Office 2000: 10-11). Issues of contention included the new €10 billion airport at Chek Lap Kok (which won Chinese approval in 1991 after tortuous negotiations), the right of abode for Hong Kong residents in Britain, and Patten's moves to introduce political freedoms in a more democratic Legislative Council than what Beijing had envisaged in 1984 (Sandschneider 2002: 35-36; Yahuda 1993: 245-66).

When the Chinese government threatened in 1994 to discriminate against the British in trade matters because of Governor Chris Patten's 'unilateral actions' on constitutional reform in Hong Kong, the EU Trade Commissioner Sir Leon Brittan warned that the EU would not condone a member state being singled out in this way. Brittan's warning staved off Chinese action against the UK.[6]

The bilateral relationship improved after the 1997 handover and with a new British Labour government in power. The Chinese Premier Zhu Rongji made Britain his first stop in Europe when he attended the second Asia Europe Meeting (ASEM) summit (and inaugural EU-China summit) in London in 1998 - the first visit by a Chinese prime minister to Britain in 13 years. A comprehensive agreement was signed by Prime Ministers Zhu and Blair to intensify their political and military dialogues. Queen Elizabeth II visited China in 1999. The British Consulate-General in Hong Kong is the largest one in the world, and strong economic, academic, social and cultural ties persist between Britain and its former crown colony. Britain closely follows Hong Kong's autonomy as a Special Administrative Region (SAR) under the 'one country, two systems' formula. Even so, overall political relations have gradually been 'Europeanized'. The future of Hong Kong has since 1997 (and Macau since 1999)

---

[6] Maull (1998: 185). One retired senior Foreign and Commonwealth Office (FCO) official however estimated British losses in trade with China at £1-2 billion on account of wrangling over Hong Kong in 1992-96 (Craddock 1999: 281). France in 1991-92 (over Taiwan) and Denmark in 1997 (over human rights) were however singled out for retaliation.

increasingly become an *EU* issue rather than the preserve of a sole EU member state (Neves and Bridges 2000). Even Chris Patten, once the bane of Beijing, became 'Brusselsized' in his toned-down human rights criticisms of Beijing when he was External Relations Commissioner.

French relations with China have witnessed even more dramatic turns than London-Beijing ties. After 1949, Paris had recognized Chiang Kai-shek and not Mao Zedong as China's legitimate national leader (unlike Britain which recognized Mao and the PRC). The close links between France and Taiwan continued after Paris and Beijing established diplomatic relations in 1964. As the first major Western country to exchange ambassadors with China, France portrayed itself as laying the foundations for a special political relationship with China. In reality, there was no coherent French policy on China for 30 years. China was a low priority in French policy up to the 1980s, and the zigzags in the bilateral relationship were symptomatic of Paris' effective 'One China-One Taiwan' policy (Mengin 1994).

The Tiananmen massacre in June 1989 triggered a series of bilateral incidents culminating in a diplomatic freeze until 1994. French Socialist leaders reacted more emotionally and with less restraint than those of other Western democracies in their support for the Chinese student demonstrators.[7] Paris gave them a special place in the bicentennial Bastille Day parade, and even allowed them to set up the Federation for Democracy in China (Foot 2000: 117; Mengin 1994: 51-52). After Tiananmen, bilateral ties sank to an even more rancorous level from 1990 with the sale of six French Lafayette frigates to Taiwan (worth \$4.8 billion; Mengin 1992: 46; Wellons 1994: 345), and Taipei's 1992 purchase of 60 Mirage 2000-5 fighter jets. The Mirage sale plunged bilateral relations into a sharp and long-drawn dispute. Beijing retaliated by closing the new office of the French Consulate-General and Economic Expansion Office in Guangzhou, and cancelled several large French contracts in China.[8]

As a consequence of the 1990-92 spats over French arms sales to Taiwan, the French share of China's total trade declined as the Chinese took punitive measures against France. The economic consequences of Chinese reprisals contributed to a shrinking French share of the Chinese market. The French share of EU exports fell from 16 per cent to 12 per cent.[9] After full diplomatic relations were restored in 1994, Prime Minister Balladur made a fence-mending visit to Beijing. President Jiang Jemin's visit to France in September 1994 finally turned the corner when trade agreements worth \$2.5 billion were signed (Foot 2000: 159; Dorient 2002).

Yet while relations with China improved under the Presidency of Jacques Chirac since 1995, political problems related to Taiwan continue to dog France-China relations. After Paris approved the sale of an observation satellite by the French-British company Matra Marconi to Taiwan in 1999 over Chinese protestations, French companies were excluded from the public tender to construct a gas terminal in southern China. The Chinese were also unhappy with the high profile accorded to the Dalai Lama's visit to France in September 2000 (*Libération* 1999; *Le Monde* 2000b, 2000c; *Beijing Review* 2000).

---

[7] Peyrefitte (1997: 296) criticized Mitterrand's post-Tiananmen policy as based on the '*émotion du moment*'.
[8] The Balladur government estimated at FF3 billion the value of contracts lost during the 'freeze' in relations. The French employers' association put it at twice that value. See *Financial Times* (1994).
[9] According to Peyrefitte (1997: 301), the French share of China's total trade shrank from 4 per cent to 1.5 per cent while the West German share rose from 3 per cent to 5 per cent between 1981 and 1990.

## Silent Diplomacy and Constructive Engagement

In contrast to Britain and France, Germany has enjoyed a far less volatile political relationship with China. As a defeated Axis power, it had no outstanding colonial issues with China at the end of World War II, and no diplomatic relations with the Republic of China in Taiwan. On the international stage, Germany shied away from taking diplomatic initiatives, and usually took the cue from its major Western allies, e.g. the recognition of the PRC in 1972 which followed on Nixon's visit to China (Kempf 2002: 6-14; Rupprecht 2000: 63-69).

In the 1980s and 1990s, Kohl's Germany adopted a policy of 'silent diplomacy' which emphasized trade with China (Sandschneider 2002: 38-39; Nesshöver 1999). Although it supported the Madrid sanctions on post-Tiananmen China, Germany under Kohl continued 'business as usual' half a year later, breaking away from the economic sanctions before they were officially lifted in September 1990. Germany was the first EU country to define a national policy towards the Asia-Pacific region, and it made China the centre of its Asia policy. Among the large EU countries, Germany is probably the most sensitive to China's sense of 'face', and thus studiously avoids situations or actions that might be construed as high-handed by the leadership in Beijing. No wonder that the Germany-China relationship is often looked upon as a 'special' one (Cabestan 1995: 42-44; Möller 1996). Without the British and French problems over Hong Kong or Taiwan, Germany has usually backed down on issues involving Beijing's sense of sovereignty and national pride. For example, Kohl refused to approve the sale of 10 submarines and 10 frigates to Taiwan in January 1993 and reaffirmed Germany's 'One China' stance (Möller 1996: 720-723).

Gerhard Schröder continued to concentrate on promoting economic relations with China while paying some lip service to German foreign policy interests in areas such as human rights and environmental protection. In 2000, the German government had cancelled an export license for a German-made satellite to Taiwan following official protests during Chancellor Gerhard Schröder's visit to Beijing (*Libération* 2000). Germany has been active in promoting cultural exchanges with China. In 2000, there were more students from China (10,000) studying in Germany than there were from Poland or France, making them the largest group in Germany. The German Foreign Ministry's 2002 policy paper on East Asia admitted that while predictions in the 1990s of an 'Asian century' had been premature, the sum of the Asia-Pacific's nations, economic, political and market potential rendered it a more prominent feature in German foreign policy, 'though also as a rival and source of critical developments with possible world wide consequences'. It also recognized that regional realignments and power shifts after the 1997 Asian crisis and September 11, 2001, made it more incumbent on Germany to work through the *EU* and other organizations, to exercise German influence in countries such as China (Auswärtiges Amt 2002: 14).

Angela Merkel's first visit to China in May 2006 continued her predecessors' pattern of cosy relations with China and downplaying human rights, although she distanced herself from Schröder's controversial attempt to lift the China arms embargo (Eyal 2006).

The EU as a whole (like Germany) has enjoyed a less problematic relationship with China than have Britain or France. Since an EC Delegation was established in Beijing in 1988, a political dialogue set up in 1994, and an annual summit started with China in 1998 (regular ministerial level meetings began in 1995), the EU as an actor has begun to challenge the traditional dominance of London, Berlin and Paris in Europe's relations with China.

The Commission's activism in China has grown in line with its rising profile in Asia. The Commission's March 1998 'Comprehensive Partnership with China' initiative which envisaged a comprehensive partnership between the EU and China, aimed to upgrade political consultation to annual summits, dialogue on human rights, support for China's accession to the WTO, and the promotion of bilateral trade and investment. The ASEM process has facilitated regular high-level contacts between Chinese and European leaders. The Commission's support for ASEM's creation in 1996 could be seen as a consequence of the need to restate the EU's credentials as a stakeholder in the region and to engage China in a multilateral political framework. ASEM was also necessary to put life into the EU's relations with the region since the EC-Association of Southeast Asian Nations (ASEAN) relationship had ceased to be a 'success story' owing to deadlocked disagreements over human rights and conditionalities for a second-generation TCA (Forster 1999). ASEM II in April 1998 provided the occasion for the first EU-China summit (held in London immediately after ASEM II).

The EU also entered into strategic linkages with China, especially in aerospace cooperation projects. A joint Sino-European satellite navigation cooperation centre was opened in Beijing in February 2003 - the same year in which China became the third nation to send a man into space - and an agreement was reached in September committing China to finance up to €230 million or one-fifth of Galileo, the EU's €1.1 billion satellite positioning system which is seen as an alternative to the US' Global Positioning System (BBC 2003; *Le Monde* 2003a; Commission 2003: 17-20). The announcement of the Galileo decision made a positive prelude to the sixth EU-China summit the following month in Beijing, although human rights, market access and the EU's growing trade deficit with China continued to be niggling issues (*Le Monde* 2003b). Evidence that China has begun to take the EU seriously as an actor can also be found in the publication of the Chinese Foreign Ministry's s first-ever 'EU policy paper' in October 2003. The paper noted that the EU was an important international player in the trend towards multipolarity, and that the euro and the EU's expansion to 25 members in 2004 served to augment the EU's weight in international affairs. Although there were 'twists and turns' in China's relations with the EU, both were not security threats to each other, but shared fundamentally similar views and interests on trade and world order (Chinese Foreign Ministry 2003).

Notwithstanding the progress in EU-China relations in 2003-4, Taiwan, Tibet, trade and human rights issues continue to be frequent bones of contention. In 2003, the European Parliament's (EP) Liberal, Democrats and Reform (ELDR) Group attempted to invite Chen Shui-bian, Taiwan's President, to address the European Parliament in Brussels (France had refused to issue a visa for the address at the EP's building in Strasbourg).[10] However, Belgium caved in to Beijing's demands when the Chinese Embassy threatened that Belgium-Chinese relations could be 'set back 10 years' if the Belgian government proceeded to issue the visa to Chen. The decision to refuse the visa was then presented as a veto by the General Affairs Council (GAC), despite support from the Foreign Ministers of Belgium, Sweden and Denmark (Wong 2006: 50).

---

[10] The EU acknowledges Taiwan as a 'Separate Customs Union'. This de facto 'economic recognition' is based on the latter being among the EU's most important trade partners (larger than Australia or Canada). The Tibetan government-in-exile opened an office in Brussels in April 2001, and the Dalai Lama campaigns actively in Europe (Finland, Sweden, etc). Taiwan's accession to the WTO in January 2002 has also helped its external relations. See Wiessla (2002: 102-105).

In 2004-5, the EU found itself under a lot of pressure from the US when Paris and Berlin prematurely announced that the EU arms embargo on China – in place since 1989 – would soon be lifted. Although the US sells more weapons to China than all the EU members states combined (€416 in 2003), the EU's response on this issue was construed as a litmus test of loyalty by Washington. The resulting dissensions within the EU scuttled the lifting of the embargo, and instead intensified US-EU joint consultations and intelligence sharing on China (Barysch 2005: 62-64; Gompert et al. 2005; Godement 2005).

EU member states' political and strategic policies towards China show clearer evidence of convergence Europeanization than economic policies. Member states have not always held together, especially when in a face-off with Beijing over Taiwan, Tibet, human rights or the arms embargo. They have sometime allowed Beijing (and sometimes Washington) to 'divide and rule' when pursuing selfish national (essentially economic) interests. But as the increasingly regular and frequent attempts at coordination show, member states realize the need to harmonize their national policies in order to maximize their collective influence in such a large and populous country.

## III. HUMAN RIGHTS

Human rights can be considered a special component of the EU-China political dialogue. It has been a major theme of EU-China relations only since the Tiananmen Square crackdown in June 1989 (Commission 2004). Until the end of the Cold War, and apart from the Netherlands, Denmark and Sweden, few member states made human rights a major plank in their relations with China (Foot 2000: 48). Tiananmen politicized the Community approach to economic relations with China. For example, the Commission which had hitherto refrained from political comments, issued a statement expressing 'consternation' and 'shock' at the 'brutal suppression' in Beijing, and cancelled Foreign Trade Minister Zheng Tuobin's scheduled visit to Brussels (Shambaugh 1996: 11). The introduction of sanctions, human rights and the United Nations Commission on Human Rights (UNCHR) issues in EC-China relations shifted much of the discussions on China to the Council and CFSP structures.

From 1989 to 1997, the EU policy on human rights in China lay principally in (i) the sanctions policy (effectively lifted in October 1990), (ii) dialogue between individual EU governments and China, and (iii) holding China accountable in multilateral fora, in particular the UNCHR by annually co-sponsoring with the US a resolution criticizing China's human rights record. Some human rights activists consider this the most 'symbolically important' EU policy in monitoring and moderating human rights in China (Baker 2002; Human Rights in China 1998). The EC-12 held together in supporting most of these sanctions from June 1989 to October 1990, the date when most of the sanctions were lifted (except the ban on military sales – see Part II). The CHR approach was adhered to each year from 1990 to 1996 (except 1991 when the US, Britain and France sought China's vote in the Security Council to endorse allied action against Iraq in the Gulf War). Although the resolution was always defeated by a no-action motion (except in 1995), the move was politically symbolic and significant in underlining the EU's commitment each spring to improvements in China's human rights record.

China is considered 'the most complex and multifaceted dialogue on human rights' which the EU has with any country (Patten 2001). Although the EU has established an important human rights dialogue with China, it has suffered from conflicting interests and coordination problems between the General Affairs Council (GAC), the member states, the European Commission and the European Parliament (Commission 2001a: 11). As the shock of Tiananmen faded away, the GAC and larger member states have tended to pay lip service to human rights in order to cultivate good political and economic relations with Beijing.

The British, conscious that their influence in the Asian region since the military pullout from Singapore in 1971 could never be more than marginal, have found it prudent after the handover of Hong Kong to 'soft-pedal their interest in human rights and democratic principles' in order to maintain a working relationship with China (Martin and Garnett 1997: 38).

The French under a Socialist president (Mitterrand) initially took a high-profile principled position on human rights after Tiananmen, but piped down considerably after the Beijing-Paris spat over Taiwan arms sales. Under President Chirac, Paris made a dramatic volte-face shielding China's human rights record from EU and international scrutiny (notably at the 1997 CHR in Geneva). In 1997, Foreign Minister Hervé de Charette remarked that it was 'preposterous for the West, which invaded and humiliated China in modern times, to "lecture" China, a country with a 5000-year old civilization, on the Human Rights Declaration and the US Constitution, which are merely 200 years old' (*Beijing Review* 1997b).

The new French position was brought to bear at the 53rd UNCHR debate in April 1997 in Geneva. Unable to persuade its EU partners and the Dutch EU Presidency to drop the resolution criticizing China, France decided to withdraw its support from the ritual EU sponsorship of the resolution. Instead France led the 'Airbus group' (France, Germany, Italy and Spain) in defecting from the common position. It was left to Denmark to draft the resolution, and the US and 14 other Western countries to co-sponsor it. With the split in EU ranks, the vote was 27 in favour of China's no-action motion, 17 against and 9 abstentions, the most stunning repudiation of the UNCHR mechanism condemning China since the campaign started in 1990 (*Beijing Review* 1997a). The UNCHR débâcle was celebrated as a spectacular victory by Chinese diplomacy. Meanwhile France was heavily criticized by many Western governments for 'kowtowing to Chinese pressure', putting short-term national economic interests over collective long-term EU interests and hence undermining the EU's credibility and its own credentials as the birthplace of human rights (Wong 2006: 95). The stage was then set for Chirac's state visit to China in May 1997, where a France-China joint declaration was issued. On human rights, it declared that both parties would 'respect diversity' and take into account the 'particularities of all sides' (French Foreign Ministry 1997; *Beijing Review* 1997c).

After the French-led defection in 1997, a new European approach to human rights in China was decided by the General Affairs Council and codified in the Commission's March 1998 strategy paper, 'Building a Comprehensive Partnership with China'. The 14 March 1998 GAC meeting agreed that at the upcoming 1998 UNCHR session, the EU would 'neither propose nor endorse, either by the organization as a whole or by individual members' any resolution criticizing China. In effect, the French position had won the day and the 'hardliners' found themselves tied to an EU position projected by France. This Europeanized position *not* to co-sponsor (albeit with reservations expressed by the 'hardliners') the UNCHR resolution with the US has been reached at the Council each March since 1998. The

Council has typically agreed that the EU should adopt the following approach at the UNCHR on China (EU General Affairs Council 2001a, 2001b):

If the resolution is put to a vote, EU members of the Commission will vote in favour, but the EU will not co-sponsor; EU members will vote against a no-action motion, should one be presented, and the EU will actively encourage other Commission members to do likewise, since in the EU's view, the very notion of no-action is itself contrary to the spirit of dialogue (Wong 2006: 96).

Pressured by the pragmatic positions taken by Germany and France, most of the EU member states and the Commission had towards the end of the 1990s toned down their critiques of the Chinese government towards a coordinated but weak common position of 'constructive dialogue'. Aside from common actions taken under the CFSP and coordinated by the Commission, individual governments regularly raise human rights concerns in their discussions with Chinese leaders. For example, German statesmen continue to voice at the CHR and other fora concerns over human rights abuses in China. Foreign Minister Joschka Fischer mentioned China at the CHR in 1999 and 2002. The German Federal government and the Bundestag have also repeatedly called upon the Chinese government to enter into a dialogue with the Dalai Lama with a view to granting Tibet substantial autonomy, and to end the suppression of Tibetan culture and religion (Auswärtiges Amt 2002: 6).

In practice, the leading actor within the EU in promoting human rights in China has been the European Parliament. It has since 1987 made regular and public criticisms of the Chinese human rights record, especially on Tibet, arbitrary detention, capital punishment, religious and political freedoms. The GAC in May 1999 supported the EP's 1994 initiative to streamline a series of budget headings under a single chapter of the EU budget (B7-70) in the 'European Initiative for Democracy and Human Rights' (EIDHR). The EP's budgetary power over the EIDHR, gives it added oversight of the Community's external relations. The EP thus holds the Commission and GAC accountable for developments 'on the ground' for the continuation of the EU-China dialogue (Commission 2001b; EU Annual Report on Human Rights 1998/99: 24-25; 2002: 131).

Aside from its powers over external assistance, the EP has leveraged on the political prestige and international publicity it can confer on foreign personalities embodying human rights struggles. The EP infuriated the Chinese in 1996 when it awarded Wei Jingsheng – then China's most celebrated dissident – the Sakharov prize for Freedom of Thought (Nathan 1999: 155). Then it invited the Dalai Lama to address a session in Strasbourg in October 2001.

Dealing with China on the subject of human rights remains a bone of contention within the EU, between member states who prefer making China publicly accountable at international fora, and those who prefer silent diplomacy or constructive engagement. While France and the 'Airbus group' defied the EU common position in 1997, they were nonetheless constrained by the general EU consensus at the GAC that China's human rights record is in need of improvement. The convergence (or compromise) of the member states' human rights policies on China since 1998 has watered down the positions of some of the more hardline countries. A combination of the hard EP and Nordic governments' unilateral approaches combined with the conciliatory EU approach of 'constructive dialogue' pioneered by France and Germany, could be viewed as a way of engaging China through a mixture of negative measures and positive incentives (Alston 1999: 578-80).

# CONCLUSION

The utility and impact of EU institutions on national foreign policy behaviour towards China is more significant than is commonly imagined or admitted. Overall there is a more coordinated European position on China today compared to 1985. The policies of each of the member states have in effect undergone significant *convergence* with each other, as well as with the Commission.

Much of this trend towards convergence has been by default rather than design. First, Europe's influence and presence in China had been on a steady and rapid decline after 1945. Only Britain and France have some residual diplomatic influence in the '*grandes négotiations politiques*' (Domenach 1990: 242). Second, the EU's role and presence in China has grown. One may argue that in the 1990s, EU policy towards China has effectively been 'Germanized', in that Germany has succeeded in exporting its model of discreet diplomacy, change through trade and non-confrontation on human rights to the EU level. In other words, Germany has 'Europeanized' what was originally one member state's national China policy. This is most patent in the economics realm, where the issue of human rights has been de-linked from trade. What exists of EU policy in China continues to be dominated by Pillar I issues. China is the focal point in a region with which in 1991 the EC traded more than with North America for the first time (Maull 1998: 57).

Convergence was also evident in the political-diplomatic arena. This was the case in ASEM's genesis, where EU member states and the Commission between 1993 and 1995 agreed on the need to engage China in a political framework, and Asian states called on the EU to participate in a summit-level dialogue with East Asia in order to counterbalance perceived excessive US (and growing Chinese) influence in the region.

Even in the area of human rights, the common EU positions built from 1989 acted as a constraint and damper on the French-German-Italian-Spanish defection in 1997. In human rights, France may have defected from the specific agreed EU action of sponsoring a resolution at the CHR, but it had to redouble its efforts urging the Chinese government along other paths desired by the EU, e.g. signing onto the International Covenant on Civil and Political Rights (ICCPR), resuming the EU-China dialogue on human rights, and in 1998 agreeing to a common GAC position to vote in favour of a resolution on China (albeit one not sponsored by the EU).

The complexities and seemingly contradictory trends in the EU's policies towards China are better understood by taking into account the foreign policy Europeanization of EU member states. EU foreign policy outputs are the result of interactions and compromises between the EU's common positions (i.e. both Community and CFSP positions) and member states' national foreign policies. Over time, European foreign policy-makers can be expected to share even more coordination reflexes on foreign policy towards China. They have similar values and interests in China's economic development, diplomatic-military power, as well as its political and social evolution. Compared to recent US-Europe disagreements over Iraq and dealing with terrorism, EU member states' policies towards China have actually been steadily converging between themselves and diverging away from Washington's preferences. The ability of the EU 25 to stay the course of pursuing a distinct and independent policy towards China may well be a litmus test of the viability of a common EU foreign policy. Unlike the US, the EU does not view China as a strategic competitor. Its positions are closer to China on the need for multilateral global governance based on the United Nations and on international law. Both need to be more active in resolving conflicts such as those in the Middle East, as they depend on imported energy. In fact, China has been hoping to use the EU as a counter-weight to the US, in areas as diverse as trade, human rights and aerospace (*Far Eastern Economic Review* 2004; Wong 2006). While an 'EU-China axis' (Shambaugh 2004) may not be apparent, the relationship is no longer the 'secondary relationship' of the past.

# REFERENCES

Aggestam, L (2004) 'Role Identity and Europeanization of Foreign Policy: a Political-cultural approach', in: Tonra, Ben and Christiansen, Thomas (eds) *Rethinking European Union Foreign Policy*, Manchester: Manchester University Press, pp. 81-98.

Alston, Philip, (ed.) (1999) *The European Union and Human Rights*, Oxford: Oxford University Press.

Andreosso-O'Callaghan, B. and Nicolas, F. (2007) 'Complementarity and Rivalry in EU-China Economic Relations in the Twenty-First Century' *European Foreign Affairs Review* 12: 13-38.

Auswärtiges Amt (2002) *East Asia: Tasks of German Foreign Policy at the Beginning of the 21$^{st}$ century*, Berlin. Available from: <http: //www.auswärtiges-amt.de/www/en> [25 May 2004].

Auswärtiges Amt (2004) *Relations between the People's Republic of China and Germany.* Available from: <http: //www.auswärtiges-amt.de/www/en>. [22 June 2004].

Baker, Philip (2002) 'Human Rights, Europe and the People's Republic of China' *China Quarterly* 169: 45-63.

Barysch, Katinka, Grant, Charles and Leonard, Mark (2005) *Embracing the Dragon: The EU's Partnership with China*, London: Centre for European Reform.

Bâtie, Hervé Dejean de la (2002) *La politique chinoise de l'Union Européenne: en progrès, mais peut mieux faire*, Available from: <http: www.ifri.org/f/Centre%20asie/articles/hdb-ue-chine.htm> [9 May 2002].

*BBC news* (2003), 'China joins EU's satellite network', 19 September. *Beijing Review* (1997a), "Anti-China Attempts foiled in Geneva" 5-11 May.

*Beijing Review* (1997b), 'Chirac- A Statesman of Pragmatism and Vision', 26 May-1 June.

*Beijing Review* (1997c), 'China, France Sign Joint Declaration', 2-8 June.

*Beijing Review* (1998), 'European Union and China to Maintain long-term Cooperation', 2-15 February.

*Beijing Review* (2000), 'Jiang meets Chirac', 6 November.

Brzezinski, Zbigniew K. (2000) *The geostrategic triad: living with China, Europe, Russia*, Washington D.C.: Center for Strategic and International Studies.

Bull, Hedley (1983) 'Civilian Power Europe: A Contradiction in Terms?' *Journal of Common Market Studies* 21: 149-170.

Cabestan, Jean-Pierre (1995) 'Sino-Western European Relations: Distant Neighbours or Distant Rivals?' *China Review*, Autumn/Winter: 42-44.

Chinese Foreign Ministry (2003) *China's EU Policy Paper*, Beijing, 13 October.

Chol, Eric (2002) 'Chine: on s'est trompé d'eldorado' *L'Express* 2678, 31 Oct-6 Nov: 72-77.

Clapham, Andrew (1999) 'Where is the EU's Human Rights Common Foreign Policy, and How is it Manifested in Multilateral Fora?', in: Philip Alston (ed.) *The European Union and Human Rights*, Oxford University Press.

Commission of the European Communities (1994.) *Towards a New Asia Strategy*, COM (94)427, Brussels, 13 July.

Commission of the European Communities (1995) *A Long-term Policy for China-Europe Relations*, COM (95)279, 15 July.

Commission of the European Communities (1998) *Building a Comprehensive Partnership with China*, COM (98)181, 25 March.

Commission of the European Communities (1999) Press Conference by Chris Patten, EU Commissioner for External Relations, Brussels, DOC/99/18, 16 December.

Commission of the European Communities (2001a) *EU Strategy towards China: Implementation of the 1998 Communication and Future Steps for a more Effective EU Policy*, COM (2001)265 final, 15 May.

Commission of the European Communities (2001b) *The EU's role in Promoting Human Rights and Democratisation in Third Countries*, COM (2001)252 final, 8 May.

Commission of the European Communities (2003) *A Maturing Partnership: Shared Interests and Challenges in EU-China Relations*, COM(2003)533 final, 10 September.

Commission of the European Communities (2004) *The EU's China Policy*. Available from: <http: //europa.eu.int/comm/external_relations/china/intro /index.htm> [22 June].

Commission of the European Communities (2006) *The EU's Relations with China*. Available from: <http://ec.europa.eu/comm/external_relations/china/ intro/index.htm> [1 September].

Craddock, Percy (1999) *Experiences of China*, new edition, London: John Murray.

Dent, Christopher M. (1999) *The European Union and East Asia: An Economic Relationship*, London: Routledge.

Domenach, Jean-Luc (1990) 'La Politique française au miroir de l'Asie', in: La Serre, Leruez and Wallace (eds) *Les politiques étrangères de la France et de la Grande Bretagne depuis 1945*, Paris.

Dorient, René (2002) 'Un septennat de politique asiatique: quel bilan pour la France?' *Politique Etrangère* 1/2002, Spring:173-188.

Dyson, K. and Goetz, K.H. (eds) (2003) *Germany, Europe and the Politics of Constraint*, Oxford, New York: Oxford University Press.

*Economist* (2000) 'Hubert Védrine, France's voice in the world', 11 November: 74.

*Economist* (2003) 'Special Report on China's Economy', 15 February.

*Economist* (2006) 'China: Struggling to keep the lid on', 27 April.

Edmonds, Richard Louis (2002) *China and Europe Since 1978: A European Perspective* (from *China Quarterly* 169. Special issue), New York: Cambridge University Press.

European Union, *Annual Report on Human Rights*, 1998.

European Union, *Annual Report on Human Rights*, 1999.

European Union, *Annual Report on Human Rights*, 2002.

European Union, *Annual Report on Human Rights*, 2003.

EU General Affairs Council (2001a) *Human Rights - Conclusions*, General Affairs Council 2338th Council meeting, Brussels, 19 March.

EU General Affairs Council (2001b) *China: EU-China Dialogue on Human Rights*, General Affairs Council 2327th Council meeting, Brussels, 22-23 January.

Eyal, Jonathan (2006) 'Merkel shows China it's not business as usual' *Straits Times*, 25 May.

*Far Eastern Economic Review* (FEER) (2001) 'EU In, U.S. Out', 7 June.

*Far Eastern Economic Review* (FEER) (2004*)* 'Sino-European Relations: It's more than love', 12 February: 26-29.

Ferdinand, Peter (1995) 'Economic and Diplomatic Interactions between the EU and China', in: Richard Grant (ed.) *The European Union and China*, pp.26-40.

*Financial Times* (1994), "Paris tries to melt Beijing ice", 7 April.

Foot, Rosemary (2000) *Rights Beyond Borders: The Global Community and the Struggle over Human Rights in China*, Oxford: Oxford University Press.

Foreign and Commonwealth Office (2000) *China: General Background Brief*, London, April.

Forster, Anthony (1999) 'The European Union in South-East Asia: Continuity and Change in Turbulent Times' *International Affairs* 75(4): 743-58.

French Foreign Ministry (2003) *Déclaration conjointe Franco-chinoise pour un Partenariat Global*, Pékin, 16 May.

Ginsberg, R.H. (1999) 'Conceptualising the European Union as an International Actor: Narrowing the Capability-Expectations Gap' *Journal of Common Market Studies*, 37(3): 429-454.

Godement, François (2004) 'Europe's China-Play: An uneasy EU, juggling human rights and business interests, may lift its arms embargo against China' *YaleGlobal*, 6 December.

Godement, François (2005) 'Europe's Second Thoughts on China Embargo: Trouble over planned arms sales may eventually result in closer US-European coordination' *YaleGlobal*, 25 March.

Gompert, D.C., Godement, François, Madeiros, Evan S., and Mulvenon, James C., (2005) *China on the Move: A Franco-American Analysis of Emerging Chinese Strategic Policies and Their Consequences for Transatlantic Relations*, Washington DC: RAND.

Grant, Richard (ed.) (1995) *The European Union and China: A European Strategy for the Twenty-First Century*, London: Routledge/RIIA.

Hill, Christopher (1993) 'The Capability-Expectations Gap, or Conceptualising Europe's International Role' *Journal of Common Market Studies* 31(1): 306-328.

Hill, Christopher and Wallace, William (1996) 'Introduction: actors and actions', in: C. Hill (ed.) *The Actors in Europe's Foreign Policy*, London: Routledge, pp.1-16.

Human Rights in China (HriC) Report (1998) *From Principle to Pragmatism: Can 'Dialogue' improve China's Human Rights Situation?*, June.

Hubler, J. and Meschi, PX (2001) 'European direct investment in China and Sino-French joint ventures' *Asia Pacific Business Review* 17(3): 157-180.

*International Herald Tribune (IHT)* (2005) 'EU stance on China arms stirs 3 nations', 4 March.

Kapur, Harish (1990) *Distant Neighbours: China and Europe*, London: Pinter Publishers.

Kempf, Gustav (2002) *Chinas Außenpolitik: Wege einer widerwillingen Weltmacht*, Munich: Oldernbourg.

*Le Monde* (1996), 'Jacques Chirac veut tripler le commerce de la France avec l'Asie', 1 March.

*Le Monde* (2000a), 'Quand la distribution française fait son marché en Asie', 26 February.

Le Monde (2000b), 'Nouveau coup de froid franco-chinois, 23 October.

Le Monde (2000c), 'Jacques Chirac, en voyage officiel en Chine, évite de justesse les écueils diplomatiques', 24 October.

*Le Monde* (2003a) 'La Chine s'associe au projet Galileo et sort de son isolement', 27 September.

*Le Monde* (2003b) 'L'Union européenne relativise ses divergences avec la Chine au nom du pragmatisme', 31 October.

*Libération* (1999), 'Ire chinoise pour un satellite français', 24 December.

*Libération* (2000), 'Pékin ne digère pas le satellite', 23 October.

Major, C. (2005) 'Europeanization and Foreign and Security Policy: Undermining or Rescuing the Nation State?' *Politics* 25(3): 175-190.

Mandelson, Peter (2005)'Challenges and opportunities for EU and China in the age of Globalisation', *SPEECH/05/484*, Beijing, 6 September.

Martin, Lawrence and Garnett, John (1997) *British Foreign Policy: Challenges and Choices for the 21st century*, London: Royal Institute of International Affairs.

Maull, H., Segal, G. and Wanandi, J. (eds) (1998) *Europe and the Asia Pacific*, London: Routledge.

Mengin, Françoise (1994) 'Relations France-Chine, quel anniversaire s'agit-il de célébrer?' *Rélations Internationales et Stratégiques* 14, été : 29-34.

Mengin, Françoise (1992) 'The Prospects for France-Taiwan Relations' *Issues and Studies* 28(3): 40-58.

Miskimmon, A. and Paterson, W.E. (2003) 'Foreign and Security Policy: On the cusp between Transformation and Accommodation', in: K. Dyson and K.H. Goetz (eds) *Germany, Europe and the Politics of Constraint*, Oxford, New York: Oxford University Press, pp. 325-345.

Möller, Kay (1996) 'Germany and China: A Continental Temptation' *The China Quarterly* 147, September: 706-725.

Nathan, A.J. (1999) 'China and the International Human Rights Regime', in: Elizabeth Economy and Michael Oksenberg (eds) *China Joins the World: Progress and Prospects*, New York: Council on Foreign Relations, pp.136-160.

Nesshöver, Christoph (1999) 'Bonn et Paris face à Pékin (1989-1997): vers une stratégie commune?' *Politique Etrangère* 1/99.

Neves, Miguel S. (1995) 'Towards a Common China Policy for the EU: a Portuguese Perspective', in Richard Grant (ed) *The European Union and China*, London: Routledge, pp.75-88.

Neves, Miguel S. and Bridges, Brian (eds) (2000) *Europe, China and the two SARs: Towards a New Era*, London: Macmillan Press.

Patten, Chris (2001) 'China's candidature for hosting the Olympic Games in 2008' Commission statements in urgency debates, by External Relations Commissioner in the European Parliament, Plenary Session, Strasbourg, SPEECH/01/33, 5 July.

Peyrefitte, Alain (1973) *Quand la Chine s'éveillera...le monde tremblera*, Paris: Fayard.

Peyrefitte, Alain (1996) *La Chine s'est éveillée*, Paris: Fayard.

Rupprecht, K. (2000) 'Germany's Policy towards China and the SARs of Hong Kong and Macau', in: Miguel S. Neves and Brian Bridges (eds) *Europe, China and the two SARs*, London: Macmillan, pp.63-69.

Sandschneider, Eberhard (2002) 'China's Diplomatic Relations with the States of Europe' *China Quarterly* 169: 33-44.

Shambaugh, D. (1996) *China and Europe 1949-1995*, London: Contemporary China Institute, SOAS.

Shambaugh, D. (2004) 'China and Europe – the emerging axis' *Current History*, September.

*Straits Times* (2006) 'China agrees to talks on car parts', 10 April.

Taube, Markus (2002) 'Economic Relations between the PRC and the States of Europe' *China Quarterly* 169, March: 78-107.

Tonra, Ben and Christiansen, Thomas (eds) (2004) Rethinking *European Union Foreign Policy*, Manchester: Manchester University Press.

Tsardanidis, C. and Stavridis, S. (2005) 'The Europeanization of Greek Foreign Policy: A Critical Appraisal' *European Integration* 27(2): 217-239.

Védrine, Hubert (1998) 'De l'utilité de la France' *Politique Internationale* 78 : 41-64.

Wellons, Patricia (1994) 'Sino-French Relations: Historical Alliance vs. Economic Reality' *The Pacific Review* 7(3): 341-348.

Wong, Reuben (2005) 'The Europeanization of Foreign Policy', in: C. Hill and M. Smith (eds) *The International Relations of the European Union*, Oxford University Press, pp. 134-153.

Wong, Reuben (2006) *The Europeanization of French foreign policy: France and the EU in East Asia*, Basingstoke and New York: Palgrave Macmillan.

Wong, Reuben (2007) 'Foreign Policy', in: P. Graziano and M. Vink (eds) *Europeanization: New Research Agendas*, Basingstoke and New York: Palgrave Macmillan, pp.321-334.

Wiessala, G. (2002) *The European Union and Asian Countries*, London: Sheffield Academic Press/UACES.

Yahuda, M.B. (1993) 'Sino-British negotiations: perceptions, organization and political culture' *International Affairs* 69(2), April: 245-66.

Yahuda, M.B. (1994) 'China and Europe: The Significance of a Secondary Relationship', in: T.W. Robinson and D. Shambaugh (eds) *Chinese Foreign Policy: Theory and Practice*, Oxford: Clarendon Press.

In: Asian Economic and Political Development
Editor: Felix Chin

ISBN: 978-1-61122-470-2
© 2011 Nova Science Publishers, Inc.

# PUBLIC PARTICIPATION, DELIBERATION AND REGIONAL IDENTIFICATION: EUROPEAN CONSTITUTIONAL PROCESS IN COMPARATIVE PERSPECTIVES

*Wang Zhanpeng*
School of English and International Studies,
Beijing Foreign Studies University

## ABSTRACT

The article departs from some theoretical hypotheses of deliberative democracy to explore the relationship between deliberation, identity construction and democratic legitimacy in the process of regional integration. The ongoing constitutional process in Europe is employed as a case to provide some empirical evidence for the study. Current literature suggests that certain elements of deliberative politics can be found in the constitution-making process in Europe. However, the constitutional crisis following the negative referendums in France and the Netherlands in spring 2005, demonstrates that this deliberative or quasi-deliberative process is a limited, even flawed process given the power-political constraints. Furthermore, it confirms that the European project, designed by its elites, has to find ways to accommodate the diverse interests of various social groups and to construct a more inclusive European identity. Moreover, this article offers a study of the emerging regionalism in East Asia so as to provide a comparative perspective that explores inspiration and wisdom, indeed lessons, from the European experience. In spite of some empirical and methodological imperfections in the study, the author argues that Europe's constitutional experience is relevant for East Asia in several ways. First, the deliberative spirit in the European experience can provide some philosophical or moral inspiration for East Asia. Second, deliberation may play some complementary role in enhancing the construction of regional identity in East Asia although it may be a very limited, incremental one in a foreseeable future. Third, the constitutional debate in Europe may help East Asian people understand the limits of the deliberative approach. In the current global and regional systems, the wisdom of the postmodernists cannot go beyond the boundaries of power-political constraints.

# INTRODUCTION

In recent years, the spread of regionalism throughout the world has posed a great challenge to the traditional notion of democratic governance based on national territories. The decision making in a regional institution has long been considered to be a bargaining process between the self-interested governments of its member states. However, as integration processes widen and deepen, people have begun to ask about the intrinsic democratic question in these arrangements. Underlying the debate is the lack of a well-developed regional identity which constitutes a bottleneck for the progress of regional integrations.

As 'deliberative turn' emerged in the landscape of political science in the 1990s (Dryzek 2004: 48-50), the renewal of some classical political thoughts has evoked the dichotomy between 'the judicial order of the political community and the cultural, historical and geographical order of national identities' (Lacroix 2002: 945). In recent years, this approach is extended to the debate on the legitimacy and political identities in the unprecedented integration efforts in Europe.[1] Some research findings demonstrate that moderate deliberative elements and their 'legitimating effects' exist in certain phases of the European constitutional process (Shaw 2003: 45-68; Magnette 2004: 207-247; Von Bogdandy 2004). However, the failures of the European constitution in France and Netherlands (through their negative referendums in spring 2005) have made it imperative for us to reconsider some deeper issues underlying the European and other regional integrations in a broader context.

In the studies of comparative regionalism, there has long been an ardent debate over whether the European Union (EU) represents a paradigm for other regions. Since the 1997-98 Asian Financial Crisis, the East Asian integration has greatly accelerated, which offers an opportunity for fostering a new collective regional identity. In this process, public participation or even deliberation may be involved for its long-term viability. There is no doubt that Europe currently stays at a much higher stage of regionalism than East Asia. For many scholars, 'Europe's immediate past is not Asia's immediate, or indeed long-term future' (Higgott 2006: 35-36; see also Breslin and Higgott 2000). Can the policy-makers and academia in East Asia learn some lessons or obtain inspiration from the controversial constitutional process in Europe? In spite of the great difficulty for analogy, a comparing and contrasting the European experience with East Asia's realities may provide us some instructive lessons on the necessity, nature, as well as limits of democratic participation or deliberation in the emerging regional integration in East Asia.

# SOME BASIC ASSUMPTIONS ON THE DELIBERATIVE APPROACH

## Deliberation: A Dichotomy between Liberal and Republican Democracy

Modern political theory on democracy contains rich traditions of liberalism/pluralism and republicanism. As a conventional explanatory paradigm, the liberal/pluralist views have long

---

[1] Habermas' constitutional patriotism has become a dominant model in understanding the political identities in European integration. See Habermas (2001: 5-26). For a good survey about Habermas' view on European integration, see Eriksen and Weigard (2003: 232-260).

dominated the discourse in political science. The political scientists in this school hold that political legitimacy stems from the free, private voting of individuals. Thus a set of formal voting arrangements are vital to the legitimacy of political institutions. The logic of the notion is based on the theories of rational choice, which argue that best outcome in the political arena can only be achieved through the compromises and free choice of individuals in the formal election process.

However such a utilitarian approach has been challenged by political theorists in the Republican tradition. For them, voting itself is insufficient; more important is citizens' participation in formal and informal discussions about the common good for the society. Moreover, such participation can be meaningful and effective only when it involves not only rights and justice, but also virtues and common interest (Sandel 1996:25-26; Michelman 1998: 281-84).

In this context, deliberative democracy has been influential in recent years. According to some political theorists, such as Jon Elster and John Dryzek, 'citizens' participation in genuine deliberation constitutes the core of democratic legitimacy' (Dryzek 2004: 51). Unlike the liberalist bargaining mechanism in which self-interested actors with fixed preferences will reach agreement through rational choice and compromises, deliberation means a process of argument, reason-giving, and compromises among equal, free individuals. In the process, some citizens may change their preferences because they are persuaded or convinced by others. Hence, this approach leaves more room to accommodate moral or ethical considerations in the policy making process of a political community (Eriksen, and Weigard 2003: 121-22).

Although such a deliberative model is theoretically desirable, critics have raised some questions about its feasibility. Empirically the pure deliberation in the republican sense only existed in ancient Greek city states with their much smaller geographical space and population. In fact, most contemporary theorists agree that the role of deliberation is to complement the existing formal voting arrangements, rather than to replace them.

## Deliberation and Regional Identification: Theorizing the EU Experience

As a traditional model of understanding domestic politics, how and why is the deliberative approach relevant for regional integration? The answer largely rests on its potential role in promoting regional identification. The emerging regionalism, particularly in Europe, has created a number of innovations not only in its market regulatory competence but also in redistributive and normative spheres. As regional integration widens and deepens, it is necessary for the regional community to establish a collective identity, i.e. a sense of belonging among individuals. Since the rise of nationalism in the late medieval ages, the common historical and cultural feelings in almost all regions have been weakened or given way to the efforts of consolidating identities of nation states. European integration can be seen as a revival of the conscious construction of regional identities. People in other regions have also been increasingly aware that overlapping identities, namely a combination of national, regional and global identities, are more and more viable and desirable in a highly interdependent world. However, rebuilding certain feelings of belonging, which are usually based on common ethnic and historical experience as well as common language, will be a long process that will last for centuries. A more feasible solution to the current deadlock appears to lie in a dissociation of ethic/historical/cultural identities and other forms of identities (e.g. economic, political, legal, and institutional ones).[2]

Inspired by the ancient Greek conception of demos and ethos, Weiler refutes the notion that the absence of a European Demos precludes democratization of the Union, but argues for a notion of regional community in which each individual may belong to 'multiple demoi' defined in different ways. Thus, the future of regional identification may rest on the coexistence of a regional, civic, and value-driven demos with a national-cultural one. In the words of Weiler (1995):

> 'Maybe the in-reaching national-cultural demos and the out-reaching supranational civic demos by continuously keeping each other in check offer a structured model of critical citizenship'.

In the debate on the European constitutional treaty, he further points out how such multi demoi may be produced in the European context: 'in many instances, constitutional doctrine presupposes the existence of that which it creates: the demos which is called upon to accept the constitution is constituted, legally by the very constitution, and often that act of acceptance is among the first steps towards a thicker social and political notion of constitutional demos' (Weiler 2002: 567). The deliberative elements in the constitutional process will provide a potential opportunity to construct such a collective identity and constitutional demos.

Habermas' constitutional patriotism, a more influential notion in this strand, further stresses the importance of values and constitutional principles a political order (or a constitution) represents in this identification process. The existence of universal values or principles may serve as the premise for decoupling individuals' political allegiance and cultural affinity in the community. Since differences in interests among various social groups are unavoidable realities in both domestic and international communities, the formation of political culture which is made in public spheres through communicative actions becomes a key factor in Habermas' theoretical construction. This deliberative process may help form a new inclusive identity based on universalistic principles. In recent years, Habermas put forward the concept of a world domestic policy. Well aware of the great constraints in the anarchical world system, he suggests that regional institutions have the potentials to serve as a middle ground between nation states and world government. Moreover, the EU may be seen as a good example of a world domestic policy where Europeans are trying to implement the values of justice and solidarity in the times of globalization (Telò and Magnette 2001: 87-89). In his recent works, Habermas explicitly sees the EU constitution as a project to realize his blueprint for a global domestic policy at the regional level. He maintains that the European constitution will produce great 'catalytic' effect on collective European identity formation. It will also help create a public sphere and shared common political culture in Europe:

> We should not forget, however, that this convergence in turn depends on the catalytic effect of a constitution. This would have to begin with a referendum, arousing a Europe-wide debate – the making of such a constitution representing in itself a unique opportunity of transnational communication, with the potential for a self-fulfilling prophecy (Habermas 2001: 16-17).

---

[2] For a good discussion on different types of regional identities, see Mayer and Palmowski (2004: 573-98).

In many cases, regional governance is confronted with the following dilemma: on the one hand, governance at transnational level is often labelled as a 'government without democracy'; on the other hand, a region-wide direct election for a full legislative body is still far from feasible. Deliberation for its flexibility and fluidity has the potential to become a middle ground.

As Habermas observes, a model for world governance should be 'intergovernmental bargaining complemented with new governance structures and deliberation in a transnational civil society', which can be 'an alternative to a world government' (Eriksen and Weigard 2003: 251). In this sense, this deliberation cannot be seen merely as procedural matters, but able to accommodate substantive, or ethical/moral considerations (Gutmann and Thompson: 31-33). This is particularly an urgent task when the welfare state is confronted with the threat of neo-liberalism in the process of globalization. On a regional level, deliberation has the potential to curb the negative impact of globalization, for it may make working people's voices better heard by elites. Among a group of people who are directly affected by a particular policy, this may complement the intergovernmental bargaining. Theoretically this bottom-up approach may be effective in certain areas that affect people's rights and well-being. If such consensus can be achieved, it will in turn increase the legitimacy of policy making. However, how can people from different nations establish an effective mechanism in which individuals can make compromises between their normative values and self-interests, particularly when their interests are highly divergent? How can members of the community be persuaded to give up their preferences when their interests are in conflict with universal values? These are some crucial questions the advocates of the deliberative democracy must answer.

## Deliberation (or Quasi-Deliberation) under Real-World Constraints: Necessity and Limits

The driving force behind the deliberative turn in Europe is not idealism, but the actual needs in the development of European regionalism. The introduction and extension of Qualified Majority Voting (QMV) in most policy areas have greatly enhanced the autonomy of the supranational institutions within the EU. Nevertheless, the question of democratic legitimacy arises. For intergovernmentalists, global or regional organizations are inherently unable to adopt direct democratic deliberation in decision making (Dahl 1999: 19-36). They argue that even for the EU polity, indirect legitimacy is adequate as long as the governments of the member states are all democratically elected, its competence clearly defined and supranational institutions confined to specified areas in strict terms (Moravcsik 2004: 348-361; Magnette 2003: 4). This line of explanation has at least two defects. First, if an elected government of a member state belongs to the minority in the Council, it usually has to accept the EU legislation at the expense of the will of its voters. Second, political elites and general public, in many cases, do not converge in their wills and interests. Therefore, it is desirable that the decisions in certain policy areas (e.g. monetary policy and working place standards) that directly affect people's well-being require more public participation at transnational level. The problem may be addressed separately within specific policy areas. However, the institutional inertia on both the national and European levels has made real change rather difficult. In this sense, a comprehensive arrangement or a region-wide debate on it might become a catalyst for increasing public interest and participation in regional affairs.

The driving force behind the constitutional experiment in Europe also comes from certain practical considerations. In recent years, the Intergovernmental Conference (IGC), as the orthodox treaty revision method, has been widely criticized for its 'inadequacy and inefficiency', or even for being a 'bad, exclusive, malfunctioning' method (Shaw 2003: 54); more IGCs have been convened with limited outcome. At the opening of the IGC in Luxembourg in 1989 Jacques Delors remarked optimistically that 'conferences like this one are not convened every five or ten years, there may not be another between now and 2000'.[3] However, there were at least three IGCs during that period. It is also the case for the Nice Treaty. When the Nice treaty was waiting for the results of national ratifications, the constitutional Convention and subsequent IGC were put on the agenda. Critics argue that the notion of governmental representatives with a clear national preference in their minds is only a myth, and that what the exhausted ministers can do at the IGCs is merely to make limited, muddling compromises at the last moment (Smith: 219-225). The Nice treaty, aimed at completing the Amsterdam IGC's unfinished work, is widely considered as another failure. Only a few months after it came into effect, its contentious institutional arrangements became a burden in the negotiations for the constitutional treaty.

However, even within the EU, the deliberative approach cannot escape real-world constraints. In the anarchical international (or regional) system today, states remain territorially sovereign and legally empowered to act on behalf of their societies. Ordinary citizens do not have much access to decision-making on foreign policies. The question of feasibility will arise when the model is applied to regional governance. The obstacles include sovereignty concerns, a gap in economic interests, geographical and cultural diversity, and difficulty in mobilizing the general public.

Currently the EU is still characterized by its in-betweenness, unlikely to become a federal state in the near future. This ambivalence is highlighted by the fact that the first proposed European constitution takes the name of a constitutional treaty. That means that the draft constitution for Europe will be closer to a public international law than a constitutional law (Weiler 2002: 565-566). The on-going constitutional process also indicates that the deliberative elements are rather weak, limited ones, which may be termed as a 'quasi-deliberation' with low public participation and heavy dependence on political elites. At the current stage, a more realistic choice is to increase policy openness and encourage public participation on the European level. Whether it can develop into a sufficient, full deliberation in the long run largely depends on the interactions among all the actors concerned.

## THE CASE OF EUROPEAN CONSTITUTION

Judged by the widely accepted criteria of modern constitutionalism, the EU has already had some constitutional features for its separation of powers, adherence to the rule of law and the protection of fundamental rights in its founding treaties. However, as a political community, what it lacks is the existence of constitutional 'demos' in Weiler's terms (2002: 565-569), or sufficient identity-construction, which may need to 'take generations and civil

---

[3] Quoted from Gazzo (1986: 23).

wars to be fully internalized'. Currently, any move towards a European constitution is unlikely to be a perfect match with a national constitution. In spite of these limitations, the proponents of the project see the constitutional process as a great chance to advance their causes.

As discussed above, constitutional patriotism in a transnational context means a kind of regional identification through the construction of universal values and principles. As Ferrajolis (1996: 157) put it, the constitution is 'the sole democratic foundation of the unity and cohesion of a political system', and that 'the future of Europe as a political entity depends to a great extent on developing a constituent process open to public debate, aimed at framing a European constitution.' Hence the deliberative method often adopted in a national constitution-making becomes necessary in the European constitutional experiment. For a long time, constitutional patriotism was criticized as utopian thinking partially for the lack of a real European constitution. In 2001, the Laeken Declaration marked an operative stage for EU's long debated constitution-making. This on-going process provides us with some valuable empirical facts in understanding the complicated relationship between public participation, deliberation, and EU's identity construction.

## THE EUROPEAN CONVENTION[4]

In the Laeken European Council, the national leaders deliberately innovated the Convention on the future of the Union to meet the democratic challenge that came both internally and externally.[5] The subsequent institutional arrangements, known as the 'Convention method', carried some important deliberative characteristics. First, unlike the traditional IGC, the 105 formal representatives were from both national and European levels, over 70 per cent of whom were directly elected members of national and European parliaments, while members from national governments accounted for only 27 per cent. In addition, 13 observers from different regions and groups attended the Convention. The participants represented interests of national or transnational groups, rather than the presupposed single national interest.

Second, the Convention commanded a good deal of institutional autonomy (Shaw 2003: 55). The Laeken Declaration set the goals and time for the Convention in general terms, but left some room for the Convention to adopt its own agenda and rules of procedure.

Third, during the Convention, its members, particularly its chairman, Giscard d'Estaing, tried to preserve a 'deliberative spirit' in rhetoric at least. His coinage of 'conventionnels', or 'conventioneers', was a good example. In an interview, he claimed that he did not like the term 'representatives' but 'conventionnels' which has fewer implications for their national or institutional connections (d'Estaing 2002a). In his introductory speech, d'Estaing (2002b: 8) asked the members of the conference to 'embark on our tasks without perceived ideas and form our vision of the new Europe by listening constantly and closely to all our partners…members of associations and civil society represented in the forum…'.

---

[4] For the basic information about the Convention, see the relevant materials from its official website http://european-convention.eu.int/.

[5] According to the Declaration, internally the EU institutions must be brought closer to its citizens, and externally it is confronted with a fast-changing, globalized world.

Fourth, the Convention took consensus rather than formal voting as its major decision-making procedure. Consensus is not only the procedure of deliberative democracy but also its ideal objective. Through such procedures, its members may do more to justify their proposals, and persuade others to accept right decisions. If broad consensus could be reached, the decisions would carry more weights in the eyes of public and thus enhance their legitimacy.

Although the Convention is criticized for being merely a case for deliberation among elites, some measures it took increased public accessibility and participation, and facilitated some transnational discussion though their impact was rather limited. For instance, all its official documents were available on its website (with average of 47,000 visitors per month); the Forum for the civil society received 1,264 contributions from Non-Governmental Organizations (NGOs), the business community, academia and others; finally there was a special session devoted to civil society convened in June 2002.[6]

In spite of these deliberative characteristics in the objectives and procedures of the Convention, we should not idealize or overestimate its importance. First in its representation, most of the representatives were officials or ex-officials of national politics, while influence of civil society was rather limited. There is an obvious 'gap between the types of moves which the Convention has made towards receptiveness ... and the creation of a genuine public sphere in relation to the politics of the EU' (Shaw 2003: 66).

Another problem with the Convention was the poor public knowledge. *Eurobarometer* results showed that the 'Yes' responses to the question on the knowledge of the Convention accounted for only 28 per cent and 48 per cent respectively in 2001 and 2002 (European Commission 2001; 2002).

Moreover, the Presidium had exerted excessive influence on the agenda and final text of the Convention report. The emphasis on consensus also constituted some hidden pressure on some representatives, some of whom gave up their dissenting opinions to avoid destroying this 'consensus'. Even so the Convention did not reach a real consensus. Ironically, the working group on the social policy was among the first to complete its work to examine the relevant part of the draft treaty, although few substantive changes have been introduced in the constitution compared with the provisions in the Treaty of Nice.[7] The debate during the French referendum indicates that social policy is far from an area where consensus has been achieved. In addition, several Eurosceptic members claimed that d'Estaing's insistence on consensus deprived them of the right for 'normal voting', and therefore was undemocratic.[8]

## The Text of the Treaty Establishing a Constitution for Europe (TeCE)

On the whole, the text of TeCE does not contain much drastic change on the existing treaties. However, some elements that may potentially promote citizens' participation and deliberation are worth noticing.

First of all, Title VI (Part I) provides participatory democracy with the same constitutional status as representative democracy in the EU. This is reflected in Article I-47,

---

[6] See 'Report from the Presidency of the Convention to the President of the European Council' (2003).
[7] See 'Final Report of Working Group XI on Social Europe' (2003).
[8] See Annex III of the report from the Presidency to the President of the European Council.

which provides that citizens' participation and deliberation at various levels are encouraged and facilitated by the Union.

Second, the role of social partners and autonomous dialogues are promoted (I-48). A most notable development in this regard is that citizens are able to initiate the drafting of EU legislation if they can collect no less than 1,000,000 signatures from required number of member states (Paragraph 4, Article I-47). Meanwhile, the involvement of national parliaments in the EU affairs is strengthened, and the European Parliament's legislative power and budgetary power further clarified or extended. Moreover, the Convention is made a standard method for EU's treaty amendment in the future.

More important than these procedural matters are the efforts in the constitutional process to build the basis for the deliberation, for both due process and values are important in exercising deliberative democracy. The reference to 'a common destiny' sends a clear message of the importance of building a community in which its members are all dependent on one another within the EU (TeCE 2004: 3). The third recital of the preamble states that 'the peoples of Europe are determined to transcend their former divisions and united ever more closely to forge a common destiny' (TeCE 2004: 3). This objective strongly indicates that the Europeans will have their fates closely bound together and therefore they need to work together for their common good.

Moreover, the basic values on which the EU is founded are openly declared in the Preamble, Part I (General Objectives), Part II (the Charter) and provisions on relevant policies. Article I-2 provides a clear definition on the values, which includes not only such traditional values as democracy, human rights, and rule of law, but also some other specific rights like tolerance and non-discrimination. Although some criticized the inclusion of these overlapping rights at the expense of the constitution's simplicity and conciseness, it appears that the drafters intended to stress the importance of the rights for minority groups and put them on an equal footing with those traditional values. The efforts are further strengthened by the inclusion of the entire Charter of Fundamental Rights as the second part of the constitutional treaty. The Charter constitutes an equivalent of the bill of rights in liberal democratic states, although its symbolic significance is greater than the actual. Moreover, the constitution further reasserts EU's uniqueness in its social model, and defines deliberation as means for the realization of social justice and solidarity in Europe.

In spite of these elements for deliberation, drawbacks of the constitutional treaty are also obvious. In those salient areas or the areas where Europeans have high expectations, the treaty only reaffirms those abstract principles rather than giving concrete measures. In the document of over 230 pages, few new relief measures are provided for people to resort to if their rights are violated. As an area that European people take great pride in, progress in social policy would have had great potential to mobilize people to participate in and give support to the constitutional process. However, most powers in this area still lie in the hands of national governments. Similar dilemmas exist in other areas such as EU taxation and budget.

## The Turbulent Ratification Process

Although the Constitutional Treaty itself is not completely analogous to a state constitution, the modifier 'constitution' or 'constitutional' has aroused great public concern on both national and European levels. Although the vetoes in France and Netherlands have endangered the whole constitutional process, possibility still exists that they may evoke great public participation in the debate, which will provide a chance for the elites and general public to reflect on the future of the Union. This will rest on the outcomes of the subsequent national and Europe-wide communications and reflections.

In the ratification process, it appears that the treaty has faced greater challenge in those countries requiring a referendum than those adopting parliamentary method. On the one hand this may be explained as a result of the divergence in the public support for the European project in different countries. On the other, it indicates that people's perceptions about the EU are more divisive than European political elites have anticipated, and that opinions of ordinary citizens do not necessarily converge with those of their elected representatives. In this sense, the involvement of people constitutes both an opportunity and a more complex challenge to the constitutional endeavour.

The vetoes from the two founding members also remind us that the huge divergence within and between member states cannot be ignored. As Weiler (2001: 67) observes, the EU is still 'a union among distinct peoples, distinct political identities, distinct political communities…The call to bond with those very others in an ever closer union demands an internalization – individual and societal – of a very high degree of tolerance.' What took place in France and Netherlands highlighted the difficulty in achieving such high level of tolerance.

Some empirical studies suggest that the factors shaping public support for European integration include cognitive mobilization, cost/benefit considerations, impact of domestic political considerations, and immigration (de Vreese 2004). The vetoes in 2005 are the result of these factors combined. For example, social Europe had been a key issue in the French debate for the Constitution, which caused the social left split over it. For the left wing Socialists, the European constitution would enforce a neo-liberal project in Europe. The painful reforms introduced by the French government convinced some voters of real danger of downward adjustment in the welfare provision. Although the mainstream Socialists supported the constitutional treaty, some party members stood firmly on the 'no' side. Moreover, the negotiations on Turkey's accession also helped the anti-treaty campaign. For the first time in the French history, the Communists and Socialists stood together with Le Pen's National Front to say 'no' to a European treaty.

According to the results of the *Eurobarometer* (European Commission 2005a) poll, the first five reasons for French voters to say 'No' were: (1) negative effects on the employment situation, (2) the weak economic situation, (3) excessive economic liberalism in the draft treaty, (4) opposition to the president/the national government/certain political parties, and (5) insufficient social Europe, while the sovereignty issue and opposition to further enlargement were much lesser concerns. In Netherlands, many voters complained that the government had not communicated sufficiently with the general public on the Constitution. The lack of information became the top reason for citizens to say 'No'. It also indicated that 'No' voters were worried about a loss of sovereignty within a political union and the possible cost of Europe for tax-payers (European Commission 2005b). It is worth noting that few voters in the two countries questioned their country's EU membership although 'no' votes won clearly in the referenda. In the opinion of 82 per cent of Dutch citizens and of 88 per cent of French citizens, their country's membership of the EU was a good thing. Of the French voters, 75 per cent even supported the idea that a Constitution for Europe was essential for European construction, and more than 60 per cent of the French believed that the 'no' victory would facilitate the renegotiation of the Constitution in order to achieve a more social constitution.

This may show that most voters in the two countries do not oppose the Union, or even the constitution-making process, but certain provisions of the text for various reasons.

On the eve of the French referendum, Habermas made several appeals to the French, arguing for a 'Yes' vote to 'strengthen Europe's power to act' (Biermann et al. 2005; Habermas 2005). However, these appeals did not receive positive responses from the French left. In fact, after the honeymoon in the Delors' era, they began to complain that the EU had been degraded into a neo-liberal project rather than a social democratic one. Their sacrifices in the ratification of the Maastricht Treaty and the 2002 presidential election were not paid off. As a summary in the Sharpener website (2005) put it,

> [T]here is no improvement in the content of the Union's policies when it comes to workers' rights, social issues, the environment or gender equality. There are some beautiful words, but no obligations made or tools created for progressive politics...'

They criticized Habermas for relying too heavily on the political elites and formal institutions in Europe but seeing 'no possibility of change from below'.

## The Aftermath of the Vetoes

During the period of reflection, the public participation in the constitutional debate is being encouraged by the EU institutions, yet its impact remains rather limited. In 2005 and 2006, the European Commission (2005; 2006) launched a number of initiatives 'to listen and communicate better to the citizens' and to trigger national and transnational discussions on certain policy areas related to the constitutional debate. These initiatives include an action plan, a 'Plan D' for democracy, dialogue and debate, and a white paper. In 2006, the Commission issued President Barroso's new 'new citizens' agenda' on the basis of the results of Plan D and relevant debates. By using this method the EU hopes to meet the expectations of its citizens in such areas as social policy, internal market and even foreign policy. However, it is greatly constrained by the fact that polices in these areas are largely decided by the members states.

Although German Chancellor Angela Merkel promised to find a solution to the constitutional impasse when Germany took over the EU presidency in January 2007, views are still highly divergent among member states. The eighteen members that have ratified constitutional treaty demand to preserve the current text, some of which even called for a declaration to include more 'Social Europe' in the Constitution. Meanwhile, other states including the UK prefer a 'mini-treaty' focused mainly on institutional reforms. The British government explicitly threatened to veto any attempt to adopt a maxi-treaty. The term 'European Constitution' is avoided in the Berlin Declaration marking the EU's 50th anniversary. If the EU countries finally compromise on a minimal-treaty solution to avoid further referenda, it will have a negative impact on a transparent and democratic debate on the future of Europe at least in the short term.

# EAST ASIAN COOPERATION[9] IN COMPARATIVE PERSPECTIVE

## The Relevance of the European Experience

The Asia-Pacific region has long been considered as an example of low-profile regionalism for its lack of high-degree institutionalization and legalization (Kahler 2000: 549-550). However, since the mid-1990s, the Asian financial crisis and China's emergence as an enthusiastic partner with Association of Southeast Asian Nations (ASEAN) have imposed great impetus for the efforts.

For a number of scholars, Europe and Asia represent two distinctive regionalisms. The political agenda in East Asia has lagged far behind that of Europe. Two major obstacles to the development of deliberative democracy in the region are the lack of a real area leader and of shared regional memory. At the current stage, 'the gradually emerging model of competitive regional cooperation or multilayered regional framework' may better reflect the realities in East Asia (Nicolas 2005: 7). Even in the foreseeable future, it is unlikely to have an East Asian constitution. However, considering the recent regional development, the EU's constitutional experience is still relevant in several ways.

Europe and East Asia may take different paths in their treaty reforms even in the long term. However, the basis of this comparative study may not be a perfect match between Europe and East Asia, but Asia may learn some useful wisdom and inspiration from the European experience. It is more on the philosophical level than on a specific policy area. What matters for East Asia are the progressive elements, deliberative spirit and even the lessons from the failures in the constitutional process. It represents a kind of quest for social justice and democratic governance in the current international system. It will be a long process that is as much socially constructed as it is economically and/or politically determined. Another useful lesson for East Asia is that a region building is not a linear process even for the highly integrated Europe. To overcome these constraints, they have to use their wisdom and find their own way. Therefore they should be well aware of those obstacles for deliberative democracy in East Asia. In the mean time, some latent but positive developments have also appeared in the region. As Acharya put it, '[t]he fact that Asia and Europe are different is not an adequate basis for celebrating European regionalism at the expense of Asia's, nor does it call for ignoring the transformative potential of the latter '(Acharya, 2006: 313 ).

## Some Negative Factors against Deliberative Democracy in East Asia

The diversity in historical and cultural experiences, as well as in economic development levels in Asia has caused great difficulty for its regional integration efforts. Strong distrust arises at various levels of society although most actors in the region hope to enjoy the benefits of economic integration. In most cases, the misunderstanding and hostility are fiercer among the general public than among political elites, which may constrain the deepening of the regional cooperation.

---

[9] Here East Asia Cooperation is a broad term denoting the on-going regional integration efforts among East Asia, Northeast Asia, and the ASEAN countries.

A major negative factor is the lack of shared historical memory in the region. A common historical experience is favourable for the development of regional identity and transnational deliberation, though whether it is a prerequisite has become controversial in recent years.[10] Unfortunately, such shared historical memory is scarce in East Asia.

For a long time in its history, China, as the strongest power in the East Asian system, held a hierarchical view of international relations and ensured a tribute system in which China's neighbouring states became vassal states of the Middle Kingdom (Fairbank 1973: 1-19). Although some researchers argue that this system was completely different from Western colonialism due to its nature of amity, mutual reciprocity and China's non-interference in the internal affairs of the vassal states (Peng 2005: 194-206), some people in Asian countries who are wary of the threat of a rising China still use it to justify their concerns about China's threat to her neighbours. Moreover, Chinese support for Communist groups within several Southeast Asian countries in the 1960s reinforced their suspicion.

Since the mid-19th century, Japan replaced China to become the leading country in the region. Within the ensuing 100 years, Japan pursued an aggressive policy to its Asian neighbours, which culminated in World War Two. For most Asians, Japan's campaign for what it called a 'greater East Asia co-prosperity sphere' in the first half of the twentieth century is merely a synonym for Japanese aggression and domination. Whether these historical problems are insurmountable barriers remains a question for the integration in East Asia.

The question of leadership is also a barrier for cooperation in the region. Given their economic and political power, China and Japan are natural leaders of the regional order in East Asia. Nevertheless, unlike France and Germany, the two powers have never achieved real reconciliation after the bitter experience of World War Two. In the 1960s and 1970s when Japan pursued a flying geese model in the region, it was out of question for Communist China to accept Japanese leadership. Since the late 1970s, China has been undergoing a process of peaceful rise in which it has successfully integrated itself into global and regional economy. Thus, the strategic competition for regional leadership has been intensified between the two countries. The situation is compounded by their different understanding of history, territorial disputes and Japan's alliance with the US.

Moreover, since the 1990s, Asian countries have witnessed a rapid deterioration of the Sino-Japanese relationship, which not only undermines their capacity to play the leading role in regional affairs, but also binds the hands of their political leaders to take radical initiatives. This is highlighted by the anti-Japanese demonstrations across China in the spring of 2005. In the same year, poll results showed that Japanese attitudes towards China continued to decline, favourability ratings hit an all-time low since 1978.[11] In this context, China and Japan are not likely to take the leadership separately or jointly. Recently China has openly supported ASEAN's leading role in the regional cooperation, though it is not clear whether ASEAN can take the responsibility effectively.

---

[10] For some scholars, European history is open for different possibilities in the story of a common European identity. In fact, since the Westphalian settlement, Europe has had more experiences of national division than that of Christendom. See Mayer and Palmowski (2004: 573-98).

[11] According to the Cabinet survey, about 32.4 per cent of respondents say 'have or tend to have an affinity towards China', while those who tend not to or don't have such affinity amount to 63.4 per cent. For more detailed results, see http://www.mansfieldfdn.org/polls/poll-05-12.htm.

## The Spillover Pressures for Public Participation in Regional Policy-Making

Since the late 1990s, a series of concrete achievements have been accomplished in East Asia Cooperation. As in Europe, the most fruitful integration occurs first in economic areas. On January 1, 2002, the ASEAN Free Trade Area (AFTA) came into force for the original six ASEAN members. ASEAN leaders also pledged to achieve an ASEAN Community by the year 2020 which would rest on the three pillars of security, economic and socio-cultural communities. As announced in 2001, the ASEAN-China Free Trade Area (FTA) is being built in stages. In 2010, an FTA of nearly two billion people with a total GDP of almost US $3 trillion will take shape.

In the region the effects of the early FTA arrangements are being spilt over to other areas. In spite of the widespread skepticism, the financial cooperation with the focus on the Chiang Mai Initiative and Asian Bond Market has been going forward smoothly. A new network of industries, trade and investment is taking shape, which lays a foundation for further development of regional cooperation. The Chiang Mai swap mechanism has been improved with a rapid expansion in its size. By May 2006, it reached US $75 billion, 90 per cent increase of a year ago. To date there have been at least twelve ministerial meeting mechanisms including public security, labour, agriculture, culture and health, which have promoted a wide range of cooperation in the areas.

On December 14, 2005, the East Asia Summit was held in Kuala Lumpur, and the leaders of ASEAN + 3 [12] countries issued a 'Kuala Lumpur Declaration', which declares that the East Asia Summit will be a 'forum for dialogue on broad strategic, political and economic issues' and that they will be committed to promoting community building in the region'.[13] In this process, regional arrangements will directly affect citizens in terms of employment, income growth, education, environmental protection, and working place safety. The demand increases for public participation in decision making at regional level.

## Some Positive Elements for Deliberation in East Asia

In both cultural and institutional senses, there are several factors that might be favourable for deliberation in East Asia. First, the influence of Asian values, which can be dated back to the origin of Confucianism and other traditions, are still present in the region, though their influence varies in different countries. These values emphasize the importance of harmonious society and consensus-building rather than that of legalism, which to some extent converge on the deliberative spirit. Common good is a kind of virtue in the society. To obtain the common good, individuals should try to balance their interests with those of others and of society. This may serve as a good starting point for the deliberative process. In recent years, a unique 'ASEAN way' has been developed in its decision-making process.[14]

Actually the ASEAN way is important not only in the intergovernmental decision making process but also in the daily operations and communications in the regional cooperation. For

[12] It refers to the proposed FTA between ten ASEAN countries plus China, Japan and Korea.
[13] See ASEAN (2005)
[14] According to Davidson (2004: 167), the ASEAN way means, 'processes including intensive informal and discreet discussions behind the scenes to work out a general consensus which then acts as the starting point around which the unanimous decision is finally accepted in more formal meeting…'

China and other countries, an informal consensus-based way in the construction of the East Asia Community is more desirable than those Western-style formal voting with rigid, binding outcome.

Second, the widespread Western influence in East Asia has counterbalanced some negative effects of traditional Asian values, particularly their inadequacy in the protection of individual rights. In fact, most countries in the region have, more or less, accepted the Western values in their path to democratization. Japan and Korea were the first groups of Asian countries that embraced the Western model in the postwar era. In the past two decades, civil society movements in some Southeast Asian countries have utilized different political and cultural schemes to advance their democratic claims. Even in China, market economy and democratic politics (though it may have different interpretations on them) have become part of its new political orthodoxy in recent years. The latent trend of increasing homogenization in the region opens way for the construction of certain 'universal' regional principles, which will be a blend of traditional Asian values, different national cultures and Western influence.

Third, China's 'peaceful development road' has the potential to provide a new driving force for the East Asia Cooperation. In the first years of this century, 'harmonious society', 'harmonious Asia' and 'harmonious world' have become buzzwords in the Chinese leadership and among its strategic thinkers. This move indicates that China has largely abandoned its traditional way of thinking based on its ideological orthodoxy. To achieve the goals of harmonious development, interests at different levels, i.e. interests on individual, group, national, regional, and international basis must be taken into account in the policy making process. Thus its domestic goals are closely interwoven with its international ones. Active involvement of international institutions, including regional ones is considered as an important part of its grand strategy. In December 2005, the State Council published a white paper entitled *China's Peaceful Development Road,* which systematically clarified the Chinese government's theory on its development model. It held that the goal of China is to build a harmonious world of sustained peace and common prosperity. In the document, the harmonious world is further defined as a 'democratic, harmonious, just and tolerant' world.[15]

China's innovations in its national strategy put new impetus on the harmonization in its relations with other countries in the region. Internally, this new strategy means a so-called comprehensive implementation of a 'scientific outlook on development', which stresses the importance of promoting social justice and fairness and of building an energy-efficient and environmental-friendly society. Moreover, it encourages consultation and inclusiveness. In the spring of 2007, some intellectuals openly suggested that China follow a Nordic model of 'social democracy' which resulted in great controversy in China's political and intellectual circles (Xie 2007). To some extent, China's new model has something in common with the welfare capitalism pursued by Japan and other Asian countries.[16]

In addition, Sino-Japan relations are undergoing certain positive changes. After Prime Minister Shinzo Abe's ice-breaking visit to China in autumn 2006, Chinese Premier Wen Jiabao called his visit to Japan an ice-thawer. Before Premier Wen's visit, the China Central Television aired a series of programmes on Japan including its culture and lifestyle of people. His speech in the Diet was televised live at home. At this moment, a dialogue on the people-

---

[15] For more details on China's policy of peaceful development, see The State Council Information Office of China (2005).

[16] The concept of 'welfare capitalism' was advanced by Ronald Dore. It is a type of capitalism that can achieve both market efficiency and individual happiness. See Dore (2001).

to-people level may be particularly valuable and helpful to break the ice. The proposed joint research activities on history and culture may be a good start in this direction. These factors combined have the potential to promote certain forms of deliberation on both national and transnational levels, in which citizens will accept some new norms and construct allegiance in the regional institutions.

## Second Track Mechanism and Citizens' Involvement in Regional Agenda Setting

Apart from the intergovernmental mechanisms such as ASEAN+3 summits, East Asian countries also set up some important Track Two unofficial coordinating mechanisms, which have taken some deliberative features. In 1998, South Korean President Kim Dae Jung proposed that two research institutes under the ASEAN+3 framework should be established to promote regional cooperation in East Asia: East Asian Vision Group (EAVG) and East Asian Study Group (EASG). In addition, an 'Industry and Commerce Forum' made up of business people and scholars was formed in the business community to discuss entrepreneurial cooperation affairs among East Asian countries. Since 2003, several Track II mechanisms have been set up under the suggestions made by the two EAVG and EASG reports: notably (1) East Asia Forum consisting of governmental and nongovernmental officials at all levels, with the purpose of promoting extensive social exchange and regional cooperation; (2) Network of East Asia Think Tanks; (3) Comprehensive Human Resources Development Program for East Asia.

The EAVG is a civilian level institution with its members consisting of outstanding intellectuals in the region. In October 2002, it completed an EAVG (2001) report entitled 'Towards an East Asian Community', which became important grounds for discussing East Asian cooperation at the 10+3 unofficial summit.[17] The report proposed 22 key recommendations in economic, financial, political/security, environmental, cultural, and institutional cooperation. In its blueprint for an East Asia Community, the report particularly stresses the importance of fostering 'the identity of an East Asian community by encouraging active exchanges and regular dialogues at both the governmental and non-governmental levels.' It also put 'shared identity', 'people focus' and 'inclusiveness' at the top list of guiding principles. The EASG report (2002) made by governmental officials endorsed the EAVG recommendations and made further concrete suggestions for the Community building in East Asia.

Currently community building has emerged as a shared future agenda in East Asia. Apart from the traditional intergovernmental mechanism, the intellectual communities in the region have shown great enthusiasm in and given vital support for the official process in various functional areas. The potential economic benefits and costs in some functional areas have created great incentives for businesses and even general public to participate in the debate about the future agenda. But generally speaking, their interest in and knowledge about East Asian cooperation are very limited. It is an important task to promote wider participation from ordinary citizens, civil societies and Nongovernmental Organizations (NGOs) in various

---

[17] For the details of the report, see EAVG (2001).

types of functional operations. Only in this process can some kind of 'we' feeling and a collective identity be gradually developed among the people in the region.

## CONCLUDING REMARKS

Theoretically dynamics of economic integration will create pressures for coordination in macro-economic policy on the regional level, which will, in turn, pose a challenge to both national and transnational governance. The tension has sparked lively debate in Europe. However this problem manifests itself in a more complex manner in other regions of the world, where more complicated constraints and deepening integration exist simultaneously. This is further compounded by the tremendous gap between the EU and other regional arrangements, which makes risky any efforts to build links between them or to take the European experience as a benchmark.

The assumptions in deliberative democracy provide a useful theoretical framework for us to reflect on this issue. As suggested by Habermas and other political scientists, deliberation in regional integration will complement rather than replace the intergovernmental approach not only because it, due to its flexibility and fluidity, is more viable than formal transnational voting arrangements, but also because it potentially has closer connections with the construction of common values and moral commitment in regional governance.

From the on-going constitutional process in Europe, we may learn:

1. At certain stages, this constitutional process may have the potential to enhance deliberation both nationally and transnationally.
2. In the process, democratic legitimacy, common identity and deliberation may be interlocking and mutually reinforcing elements.
3. The primary dilemmas for such a deliberative model are how the public can be mobilized, how they can be persuaded to give up their self interest and preference to embrace universal values, and how the broad consensus can be established in a highly diverse regional community. Theoretically, deliberation and construction of common perceptions (e.g. values) in salient areas (e.g. welfare policy) may promote public interest and consensus-building.

Under these constraints, the deliberative process in Europe has to be at a primitive stage. Moravcsik (2004: 337) argues that any assessment of transnational democracy should not be exercised in utopian thinking, and that 'any democratic metric derived from ideal theory must …be "calibrated" in order to assess whether the current arrangements are the best that are feasible under "real-world" circumstances'. This is undoubtedly a good criterion. The setback in the constitutional process seems a triumph of intergovernmentalism in the short term. However, even today the real-world constraints include both the 'No' votes in the referenda and the existing economic, political and cultural interdependence as well as the widespread concerns over the expansion of neoliberalism in Europe. In this sense, real-world circumstances should not be exclusively understood as static existence, but rather as something dynamic that can accommodate the changing realities in the world.

A comparative study may help us understand the gap between the EU's constitutional experience and the realities in East Asia. Meanwhile certain deliberative elements have emerged in East Asia cooperation, which have demonstrated the potential to address some contemporary challenges in the region.

I am well aware that this study is imperfect in several ways. It is obviously too early at this stage to assess the impact of deliberation on both EU governance and the East Asia cooperation, for its effect can only be seen over a longer period of time. Moreover, even when some changes have occurred, it is still difficult for us to measure the outcome by a social-scientific method, for it is almost impossible to determine 'when and how the actors changed their mind because of the arguments' in the deliberative process (Magnette 2004: 21).

In spite of these empirical and methodological imperfections as well as the complexity of real-world constraints, it is still worth doing, for history will not end in its status quo, but be open to different possibilities. Few people fifty-seven years ago could have imagined that European integration would have gone this far. At this moment, some wisdom may come from Robert Schuman (2000: 36): 'Europe will not be made all at once, or according to a single plan. It will be built through concrete achievements which first create a *de facto* solidarity'. At the same time, the words of Rousseau (1968: 136) are also worth remembering: 'The limits of the possible in moral matters are less narrow than we think. It is our weakness, our vices, our prejudices that shrink them'.

In the changing world, whether or not its constituent instrument will take the name of constitution, regional integration will not only be an economic but also a political, philosophical, and legal process, in which some room may be left to accommodate the spirits of modern constitutionalism. This does not necessarily mean that we must forget the real-world constraints. In this sense deliberation may play some complementary role in the East Asia cooperation although it has to be a limited, incremental one in the foreseeable future.

# REFERENCES

Acharya, Amitav (2006) 'Europe and Asia: Reflections on a Tale of Two Regionalisms', in: Bertrand Fort and Douglas Webber (eds) *Regional Integration in East Asia and Europe: Convergence or Divergence*, London: Routledge, pp. 312-321.

ASEAN (2005), 'Kuala Lumpur Declaration on the East Asia Summit', Kuala Lumpu, 14 December. Available from: <http:// http://www.aseansec.org/ 18098.htm>.

Biermann, Wolf, Buch, Hans Christoph, Grass, Günter, Habermas, Jürgen, Harpprecht, Klaus, Alexander Kluge, Alexander, Michael Naumann, Michael, Schneider, Peter, Schwan, Gesine, Zweite, Armin and Spiess, Werner (2005) 'Europe Demands Courage' *Le Monde*, 2 May 2005.

Breslin, Shaun and Higgott, Richard (2000) 'Studying Regions: Assessing the New, Learning from the Old', *New Political Economy* 5(3): 333-353.

Dahl, Robert A. (1999) 'Can International Organizations Be Democratic? A Skeptic's View', in: Ian Shapiro and Casiano Hacker-Cordon (eds) *Democracy's Edges*, Cambridge: Cambridge University Press, pp. 19-36.

Davidson, Paul J. (2004) 'The ASEAN Way and Role of Law in ASEAN Economic Cooperation', *Singapore Journal of International and Comparative Law* 8(1): 165-176.

d'Estaing, Giscard (2002a) 'La dernière chance de l'Europe unie', *Le Monde* 23 July 2002.

d'Estaing, Giscard (2002b) 'Introductory Speech to the Convention on the Future of Europe' Available from: <http://european-convention.eu.int/docs/ speeches/1.pdf.> [21 August 2006]

de Vreese, Claes H. (2004) 'Why European Citizens will Reject the EU Constitution' *Center for Europeans Studies Working Paper No. 116*. Available from:<http://www.people.fas. harvard.edu/~ces/publications/de Vreese.pdf>[14 December 2006]

Dore, Ronald (2001) *Stock Market Capitalism, Welfare Capitalism: the Anglo-Saxons versus Germany and Japan,* Oxford: Oxford University Press.

Dryzek, John S. (2004) 'Constitutionalism and its Alternatives', in: Anne Van Aaken, Christian List and Christoph Luetge (eds) *Deliberation and Decision: Economics, Constitutional Theory and Deliberative Democracy*, Burlington, VT: Ashgate Publishing Company, pp. 48-50.

Eriksen, Erik and Weigard, Jarle (2003) *Understanding Habermas*, New York: Continuum.

EASG (2002) 'Final Report of the East Asia Study Group'. Available from: <http://www. aseansec.org/viewpdf.asp?file=/pdf/easg.pdf#search='EASG>. [4 January 2007].

EAVG (2001) 'Towards An East Asian Community'. Available from: <http://www.kiep. go.kr/eng/e_sub02/sub01_1.asp?sort=andhdate=2001-11-20andseq=20011120830647 andp=7andclass=01> [4 January 2007].

European Commission (2001) *Eurobarometer 56*, Brussels: Directorate-General Press and Communication.

European Commission (2002) *Eurobarometer 57*, Brussels: Directorate-General Press and Communication.

European Commission (2005a) *Eurobarometer: The European Constitution: Post-referendum Survey in France*, Brussels: Directorate-General Press and Communication.

European Commission (2005b) *Eurobarometer: The European Constitution: Post-referendum Survey in Netherlands*, Brussels: Directorate-General Press and Communication.

European Commission (2005c) 'Listen, Communicate, Go local – New Commission Approach to Dialogue and Communication with European Citizens'. Available from: <http://europa.eu/rapid/pressReleasesAction.do?reference=IP/05/995andformat=TMLand aged=0andlanguage=ENandguiLanguage=en> [4 May 2007].

European Commission (2006) 'A Citizen's Agenda: Delivering Results for Europe'. Available from: <http://ec.europa.eu/commission_barroso/president/ pdf/com_2006_211_en.pdf> [4 May 2007].

Fairbank, John K. (1973) 'A Preliminary Framework', in: John Fairbank (ed.) *The Chinese World Order: Traditional China's Foreign Relations*, Cambridge: Harvard University Press, pp. 1-19.

Ferrajoli, Luigi (1996) 'Beyond Sovereignty and Citizenship: a Global Constitutionalism', in: Richard Bellamy (ed.) *Constitutionalism, Democracy and Sovereignty: American and European Perspectives*, Aldershot: Avebury, pp.151-160.

'Final Report of Working Group XI on Social Europe' (2003), CONV516/1/03, Brussels, 4 February. Available from:<http://register.consilium.eu.int/pdf/en/ 03/cv00/cv00516-re01en03.pdf>.

Gazzo, Marina (ed.) (1986) *Towards European Union*, vol. 2, Brussels: Agence Europe.

Gutmann, Amy and Thompson, Dennis (2003) 'Deliberative Democracy Beyond Process', in: James S. Fishkin, and Peter Laslett (eds) *Debating Deliberative Democracy*, Oxford: Blackwell Publishing, pp. 31-53.

Habermas, Jürgen (2001) 'Why Europe Needs a Constitution', *New Left Review* 11, Sep-Oct: 5-26.

Habermas, Jürgen (2005) 'The Illusionary Leftist No'. Available from: <http://print.signand singt.com/features/163.html>.

Higgott, Richard (2006) 'The Theory and Practice of Region', in: Bertrand Fort, and Douglas Webber (eds) *Regional Integration in East Asia and Europe: Convergence or Divergence*, London: Routledge, pp.17-38.

Kahler, Miles (2000) 'Legalization as Strategy: The Asia-Pacific Case', *International Organization* 54(3), Summer: 549-571.

Lacroix, Justine (2002) 'For a European Constitutional Patriotism', *Political Studies* 50: 944-958.

Magnette, Paul (2003) 'Does the Process Really Matter? Some Reflections on the European Convention', *Havard CES Working Papers*. Available from:<http://www.ces.fas.harvard.edu/working_papers/Magnette2.pdf>.

Magnette, Paul (2004) 'Deliberation or Bargaining?: Coping with Constitutional Conflicts in the Convention on the Future of Europe', in: Erik O Eriksen, John E. Fossum, and Agustin J. Menendez (eds) *Developing a Constitution for Europe?*, London: Routledge, pp. 207-247.

Mayer, Franz C. and Palmowski, Jan (2004) 'European Identities and the EU – The Ties that Bind the Peoples of Europe', *Journal of Common Market Studies*, 42(3): 573-98.

Meaders (2005) 'Another Europe is Possible: Jurgen Habermas and the EU Constitution', *Sharpener*, 25 May. Available from: <http://www.thesharpener.net/2005/05/25/another-europe-is-possible-jurgen-habermas-and-the-eu-constitution/> [12 September 2007].

Michelman, Frank I. (1998) 'Political Truth and the Rule of Law', *Tel Aviv University Studies in Law* 8: 281-291.

Moravcsik, Andrew (2004) 'Is There a 'Democratic Deficit' in World Politcs? A Framework for Analysis', *Governemnt and Opposition* 39(2): 336-363.

Nicolas, Françoise (2005) 'East Asia and Western Europe: Between Regionalism and Globalization', in: Sophie Boisseau du Rocher, and Bertrand Fort (eds) *Paths to Regionalism: Comparing Experiences in East Asia and Europe*, London: Marshall Cavendish Academic, pp.3-7.

Peng, Peng (2005) *On Peaceful Rise*, Guangzhou, PRC: Guangdong People's Press, pp. 194-206.

'Report from the Presidency of the Convention to the President of the European Council', CONV851/03, Brussels, 18 July. Available from: <http://european-convention.eu.int/docs/Treaty/cv00851.en03.pdf>.

Rousseau, Jean-Jacques (1968) *The Social Contract*, Middlesex : Penguin Books Ltd.

Sandel, Michael (1996) *Democracy's Discontent: America in Search of a Public Philosophy*, Cambridge: Belknap Press of Harvard University Press.

Schuman, Robert (2000) 'Declaration of 9 May 1950', in: Pascal Fontaine (ed.) *A New Idea for Europe*, Luxembourg: Official Publications of the European Communities.

Shaw, Jo (2003) 'Process, Responsibilities and Inclusion in EU Constitutionalism' *European Law Journal* 9(1): 45-68.

Smith, Brendan P.G. (2002) *Constitution Building in the European Union,* London: Kluwer Law International.

The State Council Information Office of China (2005) *White Paper on Peaceful Development Road.*

Telò, Mario and Paul Magnette (2002) 'Justice and Solidarity', in F. Cerutti and E. Rudolph (eds) *A Soul for Europe*, vol. I, Leuven: Peeters Publishers, pp. 73-89.

'Treaty Establishing a Constitution for Europe' (2004), *Official Journal of the European Union* C310, 16 December. Available from:<http://eur-lex.europa.eu/JOHtml.do?uri= OJ:C:2004:310:SOM:EN:HTML>[12 September 2007]

Von Bogdandy, Armin (2004) 'The European Constitution and European Identity: A Critical Analysis of the Convention's Draft Preamble', in: J.H.H. Weiler and Christopher L. Eisgruber (eds) *Altneuland: The EU Constitution in a Contextual Perspective, Jean Monnet Working Papers* 5/04. Available from: <http://www.jeanmonnetprogram.org/ papers/04/040501-07a.html>.

Weiler, J. H. H. (1995) 'The State "uber alles": Demos, Telos and the German Maastricht Decision', *Jean Monnet Working Papers* 6/95. Available from: <http://www.jeanmonnet program.org/papers/95/9506ind.html>.

Weiler, J. H. H. (2001) 'Federalism without Constitutionalism: Europe's Sonderweg', in: Kalypso Nicolaïdis and Robert Howse (eds) *The Federal Vision: Legitimacy and Levels of Governance in the US and the EU*, Oxford: Oxford University Press, pp. 54-70.

Weiler, J. H. H. (2002) 'A Constitution for Europe? Some Hard Choices', *Journal of Common Market Studies* 40(4): 563-80.

Xie, Tao (2007) 'Democratic Socialism and China's Future', *Yanhuang Chunqiu* 2: 1-8.

In: Asian Economic and Political Development
Editor: Felix Chin

ISBN: 978-1-61122-470-2
© 2011 Nova Science Publishers, Inc.

# HUMAN RIGHTS, DEMOCRACY AND FEDERALISM - PART OF THE PROBLEM OR PART OF THE SOLUTION? SECURING STABILITY IN THE EUROPEAN UNION AND THE PEOPLE'S REPUBLIC OF CHINA

### *Andreas Follesdal*
Norwegian Centre for Human Rights, University of Oslo

## ABSTRACT

Federations and human rights have a long, ambivalent and contested relationship. The paper addresses one of these concerns: whether human rights-respecting federal arrangements are sufficiently robust against claims to secession. Some fear that federal elements and human rights combine to fuel destabilizing forces. Comparative research suggests that some of these risks are real, though difficult to estimate. I argue that several elements of democratic and human rights can limit these dangers, and rather enhance the long-terms stability of federal arrangements. In particular, the contributions of human rights and political parties to the governance of sub-units and the centre merit close attention. The article has seven parts. It first presents some features of federalism and the challenge of stability. Sections 3 and 4 sketch conceptions of democracy and human rights. Sections 5 and 6 discuss how human rights may both fuel and defuse calls for secession. The concluding section brings these results to bear on attempts at alleviating the 'democratic deficit' of the European Union, and to the People's Republic of China.

## INTRODUCTION

Two global trends come together in Europe and in the People's Republic of China (PRC): the experimentation with quasi-federal, multi-level forms of governance, and increased concern for democracy and other human rights.[1] Why do these movements gain momentum and what is their relationship?

---

[1] These reflections draw on research funded by the Norwegian Research Council's 'Accommodating Difference' Project at the Norwegian Centre for Human Rights at the University of Oslo; by the Fulbright 'New Century Scholar' Program 2003, and the EUS initiatives CONNEX and NEWGOV. I am especially grateful for comments and suggestions by Maria Lundberg and Amy Verdun. The Mossavar-Rahmani Center for Business and Government, and Currier House, both at Harvard University, and the Centre for the Study of Mind in Nature (CSMN) of the University of Oslo kindly offered optimal conditions to conclude these reflections.

Regional cooperation takes place under well known acronyms – the North American Free Trade Agreement (NAFTA) and Association of Southeast Asian Nations (ASEAN), as well as Mercosur in South America , the African Union, and the European Union (EU). Some of these have lofty aspirations toward broader cooperation with federal elements, as exemplified by the European Union, whose Reform Treaty is currently being drafted.[2] Such 'coming-together' federalism of formerly independent states may also be the model for unitary states that seek to devolve powers constitutionally. Thus, in 1998 the UK decided to grant various forms of autonomy to Scotland, Wales and Northern Ireland. The Constitution of the PRC likewise grants some autonomy to certain minorities and regions, with organs of self-government (Art. 95, 113) that enjoy independence of finance and economic planning (Art. 117).

Human rights have also been gaining ground world wide. Few countries now outright reject international declarations and conventions, and violations are seldom admitted, but typically denied or excused.[3] The combination of federal forms of 'multi-level governance' and human rights raises important questions and challenges for traditions and ideals of sovereignty, democracy and human rights – all of which were largely developed for unitary states with centralized sites of political power. I shall suggest that in general, there is neither a happy coincidence nor a tragic conflict between federations and human rights. Some conflicts can be resolved, while some tensions should receive more attention by politicians and political philosophers alike. Democratic theorists must continue to reflect on the grounds for – and alternatives to – 'one-person-one-vote' and majority rule among a deeply divided citizenry (Dahl 1983; Barry 1991; Follesdal 1998; Lijphart 1999). Federal arrangements require us to reconsider the universality of human rights, especially the obligations to intervene to protect human rights within a federation. We also need a better understanding of the grounds and mechanisms for maintaining dual political loyalty among the citizenry in a multi-level political order.

The following comments address one of these concerns in particular, namely whether human rights-respecting federal arrangements are sufficiently robust against claims to secession. This is a particularly worrisome concern for those who favour devolution in order to quell calls for secession - what some scholars call 'holding-together' federalism (Stepan 1999).

Federations and human rights have a long, ambivalent and contested relationship that harks back at least to disagreements between 'Federalists' and 'Anti-federalists' about the 1789 Constitution of the United States of America. Some have argued that federal features and human rights are mutually supportive and serve to stabilize popular support for the system of governance. Federal structures are thought to safeguard human rights at both sub-unit and central levels, and human rights constraints render federations more legitimate and trustworthy.

Others fear that federal elements and human rights combine to fuel destabilizing forces. What are the grounds for such worries? Human rights norms might put a federation at risk by fuelling secessionist movements and the complex web of centre and sub-unit authority in federations is thought to more likely violate human rights. Central authorities might more

---

[2] For analyses of normative issues in the Draft Constitutional Treaty, cf. Dobson and Follesdal (2004); for an assessment of the recent 'Reform Treaty' that succeeds it, cf. Follesdal (2008).

[3] The 1993 'Bangkok Declaration' being an important exception, where representatives of Asian states dismissed civil and political rights as contrary to 'Asian values'; cf. Follesdal (2005) for references.

easily ignore citizens' human rights with impunity, and sub-units may enjoy immunity for mistreatment of their citizens, contrary to human rights requirements. So the forces that seek secession might be further fuelled by both human rights and federal arrangements that grant some powers to the sub-unit but not full political autonomy – contrary to the objective of keeping the political order together in the first place. Comparative research suggests that some of these risks are real, though difficult to estimate. I shall argue that several elements of democratic and human rights can limit these dangers, to enhance the long-terms stability of federal arrangements. In particular, the contributions of human rights and political parties to the governance of sub-units and the centre merit close attention.

The article has seven parts. First I present some features of federalism and the challenge of stability. Sections 3 and 4 sketch conceptions of democracy and human rights. Sections 5 and 6 discuss how human rights may both fuel and defuse calls for secession. The concluding section brings these results to bear on attempts at alleviating the 'democratic deficit' of the EU, and to the PRC.

# 1. ON FEDERALISM

For our purposes, federal political orders may be characterized as lacking a unique sovereign, since the centre and the territorial sub-units split or share political authority (Follesdal 2006a).

Federations have a constitutional, well-entrenched division of powers or 'competences' between central bodies and sub-units. Each level enjoys final authority with regards to some functions, and this constitutional allocation cannot be changed unilaterally. The sub-units thus enjoy immunity from central intervention in certain fields.

In what is called 'interlocking federalism' sub-units participate in central bodies of authority and influence common decisions. Indeed, sub-units can have a veto, and coalitions of small sub-units can often block decisions since they are often overrepresented. Arrangements where sub-units can veto decisions, or leave the federation are often referred to as confederations. In comparison, in other forms of decentralized government the central authorities may maintain, modify or abandon the legal powers of lower level authorities at their discretion.

## Federal and Confederal Elements in the EU

Since the 1952 European Coal and Steel Community (ECSC), what is now known as the European Union has developed both federal and confederal elements. The member states have transferred sovereignty to common institutions, and have signed away their right to veto such common decisions in an increasing number of areas. The constitutional division of authority will be made clearer in the Reform Treaty based on the 'Constitutional Treaty of Europe' (CTE) (Council of the European Union 2004). It lays out areas of exclusive competence of the Union institutions, and other exclusive competences for the member states. The shift from unanimity as the default procedure in the inter-governmental Council of Ministers and the increased power of the directly elected European Parliament (EP) further underscore that central decisions are explicitly placed beyond the control of any single sub-unit. Majority rule also increased the perception that Union decisions were beyond democratic scrutiny and control, giving fuel to the accusations that the EU suffers from a 'Democratic Deficit' (Wallace 1993; Beetham and Lord 1998; Follesdal 2006a; Follesdal and Hix 2006). Member states remain influential and exercise control, especially since they participate in central decision-making bodies in ways typical of 'interlocking' federal arrangements. As federal political orders go, Europe remains a very decentralized federal political order: for instance, it still lacks a common defence policy that is typical of federations (McKay 2001; Moravcsik 2001 and 2002). The fact that many competences remain shared between sub-units and central authorities does not make it less of a federation. Nor does the federal nature of the EU implicitly require more centralization as an objective. On the contrary, it may arguably be a bad idea to increase the powers of Union institutions, as the Reform Treaty seems to require (Schmitter 2004). The Union also has important confederal elements (Meehan 2001) - confirmed in the Reform Treaty by sub-units' right to withdraw from the Union, laid out in Article I-60 of the Constitutional Treaty. Yet some features render the 'confederation' label less appropriate: the Union's subjects are not only the member states but also citizens (Weiler 1996), and common decisions need not be unanimous.

Such 'coming together' federations typically arise when governments seek to obtain objectives beyond the reach of any single state, and that cannot be secured by treaty agreements alone. Examples include external defence, or common regulations in response to a globalizing economy that require more credible self-binding commitments than treaty agreements alone.

A dominant concern for the joining states is to prevent undesired centralization and other abuse of central authorities, thus much care goes into constraining the centre through checks by the sub-units and human rights regulations.


## Decentralising Elements in the People's Republic of China

If we use this definition of federalism strictly, the PRC is not a federation. Even so, there are some lessons to be drawn from federal experiences that might illuminate some of the issues the PRC faces, especially concerning whether to continue to grant some autonomy to certain regions and minorities, at the alleged risk of instability. The Preamble of the PRC Constitution states that 'The People's Republic of China is a unitary, multi-national state.' This could appear to be at variance with the grants to ethnic minorities of certain forms of self-government. The Constitution also recognizes regional autonomy, with organs of self-government with some independent authority for finance and economic planning (Art 95, 113, 117).

These clauses do not make the PRC a political order with federal elements in the sense defined above. The constitutionally entrenched decentralization remains – *de jure* and/or *de facto* - at the discretion of central authorities, regardless of the opinion of sub-unit authorities or an independent umpire (Ghai 2000b). As long as the constitution can be easily changed by the central authorities, they do not have the power to create a federal arrangement. They cannot credibly commit to respect the autonomy of sub-units, since they can reverse their decision to decentralize at will. To create a federal arrangement that grants autonomy to sub-units in a trustworthy way, the central authorities would have to be able to perform a constitutional act of self binding. They would have to constrain their own power of constitutional amendment.

## Why OPT for Federal Solutions?

Such opportunities foregone may seem minor and even slightly mysterious: why would a unitary sovereign create arrangements of self-binding in general? In particular, why would a state want to split authority as in a federation especially if such arrangements are likely to fuel secessionist movements? Why would a state pursue federalism in the first place? In response, I submit that the worries about instability often appear misconstrued: federal elements are often introduced as a response to perceived worries of instability and calls for secession. In these cases, to devolve some powers is the effect of popular unrest, rather than its original cause. If sub-units distrust the centre, central authorities may seek to create a federal political order. Thus, 'staying together' federations have often been created in order to order to manage multinational pressures, devolving powers to allow local variation and autonomy for separate nations who refuse a unitary structure. A federal arrangement might also give the sub-units' leaders enough political autonomy to quell upheavals, civil wars or calls for secession (Linz 1999). Thus Alfred Stepan notes that India's federal structure could accommodate minority demands for some linguistic and cultural autonomy, and thus deflate further political unrest (Stepan 1999).

Critics may still worry that even though there are some 'happy cases' such as India and Spain, there are inherent destabilizing mechanisms in federal devolution that increase the risk of secession. Is federalism as a response to instability part of the problem rather than part of the solution? Such worries may also give grounds for pause to those governments that grant local autonomy for quite other reasons than to quell secessionist movements. Thus it is surely of interest to consider whether PRC's current constitutionalized grants of regional autonomy is likely to fuel secessionists, especially when combined with human rights guarantees. The upshot of my arguments is that several of the reasons for such fears seem overdrawn. They should not dampen the PRC's endorsement of federal elements and human rights protections.

## 2. CHALLENGES OF INSTABILITY

To maintain an effective federation over time poses special challenges when compared to a unitary political order. The main concern of this article is the issue of fragmentation, but there are other challenges that must also be met – simultaneously. They therefore merit brief mention.

A stable federation must prevent secession, but also centralization – and stagnation. Yet all federations experience such long term trends toward centralizing and decentralizing decision-making that can hardly be avoided (Dehousse 1994; Tushnet 1996; Weiler 1999: 318). So there is a need for safeguards to prevent secession by one or more sub-units, and to reduce the risk of undesired, creeping centralization of all political authority. But such measures tend to reduce effectiveness and efficiency, yet those safeguards must not constrain the scope of political decision making completely.

## Preventing Centralization

To illustrate, to prevent undue centralization, the powers of the central unit are typically restricted by various checks such as specific 'lists of competences,' rules of unanimity or qualified majority voting, weighted votes, and principles of subsidiarity. Thus the Reform Treaty of the EU will provide a clearer allotment of different kinds of competences (exclusive, shared, complementary, economic policy co-ordination) and to transparency. These measures may help reduce such unintended drifts, and thus enhance trustworthiness. The proper allocation of such competences remains, however, a crucial normative issue. And some fear that a clear demarcation of competences between the sub-units and the centre will lead precisely to such stagnation (Swenden 2004).

One arrangement that offers some protection against undue centralization without causing stagnation is to include sub-unit officials in the central decision making bodies, for instance in the form of a second legislative chamber. Their institutional interests may provide some 'centrifugal' pull, while allowing decisions in response to present challenges.

## Subsidiarity

Another interesting arrangement to prevent centralization is based on the EU's 'principle of subsidiarity.' Various competing versions of the principle of subsidiarity address the contested issue of allocation of powers (Follesdal 2000). It places the burden of argument with those who seek to centralize authority. Article I-11 of the Constitutional Treaty requires that:

> 3. Under the principle of subsidiarity, in areas which do not fall within its exclusive competence, the Union shall act only if and insofar as the objectives of the proposed action cannot be sufficiently achieved by the Member States, either at central level or at regional and local level, but can rather, by reason of the scale or effects of the proposed action, be better achieved at Union level.

A new arrangement to be included in the Reform Treaty involves the national parliaments, who have an institutional interest in preventing centralization. They may voice reasoned objections against draft legislative acts that they think violate subsidiarity. If enough parliaments agree, the draft must be reviewed (CTE Protocol 2). This may prove very useful against undue centralization.

## Increased Trust in the Overarching Loyalty of Others

Another mechanism to reduce the risk of undue centralization is to build trust and trustworthiness among the citizenry at large, so that they will not seek centralization. The need for such trust has increased in the EU, where majority rule among the member states has replaced unanimity in several fields. Unanimity ensured that they would not be forced to take part in arrangements contrary to their own interests, or when they feared that others would not do their share in cooperative ventures. But the unanimity rule often prevented common action even when obviously required: this safeguard against centralization came at the cost of stagnation.

To allow for more effective common decisions, the new Reform Treaty establishes a default standard legislative procedure which requires only Qualified Majority in the Council and involves co-decision by the European Parliament and the Council together. This change increases efficient decision making, but also increases the risk of oppression of minorities and undue centralization. I return to the risk of majority tyranny below.

Stable popular support for such procedures requires a well-developed trust in other Europeans and officials (Nicolaidis 2001). Citizens and representatives must now be trusted to adjust or sacrifice their own interests and those of their voters for the sake of other Europeans in more cases. Institutions can contribute to such trust in several ways. One is by means of human rights, another one is to *socialize* citizens to the requisite normative sense of justice to consider the impact on others and to foster an 'overarching loyalty' to citizens within the whole Union (Rawls 1971; Rothstein 1998; Bellamy and Warleigh 1999; Simeon and Conway 2001: 362). One important way that institutions can facilitate such socialization is through political parties, to which I turn below.

Leaving the issues of centralization and stagnation aside, let me now turn to the main concern of this article: the risks of fragmentation. One crucial issue is how to halt and reverse such a drift and thus maintain the federal character of the political order.

## Preventing Secession

'Holding together' federations often face the opposite threat of centralization, namely creeping decentralization leading to secession. Whether federal solutions help stave off such consequences is difficult to determine, especially since many of the states that explore such options already are challenged by civil unrest, non-compliance and secessionist struggles. Comparative studies of federalism warn of a higher level of ongoing constitutional contestation concerning the constitution, its values and interpretation than in unitary political orders (Linz 1999). Stabilizing mechanisms that prevent the disintegration of the political order and citizen disenchantment are thus more important. Yet the grounds for such stability may be especially weak in federations, given their frequent genesis as solutions to intractable problems otherwise resolved by a unitary political order. Again, the maintenance of dual loyalties seems crucial (Simeon and Conway 2001).

I now hone in on a subset of these issues, i.e. whether democratic rule and human rights fosters or reduces the risk of secession in federal political orders.

## 3. DEMOCRACY

Democratic theorists disagree on many details concerning the institutional details, justification, and the proper weight of various elements of liberal representative democracy.

Some arguments for democratic governance are ultimately be based on a – possibly 'Western' – interest in self-determination and individual autonomy (Held 1995: 147). However, other arguments may defend democracy as the most reliable form of institutional arrangement to prevent risks to individuals' vital needs. Thus, Amartya Sen has argued that freedom of the press and democratic competition among political parties protect against famines (Sen 1988).

Within the Confucian tradition, Confucius' disciple Mencius' views (Mencius 1999) might be cited to provide some fragments of grounds for democratic rule:

- that it is right to replace a king who does not govern his kingdom well (51);
- that good and bad, competent and incompetent officials are best distinguished not on the basis of what aides or senior officials say, but when all the people in the kingdom say so (53);
- that the king acts as the delegate of the people when they so say (54);
- the value of scrutiny and transparency of rulers' mistakes, to permit correction and hence sustain popular support (132).

## Features of Democratic Rule

The different premises notwithstanding, I submit that there is broad agreement among Western democratic theorists on three central features of democratic rule: a) Citizens have *formal input* in decision-making in the form of voting among competing candidate rulers on the basis of informed discussion of their merits – discussions that affect their preferences. Citizens' input is what makes representative democracy 'government by the people' even when it is best described as an aristocratic oligarchy. The distinctly democratic feature of such democratic 'rule by the few' is that potential oligarchs compete for citizens' votes (Schumpeter 1976); b) This input is causally linked to *outputs* in the form of legislation and policy decisions that are held to secure and reflect the best interest of the public, however defined and determined. The substantive output is what makes representative democracy 'government for the people.' The policies are held to be in the 'best interest of the public' however that may be defined. There is an extensive theoretical debate as to this should be understood as voters' interests; their preferences over political candidates, and whether it should include preferences regarding the decision process itself (Manin, Przeworski, and Stokes 1999). The democratic quality may thus hinge on whether the outcomes are reliably close to the preferences of the median voter, whether they avoid majority dictatorship through courts and human rights protections, etc; c) Input and output are linked by means of *institutional procedures* that provide reliable causal mechanisms which give citizens reasons to comply with the outcomes. These mechanisms distinguish democracy from other ways that a population might get its voiced interests secured, for instance by a benevolent authoritarian ruler. To rule with the 'approval' of the people is insufficient to label it democratic, since non-autocratic monarchs, aristocratic or plutocratic oligarchies can do as much (Schumpeter 1976: 246). The degree of match between median voter and policy output may be an important test for evaluating constitutional arrangements (Powell 2000). But such correlation between input and output is insufficient for declaring a system democratic. The literature offers several arguments, of various empirical plausibility, for various arrangements of constrained cooperation and competition among contending parties. Even though voters may perhaps not be 'represented' by the elite, the elites are accountable to citizens (Schmitter and

Karl 1991; Dahl 1998), through mechanisms of prospective and retrospective voting for candidates or incumbents.

These mechanisms entail a range of conditions or ideals for democratic institutions (Dahl 1998): Equal effective opportunities for participation, an assumption of equal voting weight, Equal opportunities for enlightened understanding about alternative policies and their likely consequences, and agenda control.

## The Roles of Party Competition

A broad range of democratic theories insist on the important contributions provided by competition among political parties against a backdrop of free media (Key Jr. 1964: 456; Lipset and Rokkan 1967; Hall 1993). Party competition is not only a mechanism for citizens of selecting among given policy platforms on the basis of given self-interested preference maximization, parties competing for votes also question and challenge ill-directed policies. They provide a mechanism (imperfect, to be sure) for keeping politicians responsive to the interests of citizens by making threats of replacement credible (Manin, Przeworski, and Stokes 1999). They create competing, somewhat consistent platforms giving citizens a better sense of realistic alternatives and the scope of the practically feasible. They contribute to identify more sound and well-directed policies. Furthermore, parties seem especially important for maintaining stable federations: many theorists note the contributions of parties in citizens' character and political preference formation. Parties competing for votes affect voters' preferences and ultimate values. The competition crystallizes interests and perceived cleavages by giving some conflicts priority (Schattschneider 1960: 67; Lipset and Rokkan 1967). Party competition makes a limited set of policy platforms salient to voters, who shape their preferences by discussion (Schattschneider 1960: 37).

## Addressing the Risk of Majority Tyranny

One of the central weaknesses of democratic majoritarian rule is that minorities are vulnerable to majority decision making. In societies whose populations are divided in majorities and minorities along cultural, ethnic or other cleavages, individuals face a significant risk of ending in a permanent minority position on a range of important issues, without hope that they will ever get to be in the majority (Barry 1991; Follesdal 1998; Lijphart 1999; McKay 2001: 146-47). To trust a majoritarian system, the minority must be assured that the majority will not threaten the most important interests of the minority (Papadopoulos 2005). This may be done in at least three distinct ways. One is to devolve the issue to sub-units. In order to be trustworthy and function adequately as a democratic political order, a federation might thus take some policy issues away from the common policy agenda – typically language or other cultural elements – and allocate them with sub-units that have greater homogeneity regarding such issues. In this way majorities in the political order at large are prevented from harming territorially based minorities. Considerations of subsidiarity might thus hold that certain issue areas should not be regulated by central authorities, but instead be left to local units.

A second strategy is to seek to socialize individuals – majorities and minorities alike – toward commitments of solidarity. This socialization may be done instance through party platforms and education, as well as by media that informs the population in general about alternative policy options and their likely effects on vulnerable groups.

A third strategy is to limit the domain of decisions a majority may legitimately decide, so that vital interests of minorities are not left vulnerable to the misjudgements or ill will of the majority. One important set of such limits on democratic rule is human rights. We now turn to that topic.

## 4. HUMAN RIGHTS

A long-standing and broadly shared view on the responsible use of state power is that it must be used for the common good, understood as securing the basic needs of individual members of society. A government that fails in this does not have a moral claim to be obeyed or respected. Such views are found in several (but not all) Western philosophical traditions, as well as in Confucian and other traditions.

Theories of legitimacy may lay out at least two different sets of normative conditions, for a government's *internal* and *external* sovereignty respectively. The legal authority a government enjoys over individuals, and the legal immunity it enjoys vis-à-vis international bodies and other governments. Note in passing that the requirements for internal and external sovereignty may well differ. The conditions for when individuals have a moral duty to obey the government may be quite different from the conditions for when other governments and international bodies have a moral duty to not intervene by economic, diplomatic or military means in the domestic affairs of other states (Martin and Reidy 2006).

A theory of human rights typically does not deny that individuals have a duty to obey the commands of government, nor that state sovereignty should be respected. Rather, it seeks to identify the limits of such obligations. A normative theory of human rights specifies in part how governments should pursue the common good to maintain legitimate internal and external sovereignty. Such requirements may be in the form of various legal or constitutional rights and directives that regulate legislative and executive authority and discretion.

Human rights theories typically differ about which interests are significant and about what legal rights are required. Some philosophers have concentrated on the interest in being free from coercion by others, particularly from the government, to exploit one's resources according to one's own ability and interests (Hart 1955; Berlin 1969). Such premises alone would only support individuals' immunity from government interference in the form of 'negative' rights.

Other theorists recognize further interests, such as the ability to actually select certain options that they have reason to value (Gewirth 1982; Sen 1985; O'Neill 1986). Such accounts may require intervention by the state to provide the individual with the appropriate opportunities, and/or to protect them against the arbitrary will of others. The latter family of theories require a broad range of 'positive' government intervention and various social and economic rights to secure the satisfaction of basic human needs, projects and relationships (Follesdal 2005).

## A Note on Confucianism and Human Rights

I submit that Confucius and his disciple Mencius may be read as laying out some standards for legitimate internal sovereignty – though not expressed in terms of human rights. This claim might be surprising, and even contradicted by more common views often expressed: that Confucianism puts more emphasis on respecting hierarchical social structure, maintaining peace and harmonious relations, than the rights of individuals. If that is the sole acceptable interpretation of Confucianism, it would seem that human rights considerations are fundamentally inconsistent with widely held philosophical views in China. Any introduction of human rights would therefore appear as an uphill battle, fundamentally alien and incompatible with central Chinese standards of legitimate governance.

Space does not allow a detailed response to this worry and its implications. Here it must suffice to indicate that there are competing interpretive strands in Confucianism, more compatible with human rights constraints on government (Chan 1995 and 1998; Gangjian and Gang 1995; de Bary and Weiming 1998; Angle 2002). Such strands counsel against a wholesale dismissal of human rights as inconsistent with 'Asian values'.

Confucius held that for a governor to be fit to govern, he must avoid 'Terror, which rests on ignorance and murder. Tyranny, which demands results without proper warning' (Confucius 1997: 20.3). Mencius went even further, permitting tyrannicide (Mencius 1999: 55). He:

- required the king to take good care of the people, including limited taxation so as to secure that they had food and clothes, education (154-155),
- laid out the responsibility of the king to govern well in famines (121);
- held that to run a state well the king must take care of the people (154); and
- addressed the need to assess and weigh rites against human needs (381).

Mencius also provides some standards for what we would regard as legitimate external sovereignty: Unjust states may be attacked, but only by heaven (128); and humanitarian intervention is sometimes justified (190).

# 5. DEMOCRACY AND HUMAN RIGHTS FUELLING CALLS FOR SECESSION?

Human rights standards may be thought to foster unrest and trigger secession for several reasons. Firstly, systematic violation of the human rights of citizens of a sub-unit would be sufficient 'good cause' for secession, and legal acknowledgment of such rights would strengthen such calls (Baubock 2000). An express right to secede may itself be destabilizing (Sunstein 1994). Similarly, a focus on human rights may make the option of exit more salient for political entrepreneurs eager to allege mistreatment – regardless of whether such allegations are correct. What are we to make of such concerns?

To clarify what is at stake, I submit that we must distinguish the destabilizing role of human rights institutions from such effects of human rights violations. The concern here is primarily with the first, especially when conjoined with the second. Whether violations of vital interests of individuals themselves prompt secessionist movements is an important issue, but beyond the scope of our concern here. I submit that the crucial question is whether authorities' responsiveness to the best interests of citizens can be trusted and remain trustworthy in the eyes of citizens. One central mechanism in this regard is precisely arrangements that monitor and prevent human rights violations. Such human rights institutions can help provide trust and prevent calls for secession, *both* when there are no violations – because the institutions provide credible assurance thereof – *and* when there are violations. In these latter cases, human rights institutions may provide less drastic measures than secession to correct and prevent the violations. What are we to make of the fears?

First, note that the worry of unrest would seem to be even greater if citizens have no opportunities to scrutinize allegations of pervasive and long standing human rights violations, and if there is an unconditional link made between such violations and the right to secede. The former risk could be reduced by fact-finding and monitoring institutions. Both risks could be limited by arrangements that are known to replace authorities found guilty of such violations. Then secession would be only a safety valve when ordinary judicial and democratic remedies were exhausted. In such cases secession as a last resort might indeed not appear such an unacceptable option – when human rights violations actually occur.

Second, and in response, critics may worry that rights talk and democratic contestation promote self-interest rather than the proper other-regarding 'highest common concerns' of the federation as a whole. Such talk and contestation may fuel conflicts regardless of whether citizens' human rights are actually assaulted. If protesters are allowed to use democratic arenas and public media in furtherance of such objectives – regardless of their merit – debates may further fuel rather than quell unrest. However, I submit that legal human rights need not transform the public political culture into a conception of society as one of contestation among self-interest maximizers, who ignore duties and non-legal relations (Sandel 1982; Glendon 1991). Instead, human rights typically serve as aspects of the background structure securing somewhat fairer terms of day-to-day cooperation (Waldron 1988). They are safeguards that express, rather than threaten, the equal standing of all citizens (Chan 1995). Whether such legal protections are perceived as expressing a conflict view of society against the individual is not automatic, but largely a matter of the local political culture. Finally, one might worry that calls for secession in the name of democratic self-government and human rights may have a snowball effect, in that they mobilize new groups with less grounds for independence. I consider that concern below.

A preliminary conclusion is that several of these worries seem overdrawn: many fears that democracy and human rights protections will destabilize a holding-together federation seem unfounded. In particular, democratic parties, monitoring by independent media, and judiciary institutions may provide much assurance to reduce misplaced worries of human rights violations.

## 6. DEMOCRACY AND HUMAN RIGHTS QUELLING CALLS FOR SECESSION

Democratic and human rights may reduce the risk of secession in several ways, especially in a federal political order. They can safeguard the situation for minorities and political leaders within the existing state; they can limit the opportunities for ungrounded secessionist movements; and they reduce the temptations for a minority to create an independent nation state.

## Democratic Control over Constitutional Change

Recall that a federal arrangement can serve as a stable half way house with regard to sovereignty. They provide some measures of political immunity and local influence over common policies. Such credible commitment from the centre to respect sub-unit decisions in certain fields may reduce the demand for further independence. As observed in the case of the PRC, the ability to set up a credible federation that sub-unit leaders will trust requires that the central authorities cannot unilaterally revise the constitution. A federal arrangement thus requires an independent judiciary and some elements of the rule of law, including constitutional supremacy and some arrangement for the population of a sub-unit to democratically influence the content of the constitution (Ghai 2000a: 21-22).

## Human Rights-Respecting Centre Enhances Loyalty

Human rights, credibly enforced, may reduce sentiments for secession in several ways. If any human rights violations by the centre are visibly addressed once they are voiced, secession-prone minorities are less likely to be and feel oppressed within the federation. Their need to exit is less pressing. In a human rights compliant federation, minorities within a secession-seeking minority will also have their human rights protected (Simeon 1998; Zuckert 1996). They may, correctly, feel more secure within such a federal system than in a separate state where human rights mechanisms have yet to be established by what has become the majority of the new nation-state. Such internal minorities will thus not likely opt for secession.

In a society with democratic rights it may be easier for potential secessionists to voice their claims and gather supporters, as this might be thought to foster unrest. However, freedom of the press and opposition parties able to scrutinize competing claims may also serve to diffuse *unwarranted* claims by such 'ethnic entrepreneurs', for instance to check whether they indeed 'speak for the whole people' or only a vocal part of a majority; or to test whether indeed the centre has singled out a particular region for intentional mistreatment (Linz 1999: 29).

## Interlocking Democratic Federal Arrangements

In interlocking democratic federal arrangements, the sub-unit authorities participate in centre decision-making. Such arrangements have two beneficial effects. First, secession-seeking nationalists may prefer to exercise sub-unit power and such a share in central authority, realizing that they may be better of with such influence than by seceding (Baubock 2000: 379).

Second, many scholars point to the important character formation toward overarching loyalty that may occur within such mechanisms that bring central and sub-unit officials together (Kymlicka 1995; Linz 1999; Simeon and Conway 2001). Such arrangements are often recommended owing to the socialization effects when sub-unit representatives meet face-to-face to negotiate or deliberate about common concerns. Interlocking federal arrangements may thus lead officials to adjust their preferences, and include consideration of other members of the federation (McKay 2000 and 2004; Simeon and Conway 2001: 342). It also seems that federation-wide parties that are active at both sub-unit and centre levels are particularly conducive to the development of overarching loyalty (Linz 1999: 24).

## Human Rights Requirements Imposed on Any Future Independent State

Democratic and other human rights requirements imposed by the international community may also reduce the attractiveness of obtaining a separate state. Secessionist groups will know that they will be subject to human rights requirements on any future separate state that seeks external recognition. That will restrict the scope of sovereignty in ways that may diminish the perceived benefits of secession. The future political elite will for instance have to accommodate minorities and abide by democratic rule – reducing the opportunities for political gain.

The combined effect of human rights protections for citizens in interlocking federations, and on future secessionist scenarios, suggest that such rights in a federation will tend to reduce the risk of secession, rather than increase the risk. Thus, human rights may well serve a stabilizing function for federations.

## 7. CONCLUSION: SOME LESSONS

The present reflections have considered whether federal arrangements are sufficiently robust against claims to secession. Some fear that such constitutionally entrenched decentralization of authority will fuel further calls for sovereignty by some sub-units. Several elements of democratic and human rights can limit such risks, and thus enhance the long-terms stability of federal arrangements. Several features seem jointly necessary.[4] A credibly independent judiciary and mechanisms for constitutional self-binding by the centre authorities are necessary to establish a federation at all. Certain interlocking arrangements, and possibly constitutional requirements securing federation-wide parties, are conducive to stability. Moreover, important democratic and human rights may facilitate long term stability – especially freedom of the press and opposition parties. Recall also the crucial roles of political parties, beyond allowing citizens to 'kick rascals out.' Competing parties with alternative policy platforms are necessary for voters to have an informed and real prospective choice; they may stimulate creativity regarding agenda and policy options; provide scrutiny; and may enhance and constrain the option set available to the electorate. They can also maintain and foster citizens' commitment to broader societal interests. And in federations, parties can

---

[4] The list presented is not exhaustive. For instance, several authors note that timing is crucial: stability can be maintained if democracy comes first, then federal elements – while the reverse is more uncertain (Linz 1999: 35).

enhance the 'overarching loyalty' necessary among citizens of different sub-units who seek to live together – and apart – as political equals.

## Implications for the EU and for the People's Republic of China

In closing, consider some implications for the EU and the PRC. With regards to the recent developments of the EU as evidenced in the Reformed Treaty and the CTE, the increased visibility of human rights is thought to foster stability in the form of popular support. The CTE would also affirm or bolster at least three institutional mechanisms for preference formation through political parties, toward an 'overarching loyalty':

–   the political order is an interlocking federal arrangement, leading politicians to consider the impact both on individual sub-units and on other citizens of the federation;
–   national parliaments get increased opportunities for addressing issues of European integration. Publicity requirements regarding the Council's legislative work and access to documents of legislative sessions of the Council boosts national parliaments. They receive copies of suggested Treaty reforms and may – if sufficiently many agree – seek to prevent creeping centralization by claiming that proposals violate subsidiarity. Such opportunities would require discussion across sub-units, concerning precisely such central issues as the legitimate objectives of the sub-units and of the EU as a whole, and the best policies for achieving such objectives. Such discussions may foster the requisite overarching loyalty.
–   party competition is also crucial at the level of the European Union, to develop the desired 'overarching loyalty.' The Reformed Treaty will not only acknowledge some role for political parties (CTE Article I-46); it also would ensure increased transparency of the legislative process (Article I-50) and increased powers to the European Parliament (Article I-20), possibly influencing the choice of Commission President. The upshot may well be that European-level policies become contested - among European-level parties (Hix and Lord 1997; Magnette 2001; McKay 2001). Optimists may hope that these changes would make it more likely that parties will contribute to shaping Europeans' political preferences toward the requisite overarching loyalty over time. Such contestation may challenge a received view of the proper 'apolitical' role of the Commission as the guardian of 'the' European interest. But I submit that that view is flawed, and the benefits seem worth such costs. Indeed, it seems impossible to reduce the 'democratic deficit' without allowing such political contestation (Follesdal and Hix 2006). That would help citizens discover that Union decisions could be made otherwise – that 'the European interest' is indeed contestable, and that some of these decisions are indeed a matter of deliberate choice.

The Reformed Treaty will also provide additional measures that promote such negotiations in public, both by requiring publicity regarding Union institution proceedings

(CTE Article 50) and by ensuring that national parliaments get copies of legislative proposals and Commission consultation documents.

These developments should not lead to exuberance. As of yet, parties are not developed and functioning at the Union level – and it remains to be seen whether they will so develop. Elections to the European Parliament are largely 'second order' elections, a venue voters use to express their views about national government performance rather than focused on Union level political issues (Hix and Lord 1997; Hix 1999). It is difficult to guess whether such a trend will continue. Further pessimism may be fuelled by younger generations' 'postmaterialist' declining interest in party politics (Inglehart 1999).

Also, there is of course no reason to believe that the current set of political parties is optimal. They do not provide fluid platforms, but largely reflect old cleavages (Goodin 1996), and existing parties seem to force the new issues of European integration onto a traditional left-right axis. The established parties may even act as a cartel, blocking newcomers and new agenda points. Note, however, that these weaknesses are not flaws of the social functions performed by parties, but of the present crop of parties, and the difficulties of establishing and sustaining them in their multiple democratic functions. Thus these criticisms do not point to the need to abolish parties, bur rather to the challenge of how to rejuvenate their agendas and stimulate new parties.

Regarding the PRC, it too needs institutions that will foster willing support for the long term stability of the political order. Yet many of the challenges are different. The present reflections suggest that insofar as some nationalities and areas seek greater political autonomy and even secession, several recommendations may be relevant.

Federal experiments could well curb more extreme secessionist movements. A federation in the sense defined, with constitutionally entrenched division of authority, cannot be created with sufficient credibility unless the centre authorities renounce their monopoly on constitutional change, allowing sub-units some decisive role. The details of such influence must be explored elsewhere – for instance, it would seem unwise to allow each sub-unit a veto, since this easily stifles even necessary changes as long as they are detrimental to any one sub-unit.[5] Another required change is to enhance the perceived independence of the judiciary in charge of maintaining the division of powers.

Were a federation to be established, the lack of opposition parties in the PRC does not completely rule out the possibility of obtaining sufficient stability, though we may question the normative legitimacy of such an order. It might seem an open question whether the various functions secured by parties in multi-party democracies can be secured by other means. In particular, some bodies should be authorized to question and criticize government action with impunity, in order to promote good governance. Other bodies than parties and free media may do so, recall Mencius' criticisms of officials who failed in their duties and his argument that freedom of information is needed for vital feedback about government failures (Mencius 1999: 63, 121). There may also be other bodies in a one-party state that secure the various other functions outlined above, including the identification of fair policies; creative, realistic and consistent policy formulation; sustaining the right motives among the leadership; and the proper character formation of citizens.

To conclude, democratic, human rights respecting federations may not provide complete guarantees against secession by territorially clustered ethnic, linguistic, cultural or religious

---

[5] A weakness Robert Dahl identifies for the Unites States of America (Dahl 2001: 147-48).

minorities. Federal solutions may not be obtainable for all unitary states that struggle with internal conflicts along territorial lines, given their rules for constitutional change. But the alternatives modes of accommodating differences may be even less stable.

## REFERENCES

Angle, Stephen A. (2002) *Human Rights and Chinese Thought: A Cross-Cultural Inquiry*, Cambridge: Cambridge University Press.

Barry, Brian (1991) 'Is Democracy Special?' *Democracy and Power*, Oxford: Oxford University Press, pp. 24-60.

Baubock, Rainer (2000) 'Why Stay Together? A Pluralist Approach to Secession and Federation', in Will Kymlicka and Wayne Norman (eds) *Citizenship in Diverse Societies,* Oxford: Oxford University Press, pp. 366-94.

Beetham, David and Lord, Christopher (1998) *Legitimacy and the European Union*, London: Longman.

Bellamy, Richard, and Warleigh, Alex (1999). 'From an Ethics of Integration to an Ethics of Participation: Citizenship and the Future of the European Union' *Millennium: Journal of International Studies* 27(3): 447-70.

Berlin, Isaiah (1969) *Four Essays on Liberty*, London: Oxford University Press.

Chan, Joseph (1995) 'The Asian Challenge to Universal Human Rights: A Philosophical Appraisal', in James Tuck and Hong Tang (eds) *Human Rights and International Relations in the Asia-Pacific Region*, New York: St. Martin's Press, pp. 25-38.

Chan, Joseph (1998) 'A Confucian Perspective on Human Rights', in: Joanne R. Bauer and Daniel A. Bell (eds) *The East Asian Challenge for Human Rights*, New York: Cambridge University Press, pp. 212-40.

Confucius (1997) *Analects*, Simon Leys translator and notes, New York: Norton.

Council of the European Union (2004) 'Treaty Establishing a Constitution for Europe' *Official Journal of the European Union* 47, 2004/C 310/01.

Dahl, Robert A. (1983) 'Federalism and the Democratic Process', in J. R. Pennock and J. W. Chapman (eds) *Liberal Democracy,* Nomos Vol. 25, New York: New York University Press, pp. 95-108.

Dahl, Robert A. (1998) *On Democracy*, New Haven: Yale University Press.

Dahl, Robert A. (2001) *How Democratic Is the American Constitution?* New Haven: Yale University Press.

de Bary, Wm. Theodore and Weiming, Tu (eds) (1998) *Confucianism and Human Rights*, New York: Columbia University Press.

Dehousse, Renaud (ed.) (1994) *Europe After Maastricht: an Ever Closer Union?* Munchen: Law Books in Europe.

Dobson, Lynn and Andreas Follesdal (eds) (2004) *Political Theory and the European Constitution*, London: Routledge.

Follesdal, Andreas (1998) 'Democracy, Legitimacy and Majority Rule in the EU', in Albert Weale and Michael Nentwich (eds) *Political Theory and the European Union: Legitimacy, Constitutional Choice and Citizenship*, London: Routledge, pp. 34-48.

Follesdal, Andreas (2000) 'Subsidiarity and Democratic Deliberation', in Erik Oddvar Eriksen and John Erik Fossum (eds), *Democracy in the European Union: Integration Through Deliberation?* London: Routledge, pp. 85-110.

Follesdal, Andreas (2005) 'Human Rights and Relativism', in Andreas Follesdal and Thomas Pogge (eds) *Real World Justice: Grounds, Principles, Human Rights Standards and Institutions*, Berlin: Springer, pp. 265-83.

Follesdal, Andreas (2006a) 'Federalism', in Edward N. Zalta (ed.) *Stanford Encyclopedia of Philosophy*. Available from: <http://plato.stanford.edu/ entries/federalism/>.

Follesdal, Andreas (2006b) 'The Legitimacy Deficits of the European Union' *Journal of Political Philosophy* 14(4): 441-68.

Follesdal, Andreas (2008) 'How to Organize Democracy in Multi-Level and Multi-Cultural States: Can It Be Done? Should It Be Done?', in Beate Kohler-Koch (ed.), Beijing: Chinese Academy of Social Science.

Follesdal, Andreas and Hix, Simon (2006) 'Why There Is a Democratic Deficit in the EU: A Response to Majone and Moravcsik' *Journal of Common Market Studies* 44(3): 533-62.

Gangjian, Du and Gang, Song (1995) 'Relating Human Rights to Chinese Culture: The Four Paths of the Confucian Analects and the Four Principles of a New Theory of Benevolence', in Michael C. Davis (ed.) *Human Rights and Chinese Values: Legal, Philosophical, and Political Perspectives*, Oxford: Oxford University Press, pp. 35-56.

Gewirth, Alan (1982) *Human Rights: Essays on Justification and Applications*, Chicago: Chicago University Press.

Ghai, Jash (2000a) 'Chinese Minorities: Autonomy with Chinese Characteristics', in Jash Ghai (ed.) *Autonomy and Ethnicity: Negotiating Competing Claims in Multi-Ethnic States*, Cambridge: Cambridge University Press.

Ghai, Jash (2000b) 'Autonomy As a Strategy for Diffusing Conflict', in: Paul C. Stern and Daniel Druckman (eds) *International Conflict Resolution After the Cold War* , Washington DC: National Academy Press, pp. 483-530 .

Glendon, Mary Ann (1991) *Rights Talk: the Impoverishment of Political Discourse*, New York: Free Press.

Goodin, Robert E. (1996) 'Institutionalizing the Public Interest: The Defense of Deadlock and Beyond' *American Political Science Review* 90(2): 331-43.

Hall, Peter A. (1993) 'Policy Paradigms, Social Learning, and the State: the Case of Economic Policymaking in Britain' *Comparative Politics* 25(3): 275-96.

Hart, H. L. A. (1955) 'Are There Any Natural Rights?' *Philosophical Review* 64: 175-91.

Held, David (1995) *Democracy and the Global Order*, Cambridge: Polity Press.

Hix, Simon (1999) *The Political System of the European Union*, London: Macmillan Press.

Hix, Simon, and Lord, Christopher (1997) *Political Parties in the European Union*, London: Macmillan.

Inglehart, Ronald (1999) 'Postmodernization Erodes Respect for Authority, but Increases Support for Democracy', in Pippa Norris (ed.) *Critical Citizens: Global Support for Democratic Government*, Oxford: Oxford University Press, pp. 236-256.

Key Jr., Valdimer Orlando (1964) *Politics, Parties and Pressure Groups*. 5th edition, New York: Crowell.

Kymlicka, Will. 1995. *Multicultural citizenship: A liberal theory of minority rights*. Oxford: Oxford University Press.

Lijphart, Arend (1999) *Patterns of Democracy: Government Forms and Performance in Thirty-Six Countries*, New Haven: Yale University Press.

Linz, Juan J. (1999) 'Democracy, Multinationalism and Federalism', in W. Busch and A. Merkel (eds) *Demokratie in Ost Und West*, Frankfurt am Main: Suhrkamp, pp. 382-401. Available from: <http://www.march.es/ NUEVO/IJM/CEACS/PUBLICACIONES/ WORKING%20PAPERS/1997_103.pdf>.

Lipset, Seymour Martin, and Rokkan, Stein (eds) (1967) *Party Systems and Voter Alignments*, New York: Free Press.

Magnette, Paul (2001) 'European Governance and Civic Participation: Can the European Union Be Politicised?', in Christian Joerges, Yves Meny and J. H. H. Weiler (eds) *Symposium: Responses to the European Commission's White Paper on Governance*, Badia Fiesolana: European University Institute. Available from: <http://www.iue.it/ RSC/symposium/>.

Manin, Bernard, Przeworski, Adam and Stokes, Susan C. (1999) 'Introduction', in Adam Przeworski, Susan C. Stokes and Bernard Manin (eds) *Democracy, Accountability, Representation*, Cambridge: Cambridge University Press, pp. 1-26.

Martin, Rex, and Reidy, David (eds) (2006) *Rawls's Law of Peoples: A Realistic Utopia?* Oxford: Blackwell.

McKay, David (2000) 'Policy Legitimacy and Institutional Design: Comparative Lessons for the European Union' *Journal of Common Market Studies* 38(1): 25-44.

McKay, David (2001) *Designing Europe - Comparative Lessons From the Federal Experience*, Oxford: Oxford University Press.

McKay, David (2004) 'The EU as a Self-Sustaining Federation: Specifying the Constitutional Conditions', in Lynn Dobson and Andreas Follesdal (eds) *Political Theory and the European Constitution,* London: Routledge, pp. 23-39.

Meehan, Elizabeth (2001) 'The Constitution of Institutions', in: Kalypso Nicolaidis and Robert Howse (eds) *The Federal Vision: Legitimacy and Levels of Governance in the US and the EU*, Oxford: Oxford University Press, pp. 403-12.

Mencius (1999) *Mencius*, Beijing: Sinolingua.

Moravcsik, Andrew (2001) 'Federalism in the European Union: Rhetoric and Reality', in: Kalypso Nicolaidis and Robert Howse (eds) *The Federal Vision: Legitimacy and Levels of Governance in the US and the EU*, Oxford: Oxford University Press, pp. 161-87.

Moravcsik, Andrew (2002) 'In Defence of the 'Democratic Deficit': Reassessing Legitimacy in the European Union' *Journal of Common Market Studies* 40(4): 603-24.

Nicolaidis, Kalypso (2001) 'Conclusion: The Federal Vision Beyond the Nation State', in: Kalypso Nicolaidis and Robert Howse (eds) *The Federal Vision: Legitimacy and Levels of Governance in the US and the EU*, Oxford: Oxford University Press, pp. 439-81.

O'Neill, Onora (1986) *Faces of Hunger: an Essay on Poverty, Justice and Development*, London: Allen and Unwin.

Papadopoulos, Yannis (2005) 'Implementing (and Radicalising) Art. 46.4 of the Draft Constitution: Is the Addition of Some (Semi-) Direct Democracy to the Nascent Consociational European Federation Just Swiss Folklore ?' *Journal of European Public Policy* 12(3): 448-467.

Powell, G. Bingham (2000) *Elections As Instruments of Democracy: Majoritarian and Proportional Visions*, New Haven: Yale University Press.

Rawls, John (1971) *A Theory of Justice*, Cambridge: Harvard University Press.

Rothstein, Bo (1998) *Just Institutions Matter: The Moral and Political Logic of the Universal Welfare State*, Cambridge: Cambridge University Press.

Sandel, Michael J. (1982) *Liberalism and the Limits of Justice*, Cambridge: Cambridge University Press.

Schattschneider, E. E. (1960) *The Semi-Sovereign People: A Realist's View of Democracy in America*, New York: Holt, Rinehart and Winston.

Schmitter, Philippe, and Karl, Terry Lynn (1991) 'What Democracy Is ... and What It Is Not' *Journal of Democracy* 2: 75-88.

Schmitter, Philippe C. (2004) 'Is Federalism for Europe a Solution or a Problem: Tocqueville Inverted, Perverted or Subverted?', in: Lynn Dobson and Andreas Follesdal (eds) *Political Theory and the European Constitution,* London: Routledge, pp. 10-22..

Schumpeter, Joseph A. (1976 [1943]) *Capitalism, Socialism and Democracy*, London: Allen and Unwin.

Sen, Amartya K. (1985) 'Well-Being, Agency and Freedom' *Journal of Philosophy* 82(4): 169-221.

Sen, Amartya K. (1988) 'Property and Hunger', *Economics and Philosophy* 4: 57-68.

Simeon, Richard (1998) 'Considerations on the Design of Federations: The South African Constitution in Comparative Perspective' *SA Publiekreg/Public Law* 13(1): 42-72.

Simeon, Richard, and Daniel-Patrick Conway (2001) 'Federalism and the Management of Conflict in Multinational Societies', in: Alain-G. Gagnon and James Tully (eds) *Multinational Democracies*, Cambridge: Cambridge University Press, pp. 338-65.

Stepan, Alfred (1999) 'Federalism and Democracy: Beyond the U.S. Model' *Journal of Democracy* 10: 19-34.

Sunstein, Cass R. (1994) 'Approaching Democracy: a New Legal Order for Eastern Europe -- Constitutionalism and Secession', in Chris Brown (ed.) *Political Restructuring in Europe: Ethical Perspectives*, London: Routledge, pp. 11-49.

Swenden, Wilfried (2004) 'Is the European Union in Need of a Competence Catalogue? Insights From Comparative Federalism' *Journal of Common Market Studies* 42(2): 371-92.

Tushnet, Mark (1996) 'Federalism and Liberalism' *Cardozo Journal of International and Comparative Law* 4: 329-44.

Waldron, Jeremy (1988) 'When Justice Replaces Affection: the Need for Rights' *Harvard Journal of Law and Public Policy* 11: 625-47.

Wallace, Helen (1993) 'Deepening and Widening: Problems of Legitimacy for the EC', in S. Garcia (ed.) *European Identity and the Search for Legitimacy*, London: Pinter, pp. 95-105.

Weiler, J. H. H. (1996) 'European Neo-Constitutionalism: In Search of Foundations for the European Constitutional Order', in Richard Bellamy and Dario Castiglione (eds) *Constitutionalism in Transformation: European and Theoretical Perspectives*, Oxford: Blackwell, pp. 105-21.

Weiler, J. H. H. (1999) *The Constitution of Europe*, Cambridge: Cambridge University Press.

Zuckert, Michael P. (1996) 'Toward a Theory of Corrective Federalism: the United States Constitution, Federalism, and Rights', in Ellis Katz and G. Alan Tarr (eds) *Federalism and Rights*, Lanham: Rowman and Littlefield, pp. 76-100.

In: Asian Economic and Political Development
Editor: Felix Chin

ISBN: 978-1-61122-470-2
© 2011 Nova Science Publishers, Inc.

# IDENTITY CHANGE AND THE EMERGENCE OF REGIONALISM

## *Chunyao Yi*

School of Politics and International Studies,
University of Leeds

## ABSTRACT

Despite considerable research on how regional cooperation forms and how a regional integration process starts, the origin of regionalism, with particular reference to identity change and a formative regional identity, has not been fully explained. Meanwhile, although mainstream studies have acknowledged that a crisis may become the crucial catalyst for the emergence of regionalism, they have not generally analyzed how regionalism emerges in a crisis related context. This article examines the effects of international crises on one key element of the emerging regionalism – the development of collective identity. It links the question of identity change under the condition of international crisis with the emergence of regionalism, a perspective distinct from the explanations purely based on rational choice and adaptation. It further addresses the issue of identity change by referring to European and East Asian experiences, thus contributing to our understanding as to how regionalism emerged in a particular historical context.

## INTRODUCTION

Regional cooperation and regionalism have proliferated, from the remarkable regional integration in Europe since the 1950s, to a new worldwide resurgence since the late 1980s and more recent developments in East Asia. While most research efforts have been focused on the integration process, there has been renewed interest in looking at why and how regionalism emerges in particular regions from different perspectives (Milward 1984; Beeson 2004 and 2005; Stubbs 2002). Collective identity has been recognized as a key element in the making of a region as a social/political/economic entity or a regional community (Cronin 1999). 'Regional identity' is, in a way, also an interpretation of the process through which a region becomes institutionalized – a process consisting of the production of territorial boundaries, regional cohesion and institutions (Berezin and Schain 2003). Regional identity is constructed as part of the making of regions and used to maintain groupness and different exclusionary practices.

There have been quite a few descriptive, as well as normative, analyzes of what regional identity is or ought to be in the European setting (Garcia 1993; Joyce 2002; Fossum 2003).

There has also been a debate over whether and to what extent a European identity actually exists, which often links to the question of the identity-shaping potential of the European supranational institutions (Wessels 1998; Laffan 1998 and 2004). In East Asia, it is interesting to note that at the time when the Asian Financial Crisis broke out 'East Asia' remained mainly a geographic concept although the economic regionalization occurred through a market-led process without formal economic and institutional arrangements (Beeson 2004; Ando and Kimura 2003; Stubbs 2002; Saito 1999). The 'region' itself had been ill defined and there existed overlapping and competing definitions – Asia Pacific, Asia, Pacific-Rim are among those most often used (Peng 2002; Bowles 2002). There was a lack of a coherent regional voice on economic issues in East Asia. The rising regional consciousness and coherent efforts concerning East Asian regional economic governance, namely various regional economic and financial arrangements under the framework of the Association of Southeast Asian Nations Plus Three (APT), did not appear until the Asian Financial Crisis (AFC). Despite considerable research on how regional cooperation has formed and how a regional integration process has started, the origin of regionalism, with particular reference to identity change and a formative regional identity, has not been fully explained. The consolidation of a European identity and an emerging East Asian awareness raises the following question: what is the threshold at which a regional identity might emerge?

Although mainstream studies have acknowledged that a crisis may become the crucial catalyst for the emergence of regionalism, they have not generally analyzed how regionalism emerges in a crisis related context. This article focuses on the effects of international crises on one key element of the emerging regionalism – the development of collective identity shared by a group of countries. It links the question of identity change under the condition of international crisis with the emergence of regionalism, a perspective distinct from the explanations purely based on rational choice and adaptation. It further addresses the identity change with reference to the European and East Asian experiences, thus contributing to a better understanding of how regionalism emerged in particular historical contexts.

This article starts with a review of how mainstream research defines and uses the concept of 'regional identity'. This is followed by probing different theoretical approaches as to how a collective regional identity might emerge and how regional identity has been incorporated into regional integration and regionalism studies. After identifying some definitional and theoretical gaps, this article adopts an analytical framework of identity and scrutinize the emerging regional identity in relation to the European and East Asian experiences, with special attention to the mechanism active in transforming the effects of a crisis.

## ABOUT REGIONAL IDENTITY

For International Relations (IR)/regionalism scholars, regional identity is a key element to understanding regional cooperation and integration (Katzenstein 1996a and 1996b; Hall 1999; Johnston 2005). Depending on the context of the use of this concept and the theoretical approach followed what people mean when they talk about 'regional identity' and how this concept has been used are quite different. A few key uses can be identified in the literature.

First of all, regional identity is often linked to the primordial nature of a region. Narratives of regional identity consist of such elements as the nature, landscape, environment, ethnicity, language, religion and culture of a region, often implying a certain degree of homogeneity (Paasi 2003). One of the five categories of regionalism[1] in Andrew Hurrell's study is 'regional awareness and identity', which is 'often defined in terms of common culture, history or religious tradition' (1997: 41). The underlying assumption is that regional identity is contained in regional tradition and values. This argument is mostly found in literatures which trace the sources of European identity to cultural legacies such as ancient Rome and the Renaissance (Abrweiler 1993; Hale 1993; Kumar 2003), or the debates concerning the so-called 'Asian value' (Berger 1988). This is a historically and culturally deep-rooted definition which gives prominence to the particularities of each individual region and highlights the uniqueness of each. Strictly speaking, these features of nature, culture and ethnic group are used to distinguish one region from others and are actually the *identity of a region* (Paasi 2003).

Second, in contrast to the first point, regional identity is something socially and institutionally constructed. It has been argued that regional identity should not only mean 'what the world's 'natural' regions are', but also be used as 'an analytical device' to suggest what they 'ought to be' (Haas 1970: 612). In this inquiry 'one is forced to admit that geographic designations are not 'real', 'natural' or 'essential', [rather] [t]hey are socially constructed and politically contested and are thus open to change and vulnerable to the twin risks of reification and relativization' (Katzenstein 1997: 7). Moreover, in the region-building process, the 'geographical area is transformed from a passive object to an active subject capable of articulating the transnational interests of the emerging region' (Hettne and Soderbaum 2000: 461). While many studies focus on the internal construction of regions, regional identity is also regarded as a constitutive element of localized resistance to globalization (Castells 1997).

Third, regional identity is a perception of regional awareness and belonging, 'a shared perception of belonging to a particular community' (Hurrell 1997: 41). It depends on 'collective beliefs that the definition of the group and its membership is shared by all those in the group' (Zürn and Checkel 2005: 1066). Regional identity is a kind of social identity, shared by a group of states. It is not simply individual identities that are added together. It has intersubjective substance and is typically embodied in symbols, discourses and institutions. This understanding of regional identity is derived from the Social Identity Theory (SIT). In SIT, membership of a social group entails a shared identity, where individuals have a collective awareness of themselves as a group with a distinct social identity, where value and emotional significance is attached to group membership and, crucially, where the social group is constantly evaluated and compared with other social groups within a similar realm (Tajfel 1978: 63).

---

[1] Andrew Hurrell breaks up 'regionalism' into 'five different categories': (1) regionalization (autonomous economic process based on market force); (2) regional awareness and identity; (3) regional interstate co-operation; (4) state-promoted regional integration, and (5) regional cohesion. He provides an explanation of each category. However, he does not further explore how one may relate to another. See Hurrell (1997: 39-45).

# MAIN APPROACHES IN THE STUDY
# OF REGIONAL IDENTITY

Having discussed the definitions of regional identity, this section looks at how a collective regional identity might emerge and how regional identity has been incorporated into regional integration and regionalism studies. Social identity theory suggests that evidence of identity change would involve changes in conceptions of 'ingroupness', new definitions of boundaries, changes in self-valuation as new cooperative arrangements are created, and action motivated by a desire to maximize group valuation (Johnston 2005). Two general theoretical approaches in IR literature have discussed the issue of identity change and tried to analyze to what extent the formation of a collective identity is possible among international actors.

Although liberal institutionalism is more concerned with behavioural cooperation than identity change, its exponents argue that the conditions of rising interdependence increase the objective vulnerability and sensitivity of actors to each other and iterated cooperation affects mutual expectations among actors (Koehane and Kye 1977). Following this logic, increasing interdependency is a systemic condition in which an actor's identity may potentially be transformed through interactions (Sterling-Floker 2000). Moreover, in order to achieve certain goals, actors engage in 'collective practices' – involving 'persistent and connected sets of rules (formal and informal) that prescribe behavioural roles, constrain activity, and shape expectations' – as well as interacting with each other (Keohane 1990: 175). These collective practices allow for the possibility of an emerging collective identity. Once cooperation is associated with efficient interest maximization, the incentive to continue cooperating is reinforced. Repeated cooperation then produces a progressively expanding commitment to the cooperative effort. In other words, cooperative regimes can 'make a difference to actors' beliefs by helping to create a reinforcing 'feed-back' loop (Krasner 1983; Jervis 1991).

Social constructivism perceives collective identity as 'positive identification with the welfare of another, such that the other is seen as a cognitive extension of the self, rather than independent' and 'it is a basis for feelings of solidarity, community, and loyalty and thus for collective definitions of interest' (Wendt 1994: 386). They distinguish between alliances formed for instrumental reasons and collective security arrangements which are based on the commitment and willingness to act on 'generalized principles of conduct' and norms and diffuse reciprocity (Ruggie 1998; Wendt 1994; Cronin 1999). In other words, by defining a 'collective identity' and demonstrating its existence, social constructivists have tried to provide an alterative angle from which to study 'collective actions', which are not merely about rational calculations by self-interested actors and their instrumental interactions, but a process of creating new identities. Regarding the formation of a collective identity, social constructivists have argued that intersubjective structures, consisting of the shared understandings, expectations and social knowledge embedded in international institutions and threat complexes, help determine the dynamics of collective identity formation (Wendt 1994).

Although both approaches acknowledge the possibility of identity change, there are fundamental differences between them concerning the issue of collective identity. Liberal institutionalism resorts to rationalist assumptions about the actor's motivation to engage in collective actions, namely maximizing utility function. Similarly, its core implications regarding the formation of collective identity are that practices and interests may influence and redefine identity. In contrast, social constructivism, based on the assumption of an intersubjective structure, argues that collective identity is formed out of social interactions and in discursive contexts.

Both approaches have influenced views on regional identity in regionalism and regional integration studies. An early European integration theorist observed that: '…the interests and values defended by the major groups involved in the process … are far too complex to be described in such simple terms as 'the desire for Franco-German peace' or the 'will to a United Europe'… [V]alues will undergo change, that interests will be redefined in terms of a regional rather than a purely national orientation and that the erstwhile set of separate national group values will gradually be superseded by a new and geographically larger set of beliefs.' (Haas 1968: 13-14) However, even with such sensitivity to the collective identity issues, early integration theories only assumed that once the regional cooperation began to generate benefits, loyalties and expectations will gradually and naturally shift to the new regional centre (Lindberg 1963; Haas 1968). Deutsch pointed out that the key character of a 'political community' is not the establishment of organization or institution, but a sense of belonging (Deutsch 1957 and 1968). The development of a sense of community largely depends upon an effective and significant pattern of communications between units. As the intensity of communication increases, so will the sense of community.

Later research has tried to overcome the ambiguity in defining regional collective identity and explore the relations between regional integration, regional community building and regional identity. There are three tendencies in considering regional identity, which more or less overlap with the concepts and approaches identified earlier. The first is the enquiry into the nature of a potential regional collective identity (Fossum 2003; Keunen 2007). This is an approach examining the content, characteristics and components of commonly shared cultures and values. This is often either a historically and culturally rooted definition which highlights the particularities and uniqueness of an individual region, or a normatively based prescription as to what a regional identity should look like in order to facilitate further integration. The second approach, instead of emphasizing culture and traditions, argues that a regional identity results from political practices. Similar to the liberal institutionalist logic, it treats regional identity as a dependent variable and analyzes how the evolution of cooperation might lead to evolution of a collective identity and how a regional collective identity is formed in the regional integration process. Checkel has argued that the duration and intensity of exposure to an institution may lead to a higher level or more intensive identification with the institution (Checkel 2005). With its densely institutionalized regional structure, the European Union (EU) has been regarded as an ideal laboratory and 'social soil within which actor's preferences might be transformed' (Jupille and Caporaso 1999: 440). The role of regional identity has also been noted as a precondition for multilevel citizenship (Painter 2002). Considerable research has been devoted to the interplays between regional identity and national identity (for example Checkel 2001; Marcussen et al. 2001). The third approach treats regional identity as an independent variable and brings it into the explanation of the emergence of regional integration and regional community. It often tries to explore the link between regional institutional designs and particular identities. The regional group uses its acquired norms and values to compare and evaluate performances and opinions and this provides rules, standards and beliefs about what constitutes appropriate conduct and attitudes. For example, Terada argues that a particular new regional concept of East Asia has promoted substantial regional cooperation in the region (Terada 2003). However, this approach does not provide a satisfactory explanation as to how a regional collective identity is formed in the first place.

## THE GAPS

Even though we are able to identify some fundamental elements of the concept 'regional identity' and the main theoretical approaches, the ambiguity in the use of this concept as an analytical tool still exists. One question is the dichotomy between an individual-based understanding of how to define the self in relation to the region as a group and a perspective of a regional group defining its own identity (Hymans 2002). In other words, the former deals with the question of 'where do *I* belong' at the level of the individual and the latter the question of 'where do *we* belong' at the group level. The first approach answers the question to what extent an actor identifies with the region. It focuses on the central role of the individual in defining its own understanding of its group level of self. A regional identity is what an actor attributes to itself by taking the perspective of a region. From this perspective, regional identity emphasizes an individual's positive identification with the welfare of the group and the argument that the formation of a collective identity generates collective interests (Wendt 1994). The second approach looks at the self-understanding of a regional group as a unit, the collective meaning of who and what they think they are. It explains how a regional group, sometimes in the forms of regional institutions or governance, manifests itself in solidarity, in shared dispositions or consciousness, or in collective actions. This may be a product of social or institutional processes or actions, such as 'new social movement[s]' (Brubaker and Cooper 2000). While the first approach is mostly established by an analysis of the concrete social identities of actors which may be state or non-state actors, such as individual citizens, factors such as institutional thickness, social embeddness and governance are often used in understanding a regional identity in the second approach (Mackinnon et al. 2002). Meanwhile, the increase in the social identities of individual actors in the first approach may not necessarily be equal to a collective regional identity defined by the second approach.

Another question is the different emphasis of 'self' and 'other', of 'differences' and 'similarities' – whether the regional identity is expressing an intra-group or inter-group phenomenon. Social Identity Theory indicates that a collective identity cannot occur without a distinction between 'us' and the 'other' (Della Porta and Diani 1999; Neumann 1999). However, a collective identity is not only based on a differentiation between in-groups and out-groups, but rather on similarities, commonness and intra-group connections (Neumann 1996; Yuki 2003). While competition with out-groups is not irrelevant to a collective identity, it is sometimes far from the most important factor (Rich 1999). 'Individual and collective identities are created not simply in the difference between self and other but in those moments of ambiguity where one is other to oneself, and in the recognition of the other as like' (Norton 1988: 7). Actors acquire and sustain their collective identities within groups by their interactions with each other. A strongly bounded sense of groupness may rest on categorical commonality and an associated feeling of belonging together (Brubaker and Cooper 2000).

The third question is how to measure collective identity. Does collective identity have different levels consistent with the degree of actors' identification with the group? Membership is a kind of constitutive indicator to demonstrate that one individual is constitutively or legally bound to a certain social group. It is an indicator which shows a rather static status and cannot necessarily describe the intersubjective content of social identity and its change. Cronin's way of treating identity as 'a continuum from negative to positive' is useful to clarify the issue of measurement (1999: 17; Wendt 1994). This continuum ranges from the very negative end, hostility, to rivalry, indifference, cohesion, altruism, and lastly to symbiosis, the very positive end. The first three – hostility, rivalry and indifference – are negative identities, and the last three – cohesion, altruism and symbiosis – are positive identities. With this continuum, a regional identity in the majority of IR discussions lies in the positive part, either from 'indifference' (or even rivalry) to 'cohesion', or from 'cohesion' to 'altruism'.

Regionalism and integration studies seem to assume either that a primordial regional identity somehow pre-exists, or that significant identity change only occurs in the process of regional integration. An area which has been neglected is that which enquires what the emergence of regional integration schemes has to do with the identity change. The question is: will identity change occur only under the conditions of actors being 'locked in' to the cooperative arrangements and taking part into the repeated cooperation, to use liberal institutionalist terminology, or under the conditions of regional integration which is already 'taking off', to use regional integrationist terminology? Cannot identity change take place at the time of 'locking in' and 'taking off'? Since 'regional identity' has been, in a way, an interpretation of the process through which a region becomes institutionalized and socialized, examining the emerging regional identity in its threshold will also help us to understand the emergence of regional integration and regionalism.

Finally, the 'catalytic' impact ascribed to international crisis in relation to the emergence of regionalism has been widely acknowledged (Terada 2003; Bustelo 2003; Stubbs 2002). As some regional cooperation and integration processes start in a crisis or post-crisis context, it is worth examining more closely how crisis has triggered the change of a regional structure. If tackling the crisis by regional actors may advance the awareness of the regional group (Terada 2003), how has the crisis done so? Existing research has overlooked these critical historical moments which have remarkably changed the course of regional development. What is needed is an approach to understanding the identity change that incorporates the mechanism active in transforming the effects of crisis. One way to address this question is to adopt a social constructivist concept of 'social learning'. This article suggests that identity change and the emerging regional collective identity can be explained by utilizing an analytical framework based on the identity theory together with the social constructivist 'learning' process.

## EMERGING COLLECTIVE IDENTITY: AN ANALYTICAL FRAMEWORK

### Two Dimensions of Identity

This article adopts the analytical framework suggested in Abdelal et al. *Identity as a Variable* and scrutinize identity change and the emerging regional collective identity in the context of international crisis. Abdelal et al. has unpacked the content of identity into four somewhat overlapping dimensions: constitutive norms, social purposes, relational comparisons and cognitive models (Abdelal et al. 2006). This framework will be slightly modified in order to better answer the research question how a collective identity emerges and to link this to the areas of ambiguity identified in the earlier sections.

With the limited space, this article focuses only on two aspects: *normative beliefs* and *relational content. Normative beliefs*[2] are about value judgements of social and political practices. They deal with such fundamental questions as good or bad, better or worse, superior or inferior; whether a particular practice or policy is more desirable or more effective than others in dealing with human problems by maintaining and modifying security and wealth, peace and development, and whether the new form of 'human community' is superior than the old one, and it is all about a question of 'ought to' (Haas 1970: 608, 624; Nye 1968: 856-7). The normative beliefs shared by a group are a kind of 'we-mode beliefs' which are performatively and collectively accepted and committed to (Tuomela 2003). Normative beliefs are the basis for the common goals of a group and lead actors to act in ways which fulfil the group's aims. Normative beliefs, therefore, form the basis for actions. '*Relational content*' is about self and group understandings as well as views about other actors. It means an accentuation of perceived similarities between self and other in-group members and perceived differences between self and out-group members (Hogg and Abrams 1988: 21). Relational content is actually based on a 'world view', a set of ideas and beliefs through which actors try to comprehend the material world, the meaning given to a situation, the self-perception about the position in the international system or in a specific situation. Relational understandings are the basis for a social-psychological appeal, awareness and consciousness.

## Change of Identity and Crisis

Changes in identity are generally slow, as actors adapt to social competition and social evolution over the long term (Albert and Whetten 1985). However, special social events may influence the fluidity of identity and are therefore, able to expedite the change of identity. In these cases, the changes tend to be dramatic rather than gentle. 'What constitutes a crisis is an important definitional issue for ideational analysis... [and] the potential contribution of ideational analysis lies in its presumed but not yet clearly articulated ability to explain the factors that affect these perceptions in the first place...' (Campbell 2000 as quoted in Gofas 2001: 13). Here what Sahlins (1991: 43-4) calls 'the structure of meaning' defines an event as significant, in which a cognitive process is involved and determines which external events will be observed, how they will be perceived, whether they leave any lasting effects and how the information they convey will be organized for future use (Bandura 1977: 160). Moreover, the underlining ideational and normative structure cannot revert to its previous condition because the events of crisis create new understandings and attitudes (Higgs 1987). The two aspects of a collective identity often become prominent during crisis. When the existing order is widely perceived as working poorly or even breaking down, the existing normative beliefs and practices are challenged and shaken loose. Crisis also challenges beliefs about friendly or

---

[2] As 'the formal and informal rules that define group membership' appear in later stage of integration, this paper will not adopt the term of 'constitutive norms' (Abdelal et al. 2005: 8), but use the more flexible 'normative beliefs'.

adversary actors, the character of the environment and the adequacy of existing organizational and political arrangements designed to cope with that environment (Stern 1997). Accordingly, new normative beliefs and relational content are defined and applied by the group.

## Collective Social Learning

From a social constructivist perspective, the collective meaning of identities is neither fixed nor predetermined, and it is subject to a process of 'social contestation' (Abdelal et al. 2005: 16). Identity change induced by such acute events as regional crisis cannot be explained without explaining how the beliefs 'got in there', and 'why these beliefs happen to coincide' (Kratochwil 2000: 80). 'Collective social learning' serves as the main mechanism in such a cognitive process, linking identity with a changing environment (crisis), and therefore accounting for the change of identity (Wendt 1999: 321-4; Checkel 2001). Stern has argued that the conditions associated with crisis and their aftermath may facilitate learning and change, overcoming the common social and political inertia which often inhibit learning under 'normal' conditions (Stern 1997), thus making identity change possible. 'Social learning' after the crisis makes identity change possible through critical self-reflexivity and the exploration of possible identities (Brown and Skarkey 2000).

In a post-crisis regional context, reflexive consideration of the common experience tends to induce a shared understanding of the material world among regional states. Shared understandings about 'what is going on?', 'what is the situation?' entail similar beliefs about cause-effect relationships (Goldstein and Keohane 1993:10), creating similar responses and behaviours and leading to a convergence of expectations and policies. Martha Finnemore has used the 'logic of appropriateness' to predict similar behaviour from dissimilar actors, who would have acted differently if only regarded as having different utility functions and capabilities (Finnemore 1996; Sending 2002). Through reflexive consideration, the limits of existing identity are exposed and lead to the exploration of alternative future directions – a new possible identity, which enables actors to adapt, change or transform themselves according to how the future unfolds and the external environment changes (Brown and Skarkey 2000). This exploration is a kind of search for meaning, the construction of a narrative that makes sense of both past and future and the actor's as well as the group's role in creating this. The logic of 'common fate' is often produced under circumstances of uncertainty. Actors face a common fate when they perceive that their individual survival, fitness, or welfare depends on what happens to the group as a whole (Wendt 1999). Unlike the conventional formation of alliance, 'common fate' influences not only behaviour but also actors' identity. The crucial element of 'common fate' is dealing with collective uncertainty.

Western European countries after World War II and East Asian countries after the Asian financial crisis respectively shared a common reflexive understanding resulting from the shared experience of suffering and the survival of a destructive war and economic crisis, as well as a regional common fate in terms of securing economic prosperity, rebuilding social stability and dealing with regional economic and political uncertainty. Exploring new identities does not necessarily mean the resolution and integration of a mature identity, but reflects a phase of questioning existing beliefs, restructuring cognitions, searching and developing alternative models of the future through social learning mechanisms. This is a transformation process bridging 'what was' and the ideal type, 'what can be' (Ashforth and

Mael 1996). The experiences of Europe and East Asia present the critical self-reflexivity and exploration of possible identities which brought out changes along the two dimensions of a collective identity, *normative beliefs* and *relational content*.

The following sections will look at identity change and a formative regional identity in European and East Asian experiences under the suggested framework. However, making empirical arguments about collective identity is always difficult and methodologically treacherous (Cronin 1999; Abdelal et al. 2005). It is even more so when dealing with historical cases. Unlike material-based variables, social identity as an intersubjective concept is essentially constitutive rather than causal. Aware of these problems, we must rely on systematic observation and interpretation. This article looks at the nature of discourse that characterizes the interactions among states, the new concept or understandings that have been articulated and the consistent patterns in the way actors define themselves and their situations. By using historical evidences found in the literatures of European history and the hard resources in the secondary literature[3] as well as some original governmental and inter-governmental documents and reports on East Asian regional cooperation, we will unpack identity transformation and examine emerging collective regional identities.

# CASES

## Normative Beliefs and Practices

### *Europe*

International crises tend to undermine the faith of both elites and non-elites in the ideals of the old order (Higgs 1987) and make people think in a reflective way. The continuous catastrophes – the war and the economic crisis – brutally revealed the destructive results of economic protectionism and extreme nationalism in Europe from the late 1920s onwards (Dedman 2000: 32). During the economic crisis, European governments, to varying degrees, applied some similar measures – protection, import quotas, exchange control and drying-up international investment – which resulted in the economic isolation of each country from the rest and the reduction of each country's dependence on foreign trade and payment (Pollard 1974). Such an attempt by each country to solve the problem at the expense of others aggravated the tendency to national exclusiveness and the tension and hatred between nations (Aldcroft 1977a and b). The cost of this regression and the damage went far beyond material or economic factors. In contrast to the widely practiced protectionism and disintegration of the international economy in the pre-war period, the post-war period saw an attempt to explore novel solutions and establish commonly accepted norms and rules to regulate international economic relations (Milward et al. 1993). In the process of correcting the quest for extreme autarchy and self-sufficiency and stopping rampant nationalism and protectionalism, the assertions are normative rather than simply descriptive as some values are evaluated against and preferred to others. For example, the values of 'non-coercive' unification and 'self-consciously eschew(ing) the use of force' are preferred over those of the

---

[3] Moravcsik has distinguished the 'soft' and 'hard' primary sources in the secondary literature (1998). While a 'soft' primary source is one in which there is a relatively strong incentive for distortion or speculation, the 'hard' primary sources represent the basic objective facts and data.

military conqueror, colonizing or seeking hegemony as in previous unifications (Haas 1970: 608). The Schuman Plan, which saw the pooling of European coal and steel resources, made conflict between states 'not simply unthinkable, but materially impossible'.[4] This industrial sector with strategic significance was no longer viewed 'through the lens of national rivalry and relative military advantage', instead, the new supranational enterprise provided 'a foundation for a broad economic and political settlement between once-warring nations' (Hitchcock 1997: 603). The normative beliefs mapped the causal relations between regional political and economic anarchy and instability, economic chaos and war. Order, rules and commitment were the new expectations for the region. Supranationalism, not national autonomy, became the name of the game (Katzenstein 1997). The post-war European regionalism ended the old so-called 'European system' or the 'concert of great powers' and replaced it with a new stable system among but also beyond nations (Hallstein 1972).

### *East Asia*

Although some argued that the Asian Financial Crisis shattered the self-sufficient 'Asian Way' (Rüland 2000), it has also encouraged the searching for a new regional identity. The crisis has inspired fundamental re-thinking in East Asian countries of the role of strong government involvement in industrial development, a salient character of the Asian development model[5]. A discursive deconstruction of the Asian development model after the outbreak of the crisis associated the East Asian development model with 'crony capitalism' (Hall 2003; Beeson 2004). 'The discursive structures have designated the economic practices of various East Asian actors as normatively good (ethical and/or economically competent) or bad (unethical and/or economically incompetent) behaviour' (Hall 2003: 73). Although this has encountered an opposing argument that the ill-sequenced and poorly regulated financial liberalization has undermined effective governance and increased vulnerability to currency and financial crisis in the region (Nesadurai 2000; Lee 2000), there has been a new surge in re-examining the links between economic governance and economic performance in almost every country in East Asia in the years after the crisis (Drysdale 2000). A majority of governments across the region have generally kept close ties with business and played a dominant role in the banking system and corporate finance. These arrangements proved capable of supporting the extraordinary investment effort and the massive unprecedented mobilization of resources that characterized the period of outwardly oriented East Asian growth. However, as development progresses, the risks of these kinds of arrangements appear to rise, such as a lack of effective discipline, increasing allocation risk and opportunities for rent seeking (Wilson and Drysdale 2000: 6-7).

With the outbreak of the financial crisis, commitment to structural reforms and credible economic management does appear to be a prerequisite for a return of confidence and for the sharp rebound in domestic spending in the recovering economies. It has been identified that there has been a shift from 'socially justifiable' to 'degenerative' moral hazard in the

---

[4] French Foreign Minister Robert Schuman's statement on 9 May 1950. See Raymond Poidevin (1986), *Robert Schuman, homme d'Etat, 1886-1963* (Robert Schuman, man of state), Paris, pp. 261-62, cited in Hitchcock (1997).

[5] In 1993, the World Bank had coined the term 'East Asian Miracle' to appraise the successful economic development and the rapid improvement of the living standards of the people in this region. This report cited macroeconomic stability, human resource development, export orientation, and benign government-business relationships as the causes of high performance in East Asia (World Bank 1993).

'relationship banking' system (Ozawa 1999), which strongly suggests that deeper institutional reform is necessary. Tackling the relations between economic governance and economic performance and adjusting the East Asian development model has become the centrepiece of the post-crisis economic recovery. East Asian countries have reached a common understanding on the exposed regional-wide weaknesses. These include a lack of regional institutions regulating regional economic relations, especially regional monetary and financial markets, to alleviate international economic fluctuation and risk, as well as a lack of regional self-rescue mechanisms in times of crisis. In the post-crisis period, East Asia has been experiencing a proliferation of projects for improving 'governance' which signals a growing appreciation of the importance of governing capacity (Hamilton-Hart 2003).[6] There emerged a new cooperative body 'ASEAN Plus Three (APT)' (or 'ASEAN + 3') consisting of ten ASEAN countries, China, Japan and the Republic of Korea. Regional economic governance arranged by state authorities appeared for the first time in East Asia. APT post-crisis initiatives on regional governance in the financial area thus far fall into three broad categories. The first consists of peer review and formal and informal policy dialogues under the APT. A wide range of transnational regulatory issues, such as mechanisms of capital account monitoring and coordinated investment policy reform, have been considered. The second consists of more technical and substantive actions. An important regional financing arrangement (RFA), the Chiang Mai Initiative (CMI) in May 2000, established a system of swap arrangements constituted by regional liquidity funds[7] to address the goal of regional wide monetary stabilization. It enables the Central Bank of each East Asian country to resort to other countries' foreign reserves in emergency. Third, the APT Finance Ministers have agreed to the Asian Bond Market Initiative (ABMI) to develop local currency denominated bonds, aiming to establish a bond guarantee agency in the region (ADB 2005). The purpose of this initiative is to develop bond markets to mobilize savings more efficiently for the benefit of the region and to provide long-term local currency funds. In summary, the reflexivity over the crisis has remodelled the causal relations between old economic practice, economic efficiency and growth. Regional countries have pooled their sources together in order to strengthen regional economic governance and address the problems of institutional insufficiency. There seems to be a vision that in East Asia economic development and regional integration are two sides of the same coin and must proceed in tandem (Ohno 2002).

## Relational Content

### *Europe*

European governments reflected that 'international efforts to promote reconstruction were woefully inadequate after the First World War, a lesson which was appreciated by the planners responsible for the same tasks after 1945' (Aldcroft 1977a: 63). Hervé Alphand and

---

[6] Hamilton-Hart defines 'governing capacity' as 'the ability of a government to implement its own declared policy in a reasonably consistent and rule-abiding way' (Hamilton-Hart 2003: 224).

[7] In theory, the CMI provides for 33 bilateral currency swap arrangements: 30 agreements between each of the Northeast Asian countries and each of the 10 ASEAN members, plus 3 agreements among the Northeast Asian countries themselves (Henning 2002: 10 and 16). The CMI swap network, emerging between 2000 and 2002, deals with nearly $ 60 billion and the combined foreign exchange reserves at the disposal of East Asian states amounts to approximately $1 trillion. See Ministry of Finance, Japan, available from: <http://www.mof.go.jp/english/if/CMI_051109.pdf>

André Istel, de Gaulle's financial experts, stated that the 'collapse of the international economic system between 1929 and 1931 was not due to a shortage of international credit but rather to the absence of any international institutional machinery to regulate structural problems in the international economy' (as quoted in Lynch 1997: 13). When WWII was approaching its end, the allies had started to discuss how to sustain international peace and to prevent another tragedy. A common task was to establish a novel, more stable international/regional structure able to correct failed policies, to sustain peaceful relationships, to reconstruct the regional economy and to protect common prosperity. In spite of strong national differences in character, temperament, beliefs, and aims, they shared the purposive willingness to remove 'the facets that divide(d), the wasteful use of resources in fighting one another' (Hallstein 1972: 184). A new regional awareness and social purpose was evoked by this constructive attitude. Reformist economists suggested the fundamental reform of the international economy in the clear recognition that expansionary economic policies could not be sustained in isolation. From this point of view, a spirit of good neighbourliness would be easier to achieve if governments would pursue expansionary economic policies in concert to prevent another depression (Geiger 1996). The weakness and instability in one country might easily become a threat to its neighbours' prosperity. Keeping others weak had proven a notorious and self-defeating strategy. They had to cooperate with each other in order to overcome their economic difficulties. Among them, the rapprochement of France and Germany within a European framework was the basis of reorganizing intra-European political and economic affairs.

From the French point of view, the 'German Problem' was historically and psychologically generated from a deep fear of Germany's economic strength, which could boost Germany's ambition of conquering neighbouring countries (Maier 1991; Gillingham 1991; Lynch 1984). The centrepiece of the 'German Problem' was the Ruhr area, which made the French feel their economic 'inferiority' in comparison with Germany.[8] The Ruhr area is not only a symbol of German economic superiority but also a symbol of the German war industry, so that the French regarded it as material traces of Germany's imperialist and racist politics. France believed that without the Ruhr, Germany was no longer a threat (Maier 1991: 334). It was equally important that successful reconstruction and modernization of the French economy depended, to a large degree, on the guaranteed continued French access to the resources of the Ruhr (Sethur 1952; Lynch 1984). Therefore, French policy makers faced an obvious dilemma: limiting German political power while preserving, and even increasing, the Ruhr's economic importance to France and the whole of Western Europe. The French government actively searched for a solution to this dilemma. A background paper written by the chief of the *Quai*'s European desk proposed the internationalization of the Ruhr area as the first step toward a Western union and extended the Ruhr authority to the other heavy industry regions of Western Europe. They proposed a path called 'organic control' (*contrôle organique*), a system for the supervision and regulation of the Ruhr's heavy industry, 'to take precise forms over time while being adapted as closely as possible to the reorganisation of the postwar German and European economies … to integrate the productive forces of Germany into a new international order' (Gillingham 1991: 153-54, 170). This article insisted that

---

[8] The French thought that 'the difference between the French coal and steel industry and that of the Ruhr is similar to the difference between a 4 CV Renault and a heavy steam engine.' Remarks by Jacques Bardoux, cited in Müller-Härlin (2003: 269-278).

European integration without Germany was a myth, while with it prospects were unlimited. 'By the date of the Schuman Plan announcement, French expressions of interest in reconciliation with Germany had become quite commonplace' (Gillingham 1991: 170). The Schuman Plan reconciled economic and security imperatives and changed the structure and relationship of the French and German economies. It explored a new approach to untangle the problem of Franco-German relations, namely, the elimination of the 'ancient antagonism of France and Germany' through the 'establishment of common bases of industrial production' and the fusion of interests. (Willis 1968: 87).

### East Asia

'The financial crisis compelled many Asian countries to re-evaluate their place in the world' (*Financial Times* 2001) and induced fundamental changes of views on inter-regional relations and relations with the outside world. The critical reflections on the priority of foreign economic relations in East Asia exposed East Asian countries' excessive reliance on major global economies outside of the region. The lack of diversification and low level intra-regional financial flows rendered the East Asian economies susceptible to external shocks. In contrast, closer intra-regional economic interactions can act as a 'buffer attenuator' to external economic fluctuations. In the search for an alternative model for the future, East Asian countries have tried to explore their own as well as the region's role in creating it. As the Vice President of the Asian Development Bank, Mr Liqun Jin said,[9]

> 'Asia needs to address a historical weakness of inadequate collaboration in critical areas. In the absence of close cooperation, Asian economies could succeed separately, but together they could be prone to shocks as their economies become more linked to the developed world rather than each other in the region ... it cannot go on aiming at the large markets in the industrial countries, to the neglect of working together as a team to develop the regional market on the basis of better coordination in macroeconomic and financial affairs.'

Cohesion has also emerged in the attitudes and stances of the countries in this region towards actors outside the region – for example, the International Monetary Fund (IMF) in conjunction with the US government. The mainstream view in the region about the IMF's response and policy to the Asian Financial Crisis is that the IMF initially misdiagnosed the problem and chose to impose a set of solutions that only served to liberalize the East Asian market and to exacerbate the situation (Higgott 1998; Bello 1998; Bowles 2002). Some East Asian leaders also believed that the solution to the crisis proposed by the IMF was short-sighted and would worsen and prolong the economic crisis (*Business World* 2000). This situation has become the acme of change of American economic policy in this region, which has aroused resentment towards the economic intervention from outside (Haggard 2000). Therefore, regional awareness has greatly strengthened as a result of this reassessment of indigenous group strategy against the outsider's attitude in the circumstances of crisis.

By posing a question concerning the relations between regional countries and the rest of the world and delineating a boundary to differentiate insiders and outsiders, the sense of a 'group' is growing. This is what Hurrell called 'how actors interpret the world and how their understandings of where they belong are formed' (1995: 65). 'Group identities develop out of

---

[9] 'Asia-Pacific financial and monetary cooperation', Speech on the *2004 annual conference of Boao Forum for Asia* (Wu 2004).

common experiences: political actors must act together as a group before they can recognize the existence of that group' (Cronin 1999: 33). In the post-crisis era, East Asian regionalism, led by state design, has pursued the goal of restoring to the region a greater degree of political power and autonomy vis-à-vis the rest of the world (Bowles 2002). For example, the slowly evolving regional liquidity fund will give members of ASEAN Plus Three greater autonomy in their relations with global financial institutions (Nabers 2003).

Meanwhile, the crisis has also instigated a change in the self-orientation of every East Asian country. There were few signs of regional awareness in East Asia before the Asian Financial Crisis. In Southeast Asia, ASEAN countries had developed a sense of regional belonging to their own sub-regional association. In Northeast Asia, all three countries – China, Japan and South Korea – had self-orientations which were not derived from the region of 'East Asia'[10] (Li 2003). Therefore, regional economic cooperation and institutions lacked the basis of regional cohesion and a centripetal force. For example, The *White Paper on International Economy and Trade* issued by the Ministry of Economy, Trade and Industry of Japan in 2003[11] emphasizes the importance of East Asian economic cooperation and suggests that the Japanese economy must be invigorated by the economic energy of neighbouring countries. Entering the new century, China has adjusted her 'calming neighbours' (An Lin) policy and added 'enriching neighbours' (Fu Lin) as a fundamental policy in the regional area. Chinese leaders have on different occasions repeated that its ongoing economic reform and development to a great degree depends on regional stability and prosperity.[12] South Korea has planned to become the 'economic centre of Northeast Asia' as a centre of logistics and commerce.[13] This crisis made ASEAN countries realize how vulnerable they are and use 'looking East' as an opportunity for their economic recovery and sustainable development. The crisis has implanted the concept that every country is first of all rooted in the same region. A regional 'commonness', or 'we-ness', a regional consciousness appeared in this region for the first time in its history. The Asian Financial Crisis was such an extraordinary event that it developed the 'consensual knowledge' and 'inter-subjective understanding' of these countries and encouraged states to promote cooperation (Terada 2003).

## CONCLUSION

Although mainstream studies have clearly acknowledged that a crisis may become the crucial catalyst for the emergence of regionalism, they have not generally analyzed how it induces a change in identity. This article has focused on the effects of international crises on a formative regional identity. It has argued that under the conditions of international uncertainty or crisis, actors engage in a process of re-evaluating, questioning and challenging old

---

[10] Japan once defined itself as a Western developed country. South Korea believed its culture was closer to the West than to the East, although geographically it is an East Asian country. China believed itself to be an independent global power.

[11] From the website of the Ministry of Economy, Trade and Industry of Japan. Available from: <http://www.meti.go.jp/english/report/index.html> [12 March 2005].

[12] 'The China Daily's interview with Chinese Foreign Minister, Tang Jiaxuan', Chinese Foreign Ministry. Available from: < http://www.fmprc.gov.cn/chn/wjdt/wjzc/t3472.htm>; also see *Chinese Prime Minister's speech at ASEAN Plus Three Summit*, from the Sixth to Ninth Summit. Available from: < http://www.fmprc.gov.cn>.

[13] South Korea is trying to improve the FDI environment and boost the weight of foreign investment in Gross Domestic Product (GDP) to 14 per cent before 2010. See the speech on annual meeting of the Boao Asia Forum 2003 by Kim Jin-Pyo, Vice Chancellor and Minister of Finance and Economy, Republic of Korea.

normative beliefs and looking for new ones, opening up the possibilities for new identities to be formed. This often leads to shared interpretations of events, a perceived common fate and a desire to develop a means to protect peace and stability – the exploration of an alternative identity. This article echoes Wendt's point: 'there is nothing inevitable about collective identity formation in the international system', but, 'to the extent that the mechanisms are at work that promote collective identities, models that ignore them will understate the chances for international cooperation and misrepresent why it occurs' (Wendt 1994: 391).

Both Europe and East Asia can be regarded as examples of 'crisis induced' regionalism, in which particular events expedite changes in state identity and trigger the search for new ideas to guide policy-making. There exist commonalities in both cases which indicate that the crisis imposed the challenge of normative beliefs and practices. The crises created a sense of common history and common fate in both regions when the interests of each country depended on what would happen to the group as a whole. Through social learning and critical reflexivity, they have substantially altered the way in which the relationship between individual states and the region is perceived, stimulated a common understanding of the regional situation and developed a regional common fate to deal with regional economic and political uncertainty. In this process, the limits of existing identity are exposed and questioned. The social learning process enables states to adapt, change or transform their identity according to changes in the external environment. In the search for an alternative model for the future, states try to explore their own as well as the region's role in creating it.

In both cases, emerging regionalism has been characterized by the exploration for an alternative identity. It does not necessarily mean a resolution of a mature identity, but reflects a period of questioning existing beliefs, restructuring cognitions, searching and constructing alternative models of the future. In such a process of exploration, the regional policy-makers' incentives have been raised to develop collective responses to the regional threats and problems and to confirm their recognition and commitment to closer connections between neighbouring countries. The initial stage of regionalism in both regions focuses on the lessons learned from the period of the crises and addresses the main weaknesses exposed. The very first crucial initiatives in both cases are regional resolutions to address the key sources of the crises: the supranational arrangement for the coal and steel sector in Europe and the financial stabilization mechanisms in East Asia.

# REFERENCES

Abdelal, Rawi, Yoshiko Herrera, Alastair Johnston, and Rose McDermott (2006) 'Identity as a Variable' *Perspectives on Politics* 4(4): 695-711.

Abrweiler, Hélène (1993) 'Roots and Trends in European Culture', in: Soledad García (ed.) *European Identity and the Search for Legitimacy*, London: Pinter Publishers

Albert, Stuart. and David Whetten (1985) 'Organisational Identity', in: Larry Cummings and Barry Staw (eds) *Research in Organizational Behaviour* 7, Greenwich: JAI Press, pp 263-95.

Aldcroft, Derek (1977a) *From Versailles to Wall Street 1919-29*, Berkeley: University of California Press.

Aldcroft, Derek (1977b) *Studies in the Interwar European Economy,* Aldershot: Ashgate.

Ando, A and Kimumra (2003) 'The Formation of International Production and Distribution Networks in East Asia' *NBER Working Paper* no. 10167.

Ashforth, Blake and Fred Mael (1996) 'Organizational Identity and Strategy as a Context for the Individual' *Advances in Strategic Management* 13: 19-64.

Asian Development Bank (ADB) (2005) *Technical Assistance for the ASEAN+3 Regional Multicurrency Bond.* Available from: <http://www.adb.org/ Documents/TARs/REG/tar-reg-39027.pdf>.

Austria, Myrna. 'East Asian Regional Cooperation: Approaches and Process' paper presented at the '*International Conference on East Asian Regional Cooperation*' held 22-23 August 2002, Beijing, China.

Bandura, Albert (1977) *Social Learning Theory*, Englewood Cliffs: Prentice-Hall.

Beeson, Mark (2004) 'Political and Economic Integration in East Asia', in: Phillip O'Hara (ed.) *Encyclopaedia of Public Policy: Governance in a Global Age*, London: Routledge.

Beeson, Mark (2005) 'Rethinking Regionalism: Europe and East Asia in Comparative Historical Perspective' *Journal of European Public Policy* 12(6): 969-85.

Bello, Walden (1998) 'East Asia: On the Eve of the Great Transformation?' *Review of International Political Economy* 5(3): 424-44.

Berezin, Mabel and Schain, Martin (eds) (2003) *Europe Without Borders*, London: The Johns Hoskins University Press

Berger, Peter (1988) 'An East Asian Development Model?', in: Peter Berger and H.H.M. Hsiao (eds) *In Search of East Asian Development Model.* NY: Transaction Inc.

Bowles, Paul (2002) 'Asia's Post-Crisis Regionalism: Bringing the State Back In, Keeping the (United) States Out' *Review of International Political Economy* 9(2): 244-70.

Brown, Andrew and Starkey, Ken (2000) 'Organisational Identity and Learning: A Psychodynamic Perspective' *The Academy of Management Review* 25(1): 102-20.

Brubaker, Rogers and Cooper, Frederick (2000) 'Beyond "identity"' *Theory and Society* 29: 1-47.

Bustelo, Pablo (2003) 'The Impact of the Financial Crises on East Asian Regionalism', in: Fu-kuo Liu and Philippe Regnier (eds) *Regionalism in East Asia: Paradigm Shifting?*, London: Routledge/Curzon.

Campbell, John (2000) 'Convincing the Sceptics: Six Questions for Ideational Analysis,' Paper presented at the conference on *Ideational Institutionalism: Perspectives on European Politics*, University of Birmingham, 2000.

Castells, M (1997) *The Power of Identity*, Oxford: Blackwell.

Checkel, Jeffrey (2001) 'Why Comply? Social Learning and European Identity Change' *International Organization* 55(3): 553-88.

Checkel, Jeffrey (2005) 'International Institutions and Socialization in Europe: Introduction and Framework' *International Organization* 59(4): 801- 26.

Cronin, Bruce (1999) *Community Under Anarchy*, New York: Columbia University Press.

Dedman, Martin (2000) *The Origins and Development of the European Union 1945-95*, London: Routledge.

Delanty, Gerard (2005) 'Transnational Identities: Becoming European in the EU' *Perspectives on Politics* 3(1): 184-86.

Della Porta, Donatella and Diani, Mario (1999) *Social Movements*, Oxford: Blackwell.

Deutsch, Karl (1968) 'Attaining and Maintaining Integration', in: Hodges, Michael (ed.) *European Integration: Selected Readings,* Middlesex: Penguin Books, pp. 108-23.

Deutsch, Karl (ed.) (1957) *Political Community and the North Atlantic Area*, Princeton: Princeton University Press.

Drysdale, Peter (2002) 'Japan and the New Regionalism in East Asia' presentation to the Japan Economic Seminar, Washington, 22 November 2002.

Finnemore, Martha (1996) 'Norms, Culture, and World Politics: Insights from Sociology's Institutionalism' *International Organization* 50(2): 325-47.

Fossum, John (2003) 'The European Union: In Search of an Identity' *European Journal of Political Theory* 2(3): 319-40.

García, Soledad (ed.) (1993) *European Identity and the Search for Legitimacy*. London: Pinter Publishers.

Geiger, Till (1996) 'Embracing Good Neighbourliness: Multilateralism, Pax Americana and European Integration, 1945-58', in: Till Geiger and Dennis Kennedy (eds) *Regional Trade Blocs, Multilateralism and the GATT*, London: A Cassell Imprint.

Gillingham, John (1991) *Coal, Steel, and the Rebirth of Europe, 1945-1955: The Germans and French from Ruhr Conflict to Economic Community*, Cambridge: Cambridge University Press.

Gofas, Andreas (2001) 'Ideas and Interests in the Construction of EMU: Beyond the Rationalist Bias of the New Ideational Orthodoxy' *CSGR Working Paper*. Available from: <http://www2.warwick.ac.uk/fac/soc/csgr/research/working papers/2001/wp7601a.pdf>.

Goldstein, Judith and Keohane, Robert (eds) (1993) *Ideas and Foreign Policy: Beliefs, Institutions and Political Change*, Ithaca: Cornell University Press.

Graham, Andrew and Anthony Seldon (eds) (1990) *Government and Economies in the Postwar World: Economic Policies and Comparative Performance, 1945-85*, London: Routledge.

Haas, Ernst (1968) *The Uniting of Europe: Political, Social, and Economic Forces 1950-1957*, 2nd edition, Stanford: Stanford University Press.

Haas, Ernst (1970) 'The study of regional integration: reflections on the joy and anguish of pretheorizing' *International Organization* 24(4): 607-46.

Haggard, Stephan (2000) *The Political Economy of the Asian Financial Crisis*, Washington, DC: Institute for International Economics.

Hale, John (1993) 'The Renaissance Idea of Europe', in: Soledad García (ed.) *European Identity and the Search for Legitimacy*, London: Pinter Publishers.

Hall, Rodney (1999) *National Collective Identity: Social Constructs and the International System*, New York: Columbia University Press.

Hall, Rodney Bruce (2003) 'The Discursive Demolition of the Asian Development Model' *International Studies Quarterly* 47: 71-99.

Hallstein, Walter (1972) *Europe in the Making*, translated by Charles Roetter, London: George Allen and Unwin Ltd.

Hamilton-Hart, Natasha (2003) 'Asia's New Regionalism: Government Capacity and Cooperation in the Western Pacific' *Review of International Political Economy* 10(2): 222-45.

Henning, Randall (ed.) (2002) *East Asian Financial Cooperation*. Washington, DC: Institutes for International Economics.

Hettne, Björn and Söerbaum, Frederich (2000) 'Theorising the Rise of Regionness' *New Political Economy* 5(3): 57-73.

Higgott, Richard (1998) 'The Asian Economic Crisis: A Study in the Politics of Resentment' *New Political Economy* 3(3): 333-56.

Higgs, Rober (1987) *Crisis and Leviathan*, Oxford: Oxford University Press.

Hitchcock, William (1997) 'France, the Western Alliance, and the Origins of the Schuman Plan' *Diplomatic History* 21(4): 603-30.

Hogg, Michael and Dominic Abrams (1988) *Social Identifications*, London: Routledge.

Hooghe, Liesbet and Marks, Gary (2004) 'Does Identity or Economic Rationality Drive Public Opinion on European Integration?' *Political Science and Politics* 37(3): 415- 20.

Huddy, Leonie (2001) 'From Social to Political Identity: A Critical Examination of Social Identity Theory' *Political Psychology* 22(1): 127-56.

Hurrell, Andrew (1997) 'Regionalism in Theoretical Perspective', in: Louise Fawcett and Andrew Hurrell (eds) *Regionalism in World Politics -- Regional Organization and International Order*, Oxford: Oxford University Press. pp. 37-73.

Hymans, Jacques 'Applying Social Identity Theory to the Study of International Politics: A Caution and An Agenda' paper presented at the International Studies Association convention, New Orleans, Louisiana, March 24-27, 2002.

Jervis, Robert (1991) 'The Future of World Politics: Will It Resemble the Past?' *International Security* 16: 39-73.

Johnston, Alastair (2005) 'Conclusions and Extensions: Toward Mid-Range Theorizing and Beyond Europe' *International Organization* 59(4): 1031-44.

Joyce, Christopher (2002) *Questions of Identity*, London: I.B. Tauris Publishers

Jupille, Joseph and Caporaso, James (1999) 'Institutionalism and the European Union: Beyond International Relations and Comparative Politics' *Annual Review of Political Science* 2: 429-44.

Katzenstein, Peter (1996a) *The Culture of National Security: Norms and Identity in World Politics*, New York: Columbia University Press.

Katzenstein, Peter (1996b) 'Regionalism in Comparative Perspective' *ARENA Working Papers*.

Katzenstein, Peter (1997) 'Introduction: Asian Regionalism in Comparative Perspective', in: Peter Kztzenstein and Takashi Shiraishi (eds) *Network Power: Japan and Asia*, Ithaca: Cornell University Press.

Keohane, Robert (1990) 'International Liberalism Reconsidered', in: John Dunn (ed.) *The Economic Limits to Modern Politics*, Cambridge: Cambridge University Press, pp.165-94.

Keohane, Robert and Nye, Joseph (1977) *Power and Interdependence: World Politics in Transition*, Boston: Little, Brown.

Keunen, Bart (2007) 'Rethinking European Identity through a Triptych of Literary Heroes' *European Review* 15(1): 125-34.

Krasner, Stephen (ed.) (1983) *International Regimes*, Ithaca: Cornell University Press.

Kratochwil, Friedrich (2000) 'Constructing A New Orthodoxy? Wendt's 'Social Theory of International Politics' and the Constructivist Challenge' *Journal of International Studies* 29(1): 73-101.

Kumar, Krishan (2003) 'The Idea of Europe: Cultural Legacies, Transnational Imaginings, and the Nation-State', in: Mabel Berezin and Martin Schain (eds) *Europe Without Borders*, London: The Johns Hoskins University Press.

Laffan, Bridid (1998) 'The European Union: A Distinctive Model of Internationalization' *Journal of European Public Policy* 5(2): 235-53

Laffan, Bridid (2004) 'The European Union and Its Institutions as Identity Builders', in: Richard Herrmann, Thomas Risse and Marilynn Levy (eds) *Transnational Identities: Becoming European in the EU*, Boulder: Rowman and Littlefield.

Lee, Yeon-ho (2000) 'The failure of the weak state in economic liberalization: liberalization, democratization and the financial crisis in South Korea' *The Pacific Review* 13(1): 155-31.

Li, Wen (2003) 'Cooperation in Northeast China Needs a Change of Concept (Dong Bei Ya He Zuo Yu Yao Guan Nian Bian Ge' in *Northeast Asia Research (Dong Bei Ya Yan Jiu)* 4: 5-10.

Lindberg, Leon (1963) *The Political Dynamics of European Economic Integration*, Stanford: Stanford University Press.

Lynch, Frances (1984) 'Resolving the Paradox of the Monnet Plan: National and International Planning in French Reconstruction' *Economic History Review* xxxvii(2): 229-43.

Lynch, Frances (1997) *France and the International Economy: From Vichy to the Treaty of Rome*, London: Routledge.

Mackinnon, Danny, Andrew Cumbers and Keith Chapman (2002) 'Learning, Innovation and Regional Development: A Critical Appraisal of Recent Debates' *Progress in Human Geography* 26: 293-311.

Maier, Charles (1991) *The Marshall Plan and Germany: West German Development within the Framework of the European Recovery Program*, Oxford: Berg Publishers Ltd.

Marcussen, Martin, Risse, Thomas, Engelmann-Martin, Daniela, Knopf, Hans-Joachim and Roscher, Klaus (2001) 'Constructing Europe? The Evolution of Nation-State Identities', in: Thomas Christiansen, Knud Erik Jorgensen and Antje Wiener (eds) *The Social Construction of Europe*, London: Sage.

Milward, Alan (1984) *The Reconstruction of Western Europe*, London: Routledge.

Milward, Alan, Frances Lynch, Federico Romero, Ruggero Ranieri and Vibeke Soerensen (eds) (1993) *The Frontier of National Sovereignty: History and Theory, 1945-1992*, London: Routledge.

Moravcsik, Andrew (1998) *The Choice for Europe: Social Purpose and State Power From Messina to Maastricht*, London: UCL Press.

Morgan, Roger (1972) *West European Politics since 1945: The Shaping of the European Community*, London: B.T. Batsford Ltd.

Müller-Härlin, Maximilian (2003) 'The Political Reconstruction of National and European Identity in France and Germany after the Second World War' *Dialectical Anthropology* 27: 269-78.

Nabers, Dirk (2003) 'The Social Construction of International Institutions: The Case of ASEAN+3' *International Relations of the Asia-Pacific* 3(1): 113-36.

Nesadurai, Helen (2000) 'In Defence of National Economic Autonomy? Malaysia's Response to the Nancial Crisis' *The Pacific Review* 13(1): 73- 113.

Neumann, Iver (1996) 'Self and Other in International Relations' *European Journal of International Relations* 2(2): 139-74.

Neumann, Iver (1999) *Uses of the Other: 'The East' in European Identity Formation*, Minneapolis: University of Minnesota Press.

Norton, Anne (1988) *Reflections on Political Identity*, Baltimore: The Johns Hopkins University Press.

Nye, Joseph (1968) 'Comparative Regional Integration: Concept and Measurement' *International Organization* 22(4): 855-80.

Ohno, Kenichi. 'The East Asian Experience of Economic Development and Cooperation', background paper for the RIEMI/METI seminar in *the World Summit on Sustainable Development* in Johannesburg on 1 September 2002.

Ozawa, Terutomo (1999) 'The Rise and Fall of Bank-Loan Capitalism: Institutionally Driven Growth and Crisis in Japan' *Journal of Economic Issues* 33(2): 351-58.

Painter, J (2002) 'Multilevel Citizenship, Identity and Regions in Contemporary Europe', in: J Anderson (ed.) *Transnational Democracy: Political Spaces and Border Crossings*, London: Routledge, pp. 93-110.

Peng, Dajin (2002) 'Invisible Linkages: A Regional Perspective of East Asian Political Economy' *International Studies Quarterly* 46: 423-47.

Poidevin, Raymond (1986) *Robert Schuman, homme d'Etat, 1886-1963* (Robert Schuman, man of state) Paris

Pollard, Sidney (1974) *European Economic Integration 1815-1970*, London: Thames and Hudson.

Rich, Paul (1999) 'European Identity and the Myth of Islam: A Reassessment' *Review of International Studies* 25: 435–51.

Ruggie, John (1993) 'Multilateralism: Anatomy of an institution' *International Organization* 46: 561-98.

Ruggie, John (1998) *Constructing the world polity: essays on international institutionalisation*, London: Routledge.

Rüland, Jürgen (2000) 'ASEAN and the Asian Crisis: Theoretical Implications and Practical Consequences for Southeast Asian Regionalism' *The Pacific Review* 13(4): 21-51.

Sahlins, Marshall (1991) 'The Return of the Event, Again', in: Aletta Biersack (ed.) *Clio in Oceana: Toward a Historical Anthropology*, Washington, D.C.: Smithsonian Institution Press.

Saito, M (1999) 'Huaxi Jingjiquan de Zhankai jiqi Zuoyong' (The unfolding of the Chinese economic circile and its function), in: W. Chen (ed.) *Huaqiao Huaren de Jingji Toushi (The Economic Perspective of Overseas and Ethnic Chinese)*. Hong Kong: Xianggang Shehui Chubanshe.

Schwarz, Hans-Peter (1980) 'Archive Sources for the Development of European Unification politics in West Germany (1945-1955) and Their Accessibility', in: Walter Lipgens (ed.) *Sources for the History of European Integration (1945-1955): A Guide to Archives in the Countries of the Community*, Leyden-London-Boston: Sijthoff.

Sending, Olejacob (2002) 'Constitution, Choice and Change: Problems with the 'Logic of Appropriateness' and Its Use in Constructivist Theory' *European Journal of International Relations* 8(4): 443-70.

Sethur, Frederick (1952) 'The Schuman Plan and Ruhr Coal' *Political Science Quarterly* 67(4): 503-20.

Sterling-Folker, Jennifer (2000) 'Competing Paradigms or Birds of a Feather? Constructivism and Neoliberal Institutionalism Compared' *International Studies Quarterly* 44(1): 97-119.

Sterling-Folker, Jennifer (2002) 'Realism and the Constructivist Challenge: Rejecting, Reconstructing, or Rereading' *International Studies Review* 4: 73 – 97.

Stern, Eric. (1997) 'Crisis and Learning: A Conceptual Balance Sheet' *Journal of Contingencies and Crisis Management* 5(2): 69-86.

Stubbs, Richard (2002) 'ASEAN Plus Three: Emerging East Asian Regionalism?' *Asian Survey* 42(3): 440-55.

Tajfel, Henri (ed.) (1978) *Differentiation Between Social Groups*, London: Academic press.

Terada, Takashi (2003) 'Constructing an 'East Asian' Concept and Growing Regional Identity: From EAEC to ASEAN+3' *The Pacific Review* 16(2): 251-77.

Tuomela, Raimo (2003) 'Collective Acceptance, Social Institutions, and Group Beliefs', in: Wolfgang Buschlinger and Christoph Lütge (eds) *Kaltblütig, Philosophie von einem rationalen Standpunkt,* Stuttgart: Hirzel Verlag, pp.429- 46.

Wendt, Alexander (1994) 'Collective Identity Formation and the International State' *American Political Science Review* 88(2): 384-96.

Wessels, Wolfgang (1998) 'Comitology: Fusion in Action' *Journal of European Public Policy* 5(2): 209-34.

Willis, Roy (1968) *France, Germany, and the New Europe 1945-1967*, London: Oxford University Press.

Wilson, Dominic and Peter Drysdale (2000) 'Perspective', in: Peter Drysdale (ed.) *Reform and Recovery in East Asia*, London: Routledge.

World Bank (1993) *The East Asian Miracle: Economic Growth and Public Policy*, Washington D.C.

Wu, Chunhe (ed.) (2004) *What They Said in Boao: Speeches from 2004 annual conferences of Boao Forum for Asia*, Beijing: Economic Daily Press.

Yuki, Masaki (2003) 'Intergroup Comparison versus Intragroup Relations: A Cross-Cultural Examination of Social Identity Theory in North American and East Asian Cultural Contexts' *Social Psychology Quarterly* 66(2): 166-83.

Zürn, Michael and Checkel, Jeffrey (2005) 'Getting Socialized to Build Bridges: Constructivism and Rationalism, Europe and the Nation-State' *International Organization October* 59(4): 1045-79.

In: Asian Economic and Political Development
Editor: Felix Chin

ISBN: 978-1-61122-470-2
© 2011 Nova Science Publishers, Inc.

# RIDING THE ASIAN TIGER?
# HOW THE EU ENGAGED CHINA SINCE THE END
# OF THE COLD WAR

## *Benjamin Zyla*

Centre for International Relations, Queen's University

## ABSTRACT

This article examines the China-European Union (EU) relationship after the end of the Cold War. It argues that the EU uses a 'benign Wilsonian' foreign policy style and is committed to a Wilsonian worldview that is couched in promoting normative values and principles of democracy, the rule of law, freedom of people, free markets and open access to international economic markets. Brussels tries to 'entice' and engage Beijing to follow and adopt European values and principles. However, despite Europe's normative posture, the EU is not hesitant to pursue its own interests.

In this article, the theoretical 'benign Wilsonian' construct will be applied in order to examine particular components of the China-EU relationship: the push for political and social reforms, the human rights issue, economic relations, and geopolitical visions of the nature of the international system.

## INTRODUCTION

European security interests in Asia were evident throughout the Cold War and subsequently expanded in line with the post Cold War diversification of the security agenda. However, it was not until 1994 that the European Commission's policy paper 'Towards a New Asia Strategy' developed potential European Union (EU) contributions to regional stability in Asia particularly by strengthening the Union's economic presence (European Commission 1994a). The objective of the EU was to maintain the Union's leading role in the world economy and to promote economic development in the Asia-Pacific region. Second, a larger EU involvement contributed to more stability and developed greater international cooperation and understanding. The third objective was to contribute to the development and consolidation of the rule of law, respect for human rights and democratic principles, particularly in China.

Since then the relationship between the EU and China has improved considerably beyond the economic dimension. China has been the EU's largest trading partner and its economy currently attracts large sums of foreign direct investment (FDI) from companies based in the

EU. At the same time, European multinationals are not hesitant to push China to open its markets even more and to modernize its system of governance to allow the rule of law and democratic control of institutions and decision-making processes. The EU has achieved some success in this regard, but no doubt, there still are significant shortfalls particularly with regards to respecting international human rights. China, however, seems to be willing to learn from Europe's historical experiences of unifying disparate markets and developing remote areas of its continent.

The EU-China relationship is also remarkable in the sense that both have shown the willingness to shoulder more responsibility in global affairs. China is a permanent member of the United Nations Security Council and thus holds a veto power whereas the EU intends to become a member of the same council but has not achieved this goal yet. The claim of this article is that relations between the EU and China will become more important over the next few years, not only economically but also geopolitically.

## Why Is China So Important for the EU as a Global Player?

The European Union and China are continental sized economies and are thus powerful players, not only in international business. As a result, they also hold significant geopolitical weight. China had three times the population of the EU before its eastern enlargement and is four times as large as the United States in terms of its landmass. Its gross domestic product (GDP), however, is only about a tenth of the size of either the EU and the US, but with growth rates in the double digits it is encroaching on these two large Western economies.[1] In 2003, China went through an economic boom and became the third largest trading entity in the world. The EU slowly started to become aware of China's influence in international affairs and its unique position as a stakeholder in major international conflicts and problems, such as the current crisis in Darfur or Lebanon. The European Commission paid respect to the rising power by formally recognizing China's importance in global affairs in its strategic document of 2001: 'A country the size of China is both part of the problem and the solution to all major problems of international and regional co-operation' (European Commission 2001:7).The European Security Strategy of 2003 further highlights the importance of China:

> 'Our history, geography and cultural ties give us links with every part of the world: our neighbours in the Middle East, our partners in Africa, in Latin America, and in Asia. These relationships are an important asset to build on. In particular we should look to develop strategic partnerships, with Japan, China, Canada and India as well as with all those who share our goals and values, and are prepared to act in their support' (European Council 2003: 14.

In light of all this, the following research questions arise: how could one classify the EU's foreign relations with China? What style, principles, values and interests do Brussels pursue in the bilateral relationship?

I will argue in this article that, based on the European Security Strategy of 2003 and other official EU documents, the Union espouses a 'benign Wilsonian' foreign policy with regards to China. This is a foreign policy style that is closely associated with former US President

---

[1] The problem with determining China's exact GDP is the highly imprecise aggregated data published by the government.

Woodrow Wilson. Europe's Wilsonian style, however, is somewhat different from that of its closest ally, the United States, which itself enjoys a very close bilateral relationship with China. The European Union's foreign policy approach is in stark contrast to the US strategic ambition of changing regimes of sovereign countries around the world (this strategic outlook was best explained in the US National Security Strategy and its notion of pre-emption and prevention) in order to promote democratic institutions, the rule of law etc. Brussels acts passively, it attempts to 'entice' and engage other countries to follow and adopt European values and principles. Thus, one gets the impression that it appears less coercive and using its 'softer power' (See for example Nye 2004a, Nye 2004b, and Nye 2002). Meanwhile, Brussels was not hesitant to pursue its own interests, but, not as forcefully and coercively as the US.[2]

## Aim of the Article and Contribution to the Literature

This article provides an overview of developments of the EU-China relationship since after the end of the Cold War and in light of the 'strategic partnership' signed between the two countries at a joint EU–China summit in The Hague in 2004 (Crossick 2006: 1). The 'benign Wilsonian' hypothesis helps to characterize this relationship as well as to show the importance of China for EU's external relations. Its aim is also to demonstrate that China, as an evolving power in Asia, and the EU, share similar normative values of how to conduct international relations.[3] The scope of the article, however, is limited to an examination of the EU as a supranational organization including its agencies. As a result, this article excludes an examination of the relationship individual EU member states might have established with China but, nonetheless, acknowledges that such a relationship exists.

The article is novel in its contribution to the body of literature on EU external relations in two ways: first, Europe's foreign and defence policy was traditionally preoccupied with an examination of the transatlantic relationship with the United States and Canada.[4] This pre-occupation was understandable given the commitments the US and Canada made to European stability and security since World War I. Both countries committed their political, economic, and military resources to a peaceful European continent and institutionalized their relationship with Europe most chiefly in the North Atlantic Treaty Organization (NATO). Nevertheless, the European Union also enjoys external relations with other regions and states beyond those in North America. A description and evaluation of the relationship of other states in the world with the EU beyond North America have largely been marginalized in the body of literature of EU external relations. This article offers to fill this gap by choosing the EU-China relationship as a starting point of analysis. It is also novel in the sense that it offers an additional dimension of analysis in the China-EU relationship beyond the economic one. It makes reference to the political and security dimension of the relationship.[5] Third, the

---

[2] The limitation of Europe' external relationship with China will be examined form a European perspective largely because of language barriers and restricted access to government documents in China.

[3] It is recognized that it is difficult to interpret Chinese decision making processes because they are neither 'monolithic' nor 'centralized'. See for example Crossick (2006: 1).

[4] I am not arguing here the preoccupation with the economic relationship was necessarily a bad. Indeed, it was an important and significant contribution to the literature considering the large trade interests of both actors.

[5] quoted in McDougall (1997: 124).

theoretical foreign policy construct of Wilsonianism is also new to the literature of EU's external relations. However, it appears to be rather beneficial in the sense that it allows for a focus on shared norms and values.

The article is structured as follows. Section one explores the theoretical settings and assumptions of the 'benign Wilsonian' foreign policy style. In section two this construct will be used to explain four specific components of the China-EU relationship: the push for political and social reforms, the human rights issue, economic relations, and geopolitical visions of the nature of the international system and China's and the EU's role in it. The final section draws some conclusions of the EU-China relationship by allowing a discussion of the convergence of the norms and values of the bilateral relationship.

# THE THEORETICAL CONSTRUCT OF 'BENIGN WILSONIANISM'

The notion of Wilsonianism made its first appearance in the literature of International Relations and US foreign policy in reference to Woodrow Wilson's fourteen-point speech in 1919. Wilson advocated, among other things, 'political independence and territorial integrity to great and small states alike'.[6] He proposed the League of Nations, the world's first collective security agreement. Wilson himself, however, was not necessarily an idealist or a pacifist. No doubt, he was an idealist in nature but also mindful of pursuing and enhancing America's national interests. This, one might argue, put him more into the realist camp. Since then, the Wilsonian voice in international affairs has not been silent and continues to attract considerable scholarship.[7]

Wilsonianism is associated with the beliefs of promoting democracy, the rule of law, freedom of people, liberal market economies and open access to markets. Wilsonian's guiding principles are strong commitments to human rights and the rule of law. The assumption is that once the threats to liberty are removed, peace and security are more likely to flourish across the globe. It was understood that democracies would make better and more stable partners than dictatorships or monarchies.[8] This was a pursuant of strategic as well as moral objectives: strategically, poverty, crime and corruption could pose a threat to national security. Morally, poverty in the world affects Western values. As the US government put it succinctly, 'a world where some live in comfort and plenty, while half of the human race lives on less than $2 a day, is neither just nor stable' (Bush 2002).

Another characteristic of Wilsonians are their commitment to democracy as a means of preventing states from going to war with one another. This, in their view, allows for societies to prosper and to advance. Monarchies and dictatorships are seen as unpredictable forms of government where the will of the people is not reflected. Consequently, the support of democracy abroad is not only a moral duty but also a 'practical imperative'. Wilson himself said: 'We are participants, whether we would or not, in the life of the world. The interests of all nations are our own also. We are partners with the rest'.[9]

---

[6] See for example Ibid; Mead (2001).
[7] This is commonly referred to in the literature of international relations as the democratic peace theory. For an elaborate reading on the democratic peace theory see for example Doyle (1985a); Doyle (1985b).
[8] Quoted in McDougall (1997: 122).
[9] China's negotiations for a WTO membership lasted from 1985-2001.

Wilsoniansm, however, is not limited to spreading normative values of democracy and the rule of law around the globe. Based on the US tradition, international Wilsonians also believe that Wilsonianism is not only the better choice but indeed has a moral duty to the world for changing international behaviour. In this sense, based on the maximization of their national interest, Wilsonians pretend to have a natural right of projecting their values on other countries and to create global free trade regimes and producing wealthy and peaceful countries around the world. As such, the domestic politics of nation states is a fundamental concern for Wilsonians.

Taken all together, one might argue that Wilsonian's effort of trying to spread Western values and norms of democracy, the rule of law, and enhancing the governance structure of sovereign states can be understood as a nation-building effort.

## CHINA AS A CASE STUDY

As Anthony Foster argues, the EU's relationship with Asia and specifically China is not particularly strange; indeed, both parties had close relationships for a long period of time (Foster 1999: 744). After Beijing's relationship with Moscow deteriorated in the 1960s, China was forced to look for like-minded countries that did not necessarily associate with the two superpowers, the United States and the Soviet Union. Hence, China established diplomatic relations with France in 1964, with Italy in 1970 and with Great Britain and Germany in 1972. Diplomatic relations with the (then called) European Communities (EC) were formally established in 1975. Only three years later, the EC signed an economic agreement with China and included it in its preferential trading system by offering lower tariffs for importing goods and services. China, on the other hand, has seen Brussels mostly as a counterweight to other global powers, particularly the United States. However, after the end of the Cold War, the government in Beijing quickly realized that the EU was striving to become an international political actor with global aspirations that reach beyond its trade interests. Hence, Beijing opened up its relationship with the EU and its Member States in the late 1990s.

The 1985 trade and economic cooperation agreement concluded between the European Economic Community and China manifested Europe's economic interests of the bilateral relationship. Both parties to the agreement were able to concentrate on economic issues while the EC was assured that the United States would provide security for the European continent through NATO. The EC therefore could exclusively concentrate on enhancing its economic prosperity. China, however, saw the EC as a member of the 'West' and therefore was less inclined to promote overall friendly relations with the EC.

After the end of the Cold War, however, conflict over economic issues became more important and over-toned the geopolitical struggles of the Cold War. Hence, economic issues slowly found their importance in the bilateral EU-China dialogue and marked a transition from Cold War geopolitics to multipolar geo-economics (Dent 1999: 149). For its part, the EU subscribed to a policy of Chinese engagement on a multilateral and bilateral (member states) level by offering Beijing various incentives such as development aid, technical assistance for various programs, food aid, and by setting up exchange programs. Brussels also encouraged China's accession to international financial institutions such as the World Trade

Organisation (WTO).[10] All these principles and objectives, as we will see shortly, are consistent with a Wilsonian worldview of international affairs. They were laid out in the Commission's document entitled 'Building a Comprehensive Partnership with China', which was adopted in 1998 (European Commission 1998). In this document, the EU called for an upgraded political dialogue with Beijing, showed its support for socio-economic reforms in accordance with the principles of sustainable development and called for the development of a Chinese civil society that is based on the rule of law and respect for human rights. In short, the EU's objectives can be summarized as promoting sustainable development in China, support its integration into the world economy, fighting poverty by promoting democracy, human rights, and the rule of law. All these principles can be interpreted as being consistent with a Wilsonian foreign policy style.

## The Push for Political and Social Reforms

It was not until after the end of the Cold War that the China-EU relationship fully materialized and flourished. Meanwhile, a process of transformation took place in Europe. The member states ratified the Maastricht Treaty in 1993, which transformed the European Community (EC) into the European Union (EU) and gave the Union competences in the field of common foreign and defence policy (CFSP). Indeed, with Maastricht, the EU became a more influential international actor that was actively seeking representation in international organizations. This development has also left the impression with the international community that the EU is aspiring greater international responsibility.[11] The European Union gained further international influence through its enlargement process. The EU now consists of twenty-seven member states with more than 450 million people. As a result, the EU has grown to become an economic powerhouse that produces a quarter of the world's economic output. This enlarged European Union has given Brussels various new powers and instruments for engaging China bilaterally.

A major turning point in the China-EC relationship, however, was the Tiananmen Square massacre on 4 June 1989, where a large pro-democracy demonstration was repressed by armed forces. The regime in Beijing realized that if it would accommodate the striking workers was likely to lose its governing power. Mao's successor, Deng Xiaoping, himself a victim of the Cultural Revolution, had an interest in strengthening the rule of law, and an interest in relaxing political control enough to prevent a public outbreak. He intended to mobilize a democratic sentiment against the left and supported his protégé Hu Yaobang. However, when Hu refused to suppress the next great democratic demonstration at Kei Da University in 1986, Deng forced Hu's dismissal and he died only three years later. By that time Hu had already become a hero of the democratic movement. When the leadership arranged a demeaning low-key funeral for Hu, students marched to Tiananmen Square to protest and caused large demonstrations against the regime (Liang et. al. 2001). It was apparent that students and workers were inspired by the 'wave of democratization' taking

---

[10] For a good discussion about EU's new role see for example Hill (1993).

[11] According to Samuel P. Huntington a third wave of democratization started to affect the European continent back in 1974, beginning on the Iberian Peninsula. Earlier waves refer to the period between 1945 and the mid 1960s. The first wave of democracy took place in the American and French revolution. See Huntington (1991).

place in Eastern Europe.[12] The reactions of the international community and the EC to the massacre were condemning. 'Europe froze its political dealings with Beijing, cut off military contacts and banned all arms sales' (Byrysch et. al. 2005: 9). Those reactions forced the Democratic Republic of China (DRC) onto the defensive. In Europe itself, the Commission as well as the Union's member states closely examined their relationship with China. A major factor in determining a new China policy was public opinion in European capitals, which pushed the European Parliament to pass a resolution urging the Chinese government to enter into an immediate peaceful dialogue with the protestors (Weidenfeld and Wessels 1991).

When twelve member states of the EC unanimously condemned the massacre on June 6 they also suspended all high level talks between the government of China and EC officials. The EC also froze all high-level bilateral meetings, postponed new cooperation projects and cutback existing bilateral programs. The intention of those policies was to force China to resolve the conflict through dialogue rather than by using force (European Political Cooperation Bulletin 1990: 1). One day later, the EC decided to suspend all economic and cultural relations with China. By the end of the month, EC officials urged China during the Madrid European Council meeting of 26-27 June to suspend the executions of dissidents and announced to start human rights talks with the regime in Beijing. However, talks and negotiations are one thing and do not necessarily correspond to coherent policy actions. In early August, however, the EC granted China an emergency loan worth US$ 70 million for humanitarian purposes in the Suchan province. This marked a renewal of a political engagement process. This political will was endorsed unanimously by EC foreign ministers. It also helped to shape a more consistent European foreign policy towards China: the bureaucrats in Brussels preferred private diplomacy negotiations with Chinese officials and eschewed the United Nations (UN) system in this respect (Shambaugh 2005: 10). It also showed the 'benign' nature of the Wilsonian foreign policy style. This appeared to be somewhat different from the American approach, which espoused a harsher tone towards Beijing.[13] Even though the then EC was aware of China's appalling human rights record, it tried to engage the regime in Beijing also in other policy areas with the hope that they would then translate into greater democratic reforms. Contrary to the US, the EC (and later also the EU) also put emphasis on 'workplace safety, reducing gender discrimination, was decreasing state control of the media, improving prison conditions, and eliminating the death penalty' (Shambaugh 2005: 10) as well as ethnic minorities, particularly those in Tibet.[14]

In the early 1990s, the US and the EC used an engaging foreign policy style by relaxing the economic sanctions that were imposed on China after the 1989 massacre. This was done in the wake of Gulf War I when the Bush administration was seeking the support from the Chinese government for authorizing a UN chapter VII intervention mission for the liberation of Kuwait. What followed was a package put together by various international actors to engage China diplomatically and economically and tie it closer into the world trading system. In 1990 President Bush extended the most favoured nation status for another year. During the July summit meeting of the G-8 countries, Japan also pushed for a relaxation of sanctions

---

[12] This article does not examine the China-US bilateral relationship. However see for the most recent examination of the US-China relationship especially Ibid.

[13] The United States, on the other hand, places more emphasis on religious and cultural freedoms, fair treatment of political prisoners and dissidents. The literature on this aspect is vast. For the latest work see for example Delegation of the European Commission to China (2005).

[14] See for example Brodsgaard (2007).

against China and the World Bank extended Beijing's line of credit. In October, the EC foreign ministers decided to gradually resume economic cooperation as well as high-level political contacts with China (European Political Cooperation Bulletin 1990). Restrictions on high-level contacts, cultural, scientific and technical cooperation were also loosened. Nonetheless, the embargo on arms sales and military cooperation continued to be in place. The policies of engagement and enlargement were justified by the international community (mostly by Western countries) by arguing, as the French Foreign Minister, Ronald Dumas, did that the EU supported this move because of China's favourable behaviour in the United Nations Security Council during the Iraq crisis. Moreover, as Möller argues, Europe's rapprochement had to do with the fact that the continent was faced with the beginning of a recession in the early 1990s caused largely by the unification of Germany and needed access to China's economic market (Möller 2002:20). During this time of recession China became the destination for the majority of Europe's technology and industrial plants and a place that provided cheap labour conditions (Möller 2002: 23).

EU foreign policy towards China was shaped more precisely in 1995 when the EU Commission published a document entitled 'A Long-Term Policy for Relations between China and Europe' in which it called for economic and social reforms in China. At that time, the EU had become accustomed to its new role in the world and had managed to solidify its foreign policies and interests. This solidification occurred at a difficult time for Europe not only because the new competencies it acquired with the Maastricht Treaty were put for a test but also because of its preoccupation with the conflicts on the Balkans. Nevertheless, the EU tried to push Beijing to open its planned economy and to develop a social security system for its people. It labelled these two issues the 'key challenges' for a future relationship. EU bureaucrats were not short of offering their experience and advice through various programs (mostly training programs). These projects were aimed at 'assisting local authorities to build up a body of qualified legal personnel while also improving public awareness of the Chinese legal system and the legal rights of citizens.' The project promotes the EU and EU Member States legal systems as examples of best practice'(Delegation of the European Commission to China 2005). Europe's engagement found a positive response in China, which had started to introduce domestic reforms. Among those were economic market reforms and diplomatic initiatives to push China towards a greater integration into the global economic community. Brodsgard argued that these reforms were successful and have contributed to an overall transformation process. For example, the government has reduced the size of its public service trying to make it more efficient and offering a more service oriented administration.[15] The Chinese government intended to create a 'harmonious society', that is the idea of 'building a socialist new countryside'. 'This involves redistributing economic benefits to China's underdeveloped regions through establishing new infrastructures and through providing educational subsidies and better medical services' (Brodsgaard 2007).

These developments to an agreement signed by the EU and China that supported Beijing's accession to the WTO. In return, China expressed its interest and willingness to help maintaining stability and peace in the world. The EU, on the other hand, reiterated its commitment to training professionals such as lawyers and other projects to strengthen the rule of law and promote civil, political, economic and social rights (Building a Comprehensive Partnership with China 1998). On the issue of promoting the rule of law, the United States as

---

[15] See for details Byrysch, Grant and Leonard (2005: 9).

well as the EU believed that achieving this objective would be a first stepping-stone towards reaching broader goals such as a functioning market economy and legal safeguards. Brussels invested considerably more into the legal programs with China than did the United States.[16] It promoted the principles of the rule of law and good governance by setting up and maintaining EU-China legal and judicial cooperation programs, such as the EU-China intellectual property rights cooperation program.

The Commission also called for bilateral summit meetings once a year. During the third summit, which took place on 23 October 2000, bilateral discussions about human trafficking and illegal immigration were continued but ended without concrete results. 'These various common interest have provided fertile soil for a prospering EU-China relationship, which today consists of a plethora of co-operation programs, dialogues and projects' (Byrysch, Grant, Leonard 2005: 9). According to Möller, China was enthusiastic about the international attention it received, but neglected to live up to the details of the programs (Möller 2002).

The EU continued to issue policy papers on China in 1998, 2001, and 2003[17] in an effort to find a response to the vast changes that were taking place in China, particularly in its society and economy. However, all policy papers that were published after 1995 mostly reiterated previous policies and commitments while widening the scope of cooperation. It was clear that cooperation projects were desired but short term oriented (European Commission 1995). The overall strategic objective of the EU was to socialize and engage the 'Asian tiger' on various fronts and to support its modest transformation processes. The main goal was to 'help China to be a peaceful, stable, democratic, and internationally responsible country, which is internally consensus seeking and externally multilateral, and sharing broadly similar values and goals with the Union' (Crossick 2006: 2). The engagement took place in many practical policy areas: 'progress towards full integration in the world market economy, strengthening civil society, poverty alleviation, environmental protection, human resource development, scientific and technological development, progress of the information society, trade and investment cooperation' (Byrysch, Grant, and Leonard 2005: 10). In addition to functional programs and projects particularly in the economic and social sector, the EU also promoted the so called 'Human Resource Development Projects' such as the China-EU International Business School, the EU-China Managers Training program, the China-EU public administration project, and the European Studies Centre Programs, which it put considerable financial resources towards. In 1998, the Chinese Prime Minister travelled to Europe to meet with Javier Solana, the Union's High Representative for foreign and security policy as well as the President of the Union at the time and his successor held political talks and consultations. Between 2004 and 2005 more than two hundred official visits of European bureaucrats took place in China (Crossick 2006: 1). 'These annual summits have since helped

---

[16] All documents are publicly available at <http://europa.eu.int/comm/external_relations/china/intro /index.htm>.

[17] Umbach, Frank (2004). There is no doubt that the evolving relationship between China and the EU has been short in terms of long-term strategic visions and focussed only on particular areas. There are, for example, few linkages between those various programs. Part of this inconsistency results from the 'competition' the EU bureaucracy is facing from the national capitals in Berlin, London, and Paris. These three member states themselves have established bilateral programs with China, which makes a cohesive European approach difficult. As Barysch (et.al) argues, 'in practice, divisions and rivalries between individual countries often undermine EU objectives'.

to sustain momentum for the EU-China relations'.[18] Again, these were functional programs designed to socialize China and attract it to Western values.


## Human Rights

With the publication of 'A Long-Term Policy for Relations between China and Europe', the EU Commission attempted to also engage China on human rights issues by offering economic incentives in return. The aim was to engage China globally and regionally in order to promote domestic reforms (European Commission 1995). The objective of the EU's policy was to use a 'constructive engaging' approach for dealing with a rather uneasy relationship. The hope was that China would become more integrated into the international community and would refrain from using military means to solving domestic as well as international conflicts and disputes. As Möller argues, by the mid 1990s China started seeing Europe as a larger political project in international relations while acknowledging that the United States was the global hegemon (Möller 2002: 21).

At the global level issues such as disarmament, weapons of mass destruction and arms controls were raised. It was agreed that the EU would work towards opening and liberalizing Chinese society by raising human rights issues in constant dialogues as well as through the system of the UN. Nonetheless, the EU was well aware of the fact that human rights issues were a delicate topic in their bilateral relationship and that only an engagement would slowly introduce change.

The bilateral dialogue continued in 1998 when the first EU-China summit took place in London. One week earlier the EU Commission had released a new strategic paper entitled 'Building a Comprehensive Partnership with China' (EU Commission 1998). It was also endorsed by the European Council of Foreign Ministers on 29 June 1998. In this document, the EU anticipated that China would rise to be a global political and economical player in the near future. Also, the human rights problem was put into perspective and watered down. The initial long-term vision was exchanged for achieving short term objectives – to 'develop a balanced China policy that reflected China's growing international economic and political weight and to further the development of the European Union's fledging CFSP' (Byrysch, Grant, and Leonard 2005: 12). In consistence with previous documents, the aim of this document was to increase China's integration into the international community by enhancing political dialogue and supporting its membership into the world trading system. For the first time, the EU also aimed to increase its visibility in China itself by not only increasing its training programs but also by sending permanent EU representatives to China.

Internationally, the EU and the US worked jointly towards finding a common position in the UN's Geneva Human Rights Commission. The collaboration succeeded and the Commission passed resolutions condemning China's human rights records and policies. China appeared to be influenced by this international pressure and responded with concessions. It agreed to set up a panel of permanent human rights dialogues, in which the EU mostly provided technical experience and assistance for implementation. This led to a larger human rights agreement between the EU and China in which Brussels committed itself to provide technical assistance for the education of human rights lawyers, judges, and

---

[18] See also Maddison and Organisation for Economic Co-operation and Development. Development Centre (1998).

prosecutors. However, even though the EU provided China with its expertise and experience, it did not fall short of publicly criticizing Beijing for its human rights records. Shortly after the assistance agreement was reached between Brussels and the DRC, the EU member states condemned China harshly for its treatment of the dissident Wei Jingsheng (Weidenfeld and Wessels 1996: 477).

## Economic Dimension

The process of globalization in the early 1990s brought the two continents of Europe and Asia much closer together. Shortly after the end of the Cold War, China remained relatively remote in comparison to the US-Europe economic relationship (Edmonds 2002: 2). During the course of the 1990s, the Chinese-European economic relationship grew considerably, but remained secondary to other economic relations the EU enjoyed. China had also developed a much closer relationship with other economies in Asia, particularly the one in Japan. Nonetheless, the economic relationship between the two appeared to be untouched by the Tiananmen Square incident and China's violent reactions to the demonstrations. In fact, there were signs that the trade relationship was healthy and increasing.

The new EU currency also attracted considerable Chinese attention. In 1999, the euro was introduced to world financial markets as an accounting currency. One year earlier, a European Central bank opened its offices in Frankfurt. This provided the European Union with a financial institution that was responsible for 'maintaining price stability' in the eurozone. Similar to other countries, China showed considerable interest in investing parts of its foreign exchange reserves in the euro as opposed to investing it into the US dollar.

The new geo-economic dimension after the end of the Cold War had major implications for the overall China-EU economic relationship. China's export rate to Europe had soared up to 4,300 per cent after China introduced reform policies that opened its planned economy. On the contrary, Europe's sales to China over the same time span have risen up 2,000 per cent and created a serious trade deficit for the EU In 1999 the trade deficit between the EU and China amounted to $32.8 billion and rose to $106 billion in 2005 (Crossick 2006: 2). However, China remained Europe's most important export partner ranked directly after the United States (Lardy 2005: 121.). In 2004 China overtook Japan as the third largest trading economy in the world measured as the sum of exports and imports (Cooper 2005: 6.).[19] At the same time the Chinese economy grew seven per cent per year continuously for the last two decades and increased its exports by fourteen per cent annually (Cooper 2005: 7). This enormous growth rate also had an impact on the world economy, including Europe. European merchandise imports from China amounted to $2.6 billion in 1982 and grew twenty per cent by 2003 totalling $108 billion (United Nations Industrial Development Organization 2004: 151 and 83). This manifested China's position as one of the world's leading exporters of manufactured goods, which rose from one per cent in 1981 to more than six per cent in 2000 (Cooper 2005: 7). Simultaneously, Europe's exports to China also increased from $2.3 to $45 billion over the same time period (World Trade Organization 2003).

---

[19] Talks about China's entry into the world's financial system, particularly the WTO lasted from 1985-2001.

China's economic significance also resulted in its increased weight in international financial organizations. China became a member of the WTO in 2001.[20] Under the WTO rules, China gained access to the EU's €10 trillion internal market and thus guaranteed China a much larger market access. The WTO membership also forced a change in China's economy. Under the accession agreement for membership of the WTO, China became obliged to eliminate quantitative restrictions on imports and to significantly reduce tariffs by 2006.[21] These WTO regulations also apply to the EU-China trade relationship because EU member states are also member of the WTO and therefore subject to WTO regulations. These international economic structures of governance can be interpreted as the 'forceful element' of the Wilsonian tradition. Before acceding to the WTO, China mainly exported manufactured goods to the EU. In recent years, however, China grew into exporting electronic products such as laptops, digital cameras, and televisions etc. to Western countries. This new development in the Chinese economy has attracted considerable foreign direct investors in China, particularly from Europe and the United States. 'It has been the largest developing-country recipient of foreign direct investment (FDI) for more than a decade and enabled it to raise significant amounts of funds in international capital markets'(Cooper 2005: 11). By the end of 2002 the total amount of European foreign direct investment reached $34 billion and thus accounted for 7.6 per cent of all FDI in China (Shambaugh 2005: 11).

This is not to say, however, that European companies did not run into difficulties doing business in China. For example, infringements of copyrights and trademarks occurred as well as the breaching of property rights and pose a significant problem in China (Shambaugh 2005: 13). Furthermore, there was a fear amongst European investors that administrative barriers were created to distort competition. When the Chinese Prime Minister Wen Jaibao visited Europe in May 2004 he lobbied European politicians for two things. First, he asked for China's economy been awarded market status, which is particularly important for calculating anti-dumping duties. Second, he asked the European Union to lift its arms embargo sales to China, a measure that was introduced by Brussels after the Tiananmen Square massacre in 1989. Both of the demands were denied by the European Union. Brussels made it clear to Beijing that based on its human rights record the administration does not live up to its WTO obligations. The Commission examined the Chinese economy in 2004 and reported that it failed in four out of five accounts. The government was still heavily involved in steering the economy and the economy still lacked transparency. Furthermore, there has been no major progress made for ensuring property rights and a better protection of foreign capital and the Chinese financial system still does not operate independently of the state. In sum, these policies underline Europe's Wilsonian ambition of engaging China while at the same time being forceful in certain policy areas. Most recently, the EU has imposed anti-dumping duties for shoes made in China.

---

[20] However, this is not to say that China has lived up to the WTO regulations and directives. As a WTO report shows, China's domestic economy is still protected from international competition by imposed tariffs for all products. The average tariff applied on foreign goods was 12.4 per cent in 2002. For more details see Lardy (2005: 121).

[21] A most recent example of this might be China's voting behaviour in the U.N. Security Council with regards to the situation in Sudan. China has been rather quiet on this subject. For example, UN Security Council resolution 1556 called for the disarming of the Janjaweed and China abstained as did Pakistan. China has a close relationship with the non-aligned movement, which of course has a greater relevance in the UN General assembly than it has in the Security Council.

## CHINA IN THE INTERNATIONAL SYSTEM OF POWERS

China's economic power also translated into its influence as a major international political actor. As one of the permanent five members of the United Nations Security Council and by virtue of its veto power, China is a major stakeholder in decisions about international peace and security. Its performance in the Security Council during the Cold War was rather passive. The Chinese government was not allowed to sit on the Security Council until 25 October 1971. In its place the pro-Western Republic of China (Taiwan) represented China on the Security Council. To protest the exclusion of the communist Chinese government, Russia boycotted the Security Council from January to August 1950. This is why China used the veto in the Security Council only 3 times from 1946-1989 (compared with 114 for Russia and 67 for the US). The issues they vetoed all related to new memberships to the UN (Morphet 1989: 347).

In the Post Cold War Era, China has been 'passive' - it tends not to want to appear as a conflicting party unless absolutely necessary. For example, it vetoed peacekeeping missions in Macedonia and Guatemala because they had not recognized the communist Chinese government. This appears to be a tendency in Chinese foreign policy after the end of the Cold War: if China is uneasy about something, it will abstain rather than veto.[22] During the Iraq crisis in 1990, there were signs in international affairs that China would change its policies of blocking UN authorized international operations and assume a constructive role in international affairs.

Meanwhile, the international system of states underwent a process of transformation. While significant debate raged among scholars about the nature of the international system at the end of the Cold War – whether it be a unipolar or a multipolar one - they all agreed that the system had transformed. Joseph Nye has tried to 'bridge' the debate about bipolarity vs. unipolarity by offering a combination of the two concepts. He used the United States as a case study and argued that the 'new' international system indeed could be described as three-dimensional. On the military level, the United States undoubtedly became the sole global hegemon with unprecedented global-reaching capabilities. However, on the economic and cultural level the United States was faced with increased competition particularly by the European Union and Asia. This image of a three-dimensional chess-board could be translated to international relations and has significance for understanding China's role in it. Currently, China does not possess far-reaching global military capabilities that could balance the United States. However, on the economic level, China has become a major international player. It is most likely that its international economic role might translate into greater influence in global political affairs in the near future.

* Earlier versions of this article were presented at European Foreign Policy Conference, London School of Economics, London, 2-3 July 2004 and the Annual Conference of the British International Studies Association (BISA), University of Warwick, 20-22 December 2004. The author would like to thank Axel Berkofsky, Saki Dockrill, Julie Gilson, Atsuko Higashino, and Christopher Hill for helpful comments on earlier versions of this article. The author also wishes to express his gratitude to a number of officials involved in EU-Japan relations on both sides who, while anonymously, kindly agree to be interviewed.

## Convergence of EU and Chinese Strategic Values and Norms?

In general, China and Europe appear to share similar strategic objectives of how to conduct business in international affairs: both are in favour of a multipolar system of international relations and disguise a unipolar international system in which one great power is the dominant player (Shambaugh 2005: 13). Furthermore, both advocate the promotion of peace and stability in the world and prefer to solve international crises through consultation, negotiation, and resolution by making use of the UN's institutional bodies (See Byrysch, Grant, and Leonard 2005; Möller 2002). In matters of intra-state affairs, Europeans are willing to interfere in the affairs of other sovereign states for humanitarian reasons but otherwise share with the Chinese the belief of non-interference. China maintains independence and cherishes its own right and respects for independence. It upholds that any country, big or small, rich or poor, strong or weak, should be equal and its sovereignty should be respected. It appears that the EU and China share a commitment to international institutions such as the UN that shape normative behaviour. 'Europeans and Asians are much more comfortable with institutions that shape normative behaviour through consensus and the exercise of soft power. This attitude may reflect their relative weakness in hard-power terms, but it also indicates a preference for resolving differences through consensual negotiation'(Cooper 2005: 13). It also reveals that the European Union is interested in the domestic policies and developments in China whereas the United States appears to be solely concerned about geopolitical issues. Europe's intention thereby is clear: it wants to prevent China from becoming a failed state. Hence, the EU puts more emphasis on preventive engagement with China as opposed to dealing with a failed state when the process of engagement might be more difficult. The European Union, for example, is one of the leading contributors of (humanitarian) assistance to China. In addition, some of the member states such as Britain, France, Germany, Italy, and Spain have additional 'China assistance programs' in place. In 1995 the amount of assistance totalled $885 million but dropped to $258 million in 2001 (Malik 2002: 10). Concurrently, the European Union ran various China aid programs over more than 250 million euros in 2002. This amount was anticipated to double by the end of 2006.

Moreover, the fact that China is a nuclear power and a member of the UN Security Council raises important questions about the future of the international system and China's position in it. 'What will China's role and engagement be with members of the international community? China's behaviour will have an impact on Europe's preferences for multilateralism. It will also impinge on its interests such as environmental security, WMD non-proliferation, trafficking of human beings, organized crime, and money laundering. In case of the environment, for example, three quarters of Chinese energy consumption depend on coal firing plants'(Crossick 2006: 3).

Furthermore, China's geographical location, its close political relationship with North Korea, and its alignment with Pakistan since the Sino-Indian border war of 1962 could have larger implications for Europe (Shambaugh 2005: 7). China could potentially make use of its power and influence over a volatile Pakistan by, for example, supplying the regime in Islamabad with more military equipment, nuclear technology and know-how. This then would become a problem for the EU and NATO in particular as they are deployed in a NATO led mission outside of Pakistan's doorstep in Afghanistan.

Moreover, China will be an important actor wherever the EU focuses its attention to. China plays a significant role in the UN transformation process. Its position in the UN Security Council is of particular importance for Europe's ambitions of seeking a permanent seat in the Council, in which case the EU would require a Chinese endorsement. Hence, China possesses considerable voting power in one of the world's most important decision-making bodies. Also, because of its veto power, it will play an important role in deciding about the nature and form of foreign interventions that are endorsed by the United Nations under chapter VI or VII of the U.N. charter. Most recently, for example, Brussels needed the diplomatic cooperation with Beijing for solving the crisis with Iran, which is attempting to acquire nuclear technology for military purposes. Hence, the EU has an interest in making sure that it enjoys a healthy relationship with the 'Chinese dragon'. In sum, 'both partners share an interest in a strengthened, multilateral rule based international system of governance'(Crossick 2006: 4).

## CONCLUSION

According to the economic distribution of power, there seems to be no doubt that the future international system will be shaped by the European Union, the United States, and China as one of the new major international actors (Shambaugh 2005: 7 and 15). It is apparent that these three players do not only possess the bulk of the world's financial resources, but also have considerable military as well as political influences around the world. Furthermore, their power is institutionalized in the UN Security Council (even though the EU itself does not have a permanent seat in the Council but two of its largest members, the United Kingdom and France, enjoy the veto power). Shambaugh predicts that China's rise to the apex of international economics will have an influence on its role globally. If this prediction holds then a shift will have taken place – Beijing will then have transformed from a passive to an active but entangled global player. As a global player, Beijing is likely to shoulder more responsibility in international affairs and will be confronted with transnational issues such as counterterrorism, weapons of mass destruction, rogue states, international crime such as money laundering, trafficking of human beings, and peacekeeping as well as nation-building efforts in remote areas of the globe (Sandschneider 2002: 34). This plan, however, is part of the EU strategy towards China to get Beijing to engaged in international affairs and to cooperate on major international issues with the EU. It has been argued and shown that Europe's foreign policy style is driven by Wilsonian principles of international relations engagement rather than strategic competition or even military confrontation; promotion of democracy and the rule of law, freedom of people, free markets and open access to markets. This engagement, however, is taking place silently rather than publicly (Umbach 2004). The consequence of China's rise for Europe and the United States is that they will increasingly act cooperatively with Beijing rather than compete because their governments are aware of China's weight in the world. 'It is in this wider context that the European Union, as an increasingly ambitious global actor, is seeing the systematic integration of China into the international community and China's transformation into a country that respects the rule of law and international human rights'. The (strategic) objective of the EU seems to be clear: Brussels prefers to deal with a China that is entangled with a multipolar world order. This multipolar world order is anticipated to be more stable than a hegemonic or anarchical world order in which only one global hegemon rules or, in case of an anarchic world system, no power at all. The EU as a global actor also believes in the rule of international law as much as international norms and institutions for governing international affairs. These are the core elements of the European 'Weltanschauung'.

# REFERENCES

Angle, Stephen C. and Svensson, Marina (2001) *The Chinese Human Rights Reader : Documents and Commentary*, 1900-2000, Armonk: M.E. Sharpe.

Brodsgaard, Kjeld Erik (2006) 'Party Organization, Public Administration and Governing Capacity in China – Why Big Government?' Europe-China Academic Network Briefing Papers. Available from: <http://www.ec-an.eu/taxonomy/term/10> [1 May 2007].

Bush, George W. (2002), *The National Security Strategy of the United States*, September.

Byrysch, Katinka, Grant, Charles and Leonard, Mark (2005) *'Embracing the Dragon: Can the EU and China Be Friends?'* CESifo Forum 6(3), Autumn: 8-15.

Cooper, Richard N. (2005) *Sino-European Economic Relations*, Cambridge: Weatherhead Center for International Affairs, Harvard University.

Crossick, Stanley (2006) 'The Rise of China and Its Implications for the EU' *East Asian Institute Working Paper* 132(4), September.

Delegation of the European Commission to China (2005) EU-China Development and Cooperation Programmes - Legally Speaking. Available from: <http://www.delchn. cec.eu.int/newsletters/200507/002_en.htm> [1 August 2006].

Dent, Christopher M. (1999) *The European Union and East Asia : An Economic Relationship*. London and New York: Routledge.

Dorn, James A., and Cato Institute (2005) US-China Relations in the Wake of Cnooc. Available from:
<http://www.cato.org/pub_display.php?pub_id=5135>.

Doyle, Michael (1985a) *'Kant, Liberal Legacies and Foreign Affairs - Part 1'* Philosophy and Public Affairs 12(3): 205-35.

Doyle, Michael (1985b) 'Kant, Liberal Legacies and Foreign Affairs' *Philosophy and Public Affairs* 12(4): 323-53.

European Commission (1995) Communication of the Commission: A Long Term Policy for China-Europe Relations. Available from: <http://ec.europa.eu/comm/external_relations/ china/com95_279en.pdf>.

European Commission (1998) *Building a Comprehensive Partnership with China - Communication from the Commission*, Com(1998) 181, Brussels, 25 March 1998.

European Commission (2001), '*EU Strategy Towards China: Implementation of the 1998 Communication and Future Steps for a More Effective EU Policy'* Communication for the Commission to the Council and the European Parliament, COM (2001) 265.final, 15 May.

European Council (2003) *A Secure Europe in a Better World: European Security Strategy*, Brussels: European Council.

Foot, Rosemary (2000) *Rights Beyond Borders: The Global Community and the Struggle over Human Rights in China*, Oxford and New York: Oxford University Press.

Foster, Anthony (1999) 'The European Union in South-East Asia: Continuity and Change in Turbulent Times' *International Affairs* 75(4): 743-758.

Goldman, Merle (2005) *From Comrade to Citizen: The Struggle for Political Rights in China.* Cambridge: Harvard University Press.

Hasenkamp, Miao-ling (2004) Universalization of Human Rights?: The Effectiveness of Western Human Rights Policies Towards Developing Countries after the Cold War: With Case Studies on China, Frankfurt and New York: Peter Lang.

Keith, Ronald C., and Lin, Zhiqiu (2005) New Crime in China: Public Order and Human Rights, *Routledgecurzon Contemporary China Series*, New York: Routledge Curzon.

Kirby, William C. (2004) *Realms of Freedom in Modern China, The Making of Modern Freedom*, Stanford: Stanford University Press.

Lardy, Nicholas R. (2005) 'China: The Great New Challenge?', in: C. Fred Bergsten and Institute for International Economics (eds) *The United States and the World Economy: Foreign Economic Policy for the Next Decade*, Washington: Institute for International Economics.

Maddison, Angus, and the Organisation for Economic Co-operation and Development Development Centre (1998) Chinese Economic Performance in the Long Run, *Development Centre Studies*, Paris: OECD.

Malik, M. (2002) 'China, Pakistan and India: Nervous Neighbours' *The World Today* 58: 10.

McDougall, Walter A. (1997) *Promised Land, Crusader State: The American Encounter with the World since 1776*, Boston: Houghton Mifflin.

Mead, Walter Russell (2001) *Special Providence: American Foreign Policy and How It Changed the World,* 1st edition, New York: Knopf.

Mendes, Errol, and Lalonde-Roussy, Anik (2003) *Bridging the Global Divide on Human Rights : A Canada-China Dialogue*, Aldershot and Burlington: Ashgate.

Morris, Susan C. (2002) *Trade and Human Rights: The Ethical Dimension in US-China Relations,* Aldershot and Burlington: Ashgate.

Nye, Joseph S. (2002) *The Paradox of American Power : Why the World's Only Superpower Can't Go It Alone*, Oxford and New York: Oxford University Press.

Nye, Joseph S. (2004a) *Soft Power : The Means to Success in World Politics*, 1st edition, New York: Public Affairs.

Nye, Joseph S. (2004b) *The Power Game : A Washington Novel*, 1st edition, New York: PublicAffairs.

Pentikäinen, Merja (2000) EU-China Dialogue: Perspectives on Human Rights, with Special Reference to Women, Juridica Lapponica, 23, Rovaniemi: Northern Institute for Environmental and Minority Law.

Sandschneider, Eberhard (2002) 'China's Diplomatic Rekations with the States of Europe' *The China Quarterly* 169 March: 33-44.

Santoro, Michael A. (2000) *Profits and Principles: Global Capitalism and Human Rights in China,* Ithaca: Cornell University Press.

Shambaugh, David (2005) 'The New Strategic Triangle: US And European Reactions to China's Rise' *The Washington Quarterly* 28(3), Summer: 7-25.

Svensson, Marina (2002) *Debating Human Rights in China: A Conceptual and Political History,* Lanham: Rowman and Littlefield.

Umbach, Frank (2004) 'EU's Links with China Pose New Threat to Transatlantic Relations' *European Affairs*, Spring: 38-47.

United Nations Industrial Development Organization (2004) Industrial Development Report, Vienna: United Nations Industrial Development Organization.

United States Congressional-Executive Commission on China, Legislative Branch Commissioners (2002) Human Rights in China in the Context of the Rule of Law, Washington: US G.P.O. : For sale by the US G.P.O., Supt. of Docs., Congressional Sales Office.

United States Congressional-Executive Commission on China, Legislative Branch Commissioners (2002) Roundtable before the Congressional-Executive Commission on China: One Hundred Seventh Congress, Second Session, Washington: US G.P.O.: For sale by the Supt. of Docs., US G.P.O.

United States Senate, Committee on Finance (2000) US Consideration of Permanent Normal Trade Relations with China: Hearings before the Committee on Finance, United States Senate, One Hundred Sixth Congress, Second Session, on the US-China Bilateral Market Access Agreement, Human Rights, and US National Security Concerns, February 23, March 23, and April 6, 2000, Washington: US G.P.O.

World Trade Organization (2003) *World Trade 2003*, Geneva.

In: Asian Economic and Political Development
Editor: Felix Chin

ISBN: 978-1-61122-470-2
© 2011 Nova Science Publishers, Inc.

# 'EXPECTATIONS DEFICIT' IN EU-JAPAN RELATIONS: WHY THE RELATIONSHIP CANNOT FLOURISH

*Michito Tsuruoka*[*]

King's College London

## ABSTRACT

It is often argued in the study of European Foreign Policy (EFP) that there is a 'capability-expectations gap' in European Union (EU) foreign relations, which normally means the gap between excessive expectations toward the EU from abroad and the insufficient capability of the EU that cannot match the expectations. But in EU-Japan relations, a reverse gap that this article calls 'expectations deficit' can often be observed. It is a result of Japan's low expectations of Europe, which remain largely unchanged despite the growing weight and influence of the EU as an international actor. Simply put, Tokyo has yet to regard the EU to be an international (political) actor. This article analyzes the structure that generates the expectations deficit--underestimation of Europe in Japan. It argues that the existence of the 'expectations deficit' prevents EU-Japan relations from flourishing.

## INTRODUCTION

Romano Prodi, the then President of the European Commission, hailed in his address to the Japanese Diet (Japanese legislature) in April 2002 that the relationship between the European Union (EU) and Japan was 'blossoming as never before' (Prodi 2002). Indeed, it has become commonplace to describe the bilateral relations to be in good shape. The relationship in recent years has been remarkably free from trade frictions that plagued relations in the past. An ironic consequence of this, however, is that, as former European Commissioner for External Relations Sir Christopher Patten was said to have pointed out, 'the problem (in EU-Japan relations) is that there is no problem' (EPC 2004). If EU-Japan relationship is in fact something that becomes problematic when there is no urgent problem to be solved between the two sides, one may wonder what the nature of such a relationship is.

On the one hand, Prodi's claim, if somewhat exaggerated, is not wholly groundless. Economic relations have never been deeper in terms of both trade and investment, which are primarily driven by private companies. In the intergovernmental domain, Japan and the EU adopted an Action Plan for EU-Japan Cooperation at their annual summit meeting in December 2001 (EU-Japan Summit 2001). The document, which is ambitiously titled *Shaping Our Common Future*, lays out more than hundred items for bilateral cooperation ranging from security and trade to cultural and people-to-people exchanges (Shinyo 2002; Tsuruoka 2002). The overall purpose of the Action Plan, according to Prodi, was to 'make our cooperation tangible and concrete, raise its public visibility and thus make it more politically credible' (Prodi 2001). The idea of the Action Plan originated in Japanese Foreign Minister Kono Yohei's initiative launched by his speech in Paris in January 2000, in which he called for a 'millennium partnership between Japan and Europe' and declared the first decade of the twentieth-first century to be a 'decade of Euro-Japan cooperation' (Kono 2000). The Action Plan also marked the tenth anniversary of The Hague Declaration of July 1991 between Japan and the then European Community (EC), which defined the basic principle of the relations, spelled out shared values between the two parties such as the rule of law and democracy, and established consultative frameworks between the two sides most notably the annual summit meeting between the Presidents of the Commission and the Council on the one hand and the Prime Minister of Japan on the other (EC-Japan Summit 1991).[1] It is still too early to judge whether the 'decade of Euro-Japan cooperation' envisaged in the Action Plan will turn out to be a success or not. Nonetheless, the document did mark a new start for EU-Japan relations and the momentum for deepening the relationship seemed to have been reinvigorated.

On the other hand, beneath these new developments in EU-Japan relations since the early 1990s the basic structure of the relationship that dates back to the early post-war period does not seem to have changed in a fundamental way. To put it quite frankly, in terms of current issues of politics, security, and economy rather than history and culture, Japan's attention to Europe remains low, so does the public awareness of the EU as an international actor. The relations with the EU are hardly mentioned in the context of general debate on Japan's foreign policy. The same can also be said of the EU, which does not seem to give high priority to the relationship with Japan in its external relations.[2] The result is that the relations 'are conducted in a climate of relative indifference' (Nuttall 1996: 104), according to Simon Nuttall who was in charge of relations with Japan at the European Commission. He went on to admit that 'those who have a professional stake in maintaining relations do their best to overcome this indifference, but their efforts seem puny compared to the immensity of the problem' (Nuttall 1996: 104). There are obviously more reasons why EU-Japan relations remain underdeveloped in spite of more potential for cooperation. But this article shares Nuttall's assessment that mutual indifference—or put it more diplomatically, the inadequacy of mutual awareness—is one of the most fundamental problems that hinders the development of EU-Japan relations, thus preventing the two from taking advantage of the full potential of their relationship.

What follows in this article is an examination of the Japanese side of this structural problem in EU-Japan relations, namely the issue of Japan's lack of awareness of or expectations toward Europe/the EU. Seen from Europe's standpoint, it is a problem of what

---

[1] Even with the new Action Plan, The Hague Declaration provides the basic framework of EU-Japan relations. The relationship between the Declaration and the Action Plan is very similar to that between the Transatlantic Declaration of November 1990 and the New Transatlantic Agenda and the Joint Action Plan of December 1995 adopted by the EU and the United States. On The Hague Declaration, see, for example, Gilson (2000: ch. 5); Abe (1999: ch. 5); Tanaka (2000); Owada (2001). Owada was Deputy Foreign Minister at the time and actively involved in the negotiations of the Declaration. Indeed, the whole process came to be known as the 'Owada initiative'.

[2] The European Security Strategy (Solana Paper) of December 2003 states that 'In particular we should look to develop strategic partnerships, with Japan, China, Canada and India, as well as with all those who share our goals and values, and are prepared to act in their support' (European Security Strategy 2003: 14). But it does not seem to be representing a changed order of priorities or a surging interest in Japan.

this article calls 'expectations deficit'. The concept draws heavily from the argument of 'capability-expectations gap (CEG)' in European Union foreign policy that Christopher Hill introduced more than a decade ago (Hill 1993). It denotes a gap between excessive expectations for the EU from both inside and outside the Union and the insufficient capability of the EU to match them. The CEG is thought to be pervasive in a wide range of EU foreign relations. In EU-Japan relations, however, a reverse gap that I call the expectations deficit can be observed from the EU's standpoint. This emerged because Japan's expectations for the EU in the international arena remained low despite the growing weight and influence of the EU (i.e. its capability) as an international actor. I argue that the expectations deficit is harmful not only to the development of specific bilateral relations such as EU-Japan relations, but also to that of EU foreign relations as a whole, not least its desire to become a significant power in the world.

The central aim of this article is to conceptualize the expectations deficit and to explore the structure that generates the deficit in EU-Japan relations. This article will proceed in two steps. I will first revisit the concept of 'capability-expectations gap' and explain the idea of expectations deficit in relation to the CEG. Second, I will analyze the structure that generates the expectations deficit in EU-Japan relations, explore its implications for cooperation between the two sides and the EU's foreign policy as a whole. Before going into the body of the article, three points have to be clarified. First, this article is essentially diagnostic in character. It stops short of offering a prescription, which is another important task to be tackled separately. But given the fact that the structure of the problem in EU-Japan relations that this article will discuss has not been examined so far, focusing on diagnosis should be justified. Second, this article is not necessarily intended to advocate closer bilateral cooperation between Japan and the European Union. What it tries to offer is a scholarly examination of the structural problem that lies at the heart of EU-Japan relations. Third, this article will mainly discuss political and foreign policy aspect, or in other words, government-level relations between Japan and the EU. This by no means denies the fact that private business relationships are the deepest among various pillars of EU-Japan relations. However, in the light of the fact that political dialogue and cooperation are the area not only that politicians and officials are now increasingly interested in developing (at least in rhetoric), but also that is least examined by scholars, this article will rather focus on political and foreign policy aspect of the relationship.

## WHAT IS EXPECTATIONS DEFICIT?

'Capability-expectations gap (CEG)', as coined by Christopher Hill in 1993, denotes a gap between what the EU is able to deliver in the international arena through its foreign policy instruments and what people and governments both inside and outside the Union expect and demand the EU to achieve in this regard. The gap opens up because while improving the capability of the EU is always difficult, the expectations and demands to the EU are very easy to increase, often to such an extent that they become unmanageable. The gap thus is an imbalance between low capability and high expectations, which Hill argues is dangerous (Hill 1993: 315). The reasons why it is dangerous are, first, 'it could lead to debates over false possibilities both within the EU and between the Union and external supplicants' and second, 'it would also be likely to produce a disproportionate degree of disillusion and resentment when hopes were inevitably dashed' (Hill 1998: 23). As the gap is indeed detrimental to the Union's foreign policy, it should best be closed, which can only be achieved either by increasing the capability or decreasing expectations (Hill 1993: 321).

Expectations of the EU are composed of internal as well as external elements. It is, however, still important to note that the concept of CEG can be seen as an attempt to take into account what third parties think of the EU in understanding EU foreign policy: perceptions and expectations by third parties matter (Bretherton and Volger 1999: 43). This should be self-evident given the fact that the EU cannot exist in a vacuum. But the problem of CEG when applied to EU-Japan relations is that the concept does not, at least explicitly, envisage the possibility that the gap could sometimes be in the reverse.[3] The CEG always assumes that expectations outweigh capability. That is because, argues Hill, 'structural forces exist which keep expectations up just as they limit the growth of capabilities' (Hill 1998: 29). Although it may be generally the case, external expectations should not be taken for granted at all times. This article argues that in EU-Japan relations 'expectations deficit' (or reverse 'capability-expectations gap') has consistently existed and continues to exist today. In theory, the reverse gap can be a result of either excessive capability on the EU's side that should be cut or insufficient expectations to the EU on Japan's side. But the latter should certainly be the case and constitutes the starting point for discussions here.

Does the expectations deficit matter, and if so, why? I argue that it is detrimental not only to the development of EU-Japan relations, but also to that of EU foreign policy in general. First, since external expectations and demands for EU action in the world are thought to be one of the most important stimuli for its foreign policy (Smith 2003: 6-7; Ginsberg 2001: 10; Niblett 2005-06), their absence or insufficient existence would mean decreased impetus for the Union to act in the world and to develop its own foreign policy as a whole, which could result in a slow development in EU foreign policy. Indeed, from the outset, external relations of the EC/EU have in large part developed in response to international events and external demands and expectations: they have been reactive rather than spontaneous in other words. Relations with the ACP—African, Caribbean, and Pacific—countries, as a case in point, could not have developed that far without the persistent demands and expectations from the ACP side.

Second, if there are only an insufficient number of major actors in the world who regard the EU to be worth counting as an important partner, its capability and the willingness to do something in the world (assuming that the EU has both) will not be fully utilized. There may be something the Union can do by itself without having partners to work with. But in many cases, the EU needs external partners, preferably major partners, to get things done in this globalized and interdependent world. Indeed, it is the EU itself that always emphasizes the virtue of multilateralism where having partners is a fundamental prerequisite. No matter how hard the EU struggles to establish itself as an international actor, the result inevitably depends on whether the third countries regard the EU as such. The cost of being underestimated should be taken seriously. While this cost seems to be well recognized by EU diplomats who interact on a daily basis with those who regard the EU as little more than a free trade area, most scholars of European Foreign Policy (EFP) tend to overlook or underestimate it. Though I fully share the central concern of CEG that excessive and misplaced expectations are

---

[3] While Hill acknowledges that 'some outsiders have always been aware of the limitations of European foreign policy' (Hill 1998: 30), his argument does not seem to fully take into account the possibility of reverse gap.

dangerous, I argue that reverse concerns should not be discounted too easily: the expectations deficit is equally alarming to EU foreign policy.

In Japan's case, Tokyo's expectations for the EU or Europe in general seem to be much lower than what they deserve.[4] Of course, there have been some fluctuations in the degree of expectations to the EU: in the period immediately after the Cold War when there was what was called 'Europhoria' in Europe, Tokyo's expectations (or interest) to the Europe increased to some extent for a while, but it was an aberration. The problem is structural in nature, rather than cyclical, meaning that the expectations deficit cannot be seen as a result of disillusionment after excessive expectations. Nor is the problem a mere reflection of the EC/EU's lack of competence (not least in the foreign policy domain). To be sure, the EC/EU's ability to function as an international actor has been seriously limited by its lack of competence, and Tokyo's expectations for Brussels has, to some extent, evolved accordingly. But the problem is much bigger and more complex than that, because there are other— domestic and external—elements that determine Japan's expectations for the EU on which it has no control. As will be examined in the next section, Japan's expectations to the EU have remained consistently low. This has serious consequences to the development of EU-Japan relations because Tokyo has often disregarded the EU as its partner in international relations. Developing EU-Japan relations should not be easy in this circumstance.

As mentioned in the introduction, the problem is mutual in nature. Japan's lack of expectations of Europe is only one side of the coin: the other being the issue of the EU's indifference or the lack of expectations of Japan. But in this article I will focus on Japan's side of the problem, namely the expectations deficit from the EU's standpoint, because it is the aspect that has rarely been discussed in the context of European Foreign Policy (EFP) and is remarkable in the light of the seemingly pervasive existence of CEG in EU foreign relations.

Before going into details on the structure that generates the expectations deficit in EU-Japan relations, it would be worthwhile to note that the existence of this problem is not in fact a phenomenon unique to EU-Japan relations. The EC/EU has had more or less similar problem in its relations with the United States. In the history of the relations between the United States and the EC/EU, the latter has always struggled to establish itself as a dependable partner in the eyes of the US (Lundestad 1998; Cromwell 1992; Featherstone and Ginsberg 1995). Though the degree of success in this regard has varied over time, the expectations deficit in EU-US relations has certainly been a cause of concern for Brussels. A general perception that the EU is powerless remains pervasive in the US (Kagan 2003; Mead 2004). Washington has long tended to rely on the framework of NATO, where it can exert bigger influence and traditional bilateral relations with major countries of Western Europe such as Britain and Germany, which do not seem to have disappeared after the end of the Cold War (Cameron 2002: 158-9). EU-Russia relations, though in a different context, suffer from a similar set of problems, which have proven to be detrimental to the development of relations (Forsberg 2004).

In short, it can be argued that EU foreign relations have two distinct aspects: one is a set of relationships with mainly the third world where there is the capability-expectations gap;

---

[4] It is almost impossible to measure what expectations the EU deserves to attract. I will not try to quantify expectations for the EU or the capability of the EU (Hill has not tried this either). Therefore, what follows is a general argument, rather than a strictly quantified argument.

the other is the relationships with major countries such as the United States, Japan, and Russia, where the expectations deficit can be observed. China's high expectations for Europe may be remarkable in this respect. But it can largely be explained by Beijing's desire to see a multi-polar world in opposition to the US dominance. China in many ways expects the EU to be one of the major poles of the world that resists the unipolar world led by the US. These ideas are hardly shared by Japan. Reflecting the fact that the relationship with the Third World, which include many former colonies of EU member states, has been the most developed area of EC/EU external policy, not least in institutional terms, scholars in the field have been paying much attention to it. On the other hand, relations with the United State, or transatlantic relations, have tended to be dealt with in a different context with a separate framework. The major influence that the concept of CEG has enjoyed in the study of EFP could be seen as a result of this situation. But the other side of the coin, namely the expectations deficit which has rarely been discussed, must be taken more into account in EFP research.

## THE STRUCTURE THAT GENERATES EXPECTATIONS DEFICIT IN EU-JAPAN RELATIONS

It might be tempting to attribute the existence of expectations deficit in EU-Japan relations solely to Tokyo's excessive focus on relations with the United States.

**Table. Sources of the Expectations Deficit in EU-Japan Relations**

| | | ORIGINS | |
|---|---|---|---|
| | | *Japan* | *Europe / the EU* |
| **OBJECT OF LOW EXPECTATIONS** | *Europe as a whole* | Focus on the US and Asia (Japan's indifference to Europe) | Europe's indifference (and even arrogance) to Japan / Different values and principles? |
| | *The EU as an international actor* | Lack of understanding on EU policy-making / Preference for bilateral relations with major EU countries | EU's failure in its common foreign and security policy / Complexities of EU policy-making / EU's lack of competences / Different perceptions or interests? |

To be sure, it is one of the main sources of the deficit. But what lies behind the expectations deficit in EU-Japan relations is more complicated than it appears to be at first sight. I will divide the sources of expectations deficit into four through two criteria. First, in terms of the origins of the deficit, it can be divided into factors internal to Japan and those which originate on EU side. Second, in terms of low expectations, there are two kinds: one is low expectations of Europe in general, and the other is those of the EU as an international actor specifically. These four categories are illustrated in the table on the previous page, which I will explore in turn.

## (1) Japan's Focus on the US and Asia

First, not surprisingly, the lack of Japan's expectations of Europe derives from Tokyo's focus on its relations with the United States and Asian neighbours. Since the end of World War II, the mainstream élites both within and outside the government in Japan have attached the first and foremost importance to relations with the US. An alliance with Washington has always been and remains to be the only guarantee of the very survival and security of the country. The United States is the only ally that can ensure Japan's physical security in the face of any instability in the Korean Peninsula, for example. In the economic aspect as well, the US has long been the largest and the most open market to Japanese exports, on which Japan's post-war economic reconstruction and development have relied to a great extent. The result was an almost excessive focus on the US and a resultant negligence for other potentially important partners in the world, including Europe. It is sometimes criticized that in the Foreign Ministry, the influence of what might be called 'America-first-ism' has been particularly strong. The influence of post-war Americanization has also been widespread in the society as a whole. One Japanese scholar of French literature even pointed out that those who were fascinated by France in the early post-war years belonged to a camp of 'spiritual opposition', often associated with anti-Americanism (Nishinaga 1998: 17). For a country that turned almost exclusively to Europe when it sought modernization in the late nineteenth and early twentieth century, the change of orientation could not have been starker. The United States replaced Europe as the model of post-war democratization, reconstruction and development. At the same time, how to deal with its Asian neighbours has also been a top priority for Japan's foreign policy. Initially, what Japan had to do was to re-establish normal diplomatic relations after the war and settle the reparation issues. Since the 1960s and 70s economic relations with the countries in South East Asia and North East Asia have become increasingly important.[5]

At least in theory, a strong relationship with the United States and Asia should not necessarily preclude the development of close cooperation with Europe. But the mere fact that the priority given to Europe remained low has resulted in the under-development of relations between the two. Given the limited resources that Japan was able to allocate in its foreign relations, the need for close cooperation with Washington and the Asian neighbours had to crowd out relationships with other parts of the world including Europe. In this circumstance, expectations for Europe could not have increased regardless of the merits of Europe.

In recent years, however, there is a growing, if still limited, awareness in and outside the government that Japan has ignored Europe for too long and wasted the huge potential of cooperation with it, not least in political and security terms, which led to the adoption of the

---

[5] On the overall development of Japan's post-war foreign relations, Iokibe (1999) is arguably the most authoritative and popular textbook in Japan. It is telling that though the book is supposed to deal with Japan's foreign relations as a whole, it is in large part a history of US-Japan relations. In Japan, mainstream scholars who are regarded to be experts on Japanese foreign policy, not coincidentally, tend to be experts on the United States and US-Japan relations.

Action Plan between Japan and the EU in December 2001 (Tsuruoka 2002). In a report published in November 2002, Prime Minister Junichiro Koizumi's consultative body, the 'Task Force on Foreign Relations', argued that 'in a new world order, Japan needs to have a strong partner according to individual issues. In some issues, Europe can be a rational choice as such a partner' (Taigai Kankei Task Force 2002: 20). But the overall order of priorities in Japan's foreign relations is not likely to change in a short period of time. Indeed, in that report, the section on Europe comes close to the end, eighth out of eleven, though it does not explicitly say that each issue comes up in order of importance.

## (2) Japan's Lack of Understanding and Preference for Bilateral Relations

Second, on Japan's side, the lack of understanding of the EU and Tokyo's preference to deal with major countries of Western Europe bilaterally rather than talking to Brussels have contributed to Japan's low expectations for the EU as an international actor. European integration in many respects has changed the way foreign relations are conducted. In 1970, for example, the European Community (the Commission of the EC) took up large part of the competence in trade under the framework of common commercial policy (CCP), which presented a huge challenge to the third parties who now had to negotiate with a new interlocutor in Brussels rather than more familiar London or Paris. Furthermore, the division of labour between Brussels and member states did not seem very clear, particularly in the eyes of outsiders, which I will discuss later. In Japan at that time, there was simply not adequate knowledge, even in government, about how the EC was working and how Japan had to deal with it. The result was that Japan continued to prefer dealing with individual countries rather than with the EC as a whole, which in turn frustrated Brussels and aroused suspicion that Japan was employing a strategy of 'dividing' Europe (Hosoya 1993: 201-202).

Though Japan's knowledge and understanding on European integration have certainly improved in later years, the problem has not disappeared completely. In a sense, it is influenced by the press coverage in Japan. The majority of the Japanese press tends to be sceptical toward European integration in general, at least in part because they rely heavily on the British press for European news.[6] Up until just before 1999, many Japanese did not expect that the single currency would be realised as scheduled. Now, very few people in Japan are aware of the recent development of defence cooperation in the EU including the adoption of the EU's first ever Security Strategy in December 2003 and a growing number of EU led military and civilian operations under the framework of European Security and Defence Policy (ESDP).[7]

In spite of the growing experience of dealing with Brussels, the government's preference for dealing with individual countries bilaterally has not become a thing of the past. There are many reasons for this, one of the most important of which being the repeated failures of the EU to speak in a single voice in the international arena, which will be discussed later. On

---

[6] This is because English is the most accessible language for the majority of Japanese and London sees the largest concentration of the Japanese press in Europe. Many newspapers and broadcasters have their European headquarters in London, and only a handful of major ones have permanent correspondents in Brussels. At the same time, regardless of relying on English sources, journalists, by nature, prefer reporting troubles and failures to achievements and successes.

[7] The Europeans also have difficulty in recognizing these new developments. See Giegerich and Wallace (2004).

Japan's side, it is because the perception of the EU as an international actor has not been fully established. The adoption of The Hague Declaration of July 1991 between Japan and the EC helped raise the awareness of the EC/EU as an international actor in Japan, at least to some extent. But apart from trade issues where the Commission has an exclusive competence, the role of the EU in the eyes of Tokyo in the broader issues of foreign and security policy remains vague. In the light of repeated failures of the EU in its attempt to forge a common foreign and security policy, it is difficult for Japan to change its perception of the EU. The EU itself seems to recognize this problem. In its policy document (Communication) on the relations with Japan in 1995, the Commission stated that 'The EU will not improve its own image in Japan until it is seen to have political weight to match its position as an economic and technological power' (Commission of the European Communities 1995: 7). One could also argue that the concept of 'pooled sovereignty' of the EU is very different from Japan's more traditional understanding of sovereignty, which makes hard for the Japanese to make sense of the EU as an international actor without (traditional) sovereignty. Robert Keohane (2003) argues that there is a difference between the EU and the US regarding the concept of sovereignty. The same can be said, while in a different context, of Japan and the EU.

At the same time, Japan was very active in revitalizing and consolidating bilateral relations with the major countries of the EU in the rest of the 1990s after the adoption of The Hague Declaration. Though the strengthening of the relations with major countries in Europe should not have been a bad thing for the overall relations between Japan and Europe, there was a fear that these rather traditional bilateral relations would 'dilute' EU-Japan relations (Tanaka 2000: 16-17).[8] The above-mentioned report of November 2002 by the Prime Minister's 'Task Force on Foreign Relations' argues, while acknowledging the importance of cooperating with the EU, that 'it will be necessary for Japan to choose between dealing with the EU [the Commission or the Presidency] and negotiating with relevant member countries bilaterally at its own discretion to suit individual cases' (Taigai Kankei Task Force 2002: 20). Even before the release of that report, just after his inauguration, Prime Minister Koizumi visited London and Paris in June-July 2001 without calling on Brussels, which indicated the government's approach to Europe. Though Japan's degree of preference for bilateral relations with individual countries is influenced by the state of the division of labour between Brussels and national capitals and the effectiveness of EU institutions, most notably the Commission, as will be discussed later, what is important in this section is that Japan's preference for bilateral relations with individual countries is in many ways inherent in nature.

## (3) Europe's Indifference to Japan and Different Principles?

'Indifference' is a word very often used to describe the nature of EU-Japan relations. To be sure, Japan's indifference to Europe has long been obvious, as has been argued so far. But at the same time, indifference to Japan in Europe has also been consistent throughout the post-war period. The problem therefore is that of mutual indifference. To make matters

---

[8] Simon Nuttall points out that, at the time of the adoption of The Hague Declaration, there was an opposite fear in Europe that 'a strengthening of Japan's ties with the EC might lead to a corresponding weakening of links with the Member States' (Nuttall 2001: 217). It is undeniable that large member states normally prefer keeping their own distinctive relations with major countries outside the EU such as the US, Russia, China, and to a lesser extent, Japan, rather than giving a large role to the EU institutions, not least the Commission.

worse, Europe's indifference or underestimation of Japan has been felt by the Japanese involved in the relations between Japan and Europe. Murata Ryohei, a veteran diplomat who served Vice Minister for Foreign Affairs and Ambassador to the US and Germany, argues that, while acknowledging the problem of Japan's indifference to Europe, the biggest characteristic of Europe's attitude to Japan has been its indifference to Japan and expresses his concern that 'ignorance' or even 'arrogance' toward Japan has been pervasive in Europe (Murata 2004: 74-78; Kawashima 2003: 128 and 131). It is hard to deny that Europe's indifference to and underestimation of Japan influenced Japan's own perception of Europe in a negative way: the argument goes like 'given that Europeans are not interested in Japan, we do not have to pay attention to them either'. As far as the situation in Japan was concerned, there was certainly a vicious circle of what can be called mutually reinforcing indifference.

In more concrete terms as well, it is undeniable that European countries' dealings with Japan in the early post-war years did have a negative impact on Japan and its perception of Europe. In this regard, Europe has always been seen in comparison with the United States. The perceptions established after the Second World War through the 1960s in Japan was that the United States was much more open, fair, sincere, and helpful to Japan than West European countries were. In the field of trade and diplomacy, that perception was consolidated in the negotiations of Japan's accession to General Agreement on Tariffs and Trade (GATT) and the Organisation for Economic Cooperation and Development (OECD), during which West European countries were reluctant to accept Japan and tried hard to maintain discriminatory measures against the country (Akaneya 1992; Murata 2000: 14-19). Though such a European stance was not totally without legitimate grounds, it nevertheless left an impression to the Japanese that Europeans were different from the Americans and more difficult to deal with.

This sort of stereotyped perception of Europe established by the 1960s proved to be persistent. Yabunaka Mitoji, a senior Japanese trade negotiator, recalls that, even during the period of fierce trade frictions with the US in the 1980s, the Americans were much fairer and sincere to Japan in trade negotiations whereas the Europeans seemed to prefer going it alone by protecting their own market (Yabunaka 1991: 203).[9] Though Japan itself had not had a very good record in terms of trade liberalization until the 1970s and 80s, Japan almost consistently regarded Europe to be protectionist and its complaints about trade deficits to be a scapegoat for its own economic problems (Yoshimori 1986). In spite of The Hague Declaration's assertion to the contrary, people in Japan (and probably the Europeans as well) have been wondering whether the two sides really share common values and principles not least in economy and trade. This is particularly a big problem, because economy and trade have almost always been the two most dominant themes in EU-Japan relations. The overall image of Europe among the Japanese has inevitably been influenced by these negative aspects. But the situation has greatly changed since the mid-1990s, by when trade frictions between Japan and the EU had largely been solved. Receding of trade and economic problems in EU-Japan relations has allowed the EU and Japan to explore possibilities for extending dialogue and cooperation between the two parties to non-economic issues, notably foreign policy and security fields (Tsuruoka 2006). Against this background, the 'decade of

---

[9] Yabunaka, who is now Deputy Foreign Minister, was Head of Second North America Division (*Hokubei-Dainika*) in charge of economic relations with North America when he published this book.

Euro-Japan cooperation' was launched. But its long-term impact on the development of EU-Japan relations remains to be seen.

## (4) Complexity and Failures of the EU, and Different Interests?

Last but not least, the sheer complexities of EU policy-making and the EU's failures in the CFSP have often brought down Japan's expectations of Europe. First, the complexity of the EU's policy process has often dissuaded Japan from seeking more cooperation with it (Gilson 2000: 61). The Union remains, in many respects, a difficult actor in the world to deal with in the eyes of outsiders. As explained earlier, Japan's lack of understanding of how the EU works is one of the sources of the problem. The Japanese may have to learn more about how the EU works but the EU must also bear some responsibilities on this, given that the same problem can be observed in relations with other countries as well. The EU is itself aware of this problem, which is why the issue of how to make the workings of the EU less confusing to the outside world as well as to its own citizens has been one of the central objectives in successive institutional reforms. Various reforms that were to be introduced by the Constitutional Treaty, signed in October 2004, were expected to improve the situation in this respect. Introducing the posts of EU Foreign Minister and permanent President of the European Council were, among other reforms, supposed to make the EU more visible and understandable in the world stage. Scrapping the current system of rotating presidency, under which external partners see their different interlocutors every six months, would have been another important step to be of particular benefit to both the EU and the third parties. But the failure of the Constitutional Treaty, triggered by the rejection by the French and Dutch voters in their respective referenda in 2005, was a huge blow to the EU's (particularly political) profile in international relations.

Second, the EU's repeated failures to forge a common position on important international issues have often reduced the attractiveness of the EU as a partner in the international arena, not least in the field of foreign and security policy. The most infamous case was its deep division on Iraq during the run-up to the war in 2003. Prime Minister Koizumi and his government had not initially ruled out consultations with Brussels on Iraq, but found it just impossible to carry out a meaningful dialogue with EU institutions—Presidency of the Council, CFSP High Representative, or the European Commission—because of the division among major EU countries and the resultant paralysis of the EU on the issue. That was why, when Prime Minister Koizumi toured European countries immediately after the war in April-May 2003, he chose to visit London, Madrid, Paris, and Berlin before going to Athens for the EU-Japan annual summit. Substantial discussions on the issues of Iraq and other urgent matters were conducted in national capitals and the EU-Japan summit was hardly a climax of the visit, though it adopted a Joint Press Statement in which the two sides expressed their shared support to the reconstruction of Iraq. Given the deep division of opinion on the Iraq War, there was little room for EU-Japan initiative on Iraq, which had nothing to do with Tokyo's tactics or inherent bilateralism in its relations with Europe. In addition to Iraq, one more issue that has been of top priority to Japan has been the reform of the UN Security Council. Japan has been trying to become a permanent member of the Security Council for a long time (Drifte 2000), and stepped up its effort in recent years, especially in the framework of 'G-4 (Group of Four)' with Germany, Brazil, and India in 2005. On this issue again, the

EU failed to forge a single voice (mainly due to Italy's opposition to a German permanent membership in the Security Council), and as a result, the EU disappeared from Tokyo's radar screen because it was of no use from the Japanese point of view in seeking its own permanent seat of the Council. Tokyo instead sought bilateral support from individual EU member countries, not least France and Britain as permanent members of the Security Council.

A sense of frustration and uneasiness among Japanese and other Asian policymakers about Europe's (the EU's) behaviours in Asia also affect their perceptions of Europe and the EU. How to deal with North Korea, China, and Myanmar are cases in point (Kawashima 2003: 129). Especially from the viewpoint of Tokyo, which faces a set of serious problems with North Korea from the issue of abduction of Japanese citizens to that of nuclear development, the EU's more relaxed approach to Pyongyang has often been a cause for concern. The issue of lifting arms embargo on China, which has been under discussion in the EU since December 2003, is also perplexing to Japan and other countries directly involved in the region, including the United States. What was most striking and indeed worrying in the debates on this issue in the EU was that there had been few discussions, not least in initial stages, on the strategic implications and regional consequences of Brussels' decision. The issue of arms embargo thus demonstrated a huge perception gap on East Asia's security environment, which led to the launching of 'strategic dialogue' between the two parties in 2005 (EU-Japan Summit 2005). Beyond as a temporizing mechanism, the central aim of the new dialogue is to forge a common perception on security environment of East Asia between Japan and the EU, through which Tokyo expects the EU to become more attentive to the situations of the region and behave to Japan's liking in the region. But given the inevitably limited room for Europe's role in the security of the Asia-Pacific region, it remains the reality that Tokyo's expectations of the EU's role in the region seem very limited beyond expecting the EU not to do anything harmful to Japan's interest, such as lifting the arms embargo on China.

## CONCLUSION

As has been discussed throughout, the expectations deficit is a serious phenomenon that has negative impacts on the development of EU-Japan relations. The causes of the deficit are deep and often decades old on both sides. Despite the recent developments in EU-Japan relations symbolized by the adoption of the Action Plan in December 2001, the basic structure of the problem does not seem to have changed greatly. But the extent and the nature of the expectations deficit could always change. Indeed, various sets of both internal and external factors are exerting influence on the calculation of Tokyo's expectations for Europe. Economic, political and social situations in the EU and Japan, direction of US foreign policy, the state of international security and the problems of global environment are just a few examples that could influence, for better or worse, the course of expectations deficit. At the same time, much also depends on the EU, which needs to take into account the nature of the problem and its adverse implications for the development of EU foreign policy as a whole. Scholars working in the field of EFP would also have to pay more attention to the issue of the expectations deficit in addition to their customary reference to the capability-expectations gap.

In the final analysis, what is clear is that there is no easy solution to the problem of expectations deficit. The shape and the degree of the deficit is a function of many factors that are often beyond the control of government authorities including EU institutions. But any attempt to overcome the problem must start from the full understanding of the fundamental structure of the problem. There is no short cut.

# REFERENCES

Abe, Atsuko (1999) *Japan and the European Union: Domestic Politics and Transnational Relations*, London: Athlone Press.

Akaneya, Tatsuo (1992) *Nihon no GATT Kanyuu-Mondai* [The Issue of Japan's Accession to GATT], Tokyo: University of Tokyo Press.

Bretherton, Charlotte and John Volger (1999) *The European Union as a Global Actor*, London: Routledge.

Cameron, Fraser (2002) *US Foreign Policy after the Cold War: Global Hegemon or Reluctant Sheriff?* London: Routledge.

Commission of the European Communities (1995), Communication from the Commission to the Council, *Europe and Japan: The Next Steps* COM(95)73 final, Brussels, 8 March.

Cromwell, William (1992) *The United States and the European Pillar: The Strained Alliance*, Basingstoke: Macmillan.

Drifte, Reinhard (2000) *Japan's Quest for a Permanent Security Council Seat: A Matter of Pride or Justice?* Basingstoke: Macmillan.

EC-Japan Summit (1991) *The Joint Declaration on Relations between the European Community and its Member States and Japan*, The Hague, 18 July.

European Policy Centre (2004) 'EU-Asia: Prospects for the Future', a summary of a dialogue seminar held at the European Policy Centre, Brussels, 2 June.

European Security Strategy (2003) *A Secure Europe in a Better World*, Brussels, 12 December.

European Union-Japan Summit (2005) *Joint Press Statement*, Luxembourg, 2 May.

European Union-Japan Summit (2001) *Shaping Our Common Future: An Action Plan for EU-Japan Cooperation*, Brussels, 8 December.

Featherstone, Kevin and Roy Ginsberg (1995) *The United States and the European Union in the 1990s: Partners in Transition*, Basingstoke: Macmillan.

Forsberg, Tuomas (2004) 'The EU-Russia Security Partnership: Why the Opportunity Was Missed' *European Foreign Affairs Review* 9(2): 247-267.

Giegerich, Bastian and William Wallace (2004) 'Not Such a Soft Power: The External Deployment of European Forces' *Survival* 46(2): 163-182.

Gilson, Julie (2000) *Japan and the European Union: A Partnership for the Twentieth-First Century?* Basingstoke: Macmillan.

Ginsberg, Roy (2001) *The European Union in International Politics: Baptism by Fire*, Lanham: Rowman and Littlefield Publishers.

Hill, Christopher (1993) 'The Capability-Expectations Gap, or Conceptualizing Europe's International Role' *Journal of Common Market Studies* 31(3): 305-328.

Hill, Christopher (1998) 'Closing the Capabilities-Expectations Gap?' in: John Peterson and Helene Sjursen (eds) *A Common Foreign Policy for Europe?* London: Routledge, 18-38.

Hosoya Chihiro (1993) *Nihon-Gaikou no Kiseki* [The Track of Japanese Diplomacy], Tokyo: NHK Books.

Iokibe, Makoto (ed.) (1999) *Sengo Nihon-Gaikoushi* [Post-war Japanese Diplomatic History], Tokyo: Yuuhikaku.

Kagan, Robert (2003) *Of Paradise and Power: America and Europe in the New World Order*, New York: Alfred A. Knopf.

Kawashima, Yutaka (2003) *Japanese Foreign Policy at Crossroads: Challenges and Options for the Twenty-First Century*, Washington, D.C.: Brookings Institution.

Keohane, Robert (2003) 'Ironies of Sovereignty: The EU and the US' in: J.H.H. Weiler, Iain Begg, and John Peterson (eds) *Integration in an Expanding European Union*, London: Blackwell Publishing, 307-329.

Kono, Yohei (2000) 'Seeking a Millennium Partnership: New Dimensions in Japan-Europe Cooperation', a speech at the French Institute of International Relations (Ifri), Paris, 13 January.

Lundestad, Geir (1998) *'Empire' by Integration: The United States and European Integration, 1945-1997*, Oxford: Oxford University Press.

Mead, Walter Russell (2004) 'Goodbye to Berlin? Germany Looks Askance at Red State America' *National Interest* 75: 9-28.

Murata, Ryohei (2004) *Kaiko suru Nihon-Gaikou, 1952-2002* [Japan's Diplomacy in Retrospect, 1952-2002], Tokyo: Toshi-Shuppan.

Murata, Ryohei (2000) *OECD—Keizai Kaihatsu Kyouryoku Kikou: Sekai-Saidai no Shinku-Tanku* [The OECD: The World's Largest Think Tank], Tokyo: Chuukou Shinsho.

Niblett, Robin (2005-06) 'Europe Inside Out' *Washington Quarterly* 29(1): 41-59.

Nishinaga, Yoshinari (1998) *Henbou suru Furansu: Kojin, Shakai, Kokka* [A Changing France: Individual, Society, and the State], Tokyo: NHK Books.

Nuttall, Simon (2001) 'Conclusions' *Studia Diplomatica* 54(1-2): 217-229.

Nuttall, Simon (1996) 'Japan and the European Union: Reluctant Partners' *Survival* 28(2): 104-120.

Owada, Hisashi (2001) 'The Japan-EU Declaration and Its Significance Toward the Future' *Studia Diplomatica* 54(1-2): 11-26.

Prodi, Romano (2001) 'The EU and Japan: Working Together', a speech at the EU-Japan Business Round Table—Third Meeting, Brussels, 9 July.

Prodi, Romano (2002) 'Japan and Europe: Global Responsibilities in a Changing World', a speech at the National Diet of Japan, Tokyo, 26 April.

Shinyo, Takahiro (2002) 'Nihon-wa Naze EU to Teokumu-noka' [Why Japan Cooperates with the EU] *Gaiko Forum* [Forum on Diplomacy], July: 52-59.

Smith, Karen (2003) *European Union Foreign Policy in a Changing World*, Cambridge: Polity Press.

Taigai Kankei Task Force (2002) *21-Seiki Nihon-Gaikou no Kihon-Senryaku: Aratana Jidai, Aratana Bijon, Aratana Gaikou* [Basic Strategies for Japan's Foreign Policy in the 21st Century: New Era, New Vision, New Diplomacy], Tokyo, 28 November.

Tanaka, Toshiro (1998) *EU no Seiji* [The Politics of the EU], Tokyo: Iwanami Shoten.

Tanaka, Toshiro (2000) '1990-Nendai ni okeru Nihon-EU Kankei no Hatten: Kitai to Kenen' [The Development of Japan-EU Relations in the 1990s: Expectations and Apprehensions] *Hogaku Kenkyu* [Journal of Law] 73(1): 1-28.

Tsuruoka, Michito (2006) 'Rekishi no nakano Nichiou-Seiji-Kankei: Nichibeiou Sankyoku-shugi no Gainen to Nichiou-kankei' [Japan-Europe Political Relations in History: The Concept of Trilateralism and Europe-Japan Relations] *Gaiko Forum* [Forum on Diplomacy] May: 30-35.

Tsuruoka Michito (2002) 'Nichiou-Kankei eno Atarashii Shikaku: Senryakuteki Nichiou-Kyouryoku ni Mukete' [New Perspectives on EU-Japan Relations: Towards Strategic Cooperation] *Kaigai Jijou* [Journal of World Affairs] 50(7-8): 96-114.

Yabunaka, Mitoji (1991) *Taibei-Keizai-Koushou: Masatsu no Jitsuzou* [In Search of New Japan-US Economic Relations: A View from the Negotiating Table], Tokyo: Simul Press.

Yoshimori, Masaru (1986) 'Psychological Aspects of Euro-Japanese Trade Frictions: A Japanese Viewpoint', in Gordon Daniels and Reinhard Drifte (eds), *Europe and Japan: Changing Relationships Since 1945*, Woodchurch: Paul Norbury Publications, 48-58.

In: Asian Economic and Political Development
Editor: Felix Chin
ISBN: 978-1-61122-470-2
© 2011 Nova Science Publishers, Inc.

# FRANCO-GERMAN RECONCILIATION AND ITS IMPACT ON CHINA AND JAPAN: SCHOLARLY DEBATE[*]

## Min Shu

Centre for European Studies, Fudan University

## ABSTRACT

The extent to which the experience of Franco-German reconciliation is relevant in East Asia is an intriguing question to integration scholars as well as diplomatic practitioners. This article examines scholarly works on the Franco-German experience published in China and Japan during the past fifteen years. The aim is twofold. First, the analysis highlights the factual details upon which the Chinese and Japanese understandings of Franco-German reconciliation are based. Second, we identify the rhetorical patterns adopted by Chinese and Japanese scholars when they argue for the (ir-) relevance of Franco-German experience in East Asia. Based on the theory of communicative action in world politics, the article contends that, while it is unlikely that China and Japan will follow the exact path of Franco-German reconciliation, the common reference to Europe provides a useful communicative platform to reconsider the relationship between the two Asian countries.

## INTRODUCTION

The successful experience of European integration has been widely regarded as a role model of inter-state cooperation and regional integration (Mattli 1999; Laursen 2004). An oft-mentioned part of it is the post-war reconciliation between France and Germany. Considering the disastrous wars fought between the two countries over centuries, the formation of Franco-German alliance after the Second World War was an extraordinary achievement (Simonian 1985). The question is to what degree, and in which ways, the experience of Franco-German reconciliation may shed light on the inter-state relationships and regional cooperation in other contexts.

---

[*] An early version of this paper was presented at the 2nd NESCA (Network for European Studies Centres in Asia) Workshop held in Christchurch, New Zealand in July 2006. The author wishes to thank the workshop participants for comments and suggestions. The helpful comments from the editor and two anonymous reviewers are gratefully acknowledged. All the remaining errors are the responsibility of the author.

As the Sino-Japanese relationship went through a difficult period over the past few years, the postwar Franco-German reconciliation has been repeatedly raised and discussed by politicians, diplomats, scholars and even internet surfers in China and Japan. Some argue that Japan should follow the German model to acknowledge her war responsibility and manage the postwar relationship with neighbouring countries (e.g., Zhang 2003; Wu 2005; Awaya et al. 1994; Kato 1993). Others contend that East Asia is a completely different regional context to which the Franco-German experience should not apply (e.g., Jiang 2003; Kisa 2001). Interestingly, the disagreement over the relevance of European experience cuts across national borders. In China and Japan, there are people promoting the Franco-German model as well as those who dismiss the European experience as irrelevant.

How, then, does the Chinese and Japanese debate on the European experience matter in East Asia? The ongoing debate shows that many have seen the potential role-model impact of Franco-German reconciliation on East Asia. Yet, the present disagreement indicates it is unrealistic to expect that China and Japan will follow the exact path of inter-state reconciliation and cooperation as postwar Europe. After all, the historical opportunity of postwar reconciliation no longer exists in East Asia. Perhaps more importantly, the recent Sino-Japanese tension has taken a more complex form than the sole issue of history recognition.[1] However, it is equally premature to dismiss the importance of European experience. Because of the scale of the ongoing debate, the European model of inter-state reconciliation has successfully entered 'the logic of arguing' with regard to the Sino-Japanese relationship. That is, today it is almost impossible to discuss the Sino-Japanese relationship without referring to the European experience (Wu 2005).

According to Risse (2000), 'the logic of arguing' characterizes a distinct mode of social interaction. It differs not only from the logic of consequentialism in strategic bargaining (Elster 1991), but also from the logic of appropriateness in rule-guided behaviour (March and Olsen 1989, 1998). The Habermasian mode of arguing has two unique features. First, actors may redefine their interests and preferences as they argue with one another. Second, the process of argumentation helps to cultivate a common understanding about the rules of the 'world' among the arguing partners. Thus, even if there is no clear-cut answer to the issue(s) under debate, the arguing process play a critical role in (i) clarifying the underlying interests of each actor and (ii) building norms and rules to guide their further interaction.

In order to assess the argumentative impact of the ongoing debate on Europe, this article attempts to map the recent Chinese and Japanese studies on Franco-German reconciliation. Specifically, it examines scholarly analysis of the postwar Franco-German experience published in China and Japan during the past fifteen years. Here, scholarly analysis refers to serious academic studies on the European experience of postwar inter-state reconciliation, as well as sensible intellectual debate engendered by such an analysis. The decision to focus on the voices of academic intellectuals is based on three considerations. First, serious academic studies usually rely on faithful interpretation of historical facts. By examining such factual details, we can understand how the history of Franco-German reconciliation is 'reconstructed' in the scholarly analysis. Second, intellectual debate tends to employ more reasonable and less emotional argumentation. The rhetorical patterns of these arguments are therefore more easily comparable in a cross-country analysis. Third, the scholarly debate on current affairs

---

[1] The recent tension between the two countries has involved several other issues, such as the territorial dispute over the Diaoyu/Senkaku Islands and energy exploration in the East China Sea (Roy, 2005).

quite often leads political and public views. Examining scholarly works therefore provides a good starting point to make sense of the politicians and diplomats' speeches and of related popular discussions over the media and internet.

The rest of the article proceeds as follows: In the next section we trace the theoretical basis of 'the logic of arguing', highlighting the unique role of argumentative action and deliberation in world politics. The third section examines how the experience of Franco-German reconciliation is studied and interpreted by Chinese and Japanese scholars. The analysis focuses on the factual details and rhetorical patterns of each argumentation. The fourth section then tries to identify a possible communicative platform between China and Japan on the relevance of European experience in East Asia. The article concludes with a theoretical reflection in the fifth section.

## COMMUNICATIVE ACTION IN INTERNATIONAL POLITICS

The theory of 'communicative action in world politics' was first discussed at length by Thomas Risse in a seminal article published in 2000 (see also Risse 1999, 2004). Risse claims that 'processes of argumentation, deliberation, and persuasion constitute a distinct mode of social interaction to be differentiated from both strategic bargaining—the realm of rational choice—and rule-guided behaviour—the realm of sociological institutionalism' (Risse 2000: 1). That is, the theory of communicative action in world politics is advanced against the background of the rationalist-constructivist debate in international relations (see Scharpf 1997; Ostrom 1998; Wendt 1999). Rational choice theory presumes that political actors' behaviour is instrumentally oriented towards the logic of consequentialism. Sociological institutionalism, on the other hand, emphasizes the role of rules and norms in defining the appropriateness of social behavioural patterns (see March and Olsen 1989, 1998). In contrast to the former, communicative action does not require a clear definition of preferences and interests. It instead assumes 'actors' interests, preferences and the perceptions of the situation are... subject to discursive challenges' in the arguing process (Risse 2000: 7). Different from the latter, communicative action often precedes the regulatory function of social norms and rules. Actors who engage in communicative action are searching for answers to the question of what constitutes appropriateness rather than how to be appropriate (Risse 2000: 6). Communicative action thus enables actors to reach a mutual consensus on the constituting elements of social norms and rules.

From a structure-agency perspective, the logic of consequentialism supposes that the agency understands his/her interests in a given structure, whereas the logic of appropriateness highlights the structural impact of norms and rules on agency's behaviour (Hay 2002). The logic of arguing adopts a quite different analytical approach. As a starting point, it presumes that actors hold a very much fluid understanding of the structure and the agency. Actors are first of all engaging in the process of comprehending the structure—on 'reality' of the world and on the norms and rules constituting such a world. At the same time, actors are involved in the process of comprehending themselves—on their own preferences, interests and perceptions. Importantly, the comprehending process follows a specific mode of social interaction: argumentation through deliberation and persuasion. As Risse points out, human argumentation enables actors to 'engage in truth seeking with the aim of reaching a mutual understanding based on a reasoned consensus' (2000: 1-2).

Unsurprisingly, how the arguing process is conducted plays a vital role in deciding the outcomes of argumentation. It is worth noting that Risse draws theoretical inspiration mainly from Jürgen Habermas (1986). Compared with Risse's logic of arguing, the Habermasian theory of communicative action is normatively demanding. More precisely, Habermas has defined a transcendental 'ideal speech situation'[2] where the quality of arguments is the sole deciding factor and all the involved actors are open to reasonable persuasion. Three preconditions are carefully specified for the ideal speech situation. First, actors are able to inter-subjectively understand one another. Second, they must share a 'common lifeworld'[3] to ensure collective interpretations of the world and themselves. Third, everyone should share equal access to the arguing process.

To recast communicative action in world politics, Risse makes three important reinterpretations of the Habermasian 'ideal speech situation'. First, 'the degree to which a common lifeworld exists in international relations varies according to world regions and issue-areas' (Risse 2000: 16). So, it is possible to understand the existence of a 'common lifeworld' as a matter of degree. Second, the ideal speech situation can be relaxed as long as the arguing process maintains truth-tracking behaviour and argumentation leads to reasoned consensus in international affairs (Risse 2000: 19). Third, communicative behaviour in the international arena 'is likely to involve all three logics of social interaction'—that is, the logic of consequentialism, the logic of appropriateness and the logic of arguing altogether (Risse 2000: 21). The logic of arguing tends to play a key role in world politics, when actors hold uncertain views of the world and of themselves, and when existing argumentation is subject to rhetorical challenges.

Subsequent studies take seriously the reinterpretations made by Risse. One subject of particular interest is the condition(s) under which the logic of arguing may dominate the interaction in world politics. Case studies look into different international negotiations, and find that arguing is especially important during the agenda-setting phrase and in pre-negotiations, that is, a negotiation stage when the underlying issue is still under definition (Ulbert et al. 2004; Risse 2004). Another issue attracts theoretical attention is the inter-relationship between the three logics of social interaction. Several studies point out that the logic of arguing is often intricately mingled with the logic of consequentialism and the logic of appropriateness. For one thing, there are so-called 'norm entrepreneurs' who act strategically using special frames to achieve their aims without convincing others to change their preferences (Payne 2001). For another, communicative action in international negotiations cannot escape from the rules and norms shared among negotiators. To certain extent, the logic of arguing is operated within the rules of the logic of appropriateness (Müller 2004).

In summary, the logic of arguing draws attention to an oft-neglected aspect of social interaction. When actors are uncertain about their own identities and interests, and are unsure about the world and its constituting norms and rules, they are likely to engage in a process of argumentation in order to achieve mutual understanding based on reasoned consensus. It is

---

[2] Habermas discussed the 'ideal speech situation' at length in his influential two-volume work *The Theory of Communicative Action* (Habermas 1986, esp. vol. 2). Later, he further explores the normative implications of 'ideal speech situation' in deliberative politics (see Habermas 1996: 321-328).

[3] The 'common lifeworld' is an equally important concept in the Habermasian theory of communicative action. It denotes a unique communicative environment in which actors are able to use linguistic instruments to exchange inter-subjectively their views on culturally defined subjects (see Habermas 1986, vol. 2: 119-152).

necessary to point out that the outcome of argumentation depends crucially on the communicative environment, where reasoned rhetoric and shared understandings contribute to the quality of argumentation. Meanwhile, the extent to which the logic of arguing is influenced by strategic and/or rule-guided concerns plays an equally important role in shaping the communicative rationality.

In the light of the theoretical argument of communicative action in world politics, the Chinese and Japanese debate on Franco-German reconciliation offers an interesting case to explore the empirical implications of the logic of arguing in the Asian context. First of all, the debate on the relevance of European experience was motivated by the growing uncertainty over the Sino-Japanese relationship in East Asia—a vital precondition for communicative logic to take over. Furthermore, the increasing academic exchange beyond individual countries has turned scholarly debate into a special forum of the international public sphere,[4] where the logic of arguing is of particular importance. The theory of communicative action in world politics contends that the communicative logic relies on (i) reasoned rhetoric and shared understandings, and (ii) the links between the logic of arguing and the logics of consequentialism and appropriateness. Against these two criteria, we proceed to examine the scholarly debate on Franco-German reconciliation in both China and Japan.

## SCHOLARLY DEBATE ON FRANCO-GERMAN RECONCILIATION IN CHINA AND JAPAN

Postwar Franco-German reconciliation is an important chapter of European history. In the field of European integration in particular, the postwar Franco-German alliance has been widely considered as the engine of European integration for the past half a century. To examine the scholarly debate on the European experience of Franco-German reconciliation, we start from the academic enquiries conducted by the scholars specialized in European integration.

The key Chinese text on the postwar Franco-German reconciliation was written by Wu Yikang (1996). Wu argues in his article that the postwar Franco-German alliance somewhat weakened after the reunification of Germany. While the analytical focus of the article is not related to East Asia, the author provides a comprehensive overview of the historical process of Franco-German reconciliation. The theoretical orientation of the analysis is neo-realist: Wu's analysis draws special attention to the ways that both France and Germany recalculated their national interests against the background of the Cold War. In his view, Germany's intention to become a politically normal country and France's aim of building a stronger Europe were the keys to understanding the postwar Franco-German reconciliation. Despite the fact that the balance of power gradually shifted to the German side, the two countries managed to maintain their close partnership during the Cold War. However, uncertainties arose as a result of the end of the Cold War and the German reunification. Wu predicts that the Franco-German alliance would therefore enter a new phrase of weakened partnership. The analysis puts particular emphasis on the influence of political leadership on Franco-German

---

[4] The so-called 'second-track diplomacy', for example, emphasizes the roles of non-official representatives and opinion leaders in dealing with the international issues traditionally handled only by diplomats (see Davies and Kaufman 2002).

reconciliation. Yet, it is worth mentioning that the article treats Germany as a normal European country, and there is no discussion of Germany's handling of war responsibility.

By comparison, the Japanese scholar Toshiro Tanaka's discussion of Franco-German reconciliation draws tentative lessons from the European experience and dwells on how East Asia and especially Japan may learn from Europe (Tanaka 2003). With regard to the historical details of the European experience, Tanaka takes a similar approach as Wu— emphasizing the special roles of national interests and political leadership in establishing and maintaining the Franco-German alliance in the postwar era. In addition, his analysis points to some key schemes adopted by France and Germany which aimed at cultivating close friendship among the youth and improving the public images of the two countries. In the concluding section, the author argues for the relevance of European experience in East Asia and stresses the importance of improving public images in the process of inter-state reconciliation. In this way, the article has, to some extent, gone beyond neo-realist readings of the postwar Franco-German relationship. By emphasizing the impact of public images, the author has tentatively drawn the European lesson from a constructivist perspective.

The analytical approaches taken by Wu and Tanaka are not uncommon in the circle of Asian integration scholars. Although integration scholars in China and Japan normally regard the Franco-German experience as a role model of inter-state reconciliation, Chinese accounts are more often than not dominated by neo-realist explanations, particularly with regard to the calculation of national interests and the impact of the Cold War (see Liang 1998; Wu 2003; Zhang 2003). Japanese scholars, while stressing neo-realist factors, tend to pay attention to alternative analytical perspectives, for example, the declining role of the nation states in postwar Europe (Amemiya 2001), the increasing economic interdependence, and social exchanges between France and Germany (Hirota 2001; Tanaka 1998). It appears that the difference in analytical perspective plays a critical role in shaping the views of integration scholars in China and Japan.

Whilst most integration scholars tend to admire the contribution of Franco-German reconciliation to regional cooperation and integration, intellectuals working in the area of the Asian-Pacific region often disagree with one another over the relevance of European experience in East Asia. This is especially the case in China. In 2002 and 2003 two influential articles written by non-integration scholars appeared in China. Both argue that China should adopt more flexible attitudes and policies towards the Sino-Japanese relationship (Ma 2002; Shi 2003). In one of the articles, the author briefly touches upon the unusual achievement of Franco-German reconciliation in Europe (Ma 2002). In less than three lines, he compares the disastrous war experiences between France and Germany with the creation of the euro and the making of the European Union (EU) Constitution, in an attempt to draw rhetorical comparison between Europe and Asia. His reference to the European experience soon provoked a wide-ranging debate in China about the proper Chinese policy towards Japan.

On the one hand, some Chinese scholars wrote in support of the role-model impact of Franco-German reconciliation on East Asia. Zhang Tuosheng, for example, argues that China and Japan should learn from the European experience and particularly Franco-German reconciliation in order to achieve sustainable peace and development in East Asia (Zhang 2003). In making his argument, Zhang suggests that the political leadership in China and Japan has a lot to learn from Europe. On the other hand, some scholars hold a different opinion and argue against the applicability of the European experience in Asia. In his comment on the two articles mentioned earlier, Jiang Zhou launches perhaps the most comprehensive attack on the relevance of Franco-German experience in East Asia (Jiang 2003). The author first calls attention to the unsolved historical problems of war responsibility between China and Japan, challenging the argument that Japan has made sufficient public apologies about the war. He then looks into the historical context in which France and Germany managed to reach reconciliation, questioning the applicability of these conditions in today's East Asia. These historical conditions include (i) the weakening of France and Germany after the Second World War, (ii) the support of the US, (iii) the disastrous war experiences, and (iv) the unity of French and German civilizations. In Jiang's view, none of these conditions are presently met in relation to China and Japan.

On the whole, however, the non-integration scholars' discussions on the relevance of European experience are short of in-depth factual analysis and easily resort to rhetorical argumentation. Their analyses have more or less followed the same neo-realist logic as integration scholars. Notably, two arguments stand out in the debate. First, the Franco-German reconciliation worked mainly because of the special balance of power in postwar Europe. Second, whether a similar situation is applicable to China and Japan is one thing; how China may benefit from the improved Sino-Japanese relationship is another important issue. Apparently, the logic of arguing is mixed with certain elements of the logic of consequentialism in the Chinese scholarly debate on Franco-German reconciliation.

In contrast, Japanese studies on Europe often take a fact-based analytical approach. With respect to the German handling of war responsibility in particular, there is a large body of academic literature comparing Germany and Japan. This literature not only examines the general topic of the Germany and Japan's postwar responsibility, but explores related sub-fields such as war memorials, history textbook, war compensation, and the trials of war criminals. Moreover, there is even an academic journal *The Report on Japan's War Responsibility* (Sensou Sekinin Kenkyu) dedicated to the topic, which has published four issues a year since 1993.

Most Japanese scholars working in this area admit that Japan has dealt with war responsibility in a less satisfactory manner than Germany. Yamaguchi, an important Japanese scholar in the field, refers war responsibility to the activities that intend to make up for the war crimes against peace and humanity (Yamaguchi 1994). For Japanese scholars, dealing with war responsibility requires (i) war criminals be judged against their crimes, (ii) countries that committed war crimes make a sincere apology for their past, and (iii) war-committing countries make full compensation for the resulting damages (Mochida 1994). In general, the Japanese literature shows that in all these aspects Germany has made more concrete efforts to address her war responsibility. With regard to war criminals, the German Parliament passed a special resolution in 1979 to annual the time effect of Nazi crimes. According to it, war crimes are subject to legal charges in Germany without the constraint of time. So far the act has enabled legal investigations into more than 90,000 Germans, among which nearly 7,000 criminal charges were delivered (Mochida 1994). As far as war compensation is concerned, Germany not only recompensed Israel for the war crimes against Jews but also compensated for those who had died in the uprisings against Nazism. In addition, Germany paid huge amounts of money to the countries that had experienced the disastrous consequences of the war (Hirowatari 1994). Thanks to these efforts, neighbouring European countries generally agree that Germany had made serious and sincere apologies for the war.[5]

How, then, to explain Japan's inadequate response to war responsibility? Comparing the postwar history of Germany and Japan, Yamaguchi identifies four factors that have led to Japan's sluggishness in recognizing her war responsibility (Yamaguchi 1994). Firstly, the atomic bombs dropped in Japan made quite a few Japanese consider themselves as the victims of the war. This feeling has mingled with, and even blurred, the issue of Japan's war responsibility. Secondly, because of the special stance of US occupation and the influence of the Cold War, Japan had quite different domestic and international environments in the postwar period. There was much less effort to bring charges against war crimes beyond the Tokyo War Crime Tribunal. Thirdly, the long-term dominance of the Liberal Democratic Party in Japanese politics reduces the immediate pressures on the political leadership to address Japan's war responsibility. Fourthly, the postwar economic growth in Japan transformed ordinary Japanese people's perceptions of East Asia, making good neighbouring environments a less prominent political issue.

As such, Japanese scholarly works on war responsibility draw on extensive factual details of the European experience. Compared with the scholarly discussion in China, Japanese scholars regard national interests as a less important issue. International and domestic politics mattered, but there were other issues of importance for Japanese scholars. Instead of examining the European experience through the logic of consequentialism, they seem more concerned with the appropriate dealing of war responsibility. In other words, the logic of arguing is bounded by the rules of the logic of appropriateness. Another surprising finding is that the comparative studies of war responsibility have evolved into a unique academic field. It becomes even clearer when one looks into the sub-areas of war responsibility studies in Japan.

The official visits to the Yasukuni Shrine, a special symbol of Japan's handling of war responsibility, has been frequently criticized by other war-torn East Asian countries. Against this background, a detailed study of the European experience on war memorials is a welcome sign of serious scholarship. In 2002 Japanese scholar Minami published three consecutive articles on this particular topic (Minami 2002a, 2002b, 2002c). These articles examine how war memorials have been transformed in Europe over a period from the Napoleonic wars to the German reunification. According to this study, national war memorials prior to the First World War were widely characterized as a symbol of national victory (e.g., the Arc de Triomphe in Fance, Nelson's Column in the UK, and Siegessäule in Germany). Individual sacrifice in the war stood no place in these war memorials. However, such a memorial pattern was challenged by 'the tomb of unknown solider' immediately after the First World War. On the Armistice Day (11 November 1920), the opening ceremonies of the tomb of unknown solider were held in London and Paris simultaneously. Thanks to this innovative approach, national war memorials were no longer a symbol of national victory. Instead, they became the ritual sites for individual soldiers who had died for the country. Nonetheless, in contrast to the British and French practise, war memorials in Germany continued to concentrate on the war itself. Fierce debate on selecting a proper site and architectural design for the 'Imperial War Monument' (Reichsehrenmal) carried on throughout the Weimar Republic. As the Nazis

---

[5] It therefore came as a surprise when the Polish government referred to the suffering and atrocity of the Second World War during the period leading up to the renegotiation of the Constitutional Treaty in June 2007.

came to power, the German government renamed the national 'War Memorial Day' into 'Heroic Memorial Day'. More worryingly, the Nazi government decided to provide strong support to the People's Association of German War Tombs (Der Volksbund Deutsche Kriegsgräberfusorge) to promote nationalistic memorials of war heroes. As Minami (2002a: 41-42) points out, the focus of German war memorials in the inter-war period has spiritually contributed to national re-mobilization during the Second World War.

Minami also finds that war memorials remained a disputed issue in Germany even after the Second World War. In East Germany the government built official memorial sites for the domestic uprising against Nazism as well as foreign soldiers who died in the war. On the tombstone in Berlin, for instance, 'unknown combatant' was written next to 'unknown solider' as the official inscription. Meanwhile, military and civilian war casualties were kept together at the war memorial sites in West Germany. After the German reunification, the newly built national war memorial continued to be devoted to both military and civilian casualties. Yet, questions arose as to whether this kind of war memorials may have equalized those who died for the war and those who died because of the war. To address the criticism, the German government took the decision to build a new Holocaust Memorial in Berlin to reconfirm the solid stance against the violence of war. In retrospect, the European experience of war memorials has not been without controversies. Over the past centuries war memorials in Europe have transformed gradually from a heroic and nationalist symbol of victory to inclusive and transnational memorial sites whose major purpose is to condemn the violence of war.

Based on the European history of war memorials, Minami reconsiders the controversy surrounding the Yasukuni Shrine in Japan (Minami 2002c). The Yasukuni Shrine has long been a war memorial site devoted to Japanese soldiers who died for the country, regardless of the actual consequences of the war. Minami contends that heroic and nationalist ideology constitutes the public image of the Shrine. Not only have dead soldiers been memorialized as war heroes and semi-gods, but the Shrine also takes no consideration of civilian casualties of the war.[6] More worryingly, the Shine has reopened a war museum advocating a misinterpreted history of Japan's involvement in the Second World War. To deal with these problems and avoid the German inter-war history, Minami (2002c) proposes that it is necessary to build a different national war memorial site with more inclusive memorial services and an honest record of Japan's war history.

Apart from the issue of war memorials, how Germany dealt with war compensation also attracts the attention of, and the debate among, Japanese scholars (Sato 1991; Shimizu 1993; Hiriwatari 1994; Hamamoto 1995). Roughly speaking, Germany's compensation for the Second World War consists of four different categories. The first was paid according to the domestic laws in West Germany. Related legal texts include *inter alia* the Federal Assistance Law in 1950, the Federal Compensation Law (Bundesentschädigungsgesetz) in 1953, and the Federal Returning Law (Bundesrückestattungsgesetz) in 1957. Each of these has its own target group and policy instruments. For instance, the Federal Compensation Law addresses involuntary sacrifices resulting from the Nazi oppression; the Federal Returning Law regulates the return of private properties improperly appropriated by the Nazi government. By

---

[6] Different interpretations of the military casualties placed in the Yasukuni Shrine emerged again in a recently published paper containing an email exchange between a Chinese scholar based in Switzerland and a Japanese official working in the Ministry of Foreign Affairs of Japan (Chiba and Xiang 2005).

1993 the total amount of domestic compensation stood at about 75 billion deutsche marks. The second category was the war compensation that West Germany paid to other European countries. This was initially decided in 1953 according to the London Debt Agreement. The precise amount of payment was settled subsequently by the bilateral agreements between West Germany and other European countries. In total, twelve European countries received about 1 billion deutsche marks from West Germany. The compensation paid to Israel and Jewish organizations comprised the third major part of Germany's war compensation. This amounts to about 3.4 billion deutsche marks. Last but not least, some German companies were also involved in war compensation. During the war period German companies had made extensive use of forced labours (Zwangsarbeier). It is believed that there were roughly 7.91 million forced labours working in Germany towards the end of the war. To compensate for this, eight German companies paid more than 70 million deutsche marks to Jewish and humanitarian organizations over the past four decades. Put these four parts together, Germany compensated no less than 80 billion deutsche marks for the war. This amount, according to Shimizu (1993: 51), is as much as thirty times of Japan's total war compensation.

Although most Japanese scholars recognize that Germany has made substantial efforts to deal with war compensation, they disagree on the precise role-model impact. Some question the specific aspects of Germany's war compensation. First, East and West Germany's different approaches to war compensation draw the attention of several Japanese scholars (Sato 1991; Hirowatari 1994). Different from West Germany, East Germany was not put in a position to make war compensation to other European countries. Based on the bilateral treaty between East Germany and the Soviet Union, the Soviet Union renounced the right to demand war compensation in 1953. Poland later made a similar decision to give up her right of claiming war compensation. Considering the postwar settlement of war compensation in East Asia, some scholars argue that the experience of East Germany probably provides a better model for Japan. A second subject discussed by Japanese scholars concerns with the conceptual distinction between 'compensation' and 'reparation'. According to Sato (1991: 296-297), 'war reparation' is the financial burdens (sometimes unduly) imposed on the losing side of the war. In contrast, 'war compensation' aims at making compensation for improper, unjustified and immoral behaviour in the war. The latter is therefore more appropriate to address the disastrous consequences of violence and immorality in the war. Based on these conceptual understandings, some Japanese scholars point to the fact that, in contrast to the Japanese case, private demands for war compensation were widely accepted by Germany in addition to the inter-state settlements of war reparation (Sato 1991; Hirowatari 1994).

## A COMMUNICATIVE PLATFORM BETWEEN CHINA AND JAPAN?

Chinese and Japanese scholars both take the European experience of Franco-German reconciliation in a serious manner. Underlying various scholarly discussions are the questions of whether the European experience provides a role model and if yes, to what extent the European model is relevant in East Asian. With such intentions in their minds, it is fair to say that most scholarly argumentation advanced in academic works aims at 'reaching a mutual understanding based on a reasoned consensus' (Risse 2000: 1). Indeed, the logic of arguing is quite visible within the academic circles both of Japan and China. In China, what led to the postwar Franco-German reconciliation and whether the European experience is applicable to the Sino-Japanese relationship are the subjects dominating the logic of academic arguing. In Japan, the postwar experiences of Germany and Europe in terms of war responsibility, war memorials and inter-state reconciliation are the main topics that have caught the attention of the academic community. More importantly, the common reference to Europe has made it possible for the scholars of the two countries to engage in the truth-seeking process with regard to the current Sino-Japanese relationship. However, this does not mean that the other two modes of social interaction—the logic of consequentialism and the logic of appropriateness—have completely shied away from the debate. On the contrary, it is the ways the three modes of social interaction interact with one another differentiate various scholarly works in the field.

As far as the Chinese works on the postwar European experience are concerned, the argumentation is often more rhetorically oriented than factually based. This is due to three reasons. First, there is a lack of cross-disciplinary communication between scholars specialized in Europe and those working on East Asian affairs in China. European integration scholars, such as Wu Yikang (1996) and Liang Ruiping (1998), produce in-depth analyses of postwar Franco-German reconciliation. Unfortunately the main contribution of these works is limited to European studies. Until recently there are few spillover effects across the disciplinary boundary of regional focus. Second, while East-Asia-focused scholars began to pay attention to the European experience, their analysis is lacking in a solid factual basis. In most cases their references to the European model are brief and thus vulnerable to counter-argumentation. Third, as the Sino-Japanese relationship receives wider public attention, Chinese scholars start to pay more attention to the rhetorical consequences of their argumentation. Rhetorical elements are further strengthened as a result. Rhetorical action is 'the strategic use of norm-based arguments' (Schimmelfennig 2003: 48). In rhetorical argumentation, it is possible to identify the logic of consequentialism together with the logic of arguing. For some Chinese scholars, the role of national interest tends to dominate their interpretations of the postwar Franco-German alliance. The academic search for an appropriate model of the Sino-Japanese relationship, though conforming to the logic of arguing in many aspects, often stresses the strategic thinking about China's interest in East Asia. On occasion the logic of arguing is given way to the logic of consequentialism.

With regard to the Japanese debates on Europe, the analysis not only identifies serious scholarship dealing with the factual details of postwar Europe but also finds the studies of 'war responsibility' as a unique field of academic enquiries. Admittedly, these are unexpected findings against the background of official Japanese positions on postwar handlings. The logic of arguing, however, provides some insightful clues as to the reasons for the quality of Japanese scholarship. After the Second World War, Japan became engaged in a long process of political self-reidentification. As the constitution was rewritten, military power was renounced, and political institutions were re-constructed, Japan faced considerable uncertainty about her political status in the world and especially her future role in East Asia. Despite the fact that the postwar economic growth has made such a soul-searching process less urgent, many Japanese scholars took the initiative and engaged themselves in serious self-reidentification in their studies. One of the topics that caught their attention has been the status of Germany in postwar Europe. As Risse (2000: 23) points out, 'the logic of argumentative rationality and truth-seeking behaviour is likely to take over if actors are uncertain about their own identities, interests, and views of the world.' The uncertainty of postwar Japanese identity must have contributed to the rich intellectual works on war responsibility.

Nevertheless, it is worth noting that Japanese scholars tend to concern themselves more with factual details, and sometimes intentionally stay away from rhetorical argumentation. This methodological approach places them in a good position to conduct positivist enquires into the Franco-German reconciliation in postwar Europe. However, an unintended consequence is that, for some Japanese scholars, the relevance of European experience in East Asia becomes the question of whether Germany had properly dealt with her war responsibility. Depending on the depth and direction of factual enquiries, some find that the German conduct is commendable and should be relevant to Japan in the East Asian context (e.g., Yamaguchi 1994; Mochita 1994); others find problems and deficiencies in the Germany's handling of war responsibility and therefore argue against the relevance of the European experience (e.g., Sato 1991; Hirowatari 1994). In many cases the factual details of Germany's postwar conduct turns into the sole factor in deciding the relevance of European experience. This is unfortunate because the logic of arguing is quite different from the logic of appropriateness (Risse 2000: 6-7). Scholars involved in the communicative action are not to make a simple right-or-wrong factual judgement, but should engage themselves in the search for rightness (i.e., what is the right thing to do) in the context of postwar Europe. Hence, while the positivist analysis of Germany's postwar conduct is important, the logic of arguing regarding how Germany has conformed to an appropriate dealing of war responsibility is of more significance.

What are the main rhetorical patterns of the Chinese and Japanese debates on the relevance of European experience? Generally speaking, the European experience of Franco-German reconciliation has been perceived either from a nationalistic or from a post-nationalistic perspective. The nationalistic rhetoric draws on neo-realist arguments of national interests and the balance of power. Analytically, it holds that the recalculation of national interests has led to the historical reconciliation between France and Germany in postwar Europe. This view is largely shared by the Chinese and Japanese scholars working on European integration (Wu 1996; Tanaka 2003). Nationalistic rhetoric also claims that Germany's dealing with war responsibility was instrumental to regain her nationhood in postwar Europe. In the case of West Germany, war compensation was closely associated with her postwar relationships with other European countries (Sato 1991: 300). And because of this, East and West Germany have dealt with their war compensation to neighbouring countries in quite different manners. In contrast to nationalistic interpretations, post-nationalistic standpoints consider the violent and immoral war experience as the ultimate obstacle to Germany's integration into Europe. Franco-German reconciliation is only part of the European experience. A more profound transformation has taken place beyond the inter-state relationships. Minami's detailed study on the European history of war memorials is a remarkable example (Minami 2002a, 2002b, 2002c). Nationalistic and heroic war memorials were once very popular throughout Europe. But as the tomb of unknown solider came into being after the First World War, war memorials in Europe became increasingly oriented to addressing the violent nature of war. The disastrous consequences of the Second World War reinforced such a trend. In the postwar era Germany adopted a more inclusive approach to war memorials, regarding military and civilian casualties both as the undesirable consequences of war. Minami argues from a post-nationalistic perspective that only after confronting the memories of war-induced violence has Germany succeeded in finding an appropriate way to deal with the complicated issue of war memorials (Minami 2002c).

The key question is whether it is possible to reconcile the nationalistic rhetoric with post-nationalistic argumentation in the Chinese and Japanese scholars' debate on the European experience. Or, put differently, is there a communicative platform between Japanese and Chinese scholars on the European experience of dealing with postwar responsibility and reaching postwar reconciliation? The findings of our analysis are encouraging. First of all, the disagreement over the relevance of European experience in East Asia cuts across the two Asian countries. In both China and Japan, there are Europeanists who believe in the role-model impact of the European experience and Asianists who put more emphasis on the particularity of East Asian context. Thus, an initial communicative platform can be established by linking the Europeanists and the Asianists respectively across the two countries. Second, though nationalistic and postnational rhetoric may seem irreconcilable at first glance, they may complement each other and further deepen our understandings of the postwar German experience. This is because the nationalistic readings of the balance of power and the post-nationalistic understandings of the violence of war were two sides of the same coin in the German case. It also has become increasingly obvious that inter-state reconciliation in East Asia has to address simultaneously the balance of national interests and the concerns of public opinion. The former demands a delicate compromise between involved countries; the latter requires careful handling of ordinary people's war memories. The nationalistic and post-nationalistic standpoints each provide a good starting point to tackle these two imminent issues. Last but not least, the tentative optimism also lies in the belief that the academic community conforms better to the logic of arguing. As long as each side is open to reasonable persuasion, it is possible to construct a viable communicative platform between the two rhetorical perspectives and among Chinese and Japanese scholars.

## CONCLUSION

This article has examined the Chinese and Japanese scholarly debate on the European experience of Franco-German reconciliation as a possible model in East Asia. The enquiry leads to three major findings. First, there is a disciplinary division between European and Asian specialists in China. Most European specialists stress the importance of Franco-German reconciliation and argue for the relevance of European experience in East Asia. By contrast, Asian specialists are much less familiar with the European model. They often disagree with one another over the role-model impact of the European experience. Second, we have uncovered a unique academic field of war responsibility studies in Japan. This may sound strange, but the postwar self-reidentification that Japan has been engaged in provides some explanation for the abundance of scholarly works on this topic. Third, the analysis has identified two distinctive rhetorical patterns in the Chinese and Japanese scholarly debate on Europe. One is the nationalistic approach that draws attention to the calculation of national interests and the influence of balance of power in postwar Europe. The other is the postnationalistic perspective that puts more emphasis on the immorality and violence of the war and their impacts on ordinary people's memories.

Applying the theoretical framework of communicative action in world politics, the article regards the Chinese and Japanese scholarly debate on the European experience as an empirical case conforming to the logic of arguing. This working assumption finds partial support from the analysis. On the one hand, the academic enquiries into Franco-German reconciliation have contributed to the formation of a 'reasoned consensus' on the relevance of European experience in East Asia. Scholarly works in this field cover a wide range of topics such as the Franco-German alliance, Germany's war responsibility, and war memorials in Europe. These studies not only form the academic communication in question, but also enhance the communicative status of postwar Europe as an external reference. Relying on careful factual analysis and reasoned rhetorical argumentation, the scholarly debate clearly features the logic of academic arguing. On the other hand, however, the logic of arguing is not the sole mode of social interaction at work. Due to the emphasis on national interests and the overuse of rhetorical arguments, some Chinese scholars are susceptible to the logic of consequentialism in their studies. In certain cases, the European experience becomes a rhetorical instrument rather than an argumentation in itself. By comparison, some Japanese scholars pay excessive attention to the factual details of Germany's handling of war responsibility in postwar Europe. The logic of arguing sometimes is overtaken by the logic of appropriateness as the existing rules of appropriateness become the decisive factor for argumentation.

However, it is necessary to point out that the partial influences of the logics of consequentialism and appropriateness have not altered the dominant role of academic arguing in the current debate. The logic of arguing is of great value in clarifying the underlying preferences and interests and in establishing the norms and rules of social interaction. The scholarly debate on the relevance of the European experience in East Asia has followed such a direction against the growing uncertainty surrounding the Sino-Japanese relationship. It is precisely because of the necessity of understanding China's interest in the future Sino-Japanese relationship that the logic of arguing is occasionally influenced by the logic of consequentialism in the Chinese debate. Moreover, the scholarly debate has shown that the appropriate norms and rules of inter-state reconciliation in East Asia are still fluid, and indeed subject to reasonable argumentation in both China and Japan. It is remarkable that the European experience has been a focal point in the academic search for a 'reasoned consensus' on how to deal with the Sino-Japanese relationship. Based on reasoned rhetoric, scholarly works have suggested two distinctive approaches—nationalistic and post-nationalistic—to the possible rules and norms in question. Admittedly, China and Japan are unlikely to pursue the exact path of Franco-German reconciliation. It is also not clear how the scholarly debate will reshape public opinion and influence policy-makers in Japan and China. Nevertheless, the common reference to Europe following the logic of academic arguing has provided a useful communicative platform to reconsider the relationship between the two Asian countries.

## REFERENCES

Amemiya, Akihiko (2001) 'Touitu yo-roppa to kokumin kokka-----doitu niokeru syakaishi kenkyu no siten kara' (European integration and nation state: from the perspective of Germany's social history) *NIRA* 14(12), 2001.

Awaya, Kentaro, Mishima, Kenichi, Mochida, Yukio, Tanaka, Hiroshi, Hirowatari, Seigo and Yamaguchi, Yasushi (1994) *Sensou sekinin・Sengo sekinin: Nihon to Doitu ha dou*

*Chigau ka* (War Responsibility and Postwar Responsibility: How Different is Japan and Germany), Tokyo: Asahi Sinbun Sha.

Chiba, Akira and Xiang, Lanxing (2005) 'Traumatic Legacies in China and Japan: An Exchange', *Survival* 47(2): 215-232.

Davies, John L and Kaufman, Edward (eds) (2002) *Second Track/Citizen's Diplomacy: Concepts and Techniques for Conflict Transformation*, Lanham: Rowman and Littlefield Publishers.

Elster, Jon (1991) *Arguing and Bargaining in Two Constituents Assemblies, The Storrs Lectures*, New Haven: Yale Law School.

Habermas, Jürgen (1986) *The Theory of Communicative Action: Reason and the Rationalization of Society*, two volumes, Oxford: Polity Press.

Habermas, Jürgen (1996) *Between Facts and Norms*, Oxford: Polity Press.

Hamamoto, Takashi (1995) 'Sensou sekinin to sengo hosyou ni okeru nichidoku bunka hikaku' (Comparing Japanese and German culture in relation to war responsibility and postwar compensation), *Doitu to Nihon Mondai Kenkyu* (Germany and Japan Studies), No. 12.

Hay, Colin (2002) *Political Analysis: A Critical Introduction*, Basingstoke: Palgrave.

Hirota, Isao (2001) 'Wakai kara sougosinrai he----ousyu tougou to dokubutu kankei no henka'(From reconciliation to mutual trust: European integration and the changing Franco-German relationship) *NIRA* 14(12), 2001.

Jiang, Zhou (2003) 'Women Shifou Xuyao 'Duiri Guanxi Xin Siwei' huo 'Waijiao Geming' zhi Er' (Whether do we need "new thinking towards Japan" or "diplomatic revolution" II) *Guangming Guancha* (Guangming Observer), 30 July.

Kato, Shuichi (1993) *Sensou Sekinin no Uketomekata: Doitu to Nihon* (Taking War Responsibility: Germany and Japan), Tokyo: Advantage Server Co. Ltd.

Kisa, Yoshio (2001) *Sensou Sekinin to wa Nani ga* (What is 'War Responsibility'), Tokyo: Chuukou Sinsho.

Laursen, Finn (ed.) (2004) *Comparative Regional Integration: Theoretical Perspectives*, London: Ashgate Publishing.

Liang, Ruiping (1998) 'Zhanhou Fade Hejie Yuanyin Tanxi' (Exploring the reasons for postwar Franco-German reconciliation) *Xiangtan Shifan Xueyuan Xuebao* (Papers of Xiangtan Normal College), No. 4.

Ma, Licheng (2002) 'Duiri Guanxi Xin Siwei: Zhongri Minjian zhi You' (New thinking towards Japan: the worries of ordinary Chinese and Japanese) *Zhanlue yu Guanli* (Strategy and Management), No. 6.

March, James G. and Olson, Johan P. (1989) *Rediscovering Institutions: The Organizational Basis of Politics*, New York: Free Press.

March, James G. and Olson, Johan P. (1998) 'The Institutional Dynamics of International Political Orders' *International Organization* 52(4): 943-969.

Mattli, Walter (1999) *The Logic of Regional Integration: Europe and Beyond*, Cambridge: Cambridge University Press.

Minami, Morio (2002a) 'Doitu senbotusha tuitou shi to yasukuni・kokuritu boen mondai (jyou)' (The history of Germany's war memorials, the Yasukuni Shrine and the issue of national war memorial I) *Sensou Sekinin Kenkyu* (The Report on Japan's War Responsibility), No. 2.

Minami, Morio (2002b) 'Doitu senbotusha tuitou shi to yasukuni • kokuritu boen mondai (cyuu)' (The history of Germany's war memorials, the Yasukuni Shrine and the issue of national war memorial II) *Sensou Sekinin Kenkyu* (The Report on Japan's War Responsibility), No. 2.

Minami, Morio (2002c) 'Doitu senbotusha tuitou shi to yasukuni • kokuritu boen mondai (ge)' (The history of Germany's war memorials, the Yasukuni Shrine and the issue of national war memorial III) *Sensou Sekinin Kenkyu* (The Report on Japan's War Responsibility), No. 2.

Müller, Harald (2004) 'Arguing, Bargaining and All That: Communicative Action, Rationalist Theory and the Logic of Appropriateness in International Relations',*European Journal of International Relations* 10(3): 395-435.

Ostrom, Elinor (1998) 'A Behavioral Approach to the Rational Choice Theory of Collective Action' *American Political Science Review* 92(1): 1-22.

Otake, Hideo (1992) *Fudatu no Sengo: Doitu to Nihon* (Two Postwar Countries: Germany and Japan), Tokyo: Japan Broadcast Publishing Co. Ltd.

Payne, Rodger A. (2001) 'Persuasion, Frames and Norm Construction' *European Journal of International Relations* 7(1): 37-61.

Risse, Thomas (1999) 'International Norms and Domestic Change: Arguing and Communicative Behavior in the Human Rights Area' *Politics and Society* 27(4): 529-559.

Risse, Thomas (2000) '"Let's Argue!": Communicative Action in World Politics' *International Organization* 54(1): 1-39.

Risse, Thomas (2004) 'Global Governance and Communicative Action' *Government and Opposition* 39(2): 288-313.

Roy, Denny (2005) 'The Sources and Limits of Sino-Japanese Tensions' *Survival* 47(2): 191-214.

Sato, Takeo (1991) 'Doitu no sengo hosyou: nihon no hani ga?' (Germany's postwar compensation: a model for Japan?) *Sekai* (The World), No. 11.

Scharpf, Fritz (1997) *Games Real Actors Can Play*, Boulder, CO: Westview.

Schimmelfennig, Frank (2003) 'The Community Trap: Liberal Norms, Rhetorical Action, and the Eastern Enlargement of the European Union' *International Organization* 55(1): 47-80.

Shi, Yinhong (2003) 'Zhongri Jiejin yu 'Waijiao Geming'' (The close relationship of China and Japan and 'diplomatic revoluation') *Zhanlue yu Guanli* (Strategy and Management), No. 2.

Shimizu, Masayoshi (1993) 'Hosyou ni seii o simesu doitu nimanabe' (Learning from the sincerity of Germany's compensation) *Ekonomisuto* (Economist), No. 9.

Simonian, Haig (1985) *The Privileged Partnership: Franco-German Relations in the European Community 1969-1984*, Oxford: Clarendon Press.

Tanaka, Toshiro (1998) *EU no Seiji* (EU Politics), Tokyo: Iwanami Shoten.

Tanaka, Toshiro (2003) 'Peace and Reconciliation between France and Germany after the Second World War', paper presented at the 3rd ASEF Round Table, Institute of International Relations, Hanoi, Vietnam.

Ulbert, Cornelia, Risse, Thomas and Müller, Harald (2004) 'Arguing and Bargaining in Multilateral Negotiations', paper presented at the Conference on Empirical Approaches to Deliberative Politics, Florence, Italy.

Wendt, Alexander (1999) *Social Theory of International Politics*, Cambridge: Cambridge University Press.

Wu, Jianmin (2005) "Monei Gouxiang' yu Zhongri Youhao' ('Monnet's idea' and the Sino-Japanese friendship) *Renming Ribao: Haiwaiban* (People's Daily: overseas edition), 16 June.

Wu, Yikang (1996) 'Fade Zhouxin yu Ouzhou Yitihua' (The Franco-German axis and European integration) *Ouzhou* (Europe), No. 1.

Wu, Yuhong (2003) 'Fade Zhouxin Guiji Tanxi' (Exploring the development of the Franco-German axis) *Zhongguo Shehui Kexueyuan Yuanjiushengyuan Xuebao* (Papers of the Chinese Social Science Academy Postgraduate School), No. 3.

Yamaguchi, Yasushi (1994) 'Sensou sekinin mondai----doitu to nihon' (The issue of war responsibility: Germany and Japan) *Hougaku Zassi* (Law Journal), No. 3.

Zhang, Haibing (2003) 'Ouzhou Yitihua Licheng dui Dongya Yitihua de Qishi' (The lessons of European integration for regional integration in East Asia) *Shijie Jingji Yanjiu* (World Economy Studies), No. 6.

Zhang, Tuosheng (2003) 'Dui Zhongri Guanxi de Jidian Sikao' (Some comments on the Sino-Japanese relationship) *Shijie Jingji yu Zhengzhi* (World Economy and Politics), No. 9.

In: Asian Economic and Political Development  ISBN: 978-1-61122-470-2
Editor: Felix Chin  © 2011 Nova Science Publishers, Inc.

# TRADING SECURITY IN ALLIANCES: JAPANESE AND GERMAN SECURITY POLICY IN THE NEW MILLENNIUM

## *Hubert Zimmermann*
Cornell University

## ABSTRACT

Throughout the Cold War period and after, German and Japanese security and alliance policies have been frequently compared. Almost all analysts have stressed and continue to stress the basic similarities, rooted in similar histories, geopolitical circumstances, major alliance partners, constitutional limits, etc. This article claims that Germany and Japan have actually parted ways in their security and alliance policies since the early 1990s. Whereas the core function of German security policy is the 'export' of security, facilitated by the fact that there is no realistic threat to its territorial integrity, the core function of Japan's security policy is to 'import' security (from the US). These different functions explain differing attitudes regarding the necessity of nurturing the alliance with the United States, Germany's and Japan's most important military ally. Whereas norms of multilateral and peaceful conflict resolution and the search for more autonomy are strong forces in both countries, exerting a powerful pressure towards a more independent stance, structural factors, but also the self-constructed role of Japan as security importer, prevent these forces from dominating the country's security and alliance policies. The article makes a functional argument that cuts across the established dichotomy of realist and constructivist approaches.

## 1. A NEW EXPLANATION FOR GERMAN AND JAPANESE SECURITY AND ALLIANCE POLICIES

The collapse of the Soviet Union and the end of bipolarism have sparked a lively and still ongoing debate about the future direction of Germany's and Japan's security policies. In the forty years following their disastrous defeat in World War II, both countries had transformed themselves into economic powerhouses with stable political systems. Both became deeply integrated into international alliances. Their economic rise was facilitated politically as well as financially by the constraints they accepted with regard to their military forces which were limited in size and under tight international supervision. Such a low profile in military matters was made possible by a close alliance with the United States. Washington offered a security guarantee while at the same time providing reassurances for smaller neighbouring countries against potential new threats from their former nemesis.[1]

After the disintegration of the Soviet Union, the major motivation for both Germany and Japan to strive for American protection and consequentially accept American tutelage seemed gone. Would they both now transform their economic power into military might and pursue once more independent and possibly nationalist forms of foreign policies? The ensuing debate was shaped by a series of widely quoted articles by neorealist authors who claimed that the anarchic structure of the international system inherently undermined alliances between powerful countries because these, in the interest of self-protection, are forced to balance against other major powers. Rising international power and the weakening of their security dependence would push Germany and Japan towards more autonomous policies and finally even the acquisition of nuclear weapons as the ultimate guarantee for national survival (Mearsheimer 1990; Waltz 1993). Neorealist scholars argued in the early 1990s that signs for such a development were already clearly visible and detected, for example '…the beginning of a more forceful and independent course now that Japan no longer is constrained to "obey US demands"' (Layne 1993: 39). The same trend against a continuation of the vital alliance with the US was supposed to happen in the case of the united Germany.

These rather pessimistic predictions regarding the alliances, however, were refuted by most of the subsequent literature on empirical as well as theoretical grounds. The rapid militarization of Japan and Germany and the expected dissolution of the alliances did not happen. Institutionalist theories explained this with the embedding of both countries in entangling alliances. These created a common set of interests, reenforced by economic interdependence (Anderson and Goodman 1993). According to this school, alliances accumulate political capital and are able to adapt to new geopolitical situations (Wallander 1999). They do not simply wax and wane as a response to external threats (Wallander, Haftendorn and Keohane 1999). An even stronger argument was made by scholars in the constructivist tradition. According to them, norms shape the preference formation of states and these norms do not simply whither away once new circumstances appear (Katzenstein 1996b). Scholars claimed the existence of particularly strong norms in Japan and Germany which had a huge influence on how these countries interpreted the international environment. Berger wrote of a 'culture of anti-militarism' (Berger 1996: 318) which derived from the lessons of history and manifested itself in a broad societal resistance to the use of military means as instruments of foreign policy. In addition, the elites of both countries are strongly wedded to a multilateral and cooperative mode of conflict resolution. These norms were by now anchored in domestic institutions, firmly entrenched in practices and, thus, do not change easily. Rapid reorientations, such as the ones forecast by neorealists, are very unlikely. Both Japan's and Germany's post-Cold War security policy have been explained in this vein (Katzenstein 1996a; Katzenstein 1997; Berger 1998; Inoguchi 2004). Hanns Maull has popularized the term 'Civilian Power' to describe the characteristics of such policies (Maull 1990). The international policies of civilian powers are dominated by a strong preference for the use of soft power resources instead of military means. The view that Germany and Japan represented prime examples of Civilian Powers gained wide currency and came to dominate research.

---

[1] The history of Germany's and Japan's alliance with the US is well known. A few titles suffice as reference: Larres and Oppelland (1997); Schaller (1997); Iriye and Wampler (2001); Junker (2004).

This view was put to a test when Germany and Japan increasingly employed their troops abroad in multilateral missions and their leaders started to use rhetoric which emphasized the necessity of autonomous decision-making and a so-called 'normalization' of their foreign policies. However, voices claiming that neorealist predictions were now coming true remained a minority (e.g. Miller 2002; Inoguchi and Bacon 2006). Most studies still claim a basic continuity (Harnisch, Katsioulis and Overhaus 2004; Risse 2004; Maull 2004b; Nielebock and Rittberger 1999; Webber 2001; Maull 2006). The German-American clash on the Iraq War was widely interpreted as German reaction to America's violation of multilateral norms (Rudolf 2005). German and Japanese military missions abroad were seen as the results of exceptional international crises and pressures from alliance partners.

However, this still begs the question why Germany, despite similar normative predispositions, seemed to be much faster than Japan in its acceptance of sending troops abroad as part of its international strategies. In particular, how can we explain the very different responses to the Iraq War of 2003? I argue that the constructivist argument of fundamental continuity obscures the core change in German security and alliance policies and the real reasons for a Japanese policy which (against neorealist predictions) still remains very much wedded to its traditional international policy, in particular with regard to the alliance with the US. The argument advanced here also suggests that policies suggested, for example, by Prime Minister Shinzo Abe's pronouncements in his first policy addresses - to pursue a more robust diplomacy uninhibited by the historical burdens of World War II - will only go so far and not change Japan's reliance on the alliance with the US (Pilling 2006). Nor will the recent nuclear test by North Korea (October 2006), despite a flurry of speculation after that event about a nuclear Japan.

To break up the by now rather sterile dichotomy of realist and constructivist approaches, I focus on the *functional basis* of German and Japanese security policies and the consequences for their alliance policies. Like neorealists, I locate the factors determining these functional bases in constraints resulting from the position of both states in the international system. However, I do not support neorealism's mechanistic view of balancing and bandwagoning, because the motivation behind the policies of states regarding security alliances is not shaped by their relative power but rather by the function of their security policies which in turn also shapes the self-understanding of actors. The approach uses the basic insight of functional theories, i.e. that policies are determined by their function, as heuristic instrument and does not explicitly refer to any specific functional theory. The goal is to cut across entrenched ways of thinking in International Relations (IR) theory. As core functions of a state's security policies I define *security export* and *security import*. Security Importers are states which are unable to solve their fundamental security problems, such as territorial integrity and safeguarding their sovereignty, on their own. Therefore, they have to rely on direct or indirect security guarantees of more powerful states. Their security policy is focused on their own territory; activities abroad result from objectives related to the basic function of security import. Security Exporters need no partners to deal with their fundamental security problems. They try to contain threats by preventively (or pre-emptively) combating potential risks through (military, economic and cultural) engagement abroad.

These two basic functions lead to fundamentally different alliance policies. Security Importers are forced to pursue a policy which is characterized by asymmetric burden-sharing with one or several dominant security partners. Security Exporters do not need that and try to search for allies in the pursuit of their objectives within the framework of 'equal partnerships'. Security Import and Burden-Sharing were characteristic for Germany's security and alliance policies until the early 1990s, and they still shape Japanese policies. Germany, however, during the 1990s assumed rather quickly the role of a Security Exporter. One consequence was an insistence on nominal equality in its security partnerships and a more variable and ad-hoc pattern in the search for international partners.

To substantiate these claims, I will first analyze the functional basis of German and Japanese security policies and the consequences for their policies regarding security alliances until the end of the Cold War. Then I will look at the changes that occurred in the 1990s and I will derive predictions on the future of German and Japanese policies towards the US.

## 2. GERMANY AS SECURITY IMPORTER AND BURDEN-SHARER

Burden-Sharing and Security Import were the two fundamental bases of Germany's alliance and security policy after it regained its (semi-)sovereignty in 1949. Chancellor Adenauer's core goal was the consolidation of West Germany[2], at the expense of quick reunification (Schwarz 1991). The intensifying Cold War made the territorial integrity of the Federal Republic (in particular in the form of the enclave Berlin) seem very precarious. The necessity of guaranteed protection by the former adversary and now allied superpower, the United States, became an unquestioned dogma of Adenauer and his successors. After the US government had come round to the view that West Germany should become a vital part of the Western bulwark against Soviet expansionism, it was in principle ready to do so: the 1951 'troops to Europe' decision embodied the American security guarantee for West Germany and the rest of Europe (Zimmermann forthcoming). However, there was one strict condition placed on this commitment. The Europeans were expected to contribute to the sharing of the defence burden. The central component of burden-sharing as envisioned by the US (and the UK) turned out to be the contested plan for German rearmament: it was to relieve the Western allies from the burden of paying for huge conventional forces and at the same time utilize the growing West German economic potential (Zimmermann 2002). Despite intense protests in the German population and among West Germany's neighbours, the plans went ahead. The country's accession to the North Atlantic Treaty Organisation (NATO) in 1955 codified the functional basis of the German-American alliance: Bonn imported security from the US, also in the wider sense reassuring the other Europeans through the continued presence of American troops. West Germany's part of the deal was burden sharing: establishing conventional forces, paying occupation and later stationing costs, providing forward bases for US conventional and nuclear forces and extending numerous privileges to the US army. Economic burden-sharing was also part of the deal: West Germany cooperated in the US sponsored global economic institutions, it soon supported friendly regimes financially and it participated in the global ideological warfare. Nonetheless, the Americans continuously urged the Germans (and other allies) to assume more of the burden. This conflict continues to shape the diplomacy of the Western Alliance today (Duke 1993; Thies 2003; Sloan 2005: 83-86).

---

[2] The terms West Germany, Federal Republic, and Bonn (the former capital) will be used when reference is clearly made to the Western part of Germany until 1990. 'Germany' refers to the unified country.

West Germany attempted to pursue the sometimes difficult balancing act to keep its defence contribution as limited as possible and at the same time high enough to prevent the US from cancelling the overall deal. However, even in times of severe budgetary restraints and strong transatlantic disagreements on the overall strategy of the West, the pivotal importance of security import as the base line was never put into doubt. This remained stable despite a strong antimilitarist bias in large parts of the German population which advocated a demilitarized Germany (Duffield 1998). This norm certainly influenced the domestic debate and many features of German security policies, often in the form of a combination of pacifism and anti-Americanism. However, it never came to dominate during the Cold War (and after). Similarly, an important part of the German establishment argued for more German autonomy and reduced dependence on the United States. These traditional nationalists, however, were never able to escape the basic logic of German security import.

This was true for the debate on German rearmament, but also during the 1960s when the US became increasingly worried about the economic burden represented by its military commitments abroad. In a series of very controversial agreements, West Germany agreed to use its monetary strength to support the American dollar which, according to the most popular American interpretation, was under pressure not because the US had lost competitiveness vis-à-vis its European partners, but due to the foreign exchange cost of US security commitments (Zimmermann 2002). West Germany's support in this respect and the inauguration of an increasing foreign aid program, which mostly benefited needy American allies in the global ideological battle, was, like its own defence efforts, completely tied to the interest of protecting its own territory. Bonn's own international policy was relatively passive. Thus, it resisted US demands for a visible engagement in Southeast Asia. Once the American frustration with the unhelpfulness of its allies threatened to spill over into the transatlantic security guarantee, the Federal Republic agreed to important new financial concessions, such as a guarantee to support the dollar. The Vietnam War cast doubts on the stability of American security import. Thus, in the early 1970s, the Germans became more open for steps towards a more autonomous common European foreign policy. As part of their effort to get the Europeans to share more of the burden, this was acceptable for the US. However, as long as the Europeans relied on the American security guarantee, the Americans were not ready to give up their leadership role and West Germany, in the final consequence, never seriously contemplated shedding its asymmetric burden-sharing role for the sake of uncertain European cooperation. The transatlantic Ottawa declaration of June 1974 reaffirmed the basic US security guarantee and the necessity of burden-sharing (NATO 1974).

The intensification of the Cold War in the late 1970s after the Soviets invaded Afghanistan underlined the importance of German security import. Despite mass protests in the population, West German governments agreed to the stationing of medium range ballistic missiles on German soil and undertook further measures to relieve the US from some of the associated burden (Haftendorn 1991: 168). In 1982, Bonn and Washington concluded a Wartime Host Nation Agreement which regulated German support for US forces in the case of a military conflict (Duke 1993: 73). Throughout the Cold War decades the functional basis of the German American alliance never changed: West Germany was conscious of the necessity to import security from the US and agreed to an asymmetric role in the alliance characterized by burden-sharing.

## 3. JAPANESE SECURITY IMPORT AND TRANSPACIFIC BURDEN SHARING

As mentioned before, Japan's situation after World War II exhibited many parallels to the one of West Germany. First, similarly to the Federal Republic, a widely shared societal norm of non-military conflict regulation was one of the longstanding consequences of World War II in Japanese thinking about international affairs. This pacifist renunciation of military power as means for resolving conflicts was enshrined in Chapter 2, Article 9 of Japan's constitution. The constitution was imposed by the US, but large parts of the population accepted it as part of Japanese identity, as shown by the presence of strong pacifist parties. Despite this deeply engrained notion, Japan was remilitarized in the framework of an asymmetric alliance with the United States. Japanese post-war leaders were convinced that the country needed protection by the superpower, that is, it had to import security (Schoppa 2002: 103). The Japanese-American Security Treaty of 1951 granted to the US the right 'to dispose United States land, air and sea forces in and about Japan'. According to the treaty, these forces might also be used to protect Japan against outside attacks and even internal riots (if the Japanese government requested such help), and furthermore to maintain security in the Far East, an ominous reference given the ongoing war in Korea.[3] In the following years, Japanese diplomacy tried to change this agreement more in line with the logic of its interest in security import: first, to limit its validity to the Japanese territory and, second, to obtain a tight and binding security guarantee from the US.[4]

As in Europe, America's security export had two faces. It protected Japan against Communist aggression and it reassured Japan's neighbours by demilitarizing and controlling the former aggressor. This allowed Japan, like Germany, to put its energies behind economic reconstruction and rapid growth which in turn led to a ceaseless debate between the Alliance partners about the adequacy of Japanese burden-sharing. The so-called Yoshida doctrine, named after Yoshida Shigeru, Japan's most influential politician in the post-war decade, formulated the basic outlook of Tokyo's security policy: close strategic cooperation with the US, radical limits on Japan's own military potential and concentration on economic growth (Green 2001: 11). However, this caused another endless series of debates on permitted and non-permitted forms of support for the global and regional commitments of the United States (Tsuchiyama 2004: 77). In the revised Security Treaty of 1960, the notion of potential American military intervention in domestic conflicts was abolished, but the stationing rights for US forces were renewed. Japan also achieved a more binding form of the US security guarantee and, in a secret side-protocol, granted the US military the right of transit of nuclear weapons through Japanese territory (Gallicchio 2001: 124).

Japanese politicians also realized that the security import from the US entailed a very asymmetric relationship with the Americans. Nationalist politicians since have argued for more autonomy and periodically criticized Japan's dependence (Nitta 2002: 77; Green 2001: 13). From the other side of the political spectrum, the socialist opposition railed against any militarization of the country, particularly not in the framework of a close alliance with the US

---

[3] For the text of the Treaty see: American Foreign Policy 1950-1955, Basic Documents Volumes I and II Washington, DC: U.S. Government Printing Office (1957).

[4] This is shown by recently declassified documents from Japanese archives. See: 'Japan studied narrower scope of security pact with U.S' *Japan Policy and Politics*, 28 Feb. 2005.

which might get Japan involved in all kinds of international conflicts. Again, however, these forces were not able to prevail against the structural realities of Japan's geopolitical position which required security import and therefore led to a situation in which the 'logic of burden-sharing' (Katzenstein 1996a: 102) defined US-Japanese relations. Conflicts about the respective burdens emerged already during the negotiations for the 1951 Security Treaty. Japan resisted American efforts to create a conventional force of 500.000-700.000 men. Like Germany, it instrumentalized domestic opposition to limit the size of the defence contribution the Americans were able to extract (Schoppa 2002: 101-5). In the end, both sides settled for about a fifth of this ambitious figure.

The treaty of 1960 sparked intense protest in the Japanese population, resulting in the fall of Prime Minister Kishi's government. Many feared that this treaty would force Japan to participate in American military operations in Asia (Schoppa 2002). This danger became very obvious during the Vietnam War. Japan avoided any direct participation in the American effort, but it supported non-communist allies of the US financially and permitted that its territory became a major hub for US operations in South East Asia (Hughes 2004: 27-30). A State Department policy planning paper stated: 'Our object should thus be to encourage Japan to concentrate her military efforts on air and sea defence of the home islands, plus the approaches thereto, while playing a modest role in international peacekeeping, and to urge also that Japan use her growing power along economic and political lines, bilaterally and in regional groupings, to assist the development and stability of countries of the area' (Department of State 1968). However, the Japanese, like the Germans, toyed with the idea of reducing the dependence on the US as a result of the Vietnam disaster. But Japan did not have the German alternative in form of a regional alliance. Another option would have been to develop nuclear weapons. In a secret meeting with high-ranking German foreign ministry officials, the Japanese went so far as to suggest that, despite their signature of the Non-Proliferation Treaty, they were planning to develop nuclear weapons over the long run. Meanwhile they would use Article 9 of the Japanese Constitution to counter American demands for more conventional contributions. The Germans thought such outspokenness 'shocking' (AAPD 1999). However, it turned out that such speculations by Japanese officials were far removed from the reality of the Japanese situation.

The crisis of trust resulting from the Vietnam War actually sparked a reaffirmation of the alliance (Green 2001: 13). As a consequence of the War, dissatisfaction in the American Congress with the contributions of America's allies to the global struggle ran to unprecedented levels, culminating in massive demands for a reduction of commitments abroad. With the Nixon doctrine of 1969, the administration seemed to move into the same direction and demanded an end to the disproportionate share of the military burden born by the US. This debate, which lasted into the 1980s, demonstrated to the Japanese governments that the American security export was based on a quid-pro-quo and not self-evident (Maull 2004a: 323; Tsuchiyama 2004: 78). Japan had to step up its burden-sharing efforts. This resulted in the 'Guidelines for US-Japanese Defence Cooperation' of 1978, in the framework of which Tokyo and Washington intensified their military cooperation (Green 2001: 19-23). They were a first steps towards a geographic expansion of Japanese support by defining the scope of mutual cooperation as including the deterrence of an attack on Japan, common activities in the actual case of an attack, and general support of the U.S. in situations which also endangered Japan's security (Maull 1999: 293-4). As a consequence of the 'Guidelines', the cooperation between the militaries of both countries increased enormously (Katzenstein

1996a: 133). Japan became a major market for US military exports and assumed most of the cost of the American forces stationed in Japan. It also supported other US allies in the region, such as South Korea by extending trade privileges.[5] Prime Minister Nakasone's Midterm Defence Program for 1986-90 was directly placed under the heading of burden-sharing with the US (Tsuchiyama 2004: 78). At that time, also the previously fragile popular support for the alliance in Japan became more stable (Bobrow 1989).

Japan also undertook efforts to neutralize the threat to the security alliance resulting from the economic clashes of these years. It agreed to voluntary restrictions on exports and continued holding dollar reserves, enabling the US to perpetuate their twin deficits, partly caused by worldwide military commitments (Inoguchi 2004: 44). Despite the intense nature of these conflicts, Japan and the United States never principally questioned the alliance. Japan still needed the security import, and the Americans needed Japanese burden-sharing in the global conflict.

## 4. GERMAN SECURITY AND ALLIANCE POLICIES TRANSFORMED

German reunification sparked intense speculations about the future foreign policy of a bigger Germany, now liberated from the post-war restrictions on its sovereignty. However, it soon became obvious that Germany's international policies would continue within the parameters of restraint and multilateral cooperation set by the post-war diplomacy of the Bonn Republic. Nonetheless, this continuity in the means obscures the fundamental change which is going on since the early 1990s: the transformation of Germany to a Security Exporter, a transformation that was to have a strong impact on the country's alliance policies.

The first Gulf War in 1990/91 was a final manifestation of traditional transatlantic burden-sharing. Germany did not participate in the military campaign; however, it extended wide-ranging logistical support and substantial financial contributions (Duke 1993: 76-81). After the end of the Cold War and in recognition of the central role Germany played in the transformation of Eastern Europe, George Bush senior offered the German government a ‚partnership in leadership' and thus a restructuring of the relationship. However, the aspirations to change the alliance into a partnership of equals turned out to be premature. First, the United States still saw an independent European security organization as duplication and a potential waste of resources. The operations in the Balkans during the 1990s furthermore demonstrated to many decision-makers in Washington that campaigns without clear 'leadership' were militarily inefficient. In addition, the Europeans themselves were split regarding the future of the alliance. In the early 1990s, most European NATO members, including Germany, saw no urgent necessity to change the basic terms on which the alliance functioned.[6]

Thus, in the first years after the disintegration of the Warsaw Pact, due to the military superiority of the US and the security deficit in Europe, the German-American security alliance remained wedded to the terminology of burden-sharing and consequentially also the acceptance of American leadership. As argued here, this was the natural consequence of the

---

[5] Memorandum to Brzezinski from Mike Armacost regarding discussions with the Japanese government concerning an increase in Japan's cost-sharing responsibilities for the defense of South Korea, National Security Council, Jan 19, 1978, Declassified Documents Reference System.

[6] On those debates see Schmidt (2000).

different functional roles of American and German security policies. However, in a slow way, German security policy began to change during these years. The focal points which became catalysts for this change were the question of Bundeswehr deployments abroad and September 11, 2001.

Out-of-area operations of the Bundeswehr were first seriously contemplated during the first Gulf War, when the Americans asked the new Germany to participate in military campaigns even if these were not strictly related to the NATO area. Of course, this ran directly against the widespread aversion to the use of military means in Germany which had its roots in the catastrophic experience of World War II. German politicians resisted US demands by pointing to Germany's Basic Law which was interpreted as prohibiting out-of-area operations of the Bundeswehr (Baumann and Hellmann 2001: 68). However, the Gulf War made clear (not for the first time) that this norm could easily conflict with the demands placed on the country by the alliance. In particular, Conservative politicians argued that the bigger Germany could no longer afford to stay at the sidelines when its allies undertook large-scale missions in the name of the alliance. Thus, they demanded an end to the taboo regarding military deployments abroad (Baumann and Hellmann 2001: 71; Duffield 1998: 178).

Solidarity among allies became the argument which was used most frequently by the supporters of German military activities abroad. Governments in particular emphasized the necessity to bolster the German status as reliable partner in the alliance, whenever the question of Bundeswehr deployments was debated during the 1990s. This was, however, not a new argument. German activities abroad were defined here in the same way as earlier burden sharing efforts which were justified by the requirements of the transatlantic or European alliance. Thus, the traditional logic of burden-sharing was the base of this argument, and not a qualitatively new strategy (Takle 2002; Duffield 1998: 175). As we will see, this difference is essential for understanding the divergence of German and Japanese alliance policies.

In the domestic debate, the argument of solidarity with the allies clashed usually with the norm of antimilitarism. This conflict obscured the development of a de-facto qualitatively new base for German security policy which became visible only in the past couple of years. Yet it started already in 1989 as a consequence of the transformation in Eastern Europe and the break-up of Yugoslavia. Germany assumed a central role in the Western effort to stabilize the former Warsaw Pact countries, especially through massive financial transfers. Former Defence Minister Volker Rühe justified that in May 1994: '…if we do not export stability now, we will be sooner or later seized by instabilities ourselves' (Rühe 1994: 422).[7] In addition to enormous credits for East European economies, Bonn also dispensed large amounts to help scrapping obsolete nuclear weapons (Duffield 1998: 87-94). Traditional roles in the alliance were briefly reversed when Germany asked its NATO allies to participate in the cost (Duffield 1998: 94). The German government tried vehemently to multilateralize this stability export in accordance with the major characteristics of West German post-war foreign policy, that is, the use of economic instruments and the embedding of foreign policy in multilateral structures (Gardner Feldman 1999).

Stability export was also the underlying motivation of the efforts of the German government in the intensifying Yugoslav crisis 1991/92. The widely criticized rapid

---

[7] „Wenn wir Stabilität jetzt nicht ‚exportieren', dann werden wir früher oder später selbst von Instabilitäten erfasst' [This and the following translations are my own].

recognition of Slovenia and Croatia was justified on these grounds. Military instruments, however, were not yet considered. Yet, many observers thought already at that time that a strategy of stability export sooner or later could no longer renounce the use of military means. Of course, this argument flew into the face of the traditional norms of peaceful conflict resolution and the renunciation of German military out-of-area operations (Philippi 2001). The conflict was clearly exposed by the Bosnian wars. After lengthy debates, Germany slowly stepped up its participation in military peacekeeping missions, culminating in the Kosovo operation 1999. Apart from the Balkan missions, Germany also participated in the UN-Missions in Cambodia, Somalia and East Timor during these years and recently sent its Navy to help in the stabilisation of Lebanon (for details on the earlier missions, see Wagener 2004). Very soon after the decision to participate in the Kosovo campaign, Chancellor Schröder stated at the Munich Security Conference 1999, that Germany was now 'without any hesitation ready to accept responsibility as normal ally'. This role was not limited to the NATO area: 'In this sense our foreign and security policy has to be a contribution to the global safeguarding of the future. Let's call it what it is: an export of political stability' (Schröder 1999). Germany also gave up its reservations regarding the limited territorial reach of NATO after September 11 (Meiers 2006: 50). Each of these actions sparked heated domestic debates (Duffield 1998: 181-221). The argument that participation in these missions violated the Basic Law was voided by the judgment of the Federal Constitutional Court of June 1994, which held that out-of-area operations of the Bundeswehr within the framework of collective security were constitutional if the parliament gave prior authorization (or in urgent cases, post-facto authorization).

As mentioned, the political debate was shaped by the conflict of those who argued vehemently against the discarding of the anti-militaristic norm, mainly members of the Green and Social Democratic (SPD) parties, and those from the more conservative spectrum who emphasized the importance of solidarity in the alliance. Some commentators therefore argued that interests and norms related to Germany's embedding in multilateral institutions were responsible for the new policy of the Berlin Republic (Baumann 2001: 179; Duffield 1998: 175; Nabers 2004: 66). However, there are many indications, such as the German position during the war in Iraq and the new German defence guidelines, which suggest that this was one motive but not the dominant reason. In fact, what happened was that a new structurally induced function of German security policy slowly came to dominate policy despite domestic opposition and conflict. It was not a diffuse feeling of solidarity with the US and European allies but rather the transformation into a Security Exporter which explains Germany's quick embrace of military engagements abroad.

This clearly articulated change in the German understanding of its security policy has manifested itself in former Defence Minister Struck's widely quoted phrase: 'The defence of Germany starts at the Hindukush' (Struck 2003a). September 11 and the global reach of terrorism have accelerated this trend. Security export also lay at the heart of the Schröder government's most important strategy document, the Defence Policy Guidelines of March 2003:

> 'Defence as it is understood today means more, however, than traditional defensive operations at the national borders against a conventional attack. It includes the prevention of conflicts and crises, the common management of crises and post-crisis rehabilitation.

Accordingly, defence can no longer be narrowed down to geographical boundaries but contributes to safeguarding our security wherever it is in jeopardy' (DPG 2003).

'Stability transfer' and 'equal partnership' are also staples of Christian Democratic Union (CDU)/Christian Social Union (CSU) statements on security policy (CDU/CSU 2003). Not surprisingly, the Grand Coalition of Chancellor Merkel shows continuity in this respect (Meiers 2006: 58). On Oct 24, the *Financial Times* reported that according to the new 2006 White Paper 'Germany's military (would) officially abandon its primary post-war task of defending the country's borders in favour of a more robust role for German troops on international missions' (Williamson 2006). The White Paper quoted Defence Minister Jung with the words: 'We have to deal early on with crises and conflicts where they originate, to keep their negative consequences to the extent possible distant from Europe and our citizens' (Weissbuch 2006: 18). The language has not changed since the Schroeder government.

The notion of security export was also an essential part of the European Security Strategy of December 2003. Foreign Minister Fischer justified Germany's participation in the European Union (EU) peacekeeping mission in Congo (ARTEMIS), apart from humanitarian aspects and European solidarity during a speech in the parliament: 'If this continent, our direct neighbour, starts to export the horrible instability which reigns there, the security interests of all Europeans in the 21$^{st}$ century will be directly implicated. The solution of these conflicts to my mind is therefore part of a European responsibility. Germany as one of the most important EU member states has to contribute to that' (Fischer 2003).

Germany's anti-terrorism policy is also shaped by security export. The fight against terrorism is coordinated by the Ministry of the Interior and until recently it concentrated exclusively on the pre-emption of threats from within, by either right- or leftwing extremists. The terrorist attacks since 2001 showed the limits of such a geographically confined concept. Thus, European cooperation was vastly expanded in this field, in addition to German-American consultations.[8]

German security export is furthermore evident in an ideological component: transmitting the German experiences with reconciliation in Europe and the consensual modes of policy-making in the EU into the realm of international politics. This became visible in the argumentation of the Schröder government during its campaign for a permanent seat at the United Nations (UN) Security Council. In its public announcements justifying this initiative, the German foreign office quoted from an article by Karl Kaiser in 'Internationale Politik' which emphasizes German achievements after World War II in this respect.[9] All these examples are evidence of how the transfer of stability to distant regions and not the attempt to protect its own territory became the focus of German security policy.

What does the transformation from security importer to exporter mean for German alliance policies and specifically the alliance with the US? First, the functions of American

---

[8] For details see the website of the Ministry of the Interior, <http://www.bmi-bund.de>.

[9] 'The postwar foreign policy of the Federal Republic, its record on restitution and reconciliation with its former enemies, its efforts to promote European integration and East-West détente, its tradition of multilateralism and its responsible use of its growing power, its exemplary contributions to development aid, as well as its material and political involvement in the activities of the United Nations have all made Germany a natural candidate for a permanent seat. To forgo this opportunity would most surely arouse consternation abroad and be seen as an evasion of Germany's responsibilities in today's world.' See <http://www.auswaertiges-amt.de/www/en/infoservice/download/pdf/vn/global_commitment.pdf>. The article is Karl Kaiser, A Security Council Seat for Germany, in: Internationale Politik (Transatlantic Edition), 3/2004, 23-30.

and German security policy have become functionally equivalent: both see in the neutralization of potential threats outside of their own territory the central task. Of course, the extent and the means of the respective security export are vastly different, given the geopolitical positions and the enormous difference in capacities. However, the decisive factor of the argument made in this article is that both – the US and Germany with its European partners – have functionally equivalent security policies which can be described as security export.

From that follows that the reason for Germany's willingness to accept an asymmetric burden-sharing role in the transatlantic alliance, the security import from the US, has disappeared. This is a decisive change in the bilateral relationship: whereas a traditional burden-sharing role necessarily creates a hierarchy within the alliance, the new role of German security policy removes such a hierarchy. When Chancellor Schröder in the Bundestag on 13 September 2002 said that 'the existential questions of the German nation will be decided in Berlin and nowhere else' (Schröder 2002), he succinctly expressed the new situation, in contrast to the Cold War.

However, this does not necessarily lead to increasing conflict with the US or signal that the transatlantic alliance has become unimportant for Berlin. The strategies of German security policy are, contrary to neorealist speculations, still marked by an instrumental and deeply rooted multilateralism (Duffield 1998: 65). Being a security exporter does not determine whether a state pursues unilateral or multilateral strategies, as the frequent American shifts in strategy after 1945 show. Almost all official German statements on security policy emphasize the importance of the country's transatlantic and European links (White Paper 2006). Demands for a re-nationalization of German foreign policy are relegated to the extremes of the political spectrum (Varwick 2004: 18).

How then can we explain the German position in the Iraq War? Most analyzes emphasize the importance of domestic factors, in particular the 2002 national election campaign, or they see the opposition to the Iraq War primarily as a consequence of deeply rooted anti-militaristic norms in the population (Harnisch 2004: 173-4; Risse 2003: 15). While these factors certainly play an important role, they are not enough to explain the surprisingly blunt way in which Germany opposed the United States. Almost all statements by high-placed German officials on US-German relations in this period use phrases that are variants of 'equal partnership' (e.g. Struck 2003b). The *New York Times* quoted Schröder: 'But consultation cannot mean that I get a phone call two hours in advance only to be told: We're going in. Consultation among grown-up nations has to mean not just consultation about the how and the when, but also about the whether' (New York Times 2002). The Iraq War was not the first time the US has undertaken unilateral actions without consulting its allies. However, the difference is that the policy of the Bush administration not only violated the traditional norm of multilateralism, but also the new self-understanding that came with a new function of Germany's security policy which does not accept an asymmetric burden-sharing role anymore. The United States still bases its policy on such an understanding of mutual relations. However, the equivalence of US and German security policy creates German demands for a 'partnership of equals', in the sense of sovereign countries operating at eye level.[10]

Without these differences of opinion, it would not be inconceivable for Germany to participate extensively in the stabilization of the Iraq, a major potential target for security export (but not in the original military campaign which, according to most Germans, exported instability to the region). Of course, budgetary constraints and remaining doubts about the new role make any spectacular operations by the German forces rather unlikely. In addition, popular opposition to military engagements abroad remains high. However, this does not change the basic fact of the functional re-orientation.

## 5. CONTINUITY IN JAPANESE SECURITY- AND ALLIANCE POLICIES

After the collapse of the Soviet Union, the original rationale of the Japanese-American alliance seemed gone (Maull 2004a: 323-4). Many commentators now expected a quick normalization of Japanese security policy. An intense debate has started in Japan whether the geopolitical changes require a fundamental transformation of its security policies.

One of the major catalysts of this debate was the first Gulf War 1990-91. Japan pursued a similar policy as did Germany. It resisted US demands for a participation of Japanese troops on the ground and extended substantial logistical and financial help. The government tried to initiate legislation which would authorize Japan's participation in UN peacekeeping missions but it failed to win approval in November 1990 (Katzenstein 1996a: 126; Green 2001: 18). In any case, the threat to Japan's economic situation from Iraq's occupation of Kuwait was effectively removed by the US. Thus, Tokyo continued to operate within the basic logic of burden-sharing.

However, Japan's reluctance once again threatened to undermine the American security guarantee, because of intense domestic reactions in the US regarding the perceived Japanese free-riding behaviour, notwithstanding the huge financial contributions. A new wave of Japan-bashing swept the country (Reischauer Centre 1992: 10-17). Tokyo realized that its so-called check book diplomacy had not yielded any political gains and had placed the country in a rather humiliating position (Green 2002: 24). Consequentially, Japanese governments began to advocate greater participation by its forces in military missions abroad (Green 2001: 197). The main lines of the ensuing debate were drawn in a similar way as they were in Germany. Many argued for the continuation of Japan's civilian power status, stressing the pacifist traditions of the country. Some demanded participation in UN missions to prepare for the end of US protection (Ichiro Ozawa, 1994 *Nihon Kaizō Keikaku;* quoted in Mochizuki 1997b: 57-9; Green 2001: 19) or for a regional security system to lessen dependence on the US.

While this debate went on, Japan in fact moved towards direct participation in UN missions, provided its forces were not implicated in any combat activities (Katzenstein 1996a: 126-7; Aoi 2004: 116-7). In the mid-1990s Japan participated in a UN mission in Cambodia

---

[10] See already Minister of Defense Rudolf Scharping's speech of 5 July 1999 in Berlin; Europäische Sicherheitspolitik und die Nordatlantische Allianz, in: *Presse- und Informationsamt der Bundesregierung,* 1999, Stichworte zur Sicherheitspolitik 07, 56-60.

(Haar 2001: 131-44). In December 2001, the country sent troops to East Timor to support a peaceful transformation after the civil war. The most spectacular engagement, however, was the participation in the Iraq War since 2003. Tokyo thus seems to move down the same path as Berlin. However, it is not the same phenomenon: Japan did not make a conscious decision to export security.

Most Japanese decision makers do not see these activities in the framework of intrinsic strategic objectives but rather as a means to strengthen the security partnership with the US (Mochizuki 1997b: 59-61). The argument is similar to the one made by many in Germany during the 1990s regarding the importance of demonstrating solidarity in the alliance. In the final consequence, Japan's ambivalence about military engagements abroad has been trumped by the 'alliance imperative of demonstrating support for the US in Iraq to consolidate support for Japan' (Hughes 2004: 47). In a press conference on the extension of the service of Japanese Forces in Iraq in early 2005, Koizumi indicated that strengthening the alliance with the Americans was the major reason: 'Japan cannot secure its peace and independence alone in the context of international coordination and the Japan-US Alliance. I am aware of the significance of the Japan-US Security Treaty, considering the current and potential future situation regarding Japan's neighboring countries... Many people agree that the Japan-US Alliance and international coordination is the way to ensure Japan's development and prosperity. My decision this time is to implement this in concrete terms. I have no doubts about my decision' (Koizumi 2005). Koizumi's attempts to revise the constitution to enable Japan to participate more effectively in peacekeeping missions also have been explained in this vain (Pilling 2004).

For one, military cooperation with the US has become more and more extensive. The Japanese government, in the *National Defence Program Outline* (NDPO) of November 1995, stressed the security partnership more than ever and declared its willingness to participate in UN missions (Mochizuki 1997a: 13-14). In the so-called Nye-Initiative of 1995, the US emphasized the continued necessity of keeping troops in East Asia, signalling that it would not give up its role as security exporter (Funabashi 1999: 248-54).

In April 1996, the US and Japan concluded an agreement regarding the provision of military services by the Japanese for American forces (Maull 2004a: 324). This intensified cooperation resulted in the 1997 *Guidelines for US-Japan Defence Cooperation* (Guidelines 1997). These did away once and for all away with the geographic restrictions for Japanese support of American operations (Smith 2003: 122). At the same time, both countries signed an *Acquisition and Cross Servicing Agreement*, which foresaw Japanese support for American peacetime manoeuvres and in peacekeeping missions with or without UN-mandate (Hughes 2004: 99). In this context belong also the recently regularized meetings of the Japan-U.S. Security Consultative Committee.[11] The continuation of Japan's security import is also shown by its pursuit of participation in the planned Ballistic Missile Defence system of the US (Nakamoto 2006). Of course, the real threat of North Korea, dramatically displayed by its recent nuclear test and missile tests over Japanese territory, is one of the major reasons for that as well as a potential Chinese threat. Again, this will result in increased technological and strategic dependence on the US (Hughes 2004: 114). The basic logic behind these reaffirmations of the bilateral alliance remained burden-sharing.

---

[11] <http://www.mofa.go.jp/region/n-america/us/security/scc/index.html>.

Second, the necessity to import security from the US is also caused by Japan's failed attempts to establish regional security structures and cooperation mechanisms. The underlying reason for that is the dominance of the bilateral partnership with Washington:

> 'With regard to...regional multilateral frameworks, such as the Asian Regional Forum, and Japanese participation in UN peace-keeping operations and the 'war on terror', Japan's exploration of multilateralism is designed more to ultimately strengthen bilateral cooperation with the US. In no way do Japanese policymakers  seriously contemplate multilateralism as providing an alternative or even rival to the bilateralism of the security treaty' (Hughes 2004: 118).

The centrality of this alliance is stressed almost unanimously by research: 'Japan remains dependent on American hegemony for its own security in East Asia....Indeed, much of Japanese diplomacy is aimed at buttressing U.S. leadership in the United Nations and the international financial institutions' (Green 2001: 5; see also Aoi 2004: 120). Thus, there is no fundamental change in Japanese security and alliance policies. The core function remains the same as during the Cold War: stabilizing and even enhancing the Japanese-American security alliance (Maull 2004a: 335; Soeya 2005).

Of course, this means that Japan continues to be relegated to a burden-sharing role which it does not like and which strongly constrains its autonomy. Japan is still forced to import security from the US. Two structural reason of Japan's international environment are responsible for this: first, the continued threat from North Korea and China (Funabashi 1999: 254-6; Hughes 2004: 42-46). In addition, conflicts with Russia are possible, for example the Kuril and Sakhalin Island controversy; second, Japan is not integrated in trust-enhancing regional structures and it has not made a determined effort to come to terms with its past (Berger 2003; Aoi 2004). This perpetuates tensions in the region and deprives Japan of an alternative to the US security guarantee.

Thus, the US-Japanese alliance is still dominated by the logic of burden-sharing. The dynamic of bilateral relations always follows the same blueprint: 'Japan seeking both autonomy and a greater defence commitment and the United States seeking greater burden sharing' (Green 2002: 29). The imperative of security import continues to trump the norm of antimilitarism and the search for independence. Japan will continue to be confronted with American linkage strategies in bilateral economic relations (which Germany escaped through EU common trade policies and a redefinition of its security role).

## CONCLUSION

Germany's alliance policies have fundamentally changed: its security partnership with the US was defined by burden-sharing and American leadership and it is now defined by an equality of functions, causing a demand for a balanced partnership. Since the mid-1990s, Germany and the US conduct a functionally equivalent security policy - Security Export – whereas during the Cold War, Germany had to import security from the US and was constrained into a burden-sharing role. Thus, the fundamental goals and means of the US and Germany look more alike: both try to contain threats to their security by intervening politically, economically and militarily in the international system. Slowly, Germany equips itself with a similar range of instruments to fight these threats, albeit, of course, on a much lower quantitative level and under serious financial constraints. Besides normative preferences, this requires the continued integration of German security policy in multilateral structures, in particular the European Security and Defence Policy.

Although Japan on the surface seems to move towards security export, its relations with the US and its security policy are still fundamentally based on burden-sharing and security import. The latter is required because of the threat from North Korea, China, and possibly Russia. In addition, Tokyo has no regional alternative in its security policy, similar to European security cooperation. Thus, unlike Germany, Japan perpetuated and intensified its security cooperation with the US in the past 15 years and consequentially also its burden-sharing role. A more equal partnership between the US and Japan, as urged by the Armitage report of 2000 (Armitage 2000) is hardly likely, even if Japan assumes more tasks outside of its own zone of influence. This basic situation will not change in the near future.

# REFERENCES

AAPD (1999), Akten zur Auswärtigen Politik der Bundesrepublik Deutschland 1969, vol. 1, Doc. 59, Memorandum by Political Director Bahr, 13 Feb. 1969,München: Oldenbourg, pp. 196-8.

Anderson, Jeffrey J. and Goodman, John B. (1993) 'Mars or Minerva? A United Germany in a Post-Cold War Europe', in: Robert O. Keohane, Joseph S. Nye, and Stanley Hoffmann (eds) *After the Cold War. International Institutions and State Strategies in Europe, 1989-1991,* Cambridge: Cambridge University Press, pp. 23-62.

Aoi, Chiyuki (2004), 'Asserting Civilian Power or Risking Irrelevance: Japan's Policy Concerning Use of Force', in: Saori Katada, Takashi Inoguchi,, and Hanns W. Maull (eds) *Germany and Japan in International Relations*, Aldershot: Ashgate, pp. 111-28.

Armitage, Richard et.al. (2000), *The United States and Japan: Advancing Toward a Mature Partnership.* A Special Report by the Institute for National Strategic Studies (INSS) and the National Defence University (NDU), 11 October.

Baumann, Rainer (2001) 'German Security Policy within NATO', in: Volker Rittberger (ed.) *German Foreign Policy Since Unification. Theories and Case Studies*, Manchester: Manchester University Press, pp. 141- 184.

Baumann, Rainer and Hellmann, Gunther (2001) 'Germany and the Use of Military Force: 'Total War', the 'Culture of Restraint' and the Quest for Normality', in: Douglas Webber (ed.) *New Europe, New Germany, Old Foreign Policy? German Foreign Policy Since Unification*, London: Frank Cass, pp. 1-83.

Berger, Thomas U. (1996) 'Norms, Identity, and National Security in Germany and Japan', in: Peter J. Katzenstein (ed.) *The Culture of National Security. Norms and Identity in World Politics*, New York: Columbia University Press, pp. 317-356.

Berger, Thomas U. (1998) *Cultures of Antimilitarism. National Security in Germany and Japan*, Baltimore/London: Johns Hopkins University Press.

Berger, Thomas U. (2003), 'The Construction of Antagonism: The History Problem in Japan's Foreign Relations', in: John G Ikenberry and Takashi Inoguchi (eds) *Reinventing the Alliance: U.S.-Japan Security Partnership in an Era of Change*, London: Palgrave, pp. 63-90.

Bobrow, Davis B. (1989) 'Japan in the World. Opinion from Defeat to Success' *Journal of Conflict Resolution* 33(4): 571-604.

CDU/CSU (2003), Positionspapier der CDU/CSU-Bundestagsfraktion: Bundeswehr in einem geänderten sicherheitspolitischen Umfeld, 25 February. Available from: <http://www.cdu.de/doc/pdfc/25_02_03_bundeswehr.pdf> [5 August 2007].

Department of State (1968), *Intelligence Report discussing Japan's Security role in Asia* Department of State, Dec 1. Reproduced in *Declassified Documents Reference System*. Farmington Hills: Gale Group, 2006.

*DPG: Defence Policy Guidelines 2003,* Federal Ministry for Defence. Available from: <http://www.bmvg.de> [5 August 2007].

Duffield, John S. (1998) *World Power Forsaken. Political Culture, International Institutions, and German Security Policy after Unification,* Stanford, CA: Stanford University Press.

Duke, Simon (1993) *The Burdensharing Debate: A Reassessment,* New York: Macmillan.

Fischer, Joschka (2003) *Rede vor dem Deutschen Bundestag zur Beteiligung bewaffneter deutscher Streitkräfte in der Demokratischen Republik Kongo,* 18 June. Available from: <http:// www.europa-web.de/europa/03euinf/ 04AUS_BU/ficongo.htm> [5 August 2007].

Funabashi, Yoichi (1999) *Alliance Adrift,* New York: Council on Foreign Relations.

Gallicchio, Marc (2001) 'Occupation, Domination, and Alliance: Japan in American Security Policy, 1945-69', in: Akira Iriye and Robert A. Wampler (eds) *Partnership: The United States and Japan 1951-2001,* Tokyo: Kodansha, pp. 115-134.

Gardner Feldman, Lily (1999) 'The European Union's Enlargement Project and U.S.-EU Cooperation in Central and Eastern Europe', in: Frank Burwell and Ivo Daalder (eds) *The United States and Europe in the Global Arena,* London: Palgrave, pp. 44-82.

Green, Michael J. (2001) *Japan's Reluctant Realism: Foreign Policy Challenges in an Era of Uncertain Power,* New York: Palgrave.

Green, Michael J. (2002) 'Balance of Power', in: Steven K. Vogel (ed.) *US-Japan Relations in a Changing World,* Washington DC: Brookings, pp. 9-34.

Guidelines (1997) *Guidelines for Japan-U.S. Defence Cooperation, 23 September.* Available from: <www.mofa.go.jp/region/n-america/us/security/ guideline2.html>[10 May 2005].

Haar, Roberta (2001) *Nation States as Schizophrenics: Germany and Japan as Post-Cold War Actors,* Westport: Praeger.

Haftendorn, Helga, (1991) *Deutsche Aussenpolitik zwischen Selbstbeschränkung und Selbstbehauptung, 1945-2000,* Stuttgart: DVA.

Harnisch, Sebastian (2004),Deutsche Sicherheitspolitik auf dem Prüfstand: Die Nonproliferationspolitik gegenüber dem Irak', in: Harnisch, Sebastian, Katsioulis, Christos, and Overhaus, Marco (eds) (2004) *Deutsche Sicherheitspolitik. Eine Bilanz der Regierung Schröder,* Baden-Baden: NOMOS , pp. 173-200.

Hughes, Christopher W. (2004) *Japan's Re-emergence as a 'Normal' Military Power* (Adelphi Paper 368-9), London: IISS.

Inoguchi, Takashi (2004) 'The Evolving Dynamics of Japan's National Identity and Foreign Policy Role', in: Saori Katada, Takashi Inoguchi and Hanns W. Maull (eds) *Germany and Japan in International Relations,* Aldershot: Ashgate, pp. 31-49.

Inoguchi, Takashi and Bacon, Paul (2006) 'Japan's Emerging Role as a 'Global Ordinary Power' *International Relations of the Asia-Pacific* 6(1): 1-21.

Junker Detlef (ed.) (2004), *The United States and Germany in the Era of the Cold War, 1945-1990: A Handbook*, 2 vols, Cambridge: Cambridge University Press.

Katzenstein, Peter J. (1996a) *Cultural Norms and National Security. Police and Military in Post-war Japan,* Ithaca: Cornell University Press.

Katzenstein, Peter J. (ed.) (1996b), *The Culture of National Security*, New York: Columbia University Press.

Katzenstein, Peter J. (ed.) (1997) *Tamed Power. Germany in Europe*, Ithaca: Cornell University Press.

Koizumi Junichiro (2005), Press Conference: Decision on the extension of assistance of the Self Defense Forces in Iraq, January 5. Available from: <http://www.mofa.go.jp/region/middle_e/iraq/issue2003/announce_pm/press0412.html> [31 March 2007].

Larres Klaus and Oppelland, Torsten (eds) (1997), *Deutschland und die USA im 20. Jahrhundert: Geschichte der politischen Beziehungen*, Darmstadt: Wissenschaftliche Buchgesellschaft.

Layne Christopher (1993) 'The Unipolar Illusion: Why New Great Powers Will Rise?' *International Security* 17(4): 5–51.

Maull, Hanns W. (1990) 'Germany and Japan: The New Civilian Powers' *Foreign Affairs* 69(5): 91-106.

Maull, Hanns W. (1999) 'Die zwei Gesichter der japanisch-amerikanischen Sicherheitspartnerschaft', in: Monika Medick-Krakau (ed.) *Aussenpolitischer Wandel in theoretischer und vergleichender Perspektive: Die USA und die BRD*, Baden-Baden: NOMOS, pp. 285-312.

Maull, Hanns W. (2004a) 'Japan - Gescheiterte Ambitionen als globale und regionale Zivilmacht in Ostasien', in: Mir A. Ferdowsi (ed.) *Sicherheit und Frieden zu Beginn des 21. Jahrhunderts*, München: LPB, pp. 313-40.

Maull, Hanns W. (2004b) 'Germany and the Use of Force: Still a Civilian Power?', in: Saori Katada, Takashi Inoguchi, Hanns W. Maull (eds) *Global Governance – Germany and Japan in the International System*, Aldershot: Ashgate, pp. 89-110.

Maull, Hanns W. (ed.) (2006) *Germany's Uncertain Power. Foreign Policy of the Berlin Republic*, Houndmills: Palgrave.

Mearsheimer, John J. (1990) 'Back to the Future: Instability in Europe after the Cold War' *International Security* 15(1): 5-56.

Mearsheimer, John J., (2001) *The Tragedy of Great Power Politics*, New York: Norton.

Meiers, Franz Josef (2006), 'The Security and Defence Policy of the Grand Coalition", in: *Foreign Policy in Dialogue: The Foreign Policy of Germany's Grand Coalition* 6(18): 49-59. Available from: <http://www.deutsche-aussenpolitik.de/newsletter/issue18.pdf>.

Miller, John (2002) 'Japan crosses the Rubicon' *Asia-Pacific Security Studies* 1(1). Available from: <http://www.apcss.org/Publications/APSSS/Japan%20Crosses%20the%20Robicon.pdf>.

Mochizuki, Mike M. (1997a) 'A New Bargain for a Stronger Alliance', in: Mochizuki, Mike M. (ed.) *Toward a True Alliance. Restructuring US-Japan Security Relations*, Washington: Brookings, pp. 5-40.

Mochizuki, Mike M. (1997b) 'American and Japanese Strategic Debates: the Need for New Synthesis', in: Mochizuki, Mike M. (ed.) *Toward a True Alliance. Restructuring US-Japan Security Relations*, Washington: Brookings, pp. 43-82.

Nabers, Dirk (2004) 'Germany's Security Policy between Europeanism and Transatlanticism', in: Saori Katada, Takashi Inoguchi, and Hanns W. Maull (eds) *Germany and Japan in International Relations,* Aldershot: Ashgate, pp. 53-70.

Nakamoto Michiyo (2006) 'Japan plans to step up Anti-Missile Program' *Financial Times* 26 October: 3.

NATO (1974) Declaration on Atlantic Relations issued by the North Atlantic Council ('The Ottawa Declaration'), June 19. Available from:<htpp://www.nato.int/docu/basictxt/b740619a.htm> [30 September 2006].

New York Times (2002) *Interview with Chancellor Schroeder*, 4 September.

Nielebock, Thomas and Rittberger, Volker (1999) ,Die japanische und deutsche Außenpolitik in vergleichender Perspektive. Ein Tagungsbericht' *Zeitschrift für internationale Beziehungen* 6(1): 147-161.

Nitta Keith A. (2002), 'Paradigms', in: Steven K. Vogel (ed.), *US-Japan Relations in a Changing World*, Washington DC: Brookings, pp. 63-93.

Philippi, Nina (2001) 'Civilian Power and War: The German Debate about Out-of-Area Operations 1990-99', in: Sebastian Harnisch and Hanns W. Maull (eds) *Germany as a Civilian Power? The Foreign Policy of the Berlin Republic*, Manchester: Manchester University Press, pp. 49-67.

Pilling, David (2004) 'Tokyo's Defence Review names China and North Korea as Security Threats' *Financial Times* 11 December.

Pilling, David (2006) 'Abe vows to create a prouder, new Japan' *Financial Times* 30 September/1 October: 1.

Reischauer Center for East Asian Studies (1992) *The United States and Japan in 1992: A Quest for New Roles*, Washington D.C.: Paul H. Nitze School of Advanced International Studies.

Risse, Thomas (2003) *Beyond Iraq: Challenges to the Transatlantic Security Community*, (AICGS Working Paper Series). Available from: <htpp://www.aicgs.org/publications/PDF/risse.pdf> [1 May.2005].

Risse, Thomas (2004) 'Kontinuität durch Wandel. Eine 'neue' deutsche Aussenpolitik?' *Aus Politik und Zeitgeschichte* B 11: 24-31.

Rudolf, Peter (2005) 'The Myth of the 'German Way': German Foreign Policy and Transatlantic Relations' *Survival* 47(1): 133-52.

Rühe, Volker (1994) ,Deutschlands Verantwortung in und für Europa. Rede in Oxford, 19.5.1994' *Bulletin des Presse- und Informationsamts der Bundesregierung* 47: 421-4.

Schaller, Michael (1997), *Altered States: The US and Japan since the Occupation*, Oxford: Oxford University Press.

Schmidt, Gustav (ed.) (2000) *A History of NATO - The First Fifty Years. From 'Security of the West' towards 'Securing Peace in Europe'*, 3 vols., London: Palgrave.

Schoppa Leonard J. (2002) 'Domestic Politics', in: Steven K. Vogel (ed.) *U.S. Japan Relations in a Changing World*, Washington DC: Brookings, pp. 94-124.

Schröder Gerhard (1999), Deutsche Sicherheitspolitik an der Schwelle des 21. Jahrhunderts, Rede des Bundeskanzlers am 6 February. Available from: <http://www.glasnost.de/militaer/bund/990206muen.html> [5 August 2007]

Schröder Gerhard (2002), Rede vor dem Bundestag, Sept. 13. Available from:<http://archiv.bundesregierung.de/bpaexport/rede/10/440810/multi.htm> [5 August 2007].

Schwarz Hans Peter (1991) *Adenauer. Der Staatsmann, 1952-67*, Stuttgart: DVA.

Sloan Stanley R. (2005) *NATO, the European Union, and the Atlantic Community. The Transatlantic Bargain Challenged*, 2nd. ed., Lanham et.al: Rowman and Littlefield.

Soeya Yoshihide (2005) 'Japanese Security Policy in Transition: The Rise of International and Human Security' *Asia-Pacific Review* 12(1): 103-116.

Struck Peter (2003a) 'Impulse 21 - Berlin Forum on Security Policy' 23 June. Available from: <http://www.impulse21.net> [5 August 2007].

Struck Peter (2003b), 'Perspektiven einer erneuerten transatlantischen Partnerschaft' Speech by Defense Minister Struck, Nov. 3, Berlin. Available from: <http://www.nato.int/germany/reden/2003/s031103a.html> [5 August 2007]

Takle, Marianne (2002) *Towards a Normalisation of German Security and Defence Policy: German Participation in International Military Operations*, ARENA Working Papers 02/10. Available from: <htpp://www.arena.uio.no/publications/wp02_10.htm> [29 April 2005].

Thies Wallace J. (2003), *Friendly Rivals. Bargaining and Burden-Shifting in NATO* Armonk, New York: M.E.Sharpe.

Tsuchiyama, Jitsuo (2004) 'Why Japan is Allied: Politics of the US-Japan Alliance', in: Saori Katada, Takashi Inoguchi, and Hanns W. Maull (eds) *Global Governance – Germany and Japan in the International System*, Aldershot: Ashgate, pp. 71-85.

Varwick, Johannes (2004) 'Deutsche Sicherheits- und Verteidigungspolitik in der Nordatlantischen Allianz', in: Harnisch, Sebastian, Katsioulis, Christos, and Overhaus, Marco (eds) *Deutsche Sicherheitspolitik. Eine Bilanz der Regierung Schröder*, Baden-Baden: NOMOS, pp. 15-36.

Wagener, Martin (2004) 'Auf dem Weg zu einer 'normalen' Macht? Die Entsendung deutscher Streitkräfte in der Ära Schröder', in: Harnisch, Sebastian, Katsioulis, Christos, and Overhaus, Marco (eds) *Deutsche Sicherheitspolitik. Eine Bilanz der Regierung Schröder*, Baden-Baden: NOMOS, pp. 89-118.

Wallander Celeste A., 2000, 'Institutional Assets and Adaptability: NATO after the Cold War' *International Organisation* 54(4): 705-35.

Wallander Celeste A., Haftendorn, Helga, and Keohane, Robert O. (1999) 'Introduction', in: Celeste A. Wallander, Helga Haftendorn, and Robert O. Keohane (eds) *Imperfect Unions. Security Institutions over Time and Space*, Oxford: Oxford University Press, pp. 1-20.

Waltz, Kenneth N. (1993) 'The Emerging Structure of International Politics' *International Security* 18(3): 44-79.

Webber, Douglas (2001) 'Introduction: German European and Foreign Policy before and after Unification', in: Douglas Webber (ed.) *New Europe, New Germany, Old Foreign Policy? German Foreign Policy since Unification*, London: Frank Cass, pp. 1-18.

Weissbuch (2006) *Weissbuch zur Sicherheitspolitik Deutschlands und zur Zukunft der Bundeswehr*, Federal Ministry of Defence: Berlin .

Williamson Hugh (2006) 'Germany in Radical Shake-up of Military' *Financial Times* 24 October: 1.

Zimmermann, Hubert (2002) *Money and Security. Troops and Monetary Policy in Germany's Relations to the United States and the United Kingdom, 1950-71*, Cambridge: Cambridge University Press.

Zimmermann Hubert (forthcoming) 'The Improbable Permanence of a Commitment: America's Troop Presence in Europe during the Cold War' *Journal of Cold War Studies*.

In: Asian Economic and Political Development
Editor: Felix Chin
ISBN: 978-1-61122-470-2
© 2011 Nova Science Publishers, Inc.

# GLOBAL GOVERNANCE AGAINST GLOBAL WARMING AND CHINA'S RESPONSE: AN EMPIRICAL STUDY ON CLIMATE CHANGE POLICY COORDINATION IN CHINA FROM 1992 TO 2002

*Hongyuan Yu* [*]

Shanghai Institute for International Studies, China

## ABSTRACT

In coming decades, China will become the world's largest source of pollutants causing global warming and resulting in climate change. Given China's rapidly increasing emissions of pollutants, understanding the country's policies on climate change is extraordinarily important. China faces the crucial need to protect its national interests and promote development while joining in global environmental cooperation efforts. According to the fragmented-authoritarianism model of bureaucratic politics, one would expect the making of China's climate change policies to be disjointed, protracted and incremental. However, China's policy making in this area is actually highly coordinated. What variables explain this coordination of environmental – and particularly climate change – policy in China? Why have Chinese bureaucrats paid so much attention to climatic change when the regimr has given economic development prime priority? This essay addresses these questions and related concerns by focusing on domestic policy-making institutions and by linking regime theory with the behavior of Chinese bureaucracy. Both the role of China's National Coordination Committee on Climate and the influence of the United Nations Framework Convention on Climate Change (UNFCCC) on the committees' creation, development and operations will be discussed. It is concluded that China's highly coordinated policy making on climate change was in large part stimulated by the UNFCCC process.

---

[*] Send Correspondance to YU Hongyuan: Shanghai Institute for International Studies, China; 845-1 Julu Road, Shanghai 200040, P.R., China; E-mail:yuhongyuan@hotmail.com

# 1. INTRODUCTION

China is central to successful regional and global efforts to protect environmental security. Understanding China's responses to global warming and climate change is important for in the discernment of global warming and other critical environmental problems. While China has contributed to global economic growth, the country has simultaneously taken on the unenviable role of potentially the largest polluter in the world.

Since the 1980s, Chinese leaders have increasingly paid more attention to environmental protection. In 1992, at the United Nations Conference on Environment and Development, known as the Earth Summit, in Rio de Janeiro, then-premier Li Peng of China noted that environmental challenges were threatening the security of countries and regions. As a result, Li signed Agenda 21 and the UN Framework Convention on Climate Change. Since then, environmental foreign policy has been implicated in the concerns and agenda-setting of Chinese national interests and foreign policy. At the World Summit on Sustainable Development (Earth Summit 2002, or Rio+10) held in Johannesburg, South Africa, then-premier Zhu Rongji emphasised harmony between economic development and environmental protection, adhering to the human-oriented development principles. During the Summit, Zhu also declared that China had ratified the Kyoto Protocol. Currently, China's participation in international environmental institutions and processes has increased noticeably. The country has signed onto a wide range of treaties and declarations, and it has developed extensive linkages with scientific and environmental policy communities around the world. China also has hosted a variety of international conferences and workshops on the environment.

China faces the crucial need to protect its national interests and promote development while joining in the environmental cooperation movement, resulting in a dilemma for China. When On one hand, if China pursues its own interests, its immediate goal of economic development will be served in the short run. In the long run, however, China's moral reputation will be damaged and the country will lose environmental loans and technology transfers. On the other hand, if China pursues collective international environmental-protection interests, this direction may provide – in the short run -- a basis for possible future collaboration in reducing environmental disasters. In the long run, this option serves the long-term common interests of humanity.

Manion (2000) has suggested that "*policy coordinating mechanisms* are particularly important to policymaking in the Chinese system because authority is formally structured so as to require the cooperation of many bureaucratic units, nested in separate chains of authority."[108] A fragmented-authoritarianism model of China's bureaucratic politics suggests that policy making in China should be *un*-coordinated; that is, it should be disjointed, protracted, and incremental.[109] However, China's policy-making in the area of climate change

---

[108] Melanie Manion, "Politics in China," in Gabriel A. Almond; G. Bingham Powell; Kaare Strom; and Russell J. Dalton, eds., Comparative Politics Today: A World View (New York: Addison Wesley Longman, 2000), p. 449, emphasis added.

[109] See Kenneth Lieberthal, "Introduction: The 'Fragmented Authoritarianism' Model and Its Limitations." in Kenneth Lieberthal and David Lampton, eds., Bureaucracy, Politics, and Decision Making in Post-Mao China (Berkeley: University of California Press, 1992), pp. 1-30; Kenneth Lieberthal and Michel Oksenberg, "Structure and Process : An Overview" in Kenneth Lieberthal and Michel Oksenberg, Policymaking in China: Leaders, Structures, and Processes (Princeton: Princeton University Press, 1988), pp. 3-34.

is actually highly coordinated. In regard to this apparent paradox, this essay attempts to answer the following two research questions: What explains this policy coordination on climate change in China? Why have Chinese bureaucrats paid so much attention to climatic change when the regimr has given economic development prime priority?

With these considerations in mind, this article first looks at some of the consequences of climate change regime on policy coordination institution of China. After reviewing the literature on policy coordination and international regimes, UNFCCC is taken as the determinant factor for the creation of policy coordination in China. Then the article describes the policy coordination institutions and working procedures for the UNFCCC based on empirical analysis. From the empirical analysis above, conclusions on the policy coordination of China's domestic and international responses to the problem of climate change are drawn, as well as attempts to explain these bureaucratic actions. Finally, the implications of China's response to climate change for environmental security in Asia Pacific are discussed. It should be noted that although China is taking coordinated action, this article maintains that the country is still not doing enough, by waiting on the rich countries of the world to take much more concerted action. To be sure, China has a strong ethical case for expecting the developed countries to act first. However, its failure to act more robustly now may place it under greater moral scrutiny by future generations.

## 1.1 Methodology

As previously mentioned, this research has taken place through an empirical approach. Since most of necessary data, excluding the historical analysis, could be obtained from exiting literature, observing the social world and how policy coordination on climate change in China is organized and operates was necessary. Qualitative methods constitute the main research methods in this research work. These include documentary research, in-depth interviews, field research, questionnaires, and individual experience of the researcher. As a result, the research work is a procession progression of interaction between these methods. The research design is descriptive, and through the different research methods, the hypothesis of the thesis is validated.

After reviewing theoretical materials on international regimes and China's policy coordination, theories based on different approaches to the understanding international regimes are combined according to defined dependent and independent variables. Three intervening variables from international regimes (independent variables) believed to influence policy coordination (dependent variables) in China are found as follows:

1. Interests distribution;
2. Knowledge; and
3. New domestic institutions.

Based on the theoretical materials on dependent and independent variables, hypotheses about international regimes influencing the policy coordination in China are advanced.

The in-depth interviews focus on diplomatic agents, professionals and decision-makers who have a role in climate change policy making. The interviews are made up of a preparatory interview phase and an interview phase, which was based on a questionnaire. The following empirical questions are investigated using the questionnaires:

1. Does the FCCC contribute to the development of environment policy coordination in China through different intervening variables, and if so how?
2. How do these intervening variables bridge the gap between the FCCC and policy coordination in China?

Although field study will play a major role in the research work, the importance of documentary study cannot be underestimated. The document analysis focuses on the UN documents related to the UNFCCC[110], related research reports and working papers published by nongovernmental organizations (NGOs), and environmental foreign policy documents and reports related to "The State-Group National Coordination Committee for Climate" published by the Chinese government. The written material mainly consists of material from Chinese sources. This includes research publications on climate change; general information material; newsletters; newspapers; journals; and material published on web sites. It further includes related books, doctoral dissertations, Master's theses and articles.

We introduce three content-analytic indicators:

1. the homogeneity/heterogeneity of professionals and decision-makers preference/knowledge/interests expressed during policy involvement;
2. the homogeneity/heterogeneity of different sections' interests expressed during policy involvement;
3. the frequency of coordination among different sections involved in climate change before and after the founding of the UNFCCC .

The primary domestic institution for the coordination of China's climate change policies is the National Coordination Committee on Climate Change (NCCCC).[111] The discussion of the NCCCC and its implications attempt to highlight the influences of the international climate change regime, revolving around the UNFCCC, on the development of the NCCCC. Primary and tertiary documents are used to do this, as well as several in-depth interviews with officials involved in the NCCCC process. These interviews support the view that the UNFCCC has been influential in shaping the policy coordination in China, as manifested by the NCCCC.

This article is done through an empirical approach. Since most of necessary data –except the historical analysis - can't be obtained from exiting literature. We must go into the social world and observe how foreign policy coordination on climate change in China is organized and operates.The in-depth interviews focus on diplomatic agents, professionals and decision-makers who join climate change policy making. It mainly includes a preparatory interview phrase and an interview phrase.

---

[110] These   mainly include the following: (1) United Nations Conference Reports on Environment and Development held in Rio de Janeiro, Brazil in 1992; (2) UNFCCC, 1992-2000, United Nations: Report of the Conference of the Parties on its First-ninth Session.
[111] See the official Website of the National Coordination Committee on Climate Change at <http://www.ccchina.gov.cn/english/>.

The case study relies heavily on more than questionnaires and in depth interviews from 40 officials and experts from different bureaucracies and institutions. The interviews were focused, but still open-ended. The respondents were asked a set of similar questions (without fixed answering alternatives), based on my questionnaires. After he or she finished the questionnaires, specific questions were asked, varying according to their relation to foreign policy coordination of climate charge and the UNFCCC when they were interviewed. Some of the interviewees have been interviewed several times, and therefore may be described as informants. For semi-structured interviews, as those conducted in this study, the interview guide should contain the coarse features of topics to be covered, as well as suggestions for questions. Obviously, respondents interviewed late in the fieldwork were naturally asked questions based on the results from earlier interviews.

The respondents came from more than 20 bureaucracies and institutions, and include: Ministry of Development and Planning, Ministry of Foreign Affairs, Ministry of Science and Technology, State Economic and Trade Commission, China Meteorological Administration, Ministry of Finance, State Environmental Protection Administration, Ministry of Agriculture, Ministry of Communications, Ministry of Water Resources, Ministry of Construction, State Forestry Administration, State Oceanic Administration, Chinese Academy of Sciences, Chinese Academy of Social science, Tsinghua University, Peking University, Remin University, Chinese Energy Institute, and Chinese Agriculture University.

These questionnaires are embedded in my book and document quantitative independent variables (international regimes) and dependent variables employed in the book. I use three indicators: "bargaining", "consensus (Tong Yi Kou Jing)" and "making of final decision" to evaluate dependent variables (the foreign policy coordination) in China. International regimes (independent variables) are examined according to interest based, knowledge based and domestic institutions. This is indicated in practice by norms and rules in the United Nations Framework Convention on Climate Change (the UNFCCC) and related protocol, communications from Parties in the UNFCCC, and issues resolving procedures through the Conference of the Parties (COP), and Global Environmental Facility (Financial Mechanism) for climate change (GEF).

## 2. POLICY COORDINATION, INTERNATIONAL REGIMES AND DOMESTIC INSTITUTIONS

According to fragmented authoritarianism model, policy making in China is disjointed, protracted, and incremental. However, China's policymaking in climate change area takes place at a very coordinated level. What variables can explain the development of policy coordination in China best? China is a non- Annex I country, and it does not share the concrete responsibilities for reducing green house gases (GHG) in the short run. China never changes its industry and consumption structure, and related domestic laws only aiming to control its GHG emissions. In accordance, domestic variables are not enough to explain coordination phenomenon in Chinese policy. This article attempts to provide an explanation to this question by focusing on international regime theory and linking regime theory with the behavior of the bureaucracy in China.

## a. Concept of Policy Coordination

In this section, the ways in which policy coordination is influenced by international regimes, thereby resulting in internationally inspired actions by domestic policy institutions, is explored. A clarification of policy coordination, international regimes and domestic institutions using a theoretical basis follows. The policy-making process can be defined as "the entire pattern of complex interactions between officials and organizations which result in decisions and in specific courses of action."[112] According to Burns (2002), "coordination" can be "conceived of in minimalist terms to involve no more than avoiding direct conflicts among programs, and policy coordination is the process by which two or more policies or programs are matched or harmonized to achieve shared goals and objects."[113] Halpern (1980) sees coordination as involving "all (1) the management of policy decision process so that tradeoffs among policy interests and goals are recognized, analyzed, and presented to top leadership to make decisions; and (2) the oversight of official actions, especially those that follow major high-level decisions, must reflect the balance among policy goals, that the top leadership and his responsible officials have decided upon."[114] The content of policy coordination includes "(1) Independent decision-making by ministries. (2) Communication with other ministries (information exchange). (3) Consultation with other ministries (a two-way process). (4) Avoiding divergence among the ministries. (5) Inter-ministerial search for agreement (seeking consensus). (6) Arbitration of inter-organizational difference."[115]

We introduce a concept of policy coordination in this article: When the Chinese government expresses consensus (Tong Yi Kou Jing) toward some international regimes, obeys the norms of international regimes, and acquires interests according to procedures of international regimes, different bureaucratic sections try to achieve policy-making and policy implementation through communication, consultation, and bargaining. There are three basic constituents of policy coordination in China, listed as follows: consensus (Tong Yi Kou Jing) building, bargaining and the model of final policy-making. In my research case on climate change policy, the final policy-making mostly occurs at the coordination level.

Therefore, the increasing seeking of consensus (Tong Yi Kou Jing), the development of bargaining and the model of final policy-making at a coordination level are the indispensable

---

[112] Jam I. Bacchus, Foreign Policy and the Bureaucratic Process (Princeton, NJ.: Princeton University, 1974), pp. 10-11.

[113] John P. Burns, Horizontal Government: Policy Coordination in China, paper prepared for the International Conference on Governance in Asia: Culture, Ethics, Institutional Reform and Policy Change, City University of Hong Kong, Hong Kong, (December 2002), pp. 1-2.

[114] The definition is borrowed by Nina P. Halpern from " I. M. Destler, Making Foreign Economic Policy( Washington D.C.: The Brookings Institution, 1980), p. 8." Nina P. Halpern, "Information Flows and Policy Coordination in the Chinese Bureaucracy," in Kenneth G. Lieberthal and David Lampton, eds., Bureaucracy, Politics, and Decision Making in Post-Mao China (Berkeley: University of California Press, 1992), p. 126.

[115] Sally Washington of the OECD Public Management Service, 1995. On Document with the Authors.
This document was prepared by Sally Washington of the OECD Public Management Service and published on the responsibility of the Secretary-General of the OECD.. This documents represents work conducted in the Public Management Service in 1995 under the theme by the OECD:" The Impacts of Globalizations on the Work of Government". It forms part of ongoing work examining policy-making systems and issues affecting governance. It is based on issues papers prepared for discussion at two OECD meetings for officials from the centres of government; one in May 1995 at OECD Headquarters in Paries; the other in September 1995 in Copenhagen, Denmark. I get its hardcopy "OECD Documents: Policy Coordination" from China's Administration center for Agenda 21. The page number is: pp. 5-6.

explanatory variables of Chinese policy coordination , and only one or two indictors cannot explain Chinese policy-making on its own. Without "bargaining", there is no "coordination", but " harmony"; without " consensus (Tong Yi Kou Jing)", there is a lack of incentives for coordination; if the model of "final decision making" does not come about  through "coordination" but through the "top leader's intervention" or "hierarchy", then the significance of coordination diminishes.

## b. Concept of International Regimes

It is well known that international regimes may change Chinese policymaking to some extent. Krasner (1983) defines international regimes are "principles, norms, rules, and policy making procedures around which actor expectations converge in a given issue-area."[116] By way of simplification, there are three main avenues by which international regimes influence policy-making behavior: interests, institutions and ideas. There are corresponding paradigms in respect to the influence of international regimes on state policymaking. First, realism focuses on external environmental or structural factors that shape the domestic policymaking process.[117] Second, liberalism assesses different countries behaviors by considering such factors as the distribution of interests, institutional design, information flows, and the influences of domestic politics.[118] Third, from the perspective of constructivist explanations for state behavior, international identities, norms and culture can change "the nature of the policymaker's understanding, ideas, beliefs and knowledge,"[119] even shaping and defining national interests.[120] For example, Wendt (1994) argues that international regimes encourage "a convergence in preferences and a sense of shared identity."[121] This perspective fits well with the finding that the UNFCCC influenced bureaucratic behavior by helping to foster new domestic policy institutions, and continues to have a lasting impact on climate change policy coordination in China.

---

[116] Stephen D. Krasner, "Structural Causes and Regime consequences: Régime as Intervening variables," in Stephan D. Krasner, ed., International Regime ( Ithaca: Cornell University Press, 1983 ), p. 2.

[117] Jennifer Sterling-Folker, "Realist Environment, Liberal Process, and Domestic-Level Variables," International Studies Quarterly, vol. 41, no. 1 (1997), pp. 1-25.

[118] See David A. Baldwin, "Neoliberalism, Neorealism, and World Politics," in David A. Baldwin, ed., Neorealism and Neoliberalism (New York: Columbia University Press, 1993), pp. 3-25. Joseph M. Grieco, " Anarchy and The Limits of Cooperation: A Realist Critique of The Newest Liberal Institutionalism." in  David A. Baldwin, ed., Neorealism and Neoliberalism (New York: Columbia University Press, 1993), pp. 116-135.

[119] Geoffrey Garrett and Barry R. Weingast, "Ideas, Interests, and Institutions: Constructing the European Community's Internal Market," in Judith Goldstein and Robert O. Keohane, eds., Ideas and Foreign Policy (Ithaca: Cornell University Press, 1993), pp. 173-174.

[120] Martha Finnemore, National Interests in International Security (Ithaca: Cornell University Press, 1996), pp. 17-45.

[121] Alexander Wendt, "Collective Identity Formation and the International State," American Political Science Review, vol. 88, no. 2 (1994), pp. 384-396.

## c. Theoretical Approach

Referring to the Chinese domestic institution, Lieberthal and Oksenberg (1988) stress the structure of bureaucratic authority and the realities of bureaucratic practice to theorize what what is known as the "fragmented authoritarianism" model.[122] Lieberthal and Oksenberg (1988) argue that authority below the very top of the Chinese political system is fragmented and disjointed,[123] and that the fragmented, segmented, and stratified structure of the state promotes a system of negotiations, bargaining and consensus seeking among affected bureaucracies.[124] Under this model, negotiations, bargaining,[125] power exchange or reciprocity, consensus building and institutional pluralism[126] are required in Chinese domestic policymaking.[127]

Since the 1990s, many scholars have examined the influences of international regimes on China.[128] Economy (2001) and Pearson (1999) articulate four factors to understand the relation between international regimes and Chinese domestic policymaking: (1) transmission of new ideas and knowledge; (2) new domestic bureaucratic institutions; (3) training opportunities, financial transfers, and technological advances; and (4) scientific and expert communities.[129] However, Economy (2001), Pearson (1999), and other scholars do not look at the distinctive relations between international regimes and Chinese bureaucratic politics and neglect the Chinese bureaucracy's political structure, which is modeled as an authoritarian fragmented model. However, both Economy (2001) and Pearson (1999) do not sufficiently evaluate the role of international regimes in analyzing Chinese policy-making. They also neglect the Chinese bureaucratic policy-making structure, which is modeled as an authoritarian fragmented model. Even in their arguments concerning the relation between international regimes and Chinese policy-making, Economy (2001) and Pearson (1999) do not make a very detailed and deep analysis on the changes of China bureaucratic politics. Moreover, they neglect the coordination role of new bureaucratic institutions imposed by the international regimes. As is developed in the current research, most of these institutions serve as information channels and bargaining places for Chinese policy makers.

---

[122] Lieberthal, "Introduction: The 'Fragmented Authoritarianism' Model and Its Limitations." 1992, p. 11.

[123] Lieberthal, "Introduction: The 'Fragmented Authoritarianism' Model and Its Limitations." 1992, pp 2-6; Lieberthal and Oksenberg , Policymaking in China, 1988,pp. 23-24.

[124] Lieberthal and Oksenberg , Policymaking in China, 1988, pp. 23-24.

[125] Lampoon refer "bargaining" as an authority relationship of "reciprocal control ... among representatives of hierarchies.'" See David Lampton, "A plum for a Peach: Bargaining, Interest, and Bureaucratic politics in China," in Lieberthal and Lampton, Bureaucracy, Politics, and Decision Making in Post-Mao China, 1992, p.38.

[126] Carol Lee Harrin and Suisheng Zhao put forward that institutional pluralism is characterized by conflict among political leaders and bureaucrats who must be reckoned with mainly according to the institutional esources provided by their offices. Carol Lee Harrin and Suisheng Zhao, ed., Decision Making in Deng's China Perspectives from Insiders (New York :M.E. Sharpe Armonk,1995), pp. 240-242.

[127] Lieberthal and Lampton, Bureaucracy, Politics, and Decision Making in Post-Mao China, 1992, p. 12.

[128] See Samuel Kim, China and World (Boulder: Westview Press, 1989, 1992, 1998); Michel Oksenberg and Economy, China Joins the world (New York: The Foreign Relations Council, 1997); and Alistair Iain Johnston and Robert S. Ross, Engaging China: the Management of an Emerging Power (London; New York: Routledge, 1999).

[129] Economy, "The Impact of International Regimes on China's Foreign Policy-making," 2001, pp. 236-257. Margaret M. Pearson, "The Major Multilateral Economic Institutions Engage China," in Engaging China: the management of an emerging power, ed. Iain Johnston and Robert S. Ross (New York: Routledge, 1999), pp. 207-234.

The answer does not appear to be found in domestic politics alone. The international agreement that has started the process of regulating countries' emissions of GHGs, the United Nations Framework Convention on Climate Change (UNFCCC), does not require China, which classified as a developing country by the treaty, to limit its emissions in any way, neither now nor in the future. Most of China's limitations of energy use, which is the primary source of GHGs, has been motivated by domestic concerns, such as limiting energy shortages in industrial areas, mitigating China's reliance on imported fossil fuels, and occasionally reducing local air pollution. The government has hardly directed any efforts toward reducing GHGs to lower China's impact on global warming. Domestic variables are simply not powerful enough, by themselves, to drive the coordination of climate change policy in China.

Explanations for this phenomenon can be more fruitfully found in China's interactions with the outside world. As Schreurs and Economy (1997) have argued,

> The "internationalization of environmental policy formation is not just a matter of a state responding to the emergence of new kinds of problems or new ways of viewing old ones. The internationalization of environmental politics also reflects the efforts by international actors and institutions to reach down into the state to set the domestic policy agenda and influence the policy formation and implementation processes."[130]

From this perspective, it makes sense to look at international agreements on climate change in which China is a signatory party. Indeed, much of the explanation for China's high degree of domestic policy coordination on climate change reflects the impact of the UNFCCC and the international climate change regime of which it is a part. As Economy (2001) puts it, "the requirements of the regime result in the proliferation of new domestic actors or the establishment of new bureaucratic linkages that influence policy outcome." [131] Economy (2001) further argues that "International regimes spur the emergence of new bureaucratic arrangements to manage China's involvement in the regimes and encourage the introduction of new actors from the scientific and expert communities into prominent policy-making positions." [132]

## 3. THE UNFCCC AS THE DETERMINANT FACTOR FOR THE CREATION OF POLICY COORDINATION IN CHINA

The UNFCCC and global struggles against the threats of global warming now occupy a more prominent position in the Chinese political agenda. Therefore, China has to respond under UNFCCC influence carefully and seriously. China has joined the UNFCCC and its

---

[130] Elizabeth Economy and Miranda A. Schreurs, "Domestic and International Linkages in Environmental Politics." in Miranda A. Schreurs and Elizabeth Economy, eds., The Internationalization of Environmental Protection (New York: Cambridge University Press, 1997), p. 6.

[131] Elizabeth Economy, "The Impact Of International Regimes on China's Foreign Policy-Making Broading perspectives and policies but only to a point," In David Lampton, ed., the Making of Chinese Foreign and security Policy in the Era of Reform 1978-2000 (Stanford, California, Stanford University 2001), p. 236.

[132] Economy, "The Impact of International Regimes on China's Foreign Policy-Making," 2001, p. 251.

Conference Parties to the UNFCCC (COP)[133] negotiations on the mitigation of the climate change problems and set up related domestic institutions.

## 3.1. China and the International Regimes against Global Warming

How has China responded diplomatically to climate change? Broadly speaking, China's climate change diplomacy has sought to further several goals: protect Chinese sovereignty, acquire foreign aid and technical assistance, promote China's economic development,[134] and promote its role as a responsible great power and leader of the developing world, which can be can be described as the following aspects: firstly, sustainable development is the most effective response to global climate change. Secondly, the UN Framework Convention on climate change provides a fundamental and effective framework for international cooperation in response to climate change. Thirdly, developed countries should take the lead in adopting measures to reduce emission after 2012 in continued compliance with the principle of Common but Differentiated Responsibilities. Meanwhile, the international community may explore a more pragmatic and flexible mechanism, promote international technical cooperation and enhance international capacity to cope with climate change. Fourthly, China is in favor of stepping up coordination and cooperation among existing environmental protection institutions and integrating resources for higher efficiency and better-coordinated policies.[135]

Elizabeth Economy argues," China gains support within the community of developing nations. Along with India, China frequently occupies a leadership role among the developing states in international environmental negotiations." [136]She also argues, "China took a significant step forward at the UN World Summit on Sustainable Development in Johannesburg when it announced that it had ratified the Kyoto Protocol to curb greenhouse gas emissions. As a developing country, China is eligible under the Clean Development Mechanism (CDM) to earn credits by undertaking emission-reduction activities; however, it is not required to meet any emissions targets or timetables. Nonetheless, China's taking the first step means that it may later be pressured to agree to emissions reductions commitments." [137]

First and most important of all, China has joined with other developing countries in demanding that developed countries reduce their GHG emissions first and provide assistance to developing countries to help them cope with climate change and to implement sustainable development. It has usually resisted any links between financial and technical assistance from developed countries in the context of the climate change regime. Instead, it has demanded transfers of funds on non-commercial and preferential terms, and has rejected most of the

---

[133] COP: Conference Parties to the United Nations Framework Convention on Climate Change.

[134] Elizabeth, Economy, 'China's Environmental Diplomacy', in Samuel S. Kim (ed), China and the World: Chinese Foreign Policy Faced the New Millennium (Boulder: Westview Press, 1998), p. 264.

[135] "Statement by Mr.Jiang Weixin at the Joint High-level Segment of COP12", http://www.ccchina. gov.cn/cn/index.asp

[136] Elizabeth Economy, "China's Environmental Diplomacy", in Samuel Kim (ed.), China and the World: Chinese Foreign Policy faces the New Millennium (Boulder: Westview Press, 1998) (Fourth edition), p. 264.

[137] Elizabeth Economy, The River Runs Black: The Environmental Challenge to China's Future (London : Cornell University Press, 2004), p.185.

market-based international mechanisms for emissions reductions advocated by developed countries and their industries.[138] China has made some contributions to the FCCC negotiations, notably when doing so would help codify requirements that developed countries help developing countries in the context of climate change.

Second, there was spontaneous and minimal cooperation between the United States, China and many developing countries. China agreed with the United States that *adaptation* measures – transfers of funds and technology from developed to developing countries to help them cope with climate change – were the preferred ways to address the problem. As such, China joined the United States in pushing the difficult issue of cutting emissions into the future, focusing instead on garnering as many financial and other resources as possible from the world's rich. By shifting the focus of the climate talks to adaptation, and away from mitigation, both the rich and poor countries could avoid doing what they dread the most: demanding that entrenched economic interests reduce their GHG emissions.

Third is about China's identity on its dual status as a developing country (with rights to and needs for development) and its growing role as a major contributor to global environmental problems (such as GHG emissions) to acquire substantial influence in international environmental negotiations.[139] In international climate change negotiations, it has consistently sought "new and additional" funds from developed countries in return for the poor countries' support for global collective action. These efforts have paid off; China is the largest recipient of environmental aid from the World Bank and receives substantial amounts of environmental aid from other international funding agencies. Indeed, the vast majority of its environmental budget comes from abroad.[140] China is also receiving environmental technologies, such as those offered in the context of CDM, which funds climate change-related projects in developing countries.[141]

Finally is that China could and will show true leadership on climate change, Given the historical responsibility of the developed countries for the bulk of historical pollution causing global warming, China continues to ally with Asian Pacific and other poor countries in an effort to push the rich countries to reduce their carbon emissions and to provide financial and technical assistance to help vulnerable countries adapt to climate change. At many UNFCCC's conference of the parties, China has joined with India in reiterating its outright rejection of GHG emissions cuts for developing countries, instead arguing that increased emissions would be required to lift their people out of poverty.

According to the UN, "The UNFCCC was adopted on 9 May 1992, and opened for signature at the UN Conference on Environment and Development in June 1992 in Rio, where it received 155 signatures, including China."[142] The China People's Congress Council ratified the UNFCCC in November 1994. China has become involved in the foundation and negotiation of the UNFCCC since 1990. In the first Rio World Summit, China's former Premier Li Peng signed the UNFCCC. In the 2002 Second World Summit on Sustainable

---

[138] Bayer J Linnerooth, 'Climate Change and Multiple Views of Fairness', in Ference L. Toth (ed), Fair Weather? Equity Concerns in Climate Change (London: Earthscan, 1999), p.59.

[139] Economy, 'China's Environmental Diplomacy', p.265.

[140] Economy, 'China's Environmental Diplomacy', p.278.

[141] The Japan Environmental Council, Shunichi Teranishi, and Takehisa Awaji, The State of the Environment in Asia 1999/2000, p.106.

[142] The UNFCCC, "ISSUES - A brief history of the climate change process." <http://www.UNFCCC.int/ cop7/briefhistory.html>. Accessed on November 12, 2002.

Development in Johannesburg, China's former Premier Zhu Rongji annouced that China had ratified the Kyoto Protocol. [143].

Based on our fieldwork, it was found that the UNFCCC is a determinant variable in inducing China to make responsible, comprehensive and coordinative policy against the climate change through the related policy coordination institutions. First, the effectiveness of the UNFCCC depends on Chinese responsible and concrete involvement because of its huge GHG emission and fast increase. As China's GHG emissions ranks second in the World, and it is the largest developing country, it should not act as a laggard role in the UNFCCC. The goal of the UNFCCC will fail without China reducing its GHG emissions. Second, most developing counties (Group 77 and China) hope that China will protect the interests of developing countries in the negotiation of the UNFCCC. Due to differences between developing and developed countries in their economic development levels as well as their political objectives, there is a serious divergence of opinion between them on reducing the greenhouse gas emissions. Thus, China, as the important leader of "Group77 plus China," has the ability to protect all developing countries' development rights and the principle of "common but differentiated" in the COP.

## 3.2 The UNFCCC and Climate Change Policy Coordination in China

In China's Agenda 21, the China Sustainable Development and National Economic Plan from 9th to 10th 5 years, the Chinese government makes positive promises related to the UNFCCC. However, not only is the UNFCCC complex, but there are also many issues in the UNFCCC negotiation that make linking the promises to implementation troublesome. For instance, for China there remain disparities in its responsibilities to reduce GHG emissions, the equity and justice for reducing GHG, the manner in which to reduce GHG emissions, sustainable development and capacity building, climate change science, financial mechanisms, and so on. It is clear that a single bureaucracy could not handle the complex issues of the UNFCCC. Because "bureaucracies, to function, must divide knowledge, resources and policymaking authority among various departments, (i.e. program, human resources, investments, communications) there is no one person who can coordinate and control all of the actions taken by the foundation unit."[144] Thus, policy coordination is necessary. This is particularly evident in the climate change case where complexity of climate change prevents any single bureaucracy from taking charge of making all-related decisions.

Since 1991, China has built a policy coordination institution composed of 13 bureaucracies. Before 1998, the China Meteorological Administration (Zhong Guo Qi Xiang Ju) dominated in climate policy making. After the China State Council's institutional reconfiguration in 1998, China continued to improve the capacity of policy coordination on climate change,[145] and the bureaucracy transferred most of its responsibilities and authorities

---

[143] Jiang Weixin, "Presentation in the Cop8," Remin Daily[Ren Min Ri Bao], November 11, 2002.

[144] See Graham Allison, "Conceptual Models and the Cuban Missile Crisis," American Political Science Review, Vol. LXIII, No. 3(1969), pp. 690-691.

[145] Administration is much lower than Ministry in China's power configuration.

to the Ministry of Development and Planning (named Ministry of Reforming and Development after 2003).[146]

However, the Ministry of Reforming and Development does not handle climate policy making alone. Instead, many Chinese bureaucracies are involved in policy coordination toward achieving the objectives of the UNFCCC. The guiding policies of these bureaucracies are built on the goal of the coordinative development of environment, economy, and society through inter-ministerial coordination, all in the context of national plan. China's National plan for Economic and Social Development (Guo Min Jing Ji He She Hui Fa Zhan Gui Hua), a national working agenda for every five years, stipulates the working contents for China's inter-ministerial policy coordination in many aspects.

Under the pressures of international regimes against global warming, China began the national law and developmental strategy building process, following the 1992 Earth Summit, the Chinese government devised a national sustainable development plan based on the summit's 'Agenda 21' objectives. The government has issued the Energy Conservation Law (1997) and Renewable Energy Law (2005). Since the Eighth Five-year plan (1991-1995), global climate change has been listed as a priority in plans for state energy plan. In the eleventh five-year program, China will accelerate the pace of building a resource-efficient and environment-friendly society, and promote the harmonization of economic development with the population, resources, and the environment.

In our interviews with officials related to the UNFCCC, most attributed the level of policy coordination to the great demands and pressures of the UNFCCC negotiation.

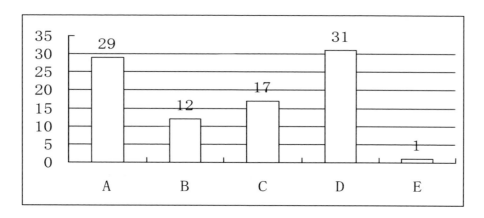

Figure 1. Factors that promote policy coordination on the UNFCCC (multi-choices)[147]
The meanings in the X axis: A: national concerns B: international organizations (UNEP, etc.) C: the working principles of the state council. D: demand of climate change negotiation E. else
The meanings in the Y axis: the number of respondents to this question.

---

[146] See China's Office of National Coordination Committee on Climate Change, ed., "China and Global Climate Change," < http://www.ccchina.gov.cn/english/source /ga/ca2003011801.htm>. Accessed on 15 October 2003.
[147] (The question is: Please choose the factors that promote policy coordination on the UNFCCC? A: national concerns B: international organizations (UNEP, etc.) C: the working principles of the state council. D: demand of climate change negotiation E. else)

Moreover, the UNFCCC requires every party to improve policy coordination capacity. According to such UN documents as the UNFCCC/CP/1995 - UNFCCC/CP/2001, national communication and national coordination regimes are very important terms in the UNFCCC and other environmental agreements, such as the Kyoto Protocol. In November 2001, the Marrakech Accords remarked on phenomenon of policy coordination.

> "National coordinating mechanisms and focal points and national coordinating entities have an important role to play in ensuring coordination at the country and regional levels and may serve as the focal point for coordinating capacity-building activities."

a.  Strengthening existing and, where needed, establishing national climate change coordination institution or focal points to enable the effective implementation of the Convention and effective participation in the Kyoto Protocol process, including preparation of national communications
b.  Developing an integrated implementation Programme which takes into account the role of research and training in capacity building

In implementing this framework, developing country Parties should promote the coordination and sustainability of activities undertaken within this Framework (UNFCCC), including the efforts of national coordinating mechanisms, focal points, and national coordinating entities."[148]Thus, China had to strengthen the policy coordintional institution buiding.

The officials from China's different bureaucracies have shown a great interest in the UNFCCC regime building to open China to the world and gain honors from top leaders. China became very isolated in the world arena after "Tian Anmen Incident" in 1989. International environmental collective action, focused on sustainable development, ozone layer depletion, and climate change, has allowed China to make breakthroughs in returning to the world as a responsible and normal state. Furthermore, Chinese top leaders believe Chinese environmental activities will win them international goodwill. For example, Premier Li Peng won an environmental protection award from the UNEP in Rio in 1992 at the height of China's international condemnation. After that, Qu Geping, Director of Environmental Bureaucracies, received a quick promotion. These positive forms of recognition encouraged Chinese officials to seek achievements in international environmental protection. For instance, in the early 1990s, the Ministry of Science and Technology became involved in environmental issues, and it soon dominated in the area of sustainable development, instead of the China's Environmental Protection Authority. However, many bureaucracies hoped make their own achievements in pursuit of UNFCCC activities. This view was reflected in interviews with officials from participating departments. All officials argued that the UNFCCC is as important as the World Trade Organization (WTO), and that their own bureaucracies should be strengthened in capacity building toward the UNFCCC.[149]

---

[148] The UNFCCC, "the Marrakech Accords and Marrakech Declaration. "<www.UNUNFCCC.int/cop7/accords_draft.pdf>. Accessed on November 12, 2002. pp. 10-14.
[149] Interview with Xu Huiyou, China   Agriculture Science and Technology Institute, 12   March 2003. Interview with Chen Enjun, China Forest Administration, 1 April 2003. Interview with Ding Yihui, former President of the IPCC, China Meteorological Administration, 3 March 2003.

## 4. POLICY COORDINATION INSTITUTIONS FOR THE UNFCCC

Economy (2004) argues, "Management of environmental protection in China is shared by many agencies and other actors, depending on the issue"[150]. The UNFCCC provides a common issue and plays a positive role in the development of policy coordination among these agencies.

### 4.1 The History of Policy Coordination Institution for the UNFCCC

In 1990, the National Group of Coordination on Climate Change, the multi-agency national Coordination Panel on Climate Change, was established by State Council to coordinate ministries and Government agencies that were related in their efforts to address climate change in scientific research. In 1992, the group was placed under the chair of State Councilor Song Jian (Former Head of Ministry of Science and Technology, and the "China Meteorological Administration was designated as the lead agency, with the office of the Climate Change Coordinating Group beneath it."[151] After China joined the UNFCCC negotiation, it split negotiation responsibilities between the Committee of Development and Planning (Committee of Reforming and Development after 2003), the Ministry of Science and Technology, the China Meteorological Administration, and the Ministry of Foreign Affairs. This delegation promoted policy coordination between bureaucratic agencies.

At the Rio UNFCCC, China tried to take a more prominent position. Soon after its adoption, the National Group of Coordination on Climate Change prepared a draft analysis of the UNFCCC's impact on China in July 1992. Ross (1998) comments, "The office convened representatives of responsible agencies- notably the State Science and Technology Commission, the Ministry of Energy, the Environmental Protection Authority, China Meteorological Administration, and the Ministry of Foreign Affairs- to draft a document analyzing China's obligations and assigning responsibility for the various components to different agencies."[152]

Thus, the growing climate change concern built into both international and national programs and situation that China's rapid integration into the world tend to make China more amenable to the UNFCCC.

After China ratified the UNFCCC and attended the Conference of Parties negotiations, its main issues became more and more complex. These issues related to politics, the economy, trade and science. Thus, it was obvious that the China Meteorological Administration lacked the ability to coordinate different bureaucracies related to the climate change policy through the National Group of Coordination on Climate Change, which was an informal and weak institution unable cope with the extent of climate change policy issues.[153] Consequently, with

---

[150] Elizabeth Economy, the River Runs Black: The Environmental Challenge to China's Future (London: Cornell University Press, 2004), p.105.

[151] Lester Ross, "China: Environmental Protection, Domestic Policy Trends, Patterns of Participation in Regimes and Compliance with International Norms," The China Quarterly, 156 (December 1998), p. 818.

[152] Ross, "China," 1998, p. 817.

[153] Interview with Ding Yihui, former President of the IPCC, China Meteorological Administration, March 3, 2003

the reconfiguration (Ji Gou Gai Ge) of Chinese State Council in the mid-1990s, China established National Coordination Committee on Climate Change.[154]

Building a policy coordination institution like the National Group of Coordination on Climate Change and China's National Coordination Committee on Climate Change was necessary for China at this time. With these institutions, different bureaucracies were able to work on a coordinated panel to make climate change policy and cope with the negotiations on UNFCCC after 1992. In support of this claim, in our questionnaires with 43 experts and officials related to the climate change policy, all agreed that it was necessary to build policy coordination institution.

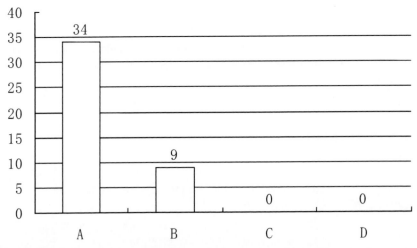

Figure 2. The Evaluation on the Foundation of Policy Coordination Institution on Climate Change [155]
The meanings in the X axis: A: very necessary   B: necessary C: unnecessary   D: else
The meanings in the Y axis: the number of respondents to this question.

## 4.2 The Function and Organizational Context of the Policy Coordination Institution for the UNFCCC

The National Coordination Committee on Climate Change is formally built to deal with any policy issues related to the global struggle against global warming (i.e., formulating policies, programs, and coordinating scientific research). Its missions include the following: (1) to improve China's capability to implement the UNFCCC, and provide the national communications and other documents as the UNFCCC required; (2) to improve China's capability to learn and coordinate toward climate change; (3) to contribute to Chinese sustainable development under the situation of climate change; and (4) to seek national

---

[154] China's Office of National Coordination Committee on Climate Change, ed., "Brief Introduction of National Coordination Committee for Climate, " <http://www.ccchina. gov.cn/index1.htm>. Accessed on November 14, 2002.

[155] The question is: Please give your the evaluation on the foundation of policy coordination institution on climate change: A: very necessary  B: necessary C: unnecessary  D: else.

interests in international negotiation in the UNFCCC.[156]The development of National Coordination Committee on Climate Change is a good indicator for the effectiveness of the UNFCCC. Besides that, Chinese bureaucracies show more and more interests in abiding the UNFCCC because of three factors below: the interests imposed by the UNFCCC through the GEF, the learning process in COP negotiation, and the norms for collective action against the climate change.

> "The Committee, chaired by the Committee of Development and Planning (Committee of Reforming and Development in 2003), includes 14 participating departments: Committee of Development and Planning, Ministry of Foreign Affairs, Ministry of Science and Technology, State Economic and Trade Commission, China Meteorological Administration, Ministry of Finance, State Environmental Protection Administration, Ministry of Agriculture, Ministry of Communications, Ministry of Water Resources, Ministry of Construction, State Forestry Administration, State Oceanic Administration and Chinese Academy of Sciences."[157]

Within the committee, the various bureacracies play different roles and serve a range of functions. The Ministry of Foreign Affairs, the Ministry of Science and Technology, the State Meteorological Administration, the Ministry of Finance, the State Environmental Protection Administration, and the Ministry of Agriculture are the vice heads of the National Coordination Committee (Fu Zu Zhang Dan Wei). The other bureaucracies that are involved with the committee, including the State Economic and Trade Commission, the Ministry of Communications, the Ministry of Water Resources, Ministry of Construction, the State Forestry Administration, the State Oceanic Administration,  and the Chinese Academy of Sciences, do not not play a central role. The general climate change policy making is chaired by the Committee of Development and Planning. The China Meteorological Administration Intergovernmental Panel on Climate Change (IPCC) manages work related to the IPCC, and the Ministry of Foreign Affairs is responsible for the international negotiations on climate change.[158]

The Office of National Coordination Committee on Climate Change in China is set up within the Committee of Reform and Development, and it is in charge of the daily issues involved in uniting the principles and status for China's climate change policy. There are five main responsibilities for the climate change coordination office. These are as follows: (1) to cope with international negotiations for global warming, while trying to protect national interest and sovereignty, by providing a coordination project based on the consensus of different bureaucracies and institutions; (2) to perform a systematic strategy study on energy and an economic development study in respect of global climate changes; (3) to arrange the

---

[156] Interviews with Zhou Hailing, Huang Jing, Duan Liping, China Ministry of Science and Technology, April 15-22, 2003; Interviews with Gao Guang Sheng and  Li Liyan, China Committee of Planning and Reform, March 1-3, 2003.

[157] See China's Office of National Coordination Committee on Climate Change, "China and Global Climate Change," 2003.

[158] Interviews with Zhou Hailing, Huang Jing, Duan Liping, China Ministry of Science and Technology, April 15-22, 2003; Interviews with Gao Guang Sheng and  Li Liyan, China Committee of Planning and Reform, March 1-3, 2003.

conferences of the China National Coordination Committee for Climate; (4) to prepare national communications; and (5) to support the activities of the four coordination groups.[159]

The China National Coordination Committee holds conferences twice a year, just before and after the Conference of Parties. Documents from June 2000 show that the conference content from that year included the following topics:

1.  The Ministry of Foreign Affairs provided some knowledge on international climate change regime negotiation, and informed participants on the main issues and China's main strategy in the next international COP negotiation;
2.  The China Meteorological Administration presented the working progress of the Intergovernmental Panel on Climate Change (IPCC);
3.  The China Ministry of Development and Planning reported on the working progress of China National Coordination Committee for Climate; And
4.  Participants discussed the next working plan of the China National Coordination Committee for Climate.[160]

These topic show that climate change issues are so complicated that knowledge from different areas is needed to support China's policy coordination in this area. Different bureaucracies should be attentive to any specific climate change issues when diverse knowledge and information coming from different aspects affect their behavior on policy coordination.

## 5. WORKING PROCEDURES OF THE CHINA NATIONAL COORDINATION COMMITTEE FOR CLIMATE

According to Li Liyan, an official in the Committee of Planning and Development, there are five main working procedures of the China National Coordination Committee for Climate : (1) to discuss important issues in climate change; (2) to coordinate different climate change policies and activities among different bureaucracies; (3) to cope with the Conference of Parties; (4) to make inter-ministerial policy in the areas of climate change; and (5) to develop consensus in climate change policy.[161]

The responsibilities for the different bureaucracies and the working procedures are clearly and definitely regulated. Most of policies are the outcomes of policy coordination among different bureaucracies. The policy coordination process can be explained from four stages based on our field work. These are as follows: (1) independent proposals or decisions; (2) the communication and consultation; (3) the inter-ministerial search for consensus; and (4) to final decisions. Each stage of the policy coordination process will now be explored.

---

[159] Interviews with Zhou Hailing, Huang Jing, Duan Liping, China Ministry of Science and Technology, April 15-22, 2003; Interviews with Gao Guang Sheng and Li Liyan, China Committee of Planning and Reform, March 1-3, 2003.

[160] "The Conference Documents in China National Coordination Committee." June 2002. Documents with the authors.

[161] Based on interviews with Li LIyan, director in Development Planning Commission, April 1, 2003. Interview with Wang Wenyuan, official in China Science Academy; March 13, 2003. Interview with LV Xuedu, official from the Ministry of Science and Technology, March 23, 2003.

In the first stage, different bureaucracies design individual policies that are within their own policy domain. For example, the Ministry of Science and Technology deals with coordinating technology projects on climate change. The Ministry of Foreign Affairs is the "window agency" in charge of the international negotiation on the UNFCCC. The Ministry of Finance is the "window agency" on the communications with the Global Environmental Facility (GEF) and manages the financial support project implementation in China. The State Environmental Protection Administration and the State Meteorological Administration copes with the climate change science. The Ministry of Agriculture handles the science of climate change and implements public education on climate change.[162]

In the second stage of the policy coordination process, communication and consultation with other bureaucracies arise. This stage is a two-way information and knowledge exchange process. Different bureaucracies communicate about what issues are airings in the UNFCCC negotiation and how they each propose to act in their own areas. Reliable and accepted channels of regular communication must exist. As well as informing other bureaucracies of issues, actions, and proposals, individual bureaucracies consult other bureaucracies in the process of formulating their own policies or positions.

According to the responses to the questionnaires, it is clear that most officials and experts agree that policy coordination improves communications among related bureaucracies.

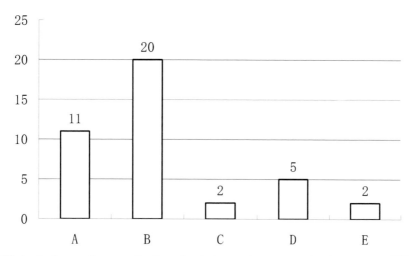

Figure 3. What role does policy coordination play in improving communications among different bureaucracies?
The meanings in the X axis: A: very large B: Large.  C. not very large  D. no  E. not clear
The meanings in the Y axis: the number of respondents to this question
(The question is what role does policy coordination plays in improving communications among different bureaucracies? A: very large B: Large.  C. not very large  D. no  E. not clear).

In the third stage of policy coordination, an inter-ministerial search for consensus occurs. Different bureaucracies try to avoid divergence among ministries and seek consensus (Tong Yi Kou Jing). The term "Tong Yi Kou Jing" indicates that different bureaucracies do not take divergent positions and that the government speaks with one voice in public and negotiation

---

[162] Interviews with Zhou Hailing, Huang Jing, Duan Liping, China Ministry of Science and Technology, April 15-22, 2003; Interviews with Gao Guang Sheng and Li Liyan, China Committee of Planning and Reform, March 1-3, 2003; Interview with Li Rui, Ministry of Finance, April 2, 2003.

in the UNFCCC. In the search for consenses, different bureaucracies work together through the defined procedures because they recognize their interdependence and their mutual interest in resolving policy differences.

Through interviews, many officials and experts observed that while climate change policy benefits some bureaucracies, it harms others mainly due to the difference between the economic development bureaucracies and the environmental scientific bureaucracies. According to the accepted principle, "What You Think Is Based on Where You Sit" [Pi Gu Jue Ding Nao Dei], every bureaucracy has its own view on agency interests and proposals. Since coping with international cooperation and negotiation is a very important component of policy coordination, it is important that international actors perceive one voice, even though policy coordination is marked by a context in which sectional conflicts of interests and views exist. Policy coordination may reduce these kinds of conflicts. According to our questionnaires, many experts and officials agree with this point.

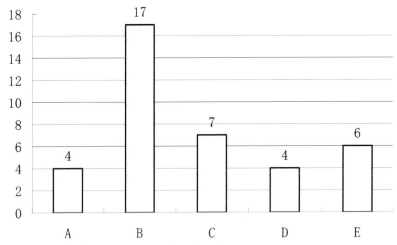

Figure 4. What role does policy coordination plays in reducing the conflicts among different bureaucracies?
The meanings in the Y axis: A. very large. B. Large. C. not very large. D. no. E. not clear
The meanings in the Y axis: the number of respondents to this question
(The question is : what role does policy coordination plays in reducing the conflicts among different bureaucracies: A: very large B: Large. C. not very large D. no E. not clear).

The fourth stage of policy coordination is the arbitration of inter-ministerial differences and outcomes in order to build consensus (Tong Yi Kong Jing). The horizontal coordination processes can resolve the difference of views, proposals, and interests. Different ministries serve unique roles in this stage. For instance, while the Ministry of Finance can arbitrate the differences in interests' caused by financial circumstances, the Ministry of Foreign Affairs unifies the different voices toward the UNFCCC negotiations. However, the Committee of Reform and Development (or the Committee of Planning and Development) plays the most significant role in producing consensus (Tong Yi Kong Jing). In the areas of the energy industry, agricultural production, the reduction the GHG emissions, economic planning remains the dominant matter of consideration. This requires a macro-planning bureaucracy to share the main responsibilities of policy coordination in climate change. Without a macro perspective, it is difficult to implement climate change policy without enough financial assistance and the layout of the national development and reform committee. This macro-planning bureaucracy is the Committee of Development and Planning, also known as Committee of Reform and Development. As the head of National Coordination Committee (Zhu Guan Dan Wei or Zu Zhang Dan Wei) for Climate Change, it is in charge of coordinating the different policies and actions related to climate change.

## SUMMARY AND CONCLUSION

According to Economy's (2001) argument, "the requirements of the regime may result in the proliferation of new domestic actors or the establishment of new bureaucratic linkages that will influence policy outcomes, and regimes often provide training opportunities, financial transfers, and technological advances that enable policy change."[163] Policy coordination is a central problem in China's climate change policy, and in the 1990s, as the focus of the international climate change discussions progressed from scientific debate to formal international political negotiations, China built and improved its policy coordination institution. From the empirical analysis above, conclusions on the policy coordination in this field may be drawn as follows:

First, China is concerned with consensus for policy coordination. Liu Jiang, and Zeng Peiyan, the former leaders of National Coordination Committee for Climate Change have stressed that policy coordination is very important for building consensus before COP conferences . In the meantime, consensus building does not always follow the model of "management by exception"[164] according to Shirk (1992). Consensus is mainly acquired by the core sections  at the policy coordination level. For example, while four bureaucracies, the Ministry of Science and Technology, the Ministry of Foreign Affairs, the Committee of Planning and Development, and the Ministry of Finance, became involved in the implementation of CDM projects supported by the Asia Bank in China, other bureaucracies in National Coordination Committee for Climate Change did not even touch upon this issue[165]. Many climate policies in China are dependent on epistemic communities from different bureaucracies, and some bureaucracies have to invite experts from Tsinghua University or the Chinese Academy for Social Sciences because they lack the ability and time to cope with the complexity of climate change issues. For example, the Ministry of Science and Technology commonly seeks assistance from Tsinghua University to deal with climate change policy issues. This relationship continues, as the Ministry maintains contact with the university for advise onits own policy. Furthermore, in some cases, immediate consensus is required to meet

---

[163] Elizabeth Economy, "The Impact of International Regimes on China's Foreign Policy-Making." 2001, p. 236.

[164] "It means that at each level of the organizational hierarchy, agency representatives make decisions by a rule of consensus. If they all agree, the decision is automatically ratified by the higher level. If the bureaucrats cannot reach consensus, then the decision is referred to the higher levels, and if the higher levels cannot agree, then either nothing happens or the ultimate principal, the Communist Party, intervenes to impose a solution." Susan Shirk, "The Chinese Political System and the political Strategy for Economic Reform," in Lieberthal and Lampton, Bureaucracy, politics, and decision making in Post-Mao China, 1992, pp. 59-91.

[165] Interviews with Zhou Hailing and Huang Jing, China Ministry of Science and Technology, April 15-22, 2003;

the need of Chinese negotiators, because international environmental negotiations have become more and more frequent than before with an increase in the environmental threat.[166]

Second, policy coordination in China does not necessarily follow the fragmented authoritarianism model according to traditional theories on policy making. According to fragmented authoritarianism model, "A unit cannot issue binding orders to another unit at the same bureaucratic rank, not even if it is at a higher territorial level."[167] However, the Committee of Development and Planning often achieves consensus among several bureaucratic bodies, of which none has authority over the others. Other "window agencies" like the Ministry of Foreign Affairs and Ministry of Finance also play a determinant role in the policy coordination process.

Third, final decision-making is not always characterized by consensus, even after policy coordination. Although a greater analysis of the final decision making processes in the context of the UNFCCC is needed, according to our in-depth interviews, consensus is not the compulsory outcome of final decision-making. In fact, there are few consensus-based understandings or strategies among different bureaucracies in climate change policy. The outcome of final decision-making is just built on "one voice" or "no voice" (Bu Biao Tai) in the process of policy coordination in climate change policy. Some officials stated that "no voice" (Bu Biao Tai) as a policy is often applied in COP (Conference of Parties 1-8) and some important summits. If different bureaucracies all agree with some points, the China National Coordination Institute for Climate automatically ratifies the policy proposals as policies of consensus and brings them to the UNFCCC level through a "window agency." If the related bureaucrats cannot reach consensus, then the decision is referred to the "window agency" instead of higher levels because the higher levels cannot cope with such complicated professional issues as climate change. The "no voice" (Bu Biao Tai) policy, therefore, acts as feedback to the UNFCCC. "No voice" (Bu Biao Tai) is not a consensus but is usually outcome of policy coordination in China.


## AUTHOR'S BIOGRAPHICAL STATEMENTS

Yu Hongyuan is an Associate Professor and Deputy Director of the Department of International Organizations and Laws at the Shanghai Institute for International Studies. He is also an honorary fellow of Center for International Energy Strategy Studies, Renmin University of China. He is the author of numerous publications including most recently "Environmental Change and Asia-Pacific," in *Journal of Global Change, Peace, and Security, Global Warming and China's Environmental Diplomacy* published by Nova Science Publishers.

---

[166] Interview with Professor Wang Yongqing, Tsinghua University, march 23, 2003.
[167] Kenneth Lieberthal, Governing China : from revolution through reform(New York : W.W. Norton,1995), p. 169.

In: Asian Economic and Political Development
Editor: Felix Chin
ISBN: 978-1-61122-470-2
© 2011 Nova Science Publishers, Inc.

# CHINA NAVAL MODERNIZATION: IMPLICATIONS FOR U.S. NAVY CAPABILITIES - BACKGROUND AND ISSUES FOR CONGRESS*

*Ronald O'Rourke*

Specialist in National Defense, Foreign Affairs, Defense, and Trade Division

## ABSTRACT

Concern has grown in Congress and elsewhere about China's military modernization. The topic is an increasing factor in discussions over future required U.S. Navy capabilities. The issue for Congress addressed in this report is: How should China's military modernization be factored into decisions about U.S. Navy programs?

Several elements of China's military modernization have potential implications for future required U.S. Navy capabilities. These include theater-range ballistic missiles (TBMs), land-attack cruise missiles (LACMs), anti-ship cruise missiles (ASCMs), surface-to-air missiles (SAMs), land-based aircraft, submarines, surface combatants, amphibious ships, naval mines, nuclear weapons, and possibly high-power microwave (HPM) devices. China's naval limitations or weaknesses include capabilities for operating in waters more distant from China, joint operations, C4ISR (command, control, communications, computers, intelligence, surveillance, and reconnaissance), long-range surveillance and targeting systems, anti-air warfare (AAW), antisubmarine warfare (ASW), mine countermeasures (MCM), and logistics.

Observers believe a near-term focus of China's military modernization is to field a force that can succeed in a short-duration conflict with Taiwan and act as an anti-access force to deter U.S. intervention or delay the arrival of U.S. forces, particularly naval and air forces, in such a conflict. Some analysts speculate that China may attain (or believe that it has attained) a capable maritime anti-access force, or elements of it, by about 2010. Other observers believe this will happen later. Potential broader or longer-term goals of China's naval modernization include asserting China's regional military leadership and protecting China's maritime territorial, economic, and energy interests.

China's naval modernization has potential implications for required U.S. Navy capabilities in terms of preparing for a conflict in the Taiwan Strait area, maintaining U.S. Navy presence and military influence in the Western Pacific, and countering Chinese ballistic missile submarines. Preparing for a conflict in the Taiwan Strait area could place a premium on the following: on-station or early-arriving Navy forces, capabilities for defeating China's maritime anti-access forces, and capabilities for

---

*This is an edited, reformatted and augmented version of Congressional Research Service Report RL33153.

operating in an environment that could be characterized by information warfare and possibly electromagnetic pulse (EMP) and the use of nuclear weapons.

Certain options are available for improving U.S. Navy capabilities by 2010; additional options, particularly in shipbuilding, can improve U.S. Navy capabilities in subsequent years. China's naval modernization raises potential issues for Congress concerning the role of China in Department of Defense (DOD) and Navy planning; the size of the Navy; the Pacific Fleet's share of the Navy; forward homeporting of Navy ships in the Western Pacific; the number of aircraft carriers, submarines, and ASW-capable platforms; Navy missile defense, air-warfare, AAW, ASW, and mine warfare programs; Navy computer network security; and EMP hardening of Navy systems.

## INTRODUCTION

### Congressional Concern

Concern has grown in Congress and elsewhere since the 1990s about China's military modernization and its potential implications for required U.S. military capabilities. China's military modernization is an increasing element in discussions of future U.S. Navy requirements. Department of Defense (DOD) officials such as Secretary of Defense Donald Rumsfeld, uniformed U.S. military leaders, Members of Congress, and defense industry representatives have all expressed concern. A May 2005 press report, for example, states that

China is one of the central issues, along with terrorism and weapons of mass destruction, in the U.S. military's 2005 Quadrennial Defense Review, a congressionally directed study of military plans.... [W]hen the chief of naval operations, Adm. Vern Clark, held a classified briefing for congressional defense committees earlier this month about threats, his focus was "mainly" on China, about which he is "gravely concerned," recalled John W. Warner, the Virginia Republican who chairs the Senate Armed Services Committee....

China has come up repeatedly in congressional debate over the size of the Navy. The 288-ship fleet of today is half the size it was three decades ago. "You never want to broadcast to the world that something's insufficient," Warner says, "but clearly China poses a challenge to the sizing of the U.S. Navy."[1]

### Issue for Congress

The issue for Congress addressed in this report is: How should China's military modernization be factored into decisions about U.S. Navy programs? Congress' decisions on this issue could significantly affect future U.S. Navy capabilities, U.S. Navy funding requirements, and the U.S. defense industrial base, including the shipbuilding industry.

## Scope of Report

This report focuses on the implications that certain elements of China's military modernization may have for future required U.S. Navy capabilities. It does not discuss the following:

- other elements of China's military modernization that may be less relevant to future required U.S. Navy capabilities;
- the potential implications of China's military modernization for — parts of DOD other than the Navy, such as the Air Force and the Missile Defense Agency, — federal agencies other than DOD, such as the Department of State, and — countries other than the United States, such as Taiwan, Russia, Japan, South Korea, the Philippines, the countries of Southeast Asia, Australia, India, and (through issues such as arms sales) countries such as Israel and U.S. allies in Europe; and
- China's foreign or economic policy, U.S. defense policy toward Taiwan, or the political likelihood of a military conflict involving China and the United States over Taiwan or some other issue.

Other CRS reports address some of these issues.[2]

## Terminology

For convenience, this report uses the term China's naval modernization, even though some of the military modernization efforts that could affect required U.S. Navy capabilities are occurring in other parts of China's military, such as the air force or the missile force.

China's military is formally called the People's Liberation Army, or PLA. Its navy is called the PLA Navy, or PLAN, and its air force is called the PLA Air Force, or PLAAF. The PLA Navy includes an air component that is called the PLA Naval Air Force, or PLANAF. China refers to its ballistic missile force as the Second Artillery.

## Sources

Sources of information for this report, all of which are unclassified, include the following:

- the 2005 edition of DOD's annual report to Congress on China's military power;[3]
- the 2004 edition of *Worldwide Maritime Challenges*, a publication of the U.S. Navy's Office of Naval Intelligence (ONI);[4]
- China's 2004 defense white paper;[5]
- the prepared statements and transcript of a July 27, 2005, hearing on China grand strategy and military modernization before the House Armed Services Committee;[6]
- the prepared statements for a September 15, 2005, hearing on China's military modernization and the cross-strait balance before the U.S.-China Economic and

Security Review Commission, an advisory body created by the FY2001 defense authorization act (P.L. 106-398) and subsequent legislation,[7] and the prepared statements and published transcript of a similar hearing before the commission on February 6, 2004;[8]

- a 2003 report on China's military power by an independent task force sponsored by the Council on Foreign Relations;[9]
- open-source military reference sources such as the Jane's Information Group; and
- news articles, including articles from the defense trade press.

## BACKGROUND

### China's Naval Modernization

#### *Maritime-Relevant Elements of China's Military Modernization*[10]

This section summarizes elements of China's military modernization that may have potential implications for required U.S. Navy capabilities. See **Appendix A** for additional details and commentary on several of these modernization activities.

#### *Theater-Range Ballistic Missiles (TBMs)*

One of the most prominent elements of China's military modernization has been the deployment of large numbers of theater-range ballistic missiles (TBMs)[11] capable of attacking targets in Taiwan or other regional locations, such as Japan.[12] Among these are CSS-6 and CSS-7 short-range ballistic missiles (SRBMs) deployed in locations across from Taiwan. DOD states that China as of 2005 has deployed 650 to 730 CSS-6 and CSS-7 TBMs, and that this total is increasing at a rate of about 100 missiles per year.[13]

Although ballistic missiles in the past have traditionally been used to attack fixed targets on land, observers believe China may now be developing TBMs equipped with maneuverable reentry vehicles (MaRVs). Observers have expressed strong concern about this potential development, because such missiles, in combination with a broad-area maritime surveillance and targeting system,[14] would permit China to attack moving U.S. Navy ships at sea. The U.S. Navy has not previously faced a threat from highly accurate ballistic missiles capable of hitting moving ships at sea. Due to their ability to change course, MaRVs would be more difficult to intercept than non-maneuvering ballistic missile reentry vehicles. According to one press report, "navy officials project [that such missiles] could be capable of targeting US warships from sometime around 2015."[15]

#### *Land-Attack Cruise Missiles (LACMs)*

China is developing land-attack cruise missiles (LACMs) that can be fired from land bases, land-based aircraft, or Navy platforms such as submarines to attack targets, including air and naval bases, in Taiwan or other regional locations, such as Japan or Guam. The U.S. Defense Intelligence Agency (DIA) states: "We judge that by 2015, [China] will have hundreds of highly accurate air- and ground-launched LACMs."[16]

### Anti-Ship Cruise Missiles (ASCMs)

China is modernizing its extensive inventory of anti-ship cruise missiles (ASCMs), which can be launched from land-based strike fighters and bombers, surface combatants, submarines and possibly shore-based launchers. Among the most capable of the new ASCMs being acquired by the PLA Navy is the Russian-made SS-N-27 Sizzler, a highly dangerous ASCM that is to be carried by eight new Kilo-class submarines that China has purchased from Russia (see section below on submarines).

### Surface-To-Air Missiles (SAMs)

China is deploying modern surface-to-air missile (SAM) systems across from Taiwan, including long-range and high-altitude systems that have an advertised range sufficient to cover the entire Taiwan Strait, which is roughly 100 nautical miles (185 kilometers) wide. Advanced SAMs may have some effectiveness against stealthy aircraft. Longer- and shorter-range SAM systems deployed along China's coast opposite Taiwan would in combination give China a multilayer defense against enemy aircraft seeking to operate over the Strait or approach that portion of China's coast.[17]

### Land-Based Aircraft

China is introducing increasing numbers of modern and capable (so-called fourth-generation) fighters and strike fighters into the PLA Air Force and PLA Naval Air Force. These include Russian-made Su-27s and Su-30s and indigenously produced FB-7s, F-10s, and F-11s. At least some of the strike fighters will be armed with modern ASCMs. China is also upgrading the ASCMs carried by its land-based maritime bombers. The effectiveness of China's combat aircraft could be enhanced by new support aircraft, including tankers and airborne warning and control system (AWACS) aircraft.

### Submarines

China's submarine modernization effort has attracted substantial attention and concern.[18] The effort currently involves the simultaneous acquisition of at least five classes of submarines, making it, in terms of number of designs involved, one of the more ambitious submarine-acquisition efforts on record by any country. China is taking delivery on eight Russian-made Kilo-class nonnuclear-powered attack submarines (SSs) that are in addition to four Kilos that China purchased from Russia in the 1990s,[19] and is building four other classes of submarines, including the following:

- a new nuclear-powered ballistic missile submarine (SSBN) design called the Type 094;
- a new nuclear powered attack submarine (SSN) design called the Shang class or Type 093;
- a new SS design called the Yuan class or Type 041; and
- another (and also fairly new) SS design called the Song class or Type 039/039G.

These five classes of submarines are expected to be much more modern and capable than China's aging older-generation submarines.

As shown in Table 1, China commissioned one to three new submarines per year between 1995 and 2003. Observers project that 11 new submarines (including six Kilos) will be commissioned in 2005, and five or more new submarines (including two Kilos) will be commissioned in 2006. The projected total of 11 new submarines in 2004 appears to be a spike produced in part by the projected delivery that year of the six Russian-made Kilos.[20]

PLA Navy submarines are armed with one or more of the following: ASCMs, wire-guided and wake-homing torpedoes, and mines.[21] Although ASCMs are often highlighted as sources of concern, wake-homing torpedoes can also be very difficult for surface ships to counter. In addition to some combination of ASCMs, torpedoes, and mines, Type 094 SSBNs will carry a new type of submarine-launched ballistic missile (SLBM), and Shang-class SSNs may carry LACMs.

China's submarine modernization effort is producing a substantially more modern and capable submarine force. As shown in **Table 1**, observers expect China to have a total of 28 Shang, Kilo, Yuan, and Song class submarines in commission by the end of 2006.

Although China's aging Ming- and Romeo-class submarines are based on old technology and are much less capable than the PLA Navy's newer-design submarines, China may decide that these older boats have continued value as minelayers or as bait or decoy submarines that can be used to draw out enemy submarines (such as U.S. SSNs) that can then be attacked by more modern PLA Navy submarines.[22]

### Table 1. PLA Navy Submarine Commissionings
Actual (1995-2004) and Projected (2005-2010)

| | Type 094 SSBN | Shang (Type 093) SSN | Kilo SS (Russian-made) | Yuan (Type 041) SS | Song (Type 039) SS | Ming (Type 035) SS[a] | Total |
|---|---|---|---|---|---|---|---|
| 1995 | | | 2 | | | 1 | 3 |
| 1996 | | | | | | 1 | 1 |
| 1997 | | | | | | 2 | 2 |
| 1998 | | | 1 | | | 2 | 3 |
| 1999 | | | 1 | | 1 | | 2 |
| 2000 | | | | | | 1 | 1 |
| 2001 | | | | | 2 | 1 | 3 |
| 2002 | | | | | | 1 | 1 |
| 2003 | | | | | 2 | | 2 |
| 2004 | | | | | 3 | | 3 |
| 2005 | | 2[b] | 6 | | 3 | | 11 |
| 2006 | | n/a | 2 | 2 | 1 | | ≥5 |
| 2007 | | n/a | | n/a | n/a | | n/a |
| 2008 | 1 | n/a | | n/a | n/a | | n/a |
| 2009 | | n/a | | n/a | n/a | | n/a |
| 2010 | 1[c] | n/a | | n/a | n/a | | n/a |

**Source:** *Jane's Fighting Ships 2005-2006*, and previous editions.
a. Figures for Ming-class boats are when the boats were launched (i.e., put into the water for final construction). Actual commissioning dates for these boats may have been later. b. Construction of a third ship may have started. c. Additional units are expected, perhaps at two-year intervals.
n/a = data not available.

ONI states that "Chinese diesel submarine force levels are stabilizing as quality replaces quantity," and has published a graph accompanying this statement suggesting that the figure may stabilize at a level between 25 and 50.[23]

Another observer states that by 2010,

> the PLA Navy could take delivery of over 20 new domestic SONG A and YUAN-class conventional submarines, 12 Russian KILO-877/636/636M conventional submarines, and five or more new indigenous Type 093 nuclear attack submarines (SSNs) — the third Type 093 is now under construction. In addition, the PLAN could retain up to 20 older Type 035 MING-class conventional [attack submarines] and about 4 older Type 091 HAN-class SSNs. This raises the prospect by 2010 of a Chinese fleet of over 50 modern-to-moderate [sic] attack submarines capable of engaging Taiwan, U.S. and Japanese naval forces.[24]

A separate observer states:

> China has been investing heavily in submarines which it sees as the poisoned arrow (Shashou jian) to the Achilles Heel of American naval might....
>
> By my count, China will have a net gain of 35 submarines over the next 15 years, with no production slow-down in sight. It is reasonable to assume that at current production levels, China will likely out-produce our shipyards and its submarines could out-number our submarines in the next 15 years. By 2020, the Chinese submarine fleet could boast nearly 50 modern attack boats....
>
> [The 2005 DOD report on China's military power] has catalogued a list of China's foreign weapons and military systems acquisitions, but in my mind none is as worrisome as the expansion of the PLA Navy's submarine fleet. China has identified America's strategic center as its maritime predominance, and its sub fleet is clearly designed to overcome U.S. supremacy at sea.[25]

One more observer states that:

> the PLA Navy now has the capability to make the antisubmarine warfare (ASW) mission very difficult for U.S. forces. With a total of more than 50 operational submarines, and with a substantial number of them new and quiet, China, quite simply, can put to sea more submarines than the U.S. Navy can locate and counter. Its older Ming and Romeo submarines are not only still lethal if ignored but also serve to disperse and dilute the efforts of the ASW forces. In other words, some, or even many, of the already large and diverse, but still rapidly growing, fleet of very capable Shang SSNs, and Kilo, Song, and Yuan SSs can reasonably expect to remain undetected as they seek to interdict the U.S. carrier strike groups. If the "shooting has started," eventually U.S. ASW forces could take a big toll against the Chinese submarine force, but the delay in sanitizing the area before the entry of carrier strike groups is what the Chinese are counting on as adequate delay to present the world with the aforementioned *fait accompli* with respect to Taiwan.[26]

Yet one more observer states:

> Evidence suggests that China is seeking to become a first-class submarine power. While the PLAN modernization shows impressive breadth with major new purchases of naval aircraft and surface combatants, submarines appear to be the centerpiece of China's strategic reorientation toward the sea. The May 2002 contract for eight additional Kilos, the likely

continuation of the Song program, and nuclear force modernization, taken together with the evident new priority on training, technological research and doctrinal development all suggest that Beijing recognizes the value of submarines as a potent, asymmetric answer to United States maritime superiority. The recent ascendance of a submariner, Adm. Zhang Dingfa, to the position of commanding officer of the PLAN underlines these tendencies. Further investments in diesel submarines, particularly when enhanced by air independent propulsion, will afford Beijing increasing near-term leverage in the East Asian littoral, while methodical nuclear modernization signifies a long-term commitment to global power projection. As one Chinese strategist recently observed, "The scale [of recent purchases] indicates that in the coming years, China will build an offshore defense system with submarines as the key point."[27]

### Aircraft Carriers

ONI states that "China's interest in aircraft carriers has not led it to build or purchase one, except as museums. Near-term focus on contingencies in the vicinity of Taiwan has minimized the importance of aircraft carriers in China's acquisition plan, but research into the ships and associated aircraft likely continues."[28] Another observer states that "while China is not yet believed to [be] building an aircraft carrier, for many years, the PLA has been developing aircraft carrier technologies. In early May [2005] the PLA moved the former Ukrainian [i.e., former Soviet] carrier Varyag, in [China's] Dalian harbor since early 2002, into a drydock, suggesting it might soon serve a military role."[29]

### Surface Combatants

China since the early 1990s has purchased four Sovremenny-class destroyers from Russia and deployed eight new classes of indigenously built destroyers and frigates that demonstrate a significant modernization of PLA Navy surface combatant technology. The introduction of eight new destroyer and frigate designs over a period of about 15 years is an undertaking with few parallels by any country in recent decades. China has also deployed a new kind of fast attack craft that uses a stealthy catamaran hull design.

### Sovremenny-Class Destroyers

China in 2002 ordered two Sovremenny-class destroyers from Russia. The ships, which reportedly are to be delivered in 2005 and 2006, are in addition to two Sovremenny-class destroyers that China ordered from Russia in 1996 and which entered service in 1991 and 2001. Sovremenny-class destroyers are equipped with the SS-N-22 Sunburn ASCM, another dangerous ASCM.[30] The SS-N-22s on the two Sovremenny-class ships ordered in 2002 are expected to be an improved version with a longer range. China reportedly has an option for two more Sovremenny-class ships, which, if exercised, would make for an eventual total of six ships.[31]

### Five New Indigenously Built Destroyer Classes

China since the early 1990s has built five new classes of destroyers. Compared to China's 16 older Luda (Type 051) class destroyers, which entered service between 1971 and 1991, these five new destroyer classes are substantially more modern in terms of their hull designs, propulsion systems, sensors, weapons, and electronics. A key area of improvement in the new destroyer designs is their anti-air warfare (AAW) technology,[32] which has been a significant PLA Navy shortcoming. Like the older Luda-class destroyers, these new destroyer classes are armed with ASCMs.

As shown in **Table 2**, China to date has commissioned only 1 or 2 ships in each of these five classes, suggesting that a key purpose of at least some of these classes may have been to serve as stepping stones in a plan to modernize the PLA Navy's surface combatant technology incrementally before committing to larger-scale series production. If one or more of these designs are put into larger-scale production, it would accelerate the modernization of China's surface combatant force.

**Table 2. New PLA Navy Destroyer Classes**

| Class name | Type | Number built | Hull number(s) | In service (actual or projected) |
|---|---|---|---|---|
| Luhu | 052 | 2 | 112, 113 | 1994, 1996 |
| Luhai | 051B | 1 | 167 | 1999 |
| Luyang I | 052B | 2 | 168, 169 | 2004 |
| Luyang II | 052C | 2 | 170, 171 | 2004, 2005 |
| n/a | 051C | 2 | 115, n/a | 2006, 2007 |

**Source:** Jane's Fighting Ships 2005-2006.
n/a = data not available.

The **Luhu-class ships** reportedly were ordered in 1985 but had their construction delayed by a decision to give priority to the construction of six frigates that were ordered by Thailand. The **Luhai-class ship** is believed to have served as the basis for the Luyang-class designs. Compared to the Luhai, the **Luyang I-class ships** appear stealthier and are believed to feature an anti-air warfare (AAW) system with a longer-ranged SAM.

The **Luyang II-class ships** appear to feature an even more capable AAW system that includes a SAM called the HQ-9 that has an even longer range, a vertical launch system (VLS), and a phased-array radar that is outwardly somewhat similar to the SPY-1 radar used in the U.S.-made Aegis combat system. Indeed, the Luyang II-class design bears some resemblance to U.S. and Japanese Aegis destroyers, though they are probably not as modern or capable in some respects as the U.S. and Japanese ships.[33] The two **Type 051C-class ships** feature a VLS and a long-range SAM, but in other respects might be less advanced in their design than the Luyang II-class destroyers. They may have been designed earlier and had their construction delayed. Even so, they are still relatively modern ships.

**Three New Indigenously Built Frigate Classes**

China since the early 1990s has built three new classes of frigates that are more modern than China's 31 older Jianghu (Type 053) class frigates, which entered service between the mid-1970s and 1989. The three new frigate classes, like the new destroyer classes, feature improved AAW capabilities. Unlike the new destroyer designs, the new frigate designs have been put into larger-scale series production. **Table 3** summarizes the three new classes.

## Table 3. New PLA Navy Frigate Classes

| Class name | Type | Number built or building | Hull number(s) | In service (actual or projected) |
|---|---|---|---|---|
| Jiangwei I | 053G H2G | 4 | 539-542 | 1991-1994 |
| Jiangwei II | 053H3 | 10 | between 521 and 567 | 1998-2005 |
| Jiangkai | 054 | 3 | 525, 526, n/a | 2004-2006 |

**Source:** *Jane's Fighting Ships 2005-2006.* n/a = data not available.

Construction of **Jiangwei I-class ships** appears to have ceased but observers believe that construction of the **Jiangwei II- and Jiangkai-class ships** is continuing and additional units beyond those shown in **Table 3** are expected. The Jiangkai-class ships feature a stealthy design that somewhat resembles France's La Fayette-class frigate, which first entered service in 1996.[34]

### New Class of Fast Attack Craft

In addition to its 190 older fast attack craft (including 37 armed with ASCMs), China in 2004 introduced a new type of ASCM-armed fast attack craft built on a stealthy, wave-piercing, catamaran hull that is one of the more advanced hull designs used by any navy in the world today. Observers believe the hull design is based on a design developed by a firm in Australia, a country which is a world leader in high-speed catamaran designs. At least three of these new fast attack craft are now in service, and additional units are expected.[35]

### *Amphibious Ships*

China is currently building three new classes of amphibious ships and landing craft, all of which began construction in 2003. Each type is being built at three or four shipyards. Between these three classes, China built a total of 19 amphibious ships and 8 amphibious landing craft in 2003 and 2004.

### *Mine Countermeasures (MCM) Ships*

China is building a new class of mine countermeasures (MCM) ship, the first unit of which is expected to enter service in 2005.

### *Naval Mines*

Regarding naval mines, ONI states:

> China is developing and exporting numerous advanced mines of all types. One example is the wireless remote controlled EM57, a mine that offers many tactical options. For example, the mine can be turned off and on remotely to prolong its life, or it can be activated and deactivated to allow safe passage for friendly vessels.[36]

DOD stated in 2003 that the PLA's mines

include bottom and moored influence mines, mobile mines, remotely controlled mines, command-detonated mines, and propelled-warhead mines. Use of propelled-warhead mines in deep waters has the potential to deny enemy naval formations large operational areas.[37]

DOD stated in 2002 that China "likely has enough mine warfare assets to lay a good defensive and a modest offensive minefield using a wide variety of launch platforms."[38] Another observer stated in a presentation that China has

> a large inventory of mines. And we see a tremendous interest in some of the most modern deadly mines going. These deep water rising mines [on the projection screen] can be purchased from Russia. They have tremendous ability to mine deeper waters where we would prefer to operate. So what we would consider to have been a haven [for U.S. Navy ships] may no longer be a haven.[39]

### Information Warfare/Information Operations (IW/IO)

China open-source writings demonstrate an interest in information warfare (IW), also called information operations (IO), as an increasingly important element of warfare, particularly against a sophisticated opposing force such as the U.S. military. Concern about potential PLA IW/IO capabilities has been heightened by recent press reports about attacks on U.S. computer systems that in some cases appear to have originated in China.[40] One observer has stated that "China even now is planting viruses in U.S. computer systems that they will activate" in the event of a military conflict with the United States.[41]

### Nuclear Weapons

Although China is not necessarily modernizing its nuclear weapon technology, it is worth noting that China, as a longstanding nuclear weapon state, could put nuclear warheads on weapons such as TBMs, LACMs, ASCMs, torpedoes, and naval mines. China could use nuclear-armed versions of these weapons (except the LACMs) to attack U.S. Navy ships at sea. China might do so in the belief that it could subsequently confuse the issue in the public arena of whose nuclear warhead had detonated,[42] or that the United States in any event would not escalate the conflict by retaliating with a nuclear attack on a land target in China. During the Cold War, analysts debated whether the use of a Soviet nuclear weapon against U.S. Navy ships during a conflict would lead to a U.S. nuclear response.

China could also use a nuclear-armed ballistic missile to detonate a nuclear warhead in the atmosphere to create a high-altitude electromagnetic pulse (EMP) intended to temporarily or permanently disable the electronic circuits of U.S. or other civilian and military electronic systems. Some observers have expressed concern in recent years over the potential vulnerability of U.S. military systems to EMP effects.[43]

### High-Power Microwave (HPM) Weapons

Some observers are concerned that China might develop or already possess high-power microwave (HPM) weapons, also called radio frequency weapons (RFWs) or E-bombs, which are non-nuclear devices that can be used to generate damaging EMP effects over relatively short distances to disable the electronic circuits of nearby enemy civilian and military systems.44 In theory, an HPM weapon could be placed on a TBM or ASCM and fired at a U.S. Navy ship. Although the effective EMP radius of such devices might be on the order of only a few hundred yards,45 such devices could be used to attack individual U.S. Navy ships without the political or escalatory risks of a high-altitude nuclear detonation.[46]

### *Military Doctrine, Education, Training, Exercises, and Logistics.*

Military capability is a product not simply of having weapons, but of having a doctrine for how to use them, well-educated and well-trained personnel, realistic exercises, and logistic support. In past years, the PLA was considered weak in some or all of these areas, and PLA military capability consequently was considered not as great as its inventory of weapons alone might suggest. The 2004 China defense white paper states an intention to improve in these areas,[47] and observers believe the PLA is acting on these intentions. DOD says that "China has stated its intentions and allocated resources to pursue force-wide professionalization, improve training, conduct more robust, realistic joint exercises, and accelerate acquisition of modern weapons."[48] The PLA in recent years has developed a doctrine for joint operations involving multiple military services,[49] improved its military education and training and conducted more realistic exercises,[50] and reformed its logistics system.[51] Improvements in these areas might be considered as important as the weapon-modernization activities discussed above. Some of these improvements may require several years to fully implement.

## China's Naval Limitations and Weaknesses

In spite of the concerns raised by the modernization effort described above, observers believe PLA military (including naval) forces continue to have limitations or weaknesses in the following areas, among others:

- sustained operations in waters and air space that are more distant from China;
- joint operations;
- C4ISR (command, control, communications, computers, intelligence, surveillance and reconnaissance) systems, including, for example, airborne warning and control system (AWACS) capabilities;
- long-range surveillance and targeting systems for detecting and tracking ships at sea — a capability needed to take full advantage of longer-ranged anti-ship weapons;
- anti-air warfare (AAW) capability for defending surface ships against air attack;
- antisubmarine warfare (ASW) capability for defending surface ships against submarine attack;
- mine countermeasures (MCM) capability; and
- logistics.

The paragraphs below elaborate on these items.

### *Weaknesses and Limitations in General*

Regarding PLA Navy limitations and weaknesses in general, DIA states:

China continues to develop or import modern weapons.... The PLA must overcome significant integration challenges to turn these new, advanced and disparate weapon systems into improved capabilities. Beijing also faces technical and operational difficulties in numerous areas.[52]

Another set of observers states:

The PLAN is limited by a lack of integration in its command, control, and communication systems; targeting; air defense; and antisubmarine warfare capabilities. PLAN ships are vulnerable to attack by aircraft, torpedoes, and antiship missiles. The navies of the ASEAN nations could, if able to operate together, exclude the PLAN from the South China Sea....

New capabilities are limited by the lack of some critical supporting systems. The PLAN is deficient in antisubmarine warfare capabilities. PLAN ships are also vulnerable to air attack by both aircraft and antiship missiles.[53]

Regarding the submarine force, one observer states that

by no means should the PLAN submarine force be considered ten feet tall. China's submarine force has some significant weaknesses: a reliance on diesel submarines that have to approach the surface to snorkel; especially in the wake of the Ming 361 accident,[54] it is evident that crew training and professionalism remain a fundamental problem; finally, there is little evidence of a robust, remote cueing capability, and probable weakness in the sphere of command and control.[55]

### *Sustained Operations in Distant Waters*

Regarding sustained operations in more distant waters, DOD states: "We assess that China's ability to project conventional military power beyond its periphery remains limited," and that

China does not appear to have broadened its concept of operations for anti-access and sea denial to encompass sea control in waters beyond Taiwan and its immediate periphery. If China were to shift to a broader "sea control" strategy, the primary indicators would include: development of an aircraft carrier, development of robust anti-submarine warfare capabilities, development of a true area anti-air warfare capability, acquisition of large numbers of nuclear attack submarines, development of effective maritime C4ISR, and increased open water training....

With its present force structure, according to the Intelligence Community, Chinese surface combatants would have difficulty projecting power into the Strait of Malacca, especially if it were conducting simultaneous blockade or invasion operations elsewhere. Similarly, although the PLA Navy occasionally patrols as far as the Spratly Islands, its limited organic air defense capability leaves surface ships vulnerable to attack from hostile air and naval forces. The PLA Navy Air Force and PLA Air Force currently lack the operational range to support PLA Navy operations. In recent years, however, the PLA Navy's South Sea Fleet, which has operational responsibility over the South China Sea, has been assigned more capable surface combatants and submarines, including two destroyers (one LUDA IV class and one LUHAI class) that provide it with its first short-range area air-defense capability, the HHQ-7C surface-to-air missile systems.[56]

## Joint Operations

Regarding joint operations, DOD states:

> Although the PLA has devoted considerable effort to develop joint capabilities, it faces a persistent lack of inter-service cooperation and a lack of actual experience in joint operations.... The lack of experience in joint operations is a subset of the overall lack of operational experience in the Chinese force.[57]

Similarly, regarding training for amphibious and other expeditionary operations, DOD states:

> Combined training for all these units is seldom conducted in a major amphibious assault exercise. Units tend to train for their missions in garrisons, local areas and regional training facilities. China's ability to integrate individual unit actions — or simulate integration — to assess accurately operational capability, is not known.[58]

Another observer states:

> There is no question that China has achieved a remarkable leap in modernization of the forces needed for these missions and that it is urgently continuing on that path. There *is* question about how China is now proceeding to exercise these new assets so as to make them truly operational in a combat environment. There is *considerable question* about China's capability to coordinate all these forces in two major simultaneous operations: (1) to bring Taiwan to its knees and (2) cause the U.S. to be tardy, indecisive, or ineffective in responding.[59]

## Anti-Air Warfare (AAW)

Regarding AAW, one observer states that China's decision to "shed its strictly coastal defense force structure in favor of acquiring larger and more modern fighting vessels capable of blue-water operations" has

> exposed a significant vulnerability — the PLAN's inability to provide a sophisticated, layered air defense for these new forces. Fleet air defense is the Achilles' heel of the 21st-century Chinese Navy....

As the PLAN's ships increased in size, capability and endurance, and with operational deployments taking them well beyond the navy's traditional mainland-based air defenses, a challenge not faced previously became apparent: having to defend these units from air attack in the event of hostilities. Response to this concern has been slow and inadequate at best, and serious consideration to providing the surface navy with the kind of air defense systems one normally associates with modern naval fleets has only begun. Not until the late 1990s was an effort made to outfit PLAN destroyers and frigates with an antiair "point defense" system, giving them some measure of self-defense.... The PLAN surface fleet, however, still lacks "modern air surveillance systems and data links required for area air defense missions. The combination of short-range weapons and lack of modern surveillance systems limits the PLAN to self-defense and point-defense [AAW] only. As a result, except in unusual circumstances, no PLAN ship is capable of conducting air defense of another ship."[60]

In a similar vein, today's PLAN naval aviation forces alone cannot provide fighter coverage for the entire Chinese coast or the fleet, so interceptor duties have ben distributed by region between naval aviation units and the PLA Air Force. This increases the number of assets available for the task, but questions remain about joint patrolling, separate chains of command, and air force overwater proficiency. When faced with training scenarios that incorporated factors likely found in a modern air combat environment, such as electronic countermeasures or even inclement weather, neither service was up to the task. In light of these facts, the potential effectiveness of the cooperation between the two services is doubtful.

Significant gaps exist in the present PLAN fleet air defense posture. Given the forces available today, China cannot adequately defend its fleet from air attack in the modern air threat environment.[61]

### Antisubmarine Warfare (ASW)
Regarding ASW, one observer states:

> The most serious deficiency of the PLAN is certainly in the area of Anti-Submarine Warfare. Good submarines, like the "Kilo" class and (possibly) the forthcoming Type-093, will play an important ASW role, but the lack of maritime patrol aircraft and of surface ships equipped with advanced acoustic sensors make the Chinese vessels vulnerable for [sic] any of the foreign high-capability submarines operating in the area.[62]

### Mine Countermeasures (MCM)
Regarding MCM, one observer writes that the PLA Navy a

> serious operational deficiency involves the mine countermeasures vessels (MCMV). Though China has an intense shipping [sic] along its coasts, the PLAN has virtually no mine-sweeping or mine-hunting capabilities. This was due, perhaps, to the consideration that the U.S. Navy is usually more concerned to keep the sea lanes open, instead of laying mines, but nevertheless the lack of MCM is simply stunning. Any hostile organisation (including, but not limited to, state-sponsored terrorists and insurgents) could play havoc with the Chinese shipping simply by laying a few mines here and there.[63]

### Logistics
Regarding logistics, DOD states:

> Since 2000, China has improved the structure, material coordination, and efficiency of its joint logistics system. However, the command system is still not compatible with the support system, and organization and planning is incompatible with supply management. The first experimental joint logistics unit was created only in July 2004.[64]

Regarding logistic support of China's new destroyers, one observer states:

> The ships' new sensors, missiles and combat systems are mainly of Russian and Western origin. However, China now is faced with the challenge of operating and maintaining these advanced systems to create a credible threat to foreign navies in Far Eastern waters....

Every piece of equipment [on China's Sovremenny-class destroyers] from hull, mechanical and electrical (HM&E) technologies to guns, sonar, communications, electronic countermeasures (ECM) and missiles are totally new to the PLAN.... [For these ships,] China is dependent on Russian advisers for training, operations and maintenance. These ships largely remain in the Russian support cocoon in Dinghai rather than at a fleet base....

Isolation from other ships and crews hurts fleet integration and coordinated operations.... It is no coincidence that the Sovremnyi and Kilo submarine home bases are in an enclave of Russian support in an isolated area near the Eastern Fleet headquarters at Ningbo.

It is unlikely that Russian advisers would be onboard during actual combat operations against Taiwan and U.S. Navy air, surface and subsurface threats. PLAN officers and crew are not expected to be able to handle operations when under fire, sustaining hits and suffering system degradation or loss. This could include problems in night or rough weather environment as well. Because all of the combat systems, except for three noted, are modern Russian equipments, China has minimal capability even to repair peacetime losses in port....

A comparison [of the AAW system on the Luyang II class destroyers] to [the] U.S. Navy Aegis [combat system] is inevitable, but Aegis was on [the U.S. Navy test ship] Norton Sound for nine years of development testing prior to the first installation on the USS Ticonderoga (CG-47) 20 years ago. Developing the software for signal processing and tracking a hundred air, surface and submarine targets will take even longer for China. Integration to various indigenous ship guns and missiles and other sensors, as well as other ships' data management and weapons, will take longer. These Chinese "Aegis" ships may be limited to 1940s era radar tasks of detecting and tracking air and surface targets for their own ship weapons. Further in the future will be an 8,000-ton DDG that is predicted to be a true area-control warship with additional Aegis capabilities. It is now in early construction stages in the new Dalian shipyard.

What kind of record is provided by prior Chinese built warships with imported Russian and Western technology? These include sensors, fire control, weapons and communications as well as HM&E. The Chinese new-construction DDGs are a mix of local designed and manufactured systems, foreign imports with production rights, illegally copied import equipment and illegal examples with no local production capability at all. The latter two represent serious training and maintenance problems. Unfortunately for the PLAN, some of them are in the highest mission-critical areas. For example, the DDGs being built have a rapid-fire Gatling gun close-in weapon system that looks like the Dutch Goalkeeper system. Signaal and the Dutch government deny exporting the equipment or production rights to China. This key weapon responsible for downing incoming cruise missiles is probably lacking documentation and training because it must be illegally obtained.[65]

## Goals or Significance of China's Naval Modernization

### PLA Navy as a Modernization Priority

The PLA Navy is one of three stated priorities within China's overall military modernization effort. China's 2004 defense white paper says three times that the effort will emphasize the navy, air force, and the ballistic missile force.[66] Consistent with this stated emphasis, the heads of the PLA Navy, Air Force, and missile force were added to the Central Military Commission in September 2004, and Navy and Air Force officers were appointed Deputy Chiefs of the General Staff.[67]

## Near-Term Focus: Taiwan Situation

DOD and other observers believe that the primary near-term focus of China's military modernization is to develop military options for addressing the situation with Taiwan.[68] DOD lists China's potential military options regarding Taiwan as follows:

- **persuasion and coercion**, which "combines the credible threat to use military force with the economic and cultural tools that China has at its disposal";
- **limited force options** that could employ "information operations, special operations forces on Taiwan, and SRBM or air strikes at key military or political sites, to try to break the will of Taiwan's leadership and population";
- **an air and missile campaign**, in which "Surprise SRBM attacks and precision air strikes could support a campaign designed to degrade Taiwan defenses, decapitate its military and political leadership, and break its will to fight rapidly before the United States and other nations could intervene";
- **a blockade**, which "Beijing could threaten or deploy... either as a 'non-war' pressure tactic in the pre-hostility phase or as a transition to active conflict";[69] and
- **amphibious invasion**, which "would be a complex and difficult operation relying upon timing and pre-conditions set by many subordinate campaigns."[70]

## Anti-Access Force for Short-Duration Conflict

More specifically, observers believe that China's military modernization is aimed at fielding a force that can succeed in a short-duration conflict with Taiwan that finishes before the United States is able to intervene, so that China can present the United States and the rest of the world with a *fait accompli*. DOD states that China is "emphasizing preparations to fight and win short-duration, high-intensity conflicts along China's periphery."[71]

Regarding the potential time line for a short-duration conflict with Taiwan, one observer states:

> The U.S. (particularly the U.S. Pacific Command/PACOM) seems to want Taiwan to focus on [acquiring] systems and defensive operational capabilities that would lengthen the amount of time Taiwan could deny the PRC from gaining air superiority, sea control, and physical occupation of Taiwan's leadership core (namely Taipei). The idea is to permit sufficient time to bring U.S. forces to bear. The amount of time needed is understood to be at least 5 days, presumably after credible warning that hostilities either are imminent or are already underway.[72]

Consistent with the goal of a short-duration conflict and a *fait accompli*, observers believe, China wants its modernized military to be capable of acting as a so-called anti-access force — a force that can deter U.S. intervention, or failing that, delay the arrival or reduce the effectiveness of U.S. intervention forces, particularly U.S. Navy forces. DOD states that, in addition to preventing Taiwan independence or trying to compel Taiwan to negotiate a settlement on Beijing's terms, "A second set of objectives includes building counters to third-party, including potential U.S., intervention in cross-Strait crises."[73]

China's emerging maritime anti-access force can be viewed as broadly analogous to the sea-denial force that the Soviet Union developed during the Cold War to deny U.S. use of the sea or counter U.S. forces participating in a NATO-Warsaw Pact conflict. One potential difference between the Soviet sea-denial force and China's emerging maritime anti-access force is that China's force could include MaRV-equipped TBMs capable of hitting moving ships at sea.

Some analysts speculate that China may attain (or believe that is has attained) a capable maritime anti-access capability, or important elements of it, by about 2010.[74] Other observers believe China will attain (or believe that it has attained) such a capability some time after 2010. DOD states that "The U.S. Intelligence Community estimates that China will require until the end of this decade or later for its military modernization program to produce a modern force, capable of defeating a moderate-size adversary."[75] The term "moderate-size adversary" would appear to apply to a country other than the United States. The issue of when China might attain (or believe that it has attained) a capable anti-access capability is significant because it can influence the kinds of options that are available to U.S. policymakers for addressing the situation.

### Broader or Longer-Term Regional Goals

In addition to the near-term focus on developing military options for addressing the situation with Taiwan, DOD and some (but not necessarily all) other observers believe that broader or longer-term goals of China's military modernization, including naval modernization, include one or more of the following:

- **asserting China's regional military leadership**, displacing U.S. regional military influence, prevailing in regional rivalries, and encouraging eventual U.S. military withdrawal form the region;
- **defending China's claims in maritime territorial disputes**, some of which have implications for oil, gas, or mineral exploration rights;[76]
- **protecting China's sea lines of communication**, which China relies upon increasingly for oil and other imports.[77]

Some PLA Navy units have recently been deployed outside China's home waters. In November 2004, for example, a Han-class SSN was detected in Japanese territorial waters near Okinawa.[78] DIA states that, as part of the same deployment, this submarine traveled "far into the western Pacific Ocean...."[79] Press reports state that the submarine operated in the vicinity of Guam before moving toward Okinawa.[80] As another example, on September 9, 2005,

> China deployed a fleet of five warships... near a gas field in the East China Sea, a potentially resource-rich area that is disputed by China and Japan. The ships, including a guided-missile destroyer, were spotted by a Japanese military patrol plane near the Chunxiao gas field, according to the [Japan] Maritime Self-Defense Forces. It is believed to be the first time that Chinese warships have been seen in that area.[81]

As a third example,

> China said on Sept. 29 [of 2005 that] it has sent warships to the disputed East China Sea, a day ahead of talks with Japan over competing territorial claims in the gas-rich waters.
>
> "I can now confirm that in the East China Sea, a Chinese reserve vessel squadron has been established," foreign ministry spokesman Qin Gang told a regular briefing....

No details were given on the size of the squadron or the area it will patrol. The establishment of the squadron follows China's creation of two naval groups in the Bohai Sea and Yellow Sea off the northern China coast, the agency said.[82]

Regarding base access and support facilities to support more distant PLA Navy operations, one press report states:

China is building up military forces and setting up bases along sea lanes from the Middle East to project its power overseas and protect its oil shipments, according to a previously undisclosed internal report prepared for Defense Secretary Donald H. Rumsfeld.

"China is building strategic relationships along the sea lanes from the Middle East to the South China Sea in ways that suggest defensive and offensive positioning to protect China's energy interests, but also to serve broad security objectives," said the report sponsored by the director, Net Assessment, who heads Mr. Rumsfeld's office on future-oriented strategies.

The Washington Times obtained a copy of the report, titled "Energy Futures in Asia," which was produced by defense contractor Booz Allen Hamilton.

The internal report stated that China is adopting a "string of pearls" strategy of bases and diplomatic ties stretching from the Middle East to southern China....[83]

# POTENTIAL IMPLICATIONS FOR REQUIRED U.S. NAVY CAPABILITIES

Potential implications of China's naval modernization for required U.S. Navy capabilities can be organized into three groups:

- capabilities for a crisis or conflict in the Taiwan Strait area;
- capabilities for maintaining U.S. Navy presence and military influence in the Western Pacific; and
- capabilities for detecting, tracking, and if necessary countering PLA Navy SSBNs equipped with long-range SLBMs.

Each of these is discussed below.

## Capabilities for Taiwan Strait Crisis or Conflict

U.S. military operations in a potential crisis or conflict in the Taiwan Strait area would likely feature a strong reliance on U.S. Navy forces and land-based U.S. Air Force aircraft.[84] If air bases in Japan and South Korea are, for political reasons, not available to the United States for use in the operation, or if air bases in Japan, South Korea, or Guam are rendered less useful by PLA attacks using TBMs, LACMs, or special operations forces, then the reliance on U.S. Navy forces could become greater.

For the U.S. Navy, a crisis or conflict in the Taiwan Strait could place a premium on the following:

- on-station or early-arriving forces;

- forces with a capability to defeat PLA anti-access weapons and platforms;
- forces with an ability to operate in an environment that could be characterized by IW/IO and possibly EMP or the use of nuclear weapons directly against Navy ships; and ! forces that can be ready to conduct operations by about 2010, or by some later date.

### On-Station and Early-Arriving Forces

In the scenario of a short-duration conflict, on-station and early-arriving U.S. Navy forces could be of particular value, while later-arriving U.S. Navy forces might be of less value, at least in preventing initial success by PLA forces.

### On-Station Forces

Given the difficulty of knowing with certainty when a Taiwan Strait crisis or conflict might occur, having forces on-station at the start of the crisis or conflict is a goal that would most reliably be met by maintaining a standing forward deployment of U.S. Navy forces in the area. Maintaining a standing forward deployment of U.S. Navy forces in the area while also maintaining U.S. Navy forward deployments in other regions, such as the Persian Gulf/Indian Ocean region and the Mediterranean Sea, would require a Navy with a certain minimum number of ships.

Although it is sometimes said that it takes three U.S. Navy ships to keep one ship forward deployed in an overseas location, the actual ratio traditionally has been higher. For example, if U.S. Navy ships are operated in the traditional manner —with a single crew for each ship and deployments lasting six months — then maintaining one U.S. Navy cruiser or destroyer continuously forward-deployed to the Western Pacific might require a total of about five San Diego-based cruisers or destroyers.[85]

Stationkeeping multipliers like these can be reduced by homeporting U.S. Navy ships at locations closer to Taiwan (such as Japan, Guam, Hawaii, or perhaps Singapore) or by deploying ships for longer periods of time and operating them with multiple crews that are rotated out to each ship. The Navy has an aircraft carrier strike group and other ships[86] homeported in Japan, and three attack submarines homeported in Guam.[87] The Navy reportedly may transfer an additional aircraft carrier from the continental United States to Hawaii or Guam, and is studying options for transferring perhaps a few additional SSNs to Hawaii or Guam. The Navy is also experimenting with the concept of deploying certain Navy ships (particularly surface combatants) for 12, 18, or 24 months and rotating multiple crews out to each ship.[88]

### Early-Arriving Forces

Having early-arriving U.S. Navy forces could mean having forces based in locations Western Pacific locations such as Japan, Guam, Singapore, or perhaps Hawaii, rather than on the U.S. West Coast.[89] **Table 4** shows potential ship travel times to the Taiwan Strait area from various ports in the Pacific, based on average ship travel speeds. All the ports shown in the table except Singapore are current U.S. Navy home ports.[90] U.S. Navy submarines, aircraft carriers, cruisers, and destroyers have maximum sustained speeds of more than 30 knots, but their average speeds over longer transits in some cases might be closer to 25 knots or less due rough sea conditions or, in the case of the cruisers or destroyers, which are conventionally powered, the need slow down for at-sea refueling. The Navy's planned Littoral Combat Ship (LCS) is to have a maximum sustained speed of about 45 knots, but its average speed over long transits would likely be less than that.[91]

As can be seen in the table, Yokosuka, Guam, and Singapore are less than half as far from the Taiwan Strait area as are Pearl Harbor, Everett, WA,[92] and San Diego. Depending on their average travel speeds, ships homeported in Yokosuka, Guam, and Singapore could arrive in the Taiwan Strait area roughly two to four days after leaving port, ships homeported in Pearl Harbor might arrive about six to nine days after leaving port, and ships homeported on the U.S. West Coast might arrive about seven to twelve days after leaving port. The time needed to get a ship and its crew ready to leave port would add to their total response times. Depending on a ship's status at the moment it was ordered to the Taiwan Strait area, preparing it for rapid departure might require anywhere from less than one day to a few days.

**Table 4. Potential Ship Travel Times to Taiwan Strait Area**

| Port | Straight-line distance to Taiwan Strait area[a] (nautical miles) | Minimum travel time in days, based on average speeds below[b] | | |
| --- | --- | --- | --- | --- |
| | | 20 knots | 25 knots | 30 knots |
| Yokosuka, Japan[c] | 1,076 | 2.2 | 1.8 | 1.5 |
| Guam | 1,336 | 2.8 | 2.2 | 1.9 |
| Singapore[d] | 1,794 | 3.7 | 3.0 | 2.5 |
| Pearl Harbor[e] | 4,283 | 8.9 | 7.1 | 5.9 |
| Everett, WA | 5,223 | 10.9 | 8.7 | 7.3 |
| San Diego | 5,933 | 12.3 | 9.9 | 8.2 |

**Source:** Table prepared by CRS using straight-line distances calculated by the "how far is it" calculator, available at [http://www.indo.com/distance/].
a. Defined as a position in the sea at 24°N, 124°E, which is roughly 130 nautical miles *east* of Taiwan, i.e., on the other side of Taiwan from the Taiwan Strait. b. Actual travel times may be greater due to the possible need for ships to depart from a straight-line course so as to avoid land barriers, remain within port-area shipping channels, etc. c. Distance calculated from Tokyo, which is about 25 nautical miles north of Yokosuka. d. No U.S. Navy ships are currently homeported at Singapore. e. Distance calculated from Honolulu, which is about 6 nautical miles southeast of Pearl Harbor.

Regarding the possible transfer of a carrier from the continental United States to Hawaii or Guam, one observer states:

> Currently the United States maintains one aircraft carrier full-time in the Western Pacific. In the event of a conflict with China over Taiwan, however, particularly given the various [PLA] threats to land-based air outlined above, having more aircraft carriers on the scene will be extremely valuable. Other than any carriers that might be transiting through the region, however, currently the closest additional carriers would be those based on the west coast of the United States. Given that a conflict with China could begin with little warning, this means that as much as two weeks could elapse before additional aircraft carriers reached the area of combat operations. The Department of Defense has already recommended forward-deploying an additional aircraft carrier in the Pacific, but it is important to note that precisely where this carrier is forward-deployed is significant. In particular, an aircraft carrier based in Hawaii would still take at least a week to reach waters near Taiwan. An aircraft carrier based in

Guam, Singapore, or elsewhere in the Western Pacific, by contrast, could arrive on the scene in about three days.[93]

Basing additional forces in Japan, Guam, Singapore, or Hawaii could increase the importance of taking actions to defend these locations against potential attack by TBMs, LACMs, or special operations forces.[94]

### *Defeating PLA Anti-Access Forces*

Defeating PLA maritime anti-access forces would require capabilities for countering:

- large numbers of TBMs, including some possibly equipped with MaRVs;
- large numbers of LACMs and ASCMs, including some advanced ASCMs such as the SS-N-27 and SS-N-22;
- substantial numbers of land-based fighters, strike fighters, maritime bombers, and SAMs, including some built to modern designs;
- a substantial number of submarines, including a few that are nuclear-powered and a significant portion that are built to modern designs;
- a substantial number of destroyers, frigates, and fast attack craft, including some built to modern designs; and
- potentially large numbers of mines of different types, including some advanced models.

### Countering TBMs

Countering large numbers of TBMs, including some possibly equipped with MaRVs, could entail some or all of the following:

- operating, if possible, in a way that reduces the likelihood of being detected and tracked by PLA maritime surveillance systems;
- attacking the surveillance systems that detect and track U.S. Navy ships operating at sea, and the network that transmits this targeting data to the TBMs;
- attacking TBMs at their launch sites;
- intercepting TBMs in flight, which in some cases could require firing two or perhaps even three interceptor missiles at individual TBMs to ensure their destruction;
- decoying MaRVs away from U.S. Navy ships.

Potential implications of the above points for Navy missile-defense programs are discussed in this next section of this report.

### Countering Submarines

Countering a substantial number of submarines would likely require a coordinated effort by an ASW network consisting of some or all of the following: distributed sensors, unmanned vehicles, submarines, surface ships, helicopters, and maritime patrol aircraft. Defeating torpedoes fired by PLA submarines would require U.S. submarines and surface ships to have systems for detecting, decoying, and perhaps destroying those torpedoes.

ASW operations against well-maintained and well-operated submarines traditionally have often been time-consuming. Acoustic conditions in waters around Taiwan are reportedly poor for ASW, which could make the task of countering PLA submarines in these areas more difficult.[95] Success in an ASW operation is highly dependent on the proficiency of the people operating the ASW equipment. ASW operational proficiency can take time to develop and can atrophy significantly if not regularly exercised.

In December 2004, the Navy approved a new concept of operations (CONOPS) a new general approach — to ASW. As described in one article,

> The Navy's new concept of operations for anti-submarine warfare calls for the use of standoff weapons, networked sensor fields and unmanned vehicles to detect and attack diesel submarines in littoral waters, rather than a reliance on "force on force" engagements.
>
> Chief of Naval Operations Adm. Vern Clark approved the CONOPS Dec. 20, according to a Navy spokesman. The five-page document will guide the development of a comprehensive ASW master plan that is expected to be classified, though it might have an unclassified version.
>
> The CONOPS envisions hundreds or thousands of small sensors that would "permeate the operating environment, yielding unprecedented situational awareness and highly detailed pictures of the battlespace." Attack submarines that today carry sensors and weapons could in the future provide logistical support to and serve as command and control bases for off-board sensors and "kill vehicles," the CONOPS states. The networking of autonomous sensor fields with manned and unmanned vehicles will change ASW from a "platform-intensive" to a "sensor-rich" operation, it adds.[96]

At a June 20, 2005, conference on the future of the Navy organized by the American Enterprise Institute (AEI), Admiral Vernon Clark, who was the Chief of Naval Operations until July 22, 2005, stated:

> [The Chinese are] building submarines at a rapid rate. They're buying them from other countries. They're building their own capabilities. And let me just to make a long story short, I published a new ASW concept [of operations] a couple of months ago. I fundamentally don't believe that the old attrition warfare[,] force on force anti-submarine warfare[,] construct is the right way to go in the 21st century. [The questioner] mentioned that I had spent part of my past life in the submarine warfare business. I have. I trailed the Soviets around. I know what that's about. And what I really believe is going to happen in the future is that when we apply the netted force construct in anti-submarine warfare, it will change the calculus in that area of warfighting forever. And it will be a courageous commander who decides that he's going to come waltzing into our network.[97]

Implementing this new ASW concept of operations reportedly will require overcoming some technical challenges, particularly with regard to linking together large numbers of distributed sensors, some of which might be sonobuoys as small as soda cans.[98]

## Countering Mines

Countering naval mines is a notoriously time-consuming task that can require meticulous operations by participating surface ships, submarines, and helicopters. The Navy's mine countermeasures (MCM) capabilities have been an area of concern in Congress and elsewhere for a number of years.[99] The Navy for the last several years has been developing several new MCM systems that are scheduled to enter service over the next few years.[100] Unmanned surface vehicles (USVs) and unmanned underwater vehicles (UUVs) are playing an increasing role in MCM operations.

### Operating Amidst IW/IO, EMP, and Nuclear Weapons.

Operating effectively in an environment that could be characterized by IW/IO and possibly EMP or the use of nuclear weapons directly against Navy ships could require, among other things:

- measures to achieve and maintain strong computer network security;
- hardening of ships, aircraft, and their various systems against EMP; and
- hardening of ships against the overpressure, thermal, and radiation effects of a nuclear weapon that is detonated somewhat close to the ship, but not close enough to destroy the ship outright.

### Forces Ready by About 2010, or by a Later Date

As mentioned earlier, some analysts speculate that China may attain (or believe that is has attained) a capable maritime anti-access capability, or important elements of it, by about 2010, while other observers believe this will happen some time after 2010. The issue of whether or when China might attain such a capability can influence the kinds of options that are available to U.S. policymakers for addressing the situation.

### Options for a Conflict Between Now and 2010

Options that could enhance U.S. Navy capabilities for a crisis or conflict in the Taiwan Strait area between now and 2010 include, among others, the following:

- increasing currently planned activities for physically surveying the physical environment around Taiwan, so as to more quickly update older data that might unreliable, and to fill in any gaps in understanding regarding how local atmospheric and water conditions might affect the performance of radars and sonars;
- increasing currently planned levels of monitoring and surveillance of PLA forces that are likely to participate in a crisis or conflict in the Taiwan Strait area;
- increasing currently planned levels of contact between the U.S. Navy and Taiwan military forces, so as to maintain a fully up-to-date U.S. understanding of Taiwan military capabilities, plans, and doctrine (and vice versa);
- increasing currently planned military exercises that are tailored to the potential requirements of a crisis or conflict in the Taiwan Strait area;
- increasing the number of ships that are assigned to the Pacific Fleet, or the number that are forward-homeported at locations such as Japan, Guam, Hawaii, and perhaps Singapore, or the numbers of both;
- deferring current plans for retiring existing ships or aircraft before 2010, particularly ships and aircraft whose nominal service lives would otherwise extend to 2010 or beyond;
- modernizing ships and aircraft now in service;
- reactivating recently retired ships and aircraft;[101]and

- procuring new items that can be completed between now and 2010, such as weapons, aircraft, and Littoral Combat Ships (LCSs).

## Options For A Conflict After 2010

Options that could enhance U.S. Navy capabilities for a crisis or conflict in the Taiwan Strait area some time after 2010 include items from the above list, plus the procurement of larger ships that take several years to build (e.g., SSNs, aircraft carriers, destroyers, and cruisers), and the development and procurement of aircraft and weapons that are not currently ready for procurement.

### *Capabilities for Maintaining Regional Presence and Influence*

For the U.S. Navy, maintaining regional presence and military influence in the Western Pacific could place a premium on the following, among other things: ! maintaining a substantial U.S. Navy ship presence throughout the region;

- making frequent port calls in the region;
- conducting frequent exercises with other navies in the region;
- taking actions to ensure system compatibility between U.S. Navy ships and ships of allied and friendly nations in the region; and
- conducting frequent exchanges between U.S. Navy personnel and military and political leaders of other countries in the region.

Factors influencing the Navy's ability to maintain a substantial U.S. Navy ship presence throughout the region include the total number of ships in the Navy's Pacific Fleet, the number of Navy ships forward-homeported at locations such as Japan, Guam, Hawaii, and perhaps Singapore, and ship-crewing and -deployment approaches (e.g., six-month deployments and single crews vs. longer deployments with crew rotation).

### *Capabilities for Tracking and Countering PLA SSBNs*

Detecting, tracking, and if necessary countering PLA Navy SSBNs equipped with long-range SLBMs could require some or all of the following:

- a seabed-based sensor network analogous to the Sound Surveillance System (SOSUS) that the U.S. Navy used during the Cold War to detect and track Soviet nuclear-powered submarines;
- ocean surveillance ships with additional sonars, which would be similar to the TAGOS-type ocean-surveillance ships that the Navy also used during the Cold War to help detect and track Soviet nuclear-powered submarines; and
- enough SSNs so that some can be assigned to tracking and if necessary attacking PLA SSBNs.[102]

# POTENTIAL OVERSIGHT ISSUES FOR CONGRESS

Potential oversight questions for Congress arising from China's military modernization and its potential implications for required U.S. Navy capabilities can be organized into three groups:

- questions relating to China's military modernization as a defense-planning priority;
- questions relating to U.S. Navy force structure and basing arrangements; and
- questions relating to Navy warfare areas and programs.

Each of these is discussed below.

## China as a Defense-Planning Priority

### DOD Planning

*Is DOD giving adequate weight in the 2005 Quadrennial Defense Review (QDR) and other planning activities to China's military modernization as opposed to other concerns, such as current operations in Iraq and Afghanistan and the global war on terrorism (GWOT) generally? Is DOD giving adequate weight in its planning to the funding needs of the Navy as opposed to those of the other services, such as the Army?*

Operations in Iraq and Afghanistan have led to increased focus on the funding needs of the Army and Marine Corps, since these two services are heavily committed to those operations. Placing increasing emphasis on China in DOD planning, on the other hand, would likely lead to increased focus on the funding needs of the Navy and Air Force, since these two services are generally viewed as the ones most likely to be of the most importance for a crisis or conflict in the Taiwan Strait area. In a situation of finite DOD resources, striking the correct planning balance between operations in Iraq and Afghanistan and the GWOT generally, and China's military modernization is viewed by some observers as a key DOD planning challenge.

### Navy Planning

*Is the Navy is giving adequate weight in its planning to China's military modernization as opposed to other concerns, such as the GWOT?*

Required Navy capabilities for participating in the GWOT overlap with, but are not identical to, required Navy capabilities for responding to China's naval modernization. In a situation of finite Navy resources, striking the correct balance between investments for participating in the GWOT and those for responding to China's naval modernization is viewed by some observers as a key Navy planning challenge.

The Navy in recent months has taken some actions that reflect an interest in increasing the Navy's role in the GWOT. In June 2005, for example, Admiral Vernon Clark, who was the Chief of Naval Operations until July 22, 2005, directed the Navy to take nine "actions to expand the Navy's capabilities to prosecute the GWOT..." Among these are the establishment of a Navy riverine force, the establishment of a reserve civil affairs battalion, the establishment of a Foreign Area Office (FAO) community in the Navy, and concept development work for a potential Navy expeditionary combat battalion composed of sailors rather than Marines. "To the extent possible," the Navy wants to implement these actions without increasing Navy active and reserve end strength.[103] In October 2005, Admiral Clark's successor as CNO, Admiral Michael Mullen, issued a guidance statement for the Navy for 2006 that contained follow-on initiatives intended to strengthen the Navy's role in the GWOT.[104] The Navy has also commissioned a study from the Naval Studies Board (an arm of the National Academy of Sciences) on the adequacy of the role of naval forces in the GWOT and options for enhancing that role.[105]

At the same time, the Navy has affirmed the importance of China's military modernization in its budget planning. At a June 20, 2005 conference on the future of the Navy organized by the American Enterprise Institute (AEI), for example, Admiral Clark was asked to comment on China. He stated in part:

> Well, I think that, you know, we're always quick to point out that China's not our enemy, but China is building a very capable maritime capability, and so we should not be blind to that.
>
> So what does it mean? Well, here's what I believe that it means. I believe that if you study the Chinese, you see that there's been some change in their thinking over the course of the last number of years. Here's this mammoth land, continent; here's — you know, it would be easy to think about this country as being land-centric in terms of its national security focus, but what we're seeing is that that really isn't where they're putting their money. They're putting their investments in, and what it looks like, if you interpret their actions, is that their primary concerns are in the area of aviation and maritime capability that other nations would bring to bear in their area, in their region of the world. And so they're trying to build a capability to make sure that they're not pushed into a corner in their own part of the world.
>
> I understand that this morning there was conjecture about their ability to build missile systems that will threaten long-range land bases and moving targets in the future, like ships at sea. And I will tell you that whether they're going to do that or not, I guarantee you that I believe that it is my duty and responsibility to expect that, based on what I understand about what they're doing, to expect that they're trying to do that. And I will tell you that the budget submit that's on the Hill is providing the kind of capability to make sure that the United States Navy can fight in that theater or exist in that theater, understanding the kind of capability that they're trying to bring to bear.[106\

## Navy Force Structure and Basing Arrangements

### Size of the Fleet

*Is the Navy planning a fleet with enough ships to address potential challenges posed by China's naval modernization while also meeting other responsibilities?*

As of November 2005, the Navy included a total of about 280 ships of various kinds. In early 2005, the Navy stated that it wanted the fleet in the future to include a total of 260 to 325 ships.[107] The Navy has stated that it will announce a successor ship force structure plan by early 2006. A key potential issue for Congress in assessing the adequacy of the Navy's ship force structure plan is whether it includes enough ships to address potential challenges posed by China's naval modernization while also meeting other responsibilities, including maintaining forward deployments of Navy ships in the Persian Gulf/Indian Ocean region and the Mediterranean Sea and conducting less-frequent operations in other parts of the world, such as the Caribbean, the waters around South America, and the waters off West Africa. If increased numbers of Navy ships are needed to address potential challenges posed by China's naval modernization, fewer ships might be available for meeting other responsibilities.

Some Members of Congress have expressed concern in recent years that the declining total number of ships in the Navy may make it difficult for the Navy to perform all if its various missions, at least not without putting undue stress on Navy personnel and equipment. In response, Navy officials in recent years have argued that the total number of ships in the Navy is no longer, by itself, a very good measure of total Navy capability over time, because of the significant increase in individual Navy ship and aircraft capabilities in recent years and the effect that computer networking technology has on further increasing the collective capability of Navy ships and aircraft. Navy officials acknowledge, however, that ship numbers are one factor in understanding Navy capabilities, particularly for conducting simultaneous operations of different kinds in multiple locations around the world.

### Division of Fleet Between Atlantic and Pacific

*Should a greater percentage of the Navy be assigned to the Pacific Fleet?* The division of the Navy's ships between the Atlantic and Pacific fleets is a longstanding question in U.S. Navy planning. Atlantic Fleet ships conduct operations in the North and South Atlantic, the Caribbean, and the Mediterranean Sea, while Pacific Fleet ships conduct operations in the Pacific Ocean, including the Western Pacific. Ships from both fleets are used to conduct operations in the Persian Gulf/Indian Ocean area. Atlantic Fleet ships homeported on the U.S. East Coast that use the Suez Canal have a shorter transit distance to the Persian Gulf than do Pacific Fleet ships homeported on the U.S. West Coast.

In recent years, roughly 45% to 47% of the Navy's ships have been assigned to the Pacific Fleet, including 46% to 50% of the Navy's SSNs and 45% to 48% of the Navy's cruisers, destroyers, and frigates. Increasing the share of the Navy assigned to the Pacific Fleet could, other things held equal, permit the Navy to maintain a larger number of ships forward deployed to the Western Pacific. Using the size of the Navy as of the end of FY2005 (282 ships, including 54 SSNs and 99 cruisers, destroyers, and frigates), increasing the Pacific Fleet's share by 5 or 10 percentage points would result in the Pacific fleet having an additional 14 to 28 ships, including roughly 3 to 5 SSNs and roughly 5 to 10 to cruisers, destroyers, and frigates.

In recent years, 7 of the Navy's 12 aircraft carriers have been assigned to the Atlantic Fleet and 5 have been assigned to the Pacific Fleet. This division reflects in part a program currently underway to conduct a mid-life nuclear refueling complex overhaul (RCOH) on each of the Navy's nuclear-powered carriers. This program results, at any given moment, in one nuclear-powered carrier being homeported at Newport News, VA, the location of the shipyard where the work is conducted. Absent the nuclear carrier RCOH program, the division of carriers between the Atlantic and Pacific might be 6 and 6, respectively, rather than 7 and 5. Whether the division of carriers between the two fleets is 7 and 5 or 6 and 6, shifting one carrier from the Atlantic to the Pacific would increase the Pacific Fleet's share of the carrier force by about 8 percentage points.

Supporters of shifting a greater share of the Navy to the Pacific Fleet could argue that responding to China's naval modernization requires, among other things, maintaining an increased number of ships forward deployed to the Western Pacific, and that the low likelihood of war in Europe and the ability of U.S. allies in Europe to deploy their own ships to the Mediterranean reduces the number of ships that the Navy needs to maintain there. Opponents of this option could argue that shifting Navy ships from the U.S. East Coast to the U.S. West Coast could make it harder to maintain deployments of a given number of ships to the Persian Gulf (due to the increase in transit distance to the Gulf for ships transferred from the East Coast to the West Coast) and could make it more difficult for the Navy to balance the maintenance demands of the fleet against the locations of repair and overhaul yards, many of which are located on the Atlantic and Gulf coasts.

### Forward Homeporting in the Western Pacific

*Is the Navy moving quickly enough to forward-homeport additional ships in the Western Pacific? Should the Navy expand the number of additional ships it is thinking of homeporting in the area?*

Increasing the number of ships forward homeported in the Western Pacific can increase both the number of ships that the Navy can maintain forward-deployed to that area on a day to day basis, and the number that can arrive in the early stages of a conflict in the Western Pacific, including the Taiwan Strait area. As mentioned earlier, the Navy may transfer an additional aircraft carrier from the continental United States to Hawaii or Guam, and is studying options for transferring perhaps a few additional SSNs to Hawaii or Guam. Observers who are concerned about deterring or responding to a conflict in the Taiwan Strait area by 2010 might emphasize the importance of implementing these actions as quickly as possible.

In addition, observers concerned about China's military modernization might argue in favor of expanding the number of ships to be transferred to Western Pacific home ports. These additional ships could include SSNs, converted Trident cruise missile submarines (SSGNs), surface combatants, and perhaps one more aircraft carrier. The final report of the 2001 Quadrennial Defense Review (QDR) stated that "The Secretary of the Navy will increase aircraft carrier battlegroup presence in the Western Pacific and will explore options for homeporting an additional three to four surface combatants, and guided missile submarines (SSGNs), in that area.[108] A 2002 Congressional Budget Office (CBO) report discussed the option of homeporting a total of up to 11 SSNs at Guam.[109] Expanding the number of ships to be homeported in the Western Pacific could require construction of additional homeporting facilities, particularly in locations such as Guam. Transferring ships from the U.S. West Coast to the Western Pacific can also have implications for crew training and ship maintenance for those ships.

### Number of Aircraft Carriers

*Should the Navy maintain a force of 12 carriers, or a smaller number?* As part of its FY2006 budget submission, the Navy proposed accelerating the retirement of the aircraft carrier John F. Kennedy (CV-67) to FY2006 and reducing the size of the carrier force from 12 ships to 11. The issue is discussed at some length in another CRS report.[110] Advocates of maintaining a force of not less than 12 carriers could argue that, in light of China's naval modernization, including the introduction of new land-based fighters and strike fighters and the possibility that the PLA might, as part of a conflict in the Taiwan Strait area, use TBMs, LACMs, or special operations forces to attack U.S. land bases in the Western Pacific, a force of at least 12 carriers is needed to deter or prevail in such a conflict. Those supporting a reduction in the carrier force to 11 or fewer ships could argue that such a reduction is acceptable in light of the increasing capabilities of individual Navy carrier air wings, the Navy's plan to transfer an additional carrier to the Western Pacific, and options for improving the defenses of U.S. bases in the Western Pacific against attack from TBMs, LACMs, and special operations forces.

### Number of Attack Submarines (SSNs)

*Should the number of nuclear-powered attack submarines be about 40, about 55, or some other number?* The Navy at the end of FY2005 operated a total of 54 SSNs. The Navy's early-2005 plan for a fleet of 260 to 325 ships includes a total of 37 to 41 SSNs plus four converted Trident cruise missile submarines, or SSGNs. The number of SSNs that will be included in the new force structure plan that the Navy is expected to announce by early 2006 is not clear. Supporters of SSNs argue that the Navy needs to maintain a force of at least 55 boats, if not more. The issue of the SSN force-level goal is discussed at length in another CRS report.[111]

Supporters of SSNs have argued in recent months that China's naval modernization, and in particular China's submarine modernization, is a significant reason for supporting a force of 55 or more SSNs rather than a lower number such as 40. The argument was an element of the successful campaign in 2005 by supporters of the New London, CT, submarine base to convince the Base Realignment and Closure (BRAC) to reject DOD's recommendation to close the base.[112]

Although the discussion is sometimes cast in terms of U.S. SSNs fighting PLA Navy submarines, this captures only a part of how U.S. SSNs would fit into potential U.S. Navy operations against PLA forces. On the one hand, ASW is conducted by platforms other than SSNs, and an SSN is not always the best platform for countering an enemy submarine. On the other hand, SSNs perform a number of potentially significant missions other than ASW.

Supporters of maintaining a larger number of SSNs in light of China's naval modernization could argue that, in addition to participating in operations against PLA Navy submarines, U.S. SSNs could do the following:

- Conduct pre-crisis covert intelligence, surveillance, and reconnaissance (ISR) of PLA Navy forces and bases. Such operations could improve U.S. understanding PLA capabilities and weaknesses.
- Covertly lay mines around China's naval bases. In light of the PLA Navy's limited mine countermeasures capabilities, the presence of mines around PLA Navy bases could significantly delay the deployment of PLA Navy forces at the outset of a crisis or conflict.
- Attack or threaten PLA Navy surface ships. In light of the PLA Navy's limitations in ASW, a threat from U.S. SSNs could substantially complicate PLA military planning, particularly for an intended short-duration conflict.
- Fire Tomahawk cruise missiles from unexpected locations.
- Tomahawks could be used to attack on PLA command and control nodes, air bases, and TBM, LACM, ASCM, and SAM launch sites.

- Covertly insert and recover special operations forces (SOF). SOF can be used to attack PLA Navy bases or other PLA coastal facilities.

Supporters of maintaining a larger number of SSNs could also argue that submerged U.S. SSNs cannot be attacked by conventionally armed TBMs and ASCMs and are less vulnerable than are U.S. Navy surface ships to EMP effects and to certain other nuclear weapon effects.

Supporters of maintaining a smaller number of SSNs could argue that U.S. SSNs, though very capable in certain respects, are less capable in others. U.S. SSNs, they can argue, cannot shoot down enemy missiles or aircraft, nor can they act as platforms for operating manned aircraft. U.S. cruisers and destroyers, they could argue, carry substantial numbers of Tomahawks. In light of the complementary capabilities of Navy platforms and the need for an array of U.S. Navy capabilities in operations against PLA forces, they could argue, the need for SSNs needs to be balanced against the need for aircraft carriers and surface combatants.

### ASW-Capable Ships and Aircraft

*Will the Navy have enough ASW-capable ships and aircraft between now and 2010? Should recently deactivated ASW-capable ships and aircraft be returned to service?* The Navy in recent years has deactivated a substantial number of ASW-capable ships and aircraft, including Spruance (DD-963) class destroyers, Oliver Hazard Perry (FFG-7) class frigates, TAGOS-type ocean surveillance ships, carrier-based S-3 airplanes, and land-based P-3 maritime patrol aircraft. Since ASW traditionally has been a platform-intensive undertaking — meaning that a significant number of platforms (e.g., ships and aircraft) traditionally has been required to conduct an effective ASW operation against a small number of enemy submarines, or even a single submarine — some observers have expressed concern about the resulting decline in numbers of U.S. Navy ASW-capable platforms.[113]

As discussed earlier, the Navy plans to shift to a new, less platform-intensive ASW concept of operations. The Navy also plans to introduce new ASW-capable platforms in coming years, including a substantial number of Littoral Combat Ships (LCSs). Fully realizing the new ASW concept of operations, however, may take some time, particularly in light of the technical challenges involved, and LCSs will not be available in large numbers until after 2010. This raises a potential question of whether the Navy will have enough ASW-capable ships and aircraft between now and 2010, and whether the Navy should reactivate recently retired ASW-capable platforms and keep them in service until the new ASW concept is substantially implemented and larger numbers of LCSs and other new ASW-capable platforms join the fleet.

Advocates of this option could argue that the recent retirements of ASW-capable platforms occurred before the dimensions of the PLA Navy submarine modernization effort were fully understood. Opponents could argue that even with these recent retirements, the Navy retains a substantial number of such platforms, including SSNs, Aegis cruisers and destroyers, remaining Oliver Hazard Perry (FFG-7) class frigates, carrier- and surface combatant-based SH-60 helicopters, and remaining P-3s. They could also argue that there are more cost-effective ways to improve the Navy's ASW capabilities between now and 2010, such as increased ASW training and exercises (see discussion below).

## NAVY WARFARE AREAS AND PROGRAMS

## Missile Defense

### Replacement for NAD Program [114]

*Should the canceled Navy Area Defense (NAD) program be replaced with a new sea-based terminal missile defense program?*

In December 2001, DOD announced that it had canceled the Navy Area Defense (NAD) program, the program that was being pursued as the Sea-Based Terminal portion of the Administration's overall missile-defense effort. (The NAD program was also sometimes called the Navy Lower Tier program.) In announcing its decision, DOD cited poor performance, significant cost overruns, and substantial development delays.

The NAD system was to have been deployed on Navy Aegis cruisers and destroyers. It was designed to intercept short- and medium-range theater ballistic missiles in the final, or descent, phase of flight, so as to provide local-area defense of U.S. ships and friendly forces, ports, airfields, and other critical assets ashore. The program involved modifying both the Aegis ships' radar capabilities and the Standard SM-2 Block IV air-defense missile fired by Aegis ships. The missile, as modified, was called the Block IVA version. The system was designed to intercept descending missiles within the Earth's atmosphere (endoatmospheric intercept) and destroy them with the Block IVA missile's blast-fragmentation warhead.

Following cancellation of the program, DOD officials stated that the requirement for a sea-based terminal system remained intact. This led some observers to believe that a replacement for the NAD program might be initiated. In May 2002, however, DOD announced that instead of starting a replacement program, MDA had instead decided on a two-part strategy to (1) modify the Standard SM-3 missile — the missile to be used in the sea-based midcourse (i.e., Upper Tier) program — to intercept ballistic missiles at somewhat lower altitudes, and (2) modify the SM-2 Block four air defense missile (i.e., a missile designed to shoot down aircraft and cruise missiles) to cover some of the remaining portion of the sea-based terminal defense requirement. DOD officials said the two modified missiles could together provide much (but not all) of the capability that was to have been provided by the NAD program. One aim of the modification strategy, DOD officials suggested, was to avoid the added costs to the missile defense program of starting a replacement sea-based terminal defense program.

In October 2002, it was reported that

> Senior navy officials, however, continue to speak of the need for a sea-based terminal BMD capability "sooner rather than later" and have proposed a path to get there. "The cancellation of the Navy Area missile defence programme left a huge hole in our developing basket of missile-defence capabilities," said Adm. [Michael] Mullen. "Cancelling the programme didn't eliminate the warfighting requirement."
>
> "The nation, not just the navy, needs a sea-based area missile defence capability, not to protect our ships as much as to protect our forces ashore, airports and seaports of debarkation" and critical overseas infrastructure including protection of friends and allies.[115]

The above-quoted Admiral Mullen became the Chief of Naval Operations (CNO) on July 22, 2005.

In light of PLA TBM modernization efforts, including the possibility of TBMs equipped with MaRVs capable of hitting moving ships at sea, one issue is whether a new sea-based terminal-defense procurement program should be started to replace all (not just most) of the capability that was to have been provided by the NAD program, and perhaps even improve on the NAD's planned capability. In July 2004 it was reported that

> The Navy's senior leadership is rebuilding the case for a sea-based terminal missile defense requirement that would protect U.S. forces flowing through foreign ports and Navy ships from short-range missiles, according to Vice Adm. John Nathman, the Navy's top requirements advocate.
>
> The new requirement, Nathman said, would fill the gap left when the Pentagon terminated the Navy Area missile defense program in December 2001. ... However, he emphasized the Navy is not looking to reinstate the old [NAD] system. "That's exactly what we are not talking about," he said March 24....
>
> The need to bring back a terminal missile defense program was made clear after reviewing the "analytic case" for the requirement, he said. Though Nathman could only talk in general terms about the analysis, due to its classified nature, he said its primary focus was "pacing the threat" issues. Such issues involve threats that are not a concern today, but could be in the future, he said. Part of the purpose of the study was to look at the potential time line for those threats and the regions where they could emerge.[116]

Reported options for a NAD-replacement program include a system using a modified version of the Army's Patriot Advanced Capability-3 (PAC-3) interceptor or a system using a modified version of the Navy's new Standard Missile 6 Extended Range Active Missile (SM-6 ERAM) air defense missile.[117]

### Aegis Radar Upgrades

*Should the radar capabilities of the Navy's Aegis cruisers and destroyers be upgraded more quickly or extensively than now planned?*

Current plans for upgrading the radar capabilities of the Navy's Aegis cruisers and destroyers include the Aegis ballistic missile defense signal processor (BSP), which forms part of the planned Block 06 version of the Navy's Aegis ballistic missile defense capability. Installing the Aegis BSP improves the ballistic missile target-discrimination performance of the Aegis ship's SPY-1 phased array radar.

In light of PLA TBM modernization efforts, including the possibility of TBMs equipped with MaRVs capable of hitting moving ships at sea, one issue is whether current plans for developing and installing the Aegis BSP are adequate, and whether those plans are sufficiently funded. A second issue is whether there are other opportunities for improving the radar capabilities of the Navy's Aegis cruisers and destroyers that are not currently being pursued or are funded at limited levels, and if so, whether funding for these efforts should be increased.

### Ships with DD(X)/CG(X) Radar Capabilities

*Should planned annual procurement rates for ships with DD(X)/CG(X) radar capabilities be increased?*

The Navy plans to procure a new kind of destroyer called the DD(X) and a new kind of cruiser called the CG(X). The Navy plans to begin DD(X) procurement in FY2007, and

CG(X) procurement in FY2011. The Navy had earlier planned to begin CG(X) procurement in FY2018, but accelerated the planned start of procurement to FY2011 as part of its FY2006-FY2011 Future Years Defense Plan (FYDP). DD(X)s and CG(X)s would take about five years to build, so the first DD(X), if procured in FY2007, might enter service in 2012, and the first CG(X), if procured in FY2011, might enter service in 2016.

The Navy states that the DD(X)'s radar capabilities will be greater in certain respects than those of Navy Aegis ships. The radar capabilities of the CG(X) are to be greater still, and the CG(X) has been justified primarily in connection with future air and missile defense operations.

Estimated DD(X)/CG(X) procurement costs increased substantially between 2004 and 2005. Apparently as a consequence of these increased costs, the FY2006-FY2011 FYDP submitted to Congress in early 2005 reduced planned DD(X) procurement to one ship per year. The reduction in the planned DD(X) procurement rate suggests that, unless budget conditions change, the combined DD(X)/CG(X) procurement rate might remain at one ship per year beyond FY2011.[118]

If improvements to Aegis radar capabilities are not sufficient to achieve the Navy's desired radar capability for countering modernized PLA TBMs, then DD(X)/CG(X) radar capabilities could become important to achieving this desired capability. If so, then a potential additional issue raised by PLA TBM modernization efforts is whether a combined DD(X)/CG(X) procurement rate of one ship per year would be sufficient to achieve this desired capability in a timely manner. If the Navy in the future maintains a total of 11 or 12 carrier strike groups (CSGs), and if DD(X)/CG(X) procurement proceeds at a rate of one ship per year, the Navy would not have 11 or 12 DD(X)s and CG(X)s — one DD(X) or CG(X) for each of 11 or 12 CSGs — until 2022 or 2023. If CG(X)s are considered preferable to DD(X)s for missile defense operations, then the earliest the Navy could have 11 or 12 CG(X)s would be 2026 or 2027.

DD(X)/CG(X) radar technologies could be introduced into the fleet more quickly by procuring DD(X)s and CG(X)s at a higher rate, such as two ships per year, which is the rate the Navy envisaged in a report the Navy provided to Congress in 2003. A DD(X)/CG(X) procurement rate of two ships per year, however, could make it more difficult for the Navy to procure other kinds of ships or meet other funding needs, particularly in light of the recent growth in estimated DD(X)/CG(X) procurement costs.

A potential alternative strategy would be to design a reduced-cost alternative to the DD(X)/CG(X) that preserves DD(X)/CG(X) radar capabilities while reducing other DD(X)/CG(X) payload elements. Such a ship could more easily be procured at a rate of two ships per year within available resources. The option of a reduced-cost alternative to the DD(X)/CG(X) that preserves certain DD(X)/CG(X) capabilities while reducing others is discussed in more detail in another CRS report.[119]

### Block II/Block IIA Version of SM-3 Interceptor

*If feasible, should the effort to develop the Block II/Block IIA version of the Standard Missile 3 (SM-3) interceptor missile be accelerated?*

The Navy plans to use the Standard Missile 3 (SM-3) interceptor for intercepting TBMs during the midcourse portion of their flight. As part of the Aegis ballistic missile defense block upgrade strategy, the United States and Japan are cooperating in developing technologies for a more-capable version of the SM-3 missile called the SM-3 Block II/Block

IIA. In contrast to the current version of the SM-3, which has a 21-inch-diameter booster stage but is 13.5 inches in diameter along the remainder of its length, the Block II/Block IIA version would have a 21-inch diameter along its entire length. The increase in diameter to a uniform 21 inches would give the missile a burnout velocity (a maximum velocity, reached at the time the propulsion stack burns out) that is 45% to 60% greater than that of the current 13.5-inch version of the SM-3.[120] The Block IIA version would also include a improved kinetic warhead.[121] The Missile Defense Agency (MDA) states that the Block II/Block IIA version of the missile could "engage many [ballistic missile] targets that would outpace, fly over, or be beyond the engagement range" of earlier versions of the SM-3, and that

> the net result, when coupled with enhanced discrimination capability, is more types and ranges of engageable [ballistic missile] targets; with greater probability of kill, and a large increase in defenses "footprint" or geography predicted.... The SM-3 Blk II/IIA missile with it[s] full 21-inch propulsion stack provides the necessary fly out acceleration to engage IRBM and certain ICBM threats.[122]

Regarding the status of the program, MDA states that "The Block II/IIA development plan is undergoing refinement. MDA plans to proceed with the development of the SM-3 Blk II/IIA missile variant if an agreeable cost share with Japan can be reached.... [The currently envisaged development plan] may have to be tempered by budget realities for the agency."[123]

In March 2005, the estimated total development cost for the Block II/Block IIA missile was reportedly $1.4 billion.[124] In September 2005, it was reported that this estimate had more than doubled, to about $3 billion.[125] MDA had estimated that the missile could enter service in 2013 or 2014,[126] but this date reportedly has now slipped to 2015.[127]

In light of PLA TBM modernization efforts, a potential question is whether, if feasible, the effort to develop the Block II/Block IIA missile should be accelerated, and if so, whether this should be done even if this requires the United States to assume a greater share of the development cost. A key factor in this issue could be assessments of potential PLA deployments of longer-ranged PLA TBMs.

### Kinetic Energy Interceptor (KEI)

*Should funding for development of the Kinetic Energy Interceptor (KEI) be increased?*

The Kinetic Energy Interceptor (KEI) is a proposed new ballistic missile interceptor that, if developed, would be used as a ground-based interceptor and perhaps subsequently as a sea-based interceptor. Compared to the SM-3, the KEI would be much larger (perhaps 40 inches in diameter and 36 feet in length) and would have a much higher burnout velocity. Basing the KEI on a ship would require the ship to have missile-launch tubes that are bigger than those currently installed on Navy cruisers, destroyers, and attack submarines. The Missile Defense Agency (MDA), which has been studying possibilities for basing the KEI at sea, plans to select a preferred platform in May 2006.[128] Because of its much higher burnout velocity, the KEI could be used to intercept longer-ranged ballistic missiles, including intercontinental ballistic missiles (ICBMs) during the boost and early ascent phases of their flights. Development funding for the KEI has been reduced in recent budgets, slowing the missile's development schedule. Under current plans, the missile could become available for Navy use in 2014-2015.[129]

Although the KEI is often discussed in connection with intercepting ICBMs, it might also be of value as a missile for intercepting TBMs, particularly longer-range TBMs, which are called Intermediate-Range Ballistic Missiles (IRBMs). If so, then in the context of this report, one potential question is whether the Navy should use the KEI as a complement to the SM-3 for countering PLA TBMs, and if so, whether development funding for the KEI should be increased so as to make the missile available for Navy use before 2014-2015.

### Ships with Missile-Launch Tubes

*Should the planned number of Navy missile-launch tubes be increased, and if so, how might this be done?*

Missile-launch tubes on U.S. Navy surface combatants, which are installed in batteries called vertical launch systems (VLSs), are used for storing and firing various weapons, including Tomahawk cruise missiles, antisubmarine rockets, air defense missiles, and SM-3 ballistic missile defense interceptors. The potential need to counter hundreds of PLA TBMs raises a potential question of whether U.S. Navy forces involved in a conflict in the Taiwan Strait area would have enough missile launch tubes to store and fire required numbers of SM-3s while also meeting needs for storing adequate numbers of other types of weapons.

Options for increasing the planned number of missile-launch tubes in the fleet include reactivating VLS-equipped Spruance (DD-963) class destroyers (61 tubes per ship), building additional Arleigh Burke (DDG-51) class Aegis destroyers (96 tubes per ship), building additional DD(X)s (80 tubes per ship), building additional CG(X)s (more than 80 tubes per ship), or designing and procuring a new and perhaps low-cost missile-tube ship of some kind. Options for a new-design ship include, among other things,

- a large ship equipped with hundreds of missile-launch tubes,[130]
- an intermediate size ship with several dozen tubes,
- a small and possibly fast ship equipped with a few dozen tubes, and
- a submarine equipped with perhaps several dozen tubes.

## Air Warfare

### Mix of F/A-18E/Fs and F-35 Joint Strike Fighters (JSFs)

*Should the Navy's planned mix of carrier-based F/A-18E/F strike fighters and F-35 Joint Strike Fighters (JSFs) be changed to include more JSFs and fewer F/A-18E/Fs?*

The Department of the Navy, which includes the Navy and the Marine Corps, currently plans to procure a total of 462 F/A-18E/F Super Hornet strike fighters and a total of 680 F-35 Joint Strike Fighters (JSFs). The F/A-18E/Fs would be operated by the Navy, and the JSFs would be operated by both services. The division of JSFs between the Navy and Marine Corps is under review, but earlier plans showed the Navy procuring a total of about 300 JSFs. Marine Corps JSFs could be operated from Navy carriers to perform Navy missions. The F/A-18E/F incorporates a few stealth features and is believed to be very capable in air-to-air combat. Compared to the F/A-18E/F, the JSF is much more stealthy and is believed to be more capable in air-to-air combat.

The growing number of fourth-generation fighters and strike-fighters in the PLA Air Force and the PLA Naval Air Force, and the growing number of modern PLA SAM systems, raises a potential question of whether the Navy should change its planned mix of carrier-based strike fighters to include more Navy JSFs and fewer F/A-18E/Fs. Such a change would produce a force with a better ability to avoid PLA SAM systems and more total air-to-air combat capability than the currently planned force.

The Department of the Navy's planned mix of F/A-18E/Fs and JSFs can be compared to the Air Force's strike fighter procurement plans. The Air Force plans to replace its current force of F-15 and F-16 fighters with a mix of 179 F/A-22 Raptor strike fighters and 1,763 JSFs. The F-22 is more stealthy and capable in air-to-air combat than the JSF. The Navy does not have an equivalent to the F-22. The Air Force argues that a mix of F/A-22s and JSFs will be needed in the future in part to counter fourth-generation fighters and strike fighters operated by other countries, including China. Supporters of the F/A-22 argue that the challenge posed by fourth-generation fighters in combination with modern integrated air defenses, is a key reason for procuring 381 or more F/A-22s, rather than 179.[131 ] Potential oversight questions include the following:

- If the Air Force is correct in its belief that a combination of F/A-22s and JSFs will be needed in part to counter fourth-generation fighters and modern SAM systems operated by other countries, including China, would the Department of the Navy's planned mix of JSFs and F/A-18E/Fs be sufficient to counter a PLA force of fighters and strike fighters that includes fourth-generation designs?
- If PLA attacks on U.S. air bases in the Western Pacific reduce the number of Air Force F/A-22s and JSFs that can participate in a conflict in the Taiwan Strait area, would the Department of the Navy's planned mix of F/A-18E/Fs and JSFs have sufficient air-to-air combat capability to counter the PLA's force of fighters and strike fighters?

## *Long-Range Air-to-Air Missile (Phoenix Successor)*

*Should the Navy acquire a long-range air-to-air missile analogous to the now-retired Phoenix missile?*

During the Cold War, when the U.S. Navy prepared to confront a Soviet sea-denial force that included land-based aircraft armed with long-range ASCMs, Navy carrier air wings included F-14 Tomcat fighters armed with Phoenix long-range (60 nautical miles to 110 nautical miles) air-to-air missiles. A key purpose of the F-14/Phoenix combination was to enable the Navy to shoot down approaching Soviet land-based aircraft flying toward U.S. Navy forces before they got close enough to launch their multiple long-range ASCMs. The strategy of shooting down the aircraft before they could launch their ASCMs was viewed as preferable because the aircraft were larger and less numerous than the ASCMs. This strategy of "shooting the archer rather than its arrows" formed part of a long-range air-to-air combat effort that was referred to as the Outer Air Battle.

Following the end of the Cold War 1989-1991, the need for waging an Outer Air Battle receded. Procurement of new Phoenixes ended in FY1990, and a planned successor to the Phoenix called the Advanced Air-To-Air Missile (AAAM) was canceled. The Phoenix was removed from service at the end of FY2004, and the F-14 is currently being phased out of service, with the last aircraft scheduled to be removed by mid-FY2007. Without the Phoenix, Navy strike fighters, like Air Force strike fighters, rely on a combination of medium- and short-range air-to-air missiles with ranges of roughly 10 nautical miles to 40 nautical miles.

In light of a potential need to counter PLA land-based strike fighters and maritime bombers protected by long-range SAMs, one question is whether a new program for acquiring a successor to the Phoenix should be initiated. The Air Force during the Cold War did not operate the Phoenix because it did not face a scenario equivalent to the Navy's scenario of shooting down a Soviet aircraft armed with multiple long-range ASCMs. In a conflict in the Taiwan Strait, however, the United States might benefit from having both Navy and Air Force strike fighters equipped with a long-range air-to-air missile for shooting down PLA strike fighters and maritime bombers equipped with ASCMs. If so, then the cost of developing a new long-range air-to-air missile could be amortized over a combined Navy-Air Force purchase of the missile.

## Anti-Air Warfare (AAW)

### Surface Ship AAW Upgrades

*Are current Navy plans for upgrading surface ship anti-air warfare (AAW) capabilities adequate?*

The PLA's acquisition of advanced and highly capable ASCMs such as the SS-N-27 Sizzler and the SS-N-22 Sunburn raises the question of whether current plans for modernizing Navy surface ship AAW capabilities are adequate. The Government Accountability Office (GAO) in previous years has expressed concerns regarding the Navy's ability to counter ASCMs.[132] Potential areas for modernization include, among other things, the following:

- ship radars, such as the SPY-1 radar on Aegis ships or the radars now planned for the DD(X) destroyer and CG(X) cruiser;
- AAW-related computer networking capabilities, such as the Cooperative Engagement Capability (CEC);[133]
- air defense missiles such as the Standard Missile,[134] the Evolved Sea Sparrow Missile (ESSM), and the Rolling Airframe Missile (RAM);
- close-in weapon systems, such as the Phalanx radar-directed gun;
- potential directed-energy weapons, such as solid state or free-electron lasers;
- decoys, such as the U.S-Australian Nulka active electronic decoy; and
- aerial targets for AAW tests and exercises, particularly targets for emulating supersonic ASCMs.[135]

### Littoral Combat Ship (LCS) AAW Capability

*Should the currently planned AAW capability of the Littoral Combat Ship (LCS) be increased?*

The Navy's planned Littoral Combat Ship (LCS) is to be armed with a 21-round Rolling Airframe Missile (RAM) launcher. The ship will also be equipped with an AAW decoy launcher.[136]

The PLA's acquisition of ASCMs that can be fired from aircraft, surface ships, and submarines raises the possibility that LCSs participating in a conflict in the Taiwan Strait area could come under attack by substantial numbers of ASCMs. Other Navy ships, such as Aegis cruisers and destroyers and, in the future, DD(X) destroyers and CG(X)s cruisers, could help defend LCSs against attacking ASCMs, but such ships might not always be in the best position to do this, particularly if ASCMs are launched at LCSs from undetected submarines or if the supporting U.S. Navy ships were busy performing other duties. If LCSs were damaged or sunk by ASCMs, the Navy's ability to counter enemy mines, submarines, and small boats —the LCS's three primary missions — would be reduced.

The possibility that the LCS's AAW system might be overwhelmed or exhausted by attacks from multiple ASCMs raises the question of whether the AAW capability planned for the LCS should be increased. Options for increasing the LCS's planned AAW capability include, among other things, adding another 21-round RAM launcher or supplementing the currently planned RAM launcher with a battery of Evolved Sea Sparrow (ESSM) missiles. In assessing such options, one factor to consider would be whether installing additional RAMs or ESSMs would require an increase in the planned size and cost of the LCS.

## Antisubmarine Warfare (ASW)

*Technologies*

*Are current Navy efforts for improving antisubmarine warfare (ASW) technologies adequate?*

In addition to the issue discussed earlier of whether the Navy between now and 2010 will have enough ASW-capable platforms, another potential issue raised by the PLA submarine modernization effort is whether current Navy plans for improving antisubmarine warfare (ASW) technologies are adequate. The Navy states that it intends to introduce several new ASW technologies, including distributed sensors, unmanned vehicles, and technologies for networking ASW systems and platforms.[137] Admiral Michael Mullen, who became the Chief of Naval Operations (CNO) on July 22, 2005, has issued a guidance statement for the Navy for 2006 which says that Navy tasks for FY2006 will include, among other things, "Rapidly prototyp[ing] ASW technologies that will: hold at risk adversary submarines; substantially degrade adversary weapons effectiveness; and, compress the ASW detect-to-engage sequences. Sensor development is key."[138]

### *Training and Exercises*

*Are current Navy plans for ASW training and exercises adequate?*

As mentioned earlier, success in an ASW operation is highly dependent on the proficiency of the people operating the ASW equipment, and ASW operational proficiency can take time to develop and can atrophy significantly if not regularly exercised. At various times since the end of the Cold War, some observers have expressed concerns about whether the Navy was placing adequate emphasis on maintaining ASW proficiency. The Navy in April 2004 established a new Fleet ASW Command, based in San Diego, to provide more focus to its ASW efforts, and since then has taken steps to enhance its ASW training and exercises:

- In April 2004, it was reported that carrier strike groups deploying from the U.S. West Coast would now stop in Hawaiian waters for three- to five-day ASW exercises before proceeding to the Western Pacific.[139]
- In March 2005, the Navy reached an agreement to lease a Swedish non-nuclear-powered submarine and its crew for a 12-month period. The submarine, which is equipped with an air-independent propulsion (AIP) system, arrived in San Diego in June 2005, where it is being used to as a mock enemy submarine in Pacific Fleet ASW exercises.[140]
- The Navy in 2005 also reached an agreement with Colombia and Peru under which one non-nuclear-powered submarine from each country deployed to the Navy base at Mayport, FL, in April 2005 to support Atlantic Fleet ASW exercises for a period of two to five months. South American non-nuclear-powered submarines have been integrated into U.S. Navy exercises since 2002.[141]
- In October 2005, the commander of the Navy's Pacific Fleet said that, upon assuming command earlier in the year, he made ASW his highest priority and instituted a cyclic approach to ASW training that includes more frequent (quarterly) assessments, as well as training exercises with other navies.[142]

In light of these actions, the potential question is whether the Navy ASW training and exercises are now adequate, or whether they should be expanded further.

### Active-Kill Torpedo Defense

*If feasible, should Navy plans for acquiring an active-kill torpedo defense system be accelerated?*

Navy surface ships and submarines are equipped with decoy systems for diverting enemy torpedoes away from their intended targets. Such decoys, however, might not always work, particularly against wake-homing torpedoes, which can be difficult to decoy. Under the Navy's surface ship torpedo defense (SSTD) development program, the U.S. Navy is developing an "active-kill" torpedo-defense capability for surface ships and also submarines that would use a small (6.75-inch diameter) anti-torpedo torpedo (ATT) to physically destroy incoming torpedoes. Current Navy plans call for the ATT to enter low-rate initial procurement (LRIP) in FY2009 and achieve initial operational capability on surface ships in FY2011.[143] In light of the modern torpedoes, including wake-homing torpedoes, that are expected to be carried by modern PLA submarines, a potential question is whether, if feasible, the current ATT acquisition schedule should be accelerated. Hitting an approaching torpedo with another torpedo poses technical challenges which could affect the potential for accelerating the ATT development schedule.

## Mine Warfare

*Are current Navy mine warfare plans adequate?*

The PLA's interest in modern mines may underscore the importance of the Navy's efforts to develop and acquire new mine countermeasures (MCM) systems, and perhaps raise a question regarding whether they should be expanded or accelerated. The Navy's MCM capabilities have been a matter of concern among members of the congressional defense committees for several years.

Conversely, the PLA Navy's own reported vulnerability to mines (see section on PLA Navy limitations and weaknesses) can raise a question regarding the less-frequently-discussed topic of the U.S. Navy's offensive mine warfare capability. To what degree can minelaying complicate PLA plans for winning a conflict, particularly a short-duration conflict, in the Taiwan Strait area? Do U.S. Navy plans include sufficient mines and minelaying platforms to fully exploit the PLA Navy's vulnerability to mines? The Navy has various mines either in service or under development,[144] and is exploring the option of starting development of an additional new mine called the 2010 Mine.[145]

## Computer Network Security

*Are Navy efforts to ensure computer network security adequate?*

The PLA's published interest in IW/IO, and concerns that recent attacks on U.S. computer networks have in some cases originated in China, underscore the importance of U.S. military computer network security. The Navy in July 2002 established the Naval Network Warfare Command in part to prevent and respond to attacks on Navy computer networks.[146] Another CRS report discusses computer network security at length.[147]

## EMP Hardening

*Are Navy efforts to harden its systems against electromagnetic pulse (EMP) adequate?*

The possibility that the PLA might use nuclear weapons or high-power microwave (HPM) weapons to generate electromagnetic pulse (EMP) effects against the electronic systems on U.S. Navy ships and aircraft raises a potential question regarding the adequacy of the Navy's efforts to harden its systems against EMP effects. A 2004 commission studying the EMP issue expressed concerns about the potential vulnerability of U.S. tactical forces to EMP.[148]

The commission's report was received at a July 22, 2004, hearing before the House Armed Services Committee. At the hearing, Representative Steve Israel asked about the role of EMP in exercises simulating operations in the Taiwan Strait:

> **Representative Steve Israel:** [Representative Roscoe] Bartlett and I just attended an NDU [National Defense University] tabletop [exercise] with respect to the Straits of the Taiwan just last week. To your knowledge, has there been any tabletop exercise, has there been any simulation, any war-game that anticipates an EMP attack, and, if there has not been, do you believe that that would, in fact, be a useful exercise for NDU, the Pentagon or any other relevant entity? Dr. Graham, do you want to answer that?
> **Dr. William R. Graham (Commission Chairman):** Thank you. Let me poll the commission and see if they have any experience with that. General Lawson?
> General Richard L. Lawson, USAF (Ret.) (Commissioner): No, sir.
> **Graham:** Dr. Wood?
> **Dr. Lowell L. Wood, Jr. (Commissioner):** I don't believe there's been any formal exercise, certainly not to my knowledge. There's been extensive discussion of what the impact

of Chinese EMP laydowns would be, not on Taiwan, which is, after all, considered by China to be part of its own territory, but on U.S. forces in the region which might be involved in the active defense of Taiwan. In particular, the consequences the EMP laydown on U.S. carrier task forces has been explored, and while, it's not appropriate to discuss the details in an open session like this, the assessed consequences of such an attack, a single-explosion attack, are very somber.

Since that is a circumstance in which the target might be considered a pure military one in which the loss of life might be relatively small, but the loss of military capability might be absolutely staggering, it poses a very attractive option, at least for consideration on the part of the Chinese military.

I would also remark that Chinese nuclear explosive workers at their very cloistered research center in northwestern China very recently published an authoritative digest and technical commentary on EMP in English, in a Chinese publication. It is very difficult to understand what the purpose of publishing a lengthy, authoritative article in English in a Chinese publication would be, if it was not to convey a very pointed message. This came not from military workers. It came from the people who would be fielding the weapon that would conduct the attack.

**Graham:** Dr. Pry on our staff has made a survey of foreign writings on EMP, and he noted that while U.S. exercises have not to our knowledge played that scenario, Chinese military writings have discussed that scenario. So it's certainly something they have thought of and it is within their mind. I have observed generally over the last 40 years that there's a tendency in the U.S. military not to introduce nuclear weapons in general and EMP in particular into exercise scenarios or game scenarios because it tends to end the game, and that's not a good sign. I think it would be a very interesting subject for the NDU group to take up and see and force them not to end the game. Time will not stop if such an event happens. Let them understand what the consequences will be.[149]

Later in the hearing, Representative Roscoe Bartlett returned to the topic of the potential effects of EMP on Navy ships:

**Representative Bartlett:** If China were to detonate a weapon high over our carrier task force, can we note in this [open] session what would the effects on the carrier task force be?

**Graham:** Mr. Bartlett, several years ago, the Navy dismantled the one simulator it had for exposing ships directly [to EMP]. It was the Empress simulator located in the Chesapeake Bay. So I don't believe any direct experimental work has been done for quite some time.

However, the general character of modern naval forces follows the other trends we've described, which is an increasing dependence upon sophisticated electronics for its functionality, and, therefore, I believe there's substantial reason to be concerned.

[Would] Any other commissioners [care to comment]?

Representative Bartlett: Dr. Wood?

**Wood:** In open session, sir, I don't believe it's appropriate to go much further than the comment that I made to [Representative] Israel that the assessments that are made of such attacks and their impacts are very somber.

The Navy generally believes — that portion of the Navy that's at all cognizant of these matters — that because they operate in an extremely radar-intensive environment, [since] they have a great deal of electromagnetic gear on board, some of which radiates pulses — radar pulses, for instance — because they can operate in that type of environment, that they surely must be EMP robust. These free-floating beliefs on the part of some Navy officers are not — repeat not — well grounded technically.[150]

# APPENDIX A: ADDITIONAL DETAILS ON CHINA'S NAVAL MODERNIZATION EFFORTS [151]

This appendix presents additional details and commentary on several of the elements of China's military modernization discussed in the Background section of this report.

## Theater-Range Ballistic Missiles (TBMs)

Regarding the potential for using TBMs against moving U.S. Navy ships at sea, DOD states that "China is exploring the use of ballistic missiles for anti-access/sea-denial missions."[152] ONI states that "One of the newest innovations in TBM weapons developments involves the use of ballistic missiles to target ships at sea. This is assessed as being very difficult because it involves much more than just a missile."[153] ONI continues:

> The use of ballistic missiles against ships at sea has been discussed for years. Chinese writings state China intends to develop the capability to attack ships, including carrier strike groups, in the waters around Taiwan using conventional theater ballistic missiles (TBMs) as part of a combined-arms campaign. The current conventional TBM force in China consists of CSS-6 and CSS-7 short-range ballistic missiles (SRBMs) deployed in large numbers. The current TBM force would be modified by changing some of the current missiles' ballistic reentry vehicles (RVs) to maneuvering reentry vehicles (MaRVs) with radar or IR seekers to provide the accuracy needed to attack ships at sea. The TBMs with MaRVs would have good defense penetration capabilities because of their high reentry speed and maneuverability. Their lethality could be increased, especially with terminally guided submunitions.

In order to attack a ship or a carrier battle group with TBMs, the target must be tracked, and its position, direction, and speed determined. This information would be relayed in near real time to the missile launchers. China may be planning ultimately to use over-the-horizon (OTH) radar, satellites, and unmanned aerial vehicles (UAVs) to monitor the target's position. Reconnaissance assets would be used to detect the ship or carrier strike group before it entered into the range of Chinese TBMs, facilitating early preparation for the engagement, and refining the target's position. Target information would be relayed through communication satellites or other channels to a command center, and then to the missile launchers. TBMs with MaRVs would then be launched at the target's projected position. The missiles would fly their preplanned trajectories until onboard seekers could acquire the ship and guide the missiles to impact.[154]

Another observer states:

> The PLA's historic penchant for secrecy and surprise, when combined with known programs to develop highly advanced technologies that will lead to new and advanced weapons, leads to the conclusion that the PLA is seeking [to] field new weapon systems that could shock an adversary and accelerate their defeat. In the mid-1990s former leader Jiang Zemin re-popularized an ancient Chinese term for such weapons, "Shashaojian," translated most frequently as "Assassin's Mace," or "silver bullet" weapons.
>
> One potential Shashoujian is identified by the [DOD's 2005 report on China military power]: a maneuvering ballistic missile design to target U.S. naval forces. In 1996 a Chinese

technician revealed that a "terminal guidance system" that would confer very high accuracy was being developed for the DF-21 [intercontinental ballistic missile, or ICBM]. Such a system could employ a radar similar to the defunct U.S. Pershing-2 MRBM or could employ off-board sensors with rapid data-links to the missile tied to satellite-navigation systems. Nevertheless, should such missiles be realized they will pose a considerable threat as the U.S. Navy is not yet ready to deploy adequate missile defenses.[155]

A separate observer states:

Land-based conventional tipped ballistic missiles with maneuverable (MarV) warheads that can hit ships at sea.... would be a Chinese "assassin's mace" sort of capability — something impossible to deal with today, and very difficult under any circumstances if one is forced to defend by shooting down ballistic missiles. The capability is dependent on Beijing's ability to put together the appropriate space-based surveillance, command, and targeting architecture necessary to make this work.[156]

One more observer states:

There is yet another exceedingly important chapter being written in the [PLA] ballistic-missile saga. China is trying to move rapidly in developing ballistic missiles that could hit ships at sea at MRBM [medium-range ballistic missile] ranges — in other words, to threaten carriers beyond the range at which they could engage Chinese forces or strike China. Among its other advantages for China, this method of attack avoids altogether the daunting prospect of having to cope with the U.S. Navy submarine force — as anti-submarine warfare is a big Chinese weakness. Along with these efforts to develop ballistic missiles to hit ships, they are, of course, working diligently to perfect the means to locate and target our carrier strike groups (CSGs). In that regard, an imperfect or rudimentary (fishing boats with satellite phones) means of location and targeting might be employed even earlier than the delay of several more years likely needed to perfect more reliable and consistent targeting of ships. Chinese missile specialists are writing openly and convincingly of MaRV'd ballistic missiles (missiles with maneuverable reentry vehicles) that maneuver both to defeat defenses and to follow the commands of seekers that spot the target ships. There seems little doubt that our naval forces will face this threat long before the Taiwan issue is resolved.[157]

## Land-Attack Cruise Missile (LACMs)

Regarding LACMs, DOD states:

China is developing LACMs to achieve greater precision than historically available from ballistic missiles for hard target strikes, and increased standoff. A first- and second-generation LACM remain under development. There are no technological bars to placing on these systems a nuclear payload, once developed.[158]

ONI states:

Land-attack cruise missiles (LACMs) are available for sale from many countries, and are marketed at arms shows around the world. Land-attack cruise missiles are becoming a significant adjunct to theater ballistic missiles in strike and deterrent roles. The number of countries manufacturing and purchasing LACMs continues to grow. Some of the systems in development are derivatives of antiship missiles, and some are dedicated designs, and a few weaponized UAVs [unmanned aerial vehicles] complete the inventory....

Israel, China, Germany, and South Africa are among he countries with LACM development programs.[159]

Another observer states:

> Since the 1970s the PLA has placed a high priority on developing an indigenous strategic land attack cruise missile (LACM). This effort has been aided by the PLA's success in obtaining advanced cruise missile technology from Russia, Israel, the Ukraine and the United States. In early June an Internet-source photo appeared of anew Chinese cruise missile with unmistakable LACM characteristics. This would tend to support revelation from Taiwan earlier this year that by 2006 the PLA will deploy 200 new land-based LACMs. With their very high accuracy such cruise missiles allow strategic targets to be destroyed with non-nuclear warheads.[160]

## Anti-Ship Cruise Missiles (ASCMs)

Regarding ASCMs, DOD states:

> The PLA Navy and Naval Air Force have or are acquiring nearly a dozen varieties of ASCMs, from the 1950s-era CSS-N-2/STYX to the modern Russian-made SS-N-22/SUNBURN and SS-N-27/SIZZLER. The pace of indigenous ASCM research, development, and production — and of foreign procurement — has accelerated over the past decade. Objectives for current and future ASCMs include improving closure speed (e.g., ramjet propulsion, such as with the SS-N-22), standoff distance (e.g., longer-range assets, such as the C-802), and stealthier launch platforms (e.g., submarines). SS-N-22 missiles may be fitted on smaller platforms in the future (e.g., the Russian Molniya patrol boat, which originated as a joint effort with China, or on the new stealth fast attack patrol boat).[161]

Regarding the SS-N-27s expected to be carried by the eight additional Kilo-class submarines China has ordered, ONI states:

> Russia continues to develop supersonic ASCMs. The most interesting is the 3M-54E design which has a cruise vehicle that ejects a rocket-propelled terminal sprint vehicle approximately 10 nautical miles from its target. The sprint vehicle accelerates to speeds as high as Mach 3 and has the potential to perform very high-g defensive maneuvers.[162]

Another observer states that "the very dangerous and lethal SS-N-27Bs [are] said by experts to be part of the best family of ASCMs in the world...."[163]

## Land-Based Surface-to-Air Missiles (SAMs)

Regarding SAM systems, DOD states:

In August 2004, China received the final shipment from Russia of four S-300PMU-1/SA-20 surface-to-air missile (SAM) battalions. China has also agreed to purchase follow-on S-300PMU-2, the first battalion of which is expected to arrive in 2006. With an advertised intercept range of 200 km, the S-300PMU-2 provides increased lethality against tactical ballistic missiles and more effective electronic counter-counter measures.[164]

Another observer states that "before 2010," China could deploy more than 300 S-300 SAM systems to locations covering the Taiwan Strait.[165]

## Land-Based Aircraft

Regarding land-based aircraft, DOD states:

China has more than 700 aircraft within un-refueled operational range of Taiwan. Many of these are obsolescent or upgrades of older-generation aircraft. However, China's air forces continue to acquire advanced fighter aircraft from Russia, including the Su-30MKK multirole and Su-30MK2 maritime strike aircraft. New acquisitions augment previous deliveries of Su-27 fighter aircraft. China is also producing its own version of the Su-27SK, the F-11, under a licensed co-production agreement with Moscow. Last year, Beijing sought to renegotiate its agreement and produce the multirole Su-27SMK for the remainder of the production run. These later generations of aircraft make up a growing percentage of the PLA Air Force inventory.

China's indigenous 4th generation fighter, the F-10, completed development in 2004 and will begin fielding this year. Improvements to the FB-7 fighter program will enable this older aircraft to perform nighttime maritime strike operations. China has several programs underway to deploy new standoff escort jammers on bombers, transports, tactical aircraft, and unmanned aerial vehicle platforms.[166]

ONI states:

China operates a force of 1950s vintage B-6D Badger dedicated naval strike bombers. Today, these aircraft are armed with the C601, an air-launched derivative of the Styx ASCM, but a program to arm them with the modern C802K is underway....

China and Russia also are working on new tactical aircraft dedicated to the antiship mission. China's FB-7 Flounder has been in development since the 1970s; its production limited by engine difficulties. The C801K-armed FB-7 entered service with the Chinese Navy, and integration of the longer-range C802K on the FB-7 is underway.[167]

Another observer states that "By 2006, in my estimation, the PLA will have 400 Sukhoi [i.e., Su-27 and Su-30] fighters and fighter-bombers."[168]

## Submarines

The paragraphs below discuss China's submarine modernization effort in more detail on a class-by-class basis.

## Type 094 SSBN

China is building a new class of SSBN known as the Type 094 class. The first two Type 094 boats are expected to enter service in 2008 and 2010. The Type 094 design may be derived from the Shang-class (Type 093) SSN design discussed below. ONI states that China "wishes to develop a credible, survivable, sea-based deterrent with the capability to reach the United States" and that the Type 094 design "benefits from substantial Russian technical assistance."[169]

The Type 094 SSBN is expected to be armed with 12 CSS-NX-5 nuclear-armed submarine-launched ballistic missiles, also known as JL-2s. Observers believe these missiles will have a range of about 8,000 kilometers to 12,000 kilometers (about 4,320 nautical miles to 6,480 nautical miles). The latter figure could permit Type 094 SSBNs to attack targets in most of the continental United States while operating in protected bastions close to China.[170]

## Shang (Type 093) SSN

China is building a new class of SSN, called the Shang (or Type 093) class. The first two Shang-class boats are expected to enter service in 2005, and construction of a third may have begun.

Observers believe the Shang-class SSNs will likely represent a substantial improvement over China's five older and reportedly fairly noisy Han (Type 091) class SSNs, which entered service between 1974 and 1990. The first Han-class boat reportedly was decommissioned in 2003, and observers expect the others will be decommissioned as Shang-class boats enter service.

The Shang class reportedly was designed in conjunction with Russian experts and is derived from the Soviet Victor III-class SSN design that was first deployed by the Soviet Union around 1978. The Victor III was the first in a series of quieter Soviet SSN designs that, by the mid-1980s, led to substantial concern among U.S. Navy officials that the Soviet Union was closing the U.S. lead in SSN technology and creating what Navy officials described an antisubmarine warfare (ASW) "crisis" for the U.S. Navy.[171]

ONI states that the Shang-class "is intended primarily for antisurface warfare at greater ranges from the Chinese coast than the current diesel force. China looks at SSNs as a primary weapon against aircraft carrier battle groups and their associated logistics support."[172] Observers expect the Shang-class boats to be armed with a modern ASCM and also with a LACM broadly similar to the U.S. Tomahawk land-attack cruise missile. One observer states:

> At first, [China's LACMs] will be launched by Second Artillery units, but soon after, they may also be used by PLA Air Force H-6 bombers and by the Navy's new Type 093 nuclear attack submarines. When used by the latter, the PLA will have its first platform capable of limited but politically useful non-nuclear power projection on a global scale....
>
> Once there is a build-up of Type 093s it should be expected that the PLA Navy may undertake patrols near the U.S. in order to draw U.S. SSNs back to defensive patrols.[173]

## Kilo-class SS

China ordered four Kilo-class SSs from Russia in 1993; the ships entered service in 1995-1999. The first two were of the less capable (but still fairly capable) Project 877 variant, which Russia has exported to several countries; the other two were of the more capable Project 636 variant that Russia had previously reserved for its own use.

China in 2002 ordered eight additional Kilos from Russia, reportedly all of the Project 636 design. The ships reportedly are to be delivered in 2005 (six boats) and 2006 (two boats).[174] ONI states that the delivery of these eight boats "will provide the Chinese Navy with a significant qualitative increase in warfighting capability,"[175] while another observer states that the Kilo-class boats are "Among the most worrisome of China's foreign acquisitions...."[176]

The eight Kilos are expected to be armed with the Russian-made SS-N-27 Sizzler ASCM, also known as the Novator Alfa Klub 3M-54E — a highly dangerous ASCM that might as difficult to shoot down, or perhaps even more difficult to shoot down, than the SS-N-22 Sunburn ASCM on China's Russian-made Sovremenny-class destroyers (see discussion below on surface combatants). China's first four Kilos (or the two Project 636 boats, if not the two Project 877 boats) might also be refitted with the SS-N-27.

## Yuan (Type 041) Class SS

China is building a new class of SS called the Yuan (or Type 041) class. The first Yuan-class boat, whose appearance reportedly came as a surprise to western observers,[177] was launched (i.e., put into the water for final construction) in 2004. Observers expect the first two Yuan-class boats to enter service in 2006.

Some observers believe the Yuan class may incorporate technology from Russia's most recent SS design, known as the Lada or Amur class, including possibly an air-independent propulsion (AIP) system.[178] One observer says the Yuan class strongly resembles both the Russian Amur 1650-class and French Agosta-class SS designs.[179]

## Song (Type 039/039G) Class SS

China is also building a relatively new SS design called the Song (or Type 039/039G) class. The first Song-class boat entered service in 1999, and a total of 12 are expected to be in service by 2006. The first boat reportedly experienced problems, resulting in design changes that were incorporated into subsequent (Type 039G) boats. Some observers believe the Song-class design may have benefitted from PLA Navy experience with the Kilo class. One report states that one Song-class boat has been equipped with an AIP system.[180] Observers are uncertain whether Song-class production will end as a result of the start of Yuan-class production, or continue in parallel with the Yuan class.

### Older Ming (Type 035) and Romeo (Type 033) Class SSs

China in 2005 also had about 20 older Ming (Type 035) class SSs and about 21 even older Romeo (Type 033) class SSs (with an additional 10 in reserve status).

The first Ming-class boat entered service in 1971 and the 20th was launched in 2002. Production may have ended in favor of Song- and Yuan-class production. In April 2003, a malfunction aboard one of the boats (hull number 361) killed its 70-man crew. Observers believe they were killed by carbon monoxide or chlorine poisoning. The boat was repaired and returned to service in 2004.

The Romeo-class boats entered service between the early 1960s and the late 1980s. A total of 84 were built. Of the 21 still in service, one is a modified boat that has been used as a cruise missile test ship. The 10 boats in reserve status may be of dubious operational condition. The total number of Romeos in service and reserve status has been declining over time.

If China decides that Ming- and Romeo-class boats have continued value as minelayers or as bait or decoy submarines that can be used to draw out enemy submarines (such as U.S. SSNs), it may elect to keep some of these older submarines in service even as new submarines enter service.

## Aircraft Carriers

An August 2005 press report states:

> Chinese shipyard workers have been repairing a badly damaged ex-Russian aircraft carrier and have repainted it with the country's military markings, raising the question once again of whether China is pursuing longer-term plans to field its first carrier.
>
> In the latest developments, images show that workers at the Chinese Dalian Shipyard have repainted the ex-Russian Kuznetsov-class aircraft carrier Varyag with the markings and colour scheme of the People's Liberation Army (PLA) Navy (PLAN). Additional new photographs show that other work, the specifics of which could not be determined, appears to be continuing and that the condition of the vessel is being improved....
>
> Still, China's ultimate intentions for the Varyag remain unclear. One possibility is that Beijing intends to eventually have it enter into some level of service. A military strategist from a Chinese military university has commented publicly that the Varyag "would be China's first aircraft carrier."
>
> It is possible that the PLAN will modify the Varyag into a training aircraft carrier. A US intelligence official said the vessel could be made seaworthy again with enough time, effort and resources. However, US defence officials said that repairing the Varyag to become fully operational would be an extraordinarily large task. The carrier was about 70 per cent complete at the time of transfer and sensitive portions were destroyed, including damage to the core structure, before China was permitted to take possession. Given the difficulty and expense, it is questionable whether Beijing would pursue the effort only to use the Varyag as a training platform; such a move could, however, mark a transitional phase en route to a fully operational capability.
>
> Another possibility is that China does, indeed, plan to repair the vessel to become its first seagoing aircraft carrier or use knowledge gained from it for an indigenously built carrier programme. The US intelligence official said such an outcome "is certainly a possibility" if China is seeking a blue- water navy capable of protecting long-range national interests far from its shores such as sea lanes in the Strait of Malacca. If this strategy were to be followed, China would have to reinstate the structural integrity degraded before delivery and study the structural design of the carrier's deck. These two activities, along with the blueprints and the ship itself, could be used to design an indigenous carrier. Such a plan would very likely be a long-term project preceded by the development of smaller vessels such as amphibious landing ships.[181]

## Surface Combatants

One observer states that by 2010, China's surface combatant force

> could exceed 31 destroyers and 50 frigates, backed up by 30 ocean-capable stealthy fast attack craft. Such a force could then be used in conjunction with submarines and attack aircraft to impose a naval blockade around Taiwan. Surface ships could also defend the

airspace around Taiwan from U.S. Naval forces, especially its P-3 anti-submarine warfare aircraft which would play a critical role in defeating a blockade.[182]

Regarding the HQ-9 SAM believed to be carried by the Luyang II-class destroyers, ONI states:

> The most challenging threat to aircraft and cruise missiles comes from high-performance, long-range [SAM] systems like the Russian SA-10/SA-20 family. The system combines very powerful three-dimensional radar and a high-performance missile with engagement ranges in excess of 100 nautical miles against a conventional target. The SA-10/SA-20 has been marketed widely and has enjoyed some success in the export market, but its high cost has limited its proliferation. Technology from the SA-10 is being incorporated into China's 50-nautical mile range HQ-9 SAM, which is intended for use on the new LUYANG destroyer. The HQ-9 will provide China's navy with its first true area air defense capability when the SAM becomes operational in the next few years.[183]

## Amphibious Ships

The three new classes of amphibious ships and craft now under construction in China, all of which began construction in 2003, are as follows:

- **Yuting II-class helicopter-capable tank landing ships (LSTs).** Three of these ships entered service in 2003 and another six in 2004. Each ship can transport 10 tanks and 250 soldiers, and has a helicopter landing platform for two medium-sized helicopters. The ships were built at three shipyards, and additional units are expected.
- **Yunshu-class landing ships (LSMs).** Ten of these ships entered service in 2004. Each ship can transport 6 tanks or 12 trucks or 250 tons of supplies. The ships were built at four shipyards, and additional units are expected.
- **Yubei-class utility landing craft (LCUs).** Eight of these landing craft entered service in 2004. Each craft can transport 10 tanks and 150 soldiers. The ships were built at four shipyards, and additional units are expected.

DOD states:

> The PLA recently increased amphibious ship production to address its lift deficiencies — although the intelligence community believes these increases will be inadequate to meet requirements — and is organizing its civilian merchant fleet and militia, which, given adequate notification, could augment the PLA's organic lift in amphibious operations.[184]

## Information Warfare/Information Operations (IW/IO)

Regarding IW/IO capabilities, ONI states, without reference to any specific country:

> IO is the combination of computer network attack, electronic warfare, denial and deception (D&D), and psychological operations (PSYOP)....
>
> Outside attack on Navy networks can take different forms depending on the attacker's goals and sophistication. Navy networks have been targeted for denial of service attacks from the Internet. More sophisticated operations, perhaps conducted by foreign military or intelligence services, might include covertly mapping Navy networks, installing backdoors to facilitate future intrusions, stealing data, and leaving behind destructive code packages to be activated in time of conflict. Malicious codes like the Melissa virus have appeared in

classified networks, demonstrating that an external attack on ostensibly protected networks could succeed. Attacks could selectively alter information in Navy databases and files, introducing errors into the system. When discovered or revealed, this corruption of trusted data could cause us to lose confidence in the integrity of the entire database.[185]

## Nuclear Weapons

Regarding the potential use of nuclear weapons against U.S. Navy forces, one study states that

> there is some evidence the PLA considers nuclear weapons to be a useful element of an anti-access strategy. In addition to the nuclear-capable [ballistic] missiles... China has nuclear bombs and aircraft to carry them, and is reported to have nuclear mines for use at sea and nuclear anti-ship missiles. At the very least, China would expect the presence of these weapons and the threat to use them to be a significant deterrent to American action.[186]

Regarding the possibility of China using a high-altitude nuclear detonation to create an EMP effect, DOD states:

> Some PLA theorists are aware of the electromagnetic effects of using a high-altitude nuclear burst to generate high-altitude electromagnetic pulse (HEMP), and might consider using HEMP as an unconventional attack, believing the United States and other nations would not interpret it as a use of force and as crossing the nuclear threshold. This capability would most likely be used as part of a larger campaign to intimidate, if not decapitate, the Taiwan leadership. HEMP causes a substantial change in the ionization of the upper atmosphere, including the ionosphere and magnetosphere. These effects likely would result in the degradation of important war fighting capabilities, such as key communication links, radar transmissions, and the full spectrum of electro-optic sensors. Additional effects could include severe disruptions to civil electric/power and transportation. These effects cannot easily be localized to Taiwan and would likely affect the mainland, Japan, the Philippines, and commercial shipping and air routes in the region.[187]

Whether China would agree with the above view that EMP effects could not easily be localized to Taiwan and surrounding waters is not clear. The effective radius of a high-altitude EMP burst is dependent to a strong degree on the altitude at which the warhead is exploded (the higher the altitude, the greater the radius).[188] China might therefore believe that it could detonate a nuclear warhead somewhere east of Taiwan at a relatively low altitude, so that the resulting EMP radius would be sufficient to affect systems in Taiwan and on surface ships in surrounding waters, but not great enough to reach systems on China's mainland.[189] Following the detonation, China could attempt to confuse the issue in the public arena of whose nuclear warhead had detonated. Alternatively, China could claim that the missile launch was an accident, and that China command-detonated the warhead at altitude as a failsafe measure, to prevent it from detonating closer to the surface and destroying any nearby ships.[190]

## High-Power Microwave (HPM) Weapons

Regarding radio-frequency weapons, ONI states:

Radio-frequency weapons (RFW) could be used against military networks since they transmit high power radio/microwave energy to damage/disrupt electronic components. RFWs fall into two categories, beam and warhead. A beam weapon is a multiple use system that can repeatedly send directional RF energy at different targets. An RF warhead is a single-use explosive device that can be delivered to the target by multiple means, including missiles or artillery shells. RFWs can be assembled with little technical knowledge from commercial off-the-shelf components, such as surplus military radars.[191]

One observer states that, "at least one U.S. source indicates the PLA has developed" non-nuclear radio frequency warheads for ballistic missiles.[192] When asked at a hearing about the possibility of China using a nuclear weapon to generate an EMP effect against Taiwan and U.S. naval forces, this observer stated:

What worries me more, Congressman, is non-nuclear electromagnetic pulse weapons. Non-nuclear explosive propelled radio frequency or EMP-like devices that could be used with far greater frequency and far more effect because they would not run the danger for China of prompting a possible nuclear response. Thereby it would be much more tempting to use and use effectively.

If you could combine a non-nuclear radio frequency weapon with a maneuvering ballistic missile of the type that the Pentagon report describes very briefly this year, that would constitute a real Assassin's Mace weapon. One that, in my opinion, we cannot defend ourselves against and would possibly effectively deny effective military — effective American military intervention in the event of — not just a Taiwan crisis, but other crises as well.[193]

# REFERENCES

[1]    John M. Donnelly, "China On Course To Be Pentagon's Next Worry," *CQ Weekly*, May 2, 2005, p. 1126. See also Anne Plummer, "Republican Senators Concerned About Timing Of Nay Force Reduction Plans," *CQ Today*, March 9, 2005. The American Shipbuilding Association, which represents the six U.S. shipyards that build the Navy's larger warships, states that a very ominous potential threat is building on the horizon. China has been officially modernizing its military for two-and-a-half decades. By 2010, China's submarine force will be nearly double the size of the U.S. submarine fleet. The entire Chinese naval fleet is projected to surpass the size of the U.S. fleet *by 2015*. In short, the Chinese military is specifically being configured to rival America's Sea Power. (Web page of the American Shipbuilding Association, located at [http://www.americanshipbuilding. com/]. Underlining as in the original.) See also Statement of Ms. Cynthia L. Brown, President, American Shipbuilding Association, Presented by Ms. Amy Praeger, Director of Legislative Affairs, Before the U.S.-China Economic and Security Review Commission On U.S.-China Trade Impacts on the Defense Industrial Base, June 23, 2005.

[2]    See, for example, CRS Report RL31555, *China and Proliferation of Weapons of Mass Destruction and Missiles: Policy Issues*, by Shirley A. Kan; CRS Report 98-485, *China: Possible Missile Technology Transfers Under U.S. Satellite Export Policy — Actions and Chronology*, by Shirley A. Kan; CRS Report RL33001, *U.S.-China Counter-Terrorism Cooperation: Issues for U.S. Policy*, by Shirley Kan; CRS Report

RL32496, *U.S.-China Military Contacts: Issues for Congress*, by Shirley Kan; CRS Report RL30427, *Missile Survey: Ballistic and Cruise Missiles of Selected Foreign Countries*, by Andrew Feickert; CRS Report RL32870, *European Union's Arms Embargo on China: Implications and Options for U.S. Policy*, by Kristin Archick, Richard F. Grimmett, and Shirley Kan; CRS Report RL30341, *China/Taiwan: Evolution of the 'One China' Policy — Key Statements from Washington, Beijing, and Taipei*, by Shirley A. Kan; CRS Report RL32804, *China-U.S. Relations: Current Issues and Implications for U.S. Policy*, by Kerry Dumbaugh; CRS Report RL30957, *Taiwan: Major U.S. Arms Sales Since 1990*, by Shirley A. Kan; CRS Issue Brief IB91121, *China-U.S. Trade Issues*, by Wayne W. Morrison; CRS Report RL32882, *The Rise of China and Its Effect on Taiwan, Japan, and South Korea: U.S. Policy Choices*, by Dick K. Nanto and Emma Chanlett-Avery; CRS Report RL32688, *China-Southeast Asia Relations: Trends, Issues, and Implications for the United States*, by Bruce Vaughn.

[3]    U.S. Department of Defense, *Annual Report To Congress [on] The Military Power of the People's Republic of China, 2005*. Washington, Office of the Secretary of Defense, released July 2005. (Hereafter cited as *2005 DOD CMP*.)

[4]    U.S. Department of the Navy, *Worldwide Maritime Challenges 2004*, Washington, prepared by the Office of Naval Intelligence. (Hereafter cited as *2004 ONI WMC*.)

[5]    The white paper is entitled *China's National Defense in 2004*. (Hereafter cited as *2004 China White Paper*.) The English-language text of the white paper can be found on the Internet at [http://www.fas.org/nuke/guide/china/doctrine /natdef2004.html].

[6]    Transcript hereafter cited as *7/27/05 HASC hearing*.

[7]    Hereafter cited as *9/15/05 USCC hearing*. The Commission's website, which includes this and other past hearings, is at [http://www.uscc.gov].

[8]    *Hearing On Military Modernization and Cross-Strait Balance, Hearing Before the U.S.-China Economic and Security Review Commission, February 6, 2004*. Washington, U.S. Govt. Print. Off., 2004. (Hereafter cited as *2/6/04 USCC hearing.* )

[9]    *Chinese Military Power, Report of an Independent Task Force Sponsored by the Council on Foreign Relations Maurice R. Greenberg Center for Geoeconomic Studies*. Washington, 2003. (Harold Brown, Chair, Joseph W. Prueher, Vice Chair, Adam Segal, Project Director) (Hereafter cited as *2003 CFR task force report*.)

[10]   Unless otherwise indicated, shipbuilding program information in this section is taken from *Jane's Fighting Ships 2005-2006*. Other sources of information on these shipbuilding programs may disagree regarding projected ship commissioning dates or other details, but sources present similar overall pictures regarding PLA Navy shipbuilding.

[11]   Depending on their ranges, TBMs can be divided into short-, medium-, and intermediate-range ballistic missiles (SRBMs, MRBMs, and IRBMs, respectively).

[12]   ONI states that "China is developing TBM systems with sufficient range to threaten U.S. forces throughout the region, to include [those] in Japan." (*2004 ONI WMC*, p. 20.)

[13]   *2005 DOD CMP*, p. 4. See also China's Military Power: An Assessment From Open Sources, Testimony of Richard D. Fisher, Jr., International Assessment and Strategy Center, Before the House Armed Services Committee, July 27, 2005, p. 9. (Hereafter cited as *Fisher 7/27/05 testimony*.)

[14]  DOD stated in 2002: "China's procurement of new space systems, airborne early warning aircraft and long-range UAV, and over-the-horizon radar will enhance its ability to detect, monitor, and target naval activity in the Western Pacific Ocean. China may have as many as three over-the-horizon (OTH) sky-wave radar systems, which China aspires to use against aircraft carriers." (Department of Defense, *Annual Report On The Military Power of the People's Republic Of China, 2002*. Washington, 2002, released July 2002. pp. 4-5. See also pp. 28-29.)

[15]  Yihong Chang and Andrew Koch, "Is China Building A Carrier?" *Jane's Defence Weekly*, August 17, 2005.

[16]  Current and Projected National Security Threats to the United States, Vice Admiral Lowell E. Jacoby, U.S. Navy, Director, Defense Intelligence Agency, Statement for the Record [before the] Senate Select Committee on Intelligence, 16 February 2005, p. 13. See also Current and Projected National Security Threats to the United States, Vice Admiral Lowell E. Jacoby, U.S. Navy, Director, Defense Intelligence Agency, Statement For the Record [before the] Senate Armed Services Committee, 17 March 2005, p. 13.

[17]  See the map entitled "SAM Area Coverage Circles," in *2004 ONI WMC*, p. 29.

[18]  For a detailed discussion of China's submarine modernization program and a strong expression of concern regarding the implications of this effort for Taiwan and the United States, see the statement of Lyle J. Goldstein as printed in *2/6/04 USCC hearing*, pp. 129-156. Goldstein's written statement was also published as a journal article; see Lyle Goldstein and William Murray, "Undersea Dragons, China's Maturing Submarine Force," *International Security*, spring 2004, pp. 161-196.

[19]  A previous CRS report discussed these four Kilo-class boats at length. See CRS Report RL30700, *China's Foreign Conventional Arms Acquisitions: Background and Analysis*, by Shirley Kan (Coordinator), Christopher Bolkcom, and Ronald O'Rourke.

[20]  ONI states that all eight Kilo-class boats are scheduled for delivery by 2005. (*2004 ONI WMC*, p. 12.) Some other sources project that the final boat or boats will be delivered by 2007.

[21]  There are also reports that the Kilos might also be armed with the Shkval, a Russian-made, supercavitating, high-speed torpedo, and that China might be building its own supercavitating torpedoes. (Statement of Lyle J. Goldstein as printed in *2/6/04 USCC hearing*, p. 139.) A supercavitating torpedo surrounds itself with an envelope of gas bubbles, which dramatically reduces its resistance as it moves through the water, thereby permitting very high underwater speeds. The Shkval has a reported speed of 200 knots or more.

[22]  One observer states that older and less sophisticated submarines will likely be employed to screen the higher-value assets. Chinese sources openly describe using certain submarines as "bait." Employing this tactic, it is conceivable that United States submarines could reveal their own presence to lurking Kilos by executing attacks against nuisance Mings and Romeos. No wonder China continues to operate the vessels, which are widely derided as obsolete by Western observers. The threat from these older submarines cannot be dismissed out of hand. Informal United States Navy testimony suggests that the PLAN can operate the older classes of diesel submarines with surprising tactical efficiency. (Statement of Lyle J. Goldstein as printed in *2/6/04 USCC hearing*, p. 153)

[23]  *2004 ONI WMC*, p. 11.  The range of 25 to 50 is based on visual inspection of the graph.

[24]  *Fisher 7/27/05 testimony*, p. 11.  On page 4, Fisher similarly states "It can be estimated that by 2010 the PLA Navy could have 50 to 60 nuclear and new conventional attack submarines...."

[25]  China's Military Power, Testimony of John J. Tkacik, Jr., Senior Research Fellow in Asian Studies, The Heritage Foundation, Before the Committee on Armed Services, United States House of Representatives, Washington, D.C., July 27, 2005.  p. 8. (Hereafter cited as *Tkacik 7/27/05 testimony*.)

[26]  [Statement of] Rear Admiral (U.S. Navy, Retired) Eric A. McVadon, Director of Asia-Pacific Studies, Institute for Foreign Policy Analysis, Consultant on East Asia Security Affairs, Before the U.S.-China Economic and Security Review Commission, [regarding] Recent Trends in China's Military Modernization, 15 September 2005, p. 5. (Hereafter cited as *McVadon 9/15/05 testimony*.)  The *fait accompli* mentioned at the end of the quote is discussed later in this report.

[27]  Statement of Lyle J. Goldstein as printed in *2/6/04 USCC hearing*, pp. 155-156.

[28]  *2004 ONI WMC*, p. 10.

[29]  *Fisher 7/27/05 testimony*, p. 4.

[30]  A previous CRS report discussed the PLA Navy's first two Sovremenny-class destroyers and their SS-N-22 ASCMs at length.  See CRS Report RL30700, op cit.

[31]  ONI puts the potential number of additional ships at two or three.  (*2004 ONI WMC*, p.

[32]  AAW is a term most frequently found in discussions of naval systems.  Discussions of systems in other military services tend to use the term air defense.

[33]  For a detailed article about the Luyang II class, see James C. Bussert, "China Debuts Aegis Destroyers," *Signal*, July 2005, pp. 59-62.  See also *Fisher 7/27/05 testimony*, p. 12.

[34]  France sold a modified version of the La Fayette-class design to Taiwan; the six ships that Taiwan built to the design entered service in 1996-1998.  See also *Fisher 7/27/05 testimony*, pp. 12-13.  One observer views the Jiangwei II-class ships as roughly comparable to France's Georges Leygues-class destroyer design, which entered service in 1979, Italy's Maestrale-class frigate design, which entered service in 1982, and the UK's Type 21 frigates, which entered service in starting in 1975 and were transferred to Pakistan in 1993-1994.  (Massimo Annati, "China's PLA Navy, The Revolution," *Naval Forces*, No. 6, 2004, pp. 66-67.)

[35]  Reference books do not show a name for this new class of attack craft, so the craft are identified by their hull numbers.  The first three ships carry numbers 2208-2210.  See also *Fisher 7/27/05 testimony*, p. 13; "PRC Appears Ready To Field New Trimaran Fast Missile Warship," *Defense & Foreign Affairs Daily*, October 5, 2004; Yihong Chang, "First Sight Of Chinese Catamaran," *Jane's Defense Weekly*, May 26, 2004.

[36]  *2004 ONI WMC*, p. 19.

[37]  U.S. Department of Defense, *Annual Report On The Military Power of the People's Republic of China, 2003*.  Washington, Office of the Secretary of Defense, released July 2003.  p. 27.

[38]  Department of Defense, *Annual Report On The Military Power of the People's Republic Of China, 2002*.  Washington, 2002, released July 2002.  p. 23.  In 2000, DOD stated: The PLAN's mine stockpiles include vintage Russian moored-contact and

bottom influence mines, as well as an assortment of domestically built mines. China currently produces the EM11 bottom-influence mine; the EM31 moored mine; the EM32 moored influence mine; the EM52 rocket-propelled rising mine; and, the EM-53 ship-laid bottom influence mine which is remotely controlled by a shore station. China is believed to have available acoustically activated remote control technology for its EM53. This technology probably could be used with other Chinese ship-laid mines including the EM52. Application of this technology could allow entire mines to be laid in advance of hostilities in a dormant position and activated or deactivated when required. China reportedly has completed development of a mobile mine and may be producing improved variants of Russian bottom mines and moored-influence mines. Over the next decade, China likely will attempt to acquire advanced propelled-warhead mines, as well as submarine-launched mobile bottom mines. (Department of Defense, *Annual Report On The Military Power of the People's Republic Of China, 2000*. Washington, 2000. See the subsection on subsurface warfare.)

[39] Statement of Lyle J. Goldstein as printed in *2/6/04 USCC hearing*, p. 133. See also p. 152.

[40] See *2005 DOD CMP*, p. 36; *2003 CFR task force report*, pp. 55-56; Peter Brookes, "The Art Of (Cyber) War, *New York Post*, August 29, 2005; Bradley Graham, "Hackers Attack Via Chinese websites," *Washington Post*, August 25, 2005: 1; Frank Tiboni, "The New Trojan War," *Federal Computer Week*, August 22, 2005: 60.

[41] Eric McVadon, as quoted in Dave Ahearn, "U.S. Can't Use Trade Imbalance To Avert China Invasion Of Taiwan," *Defense Today*, August 2, 2005, pp. 1-2.

[42] Following the April 1, 2001, collision in international airspace off China's coast of a U.S. Navy EP-3 electronic surveillance aircraft and a PLA F-8 fighter, which many observers believed was caused by reckless flying by the pilot of the F-8, China attempted to convince others that the collision was caused by poor flying by the pilot of the slower-flying and less maneuverable U.S. EP-3. For more on this event, see CRS Report RL30946, *China-U.S. Aircraft Collision Incident of April 2001: Assessments and Policy Implications*, by Shirley A. Kan, coordinator.

[43] See CRS Report RL32544, *High Altitude Electromagnetic Pulse (HEMP) and High Power Microwave (HPM) Devices: Threat Assessments*, by Clay Wilson; (Hereafter cited as CRS Report RL32544.) and John S. Foster, Jr., et al., *Report of the Commission to Assess the Threat to the United States from Electromagnetic Pulse (EMP) Attack, Volume 1: Executive Report 2004*. Washington, 2004, 53 pp. (Hereafter cited as *2004 EMP commission report*.) See also the transcripts and written statements of hearings on EMP held before the House Armed Services Committee on July 22, 2004, and before the Military Research and Development Subcommittee of the House Armed Services Committee on October 7, 1999, and July 16, 1997. (In 1997, the full committee was called the House National Security Committee.)

[44] For more on HPM weapons, see CRS Report RL32544.

[45] One source states that "a 2,000-pound microwave munition will have a minimum radius [of effect] of approximately 200 meters," or roughly 650 feet. ("High-power microwave (HPM)/E-Bomb," available on the Internet at [http://www.global security.org/military/ systems/munitions/hpm.htm].)

[46] One source states that: An electromagnetic warhead detonated within lethal radius of a surface combatant will render its air defence system inoperable, as well as damaging

other electronic equipment such as electronic countermeasures, electronic support measures and communications. This leaves the vessel undefended until these systems can be restored, which may or may not be possible on the high seas. Therefore launching an electromagnetic glidebomb on to a surface combatant, and then reducing it with laser or television guided weapons is an alternate strategy for dealing with such targets. (Section 10.4 of Carlo Kopp, "The Electromagnetic Bomb — a Weapon of Electrical Mass Destruction," op cit.)

[47]  See the sections entitled "Reducing the PLA by 200,000," "Implementing the Strategic Project for Talented People," "Intensifying Joint Training," and "Deepening Logistical Reforms," in Chapter II on national defense policy.

[48]  *2005 DOD CMP*, p. 26.

[49]  See, for example, *2005 DOD CMP*, pp. 5-6; the statement of David M. Finkelstein as printed in *2/6/04 USCC hearing*, p. 90-93; and *2003 CFR task force report*, pp. 38-39.

[50]  See, for example, [Statement of] Dennis J. Blasko, Independent Consultant, September 15, 2005, Hearing on "Net Assessment of Cross-Strait Military Capabilities" Before the U.S.-China Economic and Security Review Commission; the statement by Lyle J. Goldstein as printed in *2/6/04 USCC hearing*, pp. 131-132, 143-145; and *2003 CFR task force report*, pp. 39-41, 45-46, 49.

[51]  Regarding reformed logistics, see *2005 DOD CMP*, p. 34, and the statement of Lyle J. Goldstein as printed in *2/6/04 USCC hearing*, p. 145.

[52]  Current and Projected National Security Threats to the United States, Vice Admiral Lowell E. Jacoby, U.S. Navy, Director, Defense Intelligence Agency, Statement for the Record [before the] Senate Select Committee on Intelligence, 16 February 2005, p. 16. See also Current and Projected National Security Threats to the United States, Vice Admiral Lowell E. Jacoby, U.S. Navy, Director, Defense Intelligence Agency, Statement For the Record [before the] Senate Armed Services Committee, 17 March 2005, p. 16.

[53]  *2003 CFR task force report*, pp. 28 and 47.

[54]  This is a reference to an April 2003 fatal accident aboard a Ming-class boat with hull number 361. See Appendix A for additional details concerning this accident.

[55]  Statement of Lyle J. Goldstein as printed in *2/6/04 USCC hearing*, p. 156.

[56]  *2005 DOD CMP*, executive summary and pp. 33-34.

[57]  *2005 DOD CMP*, p. 17.

[58]  Ibid., p. 31.

[59]  *McVadon 9/15/05 testimony*, p. 6. Italics as in the original.

[60]  The passage at this point is quoting from the 2003 edition of DOD's annual report on China's military power (*2003 DOD CMP*, p. 25).

[61]  Dominic DeScisciolo, "Red Aegis," *U.S. Naval Institute Proceedings*, July 2004, pp. 56-58.

[62]  Massimo Annati, "China's PLA Navy, The Revolution," *Naval Forces*, No. 6, 2004, p. 75.

[63]  Ibid., p. 73.

[64]  *2005 DOD CMP*, pp. 34-35.

[65]  James C. Bussert, "China Builds Destroyers Around Imported Technology," *Signal*, August 2004, p. 67.

[66]  The white paper states: The PLA will promote coordinated development of firepower, mobility and information capability, enhance the development of its operational strength with priority given to the Navy, Air Force and Second Artillery Force, and strengthen its comprehensive deterrence and warfighting capabilities.... The Army is streamlined by reducing the ordinary troops that are technologically backward while the Navy, Air Force and Second Artillery Force are strengthened.... While continuing to attach importance to the building of the Army, the PLA gives priority to the building of the Navy, Air Force and Second Artillery Force to seek balanced development of the combat force structure, in order to strengthen the capabilities for winning both command of the sea and command of the air, and conducting strategic counter-strikes. (*2004 China White Paper*, op cit, Chapter II national defense policy.)

[67]  See, for example, *2005 DOD CMP*, p. 1.

[68]  Ibid., executive summary.

[69]  Analysts disagree regarding China's potential for mounting an effective blockade, particularly with its submarine force. For an analysis that casts a skeptical eye on the potential, see Michael A. Glosny, "Strangulation from the Sea? A PRC Submarine Blockade of Taiwan," *International Security*, spring 2004, pp. 125-160. For an analysis that expresses more concern about this potential, see the statement of Lyle J. Goldstein as printed in *2/6/04 USCC hearing*, pp. 132-133, 147-151.

[70]  *2005 DOD CMP*, pp. 39-42. See also *2003 CFR task force report*, pp. 2, 3, and 53.

[71]  *2005 DOD CMP*, executive summary. See also Eric A. McVadon, "Alarm Bells Ring as China Builds up its Armoury on a Massive Sale," *Jane's Defence Weekly*, March 16, 2005, p. 23; Edward Cody, "China Builds A Smaller, Stronger Military," *Washington Post*, April 12, 2005, p. 1; Bryan Bender, "China Bolsters Its Forces, US Says," *Boston Globe*, April 10, 2005, p. 1; Jim Yardley and Thom Shanker, "Chinese Navy Buildup Gives Pentagon New Worries," *New York Times*, April 8, 2005.

[72]  Testimony of Fu S. Mei, Director, Taiwan Security Analysis Center (TAISAC), Before the U.S.-China Economic and Security Review Commission [regarding] "Taiwan Straits Issues and Chinese Military-Defense Budget," September 15, 2005, p. 3.

[73]  *2005 DOD CMP*, executive summary. DOD also states that "China is developing capabilities to achieve local sea denial, including naval mines, submarines, cruise missiles, and special operations forces." (Ibid., p. 33.) Another observer states that: This mission, in essence, is to be able quickly to overwhelm Taiwan's military, cow the Taiwan government, and deter, delay, or complicate effective and timely U.S. intervention.... The concept is ... to be able very rapidly, in a matter of days, to cause Taiwan to capitulate, with such capitulation abetted by the failure of the U.S. to respond promptly and effectively. As has been said often, Beijing's concept is to be able to present to Washington and the world a *fait accompli* concerning Taiwan.... Beijing has ... developed a concept to use force, if it feels it must, to defeat Taiwan, deter or delay U.S. intervention, and at least cause Japan to think twice before introducing overt military assistance in a developing crisis.... There is, in my opinion, no question that this is Beijing's concept for overwhelming Taiwan and deterring or confronting U.S. forces. (*McVadon 9/15/05 testimony*, pp. 1, 2, 2-3, 6.)

[74]  One observer, for example, states: Because the Chinese submarine fleet will operate in nearby waters and in the mid-Pacific, China need not wait until 2020 to challenge the U.S. at sea. It will likely have a home-field advantage in any East Asian conflict

contingency as early as 2010, while the U.S. fleet will still have operational demands in the Middle East, and in tracking Russian ballistic missile submarines elsewhere. (*Tkacik 7/27/05 testimony*, p. 8.) See also *Fisher 7/27/05 testimony*, which cites the year 2010 on pages 3, 4, 7, 9 (twice), 11, and 16 in discussing China's military modernization and the resulting impact on the regional military balance, and Fisher's statement as printed in *2/6/04 USCC hearing*, p. 85, which states, "It is possible that before the end of the decade the PLA will have the capability to coordinate mass missile attacks on U.S. Naval Forces by submarines and Su-30s," and p. 88, which prints his table summarizing potential PLA anti-carrier forces by 2010.

[75] *2005 DOD CMP*, p. 26. Another observer states: "QDR [Quadrennial Defense Review] planners have recently moved forward (to 2012) their estimate of when key warfighting capabilities might be needed to fight China, and have postulated conflict scenarios lasting as long as seven years." (Loren B. Thompson, "Pentagon Fighter Study Raises Questions," August 22, 2005. Lexington Institute Issue Brief.) *2003 CFR task force report* discusses the difficulty of assessing the pace at which China's military modernization is occurring and presents a series of indicators on pages 11-15 (and again on pages 64-68) that can be monitored to help gauge the pace and direction of China's military modernization.

[76] For more on this topic, see CRS Report RL31183, *China's Maritime Territorial Claims: Implications for U.S. Interests*, Kerry Dumbaugh, coordinator.

[77] See, for example, *2005 DOD CMP*, pp. 12-13 and 33; *Fisher 7/27/05 testimony*, p. 4; *McVadon 9/15/05 testimony*, p. 1; *2003 CFR task force report*, pp. 24-25, 31-32, 62-63; Edward Cody, "China Builds A Smaller, Stronger Military," April 12, 2005, p. 1; David Lague, "China's Growing Undersea Fleet Presents Challenge To Its Neighbors," *Wall Street*

[78] Mark Magnier, "China Regrets Sub Incident, Japan Says," *Los Angeles Times*, November 17, 2004; Martin Fackler, "Japanese Pursuit Of Chinese Sub Raises Tensions," *Wall Street Journal*, November 15, 2004: 20; Kenji Hall, "Japan: Unidentified sub is Chinese," *NavyTimes.com (Associated Press)*, November 12, 2004.

[79] Current and Projected National Security Threats to the United States, Vice Admiral Lowell E. Jacoby, U.S. Navy, Director, Defense Intelligence Agency, Statement for the Record [before the] Senate Select Committee on Intelligence, 16 February 2005, p. 16-17. See also Current and Projected National Security Threats to the United States, Vice Admiral Lowell E. Jacoby, U.S. Navy, Director, Defense Intelligence Agency, Statement For the Record [before the] Senate Armed Services Committee, 17 March 2005, p. 17.

[80] Timothy Hu, "Ready, steady, go...," *Jane's Defence Weekly*, April 13, 2005: 27; "China Sub Tracked By U.S. Off Guam Before Japan Intrusion," *Japan Times*, November 17, 2004.

[81] Norimitsu Onishi and Howard W. French, "Japan's Rivalry With China Is Stirring A Crowded Sea," *New York Times*, September 11, 2005. See also "Japan Upset Over Chinese Warships Near Disputed Area," *DefenseNews.com*, October 3, 2005.

[82] "China Sends Warships to East China Sea," *DefenseNews.com*, September 29, 2005.

[83] Bill Gertz, "China Builds Up Strategic Sea Lanes," *Washington Times*, January 18, 2005, p. 1. The report stated that China is: operating an eavesdropping post and building a naval base at Gwadar, Pakistan, near the Persian Gulf; ! building a container

port facility at Chittagong, Bangladesh, and seeking "much more extensive naval and commercial access" in Bangladesh; ! building naval bases in Burma, which is near the Strait of Malacca; ! operating electronic intelligence-gathering facilities on islands in the Bay of Bengal and near the Strait of Malacca; ! building a railway line from China through Cambodia to the sea; ! improving its ability to project air and sea power into the South China Sea from mainland China and Hainan Island; ! considering funding a $20-billion canal that would cross the Kra Isthmus of Thailand, which would allow ships to bypass the Strait of Malacca and permit China to establish port facilities there.

[84]   For discussions relating to Taiwan's potential military capabilities in such a scenario, see CRS Report RL30957, *Taiwan: Major U.S. Arms Sales Since 1990*; and CRS Report RL30341, *China/Taiwan: Evolution of the 'One China' Policy — Key Statements from Washington, Beijing, and Taipei*, both by Shirley A. Kan.

[85]   For a discussion, see archived CRS Report 92-803, *Naval Forward Deployments and the Size of the Navy*, by Ronald O'Rourke.  See **Table 1**. (Out of print and available directly from the author.)

[86]   The other ships include amphibious ships and mine countermeasures ships.

[87]   One of these SSNs, the San Francisco, was significantly damaged in a collision with an undersea mountain near Guam in January 2005.  The ship was transferred to the Puget Sound Naval Shipyard at Bremerton, WA, for repairs.  The San Francisco reportedly will be replaced at Guam by another SSN, the Buffalo, in September 2006.  (David V. Crisostomo, "Guam To Receive Third Home-Ported Submarine In 2006," *Pacific Daily News (Guam)*, November 1, 2005.)

[88]   For a discussion see CRS Report RS21338, *Navy Ship Deployments:  New Approaches — Background and Issues for Congress*, by Ronald O'Rourke.

[89]   Other potential Western Pacific locations, at least in theory, include South Korea (where other U.S. forces have been based for years), the Philippines (where the U.S. Navy ships used as a major repair port until the early 1990s), and Australia.

[90]   U.S. Navy ships visit Singapore, and there is a U.S. Navy logistic group there, but no U.S. Navy ships are currently homeported at Singapore.

[91]    One version of the LCS has a sprint (i.e., high-speed) range of roughly 1,150 miles, while the other has a sprint range of about 1,940 miles.

[92]   Everett is located on the Puget Sound, about 23 nautical miles north of Seattle.

[93]   China's Military Modernization and the Cross-Strait Balance, [Statement of] Roger Cliff, September 2005, Testimony presented before the U.S.-China Economic and Security Review Commission on September 15, 2005, pp. 9-10.  (Hereafter cited as *Cliff 9/15/05 testimony*.)

[94]   For a list of recommended actions for improving the ability of bases in the Western Pacific to defend themselves from PLA attack, see *Cliff 9/15/05 testimony*.

[95]   See, for example, the statement of Lyle J. Goldstein in *2/6/04 USCC hearing*, pp. 148, 150, and 152.

[96]   Jason Ma, "ASW Concept Of Operations Sees 'Sensor Rich Way Of Fighting Subs," *Inside the Navy*, February 7, 2005.  A January 2005 article stated: The Navy cannot fight diesel subs with "force on force," such as sending one sub to defeat another sub, because that is not cost effective, [Rear Admiral John Waickwicz, chief of Fleet Anti-Submarine Warfare Command] told *Inside the Navy*.  For example, the new Virginia-class subs cost about $2 billion each, while advanced diesel subs cost hundreds of

millions of dollars each. Instead of force on force, ASW tactics will emphasize using networked sensors and communications to allow one platform — like a sub, Littoral Combat Ship, or aircraft — to defeat multiple diesel subs, he said. "You have to be able to destroy them at a very large rate, because potential enemies may have a large number" of subs, he explained. "We don't have that luxury to go one against one anymore," he added, noting that individual ASW platforms will rely on their greater capability to take on multiple subs. (Jason Ma, "Admiral: Navy's ASW Tactics To Be Aggressive And Offense-Minded," *Inside the Navy*, January 17, 2005.)

[97] Transcript of conference, as posted on the Internet by AEI at [http://www.aei.org/ events/ filter.all,eventID.1051/transcript.asp].

[98] Jason Ma, "Autonomous ASW Sensor Field Seen As High-Risk Technical Hurdle," *Inside the Navy*, June 6, 2005. See also Jason Ma, "Navy's Surface Warfare Chief Cites Progress In ASW Development," *Inside the Navy*, January 17, 2005.

[99] See, for example, General Accounting Office, *Navy Acquisitions[:] Improved Littoral War-Fighting Capabilities Needed*, GAO-01-493, May 2001; and General Accounting Office, *Navy Mine Warfare[:] Plans to Improve Countermeasures Capabilities Unclear*, GAO/NSIAD-98-135, June 1998.

[100] The Navy's mine warfare plan is available on the Internet at [http://www.exwar.org/ Htm/4000.htm]. For additional discussions of the Navy's mine warfare programs, see Department of the Navy, *Highlights of the Department of the Navy FY2006/FY2007 Budget*, Washington, 2005. (Office of Budget, February 2005) pp. 5-9; Richard R. Burgess, "New Mine Countermeasure System Designs Are Hitting the Water," *Seapower*, August 2005, p. 46, 48; Jason Ma, "Fielding Of Organic Mine Warfare Systems Slips At Least Two Years," *Inside the Navy*, March 21, 2005; William E. Landay III and Hunter C. Keeter, "Breaking the Mold," *Seapower*, March 2005, pp. 42, 44, 46; Scott C. Truver, "Mine Countermeasures And Destruction," *Naval Forces*, No. 3, 2004, pp. 63-64, 66-71; Glenn W. Goodman, Jr., "Organic Mine Countermeasures To Clear Path For Navy," *Armed Forces Journal*, January 2004, p. 36.

[101] Potential candidates include, among others, Spruance (DD-963) class destroyers, which could be reactivated as ASW platforms or missile shooters, Oliver Hazard Perry (FFG-7) class frigates and TAGOS-type ocean surveillance (i.e., towed-array sonar) ships, both of which could be reactivated as ASW platforms, and ASW-capable aircraft such as S-3 carrier-based airplanes and P-3 land-based maritime patrol aircraft.

[102] Additional measures that could assist in tracking PLA SSBNs include satellite surveillance (particularly when the SSBNs are in port or if they surface during their deployments) and human intelligence.

[103] See July 12, 2005 memorandum for distribution from Director, Navy Staff on implementation of Chief of Naval Operations (CNO) guidance — global war on terrorism (GWOT) capabilities, posted in the "Defense Plus" section of [http://www.insidedefense.com]. See also, Andrew Scutro, "Navy To Establish Expeditionary And Riverine Forces," *NavyTimes.com*, July 7, 2005; Jason Sherman, "Navy To Establish Ground Combat Units, River Force For Terror War," *Inside the Navy*, July 11, 2005; Jason Ma, "For War On Terror, Navy Could Field New 'SOF-Lite' Ground Troops," July 18, 2005; Christian Lowe, "U.S. Navy Considers New Combat Battalion," *Defense News*, July 25, 2005; "Navy Creates Riverines, Landing Unit To Lighten Marine, Army Force Load," *Seapower*, August 2005, pp. 6-7.

[104] M. G. Mullen, *CNO Guidance for 2006, Meeting the Challenge of a New Era*. Washington, 2005. 9 pp.

[105] Christopher J. Castelli, "Navy Commissions Study On 'Adequacy' Of Naval Role In War On Terror," *Inside the Navy*, July 11, 2005.

[106] Transcript of conference, as posted on the Internet by AEI at [http://www.aei.org/events/ filter.all,eventID.1051/transcript.asp].

[107] For a discussion, see CRS Report RL32665, *Potential Navy Force Structure and Shipbuilding Plans: Background and Issues for Congress*, by Ronald O'Rourke.

[108] U.S. Department of Defense, *Quadrennial Defense Review Report*, Washington, 2001 (September 30, 2001) p. 27.

[109] U.S. Congressional Budget Office, *Increasing the Mission Capability of the Attack Submarine Force*, Washington, CBO, 2002. (A CBO Study, March 2002), 41 pp.

[110] CRS Report RL32731, *Navy Aircraft Carriers: Proposed Retirement of USS John F. Kennedy — Issues and Options for Congress*, by Ronald O'Rourke.

[111] CRS Report RL32418, *Navy Attack Submarine Force-Level Goal and Procurement Rate: Background and Issues for Congress*, by Ronald O'Rourke.

[112] See, for example, Chris Johnson, "Lawmaker Points To China Buildup In Effort To Protect Sub Base," *Inside the Navy*, August 1, 2005; Anthony Cronin, "Hunter Says China Bolsters Case To Keep Sub Base Open," *New London (CT) Day*, June 28, 2005; William Yardley, "If Bases Aren't Needed, Some Fear Fleet Is Next," *New York Times*, August 22, 2005.

[113] See, for example, John R. Benedict, "The Unraveling And Revitalization Of U.S. Navy Antisubmarine Warfare," *Naval War College Review*, spring 2005, pp. 93-120, particularly pp. 104-106; and the statement by Lyle J. Goldstein in *2/6/04 USCC hearing*, pp. 149-150.

[114] This section includes material adapted from the discussion of the NAD program in CRS Report RL31111, *Missile Defense: The Current Debate*, coordinated by Steven A. Hildreth.

[115] Michael Sirak, "Sea-Based Ballistic Missile Defence: The 'Standard' Response," *Jane's Defence Weekly*, October 30, 2002.

[116] Malina Brown, "Navy Rebuilding Case For Terminal Missile Defense Requirement," *Inside the Navy*, April 19, 2004.

[117] See, for example, Jason Ma and Christopher J. Castelli, "Adaptation Of PAC-3 For Sea-Based Terminal Missile Defense Examined," *Inside the Navy*, July 19, 2004; Malina Brown, "Navy Rebuilding Case For Terminal Missile Defense Requirement," *Inside the Navy*, April 19, 2004.

[118] For more on the DD(X) and CG(X), see CRS Report RS20159, *Navy DD(X) and CG(X) Programs: Background and Issues for Congress*, by Ronald O'Rourke; and CRS Report RL32109, *Navy DD(X), CG(X), and LCS Ship Acquisition Programs: Oversight Issues and Options for Congress*, by Ronald O'Rourke.

[119] See the "Options For Congress" section of CRS Report RL32109, op cit.

[120] The 13.5-inch version has a reported burnout velocity of 3.0 to 3.5 kilometers per second (kps). See, for example, J. D. Marshall, *The Future Of Aegis Ballistic Missile Defense*, point paper dated October 15, 2004, available at [http://www.marshall.org/pdf/materials/259.pdf]; "STANDARD Missile-3 Destroyers a Ballistic Missile Target in Test of Sea-based Missile Defense System," Raytheon news release circa January 26,

2002, available on the Internet at [http://www.prnewswire.com/cgi-bin/micro_ stories.pl?ACCT=683   194&TICK=RTN4&STORY=/www/story/01-26-2002/000165 5926&EDATE =Jan+26,+2002]; and Hans Mark, "A White Paper on the Defense Against Ballistic Missiles," *The Bridge*, summer 2001, pp. 17-26, available on the Internet at [http://www.nae.edu/nae/bridgecom.nsf/weblinks/ NAEW-63BM86/$FILE/ BrSum01.pdf?OpenElement]. See also the section on "Sea-Based Midcourse" in CRS Report RL31111, *Missile Defense: The Current Debate*, coordinated by Steven A. Hildreth.

[121] Source for information on SM-3: Missile Defense Agency, "Aegis Ballistic Missile Defense SM-3 Block IIA (21-Inch) Missile Plan (U), August 2005," a 9-page point paper provided by MDA to CRS, August 24, 2005.

[122] "Aegis Ballistic Missile Defense SM-3 Block IIA (21-Inch) Missile Plan (U), August 2005," op cit, pp. 3-4.

[123] Ibid., p. 3.

[124] Aarti Shah, "U.S. Navy Working With Japanese On Billion-Dollar Missile Upgrade," *Inside the Navy*, March 14, 2005.

[125] "Cost Of Joint Japan-U.S. Interceptor System Triples," Yomiuri Shimbun (Japan), September 25, 2005.

[126] "Aegis Ballistic Missile Defense SM-3 Block IIA (21-Inch) Missile Plan (U), August 2005," op cit, p. 7.

[127] "Cost Of Joint Japan-U.S. Interceptor System Triples," Yomiuri Shimbun (Japan), September 25, 2005.

[128] Marc Selinger, "MDA TO Pick Platform For Sea-Based KEI in May," *Aerospace Daily & Defense Report*," August 19, 2005: 2.

[129] Government Accountability Office, *Defense Acquisitions[:] Assessments of Selected Major Weapon Programs*, GAO-05-301, March 2005, pp. 89-90. See also Thomas Duffy, "Northrop, MDA Working On KEI Changes Spurred By $800 Million Cut," *Inside Missile Defense*, March 30, 2005: p. 1.

[130] Such a ship might be similar in some respects to the arsenal ship concept that the Navy pursued in 1996-1997. For more on the arsenal ship, see archived CRS Report 97-455, *Navy/DARPA Arsenal Ship Program: Issues and Options for Congress*; and archived CRS Report 97-1044, *Navy/DARPA Maritime Fire Support Demonstrator (Arsenal Ship) Program: Issues Arising From Its Termination*, both by Ronald O'Rourke. Both reports are out of print and are available directly from the author.

[131] For more on the F-22, JSF, and F/A-18E/F, see CRS Issue Brief IB92115, *Tactical Aircraft Modernization: Issues for Congress*; CRS Report RL31673, *F/A-22 Raptor*, by Christopher Bolkcom; CRS Report RL30563, *F-35 Joint Strike Fighter (JSF) Program: Background, Status, and Issues*; and CRS Report RL30624, *Military Aircraft, the F/A-18E/F Super Hornet Program: Background and Issues for Congress*, all by Christopher Bolkcom.

[132] General Accounting Office, *Navy Acquisitions[:] Improved Littoral War-Fighting Capabilities Needed*, GAO-01-493, May 2001; and General Accounting Office, *Defense Acquisitions[:] Comprehensive Strategy Needed to Improve Ship Cruise Missile Defense*, GAO/NSIAD-00-149, July 2000.

[133] For more on CEC, see CRS Report RS20557, *Navy Network-Centric Warfare Concept: Key Programs and Issues for Congress*, by Ronald O'Rourke.

[134] The Navy is currently developing a new version of the Standard Missile called the SM-6 Extended Range Active Missile (ERAM) that will have a considerably longer range than the current SM-2 air defense missile. The SM-6 will also have an active seeker that will permit the missile to home in on the target on its own, without being illuminated by a ship-based radar, as is the case with the SM-2.

[135] An October 2005 report from the Defense Science Board (DSB) highlights "The dire need for several types of supersonic targets to represent existing anti-ship cruise missile threats." (Page 1) The report states: The Russians have produced and deployed a variety of supersonic, anti-ship cruise missiles. Some of these missiles are sea-skimming vehicles; others attack from high altitudes. At the time of the Task Force, the United States had zero capability to test its air defense systems such as AEGIS or Improved Sea Sparrow against supersonic targets, and the Task Force views this shortfall as the major deficiency in our overall aerial targets enterprise. Aggressive actions are needed to fix the problem. (Department of Defense, *Report of the Defense Science Board Task Force on Aerial Targets*. Washington, 2005. (October 2005, Office of the Under Secretary of Defense for Acquisition, Technology, and Logistics) pp. 2.) A cover memorandum attached to the report from William P. Delaney and General Michael Williams, USMC (Ret.), the co-chairmen of the task force, states: The area of greatest concern to the Task Force was our gap in supersonic anti-ship cruise missiles for testing. The Russians have deployed at least three such cruise missiles that involve either sea-skimming flight profiles or a high-altitude profile involving a power dive to the target. At this time, we have no test vehicles for either flight profile. See also John Liang, "DSB Highlights 'Dire' Need For Supersonic Cruise Missile Targets," *Inside the Navy*, November 14, 2005.

[136] For more on the LCS, see CRS Report RS21305, *Navy Littoral Combat Ship (LCS): Background and Issues for Congress*; and CRS Report RL32109, *Navy DD(X), CG(X), and LCS Ship Acquisition Programs: Oversight Issues and Options for Congress*, both by Ronald O'Rourke.

[137] For discussions of new ASW technologies, see Jennifer H. Svan, "Pacific Fleet Commander: Sub Threats Top Priority," *Pacific Stars and Stripes*, October 3, 2005; Jason ma, "Autonomous ASW Sensor Field Seen AS High-Risk Technical Hurdle," *Inside the Navy*, June 6, 2005; John R. Benedict, "The Unraveling And Revitalization Of U.S. Navy Antisubmarine Warfare," *Naval War College Review*, spring 2005, pp. 93-120, particularly pp. 109-110; Richard R. Burgess, "'Awfully Slow Warfare'," *Seapower*, April 2005, pp. 12-14; Jason Ma, "ASW Concept Of Operations Sees 'Sensor-Rich' Way Of Fighting Subs," *Inside the Navy*, February 7, 2005; Jason Ma, "Navy's Surface Warfare Chief Cites Progress In ASW Development," *Inside the Navy*, January 17, 2005; Otto Kreisher, "As Underwater Threat Re-Emerges, Navy Renews Emphasis On ASW," *Seapower*, October 2004, p. 15; and David Wood, "U.S. Navy Confronts Growing New Submarine Threat," *Newhouse.com*, September 10, 2004.

[138] M. G. Mullen, *CNO Guidance for 2006, Meeting the Challenge of a New Era*, Washington, 2005, p. 5.

[139] Christopher Munsey, "Fleet Anti-Sub Command Stands Up," *Navy Times*, April 19, 2004, p. 29.

[140] Jose Higuera, "Sweden's Gotland Heads For A Year With US Navy," *Jane's Navy International*, July/August 2005; 8; S. C. Irwin, "Swedish Submarine Expected To

Enhance Navy's Antisubmarine Warfare Primacy," *Navy Newsstand*, June 20, 2005; Gidget Fuentes, "Swedish Sub To Drill With U.S. Navy For A Year," *DefenseNews.com*, May 18, 2005; "U.S., Swedish Navies Sign Agreement To Bilaterally Train On State-Of-The-Art Sub," *Navy Newsstand*, March 23, 2005.

[141] Christopher Munsey, "Colombian, Peruvian Subs To Take Part In Exercise," *NavyTimes.com*, April 14, 2005; Mark O. Piggott, "South American Submarines Enhance U.S. Navy's Fleet Readiness," *Navy Newsstand*, April 14, 2005.

[142] Jennifer H. Svan, "Pacific Fleet Commander: Sub Threats Top Priority," *Pacific Stars and Stripes*, October 3, 2005.

[143] Sources: Department of the Navy, Department of the Navy Fiscal Year (FY) 2006/FY2007 Budget Estimates, Justification of Estimates, February 2005, Research, Development, Test & Evaluation, Navy Budget Activity 4, entry on Surface Ship Torpedo Defense program, PE (Program Element) 0603506N; and Pennsylvania State University Applied Research Laboratory web page on the torpedo defense programs office, available on the Internet at [http://www.arl.psu.edu/capabilities/td.html].

[144] Current information on Navy mines and mine development programs is available on the Internet at [http://www.exwar.org/Htm/4000.htm].

[145] Andrew Koch, "USN May Launch Offensive Naval Mining Mission," *Jane's Defence Weekly*, December 1, 2004, p. 10.

[146] Harold Kennedy, "Navy Command Engages In Info Warfare Campaign," *National Defense*, November 2003. See also Frank Tiboni, "DOD's 'Manhattan Project'," *Federal Computer Week*, August 29, 2005.

[147] CRS Report RL32114, *Computer Attack and Cyberterrorism: Vulnerabilities and Policy Issues for Congress*, by Clay Wilson.

[148] *2004 EMP commission report.* The report of the commission stated on page 1 that "The high-altitude nuclear weapon-generated electromagnetic pulse (EMP) is one of a small number of threats that has the potential to hold our society seriously at risk and might result in defeat of our military forces." The report stated later that been spotty, and the huge challenge of organizing and fielding an EMP-durable tactical force has been a disincentive to applying the rigor and discipline needed to do so. (Pages 47-48.)

[149] Source: Transcript of hearing.

[150] Ibid.

[151] Unless otherwise indicated, shipbuilding program information in this section is taken from *Jane's Fighting Ships 2005-2006.* Other sources of information on these shipbuilding programs may disagree regarding projected ship commissioning dates or other details, but sources present similar overall pictures regarding PLA Navy shipbuilding.

[152] *2005 DOD CMP*, p. 4. Page 33 similarly states that China is "researching the possibility of using ballistic missiles and special operations forces to strike ships or their ashore support infrastructure."

[153] *2004 ONI WMC*, p. 21. On Page 3 (Overview), ONI notes, without reference to any specific country, that "antiship ballistic missiles could be fired at our ships at sea."

[154] *2004 ONI WMC*, p. 22. Page 20 states: "Maneuvering reentry vehicles serve two purposes: one to provide an unpredictable target to complicate missile defense efforts and the other, potentially, to adjust missile flight path to achieve greater accuracy."

[155] *Fisher 7/27/05 testimony*, p. 6.

[156] Presentation entitled "Beijing Eye View of Strategic Landscale" by Mike McDevitt at a June 20, 2005, conference on the future of the U.S. Navy held in Washington, DC, by the American Enterprise Institute. Quote taken from McDevitt's notes for the presentation, which he provided to CRS.

[157] *McVadon 9/15/05 testimony*, pp. 4-5.

[158] *2005 DOD CMP*, p. 29.

[159] *2004 ONI WMC*, pp. 25, 26

[160] *Fisher 7/27/05 testimony*, p. 9. Comments about LACMs also appear on pp. 3, 4, 5, and 11.

[161] *2005 DOD CMP*, p. 29.

[162] *2004 ONI WMC*, p. 23

[163] *McVadon 9/15/05 testimony*, p. 5.

[164] *2005 DOD CMP*, p. 4. See also p. 32.

[165] *Fisher 7/27/05 testimony*, p. 4. See also p. 10.

[166] *2005 DOD CMP*, p. 4. See also pp. 23-24, 25, 31-32.

[167] *2004 ONI WMC*, p. 27. *Fisher 7/27/05 testimony*, pp. 3-4, 9-10.

[168] Statement of Richard D. Fisher, Jr., as printed in *2/6/04 USCC hearing*, p. 72.

[169] *2004 ONI WMC*, p. 37.

[170] A map published by ONI suggests that the JL-2 range is 4,300 nautical miles to 6,500 nautical miles. The caption for the map states "JL-2 range assessments extend to over 5,000 nautical miles, potentially putting all of the continental United States at risk." The map shows that range of 4,300 nautical miles would be sufficient to reach Alaska, Hawaii, and northwest Canada, that a range of 5,400 nautical miles would be sufficient to reach much or most of the continental United States, and that a range of 6,500 nautical miles would be sufficient to reach all of the continental United States with the possible exception of southern Florida. (*2004 ONI WMC*, p. 37.) China also operates a single Xia (Type 092) class SSBN that entered service in 1987, and a single Golf (Type 031) non-nuclear-powered ballistic missile submarine (SSB) that entered service in the late 1960s. The Xia-class boat is armed with 12 CSS-N-3 (JL-1) SLBMs that have a range of roughly 1,200 nautical miles. The Golf-class boat is used as an SLBM test platform.

[171] See, for example, Ronald O'Rourke, "Maintaining the Edge in US ASW," *Navy International*, July/August 1988, pp. 348-354.

[172] *2005 ONI WMC*, p. 14.

[173] *Fisher 7/27/05 testimony*, pp. 9, 11.

[174] As mentioned earlier, ONI states that all eight Kilo-class boats are scheduled for delivery by 2005 (*2004 ONI WMC*, p. 12), while some other sources project that the final boat or boats will be delivered by 2007.

[175] *2004 ONI WMC*, p. 12.

[176] *Tkacik 7/27/05 testimony*, p. 8. See also *Fisher 7/27/05 testimony*, pp. 11-12.

[177] *Jane's Fighting Ships 2005-2006*, for example, states: "It is fair to say that the intelligence community was caught completely unawares by the emergence of the Yuan class...." *Jane's Fighting Ships 2005-2006*, p. 30 (Executive Overview). See also Bill Gertz, "Chinese Produce New Type Of Sub," *Washington Times*, July 16, 2004: 1.

[178] An AIP system, such as a fuel cell system or a closed-cycle diesel engine, extends the stationary or low-speed submerged endurance of a non-nuclear-powered submarine

from a few days to perhaps two or three weeks.  AIP technology does not extend the high-speed submerged endurance of a non-nuclear-powered submarine, which remains limited, due to battery capacity, to about 1 to 3 hours of high-speed operations.

[179] *Fisher 7/27/05 testimony*, p. 11.

[180] "CHINA — Submarine Force Moving Forward," *Submarine Review*, April 2005: 106.

[181] Yihong Chang and Andrew Koch, "Is China Building A Carrier?," *Jane's Defence Weekly*, August 17, 2005.  See also Ian Storey and You Ji, "China's Aircraft Carrier Ambitions, Seeking Truth from Rumors," *Naval War College Review*, winter 2004, pp. 77-93.

[182] *Fisher 7/27/05 testimony*, p. 12.

[183] *2004 ONI WMC*, p. 29.

[184] *2005 DOD CMP*, p. 31.  See also *Fisher 7/27/05 testimony*, p. 13.

[185] *2004 ONI WMC*, p. 38.

[186] *The Chinese Military, An Emerging Maritime Challenge*, Washington, Lexington Institute, 2004, pp. 13-14.

[187] *2005 DOD CMP*, p. 40.

[188] A report by the Office of Technology Assessment (a congressional support agency that was closed in 1995), states:  "The size of the area that could be affected by EMP is primarily determined by the height of burst and is only very weakly dependent on the yield." (*MX Missile Basing*.  Washington, Office of Technology Assessment, 1981. (September 1981) p. 297.  The document is available on the Internet at [http://www.wws.princeton.edu/ota/ ns20/year_f.html].

[189] CRS Report RL32544, op cit, states that "creating a HEMP [high-altitude EMP] effect over an area 250 miles in diameter [i.e., a radius of 125 miles], an example size for a battlefield, might only require a rocket with a modest altitude and payload capability that could loft a relatively small nuclear device."

[190] Even if China does not have the capability to command the early detonation of a warhead on a ballistic missile in flight, it could claim afterward that it did.

[191] *2004 ONI WMC*, p. 39.

[192] *Fisher 7/27/05 testimony*, p. 6.  A footnote at this point in Fisher's statement says this information was: "Disclosed to the author by a U.S. source in September 2004."  See also page 9.

[193] Spoken testimony of Richard D. Fisher, Jr., in transcript of *7/27/05 HASC hearing*, in response to a question from Representative Curt Weldon.

In: Asian Economic and Political Development
Editor: Felix Chin

ISBN: 978-1-61122-470-2
© 2011 Nova Science Publishers, Inc.

# CHANGES IN CHINA'S ECONOMY, FAMILIES AND CULTURAL VALUES: EFFECTS ON STUDENT LEARNING

## *Ming Ming Chiu*
Chinese University of Hong Kong

## ABSTRACT

In the last three decades, mainland China has transformed itself from a poor, equal country to a rich, unequal country with weaker family ties and more hierarchical, individualistic cultural values. These massive changes have improved many students' learning but threaten to leave behind disadvantaged students.

China's rapid economic growth increased her children's learning both directly (educational spending on schools, books, teacher training, etc.) and indirectly (e.g., better health care). Students with more educational resources have more learning opportunities on which they can capitalize to learn more, while healthier students are more likely to capitalize on available resources to learn more.

On the other hand, economic reforms that facilitated corruption, favored coastal areas, and open markets reduced equality and reduced student learning through several inequality mechanisms: (a) less sharing among students and teachers, (b) less overall educational investment, (c) greater corruption, (d) poorer student discipline, and (e) diminishing marginal returns.

China's unequal economic growth, concentrated in its coastal cities (e.g., Shanghai), encourages large-scale urban migration. Through internal labor migration, parents earn more to give their children more physical educational resources (e.g., books) and more learning opportunities. However, internal migration worsens schooling for migrant children, increases divorces, and disrupts family ties, all of which can reduce student learning.

Meanwhile, family planning policies and programs (culminating in the one-child policy) have sharply reduced births. Smaller family size enhances learning by reducing sibling competitors for family resources. On the other hand, smaller families reduce the size of extended families and their available resources to aid children's learning.

China's greater inequality, greater internal migration, and weaker family ties have also shifted China's cultural values to become more hierarchical and individualistic. As a result, government, school, and family practices yield less sharing of resources with poorer children. Although China's economic growth and family planning improved student learning overall, her rising inequality, weaker social ties and changing cultural values threaten her poorer students' educational opportunities. Possible strategies for addressing these inequalities while maintaining economic growth include: (a) giving parents a flat, refundable tax credit for each dependent child, (b) improving relationships among students and teachers, and (c) ending urban housing subsidies.

# INTRODUCTION

In the last three decades, the People's Republic of China (henceforth "China") has transformed itself from a poor, equal nation to a rich, unequal nation. After Mao's death and the arrest of the Gang of Four, Deng Xiaoping wrestled power from Mao's successor Hua Guofeng in 1978 (Evans, 1995). Thereafter, Deng Xiaoping, Jiang Zemin, and Hu Jintao implemented many economic reforms. These included special economic zones that allowed foreign investment, foreign trade, and open markets to gradually transform and modernize China's socialist economy into a capitalist economy (Evans, 1995). Together, these reforms sharply increased China's economic growth and inequality, resulting in massive migrations into coastal cities, weaker family ties, less collectivism, and less egalitarianism. Meanwhile, social changes have reduced family ties, lowered birth rates, and altered cultural values. These massive changes have re-drawn the education landscape, improving many children's academic learning but leaving behind disadvantaged children.

# ECONOMIC GROWTH

## Reforms that Increased Economic Growth

Deng's reforms helped China acquire capital and advanced technology, motivate its labor force to work harder, and ignite its rapid economic growth. In contrast to Mao's attacks on capitalists, Deng embraced market approaches and encouraged foreign investment and trade to acquire valuable technology and management expertise (Hsü, 2000; MacFarquhar & Schoenhals, 2006). Deng also gradually replaced guaranteed jobs with open markets, which increased incentives to work hard and to improve firm profitability (Hsü, 2000).

Along with economic incentives, Deng added education incentives. The previous government's orthodox communism elevated unskilled labor and devalued education by heralding Zhang Tieshang's 1973 blank university exam in the official People's Daily (Gittings, 1999). In contrast, Deng's government repudiated Zhang's blank exam and reinstated the university exam system in 1977 to highlight the importance of learning and academic achievement (Evans, 1995).

Improved technology and labor productivity have grown China's real gross domestic product (GDP) per capita from $379 to $7,700 during 1978-2006 (US dollars, purchasing power parity [PPP], World Bank, 2007). As a result of larger government and family budgets, Chinese children's learning and literacy improved (from 70% to 91% during 1979-2000; Meng, 2002; Wang, 1985).

## Increased Government Spending

Increases in both direct and indirect government spending improved Chinese children's learning (see Figure 1). China's growing economy provided sufficient tax revenue to fund the 1986 Nine-year Compulsory Education Law. As a result, the number of students attending secondary school in China increased from 57 million to 117 million during 1978-2003 (CDO, 2007). Similarly, the number of students in China attending institutions of higher education rose from 0.3 million to 11 million during 1978-2003 (CDO, 2007). When children have more educational resources and learning opportunities, they often capitalize on them to learn more (e.g., Heyneman & Loxley, 1982).

As countries become richer, their children also benefit indirectly through better health and safety standards. In richer nations, students typically eat more nutritious food, receive better health care, and attend classes in safer school buildings (Black, 1999). Thus, they are often mentally healthier, better able to capitalize on learning opportunities, and outperform children who are malnourished, receive inadequate medical care, or are exposed to environmental hazards (e.g., Murphy et al., 1998; Neisser, et al., 1996).

## Increased Family Resources

Likewise, China's families became wealthier and more educated, allowing them to give their children more education resources and more parent time. China's poverty rate had fallen from 53% to 10% of the population during 1981-2002 (based on poverty lines of 850 or 1,200 yuan a year for rural or urban areas, respectively [about US$102 and $145 at 2002 exchange rates]; Chen & Ravallion, 2004). Richer parents can help their children learn more by giving them more education resources and higher quality educational resources (e.g., books, computers, etc.; Chiu & McBride-Chang, 2006; Entwisle & Alexander, 1995). Unlike poorer parents who work multiple jobs to pay for basic necessities, richer parents can also spend more time with their children and teach them more (Horowitz, 1995). When parents spend time with their children discussing educational or other issues (e.g., homework or dinner chats), they can serve as role models, ask provoking questions, or give explicit instructions (Pan, Perlmann, & Snow, 2000). All of these interactions can help children learn cognitive, social, and cultural skills (Pan, et al., 2000).

Due to China's rising literacy during 1979-2000 (Meng, 2002; Wang, 1985), young parents are more educated and help their children learn more (Chiu, Chow, & McBride-Chang, 2007). Compared to less educated parents, highly educated parents tend to spend more time with their children, monitor and supervise them more actively, and have more information and skills to teach them (Lareau, 1989). Furthermore, these highly educated parents have more educated people in their social network (Horvat, Weininger, & Lareau, 2003). Their more educated social network likely includes more cognitive, social, and cultural resources to help these parents' children learn more.

In short, China's rapid economic growth increased both government and family budgets, allowing them to spend more on educational resources that likely increased student learning and overall literacy rates. More educated parents and a more educated social network likely contributed additional resources that further increased children's learning.

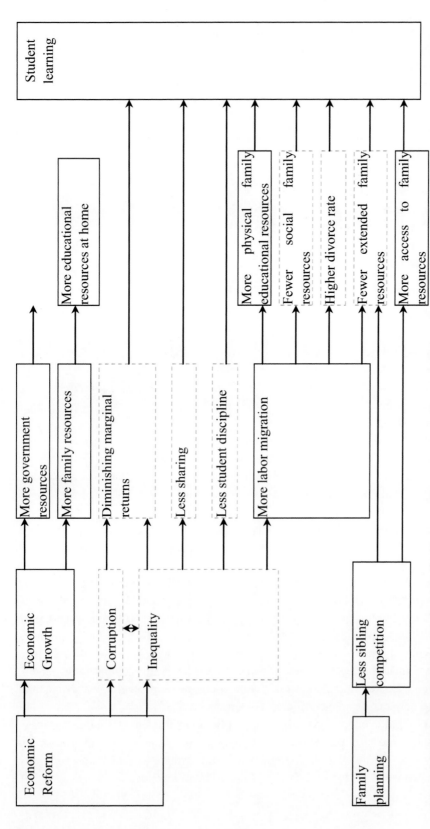

Figure 1. Effects of economic reforms and family planning on economic growth, inequality, family, and student learning. (Black, solid boxes indicate positive, overall effects on student learning. Red, dashed boxes indicate negative, overall effects on student learning.)

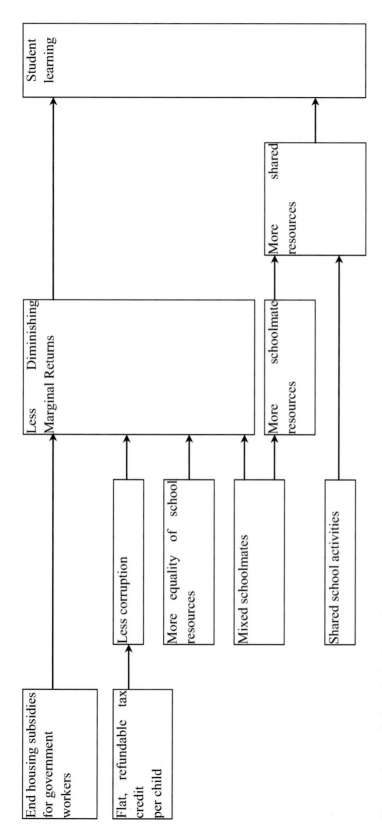

Figure 2. Proposals for reducing inequality and increasing student learning in China.

# INEQUALITY

## Economic Reforms that Reduced or Raised Inequality

Some of China's reforms increased both economic growth and equality. Privatizing agriculture (1978-1985) and letting food prices approach market rates (1995-1998) yielded the highest growth in average household income and increased equality (Keng, 2004; Chen & Ravallion, 2004). Rural and agricultural growth also increased internal trade, reduced urban-to-rural transfers of money, and reduced urban migration by the poor (Ravallion & Chen, 2004). These, in turn, largely reduced both urban and rural poverty and three types of inequality (within rural areas, within cities, and between urban and rural areas; Chen & Ravallion, 2004). Avoiding inflationary shocks and maintaining macro-economic stability protects fixed-income earners by preventing sudden price increases that often disproportionately harm poor people's real incomes (Pillai, 2004; Chen & Ravallion, 2004). Meanwhile, expansion of foreign trade increased growth without substantially affecting poverty or equality (Ravallion & Chen, 2004).

In contrast, economic reforms that facilitated corruption, favored coastal areas, and open markets reduced equality. Government reforms created many opportunities for corruption (Satō, 2006). Government officials (or their cronies) took money, used inside information to choose the best public assets, created monopolies through government regulations that limit competing firms, and so on (Zhao, 2001). Meanwhile, central and provincial government policies that favored coastal areas raised regional inequality between coastal and inland provinces from 57% to 71% during 1978-2000 (Keng, 2004; Ravallion & Jalan, 1999). For example, China created special economic zones (Park, 1997) and supported manufacturing and service industries through tax subsidies, loans, and favorable laws (Knight & Song, 2001). Furthermore, open markets and rapid growth in coastal cities created shortages of workers (especially educated workers) and sharply increased their wages far beyond those of their inland or rural peers (Knight, Li, & Zhao, 2001). Notably, economic reforms have not fully ended subsidized city housing for government employees. These housing subsidies further exacerbated the urban-rural inequality (mean urban income exceeded mean rural income by 70% in 2001; Wang, 2001). Together, these factors increased rural inequality from 25 to 37 (as measured by the Gini index) and urban inequality from 18 to 33 during 1981-2001 (Chen & Ravallion, 2004). Overall inequality rose from 25 to 46 during 1980-2006 (World Bank, 2007). As China's economic equality fell, its egalitarianism cultural values also fell (EVSG & WVS, 2006).

## Inequality Mechanisms that Hinder Learning

Greater inequality tends to reduce student learning due to several mechanisms: (a) less sharing, (b) less educational investment, (c) corruption, (d) poorer student discipline, and (e) diminishing marginal returns (Chiu, in press). As China becomes less equal, her citizenry tends to view one another as less similar, feel less solidarity, and trust one another less (less homophily, McPherson, Smith-Lovin, & Cook, 2001; EVSG & WVS, 2006). Thus, students and teachers are less likely to befriend one another, share resources, or help one another academically, so students often learn less (Chiu & Khoo, 2005).

Second, China's greater inequality increases the influence of the elite who might reduce public educational expenditures. As the rich elite have many more books and other resources at home than others, their children need fewer resources at school (Chiu, in press). As a result, they might advocate fewer public school resources and greater self-financed schooling (Chiu, in press). In school systems with substantial self-financing, poorer families cannot afford adequate educational resources for their children, so greater inequality can yield less educational investment overall (Benabou, 1996). As noted earlier, students with fewer educational resources often have fewer learning opportunities and learn less (Baker, Goesling, & Letendre, 2002). Indeed, China's public spending on education has dropped from 2.2% to 1.9% of GDP during 1991-2001, but it has remained at 13% of the government budget (UNDP, 2007).

Third, China's weaker social solidarity and falling trust (EVSG & WVS, 2006) worsens corruption (Uslaner, 2004). As people feel less connected to one another and identify less with one another, the social barriers against self-gain at the expense of others weaken, thereby facilitating corruption (Uslaner, 2004). Greater school corruption siphons off more educational resources from students, which often reduces their learning (Baker at al., 2002). Corruption can also reallocate more educational resources within the school system to the elite (typically the rich) at the expense of others (typically the poor; Uslaner, 2004), which can further exacerbate inequality within or across schools (Chiu & Khoo, 2005).

Fourth, like other countries, higher crime rates accompanied China's greater inequality (Liu, 2005; Wilkinson, 2004). For each 100,000 people in China during 1978-1999, murders increased from 0.9 to 2.2, and grand larceny skyrocketed from 0.6 to 52.4 (Liu, 2005). Furthermore, teenagers generally commit disproportionately more economic and violent crimes (Freeman, 1995; Mocan & Rees, 2005). Greater crime yields poorer student discipline, distracts student attention away from academic study, and reduces student learning (DeBaryshe, Patterson & Capaldi, 1993).

Lastly, inequality lowers student learning due to diminishing marginal returns (Chiu, in press). Consider a thirsty woman and two glasses of water. She greatly values the first glass of water and drinks it all. Her thirst quenched, she does not finish the second glass of water, showing its lower value (diminishing marginal returns, Mankiw, 2004, p. 273). In general, rich students have more educational resources than poor students do. Hence, poorer students typically benefit more from an extra book than richer students do. With greater inequality, poorer students who can derive more benefits get fewer resources, and learn substantially less. As a result, net learning effectiveness and overall learning is lower in less equal societies (Chiu & Khoo, 2005). As China shifts from a socialist, egalitarian agenda to a liberal, competitive model, local school control and local funding also increase, further exacerbating differences in geographical educational opportunities. Thus, increasing inequalities and inefficiencies due to diminishing marginal returns will likely increase among poor, rural schools in inland provinces and wealthy, urban schools on China's coastline.

In sum, some economic reforms improve economic equality, but others reduce it. Overall, economic inequality in China has increased over the last three decades, reducing egalitarianism cultural values and likely yielding negative effects on student learning. Inequality can reduce learning through less sharing among students and teachers, fewer educational resources due to corruption, poorer student discipline, and diminishing marginal returns.

# INTERNAL MIGRATION

Economic inequality creates economic incentives for labor migration, which hinders schooling for migrant children and weakens family ties that support children's learning. Government policies that favored coastal provinces, especially urban areas (e.g., special economic zones, Park, 1997), increased mean wages in these areas far above those in other areas, creating strong economic incentives for internal labor migration (Knight, Li, & Zhao, 2001). By 2006, 200 million people left their homes to find work elsewhere (Xinhua, 2006). Over 24 million moved across provinces (Huang & Pieke, 2003). Furthermore, the average migrant mailed over 4000 RMB back home in 1999, and likely brought home an equal amount during the Lunar New Year or the Autumn Harvest (Huang, 1997).

## Worse Schooling for Migrant Children

In China, many migrant children have worse schooling than other children and likely learn less than their school-attending peers. According to articles 8 and 12 of the 1986 Compulsory Education Law, local governments receive funding from central authorities and must use their budgets to provide education only for registered residents of their locality. Migrant children can go to a public school if they pay a temporary schooling fee (Jiedufei). However, many migrant parents cannot pay these fees, so about 20% of the 20 million migrant children did not attend public school in 2003 (Xin Jing Bao, 2004). Migrant parents who cannot afford the Jiedufei might send their children to poorly-equipped private schools for migrant children (Mingong Zidi Xuexiao). Still, some parents cannot afford these school fees either. In 2006, 10% of primary school-age, migrant children and 80% of middle school-age migrant children did not attend school (Xia, 2006).

China took a step toward improving schooling for migrant children by passing the 2006 Compulsory Education Law. Article 12 of the 2006 Compulsory Education Law states that local governments provide migrant children "equal conditions for receiving compulsory education." However, the law gives wide leeway to local governments; "the concrete measures shall be formulated by the provinces, autonomous regions and municipalities directly under the Central Government." Due to the modest tone of this legislation, local governments have done little to implement Article 12 (Xia, 2006).

## Migration Weakens Family Ties

Migration weakens ties both within the nuclear family (parents, siblings) and with the extended family (grandparents, aunts, uncles, cousins). By moving away from their children to get better jobs, parents earn more to give their children more physical educational resources (e.g., books) and more learning opportunities (Chiu & Zeng, in press). However, parents who live away from their children often have fewer interactions with them and give them fewer social learning opportunities, both of which typically reduce children's learning (Chiu, 2007; Putnam, 2000).

Moreover, migration increases divorce rates at both the individual and community levels. Individuals who live away from home for more years have weaker ties to their spouses and home communities, and hence are more likely to divorce (Frank & Wildsmith, 2005). In communities with higher residential mobility, divorce rates are also higher (Shelton, 1987). Similarly, as China's migration rate increased, its official divorce rate also rose from 6% of all marriages to 22% during 1985-2005 (NBSPRC, 2007). Children of divorced parents receive fewer educational resources (both physical and social), fewer learning opportunities, and often learn less (Cherlin et al., 1991).

As family members live further apart from one another, their relationships often weaken, as shown through fewer phone calls and fewer meetings (Georgas et al., 2001). In China, migrants living further from their home villages send less money home, showing how labor migration often weakens family ties (Huang & Pieke, 2003). As extended family members live farther away, children are less likely to benefit from their physical and social resources (Bengston, 2001; DeLeire and Kalil, 2002). Likewise, inamicable divorces separate children from the resources of estranged spouse's extended family members. For children living with single parents, those who receive fewer resources from their extended family often learn less than other students and are less likely to complete high school (Aquilino, 1996; Chiu, in press).

Hence, economic inequality increases labor migration, which hinders schooling for migrant children, reduces parent-child interactions, raises divorce rates, and weakens immediate and extended family ties. All of these tend to reduce family resources and learning opportunities for children, yielding less learning.

## REDUCED BIRTHS IMPROVE LEARNING BUT WEAKEN FAMILY TIES

China's family planning policies and programs have reduced both births and the number of siblings per child, yielding more learning but weaker family ties. Since its birth in 1949, China has sought to slow its fast-growing population, which grew from 0.6 billion to 1.0 billion during 1953-1982 (Scharping, 2003). Beginning in the mid-1950s, the Chinese government launched many family planning campaigns and programs, culminating in the stringent one-child birth-control policy (publicly announced in 1979; Merli & Smith, 2002). As a result of these policies, the average number of children per woman dropped from 5.4 to 1.7 during 1971-2004 (Scharping, 2003; Hasketh, Li, & Zhu, 2005).

Children with fewer siblings learn more (Steelman, Powell, Werum, & Carter, 2002). Sibling competition for parents' physical and social resources reduces the effective available resources for each child, yielding fewer learning opportunities (Downey, 2001). With fewer siblings to dilute their family resources, Chinese children born recently likely learn more than did those born in earlier decades.

However, children with fewer siblings also have proportionately fewer close relatives and more distant relatives, effectively yielding more distant extended families. As people feel greater emotional distance with more distant relatives, they tend to feel more distant from their extended family overall, and have less collectivist values (Georgas et al., 2001). Thus, China's family planning programs have yielded children with fewer siblings who face less competition for immediate family resources, but these children's children have fewer adult relatives whom they can ask for help. As a result, future children might have fewer educational resources and fewer learning opportunities, yielding less learning.

## CHANGING CULTURAL VALUES INCREASE IMPORTANCE OF IMMEDIATE FAMILY

As noted above, China's increasing economic inequality, greater migration, rising divorce rate, and falling birth rate have shifted her cultural values. Her values have become less egalitarian and collectivist, and more hierarchical and individualistic. As China's cultural values become less egalitarian, government and school practices are less likely to promote close relationships among students (Pong, Dronkers, & Hampden-Thompson, 2003). With less government, school, or schoolmate support, students rely more on themselves and on their family's resources. Thus, poorer or weaker students learn less, reducing overall learning (Chiu, in press). As China becomes more hierarchical, teachers and students also focus more on status differences, feel less social solidarity, and share fewer physical, social, or informational resources with one another, resulting in less learning (Cohen, 1994).

As China becomes more individualist, her citizens tend to rely more on themselves or their immediate family, and less on others such as extended family members (who are often physically or emotionally distant; Hofstede, 2003). Thus, children are less likely to benefit from the resources of extended families in individualistic countries (Georgas et al., 2001). With fewer extended family resources diluting the effects of immediate family resources on children's learning in China, the impact of the immediate family on learning will likely increase.

### Implications

While maintaining its economic growth and correspondingly expanding educational opportunities, China can take several steps toward addressing its inequalities (see Figure 2). These can include (a) equal educational resources for each student, (b) improving relationships among students and teachers, and (c) ending urban housing subsidies.

### Equal Educational Resources

China can devote equal educational resources for each student through direct funding, integration of richer and poor students within the same classes, and through distributed allocation of resources within a school. China's central government can reduce corruption and inequality by giving a flat, refundable tax credit to each family equal to their child(ren)'s public schooling funding (cf. Hoxby, 2001). Although this would raise administrative costs for schools to collect students' schooling fees, it would sharply reduce the corruption at each layer of government that leeches much of the money away from students (13% of the national budget devoted to education, UNDP, 2007). Negotiations between parent groups and school officials might cause short-term delays in children's schooling, but can yield long-term benefits such as better schools, principals, teachers, and more overall educational resources. Furthermore, each student would receive the same level of funding from central government revenues, which does not distort tax revenues unlike local mechanisms for funding schools (Hoxby, 2001). Also, migrant children would have the same school funds as other children. In poorer areas, the same tax credit would yield higher purchasing power and reduce inequality (Taylor & Taylor, 2004).

Schools can also reduce educational inequality by allocating students, teachers and physical resources more equally and more transparently (Chiu & Walker, 2007). To prevent clustering of richer and smarter students in the same classes, principals can assign students to classes according to sorting of students' given names (rather than by ability). This assignment of students fosters diverse friendships, sharing of resources across economic strata, and flattens the students' status hierarchy (Goldsmith, 2004; Oakes, 1990). Mixing rich and poor students together also hinders targeting of resources toward richer students, which hinders within-school corruption (Chiu & Khoo, 2005).

## Improve Relationships among Students and Teachers

Greater social solidarity among students and teachers can counter-act the impact of societal inequality and improve relationships among students and teachers. Each teacher can be assigned to a variety of grade levels and subjects. This allocation of teachers reduces the likelihood that the best teachers only teach the highest ability students in the highest grades (Darling-Hammond & Post, 2000). By teaching multiple grades, teachers instruct the same students in different classes across different years. Thus, teachers have fewer students under their charge over time and can devote more time to each student, yielding closer teacher-student relationships (Darling-Hammond, 1997). For example, a teacher teaching four 9th grade classes of 50 students over two years would have 400 students. In contrast, a teacher teaching two 9th and two 10th grade classes of 50 students over two years could teach only 200 different students. Similarly, joint activities among students with suitable teacher guidance (e.g., cooperative learning during class, extra-curricular teams, etc.) increase student contact with one another which can help foster a culture of cooperation (Gutierrez, Baquedano-Lopez, Alvarez, & Chiu, 1999).

Schools in large cities with extensive public transportation systems (e.g., Beijing) can mix students of different family backgrounds within the same school with minimal travel time. By mixing rich and poor students together in the same school, they are more likely to build friendships across economic strata, share different resources and experiences, and learn more overall as shown in a study of 41 countries (Chiu & Khoo, 2005).

## End Housing Subsidies

Lastly, ending urban housing subsides would promote market growth and reduce inequality. Government reforms have reduced housing subsidies to urban residents, but all government employees still receive free housing (28% of all employees in 2006; Cheng, 2007; Gong & Li, 2003). Privatizing government employee housing would likely increase industrial growth in the real estate sector, as suggested by the results of housing reforms in 13 socialist countries (Buckley & Tsenkova, 2001).

Gradual elimination of this free housing would help reduce inequality, especially as higher level administrators receive superior housing (Gong & Li, 2003). As government employees' wages exceed the median wage, studies show that they can afford to pay for their own housing (Duda, Zhang, & Dong, 2005; Gong & Li, 2003).

## CONCLUSION

China's economic growth and family planning improved student learning overall, but rising inequality threatens the educational opportunities of her poorer students. Rapid economic growth increased both government and family budgets, allowing them to spend more on educational resources that likely increased student learning. Also, China's reduced birth rate reduced sibling competition for family resources, which also likely increased student learning at the expense of weaker family ties.

However, China's economic reforms also increased economic inequality, which can reduce the educational opportunities of poor students. Family and school inequality can reduce learning through less sharing, less educational investment, more corruption, poorer student discipline, and diminishing marginal returns. Inequality can also reduce learning through increased labor migration and weakened family ties. As these changes have shifted China's cultural values to become more hierarchical and individualistic, they discourage government, school, schoolmate, or extended family support, thereby increasing the impact of immediate family support for children's learning. Together, these changes threaten the educational opportunities for poorer children in China, which could yield lower overall educational achievement, and undermine China's economic growth and political stability. In addition to maintaining stable economic growth and expanding educational opportunities, China can address the harmful effects of inequality on learning by (a) giving parents a flat, refundable tax credit for each dependent child, (b) improving relationships among students and teachers, and (c) ending urban housing subsidies.

## ACKNOWLEDGMENTS

I appreciate the research assistance of Sze Wing Kuo and the helpful comments by Gaowei Chen, Xiaorui Huang, Wu Jing Mavis He, Sung Wook Joh, and Sze Wing Kuo.

## REFERENCES

Aquilino, W. S. (1996). The lifecourse of children born to unmarried mothers: Childhood living arrangements and young adult outcomes. *Journal of Marriage & the Family, 58,* 293-310.

Baker, D. P., Goesling, B., & Letendre, G. K. (2002). Socioeconomic status, school quality, and national economic development: A cross-national analysis of the "Heyneman-Loxley effect" on mathematics and science achievement. *Comparative Education Review, 46*(3), 291-312.

Benabou, R. (1996). Equity and efficiency in human capital investment: The local connection. *Review of Economic Studies, 63*(2), 237-264.

Bengston, V. (2001). Beyond the nuclear family: The increasing importance of multigenerational bonds. *Journal of Marriage & the Family, 63*, 1-19.

Black, M. (1999). *Basic education: A vision for the 21st century*. Florence: UNICEF.

Bourdieu, P. (1993). *The field of cultural production*. New York: Columbia University Press.

Buckleyand, R. M., & Tsenkova, S. (2001). Housing market systems in reforming socialist economies: Comparative indicators of performance and policy. *European Journal of Housing Policy, 1*, 257-289.

Chen, S. & Ravallion, M. (2004). Learning from success. *Finance and Development, 41(4)*, 16-19.

Cheng, E. (2007, December 5). Public sector less than 40% of economy. *International News, Green Left ,* p. 734.

Cherlin, A. J., Furstenberg, F. F., Chase-Lansdale, L., Kiernan, K. E., Robins, P. K., Morrison, D. R., & Teitler, J. O. (1991). Longitudinal studies of effects of divorce on children in great Britain and the United States. *Science, 252*, 1386-1389.

China Data Online [CDO]. (2007). *National statistics*. Retrieved November 15, 2007 from http://chinadataonline.org/

Chiu, M. M. (in press). Four types of inequality reduce science achievement: A study of 41 countries. In U. Kim & Y. S. Park's (Eds.) *Asia's Educational Miracle: Psychological, Social, and Cultural Perspectives*. New York: Springer.

Chiu, M. M. (2007). Families, economies, cultures and science achievement in 41 countries: Country, school, and student level analyses. *Journal of Family Psychology, 21*, 510-519.

Chiu, M. M., Chow, B. W.-Y., & McBride-Chang, C. (2007). Universals and specifics in learning strategies: Explaining adolescent mathematics, science, and reading achievement across 34 countries. *Learning and Individual Differences, 17,* 344-365.

Chiu, M. M., & Khoo, L. (2005). Effects of resources, inequality, and privilege bias on achievement: Country, school, and student level analyses. *American Educational Research Journal, 42*, 575-603.

Chiu, M. M. & McBride-Chang, C. (2006). Gender, context, and reading: A comparison of students in 43 countries. *Scientific Studies of Reading, 10(4)*, 331-362.

Chiu, M. M., & Walker, A. D. (2007). Leadership for social justice in Hong Kong schools: Addressing mechanisms of inequality. *Journal of Educational Administration, 45*, 724-739.

Chiu, M. M., & Zeng, X. (in press). Family and motivation effects on mathematics achievement. *Learning and Instruction*.

Cohen, E. G. (1994). Restructuring the classroom. *Review of Educational Research, 64,* 1–35.

Darling-Hammond, L. (1997). *The right to learn: A blueprint for creating schools that work*. San Francisco: Jossey-Bass.

Darling-Hammond, L., & Post, L. (2000). Inequality in teaching and schooling: Supporting high quality teaching and leadership in low income schools. In R. D. Kahlenberg (Ed.), *A notion at risk: Preserving public education as an engine for social mobility* (pp. 127-168). New York: The Century Foundation Press.

DeBaryshe, B. D., Patterson, G. R., & Capaldi, D. M. (1993). A performance model for academic achievement in early adolescent boys. *Developmental Psychology, 29,* 795-804.

DeLeire, T., & Kalil, A. (2002). Single-parent multigenerational family structure and adolescent adjustment. *Demography, 39,* 393-413.

Downey, D. B. (2001). Number of siblings and intellectual development: The resource dilution explanation. *American Psychologist, 56*(6-7), 497-504.

Duda, M., Zhang, X., & Dong, M. (2005). *China's homeownership-oriented housing policy: An examination of two programs using survey data from Beijing.* Cambridge, MA: Harvard.

Entwisle, D. R., & Alexander, K. L. (1995). A parent's economic shadow: Family structure versus family resources as influences on early school achievement. *Journal of Marriage and the Family, 57,* 399-409.

European Values Study Group and World Values Survey Association [EVSG & WVS]. (2006). *European and world values surveys four-wave integrated data file, 1981-2004* [Data file]. Available from European Values Study Web site, *http://spitswww.uvt.nl/ fsw/evs/index.htm*

Evans, R. (1995). *Deng Xiaoping and the making of modern China* (2nd ed.). London: Penguin.

Frank, R., & Wildsmith, E. (2005).The grass widows of Mexico: Migration and union dissolution in a binational context. *Social Forces, 83,* 919-947.

Freeman, R. (1995). The labor market. In J. Wilson & J. Petersilia (Eds.), *Crime* (pp. 171-192). San Francisco, CA: Institute for Contemporary Studies.

Georgas, J., K. Mylonas, T. Bafiti, Y.H. Poortinga, S. Christakopoulou, C. Kagitcibasi, K. Kwak, B. Ataca, J. Berry, S. Orung, D. Sunar, N. Charalambous, R. Goodwin, W-Z. Wang, A. Angleitner, I. Stepanikova, S. Pick, M. Givaudan, I. Zhuravliova-Gionis, R. Konantambigi, M.J. Gelfand, V. Marinova, C. McBride-Chang, Y. Kodiç. (2001). Functional Relationships in the Nuclear and Extended Family: A 16-Culture Study. *International Journal of Psychology, 36(5),* 289–300.

Gittings, John. 1999. *China through the sliding door.* London: Simon & Schuster.

Goldsmith, P.A. (2004). Schools' role in shaping race relations: evidence on friendliness and conflict. *Social Problems, 51,* 587-612.

Gong, S., & Li, B. (2003). *Social Inequalities and Wage, Housing and Pension Reforms in Urban China.* Asia Programme Working Paper, No. 3. London: Royal Institute of International Affairs.

Gutierrez, K. D., Baquedano-Lopez, P., Alvarez, H. H., & Chiu, M. M. (1999). Building a culture of collaboration through hybrid language practices. *Theory into Practice, 38(2),* 87-93.

Hani. (2005). Illegal donation of 120 million won by high school seniors. *Han Kyu Rae.* Retrieved September 7, 2006, from http://www.hani.co.kr

Hasketh, T., Li, L., & Zhu, W. X. (2005). The effects of China's One-Child Family Policy after 25 Years. *New England Journal of Medicine, 353,* 1171-1176.

Heath, S. B. (1983). *Ways with words: Language, life and work in communities and classrooms.* Cambridge: Cambridge University Press.

Heyneman, S. P., & Loxley, W. A. (1982). Influence on academic achievement across high and low income countries: A re-analysis of IEA data. *Sociology of Education, 55,* 13-21.

Hofstede, G. (2003) *Cultures and Organizations*, London: Profile Books.

Horowitz, J. A. (1995). A conceptualization of parenting. *Marriage and Family Review, 20*(1-2), 43-70.

Horvat, E. M., Weininger, E. B., & Lareau, A. (2003). From social ties to social capital: Class differences in the relations between schools and parent networks. *American Educational Research Journal, 40*, 319-351.

Hoxby, C. M. (2001). All school finance equalizations are not created equal. *The Quarterly Journal of Economics, 116*, 1189 – 1231.

Hsü, I. C. Y. (2000). *The Rise of Modern China*, 6th ed., New York: Oxford University Press.

Huang, P. (1997). *Xunqiu Shengcun* [Seeking Survival]. Kunming: Yunnan Renmin Chubanshe.

Huang, P., & Pieke, F. N. (2003). *China migration country study*. London: Department for International Development.

Keng, C. W. K. (2004). *China's unbalanced economic growth*. Taipei: Himalaya Foundation.

Knight, J. & Song, L. (2001). Economic Growth, Economic Reform, and Rising Inequality in China. In C. Riskin, R. Zhao, & S. Li's (Eds.), *China's Retreat from Equality: Income Distribution and Economic Transition*. (pp. 84-124). Armonk, NY: Sharpe.

Knight, J., Li, S. & Zhao, R. (2001). A spatial analysis of wages and incomes in urban China: Divergent means, convergent inequality. In C. Riskin, R. Zhao, & S. Li's (Eds.), *China's Retreat from Equality: Income Distribution and Economic Transition*. (pp. 133-166). Armonk, NY: Sharpe.

Lareau, A. (1989). *Home advantage: Social class and parental intervention in elementary education*. London: Falmer Press.

Liu, J. (2005) Crime patterns during the market transition in China. *British Journal of Criminology, 45*, 613-633.

Lloyd, C. B., & Blanc, A. K. (1996). Children's schooling in sub-Saharan Africa: The role of fathers, mothers, and others. *Population and Development Review, 22*(2), 265-298.

MacFarquhar, R. & Schoenhals, M. (2006). *Mao's Last Revolution*. Cambridge, Mass: Belknap Press of Harvard University Press.

Mankiw, N. G. (2004). *Principles of economics*. Mason, Ohio: Thomson/South-Western.

McPherson, M., Smith-Lovin, L., & Cook, J. M. (2001). Birds of a feather: Homophily in social networks. *Annual Review of Sociology, 27*, 415-444.

Meng, H. (2002). *Literacy Assessment Practices in Selected Developing Countries: China case study*. Paris: UNESCO.

Merli, M. G. & Smith, H. L. 2002. Has the Chinese family planning program been successful in changing fertility preferences? *Demography, 39*, 557-572

Mocan, H. N., & Rees D. I. (2005). Economic conditions, deterrence and juvenile crime: evidence from micro data. *American Law and Economics Review, 7*, 319-349.

Murphy, J., Pagano, M., Nachmani, J., Sperling, P., Kane, S., & Kleinman, R. (1998). The relationship of school breakfast to psychosocial and academic functioning. *Archives of Pediatric Adolescent Medicine, 152*, 899-907.

National Bureau of Statistics of the People's Republic of China [NBSPRC] (2007). *China Statistical Yearbook*. Beijing: China Statistics Press.

Neisser, U., Boodoo, G., Bouchard, T. J., Boykin, A. W., Brody, N., Ceci, S. J., Halpern, D. F., Loehlin, J. C., Perloff, R., Sternberg, R. J., & Urbina, S. (1996). Intelligence: Knowns and unknowns. *American Psychologist, 51*, 77-101.

Oakes, J. (1990). *Multiplying inequalities: The effects of race, social class, and tracking on opportunities to learn mathematics and science.* Santa Monica, CA: Rand.

Pan, B. A., Perlmann, R., & Snow, C. E. (2000). Food for thought: Dinner table as a context for observing parent-child discourse. In L. Menn & N. B. Ratner (Eds.), *Methods for studying language production* (pp. 205–224). Mahwah, NJ: Erlbaum.

Park, J. –D. (1997). *The special economic zones of china and their impact on its economic development.* Westport, Conn : Praeger.

Pillai, N. V. (2004). *Liberalisation of rural poverty the Indian experience.* Thiruvananthapuram, Kerala : Centre for Development Studies.

Pong, S.-L., Dronkers, J., & Hampden-Thompson, G. (2003). Family policies and academic achievement by young children in single-parent families: An international comparison. *Journal of Marriage and the Family, 65(3)*, 681-699.

Putnam, R. D. (2000). *Bowling alone.* New York: Simon & Schuster.

Ravallion, M., & Chen, S. (2004). *China's (Uneven) Progress Against Poverty.* Washington DC: World Bank Policy Research Working Paper 3408.

Satō, H. (2006). From 'work-unit socialism' to hierarchical labour market in urban China. In L. Shi & H. Satō (Eds.), *Unemployment, Inequality and Poverty in Urban China Vol.1* (pp.175-211) . New York: Routledge.

Scharping, T. (2003). *Birth control in China 1949-2000: Population policy and demographic development.* London: Routledge.

Shelton, B. A. (1987). Variations in divorce rates by community size: A test of the social integration explanation. *Journal of Marriage and the Family, 49,* 827-832.

Steelman, L. C., Powell, B., Werum, R., & Carter, S. (2002). Reconsidering the effects of sibling configuration: Recent advances and challenges. *Annual Review of Sociology, 28*, 243-269.

Taylor, A. M., & Taylor, Mark P. (2004). The purchasing power parity debate. *The Journal of Economic Perspectives, 18(4)*, 135-158.

United Nations Development Programme (UNDP). (2007) *China -The Human Development Index - going beyond income.* New York: United Nations.

Uslaner, E. M. (2004). Trust and corruption. In J. Graf Lambsdorff, M. Taube, & M. Schramm (Eds.), *The new institutional economics of corruption –Norms, trust, and reciprocity* (pp. 76-92). London: Routledge.

Wang, L. (2001). Urban housing welfare and income distribution. In C. Riskin, R. Zhao, & S. Li's (Eds.), *China's retreat from equality: Income distribution and economic transition* (pp. 167-183). Armonk, NY: Sharpe.

Wang, Y. (1985). People's participation and mobilization: characteristics of the literacy campaigns in China. In G. Carron and A. Bordia (Eds.), *Issues in planning and implementing national literacy programmes* (pp.11 – 43). UNESCO: International Institute for Educational Planning.

Wilkinson, R. (2004). Why is violence more common where inequality is greater? *Annals of the New York Academy of Science, 1036*, 1–12.

World Bank. (2007). *The world development report 2006.* New York: Oxford University Press.

Xia, C. (2006). Migrant children and the right to compulsory education in China. *Asia-Pacific Journal on Human Rights and the Law, 2,* 29-74.

Xinhua (2006, Feb. 23). Urbanization is reducing China's rural population. *Xinhua,* Retrieved from http://english.peopledaily.com.cn/200602/23/eng20060223_ 245283.html

Xin Jing Bao (2004, January 15). *Hot Issues No. 4 in Beijing District and County People's Congresses (Guanzhu Beijing Quxian Lianghui Zhi Redian* (4)). Retrieved from http://news.sina.com.cn/c/2004-01-15/04551589116s.shtml.

Zhao, R. (2001). Increasing income inequality and its causes in China. In C. Riskin, R. Zhao, & S. Li's (Eds.), *China's retreat from equality: Income distribution and economic transition.* (pp. 25-43). Armonk, NY: Sharpe.

In: Asian Economic and Political Development
Editor: Felix Chin
ISBN: 978-1-61122-470-2
© 2011 Nova Science Publishers, Inc.

# CHINA EFL: WHY CHINESE UNIVERSITIES DO NOT PROVIDE AN ENGLISH SPEAKING ENVIRONMENT

## *Niu Qiang[1] and Martin Wolff[2]*
[1]Changchun University, Changchun City, P.R. China
[2]Xinyang Agricultural College, Xinyang, P.R. China

## ABSTRACT

There is a new expression in vogue on Chinese university campuses. "We must create an English speaking environment." This statement is usually uttered by a Chinese administrator using Putonghua. Chinese administrators are under the false impression that the creation of an English speaking environment simply requires providing an opportunity for oral English output.

## THE PROBLEM

Speak with any Chinese university Foreign Language Department administrator and they will extol the virtues of creating an English speaking environment (ESE) for the English majors. But take a close look and you will quickly discover that there is no ESE on campus.

First and foremost, Chinese university administrators do not have a clear and proper understanding of what constitutes an ESE. When most of them undertook their university education 20+ years ago, 2nd language acquisition research was in its infancy and comprised no more than one chapter in their textbooks and no continuing education is provided. There is a complete lack of knowledge about immersion or comprehensible input in a friendly environment.

There are two required elements to a proper ESE. A proper ESE is one where the students are inundated with comprehensible English input and where it is easier to communicate in English rather than in the native Putonghua. An English speaking environment is defined as: *"An environment where English is the_dominant language."* Or, *"an environment where people are compelled to speak English".*

Far too many Chinese Foreign Language Department administrators are under the false impression that an ESE is simply where the students are given an opportunity for English output. As a result they decry the lack of an ESE and immediately turn to speak to an English major in Putonghua; or they place all English majors in the same dormitory with Chinese speaking staff; or, they hold weekly English corners; or, they hire foreign teachers to "chat" with the Chinese students. Even at a school that does all of these things simultaneously, no ESE is created.

The administrators do not require the English majors to speak to them in English nor do they respond to them in English. There is a very simple explanation for this. The administrators are either unable to speak in English or their English is so poor that they do not want to "lose face" with the students. The administrators do not contribute to the creation of an ESE and they rarely do anything to improve their own English capability.

The administrators set a very bad example for the students.

When the Party Secretary assigned to the Foreign Language Department cannot speak or understand any English, all department business must be conducted in Putonghua, including all staff meetings and written communications. This militates against creation of an ESE.

The joint venture universities set up by foreign universities, in partnership with Chinese universities, are not exempt from this criticism. The foreign university brings its foreign curriculum and administration that usually requires that all courses be conducted in English. However, according to Chinese law, these joint ventures are required to have Chinese deans. The Chinese deans rarely speak English and hire their own Chinese speaking staff. Students find it much easier to communicate with the Chinese speaking staff in Putonghua so they bypass the English speaking staff. Eventually this leads to the Chineesing of the entire joint venture program.

The Chinese administrators who profess the need for creation of an ESE are often the primary impediment to its creation.

Thirty-eight out of forty Chinese university English teachers, who are supposed to teach in English, are incapable due to their own poor English, so they teach English in Putonghua. They are, for the most part, ignorant of the need to teach in the target language and many have inquired, "What does "target" mean?"

English majors ask their Chinese English teachers questions in Chinese and are answered in Chinese, both in the classroom and outside the classroom. Telephone text messages between teachers and students are also conducted in Putonghua.

The classrooms are littered with Chinese proverbs and political propaganda, all in Putonghua. One oral English classroom had two Chinese signs directly above the blackboard in the front of the room. The Chinese signs translated to:

> "Do not speak in this classroom" and "If you must speak, speak in Chinese." This was in an Oral English classroom where speaking English was the objective.

The Oral English classrooms have theater style row seating bolted to the concrete floor and students are thus compelled to speak to the back of the head of any other student they wish to engage in oral communication.

Modern five story libraries at universities with a 10% or higher English major population have absolutely no English books, or the English reading room is reserved for faculty only. There is no English speaking staff in the library.

The multi-media libraries offer English movies with Chinese subtitles.

The computer labs and sound labs are programmed in Chinese rather than English.

The lab support staffs and computer teachers do not speak English.

The campuses have no bi-lingual signage. Even the sign welcoming the new freshmen English majors is all in Putonghua and the freshmen orientation is all in Putonghua.

There is no English speaking staff in the canteen, post office, logistics department, dormitories, or any other service office of which the students must avail themselves.

There is no extra-curricular access to English newspapers, TV or films.

In short, there isn't even a token attempt to create a proper ESE within the pervasive native Chinese environment.

## EXCUSES

When foreign teachers complain about the lack of an ESE or make constructive suggestions for the creation of an ESE, they are net with a set of rehearsed excuses that include:

This is China.
It is my habit to speak in Chinese.
You will be gone in one year or less.
Laughter

## SOLUTIONS

The first step to creating a proper ESE on Chinese university campuses is to provide continuing education in $2^{nd}$ language acquisition to all Chinese Foreign Language Department administrators and staffs. Unless and until the administrators and staffs understand modern $2^{nd}$ language acquisition theory, all other efforts at creating a proper ESE are futile.

Second, it is imperative that all Foreign Language Department administrators and staffs be required to participate in continuing English language education programs. It is both impractical and hypocritical for Chinese teachers to demand that their students improve their English while the teachers refuse to improve their own.

Third, there must be an incentive or punishment scheme so that administrators and staffs make an honest effort to understand $2^{nd}$ language acquisition theory and to improve their English competency.

Fourth, schools must transform their Foreign Language Departments into little English enclaves, or at least bi-lingual ones.

Classrooms must be English friendly and configured to facilitate oral communication. All Chinese signage should be replaced with English signage and the desks should be configured to facilitate conversation. An example:

BEFORE / AFTER

Fifth, English competency must become an employment prerequisite for all English teachers.

Sixth, libraries must provide a diversified selection of English reading materials and English movies with English subtitles.

Without a fundamental attitude adjustment, the concept of creating an ESE is just an impossible dream.

# REFERENCES

[1]     The Second Language Acquisition Process in Immersion Contexts: Theory and Research, Smith, Samuel, Texas Papers in Foreign Language Education, v1 n2 p119-131 Fall 1988, 1988
        Abstract: Research concerning the success factors in language immersion education is reviewed, focusing on five major schools of thought. First, the traditional model for immersion research, implemented in a Montreal (Canada) suburb is examined. Then three studies of the influence of affective variables in immersion program success are examined, and it is noted that no theoretical overview of the importance of the affective aspects is known. Theorists and researchers considering the social facet of the immersion process and two works on the interrelationship between social and affective factors in the immersion setting are discussed next. Finally, Stephen Krashen's monitor model is compared with the others, and found to be the most relevant to immersion theory. A 27-item bibliography is included. (MSE)

[2]     Walking a Mile in Their Shoes: Transforming Teachers' Beliefs about English Language Learners, Grace Cho, Debra DeCastro-Ambrosetti, California State University, Fullerton, http://www.calstate.edu/ITL/ exchanges/classroom/1070_transforming_pg1.html
        "According to Krashen (1982), language is best acquired when the input is comprehensible (i.e., meaningful, interesting, little beyond current level) and when the learning environment is positive."

[3]     Creating Authentic Dialog: ESL Students as Recipients of Service Learning, Stephanie Marlow, Boise State University (Boise, Idaho, USA) "An environment where authentic dialog with native English speakers occurs on a regular basis presents ESL students with the possibility to grow both linguistically and socially". http://iteslj.org/Techniques/Marlow-ServiceLearning.html

[4]     One such administrator was bragging about how they will not answer any question from an English major unless asked in English. During this discussion the administrator received a mobile text message from an English major. The message was in Chinese. The administrator answered with a text message written in Chinese.

[5]     Xinyang Agricultural College

[6]     Shanghai Normal University. "If the students are allowed to use the English collection, the books will wear out quicker."

[7]     Jiangxi University of Economics and Finance

[8]     Shanghai Foreign Studies University, the second most important English teaching university in China.

[9]     "a teacher who gives up learning should also give up teaching." Review of Teacher Education in NSW, https://www.det.nsw.edu.au/teachrev/ submiss/contedu.htm

[10]   Xinyang Agricultural College

[11] On Target: Teaching in the Target Language. Pathfinder 5. A CILT Series for Language Teachers, 1991,

Abstract: The guide is designed to illustrate how it is realistic and possible to teach in a target foreign language, propose effective instructional strategies and techniques, and offer suggestions for inservice teacher workshops on the approach. It is proposed that language students need to experience the target language as a real means of communication, have a chance to develop their own built-in learning system, and bridge the gap between controlled, secure classroom practice and the unpredictability of real language encounters. The guide begins with a discussion of teacher concerns about teaching in the target language, sources of meaning other than verbal in communication, classroom techniques for providing messages without use of language, and providing messages using limited language. The second section offers specific strategies for implementation in the classroom, including simple instructions and other expressions, techniques for encouraging student participation and satisfaction, and areas in which teachers can cooperate. Specific activities are provided and illustrated. The final section gives ideas for departmental inservice workshops on teaching in the target language, including activities, and recommendations for troubleshooting in classroom communication. (MSE)

[12] Applying the Comprehension Hypothesis: Some Suggestions, Stephen Krashen,

Presented at 13th International Symposium and Book Fair on Language Teaching (English Teachers Association of the Republic of China), Taipei, Taiwan, November, 13, 2004. http://www.sdkrashen.com/articles/eta_paper/ index.html

"The Comprehension Hypothesis also applies to literacy: Our reading ability, our ability to write in an acceptable writing style, our spelling ability, vocabulary knowledge, and our ability to handle complex syntax is the result of reading."

Free Voluntary reading: New Research, Applications, and Controversies, Stephen Krashen

Presented at PAC5 (Pan-Asian Conference), Vladivostok, Russia, June 24, 2004, http://www.sdkrashen.com/articles/pac5/index.html

"Recreational reading or reading for pleasure is the major source of our reading competence, our vocabulary, and our ability to handle complex grammatical constructions."

In: Asian Economic and Political Development
Editor: Felix Chin
ISBN: 978-1-61122-470-2
© 2011 Nova Science Publishers, Inc.

# CHINA'S TRADE WITH THE UNITED STATES AND THE WORLD[*]

## *Thomas Lum and Dick K. Nanto*

## ABSTRACT

As imports from the People's Republic of China (PRC) have surged in recent years, posing a threat to some U.S. industries and manufacturing employment, Congress has begun to focus on not only access to the Chinese market and intellectual property rights (IPO) protection, but also the mounting U.S. trade deficit with China as well as allegations that China is selling its products on the international market at below cost (dumping), engaging in "currency manipulation," and exploiting its workers for economic gain. Members of the 109th Congress have introduced several bills that would impose trade sanctions on China for intervening in the currency market or for engaging in other acts of unfair trade, while the Bush Administration has imposed anti-dumping duties and safeguards against some PRC products and pressured China to further revalue its currency and remove non-tariff trade barriers.

China runs a trade surplus with the world's three major economic centers — the United States, the European Union, and Japan. Since 2000, the United States has incurred its largest bilateral trade deficit with China ($201 billion in 2005, a 25% rise over 2004). In 2003, China replaced Mexico as the second largest source of imports for the United States. China's share of U.S. imports was 14.6% in 2005, although this proportion still falls short of Japan's 18% of the early 1990s. The United States is China's largest overseas market and second largest source of foreign direct investment on a cumulative basis. U.S. exports to China have been growing rapidly as well, although from a low base. In 2004, China replaced Germany and the United Kingdom to become the fourth largest market for U.S. goods. China is purchasing heavily from its Asian trading partners — particularly precision machinery, electronic components, and raw materials for manufacturing. China is running trade deficits with Taiwan and South Korea and has become a major buyer of goods from Japan and Southeast Asia.

In the past decade, the most dramatic increases in U.S. imports from China have been not in labor-intensive sectors but in some advanced technology sectors, such as office and data processing machines, telecommunications and sound equipment, and electrical machinery and appliances. China's exports to the United States are taking market share from other Pacific Rim countries, particularly the East Asian newly

---

[*] This is an edited excerpted and augmented edition of a Congressional Research Service publication RL31403, Dated August 18, 2006

industrialized countries (NICS), which have moved most of their low-end production facilities to China.

This report provides a quantitative framework for policy considerations dealing with U.S. trade with China. It provides basic data and analysis of China's international trade with the United States and other countries. Since Chinese data differ considerably from those of its trading partners (because of how entrepot trade through Hong Kong is counted), data from both PRC sources and those of its trading partners are presented. Charts showing import trends by sector for the United States highlight China's growing market shares in many industries and also show import shares for Japan, Canada, Mexico, the European Union, and the Association for Southeast Asian Nations (ASEAN).

U.S. trade with the People's Republic of China (PRC) has raised several policy concerns. The trade is highly unbalanced in China's favor with a U.S. deficit of $201 billion in 2005. Many associate this deficit with the concomitant loss of American jobs in industries competing with rapidly rising imports from China. Some policymakers as well as leaders of industry and labor blame China for unfair trade practices, including deliberately undervaluing its currency, which they claim create an uneven playing field for U.S. companies when competing against imports from the PRC. U.S.-China trade issues are often driven by larger policy objectives. U.S. trade with China is but one aspect of the overall U.S. policy of engagement with the PRC, a policy that serves broader U.S. interests. Trade also underpins Beijing's development strategy and contributes to domestic support for the PRC government.

This report presents data and analysis of China's trade that shed light on various policy issues, provides an overview of recent U.S. legislative initiatives, and examines the goals and constraints of U.S. trade policy toward the PRC. Some of the specific questions addressed are how the U.S. trade balance with China compares with those of the European Union and Japan, whether imports from China are merely replacing imports from other Pacific Rim nations, and how imports from China by industry compare with imports from other countries.

## THE RATIONALE FOR U.S. POLICY AND INITIATIVES

Allowing trade with China to develop is part of the overall U.S. strategy of engagement with the PRC. The rationale behind engagement is that working with China through economic, diplomatic, informational, and military interchanges helps the United States to achieve important national security goals such as preventing nuclear proliferation, defeating global terrorism, defusing regional conflicts, fostering global economic growth, and championing aspirations for human dignity.[1] These goals are aimed at achieving U.S. national interests of security and prosperity for all Americans and projecting U.S. values abroad.

U.S. trade policy toward China is based upon the assumption that trade between the two countries has both economic and political benefits: (1) in general, trade with China benefits both sides and allows for a more efficient allocation of available resources; (2) the rapidly developing Chinese economy affords a rare opportunity for U.S. businesses to become part of a huge and rapidly expanding market; (3) China's membership in the World Trade Organization (WTO) compels the PRC to comply with international trading rules and spurs the development of market forces in the country; and (4) foreign trade and investment create a dependency on exports, imports, and foreign investment and other interaction with the outside world in China, which in turn strengthen relations with the Western world, create centers of power outside the Chinese Communist Party, and foster economic and social pressures for democracy; (5) a country as significant as China — accounting for a quarter of the world's population, armed with nuclear weapons, and a member of the U.N. Security Council — cannot be ignored or isolated. According to some experts, globalization and economic interests may be exerting a moderating influence on Beijing's policies toward protecting China's national security interests. However, the Chinese Communist Party's determination to maintain political legitimacy through economic growth also creates tensions with other countries and with emerging non-Party political actors.

The possible problems or challenges raised by the U.S. strategy of economic engagement with China include adjusting to economic competition in sectors where China has a comparative advantage, responding to PRC unfair trade practices, and the rise of an economically powerful China that is becoming more assertive in global affairs: (1) Imports from China may be entering in such increased quantities that they are a substantial cause of serious injury, or threat thereof, to competing U.S. industries;[2] (2) Imports from China may be dumped, subsidized, or unfairly aided by government entities in China, which still wield considerable influence in the economy;[3] (3) According to some economists and many policymakers, the U.S. trade deficit with the PRC stems in large part from Beijing's policy of maintaining an undervalued currency; (4) China has a poor record of adopting or enforcing internationally recognized standards for working conditions and environmental regulation which, in addition to violating human rights and harming the environment, may provide PRC businesses with unfair competitive advantages; and (5) U.S. economic engagement with China arguably contributes to the legitimacy of the socialist government and the strengthening of China's military by facilitating general economic development.

U.S. trade law and WTO regulations can deal with injury from imports and unfair trade practices. Trade disputes with China would normally be first discussed bilaterally before taking the case to the WTO for dispute resolution. China's alleged violation of international labor and environmental standards, as well as its own laws and government regulations, has fewer institutional remedies for the United States. Policy options include working to improve China's compliance through bilateral consultations and technical assistance, international organizations (such as the International Labor Organization), non-governmental organizations, and multilateral treaties (such as the U.N. Framework Convention on Climate Change and Kyoto Protocol),[4] and the threat of trade sanctions.

## Trade Policy Developments

In the past two years, the United States and China have taken some actions in response to U.S. complaints about China's "unfair trade practices."[5]

- On January 13, 2006, the Bush Administration announced that it would apply the so-called military catch-all rule to items on the Commodity Control List which could require licenses for the export of items to China that could be used to strengthen China's military power.

- On November 8, 2005, the United States Trade Representative (USTR) announced that the United States and China had, after three months of intense negotiations, reached a broad agreement on textile trade. The Agreement lasts through the life of the China WTO Textile Safeguard (through 2008), covers more than 30 individual products, and contains quotas that begin at low levels.[6]

- On July 21, 2005, the PRC government announced that its currency, the yuan, would be revalued upward (from 8.3 yuan to 8.11 yuan to the U.S. dollar) and that its future value would be "referenced" to a basket of currencies. However, China's central bank continues to intervene in the currency market in order to maintain a stable exchange rate. In its most recent action on the matter, in May 2006, the U.S. Treasury Department declined to designate China as a currency manipulator. The Treasury Department both noted some progress in China's exchange rate regime and complained of "unjustified delay" in introducing additional exchange rate flexibility.[7]

- In May 2005, the Bush Administration imposed "safeguard" quotas on 16 categories of Chinese apparel in response to a surge in such imports following the lifting of textiles and apparel quotas worldwide in January 2005.

- In December 2004, the U.S. government imposed anti-dumping duties on imported Chinese bedroom furniture. This case, the largest anti-dumping action against China, reportedly has both supporters and opponents in the U.S. furniture industry.[8]

- In September 2004, the U.S. government rejected a Section 301 complaint filed by the China Currency Coalition alleging that China's fixed exchange rate constituted currency manipulation. In November 2004, the Administration rejected a similar petition filed by Members of Congress, while continuing to press and advise China on revaluing or floating its currency.

- In April 2004, the Bush Administration rejected a Section 301 petition filed by the AFL-CIO alleging unfair trade practices based upon exploitation of labor in the PRC and calling for a tariff of up to 77% on goods imported from China. In July 2006, the USTR rejected another, similar Section 301 petition filed by the AFL-CIO.

- In March 2004, the Bush Administration filed the United States' first complaint against China under the WTO's dispute settlement mechanism, charging that the PRC unfairly taxed imported semiconductors.[9] In July 2004, China eliminated the tax breaks for domestically-produced semi-conductors.

Members of the 109th Congress have introduced several bills aimed at helping to reduce the U.S. trade imbalance with China. These bills address issues such as China's currency practices, other alleged unfair trade practices (such as dumping and export subsidies), violation of intellectual property rights, non-compliance with WTO regulations, maintaining U.S. technology leadership, and withdrawing NTR status from the PRC. The following are selected bills affecting U.S.-China trade:

- **H.R. 4808** (Jones: Introduced February 28, 2006) To prohibit the importation of motor vehicles of the PRC until the tariff rates that China imposes on motor vehicles of the United States are equal to the rates of duty applicable to motor vehicles of the PRC.

- **S. 2267** (Dorgan/Graham: Introduced February 9, 2006) To withdraw normal trade relations treatment from, and apply certain provisions of Title IV of the Trade Act of 1974 to, the products of the People's Republic of China.
- **H.R. 3283** (English: Introduced July 14, 2005) Amends the Tariff Act of 1930 to impose countervailing duties on certain merchandise from nonmarket economy countries. Passed in the House on July 27, 2005. Related bill: **S. 1421** (Collins).
- **S. 377** (Lieberman: Introduced February 15, 2005) To require negotiation and appropriate action with respect to certain countries that engage in currency manipulation.
- **H.R. 728** (Sanders: Introduced February 9, 2005) To withdraw normal trade relations treatment from the products of the People's Republic of China.
- **S. 295** (Schumer/Graham: Introduced February 3, 2005) To authorize the imposition of a 27.5% tariff on goods imported from China unless the President certifies that China has made a good faith effort to revalue its currency to reflect its fair market value. This bill, which in April 2005 had the support of 67 senators, is expected to be voted on in October 2005. Related bills: **S. 14** (Stabenow), **H.R. 1575** (Myrick), **S.Amdt. 309** (Schumer) to **S. 600**.
- **H.Con.Res. 33** (Ryan: Introduced January 26, 2005) Urging the President to take immediate steps to establish a plan to adopt the recommendations of the United States-China Economic and Security Review Commission in its 2004 Report to the Congress in order to correct the current imbalance in the bilateral trade and economic relationship between the United States and China.

## SUMMARY OF TRADE DATA

What light do the trade data shed on the controversy over economic relations with China? First, China has burst onto the U.S. trading scene in recent years. In 2003, the PRC surpassed Japan to become America's third largest trading partner, after Canada and Mexico,[10] while the United States is the PRC's second largest trading partner, after the expanded European Union (25 nations).[11] In 2005, according to PRC data, EU-China trade was valued at $217.3 billion compared to U.S.-China trade of $211.6 billion.[12] China's largest export market is the United States followed by the EU-25 and Japan. Although China is a new player in international trade, it is taking major shares of markets once dominated either by other countries and U.S. domestic industries.

China is the second largest source of U.S. imports of merchandise ($243 billion in 2005) after Canada ($287 billion). PRC imports surpassed those of Mexico in 2003 and of Japan in 2002. China now accounts for over 14% of U.S. imports (2005), up from 12% in 2003, 8% in 1999, and 3% in 1990, although this share still falls short of Japan's 18% in the early 1990s.

Second, the data show that while U.S. trade with China is unbalanced, the same is also true for Europe and Japan, although to a lesser extent. China runs a trade surplus with the world's three major economic centers. The U.S. bilateral deficit in 2005 ($201 billion), however, was 1.6 times larger than that of the EU-15 ($121.8 billion; the EU-25 deficit was $133 billion) and seven times that of Japan ($28.5 billion). (As reported by the United States, EU, and Japan.)

Third, the data show that the U.S. trade deficit with China is rising with the overall U.S. trade deficit or growing at a slightly faster rate. Between 1996 and 1998, China's share of the overall U.S. merchandise trade deficit averaged 24%; between 1999 and 2001, China's share was 18%, and between 2002 and 2004, 22%. In 2005, the United States trade deficit with China constituted 26% of its global trade deficit. Over the same period, the shares of the U.S. deficit in goods trade accounted for by Japan, the Association of Southeast Asian Nations (ASEAN), and the East Asian newly industrialized countries (NICs) have decreased while the European Union's share has increased.

Fourth, the data show that U.S. exports to China are growing faster than U.S. exports to other nations. U.S. exports to China (up 157% between 2000 and 2005) have grown faster than U.S. exports to Canada (up 19.8% over the same period), Mexico (7.5%), and Japan (-15%), although exports to China have grown from a low base.[13] In 2004, China replaced Germany and the United Kingdom to become the 4th largest market for U.S. goods, moving up from 11th place in 1999. The United States exported somewhat more to China ($41.8 billion) than it did to the United Kingdom ($38.6 billion) in 2005. According to Japanese, European, and Korean data, in 2005, Japan was the largest overseas supplier of products to China with $79.9 billion in exports. South Korea and the EU-15 and were the second and third largest exporters to China in 2005 with $69.8 billion and $61.9 billion in exports, respectively.[14]

Fifth, the U.S. industrial sectors most at risk from import competition from China are generally labor intensive, but China is moving quickly up the technology ladder. The sectors in which the United States runs the largest trade deficits are generally those that depend on abundant and low-cost labor, while the United States accrues surpluses with China in some advanced technology items, such as aircraft, as well as in some agricultural products. In China's trade with the developed countries, over two-thirds of its exports are "low-end manufactures" — appliances, toys, furniture, footwear, apparel, and plastic goods — while 85% of its imports are capital-intensive machinery and equipment, electronic goods, and natural resource-related products.[15]

The United States has incurred large trade deficits with China in some high value-added sectors as well. These sectors include office and data processing machines, telecommunications and sound equipment, and electrical machinery and appliances. In 2003, China became the third largest car market and the fourth largest maker of automobiles with an output of 4.4 million vehicles. Production of cars reached an estimated 5.5 million units in 2005, putting the PRC on par with Germany in automobile production. However, China is not a major global importer or exporter of cars and it remains heavily reliant upon foreign technology in this sector.[16]

Sixth, PRC data show much smaller bilateral trade deficits than those claimed by its trading partners. PRC trade data differ from U.S. data primarily because of the treatment of products from or to China (mainland) that pass through the Hong Kong Special Administrative Region (SAR). Other reasons include different accounting systems and a lack of transparency in China's data reporting. China counts Hong Kong as the destination of its exports sent there, even goods that are then transshipped to other markets. By contrast, the United States and many of China's other trading partners count Chinese exports that are transshipped through Hong Kong as products from China,[17] not Hong Kong, including goods that contain Hong Kong components or involve final assembly or processing in Hong Kong. Furthermore, the United States counts Hong Kong as the destination of U.S. products sent there, even those that are then re-exported to China. However, the PRC counts many of such re-exported goods as U.S. exports to China. Some analysts argue that the U.S. Department of Commerce overstates the U.S. trade deficit with China by as much as 21% because of the way that it calculates entrepot trade through Hong Kong.[18]

According to PRC data, China's trade surplus with the United States in 2005 was $114 billion — not $201 billion as reported by the United States government. In Japan's case, both countries claim to be running trade deficits with each other. According to PRC data, in 2005, China ran deficits with many of its major trading partners, including Taiwan ($57.9 billion), South Korea ($41.7 billion), Japan ($16.3 billion), Malaysia ($9.5 billion), Saudi Arabia ($8.4 billion), Philippines ($8 billion), Thailand ($6 billion), Australia ($5 billion), Brazil ($5 billion) Iran ($3.5 billion).[19]

Seventh, some trade specialists suggest that the surge of U.S. imports from China do not pose an additional threat to U.S. industries and workers because it merely represents a shift of investment and production from other Pacific Rim countries. China's share of U.S. imports has been rising while those of other Pacific Rim nations have been falling or holding steady. In terms of absolute values, until recently, U.S. imports from all major Pacific Rim countries continued to rise, although at slower rates than imports from China. In 2005, U.S. imports from the East Asian NICS — South Korea, Taiwan, Hong Kong, and Singapore — fell or barely rose from the previous year.

Eighth, the rapid growth of the Chinese economy is adding to world demand for basic commodities that is causing upward pressure on world prices. Particularly significant are Chinese net imports of crude oil, copper, and soybeans.

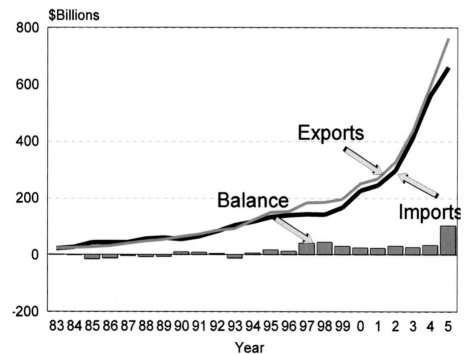

**Sources**: PRC General Administration of Customs; Global Trade Atlas (PRC data).

Figure 1. China's Exports, Imports, and Balance of Merchandise Trade, 1983-2005 (PRC data).

# CHINA'S TRADE BALANCE AND IMPORTS

As shown in Figure 1 and Appendix Table A1, according to PRC data, with the exception of 1993, China has run a global trade surplus in goods each year since 1990. That surplus emerged at the beginning of the 1990s, entered into a deficit of $11 billion in 1993 (when the government temporarily loosened controls on imports), and reached a peak of $43.3 billion in 1998 before declining to $22.6 billion in 2001. In 2005, China's global trade surplus leapt to $102 billion (PRC data).

Between 1995 and 2001, China's current account surplus (includes trade in goods, services, and unilateral transfers such as remittances and government to government payments) was smaller than its surplus in merchandise trade because of a deficit in its services trade. Since 2002, the current account surplus has exceeded the merchandise trade surplus due to large increases in services exports and remittances. In 2005, the current account surplus was $160.8 billion compared to the merchandise trade surplus of $102 billion. According to one projection, China's global current account balance will remain in surplus "for some years to come," due to continued high rates of foreign investment, strong exports, and excessive savings in the non-state sector.[20]

### Table 1. China's Imports by Major Commodity, 1999-2005
### (billions of dollars)

|                          | 1999 | 2000 | 2001 | 2002 | 2003  | 2004  | 2005  |
|--------------------------|------|------|------|------|-------|-------|-------|
| Electrical Machinery     | 35.3 | 50.7 | 55.9 | 73.3 | 104.0 | 142.1 | 174.9 |
| Machinery                | 27.8 | 34.4 | 40.6 | 52.2 | 71.6  | 91.5  | 96.4  |
| Mineral Fuel, Oil, etc.  | 8.9  | 20.7 | 17.5 | 19.3 | 29.3  | 48.0  | 64.2  |
| Optics, Medical. Instr.  | 5.0  | 7.3  | 9.8  | 13.5 | 25.1  | 40.1  | 49.9  |
| Plastic                  | 11.6 | 14.5 | 15.3 | 17.4 | 21.0  | 28.0  | 33.3  |
| Organic Chemicals        | 5.5  | 8.3  | 9.0  | 11.2 | 16.0  | 23.8  | 28.0  |
| Iron and Steel           | 7.2  | 9.6  | 10.9 | 13.2 | 22.2  | 23.6  | 26.2  |
| Ores, Slag, Ash          | 2.2  | 3.1  | 4.2  | 4.3  | 7.2   | 17.3  | 25.9  |
| Copper & Articles Thereof| 3.1  | 4.7  | 4.9  | 5.7  | 7.2   | 10.5  | 12.9  |
| Vehicles, Not Railway    | 2.4  | 3.6  | 4.5  | 6.5  | 11.8  | 12.9  | 12.2  |
| Misc. Grain, Seeds, Fruit| 1.6  | 3.1  | 3.3  | 2.8  | 5.7   | 7.3   | 8.1   |
| Cotton and Yarn, Fabric  | 2.4  | 2.8  | 2.9  | 3.3  | 4.7   | 6.9   | 7.0   |
| Aircraft, Spacecraft     | 3.2  | 2.2  | 4.4  | 4.1  | 4.5   | 4.9   | 6.6   |
| Paper, Paperboard        | 1.6  | 2.6  | 2.7  | 2.9  | 3.9   | 5.2   | 6.3   |
| Misc. Chemical Products  | 2.2  | 2.5  | 2.6  | 3.8  | 4.9   | 5.1   | 6.0   |
| Wood, Articles of Wood   | 2.9  | 3.7  | 3.5  | 4.1  | 4.6   | 5.2   | 5.7   |

**Source:** *Global Trade Atlas* using Chinese data.

As mentioned in the previous section, PRC data show much smaller bilateral trade deficits than those claimed by its trading partners. In 2005, the United States claimed it had incurred a $201 billion trade deficit with China, while China reported a trade surplus of only $114 billion with the United States. Japan reported a $28.5 billion merchandise trade deficit with China, while China likewise claimed a $16.3 billion trade deficit with Japan. In 2005, the European Union's trade deficit with China ($121.8 billion) was only $63 billion according to Chinese data. In 2005, the 156 countries categorized as the "world" by the International

Monetary Fund reported an aggregate trade deficit with China of $342 billion. This is approximately 3.3 times the $102 billion global merchandise trade deficit reported by China for that year.[21] (See Appendix Tables A1-A5.)

Not only have the surge in imports from China affected U.S. markets, but China has become a major importer of world commodities or primary goods. Table 1 shows China's imports by major commodity. Imports of machinery (including electrical) have soared from a total of $63.1 billion in 1999 to $271.3 billion in 2005. Such an increase in demand for machinery, however, has only a moderate effect on overall prices. China's imports of mineral fuel, organic chemicals, iron and steel, ores, copper, cotton, and wood, however, can affect world prices, particularly when combined with rising world demand or tightening supplies. In 2004-2005, Chinese demand for mineral fuel, in particular, including crude petroleum added to upward world price pressures.

## CHINA AND THE ASIA PACIFIC REGION

While China is gaining manufacturing prowess and its trade surplus with the United States is spiraling, the country is purchasing heavily from neighboring trading partners. In 2004, China's imports rose by 35%, including machinery, raw materials, and components for manufacturing, although this growth in imports slowed to 17% in 2005.[22] In addition, the bulk of China's exports are manufactured under foreign brand names, and over half of China's exports are produced by foreign-owned companies. According to PRC official estimates, 70% of PRC exports to the United States contain foreign components, particularly from Taiwan, South Korea, and Singapore.[23]

China has become the largest trading partner of both Taiwan and Japan. The PRC has become South Korea's largest foreign investment destination and largest export market. According to Taiwanese and Korean data, in 2005, Taiwan's estimated trade surplus with China was $31.9 billion, while South Korea's surplus was $31.2 billion.[24]

China has become a huge buyer of raw materials, agricultural commodities, industrial machinery, and electronic components from Southeast Asia, as well as an important source of foreign investment and second largest source of foreign tourists in the region.[25] China's top exports to Southeast Asia include machinery, electronic goods, iron and steel, mineral fuels, textiles and apparel, and optical, photographic, and medical equipment. Despite worries about economic competition, in 2004, ASEAN, which ran a trade surplus of $20 billion with China that year (PRC data),[26] agreed to establish a free trade zone with China which would be implemented gradually over five years.[27] In the view of many of its major trading partners in Asia, China's economic growth and open trade policies have presented both competitive challenges and economic opportunities. However, according to some analysts, China's appetite for imports is slowing, while its export production shows little sign of abating.[28] Although ASEAN accumulated a trade surplus with China again in 2005 ($19.5 billion, according to PRC data), China's exports to ASEAN grew 50% faster than its imports from Southeast Asia.

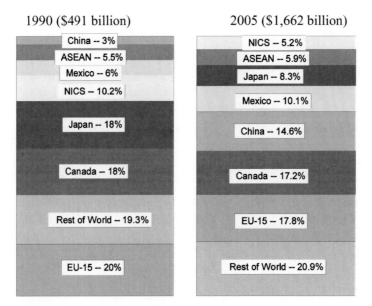

Figure 2. Shares of Total U.S. Imports by Country and Country Group, 1990 and 2005.

Some trade specialists suggest that the surge of U.S. imports from China do not pose an additional threat to U.S. industries and workers because it merely represents a shift of investment and production from other Pacific Rim countries. In other words, expanding imports from China have been offset by declining imports from other East Asian or Pacific Rim countries.[29] These countries include those at a similar level of development which are competing directly with China, such as Malaysia and Thailand, and more industrialized countries or special administrative regions that have moved their lower-end production to the PRC, such as Macao, Hong Kong, South Korea, and Taiwan. In sectors such as footwear, handbags, apparel, furniture, and building and lighting fixtures, U.S. imports from China have been displacing those from Hong Kong, South Korea, Taiwan, and Mexico and reducing imports those from other developing Asian nations.

As shown in **Figure 2**, China's share of U.S. imports grew from 3% in 1990 to 14% in 2005 (out of total U.S. imports of $491 billion and $1.66 trillion, respectively),[30] while the rest of East Asia's share (Japan, NICS,[31] and ASEAN) fell from 36% to 19%. Mexico's share of U.S. imports grew from 6% in 1990 to 11.6% in 2002. It fell to 10.6% in 2004 and further to 10.1% in 2005.

## CHINA'S TRADE WITH THE UNITED STATES, EUROPE, AND JAPAN

As shown in **Figure 3** and **Appendix Table A2**, by either Chinese or U.S. data, China runs a trade surplus with the United States. Although Chinese figures show it at only $114 billion in 2005, the United States reports it to be $201 billion. According to PRC data, China has run a trade surplus with the United States since 1993. According to U.S. data, the United States has incurred trade deficits with China since 1983.

As is the case with the United States, Japan has run a trade deficit with China since the 1980s (according to Japanese data). As shown in **Figure 4** and in **Appendix Table A3**, Japan's balance of trade with China dropped from a surplus of $6 billion in 1985 to a deficit of nearly $6 billion in 1990. Japan's trade deficit with China reached a peak of $26.5 billion in 2001, which was surpassed in 2005 ($28.5 billion). Japan's exports to China have grown dramatically in the past few years, its largest exports to the PRC being electronics, general machinery, iron and steel, optical, photographic, and medical equipment, and organic chemicals.[32]

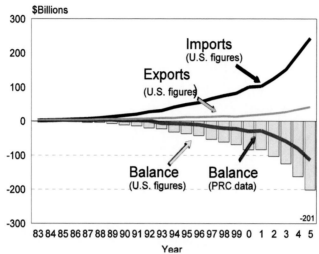

**Sources**: U.S. Department of Commerce
IMF. *Direction of Trade Statistics Yearbook*
Global Trade Atlas

Figure 3. U.S. Exports, Imports, and Balance of Trade with China, 1983-2005.

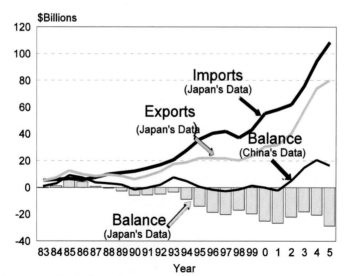

**Sources**: IMF.D irection of Trade Statistics Quarte rly
Global Trade Atlas

Figure 4. Japan's Merchandise Imports, Exports, and Balance of Trade with China, 1983-2005.

As shown in Figure 5 and Appendix Table A4, according to EU data, the European Union incurred a trade deficit with China of $947 million in 1988, which grew to $121.8 billion in 2005. According to Chinese figures, however, the EU trade deficit with China began in the late 1990s and grew to $63 billion in 2005.

Compared to the world's two other major economic centers, the U.S. trade deficit with China at $201 billion in 2005 was the largest, followed by the EU-15 deficit with China at $121.8 billion and Japan at $28.5 billion. Within the EU, according to trading partner 2005 data, Germany's trade deficit with China was $23 billion, the U.K.'s was $18.8 billion, and France's was $9.9 billion. As shown in Appendix Table A5, however, China's trade statistics indicate smaller European trade deficits or even surpluses.

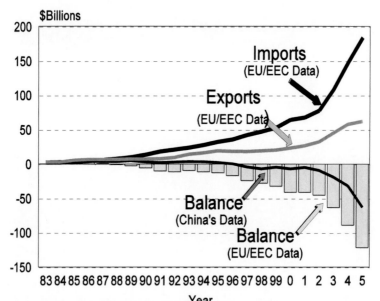

**Note**: For 1980-88, data are for the EEC12 nations. After 1988, data are for the EU 15.
**Sources**: IMF.*D irection of Trade Statistics Quarterly*
Global Trade Atlas

Figure 5. European Union Merchandise Imports, Exports, and Balance of Trade with China, 1983-2005.

# U.S. MERCHANDISE TRADE BALANCES WITH MAJOR TRADING PARTNERS

The U.S. trade deficit with China is notable for not only its size but also the large imbalance between imports from and exports to China. In 2005, Japan exported 2.5 times more to the United States than it imported, while Canada and Mexico exported 1.3 times and 1.4 times more, respectively, than they imported. China, by comparison, exported 5.8 times more to the U.S. market in 2005 than it imported from the United States. This indicates that the Chinese market has been vastly underdeveloped as a destination for U.S. exports.

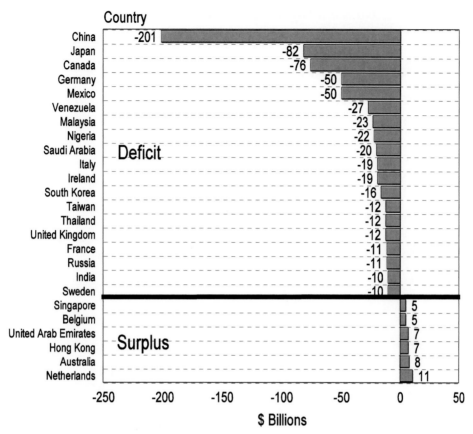

**Source**: U.S. Department of Commerce

Figure 6. U.S. Merchandise Trade Balances with Selected Countries in 2005.

## U.S. TRADE WITH CHINA BY SECTOR

### U.S. Exports to China

As shown in Table 2, among the top twenty U.S. exports to China in 2005, the top five by dollar value were electrical machinery, transport equipment, metalliferous ores, oil seeds and fruits, and general industrial machinery. Exports of metalliferous ores and oil seeds and fruits have grown by over 12 times and 6 times, respectively, since 1999, suggesting that China's appetite for raw materials and agricultural commodities has grown relative to that for general industrial machinery and office machines. Among the top 20 U.S. export items to China, textile fibers have experienced the largest growth in the past five years (969%). China's top ten imports from the world in 2005 were: electrical machinery, machinery, mineral fuels, optical and medical instruments, plastics, organic chemicals, iron and steel, iron ores, copper articles, and vehicles.

### Table 2. Top Twenty U.S. Exports to China, 1997-2005
### (millions of dollars)

| Category | 1997 | 1998 | 1999 | 2000 | 2001 | 2002 | 2003 | 2004 | 2005 |
|---|---|---|---|---|---|---|---|---|---|
| Electrical Mach. | 741 | 1,013 | 1,380 | 1,747 | 2,109 | 2,657 | 3,722 | 4,631 | 5,170 |
| Transport Equip. | 2,127 | 3,604 | 2,325 | 1,695 | 2,471 | 3,443 | 2,495 | 2,025 | 4,479 |
| Metalliferous Ores | 180 | 195 | 285 | 618 | 919 | 956 | 1,525 | 2,198 | 3,482 |
| Oil Seeds and Fruits | 419 | 288 | 354 | 1,020 | 1,014 | 890 | 2,832 | 2,332 | 2,256 |
| Gen. Ind. Mach./Equip. | 766 | 674 | 685 | 838 | 1,080 | 1,145 | 1,404 | 1,912 | 2,067 |
| Office Machines | 343 | 878 | 842 | 1,498 | 1,602 | 1,193 | 1,274 | 1,396 | 1,835 |
| Plastics in Prim. Forms | 340 | 320 | 394 | 545 | 628 | 740 | 931 | 1,342 | 1,793 |
| Prof. & Scientific Instr. | 429 | 527 | 538 | 583 | 886 | 931 | 1,167 | 1,568 | 1,710 |
| Textile Fibers | 682 | 199 | 98 | 154 | 160 | 278 | 909 | 1,638 | 1,657 |
| Organic Chemicals | 208 | 212 | 302 | 473 | 373 | 554 | 1,054 | 1,542 | 1,457 |
| Specialized Industrial Machinery | 770 | 538 | 481 | 758 | 819 | 1,124 | 1,218 | 1,744 | 1,325 |
| Telecom, Sound Recording Equip. | 644 | 655 | 573 | 817 | 1,204 | 1,110 | 978 | 1,104 | 1,299 |
| Power Gen. Equip. | 603 | 542 | 505 | 312 | 507 | 462 | 640 | 965 | 1,042 |
| Pulp and Waste Paper | 148 | 156 | 193 | 276 | 330 | 414 | 600 | 753 | 992 |
| Road Vehicles | 348 | 140 | 192 | 185 | 223 | 272 | 506 | 624 | 903 |
| Nonferrous Metals | 172 | 120 | 140 | 289 | 144 | 161 | 315 | 333 | 872 |
| Misc. Manufactures | 297 | 247 | 242 | 384 | 440 | 509 | 515 | 647 | 750 |
| Hides, Furskins | 112 | 126 | 96 | 237 | 402 | 397 | 457 | 521 | 629 |
| Chemical Materials | 124 | 143 | 177 | 247 | 285 | 312 | 403 | 582 | 604 |
| Metalworking Mach. | 173 | 190 | 162 | 211 | 265 | 367 | 304 | 618 | 547 |

**Note:** Ranked by data for 2005.
**Source:** U.S. Department of Commerce, International Trade Commission.

## U.S. Imports from China

As shown in Figure 7 and Table 3, among the top twenty U.S. imports from China in 2005 by dollar amount, the top six were office machines and automatic data processing machines, telecommunications and sound equipment, miscellaneous manufactured articles, apparel and accessories, electrical machinery, and furniture and bedding. The value of U.S.-imports of PRC office and data processing machines alone ($42.2 billion) exceeded total U.S. exports to China in 2005 ($41.8 billion). While U.S. imports in all these categories have increased, the most dramatic percentage changes have been not in traditional labor-intensive industries but in sectors that encompass advanced technology, such as office and data processing machines (up 284% between 2000 and 2005), telecommunications and sound equipment (245%), and general industrial machinery (234%).

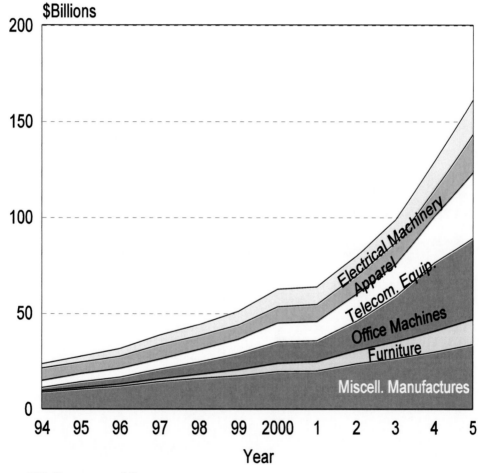

**Source**: U.S. Department of Commerce

Figure 7. Top Six Imports from China by Industry, 1994-2005.

**Table 3. Top Twenty U.S. Imports from China, 1997-2005**
**(millions of dollars)**

| Category | 1997 | 1998 | 1999 | 2000 | 2001 | 2002 | 2003 | 2004 | 2005 |
|---|---|---|---|---|---|---|---|---|---|
| Office Machines, Data Processing | 5,019 | 6,329 | 8,239 | 10,980 | 10,763 | 15,230 | 23,646 | 35,620 | 42,242 |
| Telecom and Sound Equip. | 5,126 | 6,405 | 7,382 | 9,812 | 10,118 | 14,144 | 16,937 | 24,388 | 34,249 |
| Misc. Manufactured Articles | 14,155 | 15,872 | 17,291 | 19,445 | 19,763 | 23,494 | 26,287 | 29,505 | 33,573 |
| Apparel and Accessories | 7,406 | 7,133 | 7,351 | 8,473 | 8,866 | 9,538 | 11,381 | 13,607 | 19,931 |
| Electrical Machinery, Parts, and Appliances | 4,877 | 5,707 | 7,022 | 9,037 | 9,110 | 10,217 | 11,875 | 15,270 | 18,102 |
| Furniture and Bedding | 1,545 | 2,183 | 3,261 | 4,476 | 5,018 | 6,954 | 8,749 | 10,910 | 13,187 |
| Footwear | 7,354 | 8,016 | 8,438 | 9,206 | 9,758 | 10,241 | 10,546 | 11,350 | 12,721 |
| Manufactures of Metals | 1,816 | 2,238 | 2,878 | 3,651 | 4,119 | 5,219 | 6,302 | 8,257 | 10,110 |
| General Industrial Machinery | 1,180 | 1,449 | 1,833 | 2,087 | 2,414 | 3,259 | 41,213 | 5,528 | 7,007 |
| Textile Yarn, Fabrics | 1,369 | 1,432 | 1,583 | 1,816 | 1,854 | 2,501 | 3,365 | 4,253 | 5,605 |
| Travel Goods, Handbags | 1,917 | 1,942 | 1,974 | 2,214 | 2,171 | 2,741 | 3,319 | 4,044 | 4,658 |
| Road Vehicles | 574 | 731 | 923 | 1,800 | 1,406 | 1,796 | 2,373 | 3,265 | 4,170 |
| Building Fixtures/Fittings | 1,194 | 1,444 | 2,073 | 2,555 | 2,377 | 2,962 | 3,202 | 3,700 | 4,143 |
| Nonmetallic Mineral Manufactures | 1,216 | 1,441 | 1,681 | 2,059 | 2,165 | 2,431 | 2,624 | 2,953 | 3,510 |
| Professional & Scientific Instruments | 634 | 715 | 837 | 1,025 | 1,177 | 1,301 | 1,666 | 2,180 | 2,490 |
| Iron and Steel | 314 | 398 | 349 | 623 | 439 | 441 | 483 | 1,609 | 2,354 |
| Photographic Optical Equip, Watches, Clocks | 1,211 | 1,400 | 1,600 | 2,016 | 1,935 | 1,842 | 2,030 | 2,248 | 2,176 |
| Misc. Low-Valued Items | 282 | 425 | 586 | 759 | 784 | 957 | 1,229 | 1,652 | 2,068 |
| Cork and Wood (Non-Furniture) | 335 | 445 | 568 | 710 | 792 | 990 | 1,162 | 1,612 | 2,006 |
| Organic Chemicals | 335 | 337 | 392 | 467 | 488 | 564 | 772 | 1,071 | 1,600 |
| Power Generating Machinery | 314 | 354 | 408 | 505 | 553 | 694 | 842 | 1,112 | 1,573 |
| Paper Products | 310 | 401 | 471 | 611 | 627 | 792 | 1,022 | 1,263 | 1,535 |

**Note:** Ranked by data for 2005.

**Source:** U.S. Department of Commerce, International Trade Commission.

## Balance of Trade by Sector

In modern economies, trade by sector generally follows two patterns. The first is based on traditional comparative advantage in which one country trades with another in those products in which it has an abundance of resources or in which it is comparatively productive. The United States economy is characterized by high technology, extensive farmland with high agricultural yields, expensive labor, and deep capital. As such, the United States would be expected to be strong in exports of high-technology goods, food and grains, and capital intensive products. The Chinese economy, on the other hand, is characterized by abundant and cheap labor, low capital intensity, and a mix of low, medium and high technology both in manufacturing and agriculture. As such, China would be expected to be strong in exports of not only labor-intensive manufactures, such as textiles and apparel, shoes, toys, and light manufactures, but also items produced under the tutelage of foreign companies that have invested in Chinese factories. These could include household appliances, electronics, tools, or automobile parts. One would expect trade that is conducted on the basis of comparative advantage to be unbalanced on a sector-by-sector basis. The United States, for example, would run a surplus with China in aircraft but a deficit in apparel.

The second trade pattern occurs among industrialized countries and is called intra-industry or trade within industrial sectors. This is typical of trade among North America, the European Union, and industrialized nations of Asia (e.g., Japan, South Korea, and Taiwan). The products traded usually carry brand names, are differentiated, and may be protected by intellectual property rights. For example, the United States both imports and exports items such as automobiles, machinery, electronic devices, prepared food, and pharmaceuticals. A considerable share of U.S. intra-industry trade is carried out within a multinational corporation (e.g., between Ford Motors and one of its related companies, such as Mazda in Japan, Jaguar in the United Kingdom, or with other subsidiaries abroad). A large deficit in an intra-industry trading sector in which the United States is competitive may indicate that the trading partner country is using import barriers to tip the trade balance in its favor.

Table 4 shows the U.S. balance of trade with China by major sector. Most of the sectors in which the United States runs the largest trade deficits with China are, as expected, those that depend on mostly abundant and low-cost labor. These include toys and sports equipment, furniture and bedding, footwear, textiles and apparel, and leather goods. Among the large deficit sectors, however, are machinery and mechanical appliances and electrical machinery, which reflect China's foreign investment and growing technological sophistication. In plastic articles, optical and medical instruments, books and magazines (indicated by shading in the table), the United States runs a surplus in its balance of trade with the world but a deficit with China.

The sectors in which the United States runs a trade surplus with China mirror U.S. competitive advantages and include aircraft, agricultural products, and cotton fabrics. In 2005, U.S. trade surpluses with China in aircraft, copper, iron ores, and iron and steel rose dramatically.

**Table 4. U.S. Balance of Trade with China by Sector, 2003-2005**
**(millions of dollars)**

| | 2003 | 2004 | 2005 |
|---|---|---|---|
| Total China | -123,960 | 161,977 | 201,625 |
| **Major U.S. Deficit Sectors (HTS Categories)** | | | |
| Machinery/Mechanical Appliances | -25,262 | -37,628 | -46,375 |
| Electrical Machinery | -24,007 | -34,113 | -46,249 |
| Toys and Sports Equipment | -16,070 | -17,163 | -19,074 |
| Furniture and Bedding | -11,739 | -14,339 | -16,942 |
| Footwear | -10,528 | -11,318 | -12,679 |
| Woven Apparel | -5,484 | -6,606 | -10,220 |
| Knit Apparel | -3,192 | -4,092 | -6,553 |
| Leather Art; Saddlery; Bags | -5,040 | -5,708 | -6,247 |
| Articles of Iron and Steel | -3,086 | -4,376 | -5,886 |
| *Plastic Articles* | *-3,032* | *-3,402* | *-4,380* |
| Misc. Textile Articles | -2,353 | -3,052 | -3,953 |
| Vehicles, Not Railway | -1,947 | -2,729 | -3,268 |
| Misc. Art of Base Metal | -1,414 | -1,809 | -2,243 |
| Precious Stones and Metals, Pearls | -1,391 | -1,714 | -2,065 |
| Wood and Articles of Wood | -1,019 | -1,454 | -1,847 |
| Tools, Cutlery, of Base Metals | -1,373 | -1,554 | -1,774 |
| *Optical, Medical Instruments* | *-1,650* | *-1,704* | *-1,729* |
| Rubber and Rubber Articles | -698 | -1,036 | -1,551 |
| Miscellaneous Manufactures | -1,023 | -1,203 | -1,404 |
| Ceramic Products | -1,112 | -1,203 | -1,316 |
| Artificial Flowers, Feathers | -1,091 | -1,109 | -1,145 |
| *Books, Newspapers, Manuscripts* | *-653* | *-892* | *-1,130* |
| **Major U.S. Surplus Sectors (HTS Categories)** | | | |
| Aircraft, Spacecraft | 2,388 | 1,870 | 4,296 |
| Misc. Grain, Seed, Fruit | 2,787 | 2,260 | 2,165 |
| Cotton and Cotton Fabrics | 587 | 1,260 | 1,215 |
| Wood pulp, Etc. | 599 | 752 | 990 |
| Hides and Skins | 477 | 527 | 624 |
| Copper and Articles Thereof | 436 | 344 | 545 |
| Ores | 34 | 105 | 373 |
| Iron and Steel | 879 | 45 | 336 |

**Note:** Categories in italics are those in which the United States runs a trade surplus with the world but a trade deficit with China. Classification is by Harmonized System tariff codes at the 2-digit level.
**Source:** U.S. Department of Commerce, International Trade Commission.

# U.S. Imports From China — Sector Charts and Data

This section presents charts and data on U.S. imports from China by selected industrial sectors. The charts show imports from China as compared with imports from other major exporting countries or groups of countries. These include the European Union (fifteen original countries), the Association of Southeast Asian Nations (ASEAN, which includes, Indonesia, Malaysia, Singapore, Thailand, the Philippines, Brunei, Vietnam, Laos, and Myanmar [Burma]), Taiwan, Mexico, South Korea, Japan, Hong Kong, and Canada.

The data in this section are presented according to two-digit standard international trade classification (SITC) codes as reported by the U.S. Department of Commerce. The industries selected are those in which the share of imports from China has risen to a significant level or trade policy has played a significant role (e.g. iron and steel and automobiles) even though U.S. imports from China in those industries might be relatively small.

## Iron and Steel

In iron and steel products, China is becoming a major exporter to the United States. In 2005, China was the fourth largest foreign supplier of iron and steel products to the United States (surpassing Russia, South Korea, Germany, and Japan), up from seventh place in 2003. In 2005, China also bought $445 million worth of iron and steel products from the United States, making it the third largest market for U.S. exports of iron and steel. In 2005, the United States incurred a trade deficit with China in the SITC 67 category (iron and steel), which includes semi-finished products, tubes and pipes, iron and steel rods, and ferroalloys. However, the United States attained a trade surplus with China in the HTS 72 category (iron and steel), which includes more items in "primary form."

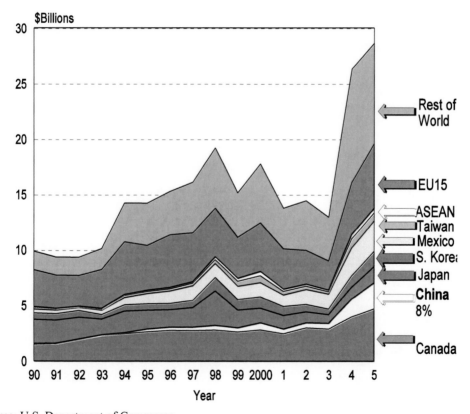

**Source**: U.S. Department of Commerce

Figure 8. U.S. Imports of Iron and Steel Products (SITC 67) by Country and Group, 1990-2005.

**Table 5. U.S. Imports of Iron and Steel Products (SITC 67) from Selected Countries and Country Groups, 1991, 2000-2005 (millions of dollars)**

|               | 1990  | 2001   | 2002   | 2003   | 2004   | 2005   |
|---------------|-------|--------|--------|--------|--------|--------|
| EU15          | 3,303 | 3,637  | 3,041  | 2,621  | 4,697  | 5,828  |
| Canada        | 1,504 | 2,437  | 2,981  | 2,885  | 3,979  | 4,699  |
| Mexico        | 357   | 1,021  | 1,340  | 1,334  | 2,530  | 2,738  |
| China         | 71    | 439    | 441    | 490    | 1,610  | 2,340  |
| Japan         | 2,097 | 1,213  | 991    | 799    | 1,072  | 1,468  |
| Korea         | 574   | 815    | 687    | 505    | 1,031  | 1,374  |
| Taiwan        | 154   | 346    | 290    | 219    | 803    | 735    |
| ASEAN         | 65    | 191    | 193    | 161    | 395    | 406    |
| Hong Kong     | 2     | 2      | 3      | 2      | 3      | 10     |
| Rest of World | 1,691 | 3,657  | 4,469  | 3,929  | 10,204 | 9,034  |
| World         | 9,818 | 13,758 | 14,436 | 12,945 | 26,324 | 28,632 |

**Source:** U.S. Department of Commerce

## Specialized Industrial Machinery

China is becoming an important supplier of specialized industrial machinery, which includes machine tools and sewing machines, but lags behind the European Union, Japan, and Canada and competes with other newly industrialized countries such as Mexico, South Korea, and Taiwan. China accounted for only 4.5% of U.S. imports in this category in 2005.

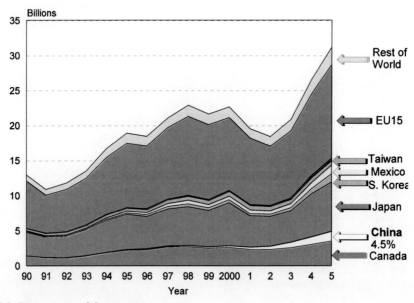

**Source**: U.S. Department of Commerce

Figure 9. U.S. Imports of Specialized Industrial Machinery (SITC 72) by Country and Group, 1990-2005.

**Table 6. U.S. Imports of Specialized Industrial Machinery (SITC 72) from Selected Countries and Country Groups, 1990, 2001-2005 (millions of dollars)**

|  | 1990 | 2001 | 2002 | 2003 | 2004 | 2005 |
|---|---|---|---|---|---|---|
| EU15 | 6,786 | 9,511 | 8,463 | 9,586 | 11,656 | 13,419 |
| Japan | 3,340 | 4,479 | 4,217 | 4,445 | 6,105 | 7,019 |
| Canada | 1,384 | 2,297 | 2,294 | 2,556 | 3,010 | 3,482 |
| China | 23 | 331 | 485 | 791 | 1,069 | 1,415 |
| Mexico | 139 | 537 | 490 | 578 | 862 | 1,241 |
| Korea | 69 | 305 | 325 | 467 | 746 | 1,159 |
| Taiwan | 313 | 626 | 638 | 623 | 730 | 684 |
| ASEAN | 13 | 101 | 113 | 145 | 250 | 287 |
| Hong Kong | 18 | 12 | 17 | 15 | 18 | 17 |
| Rest of World | 868 | 1,314 | 1,373 | 1,614 | 2,049 | 2,464 |
| World | 12,953 | 19,513 | 18,415 | 20,820 | 26,495 | 31,187 |

**Source:** U.S. Department of Commerce

## Office Machines and Computers

In U.S. imports of office machines and automatic data processing machines (including television sets, computers and computer hardware), China has quickly become the largest supplier, surpassing ASEAN. Imports of such products from China rose by over 75% between 2003 and 2005 and now account for 42% of U.S. imports in this category. Office machines and computers from other East Asian countries — Japan, Taiwan, and South Korea — have been leveling off or decreasing, although many of their high tech manufacturers have built plants in China and export from there. The top exporters of office machines and data processing machines to the United States in 2005 were China, Malaysia, Japan, Mexico, and Singapore.

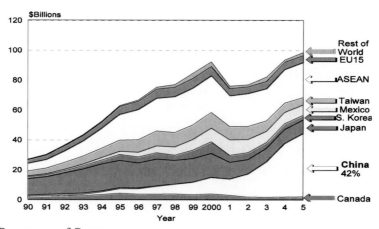

**Source**: U.S. Department of Commerce

Figure 10. U.S. Imports of Office Machines and Automatic Data Processing Machines (SITC 75) by Country and Group, 1990-2005.

**Table 7. U.S. Imports of Office Machines and Automatic Data Processing Machines (SITC 75) from Selected Countries and Country Groups, 1990, 2001-2005 (millions of dollars)**

|  | 1990 | 2001 | 2002 | 2003 | 2004 | 2005 |
|---|---|---|---|---|---|---|
| China | 117 | 10,761 | 15,230 | 23,612 | 35,579 | 42,169 |
| ASEAN | 5,150 | 20,676 | 22,043 | 21,571 | 22,460 | 23,473 |
| Japan | 11,007 | 11,055 | 9,464 | 8,978 | 9,282 | 8,936 |
| Mexico | 706 | 10,377 | 8,828 | 7,516 | 7,726 | 7,075 |
| Taiwan | 3,084 | 8,751 | 8,659 | 6,996 | 6,132 | 4,879 |
| EU15 | 2,461 | 4,676 | 4,505 | 4,815 | 4,810 | 4,516 |
| Korea | 1,347 | 4,657 | 4,632 | 3,779 | 3,885 | 3,104 |
| Canada | 1,893 | 2,942 | 1,825 | 1,644 | 1,865 | 1,966 |
| Hong Kong | 809 | 276 | 392 | 328 | 304 | 210 |
| Rest of World | 297 | 1,729 | 1,342 | 2,947 | 1,492 | 2,015 |
| World | 26,871 | 75,900 | 76,920 | 80,542 | 93,535 | 98,343 |

**Source:** U.S. Department of Commerce

## Telecommunications and Sound Equipment

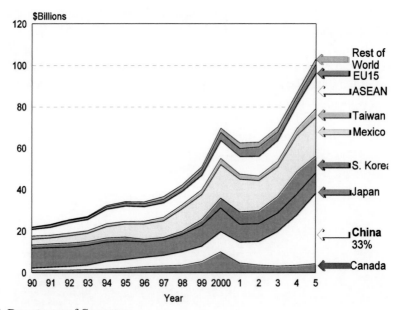

**Source**: U.S. Department of Commerce

Figure 11. Imports of Telecommunications and Sound Equipment (SITC 76) by Country and Group, 1990-2005.

China's share of U.S. imports of telecommunications and sound equipment has risen to 33%. Such imports from China rose from $1.1 billion in 1990 to $34 billion in 2005. Imports of these products from elsewhere in Asia, particularly from ASEAN countries, have also been rising rapidly. The largest suppliers of telecommunications and sound equipment to the United States in 2005 were China, Mexico, Malaysia, Japan, and South Korea.

**Table 8. U.S. Imports of Telecommunications and Sound Equipment (SITC 76) from Selected Countries and Country Groups, 1990, 2001-2005 (millions of dollars)**

|  | 1990 | 2001 | 2002 | 2003 | 2004 | 2005 |
|---|---|---|---|---|---|---|
| China | 1,142 | 10,062 | 14,144 | 16,723 | 24,311 | 34,140 |
| Mexico | 2,302 | 15,765 | 14,483 | 14,239 | 17,475 | 18,840 |
| ASEAN | 3,122 | 8,548 | 9,514 | 10,218 | 11,779 | 17,114 |
| Korea | 1,632 | 6,001 | 6,353 | 7,955 | 10,942 | 8,214 |
| Japan | 9,061 | 8,577 | 8,473 | 8,889 | 9,967 | 9,707 |
| EU15 | 890 | 3,883 | 4,559 | 4,051 | 3,707 | 4,382 |
| Canada | 972 | 4,533 | 3,543 | 3,053 | 3,435 | 4,103 |
| Taiwan | 1,426 | 2,361 | 2,137 | 2,655 | 3,261 | 4,125 |
| Hong Kong | 478 | 224 | 357 | 522 | 647 | 672 |
| Rest of World | 322 | 2,446 | 2,264 | 2,363 | 1,941 | 2,637 |
| World | 21,347 | 62,400 | 65,827 | 70,668 | 87,465 | 103,934 |

**Source:** U.S. Department of Commerce

## Electrical Machinery and Parts

U.S. imports of electrical machinery and parts (including semi-conductors) have been growing dramatically from nearly all major suppliers. At 18% of such imports in 2005, China has become a significant supplier — surpassing the EU, Japan, and ASEAN. Mexico remains the leading foreign supplier.

**Table 9. U.S. Imports of Electrical Machinery and Parts (SITC 77) from Selected Countries and Country Groups, 1990, 2001-2005 (millions of dollars)**

|  | 1990 | 2001 | 2002 | 2003 | 2004 | 2005 |
|---|---|---|---|---|---|---|
| Mexico | 4,406 | 16,290 | 16,930 | 17,547 | 19,120 | 20,671 |
| China | 652 | 9,047 | 10,217 | 11,808 | 15,197 | 17,980 |
| EU15 | 4,898 | 11,009 | 10,881 | 11,462 | 12,314 | 13,360 |
| ASEAN | 4,644 | 13,748 | 12,427 | 11,308 | 11,557 | 11,736 |
| Japan | 8,658 | 11,941 | 9,406 | 8,713 | 10,251 | 10,665 |
| Canada | 3,323 | 5,871 | 5,025 | 4,920 | 5,619 | 6,210 |
| Taiwan | 2,180 | 5,878 | 5,296 | 5,160 | 6,170 | 6,077 |
| Korea | 2,504 | 5,194 | 5,150 | 5,105 | 5,992 | 5,437 |
| Hong Kong | 792 | 1,050 | 881 | 585 | 637 | 593 |
| Rest of World | 1,080 | 4,112 | 4,359 | 4,916 | 5,414 | 5,560 |
| World | 33,137 | 84,140 | 80,572 | 81,524 | 92,271 | 98,289 |

**Source:** U.S. Department of Commerce

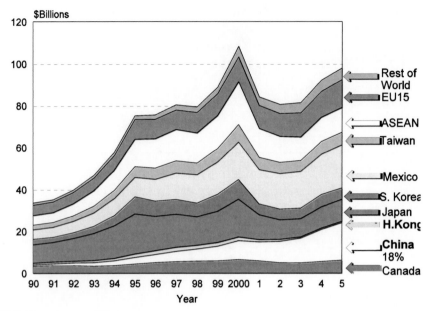

**Source**: U.S. Department of Commerce

Figure 12. U.S. Imports of Electrical Machinery and Parts (SITC 77) by Country and Group, 1990-2005.

## Road Motor Vehicles

China is the world's third largest auto market and fourth largest auto producer. China's automobile sector has absorbed heavy foreign investment — roughly 70% of the country's car market is held by Chinese-foreign joint ventures such as Shanghai General Motors (GM), Shanghai Volkswagen, and First Auto Works-Toyota — and is aimed primarily at Chinese buyers.[33] China became a net exporter of vehicles for the first time in 2005, with exports of 172,800 vehicles and imports of 161,900 units. Most of China's vehicle exports are sold in Middle Eastern, North African, and South American countries. In addition, China has become a major supplier of motorcycles to Southeast Asia. Chinese auto makers Geely and Chery reportedly have plans to begin exporting passenger cars to the United States in 2007 or 2008.[34]

Currently, China is not a significant player in the U.S. car market. U.S. road vehicle and related imports from China mainly consist of auto parts, bicycles and motorcycles, and specialty vehicles such as golf carts and beach go-carts. China has become an important supplier of auto parts to the United States, with $2 billion in selected auto parts in 2005, but trails Canada ($11.8 billion), Japan ($8.8 billion), Mexico ($7.7 billion), and Germany ($2.3 billion). China exported $290 million worth of motorcycles to the United States in 2005, accounting for 8% of U.S. motorcycle imports compared to Japan's 73%.

China is expected to continue to lower tariffs on imported automobiles, to 25% in 2006, pursuant to China's WTO accession agreement, although many non-tariff barriers reportedly remain.[35]

In U.S. imports of prefabricated buildings, sanitary, plumbing, heating and lighting fixtures and fittings, China has surged to become a main factor. The PRC accounted for over half such imports in 2005, although total imports of such products from China amounted to only $4 billion, making it the 13th largest U.S. import from China.

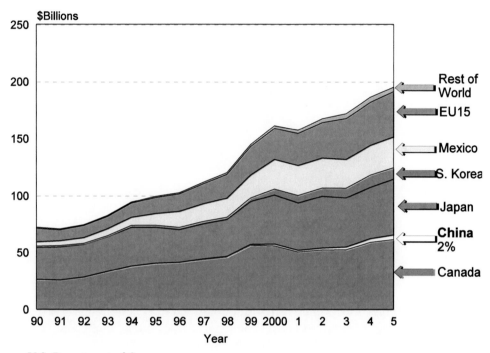

**Source**: U.S. Department of Commerce

Figure 13. U.S. Imports of Road Motor Vehicles (SITC 78) by Country and Group, 1990-2005.

**Table 10. U.S. Imports of Road Motor Vehicles (SITC 78) from Selected Countries and Country Groups, 1990, 2001-2005**
**(millions of dollars)**

|  | 1990 | 2001 | 2002 | 2003 | 2004 | 2005 |
|---|---|---|---|---|---|---|
| Canada | 26,094 | 50,477 | 52,050 | 52,448 | 58,832 | 61,332 |
| Japan | 29,839 | 41,429 | 45,449 | 43,178 | 45,033 | 48,867 |
| EU15 | 12,270 | 28,022 | 31,043 | 35,975 | 37,813 | 39,958 |
| Mexico | 4,084 | 26,246 | 26,181 | 25,222 | 26,114 | 26,744 |
| Korea | 1,275 | 6,778 | 7,382 | 8,503 | 10,773 | 10,187 |
| China | 59 | 1,404 | 1,796 | 2,369 | 3,267 | 4,198 |
| Taiwan | 871 | 1,124 | 1,239 | 1,387 | 1,522 | 1,804 |
| ASEAN | 88 | 247 | 280 | 297 | 359 | 432 |
| Hong Kong | 7 | 13 | 14 | 38 | 43 | 39 |
| Rest of World | 930 | 2,892 | 3,338 | 4,271 | 4,412 | 3,853 |
| World | 75,517 | 158,632 | 168,772 | 173,688 | 188,168 | 197,414 |

**Source:** U.S. Department of Commerce

## Building and Lighting Products

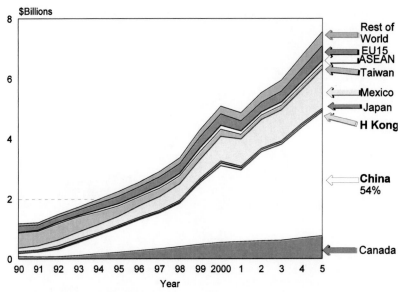

**Source**: U.S. Department of Commerce

Figure 14. U.S. Imports of Building and Lighting Products (SITC 81) by Country and Group, 1990-2005.

**Table 11. U.S. Imports of Prefabricated Buildings, Sanitary, Plumbing, Heating and Lighting Fixtures and Fittings (SITC 81) from Selected Countries and Country Groups, 1990, 2001-2005**
**(millions of dollars)**

|               | 1990  | 2001  | 2002  | 2003  | 2004  | 2005  |
|---------------|-------|-------|-------|-------|-------|-------|
| China         | 94    | 2,383 | 2,962 | 3,199 | 3,697 | 4,146 |
| Mexico        | 117   | 903   | 961   | 1,036 | 1,132 | 1,300 |
| Canada        | 80    | 572   | 598   | 617   | 693   | 762   |
| EU15          | 205   | 329   | 319   | 356   | 428   | 497   |
| Taiwan        | 495   | 156   | 152   | 151   | 154   | 142   |
| ASEAN         | 27    | 116   | 106   | 115   | 121   | 137   |
| Hong Kong     | 47    | 70    | 77    | 80    | 73    | 59    |
| Japan         | 28    | 59    | 36    | 41    | 49    | 52    |
| Korea         | 61    | 32    | 36    | 42    | 37    | 37    |
| Rest of World | 78    | 275   | 319   | 362   | 422   | 464   |
| World         | 1,232 | 4,895 | 5,566 | 5,999 | 6,806 | 7,596 |

**Source:** U.S. Department of Commerce

## Furniture

In U.S. imports of furniture and related parts, China has become a dominant supplier. The PRC accounted for over 43% of U.S. furniture imports in 2005. U.S. imports of furniture from China now exceed the combined U.S. imports from Canada and Mexico, which were the leading foreign suppliers of furniture until the late 1990s. In 2004, the Bush Administration imposed anti-dumping penalties on approximately 500 furniture manufacturers in China.

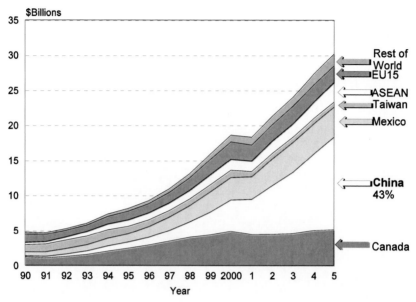

**Source**: U.S. Department of Commerce

Figure 15. U.S. Imports of Furniture and Parts (SITC 82) by Country and Group, 1990-2005.

**Table 12. U.S. Imports of Furniture and Parts (SITC 82) from Selected Countries and Country Groups, 1990, 2001-2005**
**(millions of dollars)**

|  | 1990 | 2001 | 2002 | 2003 | 2004 | 2005 |
|---|---|---|---|---|---|---|
| China | 145 | 5,017 | 6,954 | 8,742 | 10,905 | 13,179 |
| Canada | 1,209 | 4,411 | 4,423 | 4,551 | 5,007 | 5,126 |
| Mexico | 578 | 3,212 | 3,824 | 4,275 | 4,316 | 4,297 |
| ASEAN | 331 | 1,492 | 1,753 | 1,886 | 2,303 | 2,800 |
| EU15 | 1,174 | 2,309 | 2,321 | 2,489 | 2,491 | 2,371 |
| Taiwan | 1,009 | 765 | 794 | 748 | 753 | 716 |
| Japan | 162 | 141 | 107 | 135 | 181 | 210 |
| Korea | 67 | 75 | 75 | 69 | 68 | 111 |
| Hong Kong | 29 | 98 | 90 | 109 | 97 | 82 |
| Rest of World | 299 | 1,081 | 1,219 | 1,289 | 1,557 | 1,691 |
| World | 5,003 | 18,601 | 21,560 | 24,293 | 27,678 | 30,583 |

**Source:** U.S. Department of Commerce

## Travel Goods and Handbags

China has become the principal supplier of imported travel goods, handbags, and similar items, accounting for nearly 75% of U.S. imports of such merchandise in 2005. The EU has become an important supplier while China appears to have taken market shares from South Korea, Taiwan, and, more recently, ASEAN. This U.S. import category is ranked only 42[st] in total customs value.

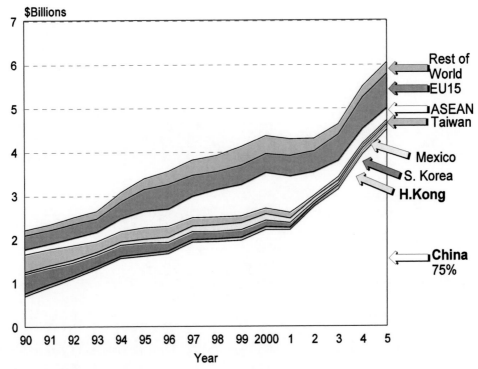

**Source**: U.S. Department of Commerce

Figure 16. Imports of Travel Goods, Handbags, and Similar Products (SITC 83) by Country and Group, 1990-2005.

**Table 13. U.S. Imports of Travel Goods, Handbags, (SITC 83) from Selected Countries and Country Groups, 1990, 2001-2005**
**(millions of dollars)**

|  | 1990 | 2001 | 2002 | 2003 | 2004 | 2005 |
|---|---|---|---|---|---|---|
| China | 692 | 2,211 | 2,741 | 3,136 | 3,936 | 4,504 |
| EU15 | 270 | 463 | 476 | 602 | 715 | 790 |
| ASEAN | 114 | 836 | 538 | 372 | 340 | 275 |
| Hong Kong | 50 | 46 | 52 | 85 | 95 | 92 |
| Mexico | 46 | 104 | 87 | 69 | 63 | 54 |
| Canada | 17 | 39 | 35 | 37 | 35 | 36 |
| Taiwan | 406 | 129 | 52 | 79 | 47 | 32 |
| Korea | 446 | 106 | 56 | 39 | 31 | 21 |
| Japan | 9 | 7 | 7 | 8 | 12 | 12 |
| Rest of World | 121 | 384 | 292 | 233 | 248 | 262 |
| World | 2,171 | 4,325 | 4,336 | 4,660 | 5,522 | 6,078 |

**Source:** U.S. Department of Commerce

## Apparel and Clothing

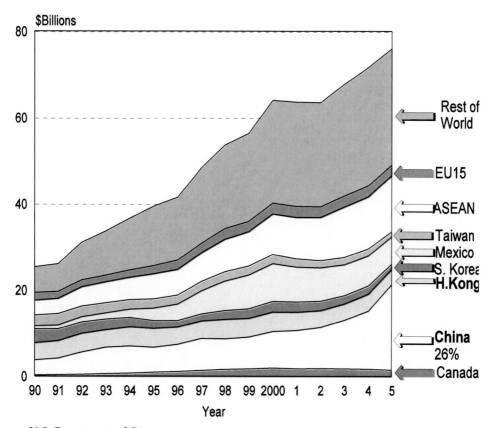

**Source**: U.S. Department of Commerce

Figure 17. U.S. Imports of Apparel and Clothing Accessories (SITC 84) by Country and Group, 1990-2005.

U.S. imports of apparel and clothing accessories from China have been rising, reaching 26% of U.S. imports in 2005. According to some estimates, more than 80% of Chinese apparel exports are produced by joint ventures, many of them involving East Asian investment.[36] Global quotas on imported textiles and apparel expired on January 1, 2005, pursuant to the Multi-Fiber Agreement, resulting in a surge in U.S. garment imports from China, which increased by 46% in 2005. Other nations with large gains in the U.S. apparel market were India (up 33%), Indonesia (20%) Bangladesh (20%), and Cambodia (20%). Although wages for low skill labor in China reportedly are rising relative to other developing countries, China's clothing manufacturers retain competitive advantages such as high labor productivity, "vertical integration" — the ability to produce all manufacturing inputs domestically — and developed infrastructure. In November 2005, the United States and the PRC signed a three-year agreement on textiles trade which imposes quotas on 21 types of Chinese textiles and clothing but which allows for a progressive increase in U.S. imports of apparel products from China through 2008.

**Table 14. U.S. Imports of Apparel and Clothing Accessories (SITC 84) from Selected Countries and Country Groups, 1990, 2001-2005 (millions of dollars)**

|               | 1990   | 2001   | 2002   | 2003   | 2004   | 2005   |
|---------------|--------|--------|--------|--------|--------|--------|
| China         | 3,422  | 8,852  | 9,538  | 11,341 | 13,567 | 19,888 |
| ASEAN         | 3,404  | 9,581  | 10,020 | 11,773 | 12,157 | 13,043 |
| Mexico        | 709    | 8,127  | 7,731  | 7,199  | 6,943  | 6,321  |
| Hong Kong     | 3,974  | 4,282  | 3,928  | 3,760  | 3,919  | 3,553  |
| EU15          | 1,790  | 2,584  | 2,473  | 2,564  | 2,586  | 2,444  |
| Canada        | 247    | 1,764  | 1,799  | 1,740  | 1,692  | 1,468  |
| Korea         | 3,244  | 2,354  | 2,206  | 1,925  | 1,936  | 1,253  |
| Taiwan        | 2,475  | 1,907  | 1,664  | 1,690  | 1,626  | 1,203  |
| Japan         | 158    | 170    | 205    | 252    | 325    | 121    |
| Rest of World | 5,891  | 24,168 | 24,150 | 25,907 | 27,438 | 26,983 |
| World         | 25,314 | 63,789 | 63,714 | 68,060 | 72,189 | 76,277 |

**Source:** U.S. Department of Commerce

## Footwear

U.S. imports of footwear from China surged during the 1990s. From $1.5 billion in 1990, they rose to over $10 billion in 2002 or two-thirds of all such imports. China has largely replaced South Korea and Taiwan as the main source of Asian-produced footwear in the United States. Other large suppliers are Italy, Brazil, and Vietnam.

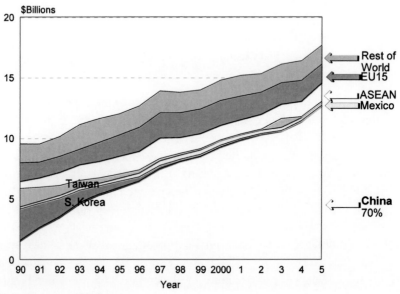

**Source**: U.S. Department of Commerce

Figure 18. U.S. Imports of Footwear (SITC 85) by Country and Group, 1990-2005.

**Table 15. U.S. Imports of Footwear (SITC 85) from Selected Countries and Country Groups, 1990, 2001-2005**
**(millions of dollars)**

| | 1990 | 2001 | 2002 | 2003 | 2004 | 2005 |
|---|---|---|---|---|---|---|
| China | 1,475 | 9,766 | 10,241 | 10,546 | 11,347 | 12,654 |
| EU15 | 1,523 | 1,950 | 1,826 | 1,763 | 1,722 | 1,558 |
| ASEAN | 579 | 1,185 | 1,237 | 1,184 | 1,259 | 1,525 |
| Mexico | 165 | 311 | 278 | 275 | 242 | 247 |
| Canada | 53 | 78 | 67 | 64 | 76 | 93 |
| Taiwan | 1,528 | 75 | 73 | 73 | 80 | 69 |
| Hong Kong | 109 | 81 | 67 | 60 | 86 | 52 |
| Korea | 2,558 | 103 | 65 | 50 | 51 | 45 |
| Japan | 5 | 2 | 2 | 2 | 2 | 3 |
| Rest of World | 1,543 | 1,698 | 1,523 | 1,542 | 1,632 | 1,588 |
| World | 9,538 | 15,249 | 15,379 | 15,559 | 16,497 | 17,834 |

**Source:** U.S. Department of Commerce

## Professional, Scientific, and Controlling Instruments

China is a minor supplier of U.S. imports of professional, scientific and controlling instruments, supplying 8% of U.S. imports in this category in 2005. Over two-thirds of such imports originate in the European Union, Mexico, and Japan.

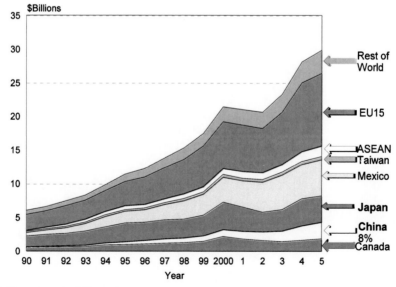

**Source**: U.S. Department of Commerce

Figure 19. U.S. Imports of Professional, Scientific, and Controlling Instruments (SITC 87) by Country and Group, 1990-2005.

**Table 16. U.S. Imports of Professional, Scientific and Controlling Instruments and Apparatus (SITC 87) from Selected Countries and Country Groups, 1990, 2001-2005 (millions of dollars)**

|               | 1990  | 2001   | 2002   | 2003   | 2004   | 2005   |
|---------------|-------|--------|--------|--------|--------|--------|
| EU15          | 2,310 | 6,887  | 6,543  | 7,744  | 10,225 | 10,802 |
| Mexico        | 513   | 3,895  | 4,436  | 5,090  | 5,082  | 5,371  |
| Japan         | 1,494 | 3,561  | 2,902  | 3,177  | 4,016  | 3,887  |
| China         | 74    | 1,172  | 1,301  | 1,660  | 2,176  | 2,483  |
| Canada        | 527   | 1,793  | 1,575  | 1,406  | 1,611  | 1,833  |
| ASEAN         | 152   | 1,027  | 1,037  | 1,139  | 1,448  | 1,571  |
| Taiwan        | 176   | 372    | 393    | 450    | 458    | 472    |
| Korea         | 89    | 152    | 156    | 153    | 177    | 230    |
| Hong Kong     | 82    | 55     | 67     | 70     | 67     | 79     |
| Rest of World | 604   | 2,287  | 2,400  | 2,675  | 3,101  | 3,433  |
| World         | 6,021 | 21,201 | 20,810 | 23,564 | 28,361 | 30,161 |

**Source:** U.S. Department of Commerce

## Photographic and Optical Equipment and Timepieces

China is a rising supplier of photographic apparatus, equipment and supplies and optical goods as well as watches and clocks. In 2005, China accounted for 17.5% of U.S. imports of such products. Japan and the European Union still dominate U.S. imports. By country, the top three suppliers of such imports for the United States are Japan, China, and Switzerland.

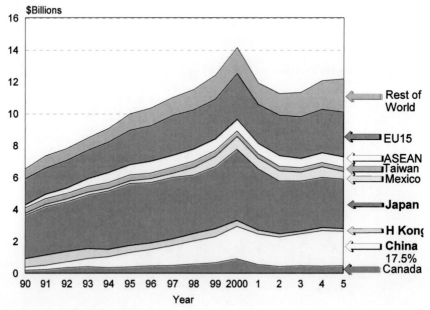

**Source**: U.S. Department of Commerce

Figure 20. U.S. Imports of Photographic Equipment, Optical Goods, Watches and Clocks (SITC 88) by Country and Group, 1990-2005.

**Table 17. U.S. Imports of Photographic Apparatus, Equipment and Supplies and Optical Goods; Watches and Clocks (SITC 88) from Selected Countries and Country Groups, 1990, 2001-2005 (millions of dollars)**

|  | 1990 | 2001 | 2002 | 2003 | 2004 | 2005 |
|---|---|---|---|---|---|---|
| Japan | 2,668 | 3,848 | 3,309 | 3,138 | 3,140 | 3,082 |
| EU15 | 1,619 | 2,439 | 2,535 | 2,612 | 2,716 | 2,807 |
| China | 191 | 1,908 | 1,842 | 2,001 | 2,239 | 2,153 |
| ASEAN | 199 | 650 | 664 | 587 | 614 | 646 |
| Mexico | 128 | 648 | 634 | 555 | 665 | 494 |
| Canada | 180 | 545 | 414 | 461 | 428 | 469 |
| Taiwan | 334 | 282 | 288 | 280 | 265 | 258 |
| Hong Kong | 526 | 236 | 200 | 164 | 182 | 178 |
| Korea | 127 | 168 | 150 | 134 | 124 | 127 |
| Rest of World | 574 | 1,348 | 1,353 | 1,510 | 1,797 | 2,072 |
| World | 6,546 | 12,072 | 11,389 | 11,442 | 12,170 | 12,286 |

**Source:** U.S. Department of Commerce

# FOREIGN DIRECT INVESTMENT IN CHINA

Fueling China's export boom is an unprecedented infusion of foreign capital in the manufacturing sector.[37] Foreign direct investment (FDI) is directed toward investments in companies in which the foreign investor has a controlling interest. It is primarily for physical plant and equipment and for the costs of establishing enterprises in China. It is not for portfolio investment on China's stock exchanges. In 2002, China overtook the United States as the world's largest recipient of foreign direct investment. In 2005, China remained in that position, despite a slight decrease from a year earlier, with $60 billion in utilized FDI.

**Table 18. China's Utilized Foreign Direct Investment Inflows, Top Foreign Investors, 2000-2005 (billions of dollars)**

| Country or Region | 2001 | 2002 | 2003 | 2004 | 2005 |
|---|---|---|---|---|---|
| Hong Kong | 16.7 | 17.8 | 17.7 | 18.9 | 17.1 |
| Virgin Islands[39] | 5.0 | 6.1 | 5.7 | 6.7 | 9.0 |
| Japan | 4.3 | 4.2 | 5.0 | 5.4 | 6.5 |
| South Korea | 2.1 | 2.7 | 4.5 | 6.2 | 5.2 |
| United States | 4.4 | 5.4 | 4.2 | 3.9 | 3.1 |
| Singapore | 2.1 | 2.3 | 2.0 | 2 | 2.2 |
| Taiwan | 2.9 | 3.9 | 3.4 | 3.1 | 2.1 |
| Germany | 1.2 | 0.9 | 0.8 | 1 | 1.5 |
| All Sources | 46.9 | 52.7 | 53.5 | 64 | 60.3 |

**Source:** U.S. & Foreign Commercial Service and U.S. Department of State, "Doing Business in China: A Country Commercial Guide for U.S. Companies," 2006.

The United States is one of the largest sources of utilized FDI in China, investing $3.1 billion in 2005. (See **Table 18.**) China relies heavily upon investment from Hong Kong and other East Asian countries and regions. A significant amount of FDI from Hong Kong comes from Taiwan or from mainland Chinese companies via their subsidiaries in Hong Kong.[38] Annual or utilized FDI from Japan and South Korea surpassed that of the United States in 2003. In 2004, South Korea surpassed Japan to be the third largest source of FDI in China. The United States remains the second largest source of cumulative FDI after Hong Kong. China's WTO commitments include allowing more foreign investment in sectors such as telecommunications, energy, banking, and insurance.

## APPENDIX

### Table A1. China's Merchandise Trade with the World, 1984-2005
### (millions of dollars)

| Year | China's Trade with the World (Chinese data) | | | World Trade with China (Partner Country Data) | | |
|------|---------------|---------------|---------------|---------------|---------------|---------------|
| | China Exports | China Imports | China Balance | World Exports | World Imports | World Balance |
| 1984 | 24,824 | 25,953 | -1,129 | 24,640 | 26,904 | -2,264 |
| 1985 | 27,329 | 42,534 | -15,205 | 38,355 | 30,867 | 7,488 |
| 1986 | 31,367 | 43,247 | -11,880 | 36,152 | 35,310 | 842 |
| 1987 | 39,464 | 43,222 | -3,758 | 39,250 | 46,654 | -7,404 |
| 1988 | 47,663 | 55,352 | -7,689 | 51,794 | 59,748 | -7,954 |
| 1989 | 52,916 | 59,131 | -6,215 | 51,666 | 72,810 | -21,144 |
| 1990 | 62,876 | 53,915 | 8,961 | 49,036 | 88,692 | -39,656 |
| 1991 | 71,940 | 63,855 | 8,085 | 61,732 | 112,372 | -50,640 |
| 1992 | 85,492 | 81,843 | 3,649 | 81,996 | 136,853 | -54,857 |
| 1993 | 91,611 | 103,552 | -11,941 | 108,406 | 156,896 | -48,490 |
| 1994 | 120,822 | 115,629 | 5,193 | 120,634 | 191,663 | -71,029 |
| 1995 | 148,892 | 132,063 | 16,829 | 145,897 | 233,614 | -87,717 |
| 1996 | 151,093 | 138,949 | 12,144 | 156,200 | 254,440 | -98,240 |
| 1997 | 182,917 | 142,163 | 40,754 | 165,230 | 286,540 | -121,310 |
| 1998 | 183,744 | 140,385 | 43,359 | 152,890 | 289,620 | -136,730 |
| 1999 | 194,932 | 165,717 | 29,215 | 162,650 | 322,080 | -159,430 |
| 2000 | 249,212 | 225,097 | 24,115 | 212,060 | 398,060 | -186,000 |
| 2001 | 266,200 | 243,600 | 22,600 | 221,450 | 413,280 | -191,830 |
| 2002 | 325,642 | 295,302 | 30,339 | 270,930 | 483,610 | -212,680 |
| 2003 | 438,472 | 413,095 | 25,377 | 422,590 | 601,920 | -179,330 |
| 2004 | 593,647 | 560,811 | 32,831 | 527,370 | 794,480 | -267,110 |
| 2005 | 762,326 | 660,221 | 102,105 | 647,690 | 989,880 | -342,190 |

**Note:** Summation of data reported by 109 of China's trading partner countries in 1983 growing to 156 countries reporting in 2005.

**Sources:** Chinese data: PRC General Administration of Customs and *Global Trade Atlas*. World Data: International Monetary Fund, *Direction of Trade Statistics Yearbook* and *Direction of Trade Statistics Quarterly*.

**Table A2. U.S. Merchandise Trade with China and China's Merchandise Trade with the United States, 1984-2005 (millions of dollars)**

| Year | U.S. Trade with China (U.S. data) | | | China's Trade with U.S. (Chinese data) | | |
|---|---|---|---|---|---|---|
| | U.S. Exports | U.S. Imports | U.S. Balance | China Exports | China Imports | China Balance |
| 1984 | 3,004 | 3,381 | -377 | 2,313 | 3,837 | -1,524 |
| 1985 | 3,856 | 4,224 | -368 | 2,336 | 5,199 | -2,863 |
| 1986 | 3,106 | 5,241 | -2,135 | 2,633 | 4,718 | -2,085 |
| 1987 | 3,497 | 6,910 | -3,413 | 3,030 | 4,836 | -1,806 |
| 1988 | 5,017 | 9,261 | -4,244 | 3,399 | 6,633 | -3,234 |
| 1989 | 5,807 | 12,901 | -7,094 | 4,414 | 7,864 | -3,450 |
| 1990 | 4,807 | 16,296 | -11,489 | 5,314 | 6,591 | -1,277 |
| 1991 | 6,287 | 20,305 | -14,018 | 6,198 | 8,010 | -1,812 |
| 1992 | 7,470 | 27,413 | -19,943 | 8,599 | 8,903 | -304 |
| 1993 | 8,767 | 31,183 | -22,416 | 16,976 | 10,633 | 6,343 |
| 1994 | 9,287 | 41,362 | -32,075 | 21,421 | 13,977 | 7,444 |
| 1995 | 11,749 | 48,521 | -36,772 | 24,744 | 16,123 | 8,621 |
| 1996 | 11,978 | 54,409 | -42,431 | 26,731 | 16,179 | 10,552 |
| 1997 | 12,805 | 65,832 | -53,027 | 32,744 | 16,290 | 16,454 |
| 1998 | 14,258 | 75,109 | -60,851 | 38,001 | 16,997 | 21,004 |
| 1999 | 13,118 | 81,786 | -68,668 | 41,946 | 19,480 | 22,466 |
| 2000 | 16,253 | 100,063 | -83,810 | 52,104 | 22,363 | 29,741 |
| 2001 | 19,234 | 102,280 | -83,046 | 54,300 | 26,200 | 28,100 |
| 2002 | 22,053 | 125,167 | -103,115 | 69,959 | 27,227 | 42,731 |
| 2003 | 26,806 | 151,620 | -123,960 | 92,510 | 33,882 | 58,628 |
| 2004 | 34,721 | 196,699 | -161,978 | 124,973 | 44,652 | 80,321 |
| 2005 | 41,836 | 243,462 | -201,626 | 162,938 | 48,734 | 114,204 |

**Sources:** U.S. data from U.S. Department of Commerce. Chinese data from PRC General Administration of Customs and *Global Trade Atlas*.

**Table A3. Japan's Merchandise Trade with China and China's Merchandise Trade with Japan, 1984-2005 (millions of dollars)**

| Year | Japan's Trade with China (Japanese Data) | | | China's Trade with Japan (Chinese Data) | | |
|---|---|---|---|---|---|---|
| | Japan Exports | Japan Imports | Japan Balance | China Exports | China Imports | China Balance |
| 1984 | 7,199 | 5,943 | 1,256 | 5,155 | 8,057 | -2,902 |
| 1985 | 12,590 | 6,534 | 6,056 | 6,091 | 15,178 | -9,087 |
| 1986 | 9,936 | 5,727 | 4,209 | 5,079 | 12,463 | -7,384 |
| 1987 | 8,337 | 7,478 | 859 | 6,392 | 10,087 | -3,695 |
| 1988 | 9,486 | 9,861 | -375 | 8,046 | 11,062 | -3,016 |
| 1989 | 8,477 | 11,083 | -2,606 | 8,395 | 10,534 | -2,139 |
| 1990 | 6,145 | 12,057 | -5,912 | 9,210 | 7,656 | 1,554 |
| 1991 | 8,605 | 14,248 | -5,643 | 10,252 | 10,032 | 220 |
| 1992 | 11,967 | 16,972 | -5,005 | 11,699 | 13,686 | -1,987 |
| 1993 | 17,353 | 20,651 | -3,298 | 15,782 | 23,303 | -7,521 |
| 1995 | 21,934 | 35,922 | -13,988 | 28,466 | 29,007 | -541 |
| 1996 | 21,827 | 40,405 | -18,578 | 30,888 | 29,190 | 1,698 |
| 1997 | 21,692 | 41,827 | -20,135 | 31,820 | 28,990 | 2,830 |

## Table A3. (continued)

| Year | Japan's Trade with China (Japanese Data) | | | China's Trade with Japan (Chinese Data) | | |
|------|------------------|------------------|------------------|------------------|------------------|------------------|
|      | Japan Exports | Japan Imports | Japan Balance | China Exports | China Imports | China Balance |
| 1998 | 20,182 | 37,079 | -16,897 | 29,718 | 28,307 | 1,411 |
| 1999 | 23,450 | 43,070 | -19,620 | 32,400 | 33,768 | -1,368 |
| 2000 | 30,440 | 55,340 | -24,900 | 41,611 | 41,520 | 90 |
| 2001 | 30,941 | 57,795 | -26,558 | 45,078 | 42,810 | 2,267 |
| 2002 | 40,001 | 61,882 | -21,881 | 48,483 | 53,489 | -5,006 |
| 2003 | 57,474 | 75,579 | -18,105 | 59,453 | 74,204 | -14,751 |
| 2004 | 73,971 | 94,446 | -20,475 | 73,536 | 94,191 | -20,655 |
| 2005 | 79,972 | 108,515 | -28,543 | 84,097 | 100,467 | -16,370 |

**Sources:** IMF, Direction of Trade Statistics Quarterly; Global Trade Atlas; PRC, General Administration of Customs.

## Table A4. European Merchandise Trade with China and China's Merchandise Trade with the European Union, 1984-2005
### (millions of dollars)

| Year | EU-15 Trade with China (EU data) | | | China's Trade with the EU-15 (Chinese Data) | | |
|------|------------|------------|------------|------------------|------------------|------------------|
|      | EU Exports | EU Imports | EU Balance | China Exports | China Imports | China Balance |
| 1984 | 2,929 | 2,639 | 290 | 2,232 | 3,323 | -1,091 |
| 1985 | 5,484 | 2,971 | 2,513 | 2,283 | 6,157 | -3,874 |
| 1986 | 6,403 | 4,106 | 2,297 | 4,017 | 7,757 | -3,740 |
| 1987 | 6,430 | 5,945 | 485 | 3,916 | 7,274 | -3,358 |
| 1988 | 6,772 | 7,719 | -947 | 4,746 | 8,176 | -3,430 |
| 1989 | 7,360 | 9,877 | -2,517 | 5,114 | 9,785 | -4,671 |
| 1990 | 7,373 | 13,289 | -5,916 | 6,275 | 9,147 | -2,872 |
| 1991 | 7,719 | 18,160 | -10,441 | 7,127 | 9,297 | -2,170 |
| 1992 | 9,604 | 20,995 | -11,391 | 8,004 | 10,863 | -2,859 |
| 1993 | 14,301 | 23,730 | -9,429 | 12,258 | 15,739 | -3,481 |
| 1994 | 16,246 | 27,644 | -11,398 | 15,418 | 18,604 | -3,186 |
| 1995 | 19,327 | 32,333 | -13,006 | 19,258 | 21,313 | -2,055 |
| 1996 | 18,387 | 35,440 | -17,053 | 19,868 | 19,883 | -15 |
| 1997 | 18,054 | 42,172 | -24,118 | 23,865 | 19,205 | 4,660 |
| 1998 | 19,298 | 47,005 | -27,707 | 28,148 | 20,715 | 7,433 |
| 1999 | 20,326 | 52,573 | -32,247 | 30,207 | 25,463 | 4,744 |
| 2000 | 23,063 | 64,022 | -40,958 | 38,193 | 30,845 | 7,348 |
| 2001 | 26,620 | 67,634 | -41,025 | 40,904 | 35,723 | 5,181 |
| 2002 | 32,208 | 77,495 | -45,227 | 48,184 | 38,552 | 9,632 |
| 2003 | 44,217 | 108,562 | -64,345 | 72,457 | 53,112 | 19,345 |
| 2004 | 57,773 | 147,111 | -89,338 | 99,843 | 68,011 | 31,832 |
| 2005 | 61,894 | 183,734 | -121,840 | 134,872 | 71,694 | 63,178 |

**Note:** From 1980-88, data are for the 12 nations of the European Economic Community and after 1988 for the 15 nations of the EU (addition of Austria, Finland, and Sweden).

**Sources:** IMF. Direction of Trade Statistics Yearbook and Direction of Trade Statistics Quarterly; Global Trade Atlas; PRC. General Administration of Customs.

**Table A5. Major Country Merchandise Exports to China, Imports from China, and Trade Balances with China, 2004 and 2005**
**(billions of dollars)**

| Partner | Trading Partner Data | | | | | | Chinese Data | | | | | |
|---|---|---|---|---|---|---|---|---|---|---|---|---|
| | 2004 | | | 2005 | | | 2004 | | | 2005 | | |
| | Exp | Imp | Bal | Exp | Imp | Bal | Exp | Imp | Bal | Exp | Imp | Bal |
| U.S. | 34.7 | 196.6 | -161.9 | 41.8 | 243.4 | -201.6 | 44.6 | 124.9 | -80.3 | 48.7 | 162.9 | -114.2 |
| Japan | 73.9 | 94.4 | -20.5 | 79.9 | 108.5 | -28.5 | 94.2 | 73.5 | 20.7 | 100.4 | 84.1 | 16.3 |
| EU-15 | 57.7 | 146.7 | -89.0 | 61.9 | 183.7 | -121.8 | 68.0 | 99.8 | -31.8 | 71.7 | 134.8 | -63.1 |
| Hong Kong | 114.2 | 118.0 | -3.8 | 130.3 | 135.1 | -4.8 | 11.8 | 101.0 | -89.2 | 12.2 | 124.5 | -112.3 |
| Taiwan | 44.9 | 16.7 | 28.2 | 51.8 | 19.9 | 31.9 | 64.7 | 13.5 | 51.2 | 74.6 | 16.7 | 57.9 |
| S. Korea | 54.9 | 29.2 | 25.7 | 69.8 | 38.6 | 31.2 | 62.0 | 27.8 | 34.2 | 76.8 | 35.1 | 41.7 |
| Germany | 26.0 | 38.4 | -12.4 | 26.4 | 49.4 | -23.0 | 30.0 | 23.7 | 6.3 | 30.6 | 32.5 | -1.9 |
| Singapore | 15.4 | 16.2 | -0.8 | 19.7 | 20.5 | -0.8 | 14.0 | 12.6 | 1.4 | 16.5 | 16.7 | -0.2 |
| U.K. | 4.3 | 19.1 | -14.8 | 5.1 | 23.9 | -18.8 | 4.7 | 14.9 | -10.2 | 5.5 | 18.9 | -13.4 |
| France | 6.7 | 14.5 | -7.8 | 8.0 | 17.9 | -9.9 | 7.6 | 9.9 | -2.3 | 9.0 | 11.6 | -2.6 |

**Sources:** IMF, *Direction of Trade Statistics Yearbook* and *Direction of Trade Statistics Quarterly; Global Trade Atlas;* Hong Kong Trade Development Council; Ministry of Economic Affairs, Board of Foreign Trade (Taiwan).

## Table A6. U.S. Merchandise Trade Balances with Selected Asian Developing Nations, 1984-2005
### (millions of dollars)

| Year | China | Indonesia | S. Korea | Malaysia | Philippines | Taiwan | Thailand |
|------|-------|-----------|----------|----------|-------------|--------|----------|
| 1984 | -377 | -4,674 | -4,188 | -9983 | -913 | -11,266 | -381 |
| 1985 | -373 | -4,152 | -4,992 | -936 | -959 | -13,295 | -804 |
| 1986 | -2,135 | -2,757 | -7,588 | -807 | -805 | -16,069 | -1,018 |
| 1987 | -3,422 | -2,955 | -10,326 | -1,159 | -898 | -19,221 | -904 |
| 1988 | -4,237 | -2,438 | -10,578 | -1,715 | -1,069 | -14,314 | -1,739 |
| 1989 | -7,094 | -2,618 | -7,115 | -2,052 | -1,102 | -14,305 | -2,343 |
| 1990 | -11,488 | -1,785 | -4,888 | -2,071 | -1,151 | -12,347 | -2,597 |
| 1991 | -14,018 | -1,675 | -2,224 | -2,446 | -1,439 | -11,038 | -2,693 |
| 1992 | -19,943 | -1,927 | -2,732 | -4,144 | -1,870 | -10,601 | -3,944 |
| 1993 | -24,927 | -3,117 | -3,003 | -4,858 | -1,646 | -10,050 | -5,214 |
| 1994 | -32,076 | -4,209 | -2,346 | -7,454 | -2,137 | -10,864 | -5,938 |
| 1995 | -36,772 | -4,599 | 523 | -9,162 | -2,070 | -10,863 | -5,452 |
| 1996 | -42,431 | -4,778 | 3,286 | -9,809 | -2,372 | -12,610 | -4,587 |
| 1997 | -53,026 | -5,222 | 1,269 | -7,695 | -3,370 | -13,331 | -5,699 |
| 1998 | -56,927 | -7,042 | -7,456 | -10,043 | -5,211 | -14,960 | -8,198 |
| 1999 | -68,668 | -7,575 | -8,308 | -12,349 | -5,153 | -16,077 | -9,340 |
| 2000 | -83,810 | -7,839 | -12,398 | -14,573 | -5,147 | -16,134 | -9,747 |
| 2001 | -83,045 | -7,605 | -12,988 | -12,956 | -3,666 | -15,239 | -8,733 |
| 2002 | -103,115 | -7,062 | -12,979 | -13,661 | -3,715 | -13,805 | -9,939 |
| 2003 | -123,960 | -6,999 | -12,864 | -14,517 | -2,068 | -14,111 | -9,338 |
| 2004 | -161,977 | -8,142 | -19,829 | -17,288 | -2,072 | -12,866 | -11,214 |
| 2005 | -201,625 | -8,971 | -16,109 | -23,252 | -2,355 | -12,788 | -12,569 |

**Source:** U.S. Department of Commerce, International Trade Commission.

# REFERENCES

[1] The White House, *The National Security Strategy of the United States of America* (March 2006), available at [http://www.whitehouse.gov/nsc/nss/2006].

[2] See Sections 201 to 204 of the Trade Act of 1974 (19 U.S.C. §§ 2251-2254).

[3] Unfair competition includes dumping (sales in the United States of an imported product at less than fair value), countervailable subsidies (excessive government subsidies of exporting industries) (see Subtitles A and B of Title VII of the Tariff Act of 1930, as added by the Trade Agreements Act of 1979 (19 U.S.C. §§ 1673 et seq.), and imports that infringe on intellectual property rights (see Section 337 of the Tariff Act of 1930, 19 U.S.C. § 1337).

[4] See CRS Report RL33602, *Global Climate Change: Major Scientific and Policy Issues*, by John R. Justus and Susan R. Fletcher.

[5] For further discussion of U.S. trade, U.S. -China trade, and U.S. trade policies toward China, see CRS Report RL33577, *U.S. International Trade: Trends and Forecasts*, by Dick Nanto; CRS Report RL33536, *China-U.S. Trade Issues*, by Wayne M. Morrison; and CRS Report RL32165, *China's Currency: Economic Issues and Options for U.S. Trade Policy*, by Wayne Morrison and Marc Labonte.

[6] Office of the United States Trade Representative. "USTR Portman Announces US-China Broad Textile Agreement." USTR Press Release, November 8, 2005.

[7] The yuan can fluctuate within a band of 0.3% per day. The exchange rate as of August 2006 was 7.98 yuan to 1.0 U.S. dollar. See United States Department of the Treasury, "Report to Congress on International and Exchange Rate Policies," May 2006.

[8] Doug Palmer, "U.S. Sets Duty of up to 198 Pct on Chinese Furniture," *Reuters News*, November 9, 2004.

[9] Chris Buckley, "China on Unfamiliar Ground in Trade Fight with U.S.," *New York Times*, March 23, 2004.

[10] In 2005, U.S.-China trade ($285 billion) nearly reached the value of U.S.-Mexico trade ($290 billion). U.S. Census Bureau, *Foreign Trade Statistics*.

[11] "EU Becomes China's Biggest Trading Partner — USDA Attache," *Reuters News*, February 25, 2005.

[12] PRC data. "China 2005 Trade Surplus Jumps to Record High," *Yahoo! Asia News*, January 11, 2006.

[13] U.S. Department of Commerce, International Trade Commission.

[14] *Global Trade Atlas*; "Economy Increasingly Dependent on Mainland Ties," *Nikkei Weekly*, June 14, 2004.

[15] Jonathan Anderson, "China, Asia's Paper Tiger?" *The Asian Wall Street Journal*, August 15, 2002.

[16] "China to Become 2nd Largest Automaker by 2010," *Asia Times Online* [http://www.atimes.com], August 25, 2005; *Xinhua News Agency*, April 11, 2005.

[17] According to the Hong Kong Trade Development Council, 55% of Hong Kong's total exports involve re-exports of Chinese (mainland) goods to markets other than China.

[18] U.S.-China Business Council, "Understanding the U.S.-China Balance of Trade," May 2003.

[19] *Global Trade Atlas*.

[20] Global Insight, "China: Interim Forecast Analysis," June 2006, and "China: Economic: Current Situation: Highlights," August 2006.

[21] U.S. Department of Commerce, International Trade Commission; Global Trade Atlas; International Monetary Fund, *Direction of Trade Statistics Quarterly*, June 2006.

[22] Robert J. Samuelson, "The World's Powerhouse," *Newsweek*, May 31, 2004.

[23] Taiwan's major exports to China include telecommunications products, computers, plastic products, steel, man-made fibers, industrial-use textiles, organic chemical products, optical and photo-taking instruments and parts, copper products, and polyester. Hong Kong Trade Development Council.

[24] Taiwan data include Hong Kong. Directorate General of Customs, Ministry of Finance, Republic of China; Korean International Trade Association.

[25] Sadanand Dhume, "Buying Fast into Southeast Asia," *Far Eastern Economic Review*, March 28, 2002.

[26] *Global Trade Atlas*

[27] "China-ASEAN Trade Surges over 40 Percent in 2003," *Thai News Service*, February 11, 2004.

[28] Keith Bradsher and David Barboza, "As Exports Boom, China Risks Global Backlash," *International Herald Tribune*, April 9, 2005.

[29] Council of Economic Advisors, *Economic Report of the President*, February 2004.

[30] U.S. Imports for Consumption, U.S. International Trade Commission.

[31] NICS — Hong Kong, Taiwan, and South Korea (Singapore is counted in ASEAN).

[32] *Global Trade Atlas*.

[33] In 2005, GM sold more than 650,000 vehicles in China compared to Volkswagen, with sales of 500,000 cars, and Toyota, with 179,000 units. "Toyota in China: Full Speed Ahead," *BusinessWeek Online*, March 9, 2006.

[34] "Chinese Automaker Geely Sets Sights on Exports to U.S." *Associated Press Newswires*, January 11, 2006.

[35] "MOC: Tariff Cut to Put Little Effect on Imported Car Price next Year," *Xinhua News Agency*, December 19, 2005.

[36] Jiang Jingjin, "China Not the Only Beneficiary," *China Daily (China Business Weekly)*, April 5, 2004.

[37] For further discussion of China's economy and foreign investment, see CRS Report RL33534, *China's Economic Conditions*, by Wayne M. Morrison.

[38] Mainland subsidiaries in Hong Kong and Macao can take advantage of investment incentives for foreign companies on the PRC mainland.

[39] Many foreign firms, including U.S. companies, are registered in the Virgin Islands, Cayman Islands, and Western Samoa for tax purposes.

In: Asian Economic and Political Development        ISBN: 978-1-61122-470-2
Editor: Felix Chin        © 2011 Nova Science Publishers, Inc.

# THE AUSTRALIA-CHINA ECONOMIC RELATIONSHIP AND PROSPECTS FOR AN FTA[*]

## *Jinmei Yang[1] and Mahinda Siriwardana[2]*

School of Economics, University of New England
Armidale, NSW 2351, Australia

## ABSTRACT

The Australia-China Free Trade Agreement (ACFTA) is already in the process of being negotiated by the two governments. This paper applies the Computable General Equilibrium (CGE) model using Global Trade Analysis Project (GTAP) database version 6 for a quantitative analysis of the economic effects of proposed ACFTA. Four scenarios are examined in this paper focusing on flexible and fixed current account positions within short run and long run. Equivalent variation (EV) and real consumption are used to measure the welfare effects resulting from the formation of the ACFTA. The results from the GTAP simulations show positive welfare effects for both Australia and China in all cases. The different magnitudes of changes in the two countries represent the relative significance and size of bilateral trade to each country. The modeling results also indicate that the ACFTA has a negligible impact on rest of the world's real GDP and welfare, and would generate trade creation greater than trade diversion for the world as a whole. Specifically, the two economies will obtain gains according to their comparative advantages. In the case of Australia, primary commodities such as grains, sugar and mining products dominate exports to China whereas in the case of China, manufactures such as wearing apparels, textiles and miscellaneous manufacturing benefit most. Labour force is estimated to move from declining sectors to growing sectors in most cases in the two economies. The sectoral adjustments of trade balance, output and demand for primary factors exhibit similar directions of changes. It is evident that an Australia-China FTA would have not only bilateral but global benefits. (JEL F13, F17).

---

[*] Paper presented to the Seventh Biennial Pacific Rim Conference, January 12-14, 2007 in Beijing. This conference is being coordinated by the Western Economic Association International in partnership with Peking University's China Center for Economic Research and the Guanghua School of Management. Conference scholarship from the University of New England is kindly acknowledged.

[1] E-mail address: jmyang@une.edu.au

[2] E-mail address: asiriwar@une.edu.au

# I. INTRODUCTION

The global trading system has seen a very substantial increase in preferential trading arrangements (PTAs) over the past decade. The number of agreement had grown from 30 in 1991 to 188 in 2005. World Trade Organization (WTO) statistics show that by 1 March 2006, 193 Regional Trade Agreements (RTAs) had been notified to the WTO (WTO 2006) and are currently in force. This increase in RTAs raises the potential for diverse and overlapping agreements with various types of preferential Rules of Origin (RoO) (Productivity Commission 2004).

Free trade agreements (FTAs), which improve market access and strengthen trade flows, are an important vehicle for enhancing bilateral trading relationships. With the worldwide proliferation of regional trade agreements, Australia shows its positive attitude to join the world trend and focuses on negotiating FTAs with selected partners where these offer the prospect of significant gains ahead of what will be achievable in the WTO process. So far, Australia has signed WTO-consistent FTAs with some major trading partners, such as the U.S. and Singapore. These bilateral trade agreements deliver great benefits where the parties are willing to move faster and undertake more profound liberalisation than can be achieved by the WTO multilateral trading system.

Australia and China commenced negotiations on an FTA following consideration of the joint FTA Feasibility Study completed in March 2005. This study concluded that there would be significant economic benefits for both Australia and China through the Australia-China FTA (ACFTA). Independent research has predicted that under full liberalisation from 2006, Australia's real GDP would rise by an additional AU$ 24.4 billion over 10 years (Mai et al. 2005). The Australian government has stressed that any FTA with China must deliver real gains for Australia businesses. Four rounds of ACFTA negotiations held so far have provided a solid basis for substantive discussions on virtually all possible provisions of the text of the FTA. The Australian side reiterated that the negotiations will be complex and challenging but Australia will approach them constructively. As Australian Deputy Prime Minister Hon Mark Vaile said, "An FTA will enable us to set the terms of our future trade with the world's fastest-growing major economy, for the benefit of all Australians" (DFAT 2006a).

This paper applies the Computable General Equilibrium (CGE) modelling approach using the Global Trade Analysis Project (GTAP) model and its database version 6 for a quantitative analysis of the economic effects of proposed ACFTA. Four scenarios with full merchandise trade liberalisation are examined in this paper focusing on flexible and fixed current account positions within short run and long run respectively.

The paper proceeds as follows. Section II reviews the Australia-China bilateral economic relations. Section III presents a brief description of the main features and database of the GTAP model used in this paper. Section IV defines simulation scenarios. The simulation results are reported and interpreted in section V. Some concluding remarks end the paper in section VI.

## II. BILATERAL ECONOMIC RELATIONS BETWEEN AUSTRALIA AND CHINA

Australia and China have a longstanding relationship with a high level of interaction on trade, investment, education and tourism. China is of great significance to Australia as a bilateral, regional and multilateral partner; it is a significant member of the WTO, a major player in APEC, Australia's second-largest trading partner in 2005, and a major source of migrants, students and tourists. Australia is also of great importance to China; in 2005 Australia was China's 11th largest merchandise trade partner. As to the two-way investment relations, China was Australia's 22nd largest investment destination (AU$ 1.2 billion in 2004), focusing on manufacturing, mineral exploration, legal, banking and education services. China also was the 17th largest investor in Australia (AU$ 2.0 billion in 2004), primarily in the resources and property sectors (DFAT 2006b).

The economies of Australia and China are of significantly different sizes, and at different stages of economic and social development. Yet the Australian and Chinese economies have already shared mutually-beneficial trade and investment relationships largely over the last two decades.

### Trends in Two-Way Merchandise Trade

Figure 1 shows the trend of total trade between Australia and China. From 1985 to 2004, the average annual increasing rate of bilateral merchandise trade was 88.8 percent. In 2004, total trade in goods and services between Australia and China reached US$ 21.2 billion, rising by 1775.7 per cent from the value of US$ 1.1 billion in 1985. The trade deficit began for Australia in 1989 and widened until the first peak of US$ 2.1 billion in 2000. Then in 2001 the deficits reached its lowest point in the last seven years (1998-2004) of the same period, at US$ 5.1 billion in 2004. The trend of trade deficit appears to be further broadening.

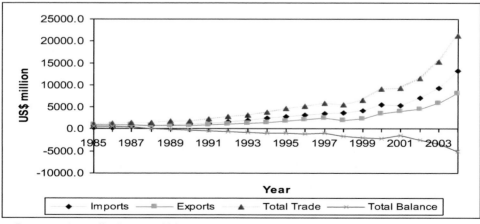

**Note**: Reporter: Australia; Partner: China.
**Source**: Comtrade database 2006.

Figure 1. Total trade between Australia and China, 1985-2004.

In 2005, Australia's trade deficit with China reached AU$ 6.8 billion, an increase of AU$ 1.4 billion on the previous year's deficit due to an AU$ 4.5 billion rise in imports partially offset by an AU$ 3.0 billion increase in exports. The main commodities contributing to the increase in imports were: Office machines and automatic data processing machines (up AU$ 0.9 billion); and Telecommunications and sound recording and reproducing apparatus and equipment (up AU$ 0.7 billion). The main increase in exports was mainly due to Metalliferous ores and metal scrap which were up AU$ 2.4 billion (Year Book Australia 2006). The sectors which contributed most to the increased deficit were: Mineral fuels, lubricants and related materials; Commodities and transactions n.e.s in the SITC; and Animal and vegetable oils, fats and waxes.

Figure 2 shows China's share in Australian merchandise exports and imports from 1996 to 2005. During the ten-year period, Australia's imports sourced from China increased substantially from 5.15 percent in 1996 to 13.25 percent in 2005, whereas its exports to China rose from 4.97 percent to 10.24 percent. In 2005, China's share in Australia's total merchandise trade was 11.87 percent, valued at AU$ 32.8 billion, whereas the total value of Australia's merchandise trade with the rest of the world was AU$ 243.4 billion. Australian merchandise imports from China increased far quicker than its exports to China; and China was Australia's 2nd largest trading partner whereas Japan ranked 1st and U.S. in 3rd in 2005.

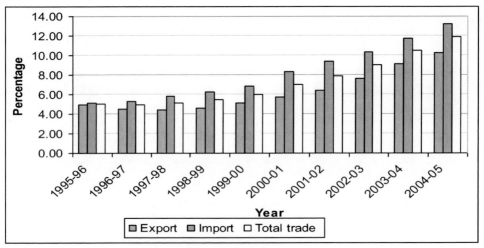

**Note**: Data are on a fiscal year basis, years ending 30 June.
**Source**: Year Book Australia (2006), ABS (various years).

Figure 2. China's share in Australian merchandise trade, 1996-2005.

On the other hand, Figure 3 demonstrates that Australia's share in China's foreign trade from 1995 to 2004 fluctuated narrowly between 1.5 and 1.77 percent and finally reached its highest at the end of the period. In sharp contrast to Figure 2, Figure 3 indicates that Australia's position in China's merchandise trade is quite stable and modest. China's imports sourced from Australia increased by 347 percent from US$ 2.58 billion in 1995 to US$ 11.55 billion in 2004, meanwhile China's exports to Australia kept rising by 443 percent from US$ 1.6 billion to US$ 8.8 billion during the same period. In 2004, there was a significant increase in both China's imports from and exports to Australia over the previous year at 58.25 percent and 41.1 percent respectively.

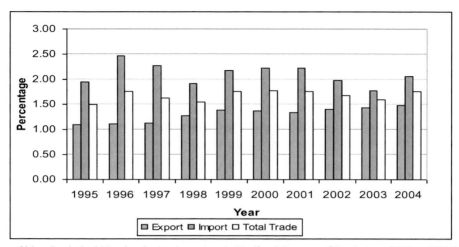

**Source**: China Statistical Yearbook (various years), National Bureau of Statistics of China (2005).

Figure 3. Australia's share in China's foreign trade, 1995-2004.

Combining Figures 2 and 3, it is evident that Australia's merchandise imports from China increased faster than its exports to China whereas its own share in China's total foreign trade shows a slight fluctuation during the same period. It is not surprising therefore that China is becoming Australia's second largest merchandise trading partner with AU$ 32.8 billion in 2005. China is playing an increasingly important role in Australia's merchandise trade compared with the role which Australia plays in China, this is probably due to the huge size of the economy China has in comparison to Australia and their different comparative advantage.

Australia imports a wide variety of goods from China. While traditional manufactured products like textile, clothing and footwear (TCF) and toys continue to grow solidly and still account for a significant share of its imports, Australia increasingly imports higher value added products from China, such as computers, telecommunication equipment, electrical machinery and sound and video recorders, which China employs its relatively abundant factor of labour to produce.

Australian imports from China rose to total AU$ 13.3 billion in 2003, up by 25.1 percent from the previous year, while Australian imports from many other major trading partners such as the U.S. and Japan fell during the same period. Chinese products have competed strongly in the Australian market, ranking the 2nd largest import source for Australia in 2004. Imports from China contribute to the Australian economy by lowering costs and offering greater choices to consumers. From 2002 to 2003, except Crude materials (inedible, except fuels), all sectors have seen increases in Australian imports from China.

The traditional trade pattern of Australia exporting primary products in exchange for manufactured goods (inter-industry trade) has increasingly given way to the exchange of goods which are differentiated products and very close substitutes. The statistics of exports and imports between Australia and China in 2002 and 2003 indicate that trade in similar products (intra-industry trade) is increasing heavily between Australia and China. It signals that international trade is playing a changing role of filling gaps in products not produced within the country (inter-industry trade).

## Bilateral Investment between Australia and China

With economic strengths, cultural diversity and stability, Australia is a very attractive business investment destination. This can be seen from the numbers: in 2005, total foreign direct investment (FDI) in Australia reached AU$ 1214 billion whereas Australian investment abroad with AU$ 653.8 billion. Meanwhile, Australia is the gateway to the world's fastest growing region — the Asia Pacific. Therefore, Australia has a particular geographic advantage to participate and play an important role in the regional economic development.

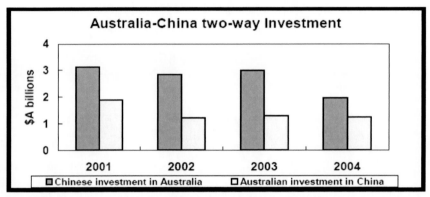

**Source**: DFAT 2006b.

Figure 4. Australia-China two-way investment, 2001-2004.

Meanwhile, as the fastest growing economy in the world, China has a stronger economic relationship with Australia. This strength is reflected through the continued growth in merchandise trade and bilateral investment. China was Australia's 22nd largest investment destination (AU$ 1.2 billion) and 17th largest investor (AU$ 2.0 billion) in 2004 (DFAT 2006b). China's investment in Australia focuses on resources and property sectors while Australia's investment in China focuses on manufacturing, mineral exploration, legal, banking and education services. A recent survey of Australia companies operating in China indicated that Australian investors in China have broadened away from manufacturing and evenly-split between the areas of manufacturing, property and business services, and other sectors including wholesale and retail trade, mining, finance and insurance, education, information services and energy supply (Maitland and Nicholas 1999).

Figure 4 demonstrates the two-way investment between Australia and China from 2001 to 2004. Table 1 further shows that Australian share in China's FDI inflows and in Australian FDI outflows during the period of 1997 to 2004. During the period, the total value of FDI in China rose by 33.97 percent from US$ 45.26 billion to US$ 60.63 billion whereas FDI from Australia went up by 111.2 percent with the total value of US$ 662.63 million in 2004. Although the share of FDI from Australia accounted for a small proportion of the total FDI in China, it does not signify a lack of real interest in the Chinese economy. On the other hand, the relatively low level of Australian direct investment in China may reflect the complementary nature of Australia and China's production patterns and resource endowments (DFAT 2002).

During the same period, Chinese investment in Australia shows a strong growth trend. According to Chinese statistics, Australia is one of the most popular destinations for Chinese investment abroad (Editorial Board of the Almanac of China's Foreign Economic Relations and Trade 2001). In the fiscal year of 2005, China invested AU$ 2.0 billion in Australia, ranking the 17th largest investor in Australia (DFAT 2006b). China's largest and highest profile Australian investments are in the resources sector. Real estate, including hotels in major metropolitan centres, farming and agricultural processing ventures and a variety of general manufacturing plants are other destinations for Chinese investment in Australia (Invest Australia 2002).

**Table 1. Australia's share in China's FDI inflows**
**and in Australia's outflows, 1997-2004, US$ million**

| Year | FDI from Australia | Total FDI in China | Percent in China's inflows (%) | Australia FDI abroad | Percent in Australia's outflows (%) |
|------|-----|-----|-----|-----|-----|
| 1997 | 313.74 | 45257.04 | 0.69 | 6431.00 | 4.88 |
| 1998 | 271.97 | 45462.75 | 0.60 | 3346.00 | 8.13 |
| 1999 | 263.31 | 40318.71 | 0.65 | -421.00 | -62.54 |
| 2000 | 308.88 | 40714.81 | 0.76 | 3162.00 | 9.77 |
| 2001 | 335.60 | 46877.59 | 0.72 | 12084.00 | 2.78 |
| 2002 | 380.70 | 52742.86 | 0.72 | 7876.00 | 4.83 |
| 2003 | 592.53 | 53504.67 | 1.11 | 15277.00 | 3.88 |
| 2004 | 662.63 | 60629.98 | 1.09 | 16288.00 | 4.07 |

**Source**: China Statistical Yearbook (various years) and UNCTAD database.

Over the long run, foreign investment may constitute an increasingly important part of the Australia-China economic relationship, but currently two-way FDI is quite modest.

## III. OUTLINES OF THE MODEL AND DATABASE

The standard GTAP model applied in this paper is a type of CGE model for comparative static analysis. Full documentation of the theoretical structure of GTAP is available in Hertel (1997). The contents of this section are largely drawn from those parts of Hertel (1997) which provide an overview of GTAP.

In GTAP model, all markets are assumed to be perfectly competitive. Demand and supply are balanced in all markets, which imply the price received by the producer the same as the producer's marginal cost. By imposing taxes and subsidies on commodities and primary factors, regional government can drive wedges between prices paid by purchasers and prices received by producers. In markets for traded commodities, buyers differentiate between domestically produced and imported products. Product differentiation is also allowed between imports by region of origin. This makes two-way trade across regions possible for each tradable product.

There are two types of inputs — intermediate inputs and primary factors used for production. In each region, each sector is assumed to mix the inputs to minimize total cost at a given output level. A three-level nested production technology constrains the sectors' inputs choice. At the first level, intermediate input bundles and primary-factor bundles are used in fixed proportions according to a Leontief function. At the second level, intermediate input bundles are formed as combinations of imported bundles and domestic goods with the same input-output name, and primary-factor bundles are obtained as combinations of labour, capital and land. In both cases, the aggregator function has a Constant Elasticity of Substitution (CES) function. At the third level, imported bundles are formed as CES composites of imported goods with the same name from each region.

Each region has a single representative household. Aggregate household expenditure is determined as a constant share of total regional income (household consumption plus government expenditure and national savings). The household buys bundles of commodities to maximize utility subject to its expenditure constraint. The bundles are CES combinations of domestic goods and import bundles, with the import bundles being CES aggregations of imports from each region.

The share of aggregate government expenditure in each region's income is held fixed. Government expenditure is allocated across commodities by a Cobb-Douglas distribution. The allocation of total expenditure on each good to domestically produced and imported versions is based on the same nesting scheme used to allocate total household expenditure on each good.

Investment in each region is financed from a global pool of savings. Each region contributes a fixed proportion of its income to the savings pool. In standard GTAP, two ways are used to allocate savings in each region. The first is to allocate according to a fixed proportion of the pool. The second is to allocate investment according to the prevalent relative rates of return.

The GTAP model captures world economic activity in 57 different industries of 87 regions (database version 6). For the purpose of analysis, we have aggregated these to 10 regions and 20 sectors (see Appendix A.1).

## IV. SIMULATION DESIGN

Table 2 shows bilateral import tariffs estimated from the GTAP database version 6. In Australia, the highest import tariffs on imports from China are recorded for Beverages and tobacco (19.0 percent), Wearing apparels (18.3 percent) and Textiles (18.1 percent). In China, the tariff level is relatively high compared with Australia. The highest import tariffs on Chinese imports from Australia are noted in Grains (89.9 percent), Beverages and tobacco (57.3 percent), Textiles (24.8 percent) and Other food products (23.2 percent). Australia's tariff rates for imports from China are almost below 5 percent whereas China's tariff rates, 15 out of 20, are above 10 percent.

The simulation scenarios examined in this paper are assumed with the full liberalisation on goods trade — that is: the removal of all bilateral tariffs on goods trade between Australia and China from the base year 2001 — while holding all other distortion levels in the system constant. As shown in Table 3, four simulations (short-run and long-run with flexible current account and fixed current account respectively) are performed to examine the proposed economic effects of the ACFTA. Different closures could have different impacts on the model results.

In scenario 1, capital, natural resources and land are fixed exogenously and their prices are endogenous. Meanwhile, skilled labour and unskilled labour are endogenous and their prices (real wage) are fixed exogenously. In scenario 2, skilled labour, unskilled labour, land and natural resources are fixed exogenously and their prices endogenous. On the other hand, capital is endogenous with its price (real rental) fixed exogenously. Scenarios 1 and 2 are both examined with the flexible current account. In scenarios 3 and 4, the current account is fixed by setting the trade balance fixed exogenously and assuming that there are no capital flows as trade is liberalised. Scenarios 3 and 4 are different from scenarios 1 and 2 respectively with the fixed current account.

**Table 2. Existing bilateral tariffs of Australia-China merchandise trade (%)**

| Sector | Australia[a] | China[b] |
|---|---|---|
| Grains | 0.0 | 89.9 |
| Other crops | 0.6 | 8.3 |
| Animal products | 0.0 | 3.3 |
| Forestry and fishing | 1.2 | 6.0 |
| Mining and energy | 2.4 | 0.4 |
| Meat products | 3.1 | 12.4 |
| Other food products | 3.1 | 23.2 |
| Dairy | 3.7 | 22.1 |
| Sugar | 0.0 | 19.5 |
| Beverages and tobacco | 19.0 | 57.3 |
| Textiles | 18.1 | 24.8 |
| Wearing apparels | 18.3 | 13.9 |
| Wood and paper products, publishing | 4.6 | 13.4 |
| Chemicals, rubber and plastic | 4.5 | 16.6 |
| Ferrous metals | 3.8 | 11.4 |
| Metal products | 5.7 | 12.0 |
| Motor vehicles and parts | 4.9 | 12.4 |
| Machinery and equipment | 2.6 | 13.3 |
| Miscellaneous manufactures | 3.7 | 18.8 |
| Services | 0.0 | 0.0 |

**Note**: a: Australian tariffs on imports from China;
   b: Chinese tariffs on imports from Australia.
**Source**: Purdue University 2005, GTAP database version 6.

**Table 3. Simulation design with zero tariff for the ACFTA in GTAP**

| | Full liberalisation | |
|---|---|---|
| Scenario | Flexible Current Account | Fixed Current Account |
| Scenario 1 | Short run | |
| Scenario 2 | Long run | |
| Scenario 3 | | Short run |
| Scenario 4 | | Long run |

# V. SIMULATION RESULTS

This section reports the results from the GTAP simulation of the ACFTA; that is: macroeconomic effects, sectoral effects and effects on trade patterns. The results will provide evidence as to whether there is trade creation and/ or trade diversion following the formation of the ACFTA and what is the estimated impact on trade flows in the international trade content due to the formation of ACFTA.

## Macroeconomic Effects

Results of the macroeconomic effects of the ACFTA are reported in Table 4. Firstly, both Australia and China are expected to increase their real GDP in all four scenarios while Australia experiences a greater increase in the range of 1.04 to 1.67 percent, compared with China's from 0.15 to 0.22 percent. This finding indicates that the ACFTA has positive effects for both countries in terms of real GDP. Meanwhile, there is little change in real GDP for any other region in all four scenarios. Generally, the increases in real GDP with the flexible current account are slightly greater than those with the fixed current account for the two countries.

Secondly, the ACFTA affects trade performance in Australia more than in China. Australia experiences export expansion ranging from 1.33 to 2.19 percent and import expansion from 2.93 to 3.69 percent. The impact on export and import volumes in China is relatively smaller (ranging from 0.84 to 0.92 percent and from 1.14 to 1.20 percent respectively) in all four scenarios. Percentage changes in trade volume show that Australia and China will experience a greater expansion in imports than exports in all cases. Moreover, in scenarios 3 and 4 with fixed current account, exports are projected to expand slightly greater than those (scenarios 1 and 2) with flexible current account. Due to the formation of the ACFTA, tariffs are reduced in a sector and domestic buyers (both final and intermediate) substitute toward imports; the domestic competing industry contracts production while foreign exporters expand. There is a trade creation resulting from the ACFTA as the two economies replace high-cost domestic products by importing more from the low-cost free trade union member.

Thirdly, the changes in the trade balance indicate that both Australia's and China's current account positions worsen in the short run (scenario 1) and improve in the long run (scenario 2). Trade balance appears to be negative with a broader deficit in Australia in the short-run (scenario 1) than in China, but this situation is changed in the long-run (scenario 2) where Australia appears to be in a trade surplus and China is still in a reduced trade deficit. There are improvements of between 0.84 and 0.99 percent in the terms of trade for Australia in all four scenarios whereas the terms of trade for China are deteriorated slightly by around 0.6 percent. It can be seen that there are negligible effects on the terms of trade on other regions with the bilateral removal of the tariffs between Australia and China.

The net welfare gains from the ACFTA are measured by equivalent variation (EV) and real consumption expenditure in this study. The EV measures the amount of income that would have to be given or taken away from an economy before trade liberalisation so as to leave the economy as well off as it would be after the policy has been changed (Brown et al. 2005 and Siriwardana 2007). Table 4 shows that there is an obvious contrast with regard to the effect on the EV. In all four cases, both Australia and China appear to experience positive EVs which indicate an improvement in economic welfare due to the trade creation resulting from the ACFTA. However, the projection suggests that the ACFTA has negative EVs for all non-member economies except Hong Kong, indicating a trade diversion effect resulting from the ACFTA. The scale is larger in the short-run scenarios (scenarios 1 and 3) than in the long-run scenarios (scenarios 2 and 4). Both Australia and China are projected to have increases in real consumption expenditure, with consumers generally benefiting more in the short-run than in the long-run. In the short-run cases (scenarios 1 and 3), the real consumption expenditure in Australia (0.68 and 0.65 percent) increases slightly more than in China (0.51 and 0.52 percent), but in the long-run cases (scenarios 2 and 4), China's real consumption expenditure increase of 0.36 percent is heavier than Australia's 0.04 percent.

## Table 4. Macroeconomic effects of ACFTA under four scenarios

| | Real GDP (%) | Export Volume (%) | Import Volume (%) | Terms of Trade (%) | Trade Balance (US$ million) | Equivalent Variation (EV) (US$ million) | Real Consumption Expenditure (%) |
|---|---|---|---|---|---|---|---|
| Scenario 1 | | | | | | | |
| AUS | 1.67 | 1.33 | 3.69 | 0.99 | -963.19 | 3919.75 | 0.68 |
| CHI | 0.22 | 0.85 | 1.20 | -0.06 | -288.78 | 3562.42 | 0.51 |
| USA | -0.01 | 0.00 | -0.01 | 0.00 | 200.73 | -459.08 | 0.01 |
| ASEAN | -0.04 | -0.04 | -0.07 | -0.02 | 35.78 | -213.05 | -0.05 |
| JPA | -0.05 | 0.08 | -0.09 | -0.04 | 537.07 | -1262.58 | -0.01 |
| KOR | -0.04 | -0.03 | -0.09 | -0.03 | 27.32 | -69.62 | 0.00 |
| TWN | -0.06 | -0.04 | -0.07 | -0.02 | -2.58 | -118.50 | -0.02 |
| KHG | 0.01 | 0.00 | 0.02 | 0.01 | -4.45 | 34.58 | 0.03 |
| EU | -0.02 | 0.00 | -0.02 | 0.00 | 201.71 | -564.89 | 0.00 |
| ROW | -0.02 | -0.02 | -0.04 | -0.01 | 256.38 | -770.52 | -0.01 |
| Scenario 2 | | | | | | | |
| AUS | 1.04 | 2.00 | 2.93 | 0.88 | 5.85 | 1608.75 | 0.04 |
| CHI | 0.16 | 0.84 | 1.16 | -0.06 | -189.83 | 2092.41 | 0.36 |
| USA | -0.01 | 0.00 | -0.01 | 0.00 | 180.60 | -148.03 | 0.01 |
| ASEAN | -0.07 | -0.08 | -0.09 | -0.01 | -51.45 | -289.32 | -0.07 |
| JPA | -0.03 | -0.03 | -0.04 | -0.02 | -70.23 | -412.79 | 0.00 |
| KOR | -0.04 | -0.05 | -0.09 | -0.03 | 4.85 | -50.45 | 0.01 |
| TWN | -0.05 | -0.03 | -0.06 | -0.03 | -8.45 | -66.92 | -0.01 |
| KHG | 0.01 | 0.00 | 0.01 | 0.01 | 2.28 | 24.93 | 0.02 |
| EU | -0.02 | 0.00 | -0.01 | 0.00 | 104.24 | -231.87 | 0.01 |
| ROW | -0.02 | -0.03 | -0.04 | -0.01 | 22.14 | -523.14 | 0.00 |
| Scenario 3 | | | | | | | |
| AUS | 1.31 | 2.19 | 3.09 | 0.84 | 0.00 | 3256.35 | 0.65 |
| CHI | 0.20 | 0.92 | 1.17 | -0.07 | 0.00 | 3481.40 | 0.52 |
| USA | -0.01 | -0.01 | 0.00 | 0.00 | 0.00 | -322.01 | 0.01 |
| ASEAN | -0.04 | -0.04 | -0.06 | -0.02 | 0.00 | -201.34 | -0.05 |
| JPA | -0.03 | -0.01 | -0.04 | -0.02 | 0.00 | -916.66 | -0.01 |
| KOR | -0.03 | -0.04 | -0.08 | -0.03 | 0.00 | -48.11 | 0.01 |
| TWN | -0.06 | -0.03 | -0.06 | -0.02 | 0.00 | -116.12 | -0.02 |
| KHG | 0.01 | 0.00 | 0.02 | 0.01 | 0.00 | 36.82 | 0.03 |
| EU | -0.01 | -0.01 | -0.01 | 0.00 | 0.00 | -440.95 | 0.00 |
| ROW | -0.02 | -0.03 | -0.03 | -0.01 | 0.00 | -645.35 | -0.01 |
| Scenario 4 | | | | | | | |
| AUS | 1.04 | 1.99 | 2.93 | 0.88 | 0.00 | 1610.49 | 0.04 |
| CHI | 0.15 | 0.88 | 1.14 | -0.07 | 0.00 | 2060.02 | 0.36 |
| USA | -0.01 | -0.01 | 0.00 | 0.00 | 0.00 | -93.53 | 0.01 |
| ASEAN | -0.07 | -0.07 | -0.10 | -0.01 | 0.00 | -302.36 | -0.07 |
| JPA | -0.03 | -0.01 | -0.04 | -0.03 | 0.00 | -428.59 | 0.00 |
| KOR | -0.04 | -0.05 | -0.09 | -0.03 | 0.00 | -48.71 | 0.01 |
| TWN | -0.05 | -0.03 | -0.06 | -0.03 | 0.00 | -68.69 | -0.01 |
| KHG | 0.01 | 0.00 | 0.01 | 0.01 | 0.00 | 28.95 | 0.03 |
| EU | -0.01 | -0.01 | -0.01 | 0.00 | 0.00 | -195.09 | 0.01 |
| ROW | -0.02 | -0.03 | -0.04 | -0.01 | 0.00 | -521.31 | 0.00 |

**Note**: All projections are percentage deviations from the base period except the trade balance and the equivalent variation (EV) which are in US$ million.

**Source**: Model simulation.

**Table 5. Decomposition of estimated equivalent variation on Australia/China under various scenarios (US $ million)**

|  | Allocative efficiency effect | Endowment effect | Change in terms of trade | Change in capital stock | Total |
|---|---|---|---|---|---|
| Australia |  |  |  |  |  |
| Scenario 1 | 1193.3 | 1992.8 | 736.7 | -3.1 | 3919.7 |
| Scenario 2 | 409.3 | 548.5 | 656.0 | -5.0 | 1608.7 |
| Scenario 3 | 973.7 | 1660.9 | 626.2 | -4.5 | 3256.4 |
| Scenario 4 | 409.9 | 549.0 | 656.7 | -5.2 | 1610.5 |
| China |  |  |  |  |  |
| Scenario 1 | 1073.0 | 2692.7 | -219.9 | 16.6 | 3562.4 |
| Scenario 2 | 928.1 | 1373.6 | -205.2 | -4.1 | 2092.4 |
| Scenario 3 | 1060.2 | 2653.9 | -258.5 | 25.8 | 3481.4 |
| Scenario 4 | 924.4 | 1364.8 | -230.4 | 1.2 | 2060.0 |

**Source**: Model simulation.

The welfare decomposition reported in Table 5 shows that in the short-run cases (scenarios 1 and 3), allocative efficiency and endowment effects contribute to the EV more than they do in the long-run scenarios 2 and 4. The terms of trade effect contributes to the EV positively for Australia, but negatively for China. Capital stock effect appears positive in all of Australia's cases, whereas for China there is positive change only in short-run scenarios 1 and 3.

## Sectoral Effects

A significant effect of trade liberalisation is that it causes reallocation of resources such as labour, capital and land which further lead to structural adjustments to some extent in the factor markets. On average, the world would gain from multilateral liberalisation since resources are reallocated to sectors in each country where there is a comparative advantage (Brown et al. 2006). The results of the sectoral effects resulting from the ACFTA are reported in Table 6, Table 7, Table 8 and Table 9.

Table 6 shows estimated changes by sector in Australia's and China's trade balance under various scenarios. In Australia, Grains and Ferrous metals show the largest improvement in trade balance followed by Chemicals, rubber and plastic, Sugar and Dairy in all scenarios. All other sectors show deteriorations in all scenarios except Machinery in scenario 3. In China, the improvement in the Wearing apparels sector is substantially large, followed by Textiles and Metal products. On the other hand, there is a large deterioration in Grains and Ferrous metals. Some other sectors, such as Meat products, Chemicals, rubber and plastic, Dairy and Animal products also show deteriorations.

Output effects by sector in Australia and China are presented in Table 7 as a percentage change in output volumes relative to initial output levels under various scenarios. The directions of change are almost the same as those in Table 6 for the trade balance by sector. However, there are some exceptions. For example, in Australia, Dairy grows faster for the trade balance, but it becomes worse for the output.

**Table 6. Estimated change in Australia/China trade balance by sector under various scenarios (US $ million)**

| Sector | Scenario 1 | Scenario 2 | Scenario 3 | Scenario 4 |
|---|---|---|---|---|
| Australia | | | | |
| Grains | 953.2 | 958.3 | 957.8 | 958.2 |
| Other crops | -158.6 | -150.6 | -151.2 | -150.6 |
| Animal products | -49.3 | -43.5 | -43.6 | -43.6 |
| Forestry and fishing | -3.8 | -2.1 | -2.8 | -2.2 |
| Mining and energy | -627.7 | -398 | -514.1 | -398.8 |
| Meat products | -31.4 | -33 | 2.6 | -33.2 |
| Other food products | -24.4 | -8.9 | -6.7 | -9 |
| Dairy | 4.1 | 17.5 | 18.2 | 17.5 |
| Sugar | 33 | 34.9 | 36.9 | 34.9 |
| Beverages and tobacco | -19.9 | -12.9 | -15.4 | -12.9 |
| Textiles | -102 | -91.2 | -92.1 | -91.3 |
| Wearing apparels | -451.1 | -438.8 | -434.4 | -439.1 |
| Wood and paper products, publishing | -50.5 | -16.4 | -17.9 | -16.7 |
| Chemicals, rubber and plastic | 61 | 133.3 | 117.1 | 133.1 |
| Ferrous metals | 740 | 854.9 | 858 | 853.9 |
| Metal products | -90 | -80 | -75.1 | -80.2 |
| Motor vehicles and parts | -256.3 | -157.6 | -152.8 | -158.1 |
| Machinery and equipment | -188.7 | -2.2 | 36.3 | -3.5 |
| Miscellaneous manufacturing | -61.5 | -48 | -39 | -48.2 |
| Services | -639.4 | -509.9 | -481.8 | -510.3 |
| China | | | | |
| Grains | -1100.2 | -1104.2 | -1100.6 | -1103.8 |
| Other crops | 6.6 | -5.9 | 8.4 | -4.5 |
| Animal products | -21.7 | -25.6 | -21.8 | -25 |
| Forestry and fishing | -16.4 | -17.4 | -15.4 | -16.9 |
| Mining and energy | 4.9 | 6.2 | 15.5 | 18.6 |
| Meat products | -90.1 | -93.2 | -90.9 | -92.2 |
| Other food products | 18.2 | 20.5 | 20.6 | 22.2 |
| Dairy | -53.8 | -53.8 | -54.1 | -53.8 |
| Sugar | -17.6 | -17.2 | -17.6 | -17.2 |
| Beverages and tobacco | 3.1 | 3.4 | 3.3 | 3.5 |
| Textiles | 501.3 | 517.7 | 513.9 | 524.9 |
| Wearing apparels | 1107.6 | 1014.3 | 1136.8 | 1034 |
| Wood and paper products, publishing | 13.1 | -4.5 | 22.5 | 2.6 |
| Chemicals, rubber and plastic | -88.2 | -59.4 | -69.8 | -47.3 |
| Ferrous metals | -543.3 | -561.6 | -546 | -556.3 |
| Metal products | 134.8 | 117.4 | 142.7 | 123.1 |
| Motor vehicles and parts | -15.6 | -7 | -0.9 | 1.6 |
| Machinery and equipment | -37.7 | 58.1 | 103.1 | 134.6 |
| Miscellaneous manufacturing | 37.2 | 157.5 | 60 | 172.6 |
| Services | -131.1 | -135.1 | -109.7 | -120.7 |

**Source**: Model simulation.

**Table 7. Estimated change (%) in output by sector in Australia and China under various scenarios**

| Sector | Scenario 1 | Scenario 2 | Scenario 3 | Scenario 4 |
|---|---|---|---|---|
| Australia | | | | |
| Grains | 24.55 | 24.70 | 24.77 | 24.70 |
| Other crops | -2.11 | -2.20 | -2.02 | -2.20 |
| Animal products | -1.51 | -1.63 | -1.31 | -1.63 |
| Forestry and fishing | 0.27 | 0.01 | 0.25 | 0.01 |
| Mining and energy | -1.07 | -0.58 | -0.73 | -0.58 |
| Meat products | -0.83 | -1.11 | -0.38 | -1.11 |
| Other food products | 0.05 | -0.17 | 0.14 | -0.17 |
| Dairy | -0.09 | 0.00 | 0.20 | 0.00 |
| Sugar | 1.92 | 1.92 | 2.24 | 1.91 |
| Beverages and tobacco | -0.19 | -0.30 | -0.16 | -0.30 |
| Textiles | -6.66 | -7.09 | -6.33 | -7.10 |
| Wearing apparels | -9.70 | -10.21 | -9.43 | -10.22 |
| Wood and paper products, publishing | 0.44 | -0.01 | 0.46 | -0.01 |
| Chemicals, rubber and plastic | 1.43 | 1.40 | 1.83 | 1.40 |
| Ferrous metals | 4.15 | 4.72 | 5.00 | 4.72 |
| Metal products | -0.28 | -0.76 | -0.28 | -0.76 |
| Motor vehicles and parts | -0.50 | -0.87 | -0.52 | -0.87 |
| Machinery and equipment | 1.06 | 0.65 | 1.44 | 0.65 |
| Miscellaneous manufacturing | 0.09 | -0.57 | -0.08 | -0.57 |
| Services | 0.98 | 0.27 | 0.71 | 0.28 |
| China | | | | |
| Grains | -3.94 | -4.06 | -3.94 | -4.06 |
| Other crops | 0.35 | 0.26 | 0.36 | 0.27 |
| Animal products | 0.53 | 0.38 | 0.52 | 0.38 |
| Forestry and fishing | 0.27 | 0.16 | 0.27 | 0.16 |
| Mining and energy | 0.26 | 0.17 | 0.25 | 0.17 |
| Meat products | 0.29 | 0.12 | 0.29 | 0.13 |
| Other food products | 0.33 | 0.24 | 0.33 | 0.24 |
| Dairy | -3.86 | -4.05 | -3.90 | -4.03 |
| Sugar | -3.35 | -3.45 | -3.39 | -3.44 |
| Beverages and tobacco | 0.33 | 0.23 | 0.32 | 0.23 |
| Textiles | 1.26 | 1.19 | 1.30 | 1.22 |
| Wearing apparels | 1.25 | 1.10 | 1.28 | 1.12 |
| Wood and paper products, publishing | 0.31 | 0.22 | 0.32 | 0.23 |
| Chemicals, rubber and plastic | 0.19 | 0.14 | 0.21 | 0.15 |
| Ferrous metals | -0.18 | -0.25 | -0.17 | -0.24 |
| Metal products | 0.47 | 0.39 | 0.47 | 0.39 |
| Motor vehicles and parts | 0.35 | 0.30 | 0.33 | 0.29 |
| Machinery and equipment | 0.30 | 0.28 | 0.33 | 0.29 |
| Miscellaneous manufacturing | 0.19 | 0.32 | 0.22 | 0.34 |
| Services | 0.33 | 0.24 | 0.30 | 0.23 |

**Source**: Model simulation.

On the other hand, Machinery performs worse for the trade balance, but shows positive output. In China, Animal products and Motor vehicles and parts are worse for the trade balance but become positive in output. The key reason for this contrast is that with the removal of bilateral tariffs, the two economies adjust their sectoral structures according to their comparative advantage. In some sectors, both imports and domestic production increase at the same time. Generally, Table 7 indicates that in sector Grains, both economies have greater structural adjustments whereas Australia at above 24 percent and China negatively at about 4 percent. Australia also has a relatively greater decrease in production in Wearing apparels (about 10 percent) and Textiles (above 6.3 percent) in all four scenarios. In China, the sectors of Grain, Dairy and Sugar appear to be hit most due to the creation of an ACFTA.

Tables 8 and 9 report the estimated changes for Australia and China in demand for the key primary factors of land, labour (including unskilled labour and skilled labour) and capital by sector under various scenarios. Once again, the directions of change are similar to the trade balance and output by sector in Table 6 and Table 7. Therefore, those results further suggest a potential need for reallocations of the primary factors among sectors. In the case of Australia, all sectors decrease the use of land except Grain in all four cases, which indicates that Grain is a relatively land-intensive sector. In the case of China, most sectors appear to increase their use of land, labour and capital except the three sectors of Grains, Dairy and Sugar, where the use of all factors appear to experience negative adjustments. In both economies, labour force is expected to move from declining sectors to growing sectors in most cases. These changes in sectoral outputs are reflected in employment impacts. For Australia, there are employment declines of above 9 percent in Wearing apparels and above 6 percent in Textiles in all four scenarios; on the other hand, there is increased employment of above 26 percent in Grains. For China, there is increased employment in almost all of the sectors except Grains, Dairy, Sugar and Beverages. The effects on China's sectoral employment, however, are comparatively negligible.

## Effects on Trade Patterns

Changes in bilateral trade flows associated with the ACFTA under four scenarios are presented in Table 10. The results demonstrate that bilateral trade would expand, with Australia's imports from China growing by around US$ 2.7 billion, and Australia's exports to China increasing by about US$ 4.3 billion (see Table 11) in all four scenarios. The results also project that all sectors except services will receive benefits from the formation of the ACFTA. The sectors benefiting most in Australia are: Grains (above 610 percent), Textiles (above 410 percent),

Miscellaneous manufacturing (above 240 percent), Wearing apparels (above 205 percent) and Dairy (above 200 percent). On the other hand, China's sectors obtain smaller gains from the ACFTA with the most benefited sectors being Textiles (about 117 percent) followed by Wearing apparels (around 73 percent) and Beverages (around 50 percent). The results also show increased opportunities for two-way trade in these sectors.

The magnitude of difference between changes in Australia's and China's bilateral export volume shows the relative significance and size of bilateral trade to each country. These differences are attributable to a combination of the relative market shares of both countries and the relative protection in both economies.Effects on trade flows in the international trade content are presented in Table 11. It can be seen that there are pervasive indications of trade diversion as shown by the reductions to a small extent in the bilateral trade flows for most other regions. For example, Australia's imports from ASEAN, KOR, TWN and ROW would all decrease. Among non-member countries or country groups, Japan, U.S. and ASEAN (6) are most adversely affected by the ACFTA in all four scenarios. The total volume of world imports increases, however, due to the formation of the ACFTA, although there is some evidence of minor trade diversion. Since trade creation is greater than the trade diversion resulting from the agreement, the ACFTA is trade creating for the world as a whole.

## Table 8. Estimated change (%) in demand for key primary factors by sector in Australia

| Sector | Scenario 1 | | | | Scenario 2 | | | | Scenario 3 | | | | Scenario 4 | | | |
|---|---|---|---|---|---|---|---|---|---|---|---|---|---|---|---|---|
| | Land | Unskilled labor | Skilled labor | Capital | Land | Unskilled labor | Skilled labor | Capital | Land | Unskilled labor | Skilled labor | Capital | Land | Unskilled labor | Skilled labor | Capital |
| Grains | 17.84 | 26.70 | 26.70 | 26.39 | 18.02 | 26.66 | 26.68 | 26.86 | 17.88 | 26.97 | 26.97 | 26.70 | 18.01 | 26.65 | 26.68 | 26.85 |
| Other crops | -3.92 | -1.51 | -1.51 | -1.76 | -3.95 | -1.76 | -1.74 | -1.61 | -3.98 | -1.40 | -1.40 | -1.61 | -3.95 | -1.77 | -1.75 | -1.61 |
| Animal products | -3.43 | -0.89 | -0.89 | -1.14 | -3.48 | -1.17 | -1.15 | -1.01 | -3.39 | -0.65 | -0.65 | -0.86 | -3.48 | -1.17 | -1.15 | -1.01 |
| Forestry and fishing | -1.96 | 0.49 | 0.49 | 0.28 | -2.23 | -0.02 | 0.00 | 0.11 | -2.12 | 0.45 | 0.45 | 0.27 | -2.23 | -0.02 | -0.01 | 0.11 |
| Mining and energy | -6.00 | -0.98 | -0.98 | -1.64 | -5.73 | -1.08 | -1.02 | -0.65 | -6.06 | -0.59 | -0.59 | -1.16 | -5.73 | -1.08 | -1.03 | -0.66 |
| Meat products | -7.59 | -0.61 | -0.61 | -1.77 | -7.43 | -1.26 | -1.17 | -0.52 | -7.78 | -0.20 | -0.20 | -1.20 | -7.43 | -1.27 | -1.17 | -0.52 |
| Other food products | -7.06 | 0.58 | 0.58 | -0.59 | -7.09 | -0.52 | -0.42 | 0.24 | -7.43 | 0.59 | 0.59 | -0.42 | -7.09 | -0.52 | -0.42 | 0.24 |
| Dairy | -7.08 | 0.53 | 0.53 | -0.63 | -7.05 | -0.42 | -0.32 | 0.34 | -7.37 | 0.74 | 0.74 | -0.27 | -7.05 | -0.42 | -0.32 | 0.34 |
| Sugar | -6.26 | 2.42 | 2.42 | 1.23 | -6.18 | 1.58 | 1.68 | 2.35 | -6.53 | 2.68 | 2.68 | 1.65 | -6.17 | 1.58 | 1.67 | 2.34 |
| Beverages and tobacco | -7.04 | 0.63 | 0.63 | -0.54 | -7.23 | -0.83 | -0.73 | -0.08 | -7.45 | 0.54 | 0.54 | -0.46 | -7.23 | -0.83 | -0.73 | -0.08 |
| Textiles | -10.32 | -6.31 | -6.31 | -7.53 | -10.31 | -7.34 | -7.24 | -6.55 | -10.58 | -6.02 | -6.02 | -7.08 | -10.31 | -7.35 | -7.25 | -6.56 |
| Wearing apparels | -11.68 | -9.47 | -9.47 | -10.65 | -11.63 | -10.38 | -10.28 | -9.62 | -11.95 | -9.23 | -9.23 | -10.25 | -11.63 | -10.39 | -10.29 | -9.63 |
| Wood and paper products, publishing | -7.29 | 1.00 | 1.00 | -0.32 | -7.39 | -0.39 | -0.28 | 0.46 | -7.71 | 0.94 | 0.94 | -0.19 | -7.39 | -0.39 | -0.28 | 0.46 |
| Chemicals, rubber and plastic | -6.87 | 2.05 | 2.05 | 0.72 | -6.83 | 0.98 | 1.09 | 1.84 | -7.13 | 2.37 | 2.37 | 1.22 | -6.83 | 0.98 | 1.09 | 1.84 |
| Ferrous metals | -5.75 | 4.85 | 4.85 | 3.48 | -5.50 | 4.26 | 4.37 | 5.14 | -5.84 | 5.61 | 5.61 | 4.42 | -5.50 | 4.25 | 4.36 | 5.13 |
| Metal products | -7.65 | 0.12 | 0.12 | -1.19 | -7.66 | -1.03 | -0.93 | -0.19 | -8.07 | 0.07 | 0.07 | -1.05 | -7.66 | -1.04 | -0.93 | -0.19 |
| Motor vehicles and parts | -7.67 | 0.08 | 0.08 | -1.23 | -7.75 | -1.25 | -1.14 | -0.41 | -8.10 | -0.02 | -0.02 | -1.15 | -7.74 | -1.25 | -1.14 | -0.41 |
| Machinery and equipment | -7.10 | 1.48 | 1.48 | 0.16 | -7.09 | 0.35 | 0.46 | 1.21 | -7.36 | 1.80 | 1.80 | 0.66 | -7.08 | 0.35 | 0.46 | 1.20 |
| Miscellaneous manufacturing | -7.49 | 0.52 | 0.52 | -0.79 | -7.59 | -0.86 | -0.75 | -0.02 | -7.97 | 0.30 | 0.30 | -0.83 | -7.58 | -0.86 | -0.76 | -0.02 |
| Services | -7.41 | 1.52 | 1.52 | 0.06 | -7.55 | -0.10 | 0.01 | 0.83 | -7.95 | 1.17 | 1.17 | -0.07 | -7.54 | -0.10 | 0.01 | 0.83 |

**Source:** Model simulation.

## Table 9. Estimated change (%) in demand for key primary factors by sector in China

| Sector | Scenario 1 | | | | Scenario 2 | | | | Scenario 3 | | | | Scenario 4 | | | |
|---|---|---|---|---|---|---|---|---|---|---|---|---|---|---|---|---|
| | Land | Unskilled labor | Skilled labor | Capital | Land | Unskilled labor | Skilled labor | Capital | Land | Unskilled labor | Skilled labor | Capital | Land | Unskilled labor | Skilled labor | Capital |
| Grains | -3.27 | -4.18 | -4.18 | -4.31 | -3.29 | -4.39 | -4.40 | -4.30 | -3.27 | -4.19 | -4.19 | -4.31 | -3.29 | -4.39 | -4.40 | -4.30 |
| Other crops | 0.41 | 0.35 | 0.35 | 0.23 | 0.43 | 0.18 | 0.17 | 0.28 | 0.41 | 0.36 | 0.36 | 0.23 | 0.43 | 0.18 | 0.18 | 0.28 |
| Animal products | 0.56 | 0.53 | 0.53 | 0.41 | 0.53 | 0.31 | 0.30 | 0.41 | 0.55 | 0.53 | 0.53 | 0.40 | 0.53 | 0.31 | 0.30 | 0.41 |
| Forestry and fishing | 0.44 | 0.40 | 0.40 | 0.29 | 0.42 | 0.21 | 0.21 | 0.29 | 0.43 | 0.39 | 0.39 | 0.28 | 0.42 | 0.21 | 0.20 | 0.29 |
| Mining and energy | 0.53 | 0.45 | 0.45 | 0.12 | 0.61 | 0.07 | 0.05 | 0.33 | 0.53 | 0.45 | 0.45 | 0.11 | 0.61 | 0.08 | 0.05 | 0.33 |
| Meat products | 0.62 | 0.58 | 0.58 | -0.01 | 0.72 | -0.10 | -0.15 | 0.35 | 0.62 | 0.58 | 0.58 | -0.01 | 0.72 | -0.09 | -0.13 | 0.36 |
| Other food products | 0.67 | 0.70 | 0.70 | 0.11 | 0.75 | -0.04 | -0.09 | 0.42 | 0.67 | 0.69 | 0.69 | 0.11 | 0.75 | -0.04 | -0.08 | 0.41 |
| Dairy | -1.36 | -3.57 | -3.57 | -4.14 | -1.28 | -4.27 | -4.32 | -3.84 | -1.38 | -3.61 | -3.61 | -4.17 | -1.28 | -4.25 | -4.29 | -3.82 |
| Sugar | -1.09 | -3.00 | -3.00 | -3.57 | -1.01 | -3.70 | -3.75 | -3.27 | -1.11 | -3.05 | -3.05 | -3.61 | -1.01 | -3.70 | -3.74 | -3.26 |
| Beverages and tobacco | 0.65 | 0.66 | 0.66 | 0.07 | 0.76 | -0.02 | -0.07 | 0.43 | 0.65 | 0.65 | 0.65 | 0.07 | 0.76 | -0.02 | -0.06 | 0.43 |
| Textiles | 1.07 | 1.61 | 1.61 | 0.94 | 1.23 | 0.93 | 0.88 | 1.44 | 1.09 | 1.64 | 1.64 | 0.98 | 1.23 | 0.95 | 0.91 | 1.46 |
| Wearing apparels | 1.02 | 1.50 | 1.50 | 0.83 | 1.22 | 0.91 | 0.86 | 1.43 | 1.04 | 1.53 | 1.53 | 0.87 | 1.22 | 0.93 | 0.89 | 1.45 |
| Wood and paper products, publishing | 0.62 | 0.59 | 0.59 | -0.07 | 0.82 | 0.01 | -0.04 | 0.52 | 0.63 | 0.60 | 0.60 | -0.06 | 0.82 | 0.02 | -0.02 | 0.53 |
| Chemicals, rubber and plastic | 0.60 | 0.54 | 0.54 | -0.12 | 0.76 | -0.12 | -0.18 | 0.39 | 0.61 | 0.56 | 0.56 | -0.10 | 0.76 | -0.11 | -0.16 | 0.40 |
| Ferrous metals | 0.39 | 0.08 | 0.08 | -0.58 | 0.62 | -0.44 | -0.49 | 0.07 | 0.40 | 0.08 | 0.08 | -0.58 | 0.62 | -0.43 | -0.48 | 0.07 |
| Metal products | 0.69 | 0.74 | 0.74 | 0.08 | 0.89 | 0.18 | 0.13 | 0.69 | 0.70 | 0.75 | 0.75 | 0.09 | 0.89 | 0.19 | 0.14 | 0.70 |
| Motor vehicles and parts | 0.66 | 0.68 | 0.68 | 0.02 | 0.84 | 0.05 | 0.00 | 0.56 | 0.66 | 0.66 | 0.66 | 0.00 | 0.83 | 0.04 | -0.01 | 0.55 |
| Machinery and equipment | 0.64 | 0.64 | 0.64 | -0.03 | 0.83 | 0.03 | -0.02 | 0.54 | 0.66 | 0.66 | 0.66 | 0.00 | 0.83 | 0.04 | 0.00 | 0.55 |
| Miscellaneous manufacturing | 0.64 | 0.63 | 0.63 | -0.03 | 0.81 | -0.02 | -0.07 | 0.50 | 0.66 | 0.66 | 0.66 | 0.00 | 0.81 | 0.01 | -0.04 | 0.51 |
| Services | 0.64 | 0.62 | 0.62 | -0.11 | 0.86 | 0.03 | -0.03 | 0.59 | 0.63 | 0.59 | 0.59 | -0.13 | 0.85 | 0.02 | -0.03 | 0.57 |

**Source**: Model simulation.

**Table 10. Estimated change of bilateral export volumes between Australia and China under various scenarios (%)**

| Sector | Scenario 1 | | Scenario 2 | | Scenario 3 | | Scenario 4 | |
|---|---|---|---|---|---|---|---|---|
| | EAC | ECA | EAC | ECA | EAC | ECA | EAC | ECA |
| Grains | 613.64 | 29.04 | 614.78 | 28.24 | 614.37 | 29.02 | 614.71 | 28.28 |
| Other crops | 33.28 | 8.73 | 33.80 | 7.95 | 33.78 | 8.57 | 33.79 | 7.98 |
| Animal products | 4.25 | 5.36 | 4.51 | 4.62 | 4.53 | 5.27 | 4.50 | 4.65 |
| Forestry and fishing | 22.11 | 5.85 | 23.35 | 4.70 | 22.87 | 5.45 | 23.32 | 4.74 |
| Mining and energy | 0.03 | 25.47 | 1.51 | 24.90 | 0.81 | 25.42 | 1.49 | 24.96 |
| Meat products | 112.15 | 39.36 | 111.95 | 38.40 | 114.16 | 38.64 | 111.90 | 38.48 |
| Other food products | 132.72 | 17.83 | 133.45 | 17.17 | 134.29 | 17.41 | 133.41 | 17.20 |
| Dairy | 199.74 | 37.90 | 201.71 | 36.71 | 202.13 | 37.20 | 201.68 | 36.78 |
| Sugar | 103.68 | 4.54 | 104.07 | 4.03 | 104.84 | 4.16 | 104.04 | 4.07 |
| Beverages and tobacco | 173.01 | 50.77 | 174.31 | 49.84 | 174.08 | 50.36 | 174.28 | 49.87 |
| Textiles | 414.32 | 117.72 | 413.93 | 116.62 | 419.71 | 117.29 | 413.85 | 116.66 |
| Wearing apparels | 207.14 | 73.67 | 205.92 | 72.71 | 209.88 | 73.08 | 205.86 | 72.74 |
| Wood and paper products, publishing | 111.85 | 33.39 | 113.03 | 32.18 | 114.02 | 32.70 | 112.98 | 32.24 |
| Chemicals, rubber and plastic | 163.42 | 34.66 | 165.10 | 33.96 | 166.09 | 34.40 | 165.06 | 34.01 |
| Ferrous metals | 97.75 | 33.86 | 99.70 | 32.86 | 99.90 | 33.62 | 99.66 | 32.92 |
| Metal products | 124.57 | 47.40 | 124.99 | 46.29 | 127.24 | 46.49 | 124.92 | 46.35 |
| Motor vehicles and parts | 104.79 | 37.99 | 105.79 | 36.76 | 106.60 | 36.92 | 105.69 | 36.82 |
| Machinery and equipment | 173.92 | 24.78 | 174.22 | 23.81 | 177.17 | 23.91 | 174.13 | 23.87 |
| Miscellaneous manufacturing | 246.66 | 25.64 | 246.40 | 25.17 | 250.53 | 24.86 | 246.30 | 25.22 |
| Services | -2.61 | 2.51 | -2.44 | 1.56 | -1.90 | 1.95 | -2.47 | 1.59 |

**Note**: EAC: Exports from Australia to China; ECA: Exports from China to Australia.
**Source**: Model simulation.

**Table 11. Effects on trade flows of Australia-China FTA (US $ million)**

|  | Scenario 1 | Scenario 2 | Scenario 3 | Scenario 4 |
|---|---|---|---|---|
| Australia's exports to |  |  |  |  |
| China | 4303.6 | 4356.9 | 4373.3 | 4355.2 |
| World | 971.2 | 1463.5 | 1605.5 | 1459.6 |
| Australia's imports from |  |  |  |  |
| USA | 84.1 | -16.2 | 0.8 | -17.8 |
| ASEAN | -76.4 | -134.6 | -117.9 | -133.8 |
| CHI | 2752.2 | 2699.9 | 2716.7 | 2702.7 |
| JPA | 72.7 | 0.0 | 8.4 | 1.3 |
| KOR | -23.1 | -42.3 | -38.4 | -42.3 |
| TWN | -37.8 | -49.6 | -47.9 | -49.5 |
| KHG | 14.7 | 6.2 | 8.4 | 6.2 |
| EU | 9.1 | -134.8 | -105.6 | -135.6 |
| ROW | -219.7 | -288.4 | -269.5 | -288.7 |
| Total | 2575.7 | 2040.1 | 2154.9 | 2042.7 |

**Source**: Model simulation.

# VI. CONCLUDING REMARKS

In summarising the bilateral economic relations between Australia and China, it is evident that there is a robust and continuing growth trend between the two economies based on a strongly complementary trading relationship. The relative importance of one to the other is stronger and more significant, especially China's significance to Australia. Primary commodities dominate Australian exports, with China demanding increasing amounts of resource commodities to fuel its industrial expansion. On the other hand, China's manufactured goods occupy a large proportion of Australian imports. The bilateral investment relationship appears relatively less developed.

In summarising the results from the simulations, it is evident that both Australia and China are projected to benefit from the ACFTA with Australia gaining more. The ACFTA generates a greater trade creation effect than trade diversion. In macroeconomic effects, there are some gains in terms of real GDP, EV and real consumption. Sectoral effects are mixed. The results show that bilateral trade would expand, with Australia's exports to China growing faster than China's exports to Australia. The bilateral removal of tariffs would cause more significant structural adjustments in the Australian economy than in the Chinese economy. The sectors that benefit most from the ACFTA are: Australia's agricultural and resource-based sectors such as Grains and Sugar; and China's manufacturing industries, especially Wearing apparels and Textiles and Miscellaneous manufactures. Consequently, this will lead to the corresponding adjustments in primary factor market in both countries.

Given these results from the GTAP model simulations, the ACFTA would benefit both economies with the abolishment of tariffs on bilateral merchandise trade. Each economy will move more closely to the sectors where they have comparative advantage. While considering the domestic income and employment impacts on each sector, the net result would be that consumers and producers have increased options of goods and inputs while importers and exporters face improved market access.

There are some limitations of this paper due to the GTAP model itself and other factors. First, the GTAP model is a comparative static model, thus it is hard to capture some dynamic effects of trade liberalisation, the simulations conducted in this paper may not reflect the true outcome. In addition, service trade liberalization and investment liberalisation have been omitted in this paper since there is very little empirical evidence available on barriers to investment and services trade. Another limitation is that only import protection liberalization is considered in this paper. The removal of export restraints may be expected to generate additional benefits for both economies and the world as a whole (Lee et al. 1997). This can be another avenue for future research.

### Appendix A.1. Aggregation of regions and commodities

| Aggregated Region | GTAP Region | Aggregated Commodity | GTAP Commodity |
|---|---|---|---|
| 1. Australia (AUS) | Australia | 1. Grains | Paddy rice; wheat; cereal grains nec |
| 2. Unites States (US) | United States | 2. Other crops | Vegetables, fruits, nuts; Oil seeds; Plant-based fibers; Crops nec Sugar cane, sugar beet, |
| | | 3. Animal products | Cattle, sheep, goat, horses; Animal products nec; Wool, silk-worm cocoons, Raw milk |
| 3. ASEAN (6) | Indonesia, Malaysia, Philippines, Singapore, Thailand, Vietnam | 4. Forestry and fishing | Forestry, fishing |
| 4. China (CHI) | China | 5. Mining and energy | Coal; Oil; Gas; Minerals nec; petroleum and coal products |

### Appendix A.1. Aggregation

| Aggregated Region | GTAP Region | Aggregated Commodity | GTAP Commodity |
|---|---|---|---|
| 5. Japan (JPA) | Japan | 6. Meat products | Meat: cattle, sheep, goats, horse; Meat products nec, |
| 6. Korea (KOR) | Korea | 7. Other food products | Vegetable oil and fats; processed rice; food products nec |
| 7. Taiwan (TWN) | Taiwan | | |
| | | 8. Dairy | Dairy products |
| 8. Hong Kong (HKG) | Hong Kong | 9. Sugar | Sugar |
| | | 10. Beverages and tobacco | Beverages and tobacco products |
| 9. European Union (EU) | United Kingdom, Germany, Denmark, Sweden, Finland, Austria, Belgium, France, Greece, Ireland, Italy, Luxemburg, Netherlands, Portugal, Spain, Cyprus, Czech Republic, Hungary, Malta, Poland, Slovakia, Slovenia, Estonia, Latvia, Lithuania | 11. Textiles | Textiles |
| | | 12. Wearing apparels | Wwearing apparel; leather products |
| | | 13. Wood and paper products, publishing | Wood products; Paper products, publishing |

**Appendix A.1. (continued)**

| Aggregated Region | GTAP Region | Aggregated Commodity | GTAP Commodity |
|---|---|---|---|
| 10. Rest of Europe (RU) | All other regions | 14. Chemicals, rubber and plastic | Chemical, rubber, plastic prods |
| | | 15. Ferrous metals | Ferrous metals; Metals nec |
| | | 16. Metal products | Metal products |
| | | 17. Motor vehicles and parts | Motor vehicles and parts; Transport equipment nec |
| | | 18. Machinery and equipment | Electronic equipment; Machinery and equipment nec |
| | | 19. Miscellaneous manufacturing | Manufacturing nec |
| | | 20. Services | Electricity; Gas manufacture and distribution; Water; construction; PublicAdministration/Defence/ Health/Education; Dwellings; Trade, Sea transport, Air transport, Communication; Financial services nec, Insurance, Business services nec, Recreation and other services |

**Source**: Purdue University 2005, GTAP database version 6.

# REFERENCES

ABS (Australia Bureau Statistics) 1998, 'International merchandise trade', Cat. No. 5422.0, Australia.

ABS (Australia Bureau Statistics) 2000, 'International merchandise trade', Cat. No. 5422.0, Australia.

ABS (Australia Bureau Statistics) 2004, 'International merchandise trade', Cat. No. 5422.0, Australia.

ABS (Australia Bureau Statistics) 2006, 'International merchandise trade', Cat. No. 5422.0, Australia.

Brown, D. K., Kiyota, K. and Stern, R. M. 2005, 'Computational analysis of the US FTAs with central America, Australia and Morocco', *World Economy*, Vol. 28, Issue 10, pp. 1441-1490, Blackwell Publishing Ltd.

Brown, D. K., Kiyota, K. and Stern, R. M. 2006, 'Computational analysis of the menu of US-Japan trade policies', *World Economy*, Vol. 29, Issue 6, pp. 805-855.

China Statistical Yearbook , various years (1996, 1999, 2001, 2003, 2005), 'Volume of Imports and Exports by Countries and Regions (Customs Statistics)', *National Bureau of Statistical of China*, China Statistics Press, Beijing.

Comtrade database (United Nations Statistics Division) 2006, *UN Commodity Trade Statistics Database*, http://unstats.un.org/unsd/comtrade/, accessed March 2006.

DFAT (Department of Foreign Affairs and Trade) 2002, 'China embraces the world market', *Commonwealth of Australia*, www.dfat.gov.au/eau, accessed March 2006.

DFAT (Department of Foreign Affairs and Trade) 2006a, *Free Trade Agreements under Negotiation/Consideration*, URL: www.dfat.gov.au/trade/, accessed May 2006.

DFAT (Department of Foreign Affairs and Trade) 2006b, *Country, Economy and Regional Information*, URL: www.dfat.gov.au/geo/, accessed May 2006.

Editorial Board of the Almanac of China's Foreign Economic Relations and Trade. 2001, *2001 Almanac of China's Foreign Economic Relations and Trade*, China Foreign

Hertel, T. W. (Editor), 1997, *Global Trade Analysis: Modeling and Applications*, Cambridge University Press.

Invest Australia, 2002, Information supplied to Economic Analytical Unit, Hongkong, April.

Lee, H., Roland-Holst, D. and Mensbrugghe, D. 1997, 'APEC trade liberalization and structural adjustments: Policy assessments', *GSID APEC discussion paper series*, No. 11.

Mai, Y., Adams, P., Fan, M., Li, R. and Zheng, Z. 2005, 'Modelling the potential benefits of an Australia-China free trade agreement', *Department of Foreign Affairs and Trade*, Australia.

Maitland, E. and Nicholas, S. 1999, 'Australian multinational enterprises in China: Motivations, technology transfer and operations', Australian Centre for International Business, University of Melbourne, Melbourne.

National Bureau of Statistics of China (NBS) 2005, URL: www.stats.gov.cn/english/statisticaldata/yearlydata, accessed April 2006.

Productivity Commission 2004, *Rules of Origin under the Australia-New Zealand Closer Economic Relations Trade Agreement*, Research Report, Canberra.

Purdue University 2005, 'GTAP database version 6', *Center for Global Trade Analysis*, URL: www.gtap.agecon.purdue.edu/databases/v6/, accessed June 2006.

Siriwardana, M. 2007, 'The Australia-United States free trade agreement: An economic evaluation', *North American Journal of Economics and Finance*, Vol. 18, Issue 1, pp. 117-133.

WTO (World Trade Organization) 2006, *Regional Trade Agreements Notified to the GATT/WTO and in Force*, WTO, Geneva, URL: www.wto.org/english/ tratop_e/ region_e/eif_e.xls, accessed June 2006.

Year Book Australia 2006, 'Merchandise exports and imports by country and country group', *Australian Bureau of Statistics* (ABS), Australia.

In: Asian Economic and Political Development
Editor: Felix Chin

ISBN: 978-1-61122-470-2
© 2011 Nova Science Publishers, Inc.

# A COMPARATIVE STUDY OF AGRICULTURAL COMMODITY'S TRADE CHINA-NIGER

## *Zakari Seydou* and *Chen Suijun*

School of Management, Zhejiang University
Center for agricultural and rural development (CARD)
Card Building, Hua-Jia-Chi Campus, Zhejiang University, 268 Kai-Xuan Road, 310029
Hangzhou, China

## ABSTRACT

This paper examines and compares the patterns of agricultural trade of China and Niger between 2000 and 2006. We find that both china and Niger agricultural imports were more than doubled in this period. Chinese imports exceed exports two years after china's accession to WTO in 2001 which opened Chinese market to world economy. There was slight decrease in the exports of Niger agricultural trade while imports increased sharply due to high population growth and deficit of food supply in the country.

Both Niger and China mainly export their farm produces to their neighboring countries. China's imports have geographically diversified sources. The study also found that there is little agricultural trading between china and Niger, which was mainly Chinese exports to Niger.

**Keywords**: Agriculture, Trade, China, Niger, Imports, Exports.

## LIST OF ABBREVIATIONS

| | |
|---|---|
| WTO: | World Trade Organization |
| CFA: | West African monetary currency, Franc zone. |
| FAOSTAT: | Food and Agricultural Organization Statistics |
| GDP: | Gross domestic product |
| SPS: | Sanitary and Phytosanitary Standards |
| TRQs: | Tariff Rate Quota |
| USA: | United Stated of America |

---

* E-mail address: zakaryaou@yahoo.com. Corresponding author: Tel: +8657186971593.

# 1. AGRICULTURAL EXPORTS OF NIGER

Between 2001 and 2005, Niger's agricultural export was estimated about 211.39 billions of CFA.

The major agricultural commodities exported by Niger are live animals, onions, cowpeas, beans, pepper, groundnuts, and so on.

From 2001 to 2005 livestock exports account about 126,949 millions of CFA. This represents 61.03% of the total Niger agricultural exports. Livestock production is the mainstay of all agricultural sectors but only 20%of Niger's population is engaged in it. Fourteen percent of Niger's GDP is generated by livestock production. The main livestock products are goat, sheep, cattle, camels, hides, skins, meat, etc...Livestock production depends on the quantity and quality of available forage, which, in turn, depends on soil fertility and land use (among other factors). In the long term, soil fertility in cropped or fallow fields is a function of the balance between nutrients added to the soil and nutrients removed through crop harvesting and grazing. A good crop production means also a good livestock raising in Niger, in the sense that crop residues are used in feeding animals during off-season. The livestock industry is vulnerable to local pasture availability and weather shocks. In the wake of the 1973–1984 droughts, which decimated herds and severely degraded natural resources in the Sahel, relations between farming and livestock production went through a difficult period. The traditional complementarity and coexistence of farmers and pastoralists turned to competition and even conflict between the two groups. This also led to such changes as further expansion of cultivated areas, the farming of marginal lands, and the steady transfer of livestock ownership from herders to better-off farmers, who would purchase the animals at distress prices.

The primary destination of livestock exports is Nigeria .About 90% of sheep, goats, and cattle are exported to Nigeria. This may be due to historic and deep economic and social links between Niger and Nigeria .The others destinations are Benin, Libya, and Cote d'Ivoire. Livestock still one of the Niger most important agricultural trade commodities. Niger livestock exports decreased sharply about 40.16 % of its volume in 2001-2005. The problem is that, this traditional activity, subject to extensive exploitation due to nomadism, suffers from a lack of professionalism and, from lack of access to veterinary products, from a nearly total absence of health monitoring of the herds. Processing activities remain embryonic due to inadequate infrastructure (transport vehicles, cold-storage slaughterhouses). Inadequate forage to feed animals is the main problem for livestock production in Niger.

Onion is the country's second most important agricultural item .From 2001 to 2005, onion exports were estimated to about 60,947 Millions of CFA. This represents about 28.83% of the total agricultural exports of Niger and increased about 15%. The main markets for Niger's onions are Ghana (41.87%), Cote d'Ivoire (25.33%) and Nigeria (18%).According to ADF e-News, August 2005, Niger is third-largest producer of onions - only Nigeria and South Africa produce more - and its bright purple and red Galmi onions are preferred by consumers across West Africa. But Niger's small-scale onion growers have long struggled to generate significant profit from their work because many cannot afford to hold on to the bulk of their harvests until prices peak at the height of the dry season in February and March. Producers living near the subsistence level often sell their yields just after harvest in August and September, when local markets are saturated with new produce and prices are extremely low. Farmers sell their crops to retire accumulated debts and purchase grain, medicine, and other basic necessities, leaving them with little cash to invest in tools, irrigation technology, hand-made storage shelters, and other inputs that would help them expand their production and profitability over time.

Niger exports also cowpeas which account about 4.67% of the total agricultural exports and experienced a net decrease of about 87.6% of its volume in 2001-2005. In Niger, cowpeas are produced mostly in the southern regions, with annual rainfall ranging from 300 to 800 mm. With 586 000 tons of dry cowpea grain produced annually, Niger Republic is the second largest world cowpea-producing country after Nigeria (over 2 million tons). Its major cowpea production period is the short raining season (June–September) according to IITA news in 18 June 2007.

Cotton lint is one of the Niger export item. Cotton production is concentrated in the Gay, Maradi, and Tahoua areas, which account for a combined 80% of Niger's cotton output (global cotton production in Niger is about 10,000 tons a year). Most cotton production activities are carried out by farmers working on small family farms using traditional methods. Cotton exports also decreased about 40.5% of its volume in 2001-2005. Its main markets are Burkina-Faso, Nigeria and Benin.

Pepper (1.06%of the total agricultural exports), Beans (1.35%), sorghum, groundnut, millet are also exported. Their main destinations are Nigeria and the other Neighboring West African Nations. See the table 1 below for more details.

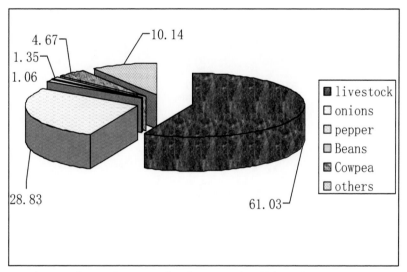

**Note**: percentage is according to the accumulated export value 2001-2005.
**Source**: institute national de statistique du Niger.

Figure 1. Major agricultural products export by Niger.

According to FEW NET report (2002), the massive purchase of cereals in Niger markets by Nigerian businessmen, resulting in a demand that is far higher than the supply. The massive exportation of food items to Nigeria is mainly due to the fact that Nigerian farmers in certain Northern States give priority to cash crop (for instance, cotton and beans) production to the detriment of food crop cultivation, resulting in an extremely high demand for cereals to feed Nigerian transformation industries and for use on poultry farms.

**Table 1. Niger major agricultural export products and their major destination markets**

| Products | Destination 1 | | Destination 2 | | Destination3 | | others |
|---|---|---|---|---|---|---|---|
| | countries | % | countries | % | countries | % | % |
| Cattle | Nigeria | 99.73% | Benin | 0.05% | Libya | 0.01% | 0.05% |
| Goat | Nigeria | 96.36% | Benin | 3.05% | Libya | 0.07% | 0.50% |
| Sheep | Nigeria | 90.64% | Benin | 6.42% | Cote d'Ivoire | 0.78% | 2.14% |
| Beans | Nigeria | 70.38 | Burkina Faso | 12.77 | China | 5.49 | 11.40 |
| Onion | Ghana | 41.87% | Cote d'Ivoire | 25.33% | Nigeria | !8.00% | 14.80% |
| Sesame seed | Nigeria | 98.82% | Burkina Faso | 1.17% | - | - | - |
| Cotton | Burkina Faso | 44.42% | Nigeria | 27.36% | Benin | 13.43% | 11.77% |
| Pepper | China | 66.66% | Nigeria | 18.5% | France | 7.4% | 7.4% |
| Garlic | Nigeria | 97.43 | Burkina Faso | 2.56 | - | - | - |
| Sorghum | Nigeria | 40.10 | India | 30.5 | USA | 14 | 15.39 |
| Millet | Nigeria | 78.30 | Mali | 12.72 | Burkina Faso | 8.87 | 0.1 |

**Note**: Percentage is according to accumulated Exports quantity of FAO World Agricultural Trade Matrix (WATM), 2001-2005

**Source**: FAOSTAT

## 1.1. Characteristics of Niger Agricultural Exports

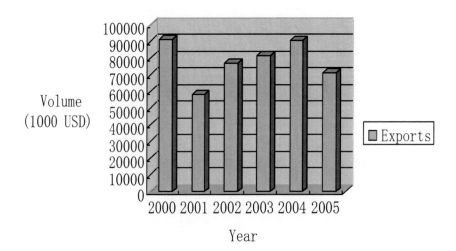

**Source**: FAOSTAT

Figure 2. Niger imports of farm products 2000-2005.

As shown by the figure2 below, Niger's Agricultural export fell sharply between 2000 - 2001, then started increasing slightly from 2001 to 2004.Between 2004 and 2005 there was a decrease in the export volume. The highest pick was recorded in 2000. In general, in 2000-2005, Niger agricultural exports decreased about 21.47% of its volume. This decrease in agricultural exports may be due to the hard agricultural environment, traditional methods of production used by farmers, climate changes, pests and diseases of crops and livestock, combined with high birth rate (one of the highest in the World) and urbanization.

## 2. AGRICULTURAL IMPORT OF NIGER

Between 2001 and 2005, Niger's agricultural import volume was estimated about 730.6 Billions of CFA.

Niger's Agricultural imports are essentially composed of edible oils which accounts about 41.94% of the total agricultural imports, cereals mainly maize and rice constitute 25.63% , sugar accounts 7.81% , wheat flour 5.34%, dried cow milk 5.57%, tobacco 5.65%, fruits, tea and other products( See the Fig 3 ).

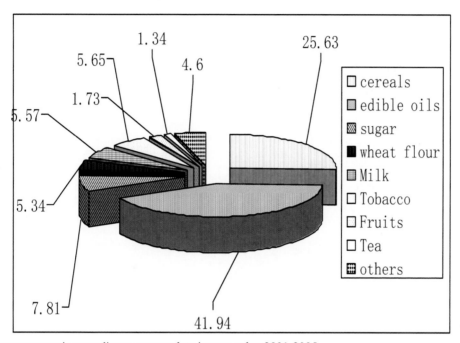

**Note**: percentage is according to accumulate import value 2001-2005
**Source**: institut national de statistique du Niger

Figure 3. Major agricultural products import by Niger.

Edible oil , cereals, sugar, tea and dried cow milk imports increased about 50.07%, 64.13%, 18.74%, 26.68% and 11.46% respectively their volumes while wheat flour volume decrease about 31.24% in 2001-2005.

The excessive increase of imports may be related to continuous decline in agricultural output due to severe environment degradation, low soil fertility, lack of access to modern technology, combine with high population growth.

In fact, despite Niger's main labor force is used in agriculture, the country cannot feed itself due to cyclic droughts which hinder increase in food production to cope with the high population growth. Niger still imports maize and rice though the farmers cultivate these two crops. The rice production is mainly under irrigation around river Niger and it is affected by high cost fertilizer (sometimes farmers cannot afford money to purchase fertilizer to increase production), use of low yielding varieties of crops, traditional methods of farming, lack of organization among farmers.

## 2.1. Sources of Niger's Agricultural Imports

Geographically, Niger imports all over the world, but its main agricultural import partners still its West African neighboring countries.

Niger imports oil palm from Cote d'Ivoire (83.38%), Malaysia (7.95%), and Togo (6.16), Wheat flour from France (49.22%), Morocco (12.55%), and Togo (10.86%), maize from Burkina Faso (42.52%), Ghana (19.58%), Benin (15.38%), dry cow milk from France (35.94%), Cote d'Ivoire (12.27%), Belgium (7.31%), food preparation nes from Tunisia (44.75), Cote d'Ivoire (13.5%), France (8.04), Cigarettes from Burkina Faso (21%), Cote d'Ivoire (19.75%), U.K (14.71%), rice from mainly from Thailand ( 42.82%), Argentine ( 34.54%), Vietnam (9.2%) and tea from China (96.09%),( See table 4 ).

As we can see contrary to agricultural exports, Cote d'Ivoire is Niger major agricultural import partner, follow by France, Burkina Faso, Benin, Togo and Tunisia.

### Table 2. Major products import by Niger and their main sources

| Products | Source 1 | | Source 2 | | Source 3 | | others |
|---|---|---|---|---|---|---|---|
| | country | % | Country | % | country | % | % |
| Cigarettes | Burkina Faso | 21.02% | Cote d'Ivoire | 19.75% | U.K | 14.71% | 32.12% |
| coffee | Cote d'Ivoire | 92.87% | France | 0.95% | Nigeria | 0.82% | 5.34% |
| Dry cow milk | France | 35.94% | Cote d'Ivoire | 12.27% | Belgium | 7.31% | 44.46% |
| Food preparation, nes | Tunisia | 44.75% | Cote d'Ivoire | 13.5% | France | 8.04% | 33.69% |
| Maize | Burkina Faso | 42.52% | Ghana | 19.58% | Benin | 15.38% | 22.5% |
| Palm oil | Cote d'Ivoire | 83.38% | Malaysia | 7.95% | Togo | 6.16% | 2.5% |
| Wheat flour | France | 49.22% | Morocco | 12.55% | Togo | 10.86% | 27.36% |
| Tea | China | 96.09% | - | - | - | - | 3.90% |
| Rice Broken | Thailand | 42.82% | Argentine | 34.54% | Vietnam | 9.2% | 13.63% |

**Note**: Percentage is according to accumulated Exports quantity of FAO World Agricultural Trade Matrix (WATM), 2001-2005
**Source**: FAOSTAT

## 2.2. Characteristics of Niger' Agricultural Imports

Niger agricultural imports doubled between the periods of 2000 - 2005 from UDS 111.69 millions to USD 269.14 millions (See Fig 6).

In the space of five years, Niger doubled its agricultural imports which are mainly food products. This makes Niger to be a net food importer. It is relatively due to food shortage in recent years and high population growth in the country.

Niger's domestic food production has for decades been outpaced by population growth, which at an annual rate of 3.3 percent is now the fastest in the world. This has encouraged an upwards trend in the demand for imported foodstuffs, though the gap between food production and needs, and the ability to purchase supplemental food on the market, varies markedly among households.

Farmers living near the subsistence level must often sell their yields in August and September, the peak months of the harvest season, when local market is flooded with grain and prices are extremely low. These farmers must then purchase addition food supplies in the "hunger month" of June and July when food is scarce and commodities traders charge exorbitant prices. This increase in food import may be also due to the fact that the sahelien region experienced the worst locust invasion in 2005 and with unfavorable weather conditions have left the region with a severe food crisis and malnutrition.

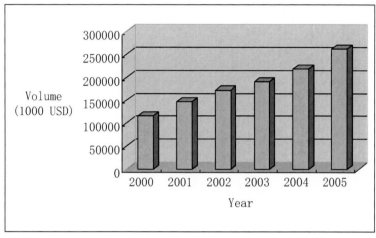

**Source**: FAOSTAT

Figure 4. Niger imports of farm products 2001-2005.


## 3. NIGER AGRICULTURAL TRADE BALANCE

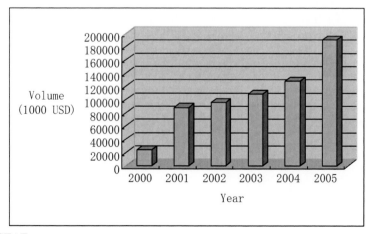

**Source**: FAOSTAT

Figure 5. Niger net imports of farm products 2000-2005.

The agricultural trade deficit, as measured by the difference between imports and exports, was widened in 2000 -2005.This pattern has become one of the permanent features of the Niger economy with negative effects on the rest of its macroeconomic fundamentals. A closer look at structural trade numbers suggests that the imports are the most dynamic component.

The uncertainty of the rains, on which agriculture in Niger remains largely dependent, the ongoing drought and poor soil are all factors limiting agricultural productivity, combining with high birth rate will attest that Niger remaining a net food importer is a long trend pattern and has a great challenge ahead to bridge the gap between its imports and exports.

## 4. CHALLENGES OF AGRICULTURAL TRADE IN NIGER

Niger finds it difficult to implement several provisions of the WTO Agreements. The main problem is lack of information on the provisions of the Agreements to be implemented and on the necessary action to be taken. The lack of officials trained in WTO-related areas, particularly experts on multilateral negotiations, as well as the lack of a diplomatic mission in Geneva (Niger does not belong to any coalition) limit Niger's opportunities for participating in the multilateral trading system (WTO, 2003). A small number of officials, principally from the Ministry of Trade, have broad knowledge of trade policy and its instruments. These difficulties are to the lack of institutional capacity in the implementing bodies, their limited knowledge of the WTO Agreements, and the lack of human and financial resources to implement them .It has proven to be very difficult to achieve satisfactory results in suppressing fraud, due in part to the very large informal sector and also to an extensive customs cordon and a highly inadequate customs infrastructure. According to the authorities, computerization of customs posts is an important step that needs to be taken. The authorities do not have the confidence to implement the provisions of the Agreement in full and abandon the national administrative values.

Development policies that promoted economic liberalization and encouraged regional integration along with specialization, commercialization of agriculture, and the withdrawal of the state from regulating the market are lacking in Niger. The monopoly power of large traders over the national grains trade has centralized control over food access, and global economic factors, such as rising cereal prices and fluctuating currency prices, have destabilized regional markets.

One of the major problems hindering agricultural trade is lack of adequate infrastructure to facilitate the connection and easy transportation of agricultural commodities to the available markets. This eventually causes several losses in most perishable crops.

Illiteracy and lack of cooperation among farmers are also obstacles to agricultural trade in Niger.

## 5. AGRICULTURAL EXPORTS OF CHINA

China's agro-exports of farm products rose 61.74 %in 2000-2005.It increased from 12.34 Billions US dollars in 2000 to 19.96 US dollars in 2005 according to FAOSTAT. China's agricultural industry has maintained a steady growth over the past years (see Fig 6 below).

China's agro-export products are much diversified as shown in the Figure 7 below. China exports are mainly composed of tea, rice, garlic, tomatoes, Chicken products, Apple, Tobacco, Maize, vegetable oil, pork and so on.

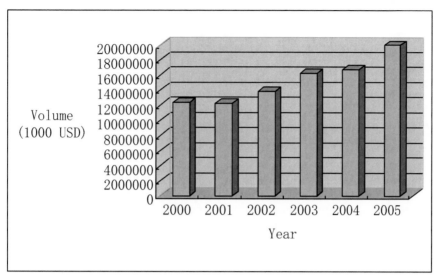

**Source**: FAOSTAT

Figure 6. China's exports of farm products.

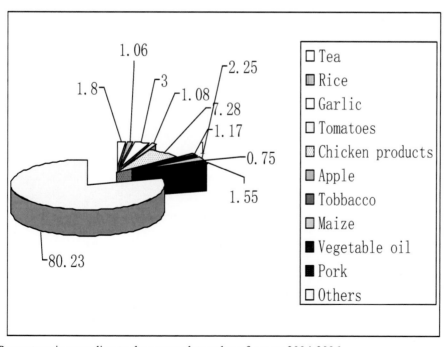

**Note**: Percentage is according to the accumulate value of export 2004-2006.
**Source**: Ministry of commerce of People's Republic of China, Department of Foreign Trade

Figure 7. Major agro-products export by China.

## 5.1. China's Major Agro-exports by Continents

China exports its farm products mainly to its neighboring Asian countries (64.98% of total agricultural exports), follow by European countries (16.46%), North America (12.38%), Africa (2.63%), South America (2.13%) and Oceania (1.36%), as shown in the Figure 8.

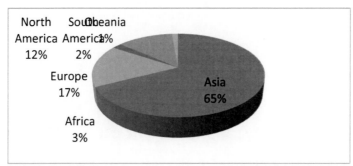

**Note**: percentage is according to accumulated export value 2002-2006
**Source**: Ministry of commerce of People's Republic of China, Department of foreign trade.

Figure 8. Chinese agro-exports by continents.

## 5.2. China's Major Agro-exports and Their Main Markets

China exports about 28.94%of its total agricultural export volume to Japan, 10.98% to USA, 9.73% to Hong Kong, 9.67% to South Korea and 40.68% to others countries (see Fig 9 below).

China exports to Japan chicken products, rice, tea, maize, vegetable oil etc... Hong Kong imports mainly pork, tea, chicken products, and vegetable oil from China.

China exports maize to South Korea, Malaysia and others countries. Tobacco is mainly exported to Belgium, Indonesia, and Philippines. Pork exported to Hong Kong, North Korea, Russia, and other countries. Tomatoes exported to Italy, Russia, Ghana, and other nations. See the Table 6 for more details.

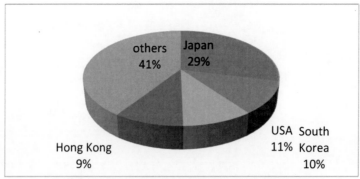

**Note**: the percentage is according to accumulated value of exports 2001-2006
**Source**: Ministry of commerce of People's Republic of China, Department of Foreign Trade.

Figure 9. China's major agro-export partners.

**Table 6. Major Agro-products export by
China and their main destination markets**

| Products | Destination 1 | | Destination 2 | | Destination3 | | Other countries |
|---|---|---|---|---|---|---|---|
| | country | % | country | % | country | % | % |
| Tea | Morocco | 20% | Japan | 15.62% | Hong Kong | 7.21% | 57.17% |
| Rice | Japan | 18.57% | Russia | 14.56% | S.Korea | 13.4% | 53.47% |
| Garlic | Indonesia | 16.52% | U.S.A | 13.23% | Malaysia | 7% | 63.25% |
| Tomato | Italy | 13.78% | Russia | 11.17% | Ghana | 8.2% | 66.85% |
| Chicken products | Japan | 26.95% | S.Korea | 1.17% | Hong Kong | 0.62% | 71.26% |
| Apple | Indonesia | 12.92% | Russia | 12.86% | Philippines | 9.35% | 64.87% |
| Tobacco | Belgium | 14.76 | Indonesia | 12.28 | Philippines | 10.74 | 62.22 |
| Maize | S.Korea | 64.5 | Japan | 14.71 | Malaysia | 8.67 | 12.12 |
| Vegetable oil | Hong Kong | 19.37 | Japan | 12.92 | Netherlands | 10.75 | 56.96 |
| pork | Hong Kong | 35.17 | N.Korea | 26.76 | Russia | 16.27 | 21.8 |

**Note**: Percentage is according to the accumulated export value from 2001-2006
**Source**: Ministry of commerce People's Republic of China, Department of Foreign Trade

According to Shunli Yao (2006),If comparison is made between labor/land and capital, China certainly has comparative advantages in agriculture and that's why China exports mainly agricultural products (as well as labor-intensive manufacturing goods) to Japan, Hong Kong and South Korea (and imports capital- and technology-intensive industrial goods from those countries in return) .

As we can see, China has diversified agro-trade partners. One single product has several destination markets. This is due to the huge Chinese market and more involvement of China in international trade.

# 6. CHINA'S IMPORTS OF FARM PRODUCTS

China's imports of agricultural products increased dramatically in 2001-2005. The volume of the imports was shifted from 10955972 US dollars to 27813943 US dollars. In five years, China has more than doubled its imports of farm products. The massive increased was experienced between the period 2002 and 2003.This was immediately after China joined WTO whereby trade tariffs were lowering and opening up Chinese market to international trade., ( See Fig 10 for more details).

A combination of rapid economic growth and income growth, population growth and urbanization is likely behind the major increase in food consumption expenditures. The fast import in farm products is a reflection of country's growing economic strength and increasing international influence.

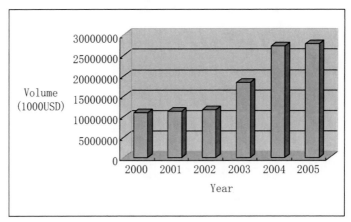

**Source**: FAOSTAT

Figure 10. China's imports of farm products 2000-2005.

The combination of spectacular economic growth, lower barriers to imports, higher commodity prices, and tightening domestic commodity supplies led to a more-than-doubling of China's agricultural imports between 2002 and 2004（Gale Fred, 2005）.

According to the Chinese economists in people's daily online news in 9th December, 2004, growth in food imports is a long-term trend in China as the Nation further integrates itself into global trade and becomes wealthier.

## 6.1. Types and Origin of China's Agro-imports

The major farm products import by China are wheat (2.86%of the total volume of imports), soybean (3.67%), palm oil (4.81%), sugar (1.36), wool (4.01%), cotton (12.68%), soybean oil (25.1%), natural rubber (7.23), leather (10.45%), broilers (1.05%) and other products (26.76%) in 2004-2006.

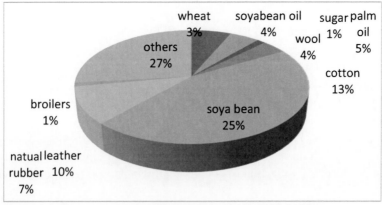

**Note**: percentage is according to the accumulated import volume 2004-2006
**Source**: Ministry of commerce of People's Republic of China, Department of foreign trade.

Figure 11. Major farm products import by China.

According to Gale and James (2003), China will remain a large importer of soybean and its serious problem with water scarcity in wheat growing regions is another factor favoring rising wheat imports in the long run. China was the World top soybean importer in 2004, according to FAOSTAT.

**Table 8. Major Chinese Agro-import products and the main sources**

| Products | Source 1 | | Source 2 | | Source 3 | | Other sources |
|---|---|---|---|---|---|---|---|
| | Country | % | Country | % | Country | % | % |
| Wheat | Canada | 38.01 | Australia | 24.52 | France | 6.89 | 30.58 |
| Soybean oil | Argentine | 73.37 | Brazil | 26.06 | U.S.A | 0.5 | 0.63 |
| Palm oil | Malaysia | 72.26 | Indonesia | 26.97 | Papua Guinea | 0.51 | 0.28 |
| Sugar | Cuba | 35.37 | Guatemala | 18.07 | Thailand | 11.74 | 34.89 |
| Wool | Australia | 81.80 | New Zealand | 8.98 | Paraguay | 1.93 | 7.29 |
| Cotton | U.S.A | 49.15 | India | 10.82 | Uzbekistan | 10.66 | 29.37 |
| Soybean | U.S.A | 41.47 | Brazil | 33.61 | Argentine | 24.03 | 0.90 |
| Natural Rubber | Thailand | 42.72 | Malaysia | 27.83 | Indonesia | 19.95 | 9.5 |
| Cow leather | Thailand | 15.65 | S.Korea | 13.32 | -- | - | 71.03 |
| Bb Broilers | U.S.A | 56.94 | Brazil | 32.58 | Argentine | 8.68 | 1.8 |

**Note**: Percentage is according to accumulated value from 2003-2006
**Source**: Ministry of Commerce of People's Republic of China, Department of foreign trade.

China's imports of farm products are not only food in nature but included raw materials such cotton, leather, natural rubber, wool to supply the fast growing industries.

China imports wheat mainly from Canada, Australia and France, soybean oil from Argentine (73.37%), Brazil (26.06%) and USA, palm oil from Malaysia (72.26%), and Indonesia (26.97%), sugar from Cuba (35.37%), Guatemala (18.07%) and Thailand (11.74%) , wool from Australia (81.80%) and New Zealand (8.98%), cotton from USA (49.15%), India (10.82%) and Uzbekistan (10.66%), soybean from USA (41.47%), Brazil (33.61%) and Argentine (24.03%), natural rubber from Thailand (42.72%), Malaysia (27.83%) and Indonesia (19.95%), leather from Thailand ( 15.65%) and South Korea (13.32%0, broilers from USA (56.94%), Brazil (32.58%) and Argentine ( 8.68%) . See Table 8 for more details.


## 6.2. China's Agro-product Imports by Continent and Countries

North America is where China imports more its agro-products (28.74%), followed by South America (24.60%), Asia (21.52%), Oceania (10.64%), Europe (10.87%) and Africa (3.60) as shown in Fig 12.

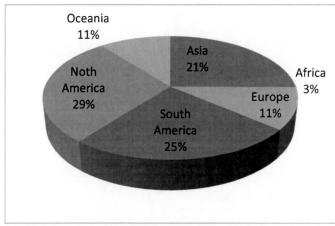

**Note**: percentage is according to the accumulated agro-import volume 2004-2006.
**Source**: Ministry of commerce of People Republic of China, Department of Foreign Trade.

Figure 12. China's agricultural imports by continents.

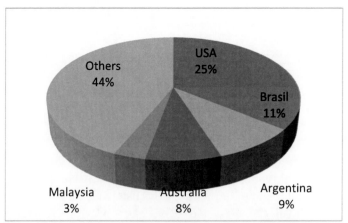

**Note**: percentage is according to the accumulated volume of agro-imports 2004-2006.
**Source**: Ministry of commerce of People's Republic of China, Department of Foreign Trade.

Figure 13. China's major agro-imports partners.

China's main agro-import partners are USA (24.82%), Brazil (10.9%), Argentine (9.14%), Australia (8.08%), and Malaysia (3.36%), as shown in Fig 13.

With one-fifth of the world's consumers and one of the world's fastest growing economies, China is a key player in world agricultural trade.

## 7. CHINA'S AGRICULTURAL TRADE BALANCE

Chinese overall agricultural trade has been expanding significantly in the period 2000-2006. Exports of farm products rose 61.74% while imports rose almost 2.5 times within five years.

Since 1949, agricultural exports for most years have exceeded agricultural imports till 2003 whereby the imports over passed exports. As shown in the Fig 14below after China joined the WTO in 2001, it has witnessed increasing net import of farm products.

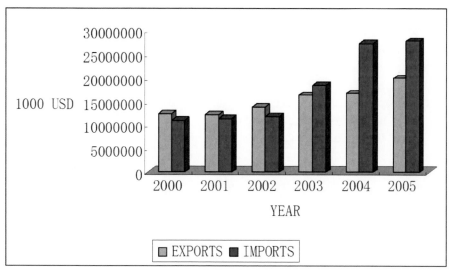

**Source**: FAOSTAT

Figure 14. China's agro-trade.

According to People's daily online, February 17, 2005, the higher trade deficit in agricultural produces finds its main cause in the following categories of grain, cotton and sugar as industrial materials and animal and fowl products. The occurrence of trade deficit in these three major agricultural produces has different reasons:
-In 2003, the grain output dropped to the lowest level in recent a few years and a series of measures were taken to stimulate the grain production in 2004. In the meanwhile the quota for the export of agricultural produces was reduced in the agricultural produce trade while encouraging measures were also taken to stimulate the import of agricultural produce. In addition, there occurred domestically a recovery price increase for major agricultural produces in 2004 with the increasing rate to reach some 30 - 40 percent, while the government and enterprises had a large amount of grain import of their own accord. This has incurred an extraordinary scale in the increase of grain import in 2004 and it is a very important factor in causing the huge trade deficit in agricultural produce.
-The global quota for textile garment products was fully cancelled at the beginning of 2005. The domestic textile enterprises all took it a favorable opportunity for increasing their export and increased one after another their cotton reserve. Though 2004 year saw a rich harvest in cotton production in China yet the supply still fell short of the demand in domestic market, therefore, a very big increase in cotton import.
-With regard to the trade deficit in animal and fowl products this was closely related with the disastrous influence of the explosive bird-flu at the beginning of 2004.

The fast rise of export and import in farm products is a reflection of country's growing economic strength and increasing international influence. After the accession of China to the

WTO, there is drop in the average tariffs for farm products (15.3% in 2002 against 23.2% in 2000). The Chinese agricultural reform also allow farmers to sell above quota production at market prices ,lowering grains quotas, increasing grains imports and expanding inter provincial trade.

China's agricultural imports and exports are both likely to grow in coming years. Strong income growth and rapid urbanization in China will increase demand for food products, generating demand for imports. The rapid growth of its manufacturing industries will also generate demand for industrial inputs like cotton, animal hides, rubber, and food ingredients. At the same time, China will become an increasingly important source of inexpensive vegetables, fruits, fish, and processed foods, such as instant noodles, for other land-scarce, middle- and high-income Asian countries (Fred Gale and James Hansen, 2003).

China's exports of horticultural, livestock, and manufactured food products are likely to continue growing, since China can produce these products at relatively low cost (Fred Gale and James Hansen, 2003).

According to Hyatt (2007), almost 90 percent of China's agricultural exports are labor-intensive products, such as fruits, meats and aquaculture products. Most of China's agricultural imports are land-extensive products such as soybeans and cotton. Despite its massive current account surplus, China has been a net agricultural importer since 2004, a trend that is likely to continue as the country develops, and household incomes rise.

## 8. PROBLEMS OF AGRICULTURAL IN CHINA

China faces mainly sanitary and phytosanitary standard (SPS) problems in trading its farm products.

Chinese farmers and exporters had anticipated a large, positive impact on domestic production with accession to the WTO, especially for labor-intensive agricultural products such as vegetables, fruits, livestock and poultry products, and seafood, but these expectations proved unrealistic. In fact, these products have been hardest hit by the need to meet significant sanitary and phytosanitary (SPS) standards, and this has prevented substantial growth in these agricultural exports. According to an investigation by China's Ministry of Commerce, about 90 percent of China's exporters of foodstuffs, domestic produce, and animal by-products were affected by foreign technical trade barriers, and China suffered losses totaling U.S$9 billion in 2002, (Fengxia Dong and Helen Jesen, 2004).

China's recent experiences with SPS barriers have been mainly with the European Union, Japan, and the United States.

These three countries accounted for 41, 30, and 24 percent, respectively, of the trade losses attributable to SPS measures in 2002. And, because failure to pass SPS inspections often leads to closer inspection of future exports, China's agricultural products have confronted much stricter inspection in these markets following several of the SPS-related problems (Fengxia et al, 2004)

According to Fengxia Dong and Helen Jesen, SPS problems have existed in agricultural production in China for a long time but have only received worldwide attention since China's accession to the WTO. The causes of China's SPS problems can be attributed to many factors, most of which are common to developing countries.

First, China's food quality regulatory and supervisory system does not yet provide the necessary guidelines for agricultural and food production. Current regulations in China, which are outdated and inconsistent with international standards, are insufficient to meet the present requirements of international trade.

Second, the lack of effective regulation and supervision to control agricultural production and processing, coupled with noncompliance with regulations, has resulted in Chinese producers often misusing or abusing chemical fertilizers, pesticides, and antibiotics. Antiquated production techniques and technology also have an impact. In animal production, there are persistent violations of regulations on drug additives and quality standards. According to a report for sample inspections by China's Ministry of Agriculture in 2002, besides prohibited drug additives, lead, aflatoxin B1, and Salmonella were the most common adulterants or types of contamination found in animal feed. Another problem facing by china's agricultural trade is lack of adequate infrastructure.

According to Shunli Yao, 2006, poor transport infrastructure has often been cited as a reason for the lack of integrated domestic agricultural market. Cotton producers in Chinese northwestern Xinjiang autonomous region have difficulties shipping their produce to the textile and clothing factories in the eastern region and transportation subsidies they received have become a controversial issue in the WTO agriculture negotiations. Similarly, soybeans produced in Chinese northeastern provinces have a hard time reaching the coastal oil crushing facilities. Needless to say, the weak transport infrastructure also serves as a natural barrier to the expansion of Chinese agricultural trade. So do the grains reserve system and the low degree of marketing in Chinese agriculture.

## 9. BASIC COMPARATIVE DATA ON NIGER AND CHINA

| Indicators | China | | Niger | |
|---|---|---|---|---|
| | 2000 | 2005 | 2000 | 2005 |
| Population, total | 1.3 billion | 1.3 billion | 11.8 million | 14 million |
| Pop. growth | 0.7 | 0.6 | 3.4 | 3.3 |
| Life expectancy | 70.3 | 71.8 | 43.6 | 44.9 |
| Surface area (Sq.km) | 9.6 million | 9.6 million | 1.3 million | 1.3 million |
| Forest area (Sq.km) | 1.8 million | 2.0 million | 13,280 | 12,660 |
| Agric. Land(% of land area) | 58.8 | - | 29.6 | - |
| GDP (current US %) | 1.2 trillion | 2.3 trillions | 1.8 billion | 3.8 billion |
| GDP growth (annually) | 8.4 | 10.2 | -1.4 | 6.8 |
| Inflation (annually) | 2.1 | 4.4 | 4.5 | 8.0 |
| Agric, value added( %of GDP) | 14.8 | 12.5 | 37.8 | |
| Industry ,value added (%of GDP) | 45.9 | 47.3 | 17.8 | |
| Services, etc...value added (%of GDP) | 39.3 | 40.1 | 44.4 | |
| Exports of goods and services(%of GDP) | 23.3 | 37.3 | 17.8 | |
| Imports of goods and services (of GDP) | 20.9 | 31.7 | 25.7 | |

**Source**: World development indicators database, April 2007

## 10. COMPARISON BETWEEN THE CHARACTERISTICS OF AGRICULTURAL TRADES OF CHINA AND NIGER

Both China and Niger agricultural imports almost rose 2.4 times during the period 2000-2005.

Chinese imports of farm products experienced a rapid growth especially after its accession to WTO which opened up Chinese market to the world.

Both China and Niger import edible oils such as palm oil and soybean oil, and also sugar and wheat. China imports raw materials such as wool, cotton, leather and natural rubber to supply the growth of manufacturing industries. Niger is net importer of cereals which accounted about 25.63 percent of the total imports. Niger imports of farm products are mainly food in nature .Because the Niger industry still at enfant stage, it does not import raw materials.

China's partners of agricultural imports are geographically diversified. China is USA major market for agricultural products mainly soybean and wheat, which accounted about 24.82 percent of the total imports, followed by Brazil, Argentina and Australia which accounted about 10.9, 9.14 and 8.08 percent respectively. The main source of Niger imports of farm products is Cote d'Ivoire, France and other neighboring countries.

The rapid growth in Chinese imports of farm products is due to a combination of rapid economic and income growth, population growth and urbanization which are behind a major increase in food consumption expenditures. It is also due to the fact that, China's increasing market driven economy, limited domestic production capacity and a more open foreign trade environment.

Increase in Niger's imports of farm products is due to a high population growth, urbanization, hard climatic conditions which is lagging agricultural production causing food shortage in the country.

Chinese exports rose about 61.74 percent during the period 2000-2005, while that of Niger experienced a decrease of 21.47 percent of its volume in the same period. Chinese exports are diversified while that of Niger comprised mainly of animal products (61 percent of the total exports) and onion (28.83 percent).

Japan is the largest market for Chinese agricultural exports, accounting for about 28.94 percent of the total. Most of the China's other major export markets are USA and neighboring countries or regions including Hong Kong and South Korea. The main destination of Niger's exports of farm products is Nigeria, accounting almost 90 percent of the total and other go to other neighboring countries.

Environment degradation, lack of efficient policies in agriculture may be the cause of decrease in Niger's exports of farm products.

Both Niger and China have deficit in their trade of farm products. China was a net exporter till 2002, while Niger remains traditionally a net importer of agricultural products.

For a country with nearly 1.3 billion consumers and limited natural resources, China's level of food imports is surprisingly low. China is nearly self-sufficient in food compare to Niger.

## 11. ANALYSIS OF AGRO-TRADE BETWEEN CHINA AND NIGER

In 2002-2005, Chinese agricultural exports to Niger were almost stagnant. Then in 2006 it rose from 4.37 millions US dollars to 6.30 millions US dollars (See Fig 15). As shown in the same figure, in the period 2002-2005, china did not import farm products from Niger. It is only by 2006 that there were a few imports from Niger which accounted about 980,000 US dollars.

The Chinese exports are almost 7 times that of import volume in 2006.

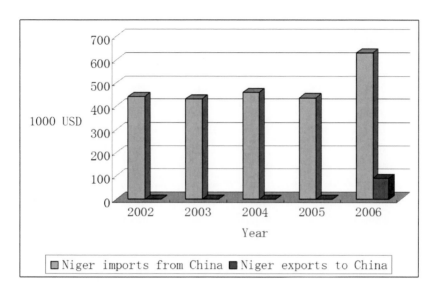

**Source**: Ministry of commerce of People's Republic of China, Department of foreign trade.

Figure 15. China and Niger agro-trade.

According to the Chinese embassy in Niger in 2004-12-22 report, there were no Chinese imports from Niger because, Niger mainly exports its farm products to its neighboring countries (Nigeria, Benin and others), which can hardly meet demand. According to the same report, Niger import mainly rice and tea from China. Rice and tea imports represented respectively 43.29% and 5.1% of the total Niger imports from china including non farm products in 2000. This makes Niger a net importer agricultural trade.

In general, China agricultural trade with African countries is very limited compared to the other continents. African countries do not have a strong comparative advantage in the production of any of China's main agricultural imports (Ali Zafar, 2007).High Asian tariff rates on some African products appear to discourage their export to Asian countries.

### 11.1 Prospects of Agro-Trade between China and Niger

The two countries since the resumption of diplomatic relations in 1996, the bilateral friendly cooperative relations continue to be consolidated, the development and expansion of bilateral trade between the two countries have laid a good foundation.

Both China and Niger expanded their agricultural trade between the period 2001-2005.

Although China's agricultural trade with Niger is relatively small by comparison with its trade with other countries like Japan and USA, it has grown rapidly especially in 2006.

China traditionally exports rice to Niger, but remains competitive product due to the fact, Niger imports also rice from Vietnam, Thailand and Argentine. Niger will continue to import rice to supply its grain deficit caused by severe soil degradation and desertification which hinder agricultural production in the country. In fact, rice is cultivated around Niger's river through irrigation but still rudimentary due to lack of irrigations facilities, high cost of fertilizers, lack of improved technology and farming systems, lack of management among farmers. Rice production is extremely costly and the output is very marginal and insufficient to meet the demand of the populations. Rice is mainly consumed daily by urban people in Niger. Under the high population growth and dramatic climate conditions, Niger will continue to import rice to cope its deficit in food shortage.

China also exports tea to Niger and it's the only supplier. Tea is mostly consumed among the youth in Niger.

Niger's population constitutes of more 50% of youth. The pattern of tea export by China will be a long trend business.

The only way out for Niger to overcome its agricultural trade deficit with china is to develop its livestock sector as the country possesses the favorable environment for raising livestock to be able to export meat, skin and hikes to Chinese huge market. China needs hides and skins for use in leather products manufacturing. Niger has the potentiality to improve its cotton production by using high yielding varieties of crops, and good farming methods to increase output to be able a part of Chinese market supplier.

As income grows and urbanization occurs, diets are diversified and additional services embodied in food and agricultural products are demanded.

With the dramatic expansion and investment between China and Niger, the regular exchange between the policy makers will permit china and Niger to know more of their complementary in agricultural trade.

## 11.2. Major Challenges and Constraints in Agricultural Trade between China and Niger

### 11.2.1 Niger is Landlocked Country

Situated in the heart of African continent, the country suffers from being landlocked, which drives up the cost of imports and exports. The nearest ports are more than 1,000 km distant and there is no interconnecting rail infrastructure. Trading with Niger demands high transportation and time consuming efforts.

### 11.2.2 Severe Climatic Conditions

Severe climatic conditions hinder agricultural production. The unfavorable weather conditions cause food shortage and no surplus for trade.

Niger is one of the poorest countries in the World and droughts and famine are recurrent problems affecting the country. Natural resources-water, soil and vegetations-that constitute the foundation for all agricultural production are rather limited in Niger. Rainfall is very low and erratic with periods of drought often followed by devastating flash floods. Water resources are limited, unevenly distributed and not easily accessible. Soils are poor, temperature high, and natural vegetation is sparse. As result, a large part of the country is unsuitable for rainfed agriculture, natural pastures are being depleted, and fuel wood which represents the main source for energy for Niger's households is scarce.

### 11.2.3. Poverty

Niger is a lower income country which comes under sub Saharan African region, according to the classification made by the World Bank on the basis of income and region for the year 2006

Niger is one of the world poorest countries, with the per capita purchasing power very limited; the country has 63% of poor population. In rural areas, the poor and extremely poor represent 66 percent and 36 percent respectively.

Niger's market capacity is limited with capital city of less than 1 million of population only.

Sixty-three percent of Niger's population lives on less than a dollar a day, and the per capita gross domestic product (GDP) was $280 in 2005. For rural people, access to scarce arable land was the most pressing issue. The poor were described as having little or no land and many young or elderly dependents; the non-poor have land and able-bodied family members to work it. Land tenure rights are currently not protected and will be codified once the complementary regulations to the Rural Code are enacted. The poor work for others or migrate, although getting by during hard times was described as being increasingly difficult, with deteriorating returns to migrating. Many rural people try to diversify their income source, but the options are limited and poorly paid. Even better-off farmers are vulnerable to bad weather, lack of proper storage, and other threats to stock. Many farmers get into debt, sell crops to repay, and then are short of food in the months before the harvest.

### 11.2.4. Increasing Demand of Grain in China

Increasing demand of grains in China may be one of the factors that can affect Sino-Niger trade of farm products. China traditionally exports rice to Niger and this may be affected by the high demand of grain in the country.

China's 1.2 billion people represent 21 percent of the world's population, even with the country's thourough planning and birth control policy, its numbers increase by 16 million people annually. Such growth is placing a heavier demand on the nation's supply of various agricultural products. An added 16 million people translates into demand for an extra four million metric tons of grain per year. According to Zhang G. Li and Diana E. Eadinglin (1999), during the first half of the 1990s, China went from being a net exporter of grains to a net importer and by 2030; its annual grain demand could reach 479 million metric tons, up from 335 million in 1990. They continue to state that changes in Chinese dietary habits have increased the amount of fodder required to feed the growing number of livestock raised for food, thereby affecting demand for grains and other agricultural products.

### 11.2.5. Impact of Chinese Trade Policies

According to U.S report published in April 2004, in Asian Economic news, attested that China still has substantial barriers to trade. Agricultural trade with China remains among the least transparent and predictable of the world's major markets. Capricious practices by

Chinese customs and quarantine officials can delay or halt shipments of agricultural products into China, while sanitary and phytosanitary standards with questionable scientific bases and a generally opaque regulatory regime frequently are devil traders in agricultural commodities.

Those who export to China express concerns as to the lack of transparency in the quota allocation process, since no information on the quantities and destinies of the TRQs is provided. Another problem reported is that TRQs allocated to some commodities are too small to be commercially viable. A potential importer holding a quota for a few thousand metric tons of grains has to pool the quota with other shipments in order to fill a large grain cargo ship (which generally holds between 10 and 55 thousand tons),( Shunli Yao , 2006). China is still practicing a protectionist policy in grain trade.

China also maintains a variety of nontariff barriers that restrict imports, including import licenses, and state trading. Phytosanitary and food safety measures, such as China's regulations on genetically modified agricultural products, should be science based, according to WTO rules, but many observers are concerned that China will use such measures to block imports.

## CONCLUSION

China and Niger agro-trades have experienced a growth during the period 2001-2005.

Niger agriculture is facing with severe environmental degradations, low productivity combine with high population growth causing the country to rely on imports to cope with its population needs. China's ascension to WTO opened its market to World. This has caused China's imports to exceed exports. It is also related to the high income growth which causes increase in food consumption.

There is a little trading of farm produce between Niger and China which is mainly Chinese exports to Niger. This shows that there is little complementarities of agricultural trade between the two countries. For improvement of bilateral trade, they should provide a common institutional framework for conducting trade relations. They should try to conform to the international sanitary and phytosanitary standards to permit full integration in to world market (especially exports to developed countries). China should establish a Food Safety Commission that centralizes food safety administration and quality control to minimize trade losses caused by SPS.

On the other hand, as China faces more SPS conflicts, the government should participate in bilateral negotiations to resist unfair trade restrictions and discrimination and could use the WTO to coordinate and resolve trade disputes. As a member of the WTO, China and Niger can participate in the negotiation and establishment of international regulations and standards to obtain a more equal position for its agricultural exports.

## REFERENCES

[1]  "Agricultural trade deficit implies food crisis", people's daily online, September 12, 2004.

[2]  Ali Zafar, "The growing relationship between China and Sub-Sahara Africa: Macroeconomic trade, trade, investment and aids links", Oxford University press, 2007.

[3] "China still has substantial barriers to trade", U.S report, Asian Economic News, April 5, 2004.

[4] "Chinese agriculture, how to cope with trade deficit", People's daily online, February 17, 2005: http://english.peopledaily.com.cn/200502/17/eng 20050217_173848.html

[5] FAOSTAT,detailedTradeMatrix:http://faostat.fao.org/site/535/DesktopDefault.aspx?PageID=535

[6] FAOSTAT,TradeStat:http://faostat.fao.org/Portals/_Faostat/documents/xls/Total_Agricultural_Exports.xls

[7] Fengxia Dong and Helen H. Jensen, "China's challenges conforming to sanitary and phytosanitary measures for agricultural exports", Center for agricultural and rural development, Iowa Ag-review, spring 2004, vol.10 N0 2.

[8] "Farmers embrace dry season cowpea production technology in Niger Republic", international institute of tropical agriculture (IITA), 18 June 2004.

[9] Fred Gale, "China's agricultural imports boomed during 2003-04", USDA, WRS-05-04, May 2005.

[10] Fred Gale and James Hansen, "China's exports outpaced imports during WTO year one", USDA, FAU-79-02, 2003.

[11] "Focus on Niger: helping onion growers capitalize on the power of purple", ADF-e news (US-African Development Foundation), August 2005.

[12] Grand Hyatt, "China's agricultural trade: issues and prospects", IATRC summer symposium, Beijing, China, July 8-9, 2007.

[13] InstitutNationaldelaStatistiqueduNiger,commerceexterieur:http://www.stat-niger.org/frame/commerce.htm。

[14] Shunli Yao (2007), "Persistence of Chinese agricultural trade patterns: some national and regional evidences", China Center for Economic Research, Peking University.

[15] Tradeoverview,WorldBankreport,2007:hpp//www.worldbank.org/WBSITE/EXTERNAL/TOPICS/trade/o.content TMDK:2009808~page

[16] Trade policy review: Niger, World Trade Organization report, WT/TPR/S/118, 30 June 2003.

[17] USAID/FEWS NET, "Monthly report on food security in Niger", 26th February, 2002.

[18] WorldBankGroup:http://devdata.worldbank.org/external/CPProfile.asp?PTYPE=CP&CCODE=CHN

[19] Zhan G.Li and Diana E. Eadington, Marketing agricultural product to China, Business Horizons, March-April 1999.

[20] Foreign Trade Division of Ministry of Commerce of the People's Republic of China import and export of agricultural products, monthly statistical report, 2007-12-27: http://wms.mofcom.gov.cn/aarticle/subject/ncp/subjectbb/2006 03/20060301783733.html。

[21] Republic of China in Economic and Commercial Counsellor at the Embassy of the Republic of Niger, in the bilateral relations,2004-12-22: http://ne.mofcom.gov.cn/zxhz/zxhz.html。

In: Asian Economic and Political Development
Editor: Felix Chin

# THE HICKSIAN NATIONAL INCOME OF CAMBODIA, 1988-2004

## *Nyda Chhinh[1,*] and Philip Lawn[2,♦]*

[1]Faculty of Environmental Sciences, Royal University of Phnom Penh,
Phnom Penh, Cambodia
[2]Faculty of Social Sciences, Flinders University, Adelaide, Australia

## 1. INTRODUCTION

This chapter aims to demonstrate that a green measure of GDP, or what might be better termed as a measure of Hicksian national income, should be included in the formal system of national accounts primarily as an alternative or satellite indicator to GDP. The reason for this is that GDP overstates the national product available for consumption yet is increasingly deployed as a guide to the prudent conduct of national governments (Daly 1989). Since, as we aim to show, Hicksian national income constitutes a more appropriate measure of the sustainable national product available for consumption, it can be used as an indispensable tool for both policy-makers and international donor organisations to design the policies required to achieve sustainable development (SD). Although specific policies to achieve SD is not the main aim of this chapter, the results to be later revealed make it possible to: (a) shed some useful light on the nature of Cambodia's recent economic development — a country still recovering from past wars and the devastating impact of the Pol Pot dictatorship; (b) identify what factors have contributed most to the fall or the lack of increase in Cambodia's Hicksian national income; and (c) outline the nature of the policies that are necessary to increase Cambodia's sustainable national product without having to involve the depletion of its income-generating capital.

To achieve its aims, this chapter is organised as follows. Section 2 provides a brief historical overview of Cambodia's social and economic development. In Section 3, a theoretical and empirical overview of green GDP is outlined. In this section, the inadequacies of GDP as a measure of national income are exposed as is the theoretical basis behind the use of green GDP as an alternative measure of sustainable national income. Section 4 presents the methodology employed to calculate the environmental costs and defensive and rehabilitative expenditures associated with the growth of Cambodia's national product. In Section 5, the

---

[*] Send Correspondance to Nyda Chhinh: Faculty of Environmental Sciences, Royal University of Phnom Penh, Room 112, RUPP Main Building, Russian Confederation Blvd. Phnom Penh, Cambodia; Phone : 855 12 955 169; E-mail: nydachhinh32@yahoo.com

[♦] Send Corrspondance to Philip Lawn: Faculty of Social Sciences, Flinders University, GPO Box 2100, Adelaide, SA, 5001, Australia, Phone: 61 8 8201 2838, Fax: 61 8 8201 2644, E-mail: phil.lawn@flinders.edu.au

various costs are deducted from GDP to reveal the Hicksian national income of Cambodia for the period 1988 to 2004. Some general conclusions are outlined in Sections 6 and 7.

## 2. CAMBODIA'S ECONOMIC DEVELOPMENT: HISTORICAL BACKGROUND AND RECENT DEVELOPMENTS

### 2.1. Pre-1953 Independence

The first recognised forms of civilisation in present day Cambodia appeared in the 1st century AD (Tully, 2005). During the 4th and 5th centuries, the Indianised states of Funan and Chenla gradually merged in a region which now constitutes present-day Cambodia and southwestern Vietnam (Chandler, 1983). The process of Indianisation in the region eventually came to a halt following the subjugation of Funan in the 6th century by the rulers of Chenla (Tully, 2005).

In the 9th century, Jayavarman II, a Khmer prince, founded what is conventionally known as the Angkor Empire in an area north of the Tonle Sap (Great Lake) (Chandler, 1983). During the 11th century, Angkor reached its zenith under Suryavarman II, who consolidated Khmer hegemony over the majority of modern Cambodia, Thailand, Laos, and Vietnam. Whilst a succession of battles with neighbouring kingdoms led to a decline in Khmer rule, it remained dominant for the next four centuries until Angkor was politically weakened by Siamese incursions and eventually sacked in the 15th century (Tully, 2005).

It was during the 15th century that the Khmer kingdom sought to regain its former glory through the agency of maritime trade. However, ongoing wars with Thailand and Vietnam continued to result in the loss of Cambodian territory. For the next three centuries, the Khmer kingdom alternated as a vassal state of the Thai and Vietnamese kingdoms with only brief periods of relative independence (Tully, 2005).

In 1863, King Norodom, who had previously been installed by Thailand, appealed to France for protection. The plea proved to be successful with the Thai king in 1867 forced to sign a treaty with France forsaking suzerainty over Cambodia in exchange for control of the Cambodian provinces of Battanbang and Siem Reap (Herz, 1958).[1] Except for the Japanese war-time occupation between 1941 and 1945, Cambodia remained a protectorate of France until 1953, effectively administered in conjunction with the latter's sovereignty over French Indochina (Vietnam).

### 2.2. Post-1953 Independence to the 1993 Elections

Cambodia finally gained independence from France on November 9, 1953. In the process, it became a constitutional monarchy under King Norodom Sihanouk (Tully, 2005). In 1955, Sihanouk relinquished the throne to his father in order to secure the Prime

---

[1]  The two provinces were eventually returned to Cambodia following a border treaty between France and Thailand in 1906.

Ministership of Cambodia. Upon his father's death in 1960, Sihanouk returned as Head of state, this time as the Prince of Cambodia (Osborne, 1973).

With war escalating in neighbouring Vietnam during the 1960s, Sihanouk adopted a neutral stance but was deposed in 1970 by a military coup led by Prime Minister Lon Nol and Prince Sisowath Sirik Matak (Tully, 2005). Safely stationed in Beijing, Sihanouk openly declared his support for the communist Khmer Rouge rebels whom had gradually acquired territory in the remote highland regions of Cambodia.[2] Sihanouk also urged his followers to overthrow the US-supported government of Lon Nol (Tully, 2005). Through his provocative actions, Sihanouk succeeded in triggering a civil war in Cambodia.

Having discovered that the Viet Cong was operating inside the Cambodian border, the USA compounded the deteriorating circumstances in Cambodia by conducting a series of bombing raids on suspected Viet Cong bases and supply routes. Following a brief invasion of Cambodia, the USA expanded its bombing missions to include strikes on the Khmer Rouge (Kiernan, 2002). In 1973, the American bombing ceased. This provided an ideal opportunity for the advancing Khmer Rouge to reach Phnom Penh and seize power, which it accomplished in 1975 (Kiernan, 2002).

Under the dictatorial leadership of Pol Pot (1975-1979), the Khmer Rouge had a devastating impact on Cambodia. Education, religion, and political opposition were almost entirely subverted, while an estimated 1.7 million Cambodians died from execution, starvation, or forced labour (Tully, 2005).[3] Thousands more fled across the border into neighbouring Thailand. Many of the executed were deemed 'enemies of the state' simply by being a civil servant, a person of education or religion, or having had a past association with the previous regime.

Towards the latter stages of Pol Pot's rule, Vietnam invaded Cambodia in an attempt to curtail Khmer Rouge incursions into Vietnam and halt the genocide of Vietnamese Cambodians (Vickery, 1984). Warfare between the two countries continued throughout the 1980s until a peace deal, negotiated in 1989, was finally put into effect in 1991 (Tully, 2005). The peace settlement included a United Nations mandate to enforce a ceasefire as well as mechanisms and institutions, such as the United Nations Transitional Authority in Cambodia (UNTAC), to deal with disarmament and the resettlement of refugees.

## 2.3. Post-1993 Elections

During 1992, UNTAC arrived in Cambodia to oversee the negotiated ceasefire, disarm combatants, and engage in humanitarian aid and economic reconstruction. UNTAC was also assigned the task of conducting general elections, which were held in May of 1993 (Tully, 2005). Despite threats of Khmer Rouge violence, nearly 90% of enrolled voters exercised their newly conferred voting rights. Of the 120 National Assembly seats, 58 were won by FUNCINPEC candidates and 51 by the Cambodian Peoples Party (CPP). Owing to the lack of a decisive winner, an interim coalition administration was formed. The National Assembly again recognised Sihanouk as the King of Cambodia while, in order to maintain political

---

[2]  The intellectual origins of the Khmer Rouge are detailed in Jackson (1989).

[3]  April 17, 1975, the day on which the Khmer Rouge took charge of Cambodia, is often referred to as 'year zero', such was the impact it had on the country and culture (Ponchaud, 1977).

harmony, two Prime Ministers were appointed — Prince Norodom Ranariddh (FUNCINPEC) as 'First' Prime Minister and Hun Sen (CPP) as 'Second' Prime Minister (Tully, 2005).

During a period of relative political and economic stability between 1993 and 1997, Cambodia's real GDP rose quite steadily, largely fuelled by the rapid increase in foreign investment and international tourism. However, the growth in real GDP was eventually impeded by two major events. The first was the 1997 Asian financial crisis. The second was the power struggle between the Prime Ministers Ranariddh and Hun Sen which led to a fracture in the relationship between the FUNCINPEC and CPP (Tully, 2005). With the coalition government in turmoil, Ranariddh was forced to flee into temporary exile.

As a consequence of the rising political instability, threats were made by foreign donors to withdraw much needed aid to Cambodia. Pleas were also made for political reconciliation by King Sihanouk. In response, Hun Sen and the CPP agreed to new elections in July 1998. Tarnished by violence and allegations of vote-rigging, the elections resulted in a comfortable victory for the CPP (Tully, 2005). Despite protests emanating from opposition political forces, international agencies proclaimed the poll to be free, fair, and representative of the electorate's preferences.

In 1999, the first full year of relative peace in Cambodia in thirty years, a series of economic reforms were implemented. Real GDP proceeded to grow by 5.0% in both 1999 and 2000. Peace and stability was, however, briefly thrown into chaos in late 2000 by a terrorist attack on government buildings in Phnom Penh involving members of the opposition Sam Rainsy Party. In addition, a coup to oust Prime Minister Hun Sen was attempted by the Cambodian Freedom Fighters (CFF).

Stability was somewhat restored with the strengthening of the CPP's political power following communal elections in February, 2002. Nevertheless, with the CPP winning 1,600 of the 1,621 communes, accusations were again raised regarding voter registration irregularities, vote-buying, intimidation, and media partiality. Violence was also seen to play a part in the unbalanced result with the killing of as many as twenty candidates and activists, mostly from the opposition Sam Rainsy Party (SBS, 2002).

Further instability emerged in Cambodia in 2004 following the shock abdication of King Sihanouk. In order to quell disunity, a special nine-member throne council was hastily formed. The council proceeded to elect Norodom Sihamoni to the position of King of Cambodia on October 14, 2004. In the face of ongoing instability and the fear of renewed political unrest, Cambodia's real GDP managed to increase by 6.3% in 2001 and 5.2% in 2002. In all, Cambodia's real GDP grew at an average annual rate of 6.9% between 1995 and 2004 (World Bank, 2006).

In spite of this decade of rapid growth, the Cambodian economy continues to suffer from internal unrest and the legacy of past wars. Furthermore, the overwhelming majority of the Cambodian population lacks essential education and productive skills. This is particularly so in the poverty-ridden rural areas where basic infrastructure is in short supply.

Due, in part, to the skill shortages just mentioned, the primary industries of fishing, forestry, and agriculture continue to form the backbone of the Cambodian economy. Since many of these industries provide a relatively low financial return, Cambodia possesses one of the highest poverty rates in the Asia-Pacific region (77.7% in 2004).[4]

---

[4]  The poverty rate revealed here refers to the percentage of the population living on less than $US2 per day.

International concerns over corruption and the possibility of renewed political instability in Cambodia have also kept foreign investment to lower than anticipated levels (Tully, 2005).[5] Moreover, both factors have constantly delayed the receipt and appropriate distribution of foreign aid to needy Cambodians. Recent reports suggest that corruption has led to the illegal transfer of international aid into the private coffers of the Cambodian elite. As a consequence, corruption contributes significantly to the enormous disparity of income within the Cambodian population.

However, the recent economic reforms together with the relative political and economic stability over the past decade (as compared to the pre-1993 circumstances) have no doubt contributed to the increase in Cambodia's average life expectancy and adult literacy rate, as well as the 23% reduction in the number of undernourished citizens as a proportion of the Cambodian population (World Resources Institute, Earthtrends). But with a poverty rate of around 70% (i.e., people living on less than $2US per day) and a population expected to almost double by 2050, Cambodia still has a long way to go to combat widespread impoverishment. What's more, it must approach the poverty issue in the knowledge that its energy consumption and $CO_2$ emissions are rising steeply and its forest and fish stocks are dramatically in decline. Collectively, these environmental concerns impose a significant constraint on Cambodia's future genuine progress of which the latter will only be sustainably achieved through appropriate and well considered policy measures.

# 3. THEORETICAL AND EMPIRICAL OVERVIEW OF GREEN GDP

This section of the chapter details the methodological approach used to calculate the Hicksian national income of Cambodia for the period 1988-2004. The study period thus begins towards the end of the reign of the Khmer Rouge regime and the war with Vietnam. It also includes the decade following the democratic elections in 1993, the relative stability in Cambodia from 1993 to 1997, the Asian financial crisis, Cambodia's own political instability towards the end of 1997, and the high growth period between 1995 and 2004. This Hicksian national income study therefore documents the impact of Cambodia's recent economic development in what can be described as a recovery period in Cambodia's history, yet one frustrated by sporadic instability and a lack of critical infrastructure and civil institutions.

## 3.1. Theoretical Developments

The theory behind measures of green GDP has developed considerably since the concept first emerged in the early 1970s. The majority of the theoretical developments centre on proposed adjustments to GDP to incorporate the long-term sustainability implications of natural resource depletion and other forms of environmental deterioration. Early on in the development of a green GDP, Weitzman (1976) utilised a dynamic optimisation model to derive a welfare measure called Net National Product (NNP) — in effect, a variation on the

---

[5] In terms of the Corruption Perceptions Index (Transparency International, www.transparency.org), Cambodia is ranked 151 out of 163 countries.

concept of Net Domestic Product (NDP). Weitzman's approach was later translated into a green measure of GDP by Dasgupta and Mäler (2000).

Many other approaches have since been adopted to obtain a measure of green GDP. In the early 1990s, Mäler (1991) suggested that three costs categories should be subtracted from GDP:

- defensive expenditures;
- forms of environmental degradation;
- and the change in the value of stocks of environmental resources.

Asheim (1994) was also prominent in the theoretical developments of green GDP having established indicators of welfare equivalent income, sustainable income, and net social profit. More recently, Cairns (2000) has developed a useful green accounting model to mirror the mismanagement of natural resources in developing countries.

As for the formal national accounting procedures employed by national statistical agencies to calculate, for example, GDP, they are based on the United Nations System of National Accounts (SNA). Introduced more than half a century ago to measure national production levels, the SNA fails to incorporate the impact of environmental damage on national productivity. Stimulated by criticisms levelled at it by the Brundtland Commission in the 1980s (WCED, 1987), the United Nations (UN) revised the SNA in 1993 (UN, 1993). The revised framework is called the System of Integrated Environmental and Economic Accounts (SEEA) and its central aim is to record the stocks and flows of all natural resource assets into the conventional national accounting framework (UN, 1993).

However, the SEEA does not require environmental cost adjustments to measurements of GDP. As such, the SEEA is merely a satellite accounting report to accompany the original SNA framework in readiness for any future estimation of environmentally-adjusted income. To date, environmental cost adjustments to GDP have not been mandated by the United Nations.

## 3.2. The Green GDP Methodology Used in the Cambodian Study

The methodology used in this chapter for the calculation of Cambodia's true national income is based on the definition of income first posited by Hicks (1946) — namely, that income ought to reflect the maximum quantity of goods a nation can consume without undermining its capacity to consume the quantity of goods over time. One of the essential requirements of the Hicksian concept of income is the need to keep income-generating capital intact. Indeed, any measure of income that counts, as income, the depletion of income-generating capital, effectively overstates 'true' income in the Hicksian sense.

With this in mind, it is worth considering the extent to which GDP constitutes a measure of Hicksian income and, should it not, what adjustments ought to be made to bring GDP into line with this more appropriate definition. GDP is a monetary measure of the goods and services annually produced by domestically *located* factors of production (i.e., by the natural and human-made capital located in a particular country). By natural capital, we mean forests, sub-soil assets, fisheries, water resources, and critical ecosystems. Human-made capital, on the other hand, includes the stock of producer goods (e.g., plant, machinery, and equipment) that are used to produce consumer goods and replacement producer goods.

GDP can be measured in *nominal* or *real* values. If GDP is measured in nominal values, it is measured in terms of the prices at the time of production. On the other hand, if GDP is measured in real values, it is measured in terms of the prices of all goods and services in a particular year — often referred to as the *base* year.

The best way to embark on an assessment of GDP is to first consider whether it would be possible for a nation to consume its entire output and still be in a position to consume at least as much output in the following year and beyond. The answer to this is, of course, no. To begin with, some of a nation's output must be set aside to replace worn out and depreciated human-made capital. Secondly, the generation of a nation's GDP also involves the depletion of natural capital. If a nation failed to replace or maintain these forms of capital, it would be unable, eventually, to maintain its productive capacity at a level necessary to sustain the same consumption stream over time. Clearly, the portion of a nation's output that is required to maintain income-generating capital intact ought not to be used for current consumption purposes. This portion cannot, therefore, be classed as true income.

In addition to this, there are other elements of a nation's annual output that are used for defensive and rehabilitative purposes that, in turn, assist in sustaining output over time (Leipert, 1986). For example, vehicle accident repairs and some medical procedures take place to restore human beings and their productive instruments to something approximating their previous condition. In doing so, the output generated in both instances is not used directly for consumption purposes — it is produced merely to maintain the productivity of human beings, as labour, and the existing stock of human-made capital.

Examples of output produced for defensive purposes include flood mitigation projects and crime prevention measures. Somewhat differently, however, output generated in these circumstances occurs to prevent future economic activity from impacting deleteriously on the existing stock of natural and human-made capital (i.e., to minimise future rehabilitative expenditures).

Not unlike the depreciation of human-made and human-made capital, the value of all output produced for rehabilitative and defensive purposes cannot be directly consumed without undermining the capacity to sustain future output. Nor, then, can it be classed as true income.

In all, it has been suggested that a better measure of national income can be calculated by subtracting from GDP the value of depreciated human-made capital and depleted natural capital as well as all defensive and rehabilitative expenditures. Thus, for the purposes of this study, Cambodia's Hicksian national income has been calculated by adhering to the following equation (Daly, 1996):

Hicksian national income = GDP – DHK – DNK – DRE                    (1)

where:

- GDP = Gross Domestic Product
- DHK = depreciation of human-made capital (producer goods)
- DNK = depletion of natural capital

- DRE = defensive and rehabilitative expenditures.

As mentioned at the beginning of this section, a key aspect of the Hicksian income concept is the need to keep income-generating capital intact. If it is assumed that human-made capital can be substituted for natural capital, it is only necessary to maintain intact a combined stock of human-made and natural capital. This form of sustainability is known as *weak sustainability*. If, however, it is assumed that the two forms of capital are complementary, it is necessary to ensure both forms of capital individually do not decline over time, particularly natural capital. This alternative form of sustainability, which is advocated by ecological economists, is known as *strong sustainability* (Pearce, 1993; Daly, 1996; El Serafy, 1996; Lawn, 2003 and 2007).

For the purposes of this chapter, the strong sustainability concept will be followed. This is based on arguments put forward by Georgescu-Roegen (1979) and Daly (1996) which, in our view, have successfully demonstrated that human-made capital is not a long-term substitute for natural capital. The adoption of the strong sustainability approach has significant implications for the way in which the category of natural resource depletion is calculated prior to its subtraction from GDP. Owing to the limited availability of Cambodian data, many of the valuation methods used in the adoption of a strong sustainability approach to Hicksian national income cannot be employed in a practical sense. Alternative methods have therefore been employed.

## 3.3. Empirical Overview of Green GDP Studies

In the early 1970s, and in response to the *Limits to Growth* thesis by the Club of Rome (Meadows et al., 1972), Nordhaus and Tobin (1972) adjusted GDP in order to calculate a Measure of Economic Welfare (MEW) for the United States between 1929 and 1965. This work was lauded but also heavily critiqued by Daly and Cobb (1989) who argued that the MEW failed to go far enough in its attempt at calculating a true measure of national income.

Many empirical studies involving environmental adjustments to GDP have since been calculated. They include estimates for Germany (Leipert, 1989), Mexico (Van Tongeren et al., 1993), Ecuador (Kellenberge, 1996), Sweden (Skanberg, 2001), the Netherlands (Gerlagh et al., 2002), and India (Atkinson and Gundimeda, 2005). However, three additional and more comprehensive empirical studies have contributed most to the methodology used in this chapter. They have been performed by Repetto et al. (1989), Young (1990) and Foy (1991).

In the well known Repetto et al. (1989) study on Indonesia, an adjustment to the GDP was undertaken by deducting the costs of three natural capital assets: forests, petroleum, and soil erosion. This study enabled Repetto et al. to conclude that, having subtracting estimates of net natural resource depletion, the conventional measure of Indonesia's GDP overstated the country's Hicksian income. The results of the study showed that the average annual rate of growth in GDP between 1971 and 1984 was 7.1%, while Net Domestic Product — the term given by Repetto et al. for the green GDP estimate — grew by an average annual rate of just 4.0% (Repetto et al., 1989, p. 4). Significantly, the adjustment to Indonesia's GDP was very conservative since the environmental cost deduction was confined to the depletion of three natural resource assets. In addition, there were no calculations and subsequent adjustments for both human-made capital depreciation (HCD) and defensive and rehabilitative expenditures (DRE).

A year later, Young (1990) suggested that environmental and natural resource accounts should be integrated into Australia's national accounting framework in order to provide a more accurate estimate of Australia's national income. The study conducted by Young incorporated a greater range of natural resources than Repetto et al. and included such environmental costs as land degradation, deforestation, and mineral depletion. Young concluded from his study, which revealed a difference in the growth rates of conventional GDP and green GDP, that necessary steps should be taken by the Australian Government to arrive at a more reliable and meaningful national economic indicator than GDP.

In 1991, Foy (1991) adjusted the Gross State Product (GSP) of the US state of Louisiana for the period 1963 to 1986. Foy concluded that, when non-renewable resource depletion was taken into account, the average annual reduction in Louisiana's GSP was 3.3% lower using a depreciation approach, yet as much as 13.8% lower when using the El Serafy (1989) user cost approach. Only two non-renewable resource items — namely, oil and gas — were calculated and incorporated into the study. Again, the adjustment to income, this time at the state level, was very conservative and likely to have underestimated the full cost of environmental damage.

Based on the theoretical and empirical reviews of Hicksian income conducted above, it can be seen that adjustments made to GDP, albeit arbitrary in many cases, constitute a significant step towards: (a) the development of a better measure of green GDP and, therefore, a better indicator of sustainable development, and (b) a more appropriate economic compass for policy-makers to use than GDP. Although, many scholars (e.g., Repetto et al., Young, and Foy) have incorporated only some of the adjustments to GDP suggested by Daly (see equation 1), there is little doubt that GDP is a poor representative of Hicksian national income (likewise GSP at the state or provincial level).

# 4. VALUATION METHODS USED TO CALCULATE CAMBODIA'S HICKSIAN NATIONAL INCOME

This study employs a number of valuation approaches to calculate Cambodia's Hicksian national income. The basic doctrine used to compute Hicksian income is modified given the Cambodian data limitations. Moreover, to arrive at the imputed environmental cost attributed to resource depletion, a conservative approach is adopted that is primarily based on the methods and results from other studies, as detailed below.

## 4.1. Human-Made Capital Depreciation (HCD)

The first of the deduction items in equation (1) is the depreciation of human-made capital. Human-made capital depreciation is often referred to in conventional national accounts as the 'consumption of fixed capital' and equals the amount charged for the use of both private sector and government fixed capital located within a country (e.g., plant, machinery, buildings, etc.). Consumption of fixed capital is invariably estimated by computing the decline in the value of fixed assets due to wear and tear, obsolescence, accidental damage, and aging.

Because the consumption of fixed capital has not been regularly calculated by the Cambodian statistical bureau, this value had to be estimated. For the year 2000, the World Resources Institute (WRI) argued that the Cambodia's consumption of fixed capital was equivalent to 7% of its Gross National Income (GNI) (WRI, 2003). In 2000, Cambodia's GNI was 11,815.0 billion riels[6] (UNSD, 2005). Using equation (2) below, the consumption of fixed capital in 2000 was 827.0 billion riels. Unfortunately, there are no GNI estimates available for the remaining years of the study period. Instead, GDP was used to determine the values for the consumption of fixed capital. GDP can be used because there is a close association between GDP and GNI.[7]

**Table 1: Human capital depreciation (HCD) - Cambodia, 1988-2004**

| Year | GNI at 2000 prices (billion riels) $a$ | CFC at 7% of GNI in 2000 (billion riels) $b$ $(0.07 \times a)$ | GDP at 2000 prices (billion riels) $c$ | CFC as % of GDP $d$ $(b/c)$ | CFC (HCD) (billion riels) $e$ $(c \times d)$ |
|---|---|---|---|---|---|
| 1988 | - | - | 6,688 | 0.059 | 391.45 |
| 1989 | - | - | 6,900 | 0.059 | 405.07 |
| 1990 | - | - | 6,981 | 0.059 | 409.78 |
| 1991 | - | - | 7,511 | 0.059 | 440.89 |
| 1992 | - | - | 8,038 | 0.059 | 471.83 |
| 1993 | - | - | 8,496 | 0.059 | 498.73 |
| 1994 | - | - | 9,277 | 0.059 | 544.58 |
| 1995 | - | - | 9,883 | 0.059 | 580.15 |
| 1996 | - | - | 10,411 | 0.059 | 611.14 |
| 1997 | - | - | 10,999 | 0.059 | 645.66 |
| 1998 | - | - | 11,545 | 0.059 | 677.71 |
| 1999 | - | - | 12,994 | 0.059 | 762.77 |
| 2000 | 11,815.0 | 827.1 | 14,089 | 0.059 | 827.05 |
| 2001 | - | - | 14,863 | 0.059 | 872.49 |
| 2002 | - | - | 15,643 | 0.059 | 918.27 |
| 2003 | - | - | 16,745 | 0.059 | 982.96 |
| 2004 | - | - | 18,032 | 0.059 | 1,058.51 |

**Sources:** World Bank (1994 and 2006); WRI (2003); UNSD (2005)

At 827.0 billion riels, the consumption of fixed capital constitutes 5.9% of GDP (equation 3). The values of the consumption of fixed capital were therefore assumed to equal 5.9% of GDP in all remaining years of the study period. The value of consumption of fixed capital or human-made capital depreciation is found in Table 1. The negative value of human-made capital depreciation indicates that this item is a *cost* and should be subtracted from GDP when calculating a nation's Hicksian national income.

$$HCD_{2000} = GNI_{2000} \times 0.07 \qquad (2)$$
$$= 11,815 \text{ billion riels} \times 0.07$$

---

[6]  The Cambodia currency is referred to as 'riels'. In 2002, US$1 = 3,850 riels.

[7]  Gross national Income (GNI) measures the total income of all people who are citizens in a given country while GDP measures the value of the total output of all persons living in that country.

$$= 827.0 \text{ billion riels}$$

$$\frac{HCD_{2000}}{GDP_{2000}} = \frac{827}{14,089} = 0.059 \tag{3}$$

## 4.2. Defensive and Rehabilitative Expenditures (DRE)

Like most studies involving the subtraction of defensive and rehabilitative expenditures (e.g., Daly and Cobb, 1989; Lawn, 2001; Clarke and Lawn, 2005), it was assumed for this study that half of all government expenditure on education and health is required to help maintain the nation's productive capacity due to the ongoing negative impacts of past and present economic activities.

The data available on government health and education expenditure only exists for the period 1996 to 2004. To estimate the data for the missing years (1988-1995), a number of steps were undertaken. Firstly, government health and education expenditure as a percentage of GDP was computed for each year from 1996 to 2004. Secondly, the average percentage value for this period was calculated. It was then assumed that this average (2.1%) was the same percentage value for the missing years. Finally, as explained above, the annual value of defensive and rehabilitative expenditure (DRE) was assumed to be 50% of government expenditure on health and education (Daly and Cobb, 1989; Lawn 2001). That is:

$$\text{DRE} = 0.5 \times \text{Government expenditure on health \& education} \tag{4}$$

The calculations and the annual DRE values for Cambodia are revealed in Table 2 below.

**Table 2: Defensive and rehabilitative expenditure (DRE) - Cambodia, 1988-2004**

| Year | Govt. health & education exp. (billion riels) | DRE (billion riels) | GDP (billion riels) | DRE as % of GDP |
|---|---|---|---|---|
| | $a$ | $b$ $(0.5 \times a)$ | $c$ | $d$ $(b/c)$ |
| 1988 | 134.03 | 67.01 | 6,668 | 0.010 |
| 1989 | 138.69 | 69.34 | 6,900 | 0.010 |
| 1990 | 140.30 | 70.15 | 6,981 | 0.010 |
| 1991 | 150.95 | 75.48 | 7,511 | 0.010 |
| 1992 | 161.55 | 80.77 | 8,038 | 0.010 |
| 1993 | 170.76 | 85.38 | 8,496 | 0.010 |
| 1994 | 186.45 | 93.23 | 9,277 | 0.010 |
| 1995 | 198.63 | 99.32 | 9,883 | 0.010 |
| 1996 | 140.46 | 70.23 | 10,411 | 0.007 |
| 1997 | 138.98 | 69.49 | 10,999 | 0.006 |
| 1998 | 130.04 | 65.02 | 11,545 | 0.006 |
| 1999 | 271.35 | 135.68 | 12,994 | 0.010 |
| 2000 | *344.00* | *172.00* | *14,089* | *0.012* |
| 2001 | 343.07 | 171.53 | 14,863 | 0.012 |
| 2002 | 444.04 | 222.02 | 15,643 | 0.014 |
| 2003 | 445.93 | 222.96 | 16,745 | 0.013 |
| 2004 | 429.90 | 214.95 | 18,032 | 0.012 |

**Sources:** World Bank (1994 and 2006); Cambodian Development Review (2005)

## 4.3. Natural Capital Depletion (NCD)

The El Serafy (1989) user cost method was employed to calculate the true income and the set-aside components from the net receipts generated from the depletion of Cambodia's natural resource assets. The formula used to calculate the income and set-aside components is:

$$R - X = R\left(\frac{1}{(1+r)^{n+1}}\right) \tag{5}$$

where:

- $X$ = income (resource rent);
- $R$ = total receipts (the value of harvesting minus the costs incurred from harvesting the resource in excess of the sustainable harvesting rate);
- $R - X$ = the user cost or depletion factor that should be set aside as a capital investment to establish a suitable replacement asset. This amount must be deducted from GDP when calculating a nation's Hicksian national income;
- $r$ = discount rate or regeneration rate of the replacement asset (alternative renewable resource);
- $n$ = number of periods over which the resource would be exhausted if extracted at the current rate.

The user cost formula is normally applied to a non-renewable resource. However, it can be employed to calculate the user cost of a renewable resource if harvesting of the resource exceeds its natural regeneration rate. Excessive harvesting implies that the resource will eventually be exhausted. In these circumstances, harvesting of a renewable resource is no different to the extraction of a non-renewable resource.

Choosing the appropriate discount rate ($r$) is very critical.[8] Ultimately the discount rate chosen depends on whether one adopts the *weak* or *strong sustainability* objective. If a weak sustainability approach is adopted, the asset established to replace the depleted natural resource can be in the form of human-made capital. The interest rate generated by a typical human-made capital asset is around 7%. However, if a strong sustainability approach is embraced, the replacement asset must be a renewable resource. The interest rate on a renewable resource is effectively its natural regeneration rate. This is typically in the order of 1 to 2%.

The significance of the chosen discount rate can be illustrated by the following. Consider a scenario where the life expectancy of a resource is 60 years ($n = 60$ years). At a discount rate of $r = 1\%$ (strong sustainability), 54.5% of the net receipts from resource depletion must be set aside to establish a replacement resource asset (i.e., a cultivated renewable resource). In other words, for every 100 riels received, 45.5 riels would constitute genuine income that could be used for consumption purposes. The remaining 54.5 riels would constitute the user

---

[8] The discount rate deployed when using the El Serafy user cost approach is rationally explained in Lawn (1998, 2001, and 2007).

cost of the resource to be subsequently subtracted when calculating a nation's Hicksian national income. Conversely, at a discount rate of $r = 7\%$ (weak sustainability), just 1.6% of all net receipts would have to be set aside to establish a replacement asset which, under weak sustainability conditions (although incorrectly in our view), can exist in any form. In the weak sustainability case, 98.4 riels would constitute income while only 1.6 riels would need to be set aside for reinvestment. As indicated earlier, this empirical study of Cambodia has employed the strong sustainability approach. A discount rate of 1% was therefore used to calculate the user cost of forest and fish depletion.

## *Valuing the Cost of Deforestation*

The environmental cost of deforestation represents the 'opportunity cost' of forest depletion. It equals the value of the forest that could be obtained over time if the deforestation had not taken place. The larger is the rate of forest clearance, the higher is the opportunity cost of forest depletion. The opportunity cost of forestry operations is negligible if the rate of harvesting does not exceed the regeneration rate of the forest.

To arrive at the imputed environmental cost on deforestation, two variables are required. The first variable is the 'regeneration rate' of Cambodia's forest stocks. This, according to the Department of Fisheries (2001a), is 0.33 m$^3$ per hectare per year. Given the assumption that the 'volume over bark'[9] of Cambodia's forests is the same as it is for Indonesia's forests — that is, 219 m$^3$ per hectare (Repetto el al., 1989) — the regeneration rate amounts to:

$$(0.33 \text{m}^3 / 2129 \text{m}^3) \times 100\% = 0.155\% \qquad (6)$$

The second variable is the 'harvesting rate' of Cambodia's forests. According to the Department of Fisheries (2001a), the harvesting rate was 0.57% from 1988 to 1994, but 3% from 1995 and 2004 (World Bank, 2003). Based on the estimated regeneration rate and the 2004 harvesting rate, Cambodia's major forest areas are likely to be fully exhausted in 26 years. Hence, the variables employed to calculate the user cost of deforestation were:

- $R$: Total receipts = Value of the change in forest area
- $r$: Regeneration rate = 0.155 %
- $n$: Number of year to completely deplete the forest (26 years).[10]

The calculations and user cost values of Cambodia's forest depletion are revealed in Table 3 below.

---

[9] *Volume over bark* is the gross volume in cubic metres per hectare over bark of free bole (from stump or buttresses to crown point of first main branch) of all living trees more than 10 centimetres in diameter at breast height (Repetto et al. 1989, p. 29).

[10] The value of $n = 31$ years is derived on the assumption that the total of harvestable forest areas will be exhausted except for protected areas.

**Table 3: User cost of forestry assets - Cambodia, 1988-2004**

| Year | Annual change in forest area (cubic metres) | Forest value per hectare (riels) | Value of change in forest area (billion riels) | User cost (1 - X/R) | User cost (R - X) (billion riels) |
|---|---|---|---|---|---|
| | $a$ | $b$ | $c$ | $d$ | $e$ |
| | | | $(a \times b)$ | | $(c \times d)$ |
| 1988 | -10,667,946 | 6,149 | -65.59 | 0.959 | -62.91 |
| 1989 | -10,623,152 | 6,149 | -65.32 | 0.959 | -62.64 |
| 1990 | -10,578,547 | 6,149 | -65.04 | 0.959 | -62.38 |
| 1991 | -10,534,129 | 6,149 | -64.77 | 0.959 | -62.12 |
| 1992 | -10,489,898 | 6,149 | -64.50 | 0.959 | -61.86 |
| 1993 | -10,445,852 | 6,149 | -64.23 | 0.959 | -61.60 |
| 1994 | -10,401,991 | 6,149 | -63.96 | 0.959 | -61.34 |
| 1995 | -86,358,607 | 6,149 | -530.98 | 0.959 | -509.24 |
| 1996 | -83,335,490 | 6,149 | -512.39 | 0.959 | -491.41 |
| 1997 | -80,418,202 | 6,149 | -494.46 | 0.959 | -474.21 |
| 1998 | -77,603,038 | 6,149 | -477.15 | 0.959 | -457.61 |
| 1999 | -74,886,423 | 6,149 | -460.44 | 0.959 | -441.59 |
| 2000 | -72,264,907 | 6,149 | -444.33 | 0.959 | -426.13 |
| 2001 | -69,735,162 | 6,149 | -428.77 | 0.959 | -411.21 |
| 2002 | -67,293,974 | 6,149 | -413.76 | 0.959 | -396.82 |
| 2003 | -64,938,244 | 6,149 | -399.28 | 0.959 | -382.93 |
| 2004 | -62,664,980 | 6,149 | -385.30 | 0.959 | -369.52 |

**Sources:** World Bank (2003); Department of Fisheries (2001b)

## Valuing the Cost of Overfishing

The methodology used to calculate the imputed environmental cost or opportunity cost of overfishing is the same used for deforestation. Obviously, the variation in the two calculations relates to the different regeneration rate of fish and as well as the number of years it would take to deplete fish stocks if they were harvested at present rates. The regeneration rate was assumed to be one percent ($r = 1\%$). This regeneration rate is based on evidence showing that, although "reproductive female fish generate large numbers of eggs, in some cases numbering in the millions per female, very few of these eggs grow and survive to reproductive maturity" (Kahn, 2005).

The estimate of the stock changes revealed in Table 4 was based on: (a) the increase in 'catch per units' and fish production claimed by Khy (2005), and (b) the annual harvest report by the Department of Fisheries (2001b). Given current fish demands in Cambodia, it was assumed that it would take thirty years ($n = 30$ years) to exhaust existing fish stocks at current harvesting rates. Hence, the variables employed to calculate the user cost of fish stock depletion were:

- $R$:  total receipts = Value of the change in fish stocks
- $r$:  Discount rate = regeneration rate = 1.0% per annum
- $n$:  Number of years to completely deplete fish stocks at the current rates of harvesting (assumed to equal 30 years).

**Table 4: User cost of fishery assets - Cambodia, 1988-2004**

| Year | Annual change in fish stocks (tonnes) | Fish value per tonne (billion riels) | Value of change in fish stocks (billion riels) | User cost (1 - X/R) | User cost (R - X) (billion riels) |
|---|---|---|---|---|---|
| | a | b | c | d | e |
| | | | (a × b) | | (c × d) |
| 1988 | -6,800 | 0.01114 | -75.78 | 0.795 | -60.28 |
| 1989 | -2,156 | 0.01114 | -24.03 | 0.795 | -19.11 |
| 1990 | -31,490 | 0.01114 | -350.94 | 0.795 | -279.15 |
| 1991 | -38,504 | 0.01114 | -429.11 | 0.795 | -341.33 |
| 1992 | -33,990 | 0.01114 | -378.80 | 0.795 | -301.31 |
| 1993 | -29,529 | 0.01114 | -329.09 | 0.795 | -261.77 |
| 1994 | -24,065 | 0.01114 | -268.19 | 0.795 | -213.33 |
| 1995 | -33,444 | 0.01114 | -372.72 | 0.795 | -296.48 |
| 1996 | -25,710 | 0.01114 | -286.52 | 0.795 | -227.91 |
| 1997 | -36,540 | 0.01114 | -407.22 | 0.795 | -323.92 |
| 1998 | -44,622 | 0.01114 | -497.29 | 0.795 | -395.57 |
| 1999 | -35,168 | 0.01114 | -391.94 | 0.795 | -311.76 |
| 2000 | -59,451 | 0.01114 | -662.55 | 0.795 | -527.02 |
| 2001 | -118,515 | 0.01114 | -1,320.79 | 0.795 | -1,050.61 |
| 2002 | -349,600 | 0.01114 | -3,896.12 | 0.795 | -3,099.14 |
| 2003 | -354,338 | 0.01114 | -3,948.92 | 0.795 | -3,141.14 |
| 2004 | -257,739 | 0.01114 | -2,872.38 | 0.795 | -2,284.81 |

**Sources:** World Bank (2006); MAFF (undated)

## *Valuing the Cost of Soil Erosion*

The environmental cost of soil erosion equals the monetary value associated with soil degradation. Given the nature of the Cambodian environment, soil degradation not only reduces agricultural productivity, but also the productivity of its forests.

Unfortunately, there is no reliable study of soil erosion costs in Cambodia. Nonetheless, Khor (undated) has argued that, in the East Asia region, soil degradation comprises 7% of agricultural losses. Moreover, an empirical study by Yang (undated) on the impact of soil erosion on crop yields reveals a 40% decline in agricultural productivity in the northeast region of Cambodia. This study conservatively assumes that the soil erosion cost in Cambodia over the study period equates to 7% of agricultural output. This is relatively small when compared to the estimated cost of soil erosion in Java at 40% of GDP (Magrath et al. in Barbier, 1991). The cost of soil erosion in Cambodia was therefore calculated by adopting the following equation:

Soil erosion cost = Total value of agriculture × 0.07          (7)

The total value of Cambodia's agricultural product was derived from the World Bank (1994 and 2006). It is revealed in Table 5 along with the estimated cost of soil erosion in Cambodia.

**Table 5: Cost of soil erosion - Cambodia, 1988-2004**

| Year | Value of agricultural output (billion riels) | Soil erosion cost as 7% of agric. value | Cost of soil erosion (billion riels) |
|------|------|------|------|
| | a | b | c |
| | | | (a × b) |
| 1988 | 1,850.63 | -0.07 | -129.54 |
| 1989 | 2,044.94 | -0.07 | -143.15 |
| 1990 | 2,000.53 | -0.07 | -140.04 |
| 1991 | 2,106.02 | -0.07 | -147.42 |
| 1992 | 2,144.88 | -0.07 | -150.14 |
| 1993 | 2,354.00 | -0.07 | -164.78 |
| 1994 | 2,375.00 | -0.07 | -166.25 |
| 1995 | 2,605.00 | -0.07 | -182.35 |
| 1996 | 2,673.00 | -0.07 | -187.11 |
| 1997 | 2,646.00 | -0.07 | -185.22 |
| 1998 | 2,846.00 | -0.07 | -199.22 |
| 1999 | 3,146.00 | -0.07 | -220.22 |
| 2000 | 3,085.00 | -0.07 | -215.95 |
| 2001 | 3,178.00 | -0.07 | -222.46 |
| 2002 | 3,059.00 | -0.07 | -214.13 |
| 2003 | 3,668.00 | -0.07 | -256.76 |
| 2004 | 3,612.00 | -0.07 | -252.84 |

**Sources:** World Bank (1994 and 2006); Khor (undated)

## *Valuing the Cost of Air Pollution*

Air pollution constitutes a form of natural capital depletion in the sense that it reflects the erosion of a nation's waste assimilative capacity. The imputed air pollution cost should thus equal the amount a nation spends to rehabilitate the health of affected citizens, to repair buildings and other structures, plus the cost of reduced agricultural production as a consequence of any reduced assimilative capacity.

No empirical study has been conducted on air pollution costs in Cambodia. The imputed cost of air pollution in Cambodia used for this chapter was therefore based on a case study in China by Deng (2006) using two methods of valuation. For the year 2000, Deng found that the air pollution cost for China was 3.26% of GDP based on a willingness-to-pay approach, and 0.7% of GDP based on a human capital approach.

For this chapter, the latter estimation of the imputed cost of air pollution was adopted — that is, 0.7% of a nation's GDP. It is conservatively low compared to other studies. For example, Kan and Chen (2004) found that the air pollution cost was 1.03% of GDP in Shanghai, and between 3 to 6% of GDP in India (Lvovshy, 1998). The lower value of 0.7% was chosen because the health cost of air pollution is to some extent already deducted in terms of the item capturing defensive and rehabilitative expenditures. This approach avoids double-counting.

Because the Deng (2006) study is based on China, it was assumed that the per unit GDP cost of air pollution is the same in both Cambodia and China. Thus, in order to impute the air pollution cost in Cambodia, a number of steps were required. Firstly, the cost of air pollution in China for the year 2000 was calculated. In 2000, China's GDP was US$1,080.7 billion (Deng, 2006). At 0.7% of GDP, the total air pollution cost in China amounts to US$7,565.2 million. Secondly, the unit cost of air pollution per metric tonnes of $CO_2$ emissions in China was only calculated for the year 2000.[11] In this particular year, China's $CO_2$ emissions were 3,469,117 metric tonnes (WRI, 2006). By dividing the total pollution cost by total $CO_2$ emissions, one obtains a pollution cost for China in 2000 equal to US$2,180 per metric tonne of $CO_2$ emissions.

To calculate the total air pollution cost in Cambodia in 2000 (see Table 6), the unit cost of air pollution in China was converted to Cambodian currency (*riels*) at the prevailing exchange rate in the year 2000 (3,850 riels per US dollar). By performing this calculation, the air pollution cost for Cambodia amounted to 8.415 million riels per metric tonne of $CO_2$ emissions. This unit price was applied to the remaining years of the study period, as shown in equation (8).

Air pollution cost = total emissions of $CO_2$ × 8.415 million riels          (8)

**Table 6: Cost of air pollution - Cambodia, 1988-2004**

| Year | Total $CO_2$ emissions (000s of metric tonnes) | Unit price per tonne of $CO_2$ emissions (riels) | Cost of air pollution (billion riels) |
|---|---|---|---|
| | $a$ | $b$ | $c$ $(-a \times b)$ |
| 1988 | 450.70 | 8,415 | -3.79 |
| 1989 | 450.70 | 8,415 | -3.79 |
| 1990 | 450.70 | 8,415 | -3.79 |
| 1991 | 461.70 | 8,415 | -3.89 |
| 1992 | 476.30 | 8,415 | -4.01 |
| 1993 | 476.30 | 8,415 | -4.01 |
| 1994 | 588.50 | 8,415 | -4.95 |
| 1995 | 599.50 | 8,415 | -5.05 |
| 1996 | 700.60 | 8,415 | -5.90 |
| 1997 | 661.00 | 8,415 | -5.56 |
| 1998 | 661.00 | 8,415 | -5.56 |
| 1999 | 524.00 | 8,415 | -4.41 |
| 2000 | 531.30 | 8,415 | -4.47 |
| 2001 | 581.90 | 8,415 | -4.90 |
| 2002 | 596.50 | 8,415 | -5.02 |
| 2003 | 620.67 | 8,415 | -5.22 |
| 2004 | 650.46 | 8,415 | -5.47 |

**Sources:** WRI (2006a); Deng (2006)

# 5. RESULTS OF THE SNDP STUDY

## 5.1. Cambodia's Real GDP and Hicksian National Income

The Hicksian national income results for Cambodia for the period 1988-2004 are summarised in Table 7. As the table reveals, Cambodia's real GDP was 6,668 billion riels in 1988 (column $a$) while its Hicksian income was 5,953 riels (column $e$). By the end of the study period, real GDP had grown to 18,032 billion riels. Although Cambodia's Hicksian income also increased over the study period, it was considerably lower at 13,846 billion riels.

---

[11] The unit price of year 2000 is calculated because year 2000 is the year base of real GDP.

**Table 7: Per capita real GDP versus per capita Hicksian income - Cambodia, 1988-2004**

| Year | Real GDP (billion riels) a | HCD (billion riels) b | NCD (billion riels) c | DRE (billion riels) d | Hicksian income (billion riels) e (a - b - c - d) | Population (000s) f | Per capita real GDP (riels) g (a/f) | Per capita Hicksian income (riels) h (e/f) |
|---|---|---|---|---|---|---|---|---|
| 1988 | 6,668 | 391.45 | 256.52 | 67.01 | 5,953.48 | 6,463.0 | 1,031,792.0 | 921,164.0 |
| 1989 | 6,900 | 405.07 | 228.69 | 69.34 | 6,197.38 | 6,978.4 | 988,839.0 | 888,083.5 |
| 1990 | 6,981 | 409.78 | 485.36 | 70.15 | 6,015.41 | 7,493.8 | 931,535.0 | 802,722.6 |
| 1991 | 7,511 | 440.89 | 554.76 | 75.48 | 6,439.50 | 8,009.1 | 937,756.9 | 804,019.4 |
| 1992 | 8,038 | 471.83 | 517.32 | 80.77 | 6,967.77 | 8,524.5 | 942,890.5 | 817,379.9 |
| 1993 | 8,496 | 498.73 | 492.16 | 85.38 | 7,419.73 | 9,039.9 | 939,833.8 | 820,776.3 |
| 1994 | 9,277 | 544.58 | 445.87 | 93.23 | 8,193.33 | 9,555.3 | 970,877.3 | 857,466.2 |
| 1995 | 9,883 | 580.15 | 993.11 | 99.32 | 8,210.42 | 10,070.7 | 981,366.2 | 815,282.0 |
| 1996 | 10,411 | 611.14 | 912.33 | 70.23 | 8,817.30 | 10,586.0 | 983,465.6 | 832,918.0 |
| 1997 | 10,999 | 645.66 | 988.91 | 69.49 | 9,294.94 | 11,101.4 | 990,774.7 | 837,275.3 |
| 1998 | 11,545 | 677.71 | 1,057.96 | 65.02 | 9,744.31 | 11,616.8 | 993,819.9 | 838,812.4 |
| 1999 | 12,994 | 762.77 | 977.98 | 135.68 | 11,117.57 | 12,132.2 | 1,071,036.6 | 916,371.1 |
| 2000 | 14,089 | 827.05 | 1,173.57 | 172.00 | 11,916.38 | 12,351.4 | 1,140,682.1 | 964,780.8 |
| 2001 | 14,863 | 872.49 | 1,689.18 | 171.53 | 12,129.80 | 12,573.6 | 1,182,081.8 | 964,705.4 |
| 2002 | 15,643 | 918.27 | 3,715.10 | 222.02 | 10,787.60 | 12,803.0 | 1,221,824.7 | 842,585.3 |
| 2003 | 16,745 | 982.96 | 3,786.05 | 222.96 | 11,753.03 | 13,040.7 | 1,284,060.0 | 901,259.5 |
| 2004 | 18,032 | 1,058.51 | 2,912.64 | 214.95 | 13,845.89 | 13,287.1 | 1,357,110.6 | 1,042,059.0 |

Note: All values in billions of riels except where indicated

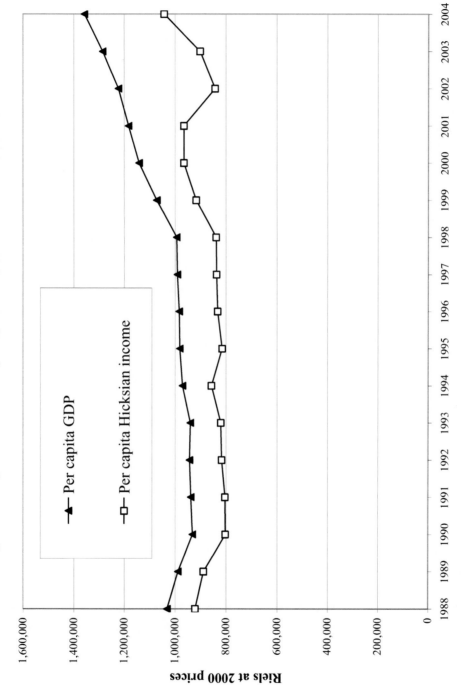

Figure 1: Per capita real GDP versus per capita Hicksian income - Cambodia, 1988-2004

Crucially, the disparity between real GDP and Hicksian national income increased from 715 billion riels in 1988 to 4,186 billion riels by 2004. This, in effect, constitutes a 6-fold increase in the gap between Cambodia's real GDP and Hicksian national income over the study period. It is therefore clearly apparent that Cambodia's real GDP substantially overstated Cambodia's sustainable income throughout the study period. Indeed, it was an average of 20.6% higher than Hicksian national income over the entire study period, but a more substantial 30.2% higher in 2004.

Figure 1 provides a comparison between Cambodia's per capita real GDP and per capita Hicksian income (columns $g$ and $h$ in Table 7). Between 1988 and 1998, there was very little increase in the per capita value of both indicators. In addition, the difference between the two remained steady until 1994 upon which there was a sharp decline in per capita Hicksian income in 1995.

From 1998 to the end of the study period in 2004, Cambodia's per capita real GDP rose significantly. Whilst, in 1999 and 2000, per capita Hicksian income also increased steeply, there was a marked downturn in per capita Hicksian income in 2001 and 2002. Per capita Hicksian income recovered in 2003 and 2004, however, the disparity between Cambodia's per capita real GDP and per capita Hicksian income was more substantial than it was pre-2001. This suggests that the per capita GDP growth spurt between 1988 and 2004 did not genuinely equate to a similar increase in sustainable per capita income and that, relative to the early part of the study period, the much higher per capita level of GDP after 2001 was fuelled by an increased consumption of income-generating capital. Interestingly, this latter phenomenon occurred not long after the implementation of the 1999 economic reforms. This evidence does not imply that each reform had a negative impact and that Cambodia would have fared better towards the end of the study period had they not been introduced. But it does suggest that their full impact should be closely examined to determine which reforms ought to remain and which should perhaps be abandoned, or at least be modified.

## 5.2. Component Items of Cambodia's Hicksian National Income

To obtain a better understanding of the trend movement of Cambodia's Hicksian income, it is necessary to examine the individual cost items subtracted from GDP. Table 7 (column $c$) and Figure 2 show that the dominant item influencing Cambodia's Hicksian income was the cost of natural capital depletion (NCD). This was followed in importance by the depreciation of human-made capital (HCD) (column $b$) and, finally, DRE (column $d$). In 2004, the cost of NCD was 2,912.6 billion riels, while HCD and DRE were 1,058.5 billion riels and 215.0 billion riels respectively. The cost of NCD was therefore nearly three times greater than HCD and almost 13.6 times bigger than DRE.

There are two other very important aspects about NCD worth noting. Between 1988 and 1994, NCD remained relatively steady. In 1995, however, NCD rose considerably and remained at the much higher level through to 2000. It was in 1995 that Cambodia's per capita Hicksian income dipped. Secondly, NCD increased dramatically in 2001 and 2002. This coincided with the rapid increase in Cambodia's per capita GDP but the sharp decline in per capita Hicksian income.

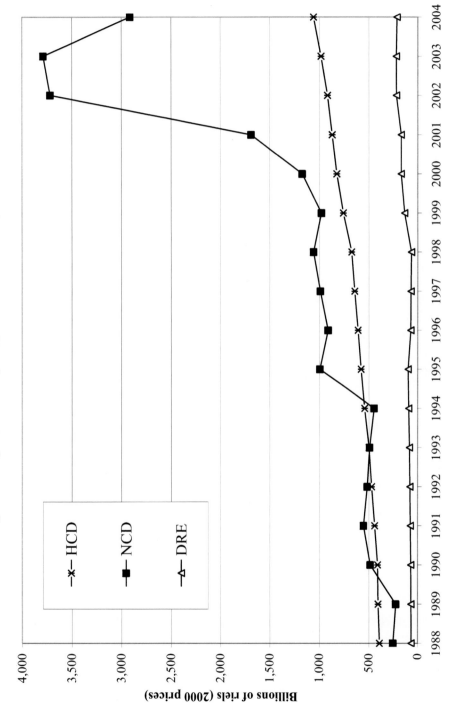

Figure 2: Comparison of NCD, HCD, and DRE - Cambodia, 1988-2004

Of the individual environmental cost items that have been used to calculate the annual value for NCD, the cost of fish and forest depletion made the greatest contribution. Air pollution costs were relatively minor, but rising, while the cost of soil erosion effectively doubled over the study period. Both air pollution and land degradation are environmental issues that should not be overlooked by Cambodian policy makers. However, as we see it, the future management of fish and forest resources is likely to have the most significant implications for Cambodia's short-term and long-term development. For this reason, the following section will concentrate on these two important resource assets.

## 6. RESOURCE DEPLETION ISSUES

### 6.1. Forestry Issues

Between 1988 and 2004, Cambodia's total forest area was reduced from 11.9 million to 8.4 million hectares. This amounts to a 30% reduction in forests over the study period. For management purposes, Cambodia's forests are classified as either 'protected' forest or forest that exists within management concession zones. The protected areas cover about 18% of the total land area (3.3 million hectares) while the rest is reserved for concession areas (Ministry of Environment, 1998). At current rates of deforestation, the forest area in Cambodia will effectively be reduced to protected areas only by 2030 and, if the situation persists, desertification is likely to occur in less than 5 decades.

Exactly what are the major factors behind the rapid rate of deforestation in Cambodia? In the first instance, there is a strong and increasing demand for fuelwood. Fuelwood is currently the primary source of energy for most Cambodians. As the situation presently stands, Cambodians are permitted to collect fuelwood from any forest area, including protected areas. The fuelwood extracted from forest areas is estimated at 0.3 cubic meters per capita per year (Ministry of Environment, 1998). This consumption rate exceeds the regeneration rate of Cambodia's forests. Thus, commercial logging aside, the local demand for fuelwood is itself contributing to the depletion of Cambodia's forest resources.

The impact of fuelwood demand on Cambodia's forests cannot be underestimated. In 2005, for example, Cambodians were expected to consume up to 19,083 hectares of forest area for fuelwood while forest regeneration was estimated to be 12,577 hectares. This constitutes a forest deficit of 6,506 hectares or a rate of fuelwood demand that exceeds the rate of forest regeneration by 52%.

Secondly, forest stocks have been extensively reduced by commercial logging. Excessive logging has occurred largely as a consequence of the Cambodian Government's desire to generate royalties from commercial logging in concession forest areas for economic rehabilitation and development purposes. On a positive note, the number of concession forest areas has fallen from 33 in 1997 (covering 7 million hectares) to 15 in 2002 (covering 2.5 million hectares). Whilst this has helped to reduce the annual harvest of forests by around 25% since the mid-1990s, it has not been anywhere sufficient to prevent continuing high rates of deforestation.

Clearly, to prevent further deforestation in Cambodia, it will be necessary to deal with the problem of excessive commercial logging, undoubtedly the main offending area. Continued economic development in Cambodia should help alleviate the fuelwood issue since greater access to electricity should follow. Of course, any natural decline in fuelwood demand will depend very much upon how equitably the gains from further rises in real GDP are distributed among the Cambodian population. Hence, a more equitable distribution of income should be a top policy priority for the Cambodian Government.

Returning to the commercial sector, policy makers must ensure that timber is harvested in concession areas in line with sustainable harvesting practices. This means restricting the harvest to a rate that does not exceed the natural regeneration rate of the forests. Access to forests should be contingent upon logging companies meeting such a condition and leases should be revoked if the condition is violated.

To avoid 'hit-and-run' harvesting, logging companies should also be contracted over a lengthy period (i.e., long-term rather than short-term leases). Short-term leases provide a distorted incentive for logging companies to rapidly deplete the resource stock, whereas long-term leases tied to the quantity of timber harvested rather than the area available for harvest guarantee 'resource security'. Long-term leases tied to the quantity of timber harvested also provide two additional benefits. Being quota-based, they allow the relevant government authority to better control the overall quantity of timber harvested by all logging companies. Secondly, the amount paid for a lease equates to a harvest tax which would provide logging companies with an incentive to optimise the harvesting process. It would also encourage the use of quality harvesting techniques that could be provided by expert government advice (Kahn, 2005).

## 6.2. Fisheries Issues

Based on the methodology employed in this chapter, Cambodian fish stocks have declined over the study period from 8.0 million tonnes to 6.7 million tonnes. The annual harvest has grown rapidly from 86,800 tonnes in 1988 to 325,500 tonnes in 2004. It should be noted that the 2004 harvest was much lower than the peak harvest in 2003 of 425,642 tonnes.[12] The amount of fish harvested from 1988 to 2000 rose quite steadily at an average annual rate of 3.9% but increased dramatically in both 2001 (43.0%) and 2002 (118.2%).

Broadly speaking, there are three management strategies employed in Cambodia in relation to fish resources. The first involves seasonal limits and restrictions on fishing equipment; the second involves the existence of fish sanctuaries in protected areas; and the third involves the establishment of fishing lots (areas designated for commercial fishing only). Fishing lots are granted in such a way as to ensure the access to fish stocks is shared amongst the general community and fishing lot owners. However, while lot owners are permitted to catch fish outside their fishing lots, the general community is prohibited from accessing fishing lots under commercial ownership.

Under current government policy, fishing rights are subject to a public bidding process every two years. In many instances, local communities have difficulty raising the financial capital necessary to participate in the bidding process. Their access to fish stocks is consequently limited, which again raises the equity issue.

---

[12] It is too early to ascertain whether the decline in the 2004 harvest was due to reduced effort or plummeting fish stocks.

Since the fishing lots are a form of commercial property, commercial operators have an incentive to bulk harvest in order to maximise returns from their initial investment. This gives the fishing lot owners the opportunity to engage in excessive harvesting despite the restrictions placed upon them in terms of fishing equipment and closed harvesting seasons. In all, the establishment of fish lots has brought about a massive increase in harvest rates which is clearly unsustainable.

The Cambodia Government, which is the ultimate owner and manager of all fish stocks under the Cambodian Constitution, has recently expressed a strong commitment towards the sustainable management of all fish stocks. It envisages enforcing such a policy by 2010. However, the details of such a policy are yet to be released.

We believe a sustainable management plan will only be successful if it follows a few very basic principles. Firstly, it will need to ensure that access to fish stocks is equitably shared between local communities and commercial operators. This could be achieved by: (a) freely distributing a certain percentage of all fishing rights or permits to local communities via local government agencies; (b) restricting commercial operators to fishing lots; and (c) making all freely distributed permits non-tradeable. Only permits sold through auction would be tradeable. Secondly, fishing rights must be quantity based — that is, act as quotas — in order to restrict catch numbers to sustainable levels. Thirdly, large financial penalties must be imposed on transgressors since only then will permit holders face a disincentive large enough to deter over-fishing.

As an added bonus, the fee paid to acquire fishing rights at auction can serve as a tax to bring the private cost of fishing into line with the full social cost. Because fisheries possess two features typically characteristic of open access resources (see Khan, 2005), there is invariably a disparity between the private cost of fishing and the cost incurred by society as a whole. The fee paid to acquire fishing rights would bridge this gap and ensure an efficient number of operators in the industry. Competition between operators would also induce them to utilise the best available fishing technology, thereby further increasing efficiency. Meanwhile, the government could also use the revenue earned from the auctioning process to restock rivers and lakes or compensate affected parties.

## CONCLUDING REMARKS

Although Cambodia's per capita GDP has increased moderately in recent years, the same cannot be said for Cambodia's per capita Hicksian income. Indeed, this study indicates that per capita GDP was stimulated to a very large extent by the liquidation of Cambodia's natural capital — in particular, its forest and fishery assets. Having said this, Cambodia's per capita Hicksian income was slightly higher in 2004 than it was in 1988 and increased over the last two years of the study period.

Does this mean that Cambodia is on a sustainable economic pathway? No, it simply indicates that Cambodia's per capita income would have risen slightly over the study period had it taken the necessary steps to operate in accordance with the strong sustainability requirement to keep natural capital intact. But it clearly did not do this. It is therefore incumbent upon Cambodian policy makers to limit the rate of resource extraction to rates consistent with their regenerative capacities and, where possible, invest in natural capital as well as human-made capital assets. Although the Cambodian Government has expressed a desire to utilise the nation's natural resources sustainably by 2010, it has yet to indicate how it will achieve this. We believe the policies implemented will need to adhere to some basic principles, some of which we have sketched in this chapter.

If there is one positive aspect to emerge from this study, it is the message that a transition to a sustainable economic pathway need not, at least for the time being, result in a radical decline in Cambodia's per capita income. Cambodian policy makers should therefore seize the opportunity while it exists. After all, there is no telling when it might cease or how costly the transition could eventually become should appropriate action not be immediately taken.

## REFERENCES

Asheim, G. (1994), 'Net national product as an indicator of sustainability?', *Scandinavian Journal of Economics*, 96: 257-265.

Atkinson, G. and Gundimeda, H. (2005), *Accounting for India's forest wealth*, (online), Available: http://www.sciencedirect.com/science/article/
B6VDY-4J4B9CJ-1/2/f67d94c6e244d22414a647f416423c3f (4 July 2006).

Barbier, E. (1991), 'Environmental Degradation of the Third World', in D. Pearce (ed.), *Blueprint 2: Greening the World Economy*, London: Earthscan.

Cairns, R. D. (2000), 'Sustainability accounting and green accounting', *Environment and Development Economics*, 5(1): 49-54.

Chandler, D. (1983), *A History of Cambodia*, Boulder: Westview Press.

Clarke, M. and Lawn, P. (2005), 'Measuring Victoria's Genuine Progress: A Genuine Progress Indicator (GPI) for Victoria', *Economic Papers*, 24(4): 368-389.

Daly, H. (1996), *Beyond Growth*, Boston: Beacon Press.

Daly, H. and Cobb, J. (1989), *For the Common Good*, Boston: Beacon Press.

Dasgupta, P. and Mäler, K. (2000), 'Net national product, wealth, and social well-being', *Environment and Development Economics*, 5(1): 69-93.

Deng, X. (2006), 'Economic costs of motor vehicle emissions in China: A case study', *Transportation Research Part D: Transport and Environment*, 11(3): 216-226.

Department of Fisheries (2001a), *Natural Resources Evaluation*, (online), Available: http://www.maff.gov.kh/pdf/NaturalResorcesEvaluation.PDF (15 June 2006).

Department of Fisheries (2001b), *Inland Fisheries Review*, Phnom Penh: Ministry of Agriculture, Forestry and Fisheries.

El Serafy, S. (1989), 'The proper calculation of income from depletable natural resources', in Y. Ahmad, S. El Serafy, and E. Lutz, E. (eds), *Environmental Accounting for Sustainable Development*, World Bank, Washington DC, pp. 10-18.

El Serafy, S. (1996), 'Weak and strong sustainability: natural resources and national accounting - Part I', *Environmental Taxation and Accounting*, 1(1): 27-48.

Foy, G. (1991), 'Accounting for non-renewable natural resources in Louisiana's gross state product', *Ecological Economics*, 3(1): 25-41.

Georgescu-Roegen, N. (1979), 'Comments on the papers by Daly and Stiglitz', in V. K. Smith (ed.), *Scarcity and Growth Reconsidered*, Baltimore: John Hopkins University Press.

Gerlagh, R., Dellink, R., Hofkes, M. and Verbruggen, H. (2002), 'A measure of sustainable national income for the Netherlands', *Ecological Economics*, 41(1): 157-174.

Herz, M. (1958), *A Short History of Cambodia: From the Days of Angkor to the Present*, London: Atlantic Book Publishing Company.

Hicks, J. (1946), *Value and Capital*, Second Edition, London: Clarendon.

Jackson, K. (1989), 'The intellectual origins of the Khmer Rouge', in K. Jackson (ed.), *Cambodia 1975-1978: Rendezvous with Death*, New Jersey: Princeton University Press.

Kahn, J. (2005), *The Economic Approach to Environmental Natural Resources*, Ohio: Thomson.

Kan, H. and Chen, B. (2004), 'Particulate air pollution in urban areas of Shanghai, China: health-based economic assessment', *Science of the Total Environment*, 322(1-3): 71-79.

Kellenberge, J. (1996), *Accounting for Natural Resources in Ecuador: Contrasting Methodologies, Conflicting Results*, Washington DC: World Bank.

Khor, M. (undated), *Land Degradation Cause $10 Billion Loss to South Asia Annually*, (online), Available: http://www.twnside.org.sg/title/land-ch.htm (7 August 2006).

Khy, T. (2005), 'Fishery management in Cambodia: A case study in Anlong Rang and Kompong Tralach fishing community', *Economic Institute of Cambodia*, 1(6): 13-15.

Kiernan, B. (2002), *The Pol Pot Regime*, Second Edition, New Haven: Yale University Press.

Lawn, P. (1998), 'In defence of the strong sustainability approach to national income accounting', *Environmental Taxation and Accounting*, 3(1): 29-47.

Lawn, P. (2001), *Toward Sustainable Development: An Ecological Economics Approach*, Boca Raton: Lewis Publishers.

Lawn, P. (2003), 'How important is natural capital in terms of sustaining real output? revisiting the natural capital/human-made capital substitutability debate', *International Journal of Global Environmental Issues*, 3(4): 418-435.

Lawn, P. (2007), *Frontier Issues in Ecological Economics*, Cheltenham, UK: Edward Elgar.

Leipert, C. (1989), 'Social costs of the economic process and national account: The example of defensive expenditure', *Journal of Interdisciplinary Economics*, 3(2): 27-46.

Lvovshy, K. (1998), *Economic Cost of Air Pollution with Special Reference to India*, (online), Available: http://lnweb18.worldbank.org/ SAR/sa.nsf/Attachments/EconomicCost/$File/Economic+costs+of+air+pollution+KL.pdf . (30 August 2006).

Mäler, K. (1991), 'National accounts and environmental resources', *Environmental and Resource Economics*, 1(1): 1-15.

Meadows, D. H., Meadows, D. L., Randers, J., and Behrens, W. III., Eds. (1972), *The Limits to Growth*, New York: Universe Books.

Ministry of Environment (1998), *National Environment Plan 1998-2002*, Phnom Penh, Cambodia.

Nordhaus, W. and Tobin, J. (1972), 'Is economic growth obsolete?', in The National Bureau of Economic Research (ed.), *Economic Growth*, New York: Columbia University Press.

Osborne, M. (1973), *Politics and Power in Cambodia*, Camberwell: Longman.

Pearce, D. (1993), *Blueprint 3: Measuring Sustainable Development*, Earthscan: London.

Ponchaud, F. (1977), *Cambodia: Year Zero*, New York: Holt, Rinehart and Winston.

Repetto, R., Magrath, W., Wells, M., Beer, C. and Rossini, F. (1989), *Wasting Assets: National Resources in the National Income Accounts*, Washington DC: World Resources Institute.

SBS (2002), *World Guide: The Complete Fact File on Every Country*, Tenth Edition, South Yarra: Hardie Grant Books.

Skanberg, K. (2001), *Constructing a Partially Environmentally Adjusted Net Domestic Product for Sweden, 1993 And 1997*, Working Paper 76, Konjunktur Institute.

Transparency International (various), www.transparency.org

Tully, J. (2005), *A Short History of Cambodia: From Empire to Survival*, Crows Nest: Allen & Unwin.

United Nations (UN) (1993), *Integrated Environmental and Economic Accounting (interim version)*, New York: World Bank.

United Nations Statistics Division (UNSD) (2005), *Cambodia*, (online), Available: http://unstats.un.org/unsd/snaama/resultsCountry.asp?Country=116&Year=0&SLevel=99 &Disp=Million (18 August 2005).

Van Tongeren, J., Schweinfest, S., Lutz, E., Gomez Luna, M. and Martin, G. (1993), 'Integrated economic and environmental accounting: a case study for Mexico', in E. Lutz (ed.), *Toward Improved Accounting for the Environment*, Washington DC: World Bank.

Vickery, M. (1984), *Cambodia 1975-1982*, Sydney: Allen & Unwin.

Weitzman, M. (1976), 'On the welfare significance of national product in a dynamic economy', *Quarterly Journal of Economics*, 90(1): 156-162.

World Bank (1994), *Cambodia: From Reconstruction to Rehabilitation*, Report No. 12667, Phnom Penh, Cambodia.

World Bank (2003), *Cambodia Environment Monitor*, Phnom Penh: World Bank.

World Bank (2006), *2006 World Development Indicators*, Washington, DC: World Bank.

World Commission on Environment and Development (WCED) (1987), *Our Common Future*, Oxford: Oxford University Press.

World Resources Institute (WRI) (2003), *EarthTrends: Economic Indicators, Cambodia*, (online), Available: http://earthtrends.wri.org (3 April 2006).

World Resources Institute (WRI) (2006), *EarthTrends: Climate and Atmosphere, CO2: Total Emissions, Cambodia*, (online), Available: http://earthtrends.wri.org (3 August 2006).

Yang, S. (undated), *Sustainable Agricultural Development Strategies for the Least Developed Countries of the Asian and the Pacific Region, Cambodia*, (online), Available: http://www.unescap.org/rural/doc/sads/cambodia.PDF (12 May 2006).

Young, M. (1990), 'National resource accounting', in M. Common and S. Dovers (eds), *Moving Toward Global Sustainability: Policies and Implication for Australia*, Canberra: Australian National University Press.

In: Asian Economic and Political Development
Editor: Felix Chin

ISBN: 978-1-61122-470-2
© 2011 Nova Science Publishers, Inc.

# AFGHANISTAN: NARCOTICS AND U.S. POLICY*

## *Christopher M. Blanchard*

Analyst in Middle Eastern Affairs, Foreign Affairs, Defense, and Trade Division, USA

## ABSTRACT

Opium poppy cultivation and drug trafficking have become significant factors in Afghanistan's fragile political and economic order over the last 25 years.   In 2005, Afghanistan remained the source of 87% of the world's illicit opium, in spite of ongoing efforts by the Afghan government, the United States, and their international partners to combat poppy cultivation and drug trafficking.   U.N. officials estimate that in-country illicit profits from the 2005 opium poppy crop were equivalent in value to 50% of the country's legitimate GDP, sustaining fears that Afghanistan's economic recovery continues to be underwritten by drug profits.

Across Afghanistan, regional militia commanders, criminal organizations, and corrupt government officials have exploited opium production and drug trafficking as reliable sources of revenue and patronage, which has perpetuated the threat these groups pose to the country's fragile internal security and the legitimacy of its embryonic democratic government. The trafficking of Afghan drugs also appears to provide financial and logistical support to a range of extremist groups that continue to operate in and around Afghanistan, including remnants of the Taliban regime and some Al Qaeda operatives. Although coalition forces may be less frequently relying on figures involved with narcotics for intelligence and security support, many observers have warned that drug related corruption among appointed and newly elected Afghan officials may create new political obstacles to further progress.

The initial failure of U.S. and international counternarcotics efforts to disrupt the Afghan opium trade or sever its links to warlordism and corruption after the fall of the Taliban led some observers to warn that without redoubled multilateral action, Afghanistan would succumb to a state of lawlessness and reemerge as a sanctuary for terrorists. Following his election in late 2004, Afghan president Hamid Karzai identified counternarcotics as the top priority for his administration and since has stated his belief that "the fight against drugs is the fight for Afghanistan." In 2005, U.S. and Afghan officials implemented a new strategy to provide viable economic alternatives to poppy cultivation and to disrupt corruption and narco-terrorist linkages. According to a U.N. survey, these new initiatives contributed to a 21% decrease in the amount of opium poppy cultivation across Afghanistan in the 2004-2005 growing season. However, better weather and higher crop yields ensured that overall opium output remained nearly static

---

* Excerpted from CRS Report RL32686.

at 4,100 metric tons. Survey results and official opinions suggest output may rise again in 2006.

In addition to describing the structure and development of the Afghan narcotics trade, this report provides current statistical information, profiles the trade's various participants, explores alleged narco-terrorist linkages, and reviews U.S. and international policy responses since late 2001. The report also considers current policy debates regarding the role of the U.S. military in counternarcotics operations, opium poppy eradication, alternative livelihood development, and funding issues for Congress. For more information on Afghanistan, see CRS Report RL30588, *Afghanistan: Post-War Governance, Security, and U.S. Policy.* and CRS Report RS21922, *Afghanistan: Presidential and Parliamentary Elections.*

## INTRODUCTION

In spite of ongoing international efforts to combat Afghanistan's narcotics trade, U.N. officials estimate that Afghanistan produced a massive opium poppy crop in 2005 that supplied 87% of the world's illicit opium for the second year in a row.[1] Afghan, U.S., and international officials have stated that opium poppy cultivation and drug trafficking constitute serious strategic threats to the security and stability of Afghanistan and jeopardize the success of post-9/11 counterterrorism and reconstruction efforts there. In light of the 9/11 Commission's recommendation that the United States make a long-term commitment to the security and stability of Afghanistan, counternarcotics policy has emerged as a focal point of recurring debate in the Bush Administration and in Congress concerning the United States' strategic objectives in Afghanistan and the global war against terrorism.

Concerns include the role of U.S. military personnel in counternarcotics activities and strategies for continuing the simultaneous pursuit of counterterrorism and counternarcotics goals, which may be complicated by practical necessities and emerging political realities. Coalition forces pursuing regional security and counterterrorism objectives may rely on the cooperation of commanders, tribal leaders, and local officials who may be involved in the narcotics trade. Similarly, U.S. officials and many observers believe that the introduction of a democratic system of government to Afghanistan has likely been accompanied by the election and appointment of narcotics-associated individuals to positions of public office.

Efforts to combat the opium trade in Afghanistan face the challenge of ending a highly-profitable enterprise that has become deeply interwoven with the economic, political, and social fabric of a war-torn country. Afghan, U.S., and international authorities are engaged in a campaign to reverse an unprecedented upsurge of opium poppy cultivation and heroin production: they have begun implementing a multifaceted counternarcotics initiative that includes public awareness campaigns, judicial reform measures, economic and agricultural development assistance, drug interdiction operations, and more robust poppy eradication. The Bush Administration and Congress continue to consider options for upgrading U.S. support for counternarcotics efforts in Afghanistan in order to meet the challenges posed by the Afghan opium economy to the security of Afghanistan and the international community. Questions regarding the likely effectiveness, resource requirements, and implications of new counternarcotics strategies in Afghanistan are likely to arise as such options continue to be debated.

# AFGHANISTAN'S OPIUM ECONOMY

Opium production has become an entrenched element of Afghanistan's fragile political and economic order over the last 25 years in spite of ongoing local, regional, and international efforts to reverse its growth. At the time of Afghanistan's proCommunist coup in 1978, narcotics experts estimated that Afghan farmers produced 300 metric tons (MT) of opium annually, enough to satisfy most local and regional demand and to supply a handful of heroin production facilities whose products were bound for Western Europe.[2] Since the early 1980s, a trend of increasing opium poppy cultivation and opium production has unfolded during successive periods of insurgency, civil war, fundamentalist government, and recently, international engagement (Figures 1 and 2). In 2004, Afghanistan produced a world record opium poppy crop that yielded 4200 MT of illicit opium — an estimated 87% of the world's supply. A slightly smaller crop in 2005 produced a similar volume of opium, and estimated 4,100 MT, due to improved weather and environmental conditions.

Narcotics experts describe Afghanistan's opium economy as the backbone of a multibillion dollar drug trade that stretches throughout Central and Southwest Asia and supplies heroin to consumption markets in Europe, Russia, the Middle East, and the United States. Millions of Afghans remain involved with various aspects of the opium trade, including farmers, laborers, traffickers, warlords, and government officials. Some experts have warned that the consolidation of existing relationships between these groups supports negative trends such as warlordism and corruption and threatens to transform Afghanistan into a failed narco-state.

# CURRENT PRODUCTION STATISTICS

According to the 2005 Afghanistan Opium Survey conducted by the United Nations Office on Drugs and Crime (UNODC) and the Afghan Ministry of Counternarcotics (MCN):

- Opium poppy cultivation took place in fewer Afghan provinces in 2005 than in 2004, with significant decreases occurring in some provinces and significant increases occurring in others (see Figure 3). Afghan farmers cultivated opium poppy on 104,000 hectares of land during the 2004-2005 growing season, a 21% decrease from the 131,000 hectares cultivated in 2004. The area under cultivation was equal to 2.3% of Afghanistan's arable land. U.S. government estimates placed the area under cultivation at a similar level of 107,400 hectares.
- The 2005 opium poppy crop produced 4,100 MT of illicit opium, a small decrease from the 4,200 MT produced in 2004. Although the area of land dedicated to opium poppy cultivation decreased by 21%, crop yields improved due to better weather and other environmental factors. A range of accepted opium to heroin conversion rates indicate that the 2005 opium yield of 4,100 MT could have produced 400 to 650 MT of refined heroin.[3] U.S. government estimates placed overall opium output lower at 3,375 MT.
- Approximately 309,000 Afghan families cultivated opium poppy in 2005, a number equal to roughly 2.0 million people or 8.7% of the Afghan population. An estimated

500,000 laborers and an unknown number of traffickers, warlords, and officials also participate.

- The estimated $2.7 billion value of Afghanistan's 2005 illicit opium harvest is equivalent to approximately 50% of the country's licit GDP. Many licit and emerging industries are financed or supported by profits from narcotics trafficking.[4]

The 2005 UNODC report credits the public outreach efforts of President Karzai, who has characterized opium as shameful and demanded that regional and local officials take direct action to curb poppy cultivation and opium trafficking. The report also indicates that farmers fear crop eradication and notes that the largest declines in opium poppy cultivation occurred in provinces that received the largest investments of alternative livelihood assistance. Other observers have pointed to the steady increase in opium production volume that has occurred since late 2001 and argued that excess opium supply had reduced raw opium price levels (Table 1) and price incentives for farmers to cultivate poppy. Price levels have shown signs of increase since late 2005 which may reinvigorate price incentives in some areas.

Experts have identified two factors that may affect Afghanistan's future opium output regardless of reported declines in cultivation. Intensified interdiction and eradication efforts by Afghan authorities may fuel a renewed increase in opium prices that could enrich traffickers who control large existing stocks of opium and encourage farmers to resume cultivation in the future. In addition, drought and crop disease problems that limited the output of the 2004 poppy crop may not affect the output of future poppy crops. Smaller nationwide poppy crops may yield higher opium outputs if weather and irrigation improve productivity in cultivated areas.

**Note:** The following figures display trends in poppy cultivation and opium production in Afghanistan over the last 25 years. The sharp decline in cultivation and production in the 2000-2001 growing season is related to the Taliban regime's decision to ban opium poppy cultivation. According to U.S. officials, opium trafficking continued unabated during this period, and Taliban authorities and their allies collected higher profits from the sale of opium and heroin stockpiles.[5] Note view graphing on CRS-4,5,& 6.

## Table 1. Recent Opium Prices in Afghanistan
(regionally weighted fresh opium farmgate[a] price US$/kilogram)

|             | 1999 | 2000 | 2001[b] | 2002 | 2003 | 2004 | 2005 |
|-------------|------|------|---------|------|------|------|------|
| Opium Price | $40  | $28  | $301    | $350 | $283 | $92  | $102 |

**Source:** United Nations Office on Drugs and Crime, Afghanistan Opium Survey 2004-5.
a. Farmgate price for fresh opium is the price paid to farmers for non-driedopium. b. Dry opium prices skyrocketed to nearly $700/kg immediately following the September 11, 2001 terrorist attacks and fell to $93/kg after U.S. airstrikes began.

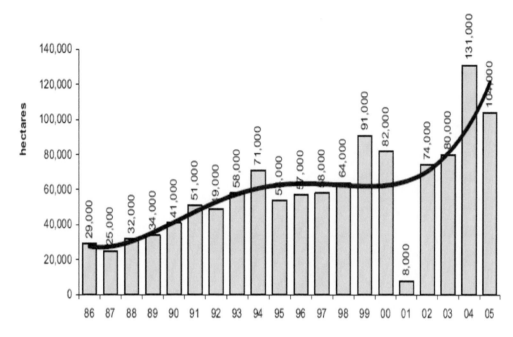

Figure 1. Opium Poppy Cultivation, 1986-2005 (hectares).

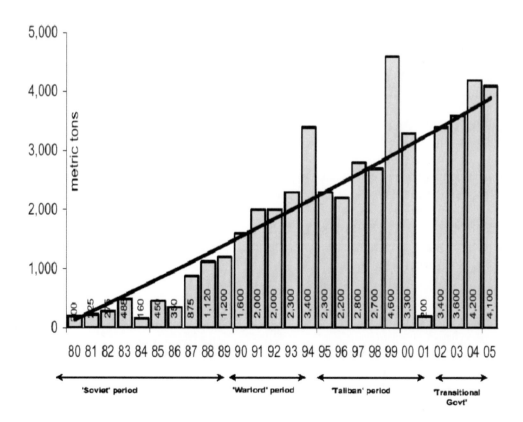

Figure 2. Opium Production, 1980-2005 (metric tons).

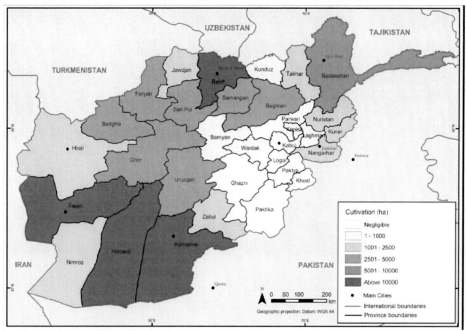

Figure 3. Opium Poppy Cultivation by Province, 2005.

# HISTORICAL DEVELOPMENT

During the more than two decades of occupation, foreign interference, and civil war that followed the 1979 Soviet invasion, opium poppy cultivation and drug trafficking served as central parts of Afghanistan's war economy, providing revenue to individuals and groups competing for power and an economic survival mechanism to a growing segment of the impoverished population. In December 2001, Afghan leaders participating in the Bonn conference that formed Afghanistan's interim post-Taliban government echoed pleas issued by their pro-Communist predecessors decades earlier:[6] They strongly urged that "the United Nations, the international community, and regional organizations cooperate with the Interim Authority to combat international terrorism, cultivation, and trafficking of illicit drugs and provide Afghan farmers with financial, material and technical resources for alternative crop production."[7] In spite of renewed efforts on the part of Afghan and international authorities to combat opium poppy cultivation since the fall of the Taliban, Afghanistan remains the world's leading producer of opium.

## Opium and Afghanistan's War Economy

Following the Soviet invasion of 1979 and during the civil war that ensued in the aftermath of the Soviet withdrawal, opium poppy cultivation expanded in parallel with the gradual collapse of state authority across Afghanistan. As the country's formal economy succumbed to violence and disorder, opium became one of the few available commodities capable of both storing economic value and generating revenue for local administration and military supplies. Some anti-Soviet mujahideen commanders encouraged and taxed opium poppy cultivation and drug shipments, and, in some instances, participated in the narcotics trade directly as a means of both economic survival and military financing.[8] Elements of Pakistan's Inter-Services Intelligence (ISI) agency and Afghan rebel commanders to which the ISI channeled U.S. funding and weaponry are also alleged to have participated in the Afghan narcotics trade during the Soviet occupation and its aftermath, including in the production and trafficking of refined heroin to U.S. and European markets.[9] After the withdrawal of Soviet troops and a drop in U.S. and Soviet funding, opium poppy cultivation, drug trafficking, and other criminal activities increasingly provided local leaders and military commanders with a means of supporting their operations and establishing political influence in the areas they controlled.

## Taliban Era

The centralization of authority under the Taliban movement during the mid-to-late 1990s further fueled Afghan opium poppy cultivation and narcotic production, as Taliban officials coopted their military opponents with promises of permissive cultivation policies and mirrored the practices of their warlord predecessors by collecting tax revenue and profits on the growing output.[10] In 1999, Afghanistan produced a peak of over 4500 MT of raw opium, which led to growing international pressure from states whose populations were consuming the end products of a seemingly endless supply of Afghan drugs. In response, the Taliban announced a ban on opium poppy cultivation in late 2000, but allowed the opiate trade to continue, fueling speculation that the decision was designed to contribute to their marginalized government's campaign for international legitimacy. Under the ban, opium poppy cultivation was reduced dramatically and overall opium output fell to 185 MT, mainly because of continued cultivation and production in areas under the control of Northern Alliance forces. Individual Northern Alliance commanders also taxed opium production and transportation within their zones of control and continued producing opium and trafficking heroin following the Taliban prohibition.[11] Although U.S. and international officials initially applauded the Taliban policy shift, many experts now believe that the ban was designed to increase the market price for and potential revenue from stocks of Afghan opium maintained by the Taliban and its powerful trafficking allies within the country.[12]

## Post-Taliban Resurgence

Following 9/11, Afghan farmers anticipated the fall of the Taliban government and resumed cultivating opium poppy as U.S.-led military operations began in October 2001. International efforts to rebuild Afghanistan's devastated society began with the organization of an interim administration at the Bonn Conference in December 2001, and Afghan leaders committed their new government to combat the resurgence of opium poppy cultivation and requested international counternarcotics assistance from the United States, the United Kingdom and others.[13]  The United Kingdom was designated the lead nation for international counternarcotics assistance and policy in Afghanistan. On January 17, 2002, the Afghan Interim Administration issued a ban on opium poppy cultivation that was enforced with a limited eradication campaign in April 2002.  In spite of these efforts, the 2001-2002 opium poppy crop produced over 3400 MT of opium, reestablishing Afghanistan as the world's leading producer of illicit opium. Since 2002, further government bans and stronger interdiction and eradication efforts failed to reverse an overall trend of increasing opium poppy cultivation and opium output, although year-on-year reductions occurred in 2005.

# ACTORS IN AFGHANISTAN'S OPIUM ECONOMY

Farmers, laborers, landowners, and traffickers each play roles in Afghanistan's opium economy. Ongoing field research indicates that the motives and methods of each group vary considerably based on their geographic location, their respective economic circumstances, their relationships with ethnic groups and external parties, and prevailing political conditions.[14] Studies suggest that profit is not the universal motivating factor fueling opium poppy cultivation in Afghanistan: opium trade field researcher David Mansfield argues that the "great diversity in the socio-economic groups involved in opium poppy in Afghanistan and the assets at their disposal" ensures that "there is great disparity in the revenues that they can accrue from its cultivation."[15] Household debt and land access needs also motivate opium poppy cultivation.

## Farmers

Field studies have identified several structural barriers that limit the profitability of opium poppy cultivation for the average Afghan farmer. Many Afghan farming households cultivate opium poppy in order to improve their access to land, water, agricultural supplies, and credit — inputs that remain in short supply in many of the rural areas where opium poppy is grown. Experts have identified high levels of household debt as a powerful structural determinant of the continuation of opium poppy cultivation among some Afghan farmers. An opium-for-credit system, known as *salaam*, allows farmers to secure loans to buy necessary supplies and provisions if they agree in advance to sell future opium harvests at rates as low as half their expected market value. Crop failures that occurred as a result of a severe four-year nationwide drought (1998-2001) reportedly caused many farming households to accumulate large amounts of debt in the form of *salaam* loans based on future cultivation of opium poppy. In some cases, the introduction of strict poppy cultivation bans and crop eradication policies by the Taliban in 2001 and the Afghan Interim Authority in 2002 and 2003 increased the debt levels of many Afghan farmers by destroying opium crops that served as collateral for *salaam* arrangements.

Although the Afghan government issued a decree banning opium-based loans and credit in April 2002, the 2005 UNODC/MCN opium survey reports that *salaam* lending has continued. Increased debt has led some farmers to mortgage land and to agree to cultivate opium poppy in the future through sharecropping arrangements. Other landless farmers have reportedly been forced to accept the crop selection choices of landowners who control their access to land and water and who favor opium poppy over other traditional crops. According to experts, this combination of drought-induced debt, predatory traditional lending systems, and the unintended side-effects from government cultivation bans and eradication programs has fueled opium poppy cultivation in Afghanistan. The 2005 UNODC/MCN opium survey warns that in areas where farmers carry high salaam and other loan debt, significant decreases in opium poppy cultivation and associated revenue may be "potentially problematic" and could create "severe financial pressure on to farmers to resume opium production [in 2006] in order not to default."

## Land Owners

Afghan land owners are better positioned to profit from opium poppy cultivation because of the labor intensive nature of the opium production process. Land owners who control vital opium cultivation inputs like land, water, and fertilizers enjoy an economic advantage in the opium production cycle, which places heavy demands on Afghanistan's rural agricultural labor market during annual opium poppy planting, maintenance, and harvesting seasons. Wealthy land owners secure the services of skilled itinerant laborers to assist in the complex opium harvesting process, which improves their crop yields and profits. Itinerant laborers, in turn, contribute to the spread of opium cultivation expertise around Afghanistan.[16] Although opium prices have fallen since reaching a peak of $350/kg in 2002, farmers have experienced greater profit loss than land owners.[17] Land owners also have benefitted from consolidation of property related to rising debt levels among Afghan farmers. Land valuation based on potential opium yields also benefits land owners.

## Traffickers

International market prices for heroin and intermediate opiates such as morphine ensure that individuals and groups engaged in the shipment and distribution of refined opium products earn substantially higher profits than those involved with cultivating and producing raw opium gum.[18] Although opium refining facilities that produce morphine base and heroin traditionally have been located in tribal areas along the Afghan border with Pakistan, the growth and spread of opium cultivation in recent years has led to a corresponding proliferation of opiate processing facilities, particularly into northeastern Badakhshan province.[19] The large proportion of heroin in the composition of drugs seized in countries neighboring Afghanistan reflects this proliferation and suggests that the profitability of opiate trafficking for Afghan groups has increased significantly in recent years.

Although Afghan individuals and groups play a significant role in trafficking opiates within Afghanistan and into surrounding countries, relatively few Afghans have been identified as participants in the international narcotics trafficking operations that bring finished opiate products such as heroin to Middle Eastern, European, or North American consumer markets.[20] Ethnic and tribal relationships facilitate the opium trade within Afghanistan, while relationships between ethnic Tajik, Uzbek, Pashtun, and Baluchi Afghans and their counterparts in Central Asia, Pakistan, and Iran provide a basis for the organization and networking needed to deliver Aghan opiates to regional markets and into the hands of international trafficking organizations.[21] Some observers argue that trafficking profits are a source of economic and political instability and that interdiction and prosecution should precede eradication efforts so that increased post-eradication opium prices do not enrich trafficking groups further. Multilateral intelligence gathering and interdiction operations have been initiated since 2001 and are described in further detail below.

## NARCOTICS AND SECURITY

Experts and officials have identified three areas of concern about the potential impact of the Afghan narcotics trade on the security of Afghanistan, the United States, and the international community. Each is first summarized, and then more fully developed below.

- **Prospects for State Failure:** Afghan, U.S., and international officials have identified several correlations between the narcotics trade and negative political and economic trends that undermine efforts to stabilize Afghanistan, establish the rule of law, and restore a functioning and licit economy. These trends include corruption and the existence of independent armed groups opposed to the Afghan government's reform and counternarcotics agendas. Similar drug-related trends threaten countries neighboring Afghanistan. Political observers have warned that figures involved with the drug trade have been elected or appointed to public office and may oppose or undermine current and future counternarcotics initiatives.
- **"Narco-Terrorism":**  Afghan and U.S. officials believe that Taliban insurgents and regional groups associated with Al Qaeda continue to profit from Afghanistan's burgeoning narcotics trade. Officials also suspect that drug profits provide some Al Qaeda operatives with financial and logistical support.  U.S. officials believe that financial and logistical relationships between narcotics traffickers, terrorists, and criminal groups pose threats to the security of Afghanistan and the wider international community.
- **Consumption and Public Health:** World health officials believe that Afghan narcotics pose social and public health risks for populations in Afghanistan, its neighbors, Russia, Western Europe, and, to a limited extent, the United States. Increased use of Afghan opiates has been closely associated with increased addiction and HIV infection levels in heroin consumption markets.

## NARCOTICS AND PROSPECTS FOR STATE FAILURE IN AFGHANISTAN

Afghan authorities and international observers have identified negative trends associated with the narcotics trade as barriers to the reestablishment of security, the rule of law, and a legitimate economy throughout Afghanistan — goals which U.S. and Afghan authorities have characterized as essential for the country's long term stability. In a September 2004 report on Afghanistan's economic development, the World Bank described these related trends as "a vicious circle" **(Figure 5)** that constitute "a grave danger" to the "entire state-building and reconstruction agenda."[22]

## Anti-Government Elements and Popular Violence

Authorities fear that heavily armed trafficking groups and regional militia may join Afghan farmers in violently resisting expanded drug interdiction and crop eradication efforts. Opium production remains a source of revenue and patronage for some armed groups and militia leaders seeking to maintain their power and influence over areas of the country at the expense of the extension of national government authority.[23] According to U.N. and Afghan officials, some armed groups impose informal taxes and checkpoint fees of 10% to 40% on farmers, traffickers, and opiate processing laboratories within their areas of control, receiving cash or payment in opium.[24] Although much of the outright conflict between regional and factional militias that motivated opium cultivation in the past has ended, long-established political and commercial networks linking armed groups, landowning elites, transportation guilds, and drug syndicates continue to constitute the foundation of the opium economy. Note: View Table on CRS-13.

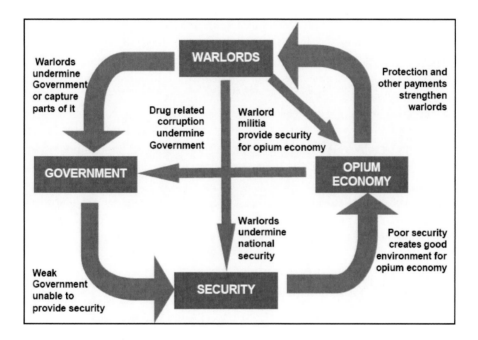

Figure 4. Narcotics and Security in Afghanistan.

Fears of widespread violence are based in large part on patterns of clashes between Afghan farmers and counternarcotics authorities seeking to eradicate crops. In April 2005, a large government eradication force clashed with approximately 2,000 villagers demonstrating against the destruction of opium crops in the southern district of Maiwand, leading to the death of one security officer and the wounding of several civilians. Afghan soldiers and police also were killed during 2005 by attackers firing on government eradication forces in Uruzgan and Kandahar. These clashes and attacks follow a pattern evident in previous years, in which eradication teams employed by provincial authorities faced demonstrations, small arms fire, and mined poppy fields.[25] At the outset of the Afghan government's first eradication campaign in April 2002, for example, Pashtun farmers barricaded the major highway linking Pakistan and Afghanistan, and clashes between opium farmers and Afghan eradication teams killed 16 people.[26]

## Corruption and Challenges to Afghan Democracy

According to the State Department, national government officials are generally "believed to be free of direct criminal connection to the drug trade," although among provincial and district level officials, "drug-related corruption is pervasive."[27] In December 2004, Afghan counternarcotics official Mirwais Yasini indicated that "high government officials, police commanders, governors are involved" in the drug trade.[28]  Government authorities and security forces in Afghanistan have accused each other of involvement in opium production and trafficking, and militia commanders have clashed over opium production and profits in various regions of the country, threatening the country's stability and the lives of civilians.[29]  Although most of Afghanistan's prominent political figures have publicly condemned the country's opium economy, some political figures and their powerful supporters are alleged to have links with the trade or hold responsibility for areas of Afghanistan where opium poppy cultivation and drug trafficking take place.  Commanders under the control of former cabinet members and former presidential candidates are alleged to participate in the opium trade.[30]

Some observers fear that as the Afghan government develops stronger counternarcotics policies and capabilities, groups that are involved with the opium trade will join others in seeking to corrupt or subvert Afghanistan's democratic process.  Although no major attempts were made to disrupt the Afghan national presidential or parliamentary elections, armed factions and local militia leaders continue to exert political influence across Afghanistan.[31] With regard to recent parliamentary elections, some experts have argued that drug money may have financed the campaigns of candidates, and at least one expert warned that "drug lords" were candidates.[32]

## Opium Profits and Afghanistan's Economic Recovery

Reports continue to indicate that profits from Afghanistan's opium trade may be overwhelming efforts to reestablish a functioning, licit economy.  According to the UNODC/MCN 2005 opium survey, the value of the 2005 opium harvest, an estimated $2.7 billion, was equal to 50% of the country's licit GDP from 2004.  The World Bank reports that the opium economy has produced significant increases in rural wages and income and remains a significant source of credit for low income rural households. Opium profits fuel consumption of domestic products and support imports of high value goods such as automobiles and appliances from abroad.  Funds from the drug trade are also a major source of investment for infrastructure development projects, including major projects in "building construction, trade, and transport."[33]  Analysts argue that efforts to combat narcotics must address Afghanistan's economic dependence on opium and replace drug profits with licit capital and investment.  In February 2005, the IMF warned that new counternarcotics efforts, if successful, "could adversely affect GDP growth, the balance of payments, and government revenue" by lowering drug income and weakening its support for domestic consumption and taxed imports.[34]

## NARCOTICS, INSURGENCY, AND TERRORISM

Afghan and U.S. officials believe that linkages between insurgents, terrorists, and narcotics traffickers threaten the security of Afghanistan and the international community. In addition to moving deadly opiates, sophisticated drug transportation and money laundering networks may also facilitate the movement of wanted individuals and terrorist funds and support illicit trafficking in persons and weapons. Although some U.S. officials have made unequivocal statements about the existence of narco-terrorist linkages, most officials address the issue in general terms and indicate that intelligence agencies are continually developing more complete pictures of these relationships. In late 2005 and early 2006, Afghan president Hamid Karzai made several statements indicating that drug profits were providing financial support to the ongoing Taliban insurgency, including funding suicide bombing operations that killed Afghan civilians. According to U.S. officials, senior Al Qaeda leaders considered and subsequently rejected the idea of becoming directly involved in managing and profiting from aspects of Afghanistan's narcotics trade. Ideological considerations and fear of increased visibility and vulnerability to foreign intelligence and law enforcement services reportedly were the predominant factors in their decision.[35] Al Qaeda operatives and the local tribal and criminal networks in the Afghanistan-Pakistan border region that are suspected of supporting and sheltering them are thought to have some involvement with the regional narcotics trade. **Table 2** describes known linkages between groups involved in terrorism and the drug trade as presented by State Department officials to Members of Congress in April 2004 and February 2005.

### Taliban and Al Qaeda Financiers

Afghan individuals serve as middlemen between the groups described in **Table 2** and narcotics producers and traffickers. Press reports and U.S. officials have identified two prominent figures involved in Afghanistan's drug trade that reportedly have financed Taliban insurgents and some low-level Al Qaeda operatives:

- **Haji Bashir Noorzai** is a former confidant of ousted Taliban leader Mullah Omar who served as a military commander during the Taliban era and was reportedly a "major financial supporter of the Taliban."[36]  In June 2004, the Bush Administration added Haji Bashir Noorzai to the U.S. government's drug kingpin list.  In April 2005, Noorzai was arrested by DEA officials and charged with conspiracy to import heroin into the United States over a 15-year period. The indictment charges that Noorzai and his organization "provided demolitions, weaponry, and manpower to the Taliban" in return for "protection for its opium crops, heroin laboratories, drug-transportation routes, and members and associates." [37]

- **Haji Baz Mohammed** is an alleged drug organization leader from the eastern province of Nangarhar who was extradited to the United States in October 2005 to face charges of importing Afghan heroin into the United States. According to his indictment, Mohammed's organization was "closely aligned with the Taliban" and "provided financial support to the Taliban and other associated Islamic-extremist organizations in Afghanistan" in return for protection.[38]
- **Haji Juma Khan** has been identified as an alleged drug lord and Al Qaeda financier. In August 2004, then-U.S. Assistant Secretary of State for International Narcotics and Law Enforcement (INL) Robert Charles told *Time Magazine* that Haji Juma Khan is "obviously very tightly tied to the Taliban." Afghan Counter Narcotics Directorate chief Mirwais Yasini added that "there are central linkages among Khan, Mullah Omar and [Osama] Bin Laden."[39]

U.S. forces reportedly detained and released both Haji Juma Khan and Haji Bashir Noorzai in late 2001 and early 2002. Press accounts state that Noorzai voluntarily provided intelligence about his Taliban and Al Qaeda colleagues during questioning at Kandahar's airport prior to his release.[40] DEA officials reportedly were unable to question him at the time.[41] Noorzai's forces later surrendered a large number of weapons to coalition and Afghan authorities and provided security for Qandahar province governor Gul Agha Sherzai.[42] Juma Khan remains at large, and Department of Defense officials indicate that U.S. military forces are not directly pursuing major figures in the Afghan opium trade, although U.S., Afghan, and coalition authorities continue to monitor and collect intelligence on their activities and support Afghan authorities and their operations.[43]

## CONSUMPTION MARKETS

Afghan opium presents significant public health and internal security challenges to downstream markets where refined heroin and other opiates are consumed, including the United States. Russia and Europe have been the main consumption markets for Afghan opiates since the early 1990s, and estimates place Afghan opium as the source of over 90% of the heroin that enters the United Kingdom and Western Europe annually. Russian and European leaders have expressed concern over the growth of Afghanistan's opium trade as both a national security threat as well as a threat to public health and safety.

### Trafficking to the United States

Heroin originating in southwest Asia (Afghanistan, Pakistan, Iran, and Turkey) "was the predominant form of heroin available in the United States" from 1980 to 1987,44 and the DEA's Heroin Signature Program has indicated that southwest Asia-derived heroin currently constitutes up to 10% of the heroin available in the United States.[45] Since the 1980s, several figures involved in the Afghan drug trade have been convicted of trafficking illegal drugs, including heroin, into the United States.[46] Afghan and Pakistani nationals have been

**Table 2. Afghan Extremists' Links to the Drug Trade**

| Afghan Extremists | Are they receiving money from the trade? | Do traffickers provide them with logistical support? | Are they telling farmers to grow opium poppy? |
|---|---|---|---|
| Hizb-i Islami/ Gulbuddin (HIG)[a] | **Almost Definitely:** HIG commanders involved in trafficking have led attacks on Coalition forces, and U.S. troops have raided labs linked to the HIG. | **Most Likely:** HIG commanders involved in the drug trade may use those ties to facilitate weapons smuggling and money laundering. | **Probably:** Afghan government officials say the Taliban encourage and in some instances force poppy cultivation. Existing State Department estimates suggest other groups interested in weakening the government in Kabul — like the HIG — may have followed suit. |
| Taliban | **Almost Definitely:** U.N. and Afghan Transitional Authority officials report the group earns money from trafficking and gets donations form drug lords. | **Most Likely:** Major drug barons who supported the Taliban when it was in power remain at large, and may be moving people, equipment, and money on the group's behalf. | |
| Islamic Movement of Uzbekistan (IMU) | **Probably:** Uzbek officials have accused the group of involvement in the drug trade, and its remnants in Afghanistan may turn to trafficking to raise funds. | **Probably:** Members with drug ties may turn to traffickers for help crossing borders. | **Possibly:** No reports, and these groups — as foreigners in Afghanistan — may lack the moral and political authority needed to influence farmers' planting decisions. |
| Al Qaeda | **Possibly:** Only scattered reports, but fighters in Afghanistan may be engaged in low-level — but still lucrative — drug deals. | **Probably:** Traffickers stopped during December 2003 in the Arabian Sea were linked to Al Qaeda. Al Qaeda may hire criminals in South Asia to transfer weapons, explosives, money, and people through the region. | |

indicted and convicted on heroin trafficking and money laundering charges in U.S. courts as recently as April 2005. In addition to the cases of Haji Bashir Noorzai and Haji Baz Mohammed noted above, the following other recent cases involve links to the Taliban and Al Qaeda:

- In the mid-1990s, several Pakistani nationals were extradited to the United States and convicted of heroin and hashish trafficking, including Haji Ayub Afridi, a former member of Pakistan's Parliament and alleged drug baron.[47]
- Since 2001, DEA and FBI investigators have prosecuted several Afghan and Pakistani nationals in connection with heroin trafficking and money laundering charges, including members of Pakistan's Afridi clan.[48] Officials have indicated that some of the individuals involved in these recent cases may have relationships with Taliban insurgents and members of Al Qaeda.[49]
- Al Qaeda operatives and sympathizers have been captured trafficking large quantities of heroin and hashish and attempting to trade drugs for Stinger missiles.[50]

## Russia

Afghan opiates have been a concern for Russian leaders since the 1980s, when Afghan drug dealers targeted Soviet troops and many Russian soldiers returned from service in Afghanistan addicted to heroin.[51] More recently, the Russian government has expressed deep concern about "narco-terrorist" linkages that are alleged to exist between Chechen rebel groups, their Islamist extremist allies, and Caucasian criminal groups that traffic and distribute heroin in Russia. Since 1993, HIV infection and heroin addiction rates have skyrocketed in Russia, and these trends have been linked to the influx and growing use of Afghan opiates. These concerns make the Afghan narcotics trade an issue of priority interest to Russian decision makers, and motivate attention and initiative on the part of Russian security services in the region. The head of Russia's counternarcotics service has announced plans to open a counternarcotics field office in Kabul.[52]

## Western Europe

In Europe, press outlets and public officials in several countries have devoted significant attention to Afghanistan's opium trade since the 1990s. In the United Kingdom, where British officials estimate that 90-95% of the heroin that enters the country annually is derived from Afghan opium, the public places a high priority on combating the Afghan opiate trade. In October 2001, British Prime Minister Tony Blair cited the Taliban regime's tolerance for opium cultivation and heroin production as one justification for the United Kingdom's involvement in the U.S.-led military campaign in Afghanistan. Some British citizens and officials have criticized the Blair Administration's counternarcotics efforts in Afghanistan and argued that more should be done to stem the flow of Afghan opiates in the future.[53] The United Kingdom currently serves as the lead nation for international counternarcotics efforts in Afghanistan, and British government officials assist Afghan counternarcotics authorities in intelligence gathering and targeting operations for interdiction and eradication. British defense officials have announced plans to send up to 4,000 British troops to the key opium-producing province of Helmand province in southern Afghanistan, where their mission reportedly will include efforts to support security operations and target narcotic traffickers.

## REGIONAL SECURITY IMPLICATIONS

Afghanistan's opiate trade presents a range of policy challenges for Afghanistan's neighbors, particularly for the Central Asian republics of the former Soviet Union. As a security issue, regional governments face the challenge of securing their borders and populations against the inflow of Afghan narcotics and infiltration by armed trafficking and terrorist groups. Regional terrorist organizations and international criminal syndicates that move Afghan opiates throughout the region have been linked to insecurity, corruption, and violence in several countries.[54] As a public health issue, Afghan narcotics have contributed to a dramatic upsurge in opiate use and addiction rates in countries neighboring Afghanistan, a factor that also has been linked to dramatic increases in HIV infection rates in many of Afghanistan's neighbors. According to the UNODC, by 2001, "Afghan opiates represented: almost 100% of the illicit opiates consumed in... Iran, Pakistan, Turkey, Kazakhstan, Turkmenistan, Kyrgyzstan, Tajikistan, Uzbekistan, Azerbaijan, and the Russian Federation." [55] With the exception of Turkey, intravenous use of Afghan opiates is the dominant driver of growing HIV infection rates in each of these countries.[56] These destabilizing factors could provide a powerful pretext for increased attention to and possible intervention in Afghan affairs on the part of regional powers such as Iran and Pakistan.

## Central Asia [57]

The emergence of the so-called "Northern Route" of opiate trafficking through Central Asia and the Caucasus in the mid-1990s transformed the region's previously small and relatively self-contained opiate market into the center of global opium and heroin trafficking. Ineffective border control, civil war, and corruption facilitated this trend, and opiate trafficking and use in Kazakhstan, Uzbekistan, Turkmenistan, and Kyrgyzstan now pose significant security and public health threats to those countries. U.S. officials have implicated the Islamic Movement of Uzbekistan in the regional drug trade, as well as well-organized and heavily armed criminal syndicates that threaten U.S. interests.

Tajikistan has emerged as the primary transit point for Afghan opiates entering Central Asia and being trafficked beyond. From 1998 to 2003, Tajikistan's Drug Control Agency seized 30 MT of drugs and narcotics, including 16 MT of heroin. U.N. authorities estimate that the European street value of the 5,600 kg of heroin seized by Tajik authorities in 2003 was over $3 billion.[58] The 201st Russian Army Division stationed troops along the Afghan-Tajik border to disrupt the activities of criminals, narcotics traffickers, and terrorist groups from 1993 through late 2004. Tajik and Russian authorities have begun replacing these Russian military forces with Tajik border security guards and are scheduled to complete the process by the end of 2006.[59] Some observers have expressed concern that the relatively poor training and inexperience of the Tajik forces may result in an increase in the flow of opium and heroin into Central Asia and onward to Russia and Europe. Others fear that Tajik security forces may prove more vulnerable to corruption than their Russian counterparts.[60] In January 2005, Russian press sources reported that Russian border guards seized 2.5 MT of heroin on the Tajik-Afghan border in 2004. A Russian-led Collective Security Treaty Organization interdiction effort known as Channel-2005 seized close to 9 MT of drugs in 2005, including over 200 kg of heroin.[61]

## Pakistan

According to the 2005 State Department International Narcotics Control Strategy Report (INCSR), "Pakistan remains a substantial trafficking country for heroin, morphine, and hashish from Afghanistan," and Pakistani narcotics traffickers "play a very prominent role in all aspects of the drug trade" in regions of Afghanistan that border Pakistan. Trafficking groups routinely use western areas of Afghanistan and Pakistan as staging areas for the movement of opiates into and through Iran. Efforts to control the narcotics trade in Pakistan have historically been complicated by the government's limited ability to assert authority over autonomous tribal zones, although recent cooperative border security efforts with the United States have increased the presence of government authorities in these regions. The Pakistani government's efforts to reduce opium poppy cultivation and heroin production since 2001 have been moderately successful; however, drug usage remains relatively high among some elements of Pakistani society. In March 2003, former U.S. Ambassador to Pakistan Wendy Chamberlain told a House International Relations Committee panel that the role of Pakistan's Inter-Services Intelligence (ISI) agency in the heroin trade from 1997-2003 had been "substantial."[62] The 2003 State Department INCSR stated that U.S. officials have "no evidence" that any senior government officials were involved with the narcotics trade or drug money laundering, although the report also stated that narcotics remained a source of "persistent corruption" among lower level officials.

## Iran

Narcotics trafficking and use continue to present serious security and public health risks to Iran, which the State Department has called "a major transit route for opiates smuggled from Afghanistan." According to the 2003 State Department INCSR, over 3200 Iranian security personnel have been killed in clashes with heavily-armed narcotics trafficking groups over the last twenty years, and 67% of HIV infections in Iran are related to intravenous drug use by the country's more than 1 million estimated addicts. Iran's interdiction efforts along its eastern borders with Afghanistan and Pakistan are widely credited with forcing opiate traffickers to establish and maintain the "Northern Route" through Central Asia. According to the State Department, Iranian officials seized 181 MT of opiates in the first six months of 2004.

The 2005 INCSR states that the Iranian government "has demonstrated sustained national political will and taken strong measures against illicit narcotics, including cooperation with the international community." Although the absence of bilateral diplomatic relations prevents the United States from directly supporting counternarcotics initiatives in Iran, the INSCR indicates that United States and Iran "have worked together productively" in the UN's multilateral "Six Plus Two" group. Shared interest in interdiction has led the United Kingdom to support the Iranian government's counternarcotics efforts since 1999 by providing millions of dollars in grants for security equipment purchases, including bullet-proof vests for Iran's border patrol guards.[63]

## THE INTERNATIONAL POLICY RESPONSE

The Bonn Agreement that established the Afghan Interim Authority committed Afghanistan's new government to cooperation with the international community "in the fight against terrorism, drugs and organized crime."[64] After taking office in early 2002, Hamid Karzai's transitional administration took a series of steps to combat the growth of the Afghan narcotics trade, including issuing a formal ban on opium cultivation, outlining a national counternarcotics strategy, and establishing institutions and forces tasked with eradicating poppy crops and interdicting drug traffic. Karzai's government places a high priority on creating alternative livelihoods and sources of income for opium growing farmers. Many countries have contributed funding, equipment, forces, and training to various counternarcotics programs in Afghanistan, including crop eradication and judicial reform. The United States and others work closely with Afghanistan's neighbors in an effort to contain the flow of narcotics and strengthen interdiction efforts.

The United Kingdom serves as the lead coalition nation for international counternarcotics policy and assistance in Afghanistan. Under British leadership, basic eradication, interdiction, and alternative livelihood development measures began in the spring of 2002. The State Department's International Narcotics and Law Enforcement (INL) Bureau administers U.S. counternarcotics and law enforcement assistance programs in Afghanistan and coordinates with the U.S. Agency for International Development (USAID), the Drug Enforcement Administration (DEA), the Government of Afghanistan, the United Kingdom, Italy, Germany, and the United Nations Office on Drugs and Crime (UNODC). To date, U.S. forces in Afghanistan have engaged in some counternarcotics activities based on limited rules of engagement, although military officials indicate that the role of the U.S. military in counternarcotics has expanded in 2005 to include police training and interdiction mission support. British military units carry out interdiction missions in cooperation with Afghan authorities that target drug production laboratories and trafficking infrastructure. The United States also provides counternarcotics assistance to other countries in the region.

The Bush Administration has begun a "five pillar" inter-agency initiative to reinvigorate U.S. support for the implementation of Afghanistan's national counternarcotics strategy. The initiative has been accompanied by a substantial increase in spending on counternarcotics programs, with particular emphasis on alternative livelihood development and greater U.S. support for crop eradication efforts. Training of and equipment for Afghan counternarcotics forces and prosecution teams also have figured prominently in the new strategy. Most observers and officials expect that a long-term, sustained international effort will be necessary to reduce the threat posed by the opium trade to the security and stability of Afghanistan and the international community.

# AFGHAN COUNTERNARCOTICS POLICIES, PROGRAMS, AND FORCES

## Bans, Prohibitions, and Policy Statements

Among the first acts of the newly established Afghan Interim Authority created by the Bonn Agreement was the issuance of a decree that banned the opium poppy cultivation, heroin production, opiate trafficking, and drug use on January 17, 2002. On April 3, 2002, Afghan authorities released a second decree that described the scope and goals of an eradication program designed to destroy a portion of the opium poppy crop that had been planted during late 2001. In order to prevent further cultivation during the autumn 2002 planting season, the government issued a third, more specific decree in September 2002 that spelled out plans for the enforcement of bans on opium cultivation, production, trafficking, and abuse.

Religious and political leaders have also spoken out adamantly against involvement in the drug trade. Islamic leaders from Afghanistan's General Council of Ulema issued a *fatwa* or religious ruling in August 2004 that declared poppy cultivation to be contrary to Islamic *sharia* law.[65] Following his election in October 2004, President Hamid Karzai has made a number of public statements characterizing involvement in opium cultivation and trafficking as shameful and stating that provincial and district leaders would be held accountable by the central government for failure to combat drug activity in areas under their control.

Afghan authorities developed a national counternarcotics strategy in 2003 in consultation with experts and officials from the United States, the United Kingdom, and the UNODC.[66] The strategy declares the Afghan government's commitment to reducing opium poppy cultivation by 70% by 2008 and to completely eliminating poppy cultivation and drug trafficking by 2013. The strategy identifies five key tactical goals to support its broader commitments: "the provision of alternative livelihoods for Afghan poppy farmers, the extension of drug law enforcement throughout Afghanistan, the implementation of drug control legislation, the establishment of effective institutions, and the introduction of prevention and treatment programs for addicts." In 2005, the Afghan government released an implementation plan for the strategy that outlines specific initiatives planned in each of the five policy areas, as well as for regional cooperation, eradication, and public information campaigns.[67] Afghanistan's new counternarcotics law clarifies administrative authorities for counternarcotics policy and establishes clear procedures for investigating and prosecuting major drug offenses.

## Institutions and Forces

In October 2002, then-Interim President Hamid Karzai announced that the Afghan National Security Council would take responsibility for counternarcotics policy and would oversee the creation and activities of a new Counternarcotics Directorate (CND). The CND subsequently established functional units to analyze data and coordinate action in five areas: judicial reform, law enforcement, alternative livelihood development, demand reduction, and public awareness. Following its establishment in late 2002, the CND worked with other Afghan ministries, local leaders, and international authorities develop counternarcotics policies and coordinate the creation of counternarcotics institutions and the training of effective personnel. The CND was transformed into a new Ministry of Counternarcotics (MCN) in December 2004. Habibullah Qaderi currently serves as Afghanistan's Minister for Counternarcotics.

Counternarcotics enforcement activities have been directed from within the Ministry of Interior since 2002. General Mohammed Daud was named Deputy Ministry of Interior for Counternarcotics in December 2004. General Daud and his staff work closely with U.S. and British officials in implementing the Afghan government's expanded counternarcotics enforcement plan. The Ministry of Interior directs the activities of the following Afghan counternarcotics and law enforcement entities.

- **Counternarcotics Police-Afghanistan (CNP-A).** The CNP-A consists of investigative and enforcement divisions whose officers work closely with U.S. and British counternarcotics authorities. CNP-A officers continue to receive U.S. training to support their ability to plan and execute counternarcotics activities independently.

- **National Interdiction Unit (NIU).** The NIU was established as an element of CNP-A in October 2004 and continues to conduct significant raids across Afghanistan. Approximately 200 NIU officers have received U.S. training and now operate in cooperation with DEA Foreign Advisory Support Teams (FAST teams, for more see below).[68]

- **Central Eradication Planning Cell (CPEC).** The CPEC is a U.K.-supported targeting and intelligence center that uses sophisticated technology and surveying to target poppy crops and monitor the success of eradication operations. The CPEC provides target data for the Central Poppy Eradication Force (CPEF).

- **Central Poppy Eradication Force (CPEF).** The U.S.-supported CPEF conducts ground-based eradication of poppy crops throughout Afghanistan based on targeting data provided by the Central Eradication Planning Cell (CPEC). The force is made up of approximately 1,000 trained eradicators and is supported by security personnel. Plans called for 3,000 CPEF officers to be trained by the end of 2005; however, Afghan and U.S. officials have expressed a preference for locally led and administered eradication efforts for 2006, after the CPEF failed to meet its targets for 2005.[69]

- **Afghan Special Narcotics Force (ASNF).** The elite ASNF, or "Force 333," has received special training from the British military and carries out interdiction missions against high value targets and in remote areas. The U.S. military provides some intelligence and airlift support for the ASNF. According to the Ministry of Counternarcotics, the ASNF has destroyed over 150 MT of opium, 45 MT of precursor chemicals, and 191 drug laboratories.

- **Border Police, National Police, and Highway Police.** Approximately 27,000 Afghan police have graduated from U.S.-sponsored training facilities, and elements of all three forces have received training, equipment, and communications support from British, German, and U.S. authorities to improve their counternarcotics enforcement capabilities. U.S. and German authorities planned to train 50,000 border and national police by December 2005.

# U.S. POLICY INITIATIVES: THE "FIVE-PILLAR" PLAN

In spite of limited efforts on the part of Afghan, U.S., and international authorities, the land area used for opium poppy cultivation in Afghanistan and Afghanistan's corresponding opiate output increased annually from late 2001 through 2004. Although public awareness of government opium poppy cultivation bans and laws outlawing participation in the narcotics trade is widespread, until recently, counternarcotics enforcement activities have been hindered by the Afghan government's tactical inability to carry out nationwide, effective eradication and interdiction campaigns as well as a lack of adequate legal infrastructure to support drug-related prosecutions. International development agencies have made positive, but limited, efforts to address structural economic issues associated with rural livelihoods and drug production, such as household debt and the destruction of local agricultural market infrastructure. These efforts were not centrally coordinated or linked directly to counternarcotics goals and initiatives until late 2004.

Substantial growth in opium poppy cultivation and narcotics trafficking led U.S. officials, in consultation with their Afghan and coalition partners, to develop a more comprehensive, complementary plan to support the implementation of the Afghan national counternarcotics strategy. The evolving policy initiative developed by U.S. agencies consists of five key elements, or pillars, that mirror Afghan initiatives and call for increased interagency and international cooperation.[70] The five pillars of the U.S. initiative are public information, judicial reform, alternative livelihood development, interdiction, and eradication. New initiatives in these areas are building upon a range of preexisting policy initiatives being implemented by U.S., Afghan, and coalition authorities.

## Public Information

Afghan and U.S. authorities have initiated public information campaigns to reach out to ordinary Afghans and raise public awareness about the threat of narcotics and the danger of participation in the illegal drug trade.[71] The efforts build on the Afghan government's public awareness strategy, which enlists local community and religious leaders to support the government's counternarcotics policies and encourages them to speak out in their communities against drug use and involvement the opium trade. As noted above, Islamic leaders from Afghanistan's General Council of Ulema have supported this effort by publicly condemning poppy cultivation and involvement in the drug trade.[72]

The U.S. campaigns supplement existing public information efforts designed to reduce demand for illegal drugs within Afghan society and spread awareness of the Afghan government's opium poppy cultivation bans and drug laws. The UNODC/MCN 2005 Opium Survey found that farmers across Afghanistan were well aware of the government's ban on opium poppy cultivation and that many farmers who declined to cultivate opium poppy did so because they feared eradication or incarceration. An earlier survey also reported that farmers in provinces where opium poppy cultivation was found to have increased believed that the government could not or would not enforce the ban.

## Judicial Reform

Department of State (INL office) and Department of Justice personnel are undertaking judicial reform efforts to further enable Afghan authorities to enforce counternarcotics laws and prosecute prominent individuals involved in narcotics trafficking. A Counternarcotics Vertical Prosecution Task Force (CNVPTF) is under development and will feature integrated teams of Afghan judges, prosecutors, and enforcement officials that are being specially trained to handle complex, high-profile cases.  Some U.S. federal prosecutors are participating in CNVPTF training activities in Afghanistan.  In 2005, an Afghan team of ten investigators, seven prosecutors, and three judges began serving under the jurisdiction of the Kabul criminal court and are currently processing cases against narcotics suspects and detainees.  The U.S. Department of Defense is supporting construction activities for a maximum-security wing at the Pol-i-Charki prison near Kabul to hold narcotics offenders prosecuted by the Task Force.  Afghan and coalition officials are currently working to identify targets for prosecution, although, according to U.S. officials, political concerns and security considerations will play a role in the targeting of individuals.

The April 2005 arrest of Haji Bashir Noorzai by U.S. officials and the extradition of Haji Baz Mohammed raised concern about the readiness and ability of Afghan authorities to investigate, prosecute, and incarcerate drug suspects independently.  According to an Afghan Interior Ministry official, "Afghan police had no role in [Noorzai's] arrest," and Afghan authorities were constrained because of "a lack of concrete evidence against him."[73] Discussion of a limited amnesty program for prominent narcotics traffickers surfaced in January 2005 but is reportedly no longer under consideration.[74] With U.S. and coalition support, the government of Afghanistan drafted and issued a new counternarcotics law in December 2005 that clarifies administrative authorities for counternarcotics policy and establishes clear procedures for investigating and prosecuting major drug offenses.

## Alternative Livelihood Development [75]

In order to provide viable economic alternatives to opium poppy cultivation and drug production, U.S. officials have developed a three-phased plan that directly links development initiatives to overall counternarcotics efforts through a comprehensive program targeted to opium producing areas.  The first phase of the alternative livelihoods plan accelerated existing agricultural development initiatives, including improvements to agricultural market infrastructure, farmer education programs, and micro-credit lending systems to support rural families.  The new efforts build on existing USAID programs to develop integrated systems of crop processing facilities, storage areas, roads, and markets, and to restore wheat and other cereal crop production levels.  Work began on phase one projects in early 2005 and will continue through 2006.

The second phase of the plan consists of a one-year "immediate needs"/ "cash-for-work" program that is sponsoring labor intensive work projects to provide non-opium incomes to rural laborers and to rehabilitate agricultural infrastructure.  The program began in December 2004 and has been renewed for 2006.  USAID personnel design "immediate needs" projects in consultation with local councils and tribal leaders in districts where crop eradication has been planned or where farmers have agreed to cease poppy cultivation.[76]  According to USAID, in main opium producing provinces, USAID-sponsored alternative livelihood cash-for-work programs generated 4.5 million work days in 2005 and paid $15.7 million in salaries to 194,000 people who otherwise may have engaged in or supported opium poppy cultivation. Over 6,00 km of irrigation canals, drainage ditches, nd traditional water transportation systems were repaired and cleaned in a number of provinces, improving irrigation and supporting high value agriculture on an estimated 290,000 hectares of land.[77]

The third, "comprehensive development" phase of the plan began in six key poppy-producing provinces during 2005 and is scheduled to be implemented through 2009. Current and planned projects include long-term infrastructure development for urban and rural areas, credit and financial services expansion, agricultural diversification, and private investment support. The Afghan government requested that USAID expand alternative livelihood programs into the provinces of Ghor, Dai Kundi, Konar, Farah, and Uruzgan, and USAID personnel have consulted with contractors and security officials and initiated preliminary projects in some of those provinces.

**Table 3. Alternative Livelihood Proposed Spending Targets by Province, FY2005-2007**
**($ millions)**

| Province | Immediate Needs | Comprehensive Development | 2004 Province Share of Nationwide Poppy Cultivated Area |
|---|---|---|---|
| Nangarhar and Laghman | $18 | $110 | 21.1% |
| Helmand and Kandahar | $19 | $120 | 34.2% |
| Badakhshan and Takhar | $1.5 | $60 | 8.6% |

Accountability standards have been built into the USAID alternative livelihood programs, including seed and fertilizer distributions and cash-for-work programs. Seed and fertilizer recipients, including government officials, are required to agree in writing not to grow poppy in exchange for program support. Cash-for-work program participants must make similar commitments, and program staff monitor participant activities outside of the program to ensure compliance. According to USAID, all alternative livelihood program assistance is 100% conditional on the reduction of poppy cultivation within one year of the receipt of assistance.[78] For example, alternative livelihood assistance was denied to the border district of Achin in eastern Nangarhar province during 2005 because its inhabitants refused to halt poppy cultivation. Some villages in Achin that subsequently agreed to abandon poppy farming during the current season are scheduled to receive alternative livelihood assistance on a conditional basis in 2006.

## Interdiction

Reflecting on the absence of effective counternarcotics institutions and authorities in post-Taliban Afghanistan, international authorities led by the United States Drug Enforcement Administration (DEA) established a series of cooperative interdiction initiatives in countries neighboring Afghanistan beginning in early 2002. The primary U.S.-led effort, known as "Operation Containment," is designed to "implement a joint strategy to deprive drug trafficking organizations of their market access and international terrorist groups of financial support from drugs, precursor chemicals, weapons, ammunition and currency."[79] Operation Containment has continued since early 2002 and currently involves "nineteen countries from Central Asia, the Caucasus, Europe and Russia."[80] According to the DEA, Operation Containment activities were responsible for the seizure of "2.4 metric tons of heroin, 985 kilograms of morphine base, three metric tons of opium gum, 152.9 metric tons of cannabis, and 195 arrests" in the first quarter of 2005.[81] A similar multinational DEA-led effort named Operation Topaz has focused on interdicting acetic anhydride — a primary heroin production precursor chemical — to Afghanistan.

In addition to ongoing international narcotics and precursor interdiction initiatives under Operation Containment and Operation Topaz, U.S. officials are providing increased support to Afghan government interdiction efforts through intelligence cooperation, training programs, equipment transfers, and joint operations. The DEA has expanded its presence in Afghanistan since January 2003, although in the past DEA officials have cited restrictions on the capabilities and freedom of movement of their staff in Afghanistan due to a general lack of security outside of Kabul. DEA Foreign Advisory and Support Teams (FAST) have been deployed to Afghanistan "to provide guidance and conduct bilateral investigations that will identify, target, and disrupt illicit drug trafficking organizations." The FAST teams receive Defense Department support and are currently conducting operations and providing mentoring to newly-trained Afghan recruits. DEA received new FY2006 funding to expand its operational presence in Afghanistan and Central Asia, including support for FAST teams, Operation Containment activities, and new field officers.

Current U.S. Department of Defense directives state that U.S. military forces in Afghanistan do not and will not directly target drug production facilities or pursue drug traffickers as a distinct component of ongoing U.S. counternarcotics initiatives.[82] Current rules of engagement allow U.S. forces to seize and destroy drugs and drug infrastructure discovered during the course of routine military operations carried out in pursuit of conventional counterterrorism and stability missions.[83] U.S. forces continue to provide limited intelligence and air support to Afghan and British forces during interdiction missions, including the destruction of heroin laboratories and opiate storage warehouses. U.S. initiatives that supply Afghan police with tents, boots, communication equipment, mobility support, infrastructure improvements, and training are expected to continue. Defense Department and military personnel plan to focus future efforts on further improving Afghanistan's border security and providing greater intelligence support to Afghan law enforcement officials through joint military/DEA/Afghan "intelligence fusion centers" located at U.S. facilities in Kabul and the Afghan Ministry of Interior.[84]

British forces currently contribute to a central targeting operation that identifies opiate warehouses and processing facilities for destruction. British Customs and Excise authorities also work with Afghan officials through mobile heroin detection units in Kabul. British military forces reportedly will operate under more permissive rules of engagement that will allow them to carry out "opportunistic strikes" against narcotics infrastructure and to support Afghan eradication teams with a "rapid-reaction force." British defense officials have announced plans to send up to 4,000 British troops to the key opium-producing province of Helmand province in southern Afghanistan, where their mission reportedly will include efforts to support security operations and target narcotic traffickers. [85]

## Eradication

Critics have cited growth in opium poppy cultivation figures as evidence that manual eradication campaigns have failed to serve as a credible deterrent for Afghan farmers. Plans developed by the Department of State, in consultation with Afghan authorities, called for early and more robust opium poppy eradication measures for the 2004-2005 growing season to provide a strong deterrent to future cultivation. The Afghan Central Poppy Eradication Force (CPEF) carried out limited operations with support from U.K. intelligence officers, U.S. advisors, and international contractors in early 2005. Field reports indicated that CPEF personnel met violent resistance from farmers in some instances and largely failed to meet their eradication targets for the 2004-2005 season.[86]

The centrally organized and executed eradication plan marked a departure from previous eradication campaign strategies, which largely relied upon governors and local authorities to target and destroy crops. Most governors pledged to support President Karzai's eradication initiatives in 2005, and U.S. officials report that areas where governors and local leaders embraced and enforced the central government's eradication demands saw significant reductions in poppy cultivation. During the current season, "poppy elimination programs" (PEPs) are being established in select Afghan provinces. The PEPs are led by small U.S. interagency and international teams that will direct and monitor locally led and administered counternarcotics activities, including eradication. U.S. officials have stressed the importance of early season, locally executed eradication in order to minimize violent farmer resistance and give Afghan farmers time to plant licit replacement cash crops.

## ISSUES FOR CONGRESS

Experts and government officials have warned that narcotics trafficking may jeopardize the success of international efforts to secure and stabilize Afghanistan. U.S. officials believe that efforts to reverse the related trends of opium cultivation, drug trafficking, corruption, and insecurity must expand if broader strategic objectives are to be achieved. A broad interagency initiative to assist Afghan authorities in combating the narcotics trade has been developed, but the effectiveness of new U.S. efforts will not be apparent until later this year. Primary issues of interest to the Congress include program funding, the role of the U.S. military, and the scope and nature of eradication and development assistance initiatives. The 108th Congress addressed the issue of counternarcotics in Afghanistan in intelligence reform proposals, and the first session of the 109th Congress considered new counternarcotics policy proposals in relation to FY2006 appropriation and authorization requests.

## BREAKING THE NARCOTICS-INSECURITY CYCLE

As noted above, narcotics trafficking and political instability remain intimately linked across Afghanistan. U.S. officials have identified narcotics trafficking as a primary barrier to the establishment of security and consider insecurity to be a primary barrier to successful counternarcotics operations. Critics of existing counternarcotics efforts have argued that Afghan authorities and their international partners remain reluctant to directly confront prominent individuals and groups involved in the opium trade because of their fear that confrontation will lead to internal security disruptions or armed conflict with drug-related groups. Afghan authorities have expressed their belief that "the beneficiaries of the drugs trade will resist attempts to destroy it," and have argued that "the political risk of internal instability caused by counternarcotics measures" must be balanced "with the requirement to project central authority nationally" for counternarcotics purposes.[87] Conflict and regional security disruptions have accompanied recent efforts to expand crop eradication programs and previous efforts to implement central government counternarcotics policies.

U.S. officials have identified rural security and national rule of law as prerequisites for effective counternarcotics policy implementation, while simultaneously identifying narcotics as a primary threat to security and stability.[88] Although an increasing number of Afghan police, security forces, and counternarcotics authorities are being trained by U.S. and coalition officials, the size and capability of Afghan forces may limit their power to effectively challenge entrenched drug trafficking groups and regional militia in the short term. Specifically, questions remain as to whether Afghan security and counternarcotics forces alone will be able to establish the security conditions necessary for the more robust eradication, interdiction, and alternative livelihood programs planned by U.S. and Afghan officials. From a political perspective, U.S. officials expect that parliamentary and provincial elections will contribute to the political legitimacy of government counternarcotics initiatives; however, the creation of sufficient political and military stability for effective counternarcotics operations is likely to remain a significant challenge. The death of several local contractor employees working on USAID alternative livelihood projects in May 2005 brought renewed urgency to these concerns.

## BALANCING COUNTERTERRORISM AND COUNTERNARCOTICS

In pursuing counterterrorism objectives, Afghan and coalition authorities also must consider difficult political choices when confronting corrupt officials, militia leaders, and narcotics traffickers. Regional and local militia commanders with alleged links to the opium trade played significant roles in coalition efforts to undermine the Taliban regime and capture Al Qaeda operatives, particularly in southeastern Afghanistan. Since late 2001, some of these figures have been incorporated into government and security structures, including positions of responsibility for enforcing counternarcotics policies.[89] According to Afghanistan scholar Barnett Rubin, "the empowerment and enrichment of the warlords who allied with the United States in the anti-Taliban efforts, and whose weapons and authority now enabled them to tax and protect opium traffickers," have provided the opium trade "with powerful new protectors."[90]

Pragmatic decisions taken since 2001 to prioritize counterterrorism operations and current plans to enforce counternarcotics policies more strictly may conflict with each other, forcing Afghan and coalition authorities to address seemingly difficult contradictions. "Tactical" coalition allies in militia and other irregular forces with ties to the drug trade may inhibit the ability of the central government to extend its authority and enforce its counternarcotics policies. These issues may weigh strongly in decision concerning the feasibility and prospects for success of continuing counterterrorism and counternarcotics operations. One senior Defense Department official has argued that U.S. counternarcotics strategy in Afghanistan must recognize "the impact the drug trade has on our other policy objectives, while complementing (and not competing with) our other efforts in furtherance of those objectives."[91]

## DEFINING THE ROLE OF THE U.S. MILITARY

Some observers have argued that U.S. and coalition military forces should play an active, direct role in targeting the leaders and infrastructure of the opiate trade. Although U.S. Central Command (CENTCOM) officials have indicated that "the DoD counter-narcotics program in Afghanistan is a key element of our campaign against terrorism,"[92] military officials reportedly have resisted the establishment of a direct counternarcotics enforcement role for U.S. forces in Afghanistan. Critics claim that a direct enforcement role for U.S. or coalition forces may alienate them from the Afghan population, jeopardize ongoing counterterrorism missions that require Afghan intelligence support, and divert already stretched military resources from direct counter-insurgent and counterterrorism operations. According to the Defense Department, U.S. military forces are authorized to seize narcotics and related supplies encountered during the course of normal stability and counterterrorism operations.

Current U.S. policy calls for an expanded role for U.S. military forces in training, equipping, and providing intelligence and airlift support for Afghan counternarcotics teams but stops short of elevating narcotics targets to a direct priority for U.S. combat teams. Defense Department officials agreed in March 2005 to provide limited airlift assistance (four operations per month) to U.S. and Afghan interdiction teams using U.S. Blackhawk and Soviet-era Mi-8 helicopters. Successful interdiction operations in remote areas have been carried out on this basis since mid-March 2005, and further helicopter leasing and pilot training arrangements have been made.

The conference report (H.Rept. 109-360) on the National Defense Authorization Act for Fiscal Year 2006 (P.L. 109-163) did not include a provision included in the Senate version of the bill (S. 1042, Section 1033) that would have allowed the Defense Department to provide a range of technical and operational support to Afghan counternarcotics authorities based on an element of the National Defense Authorization Act for Fiscal Year 1991 (P.L. 101- 510, Section 1004). The Senate version would have authorized "the use of U.S. bases of operation or training facilities to facilitate the conduct of counterdrug activities in Afghanistan" in response to the Defense Department's request "to provide assistance in all aspects of counterdrug activities in Afghanistan, including detection, interdiction, and related criminal justice activities."[93] This would have included transportation of personnel and supplies, maintenance and repair of equipment, the establishment and operation of bases and training facilities, and training for Afghan law enforcement personnel.

## REDEFINING ERADICATION

Proponents of swift, widespread eradication argued that destroying a large portion of the 2004-2005 opium poppy crop was necessary in order to establish a credible deterrent before opium production in Afghanistan reaches an irreversible level. Critics of widespread, near-term eradication argued that eradication in the absence of existing alternative livelihood options for Afghan farmers would contribute to the likelihood that farmers would continue to cultivate opium poppy in the future by deepening opium based debt and driving up opium prices.[94] U.S. and Afghan authorities maintain that the Central Poppy Eradication Force and governor-led eradication programs were effective in deterring and reducing some opium poppy cultivation in 2005. However, given recurrent clashes between eradication forces and farmers, some observers and officials have expressed concern about the safety and effectiveness of current ground-based eradication efforts. During the 2006 season, "poppy elimination program" teams will be in place in key opium poppy growing provinces to monitor and direct early season, locally-executed eradication activities. This strategy is designed to minimize violent farmer resistance to central government forces and give farming families time to plant replacement cash crops.

## Aerial Eradication

Policy makers are likely to engage in further debate concerning the option of aerial poppy eradication and its possible risks and rewards. Afghan and U.S. authorities discussed the introduction of aerial eradication to Afghanistan in late 2004, but decided against initiating a program in early 2005 due to financial, logistical, and political considerations. Afghan President Hamid Karzai has expressed his categorical opposition to the use of aerial eradication, citing public health and environmental safety concerns.[95] Proponents of aerial eradication argue that the large amount of rural land under poppy cultivation in Afghanistan and poor road infrastructure makes ground-based eradication inefficient and subjects eradication teams to unnecessary security threats. Critics of aerial eradication argue that the mixed-crop cultivation patterns common throughout Afghanistan will expose legitimate food crops to damage and warn that aerial spraying may produce widespread, possibly violent resistance by villagers with vivid memories of centrally directed Soviet military campaigns to destroy food crops and agricultural infrastructure. The Senate report on the FY2005 supplemental appropriations bill (H.R. 1268) specifies that "none of the funds recommended by the Committee may be available for aerial eradication programs within Afghanistan absent a formal request by the President of Afghanistan seeking such support."

Reports of unauthorized aerial spraying in eastern Nangarhar province in mid-November 2004 angered Afghan officials and led to an investigation by the Afghan Ministries of Agriculture and Health of claims that crops had been sprayed with herbicides by unidentified aircraft. The government investigation reportedly revealed that unidentified chemicals were present in soil samples, that non-narcotic crops had been destroyed, and that an increase in related illnesses in local villages had occurred. Afghan officials cited U.S. control of Afghan airspace in their subsequent demands for an explanation. U.S. and British officials have denied involvement in the spraying and assured Afghan authorities that they support President Karzai's position.[96] In early December 2004, then-U.S. Ambassador to Afghanistan Zalmay Khalilzad suggested that "some drug-associated people" may have sprayed the crops "in order to create the sort of distrust and problem between Afghanistan and some of its allies."[97] Observers noted that the vocal negative reaction of the Afghan population and government to an alleged isolated spraying incident illustrates the type of popular opposition that may accompany any future aerial eradication program.

Afghan government officials would have to approve any future aerial spraying operations undertaken by U.S. or coalition forces in Afghanistan. Any future aerial eradication in Afghanistan also would require specific funding and the introduction of airframes and military support aircraft that exceed current U.S. capabilities in the region. Aerial eradication programs, if employed in the future, could feature the use of chemical herbicide such as the glyphosate compound currently approved for use in Colombia. The use of *mycoherbicides*, or fungal herbicides, also has been discussed. Opium poppy-specific mycoherbicide has been developed with U.N., U.K., and U.S. support at the Institute of Genetics and Experimental Biology, a former Soviet biological warfare facility in Tashkent, Uzbekistan.[98] Mycoherbicide tests continue, including efforts by USDA's Agricultural Research Service , although USDA officials and others have expressed various concerns about the use of mycoherbicides for counternarcotics purposes.[99]

## PENDING LEGISLATION AND COUNTERNARCOTICS FUNDING

Several intelligence reform proposals in the 108th Congress sought to address the 9/11 Commission's recommendation on expanding the U.S. commitment to Afghanistan's security and stability, including U.S. counternarcotics efforts. Section 7104 of the Intelligence Reform and Terrorism Prevention Act of 2004 (P.L. 108 —458) states the sense of Congress that "the President should make the substantial reduction of illegal drug production and trafficking in Afghanistan a priority in the Global War on Terrorism" and calls on the Administration to provide a secure environment for counternarcotics personnel and to specifically target narcotics operations that support terrorist organizations. The act also required the submission of a joint Defense and State Department report within 120 days of enactment that described current progress toward the reduction of  poppy cultivation and heroin production in Afghanistan and provided detail on the extent to which drug profits support terrorist groups and anti-government elements in and around Afghanistan.

In the 109th Congress, H.R. 1437, the "Afghan Poppy Eradication and Prosperity Act of 2005," would authorize $1 billion to support a two-year USAID-led cash-for-work and poppy eradication pilot program in Afghanistan. Under the program, Afghan laborers would receive $10 per day of work.  As noted above, cash-for-work programs are currently being administered by USAID and British authorities in Afghanistan. The bill would require an annual report from USAID on progress toward poppy eradication and alternative livelihood creation. The bill has been referred to the House Committee on International Relations.

### Counternarcotics Funding

Funding for U.S. counternarcotics operations in Afghanistan consists of program administration costs and financial and material assistance to Afghan counternarcotics authorities. Table 4 displays the funding appropriated for U.S. counternarcotics activities in Afghanistan and related regional programs from FY2002 through FY2006.

## Table 4. U.S. Counternarcotics Funding for Afghanistan by Source, FY2002-FY2006
($ million)

| | FY2002 | | FY2003 | | FY2004 | | | FY2005 | | FY2006 | |
|---|---|---|---|---|---|---|---|---|---|---|---|
| | Appropriated Funds | P.L. 107-206 | Appropriated Funds | P.L. 108-11 | Appropriated Funds | P.L. 108-106 | P.L. 107-38 | Appropriated Funds | P.L. 109-13 | P.L. 109-13 | Appropriated Funds |
| Department of State | $3.00[a] | $60.00 | $3.00[a] | $25.00 | - | $170.00[b] | $50.00[c] | $89.28 | $260.00 | | $235.00 |
| Department of Defense | - | - | - | - | - | $73.00 | - | $15.40 | $242.00 | | - |
| Drug Enforcement Agency[d] | ($0.58) | - | ($2.92) | - | ($3.96) | | | ($7.67) | $7.65 | | $17.60[e] |
| USAID[f] | - | $9.99 | $14.29 | - | $53.55 | | | $95.69 | $248.50 | | $90.50[g] |
| **Annual Total** | **$73.57** | | **$45.21** | | **$350.51** | | | **$966.19** | | | **$343.10** |

**Sources:** U.S. Agency for International Development - Budget Justifications to the Congress, Department of State - Congressional Budget Justifications for Foreign Operations, Office of the Secretary of Defense - Defense Budget Materials, Office of Management and Budget, and Legislative Information System. [a] $3 million funding for Southwest Asia Initiative counternarcotics programs in Pakistan partially designed to restrict the flow of Afghan opiates. [b] Of the $170 million funding for Southwest Asia Initiative counternarcotics programs in Pakistan, $110 million was channeled toward police training and judicial reform programs. [c] Reprogrammed funds appropriated as part of $40 billion Emergency Response Fund established in the aftermath of the September 11th attacks. [d] On May 8, 2002, Congress approved a reprogramming of 17 positions and $15,125,000 in Violent Crime Reduction Fund prior year funds to support the Drug Enforcement Administration's 'Operation Containment', which targets heroin trafficking in Southwest Asia. The figures for FY2002-FY2005 reflect annual expenditure of the reprogrammed obligated funds. (DEA response to CRS request, October 2004.) [e] FY2006 funds include $7.72 million for Operation Containment, $4.3 million to support Foreign Advisory Support Teams (FAST) teams, and $5.58 million for DEA offices in Kabul and Dushanbe, Tajikistan. New funds were not appropriated for the creation of a DEA office in Dubai, United Arab Emirates authorized in House Report 109-272. [f] USAID figures for FY2002-FY2005 reflect funds applied to USAID's "Agriculture" and "Agriculture and Alternative Livelihoods" programs (Program #306-001). [g] USAID will shift activities currently funded through its"Agriculture and Alternative Livelihoods" program to a "Thriving Economy Led by the Private Sector" program (Program #306-YYY). Relevant funds include $90.5 million to "Develop and Expand Alternative Development."

**Table 5. Planned Use of FY2005 Supplemental Appropriations, P.L. 109-13**

($ million)

| Agency | Amount | Proposed Purpose |
|---|---|---|
| Department of Defense (Drug Interdiction and Counter-Drug Activities) | $242 | Funds for training, equipment, intelligence, infrastructure, and information operations related to the campaign against narcotics trafficking and narcotics-related terrorist activities in Afghanistan and the Central Asia area. Of this amount, $70 million restored funding to other DoD counternarcotics activities from which funds were used to finance counter-drug assistance to Afghanistan. P.L. 109-13 limited the provision of assistance to $34 million for the Afghan government and allows for the delivery of individual and crew-served weapons for counter-drug security forces. (Note: The Administration's original request was for $257 million.) |
| Department of State (International Narcotics Control and Law Enforcement Account) | $260 | Funds to continue the expanded counternarcotics effort in Afghanistan begun in FY2005. Of the total amount requested, $95 million replenished funding advanced to start expanded crop eradication, establishment of a National Interdiction Unit, prosecution of drug traffickers, and public information programs. The remaining $165 million supported the Department of State's contribution to expanded efforts in eradication ($89 million), interdiction ($51 million), law enforcement ($22 million), and public information ($3 million). |
| United States Agency for International Development (Economic Support Fund) | $248.5 | Funds to support alternative livelihoods programs. A portion ($138.5 million) of the amount replenished reconstruction and development aid accounts that had been drawn on previously to create alternative livelihood programs in late 2004 and early 2005. The balance ($110 million) is being used to expand alternative livelihood programs beyond pilot provinces. |
| Drug Enforcement Agency | $7.65 | Funds to support and equip DEA's Foreign Advisory Support Teams (FAST) and to provide operational support for a 100-member Afghan Narcotics Interdiction Unit (NIU). |
| **Total FY2005 Supplemental Appropriation** | **$758.15** | |

**Source:** P.L. 109-13 and Office of Management and Budget, Estimate #1: Emergency Supplemental — Ongoing Military Operations in the War on Terror; Reconstruction Activities in Afghanistan; Tsunami Relief and Reconstruction; and Other Purposes, February 14, 2005.

Table 5 describes the Administration's planned use for the counternarcotics funding included in the FY2005 supplemental appropriation (P.L. 109-13), which provided $758.15 million of the $773.15 million in supplemental FY2005 counternarcotics funding originally requested by the Administration. Under the terms of P.L. 109-13, the Comptroller General must conduct an audit of the use of all Economic Support Fund and International Narcotics Control and Law Enforcement funds for bilateral counternarcotics and alternative livelihood programs in Afghanistan obligated and expended during FY2005. The General Accounting Office is currently conducting this audit. Requests for further funding for Department of Defense counternarcotics activities in Afghanistan will likely be made as part of future supplemental funding requests.

## APPENDIX A

### Cited Field Surveys

Jonathan Goodhand, "From Holy War to Opium War: A Case Study of the Opium Economy in North Eastern Afghanistan," Peacebuilding and Complex Emergencies Working Paper Series, Paper No. 5, University of Manchester, 1999.

Frank Kenefick, and Larry Morgan, "Opium in Afghanistan: People and Poppies —The Good Evil," Chemonics International Inc. for USAID, February 5, 2004.

Aga Kahn Foundation, "Badakhshan Province: Suggestions for an Area Development Based Counter-narcotics Strategy," April 2004.

David Mansfield, "Coping Strategies, Accumulated Wealth and Shifting Markets: The Story of Opium Poppy Cultivation in Badakhshan 2000-2003," Agha Khan Development Network, January 2004.

David Mansfield, "Alternative Development in Afghanistan: The Failure of Quid Pro Quo," International Conference on the Role of Alternative Development in Drug Control and Development Cooperation, January 2002.

Adam Pain, "The Impact of the Opium Poppy Economy on Household Livelihoods: Evidence from the Wakhan Corridor and Khustak Valley in Badakhshan," Aga Kahn Development Network, Badakhshan Programme, January 2004.

UNODC, "An Analysis of the Process of Expansion of Opium Cultivation to New Districts in Afghanistan," Strategic Study #1, June 1998.

UNODC, "The Dynamics of the Farmgate Opium Trade and the Coping Strategies of Opium Traders," Strategic Study #2, October 1998.

UNODC, "The Role of Opium as an Informal Credit," Preliminary Strategic Study #3, January 1999.

UNODC, "Access to Labour: The Role of Opium in the Livelihood Strategies of Itinerant Harvesters Working in Helmand Province, Afghanistan," Strategic Study #4, June 1999.

UNODC, "The Role of Women in Opium Poppy Cultivation in Afghanistan," Strategic Study #6, June 2000.

# REFERENCES

[1]    United Nations Office on Drugs and Crime (UNODC)/Government of Afghanistan Counternarcotics Directorate (CND), Afghanistan Opium Survey 2004, Nov. 2004.

[2]    See Jonathan C. Randal, "Afghanistan's Promised War on Opium," *Washington Post*, Nov. 2, 1978, and   Stuart Auerbach, "New Heroin Connection: Afghanistan and Pakistan Supply West With Opium," *Washington Post*, Oct. 11, 1979.

[3]    UNODC/Afghan Gov., Afghanistan Opium Survey 2004, Nov. 2004, pp. 105-7.

[4]    See Barnett Rubin, "Road to Ruin: Afghanistan's Booming Opium Industry," Center for International Cooperation, Oct. 7, 2004, and the World Bank Country Economic Report -Afghanistan: State Building, Sustaining Growth, and Reducing Poverty, Sept. 9, 2004.

[5]    Author interviews with U.S., U.N., and coalition officials, Kabul, Afghanistan, Jan. 2005.

[6]    In 1978, pro-Communist Afghan officials reportedly requested "a lot of assistance from abroad, especially economic help, to help replace farmers' incomes derived from opium poppy cultivation." Randal, Washington Post, Nov. 2, 1978.

[7]    Agreement on Provisional Arrangements in Afghanistan Pending the Re-establishment of Permanent Government Institutions [The Bonn Agreement], Dec. 5, 2001.

[8]    See Arthur Bonner, "Afghan Rebel's Victory Garden: Opium," *New York Times*, June 18, 1986, and Mary Thornton, "Sales of Opium Reportedly Fund Afghan Rebels," *Washington Post*, Dec. 17, 1983.

[9]    See James Rupert and Steve Coll, "U.S. Declines to Probe Afghan Drug Trade: Rebels, Pakistani Officers Implicated," *Washington Post*, May 13, 1990; Jim Lobe, "Drugs: U.S. Looks Other Way In Afghanistan and Pakistan," *Inter Press Service*, May 18, 1990; John F. Burns, "U.S. Cuts Off Arms to Afghan Faction," *New York Times*, Nov. 19, 1989; Kathy Evans, "Money is the Drug" *The Guardian* (UK), Nov. 11, 1989; and Lawrence Lifschultz, "Bush, Drugs and Pakistan: Inside the Kingdom of Heroin," *The Nation*, Nov. 14, 1988.

[10]   The Taliban government collected an agricultural tax (approximately 10%, paid in kind), known as *ushr,* and a traditional Islamic tithe known as *zakat* (variable percentages).  The Taliban also taxed opium traders and transport syndicates involved in the transportation of opiates.  UNODC, "The Opium Economy in Afghanistan," pp. 92, 127-8.

[11]   UNODC, "The Opium Economy in Afghanistan," p. 92.

[12]   In December 2001, then Assistant Secretary of State for International Narcotics and Law Enforcement Affairs Rand Beers stated that the Taliban had not banned opium cultivation "out of kindness, but because they wanted to regulate the market: They simply produced too much opium." Marc Kaufman, "Surge in Afghan Poppy Crop Is Forecast," *Washington Post*, Dec. 25, 2001.  See Table 1 and UNODC, Opium Economy in Afghanistan,  p. 57.

[13]   The Bonn Agreement, Dec. 5, 2001.

[14]   Analysis in this report relating to the motives and methods of Afghan farmers, land owners, and traffickers is based on the findings of the UNODC's "Strategic Studies" series on Afghanistan's opium economy and a series of commissioned development

reports by David Mansfield, the Aga Khan Foundation, Frank Kenefick and Larry Morgan, Adam Pain, and others. UNODC Strategic Studies reports are available at [http://www.unodc.org/ pakistan/en/publications.html]. Complete citations are provided in Appendix A.

[15] David Mansfield, "The Economic Superiority of Illicit Drug Production: Myth and Reality," International Conference on Alternative Development in Drug Control and Cooperation, Aug. 2001.

[16] See UNODC, "An Analysis of the Process of Expansion of Opium Poppy Cultivation to New Districts in Afghanistan," June 1998.

[17] UNODC, "Afghanistan Opium Survey 2003," p. 8.

[18] See UNODC, "The Opium Economy in Afghanistan," pp. 129-40, 165-8.

[19] UNODC, "The Opium Economy in Afghanistan," pp. 139, 158.

[20] "The involvement of Afghan groups/individuals is basically limited to the opium production, the trade of opium within Afghanistan, the transformation of some of the opium into morphine and heroin, and to some extent, the trafficking of opiates to neighboring countries." UNODC, The Opium Economy in Afghanistan, p. 64.

[21] See Tamara Makarenko, "Bumper Afghan Narcotics Crop Indicates Resilience of Networks," *Jane's Intelligence Review*, May 1, 2002.

[22] Testimony of Robert B. Charles, Assistant Secretary of State for International Narcotics and Law Enforcement Affairs, House International Relations Committee, Sept. 23, 2004.

[23] See UNODC, "The Opium Economy in Afghanistan," p. 69, and Report of the Secretary-General on the Situation in Afghanistan and its Implications for International Peace and Security, Aug. 12, 2004.

[24] UNODC/CND, Afghanistan Opium Survey 2004, p. 66.

[25] The Afghan government's Central Eradication Force reportedly was "rocketed by furious villagers" during a 2004 eradication mission in Wardak province outside of Kabul. *Reuters*, Pressure on Karzai as Afghan Drug Problem Worsens, Oct. 5, 2004.

[26] See *Agence France Presse*, "Afghanistan Deploys 67 Million Dollars in War on Drugs," Apr. 11, 2002, and Anwar Iqbal, "War on Dug Begins in Afghanistan," *United Press International*, Apr. 10, 2002.

[27] Department of State, International Narcotics Control Strategy Report, Mar. 2005.

[28] *Agence France Presse*, "Curbing Rampant Afghan Opium Trade Will Take Karzai Years," Dec. 5, 2004.

[29] See *New York Times*, "7 Are Killed in a Clash of Afghan Militias," Feb. 9, 2004, and FBIS IAP20040707000101 - Afghanistan Briefing, July 5-7, 2004.

[30] See Victoria Burnett, "Outlook Uncertain: Can Afghanistan Take the Next Step to Building a State?" *Financial Times*, Aug. 19, 2004; Carol Harrington, "Ruthless Dostum a Rival for Karzai," *Toronto Star*, Sept. 20, 2004; and Jurgen Dahlkamp, Susanne Koelbl, and Georg Mascolo, (tr. Margot Bettauer Dembo), "Bundeswehr: Poppies, Rocks, Shards of Trouble," *Der Spiegel* [Germany], Nov. 10, 2003.

[31] Human Rights Watch, "The Rule of the Gun." Sept. 2004.

[32] Anne Barnard and Farah Stockman, "U.S. Weighs Role in Heroin War in Afghanistan," *Boston Globe*, Oct. 20, 2004.

[33] World Bank, State Building..., p. 87.

[34] International Monetary Fund, IMF Country Report No. 05/33 - Islamic State of Afghanistan: 2004 Article IV Consultation and Second Review, Feb. 2005.

[35] Author interviews with U.S. officials in Kabul, Afghanistan, Jan. 2005.

[36] Liz Sly, "Opium Cash Fuels Terror, Experts Say," *Chicago Tribune*, Feb. 9, 2004; John Fullerton, "Live and Let Live for Afghan Warlords, Drug Barons," *Reuters*, Feb. 5, 2002.

[37] See U.S. v. Bashir Noorzai, U.S. District Court, Southern District of New York, S1 05 Cr. 19, Apr. 25, 2005.

[38] See U.S. v. Baz Mohammed, U.S. District Court, Southern District of New York, S14 03 Cr. 486 [DC], Oct. 25, 2005.

[39] Tim McGirk, "Terrorism's Harvest," *Time Magazine* [Asia], Aug. 2, 2004.

[40] Haji Bashir reportedly described his time with U.S. forces in the following terms: "I spent my days and nights comfortably... I was like a guest, not a prisoner." *CBS Evening News*, "Newly Arrived US Army Soldiers Find it Difficult to Adjust...," Feb. 7, 2002.

[41] Steve Inskeep, "Afghanistan's Opium Trade," *National Public Radio*, Apr. 26, 2002.

[42] See Mark Corcoran, "America's Blind Eye," Australian Broadcasting Corporation, *Foreign Correspondent*, Apr. 10, 2002.

[43] Defense Department response to CRS inquiry, Nov. 12, 2004.

[44] Drug Enforcement Agency, "The Availability of Southwest Asian Heroin in the United States," May 1996.

[45] Drug Enforcement Agency, "Heroin Signature Program: 2002," Mar. 2004.

[46] In 1985, the DEA developed evidence against a wealthy Afghan national alleged to have been "involved in supplying Afghan rebels with weapons in exchange for heroin and hashish, portions of which were eventually distributed in Western Europe and the United States." See Select Committee on Narcotics Abuse and Control - Annual Report 1985, Dec. 19, 1986, p. 58; See U.S. v. Roeffen, et al. [U.S. District Court of New Jersey (Trenton), 86-00013-01] and U.S. v. Wali [860 F.2d 588 (3d Cir.1988)].

[47] Marcus W. Brauchli, "Pakistan's Wild Frontier Breeds Trouble — Drugs, Terrorism Could Overflow Into Other Regions," *Wall Street Journal*, June 3,1993; Kathy Gannon, "Pakistan Extradites Suspected Drug Dealers to U.S.," *Associated Press*, Oct. 16, 1993; Jeanne King, "U.S. Denies Bail to Alleged Pakistani Drug Baron," *Reuters*, Dec. 21, 1995; and Ron Synovitz, "U.S. Indicts 11 In Connection With Drug Ring," *RFE/RL*, Sep. 17, 2003.

[48] U.S. v. Afridi, et. al., [U.S. District Court of Maryland, (Baltimore), AW-03-0211].

[49] Testimony of DEA Administrator Karen Tandy before the House International Relations Committee, Feb. 12, 2004.

[50] James W. Crawley, "U.S. Warships Pinching Persian Gulf Drug Trade," *San Diego Union-Tribune*, February 9, 2004, and Tony Perry, "2 Convicted of Seeking Missiles for Al Qaeda Ally," *Los Angeles Times*, Mar. 4, 2004.

[51] Defense Department officials report that steps are taken to educate U.S. troops serving in Afghanistan about the dangers of narcotics use and to monitor and prevent drug use. Testimony of Lt. Gen. Walter L. Sharp, Director of Strategic Plans (J-5), Before the House International Relations Committee, Sept. 23, 2004.

[52] *Agence France Presse*, "Russia plans anti-drug centre in Kabul," Mar. 29, 2005.

[53] House of Commons (UK) - Foreign Affairs Committee, Seventh Report, July 21, 2004.

[54] For more information see Tamara Makarenko, "Crime, Terror and the Central Asian Drug Trade," Harvard Asia Quarterly, vol. 6, no. 3 (Summer 2002), and Integrated Regional Information Networks (IRIN) Report, "Central Asia: Regional Impact of the Afghan Heroin Trade," U.N. Office for the Coordination of Humanitarian Affairs (OCHA), Aug. 2004. Available at [http://www.irinnews.org/webspecials/opium/regOvr.asp].

[55] UNODC, "The Opium Economy in Afghanistan," p. 33, 35.

[56] For more information, see the World Health Organization's Epidemiological Fact Sheets on HIV/AIDS at [http://www.who.int/GlobalAtlas/PDFFactory/HIV/index.asp], and Julie Stachowiak and Chris Beyrer, HIV Follows Heroin Trafficking Routes," Open Society Institute - Central Eurasia Project, Available at [http://www.eurasianet.org/health.security/presentations/hiv_trafficking.shtml].

[57] For more on Central Asian security and public health, including information on narcotics trafficking, organized crime, and terrorism see CRS Report RL30294, *Central Asia's Security: Issues and Implications for U.S. Interests*, and CRS Report RL30970, *Health in Russia and Other Soviet Successor States: Context and Issues for Congress*, both by Jim Nichol.

[58] IRIN Report, "Tajikistan: Stemming the Heroin Tide," OCHA, Sept. 13, 2004. Available at [http://www.irinnews.org/webspecials/opium/regTaj.asp].

[59] *Agence France Presse*, "Tajiks to Take Over Patrolling Half of Tajik-Afghan Border From Russians," Oct. 1, 2004.

[60] See Rukhshona Najmiddinova, "Tajikistan Arrests Anti-Drug Agency Head," *Associated Press*, Aug. 6, 2004.

[61] *Moscow Interfax*, "Russia Says Around 9 Tonnes of Afghan Drugs Seized in International Operation," Nov. 13, 2005. FBIS Document CEP20051113029009.

[62] Ambassador Wendy Chamberlain, "Transcript: Hearing of the Subcommittee on Asia and the Pacific of the House International Relations Committee," Federal News Service, Mar. 20, 2003. See also, Ahmed Rashid, Taliban, Yale University Press, 2000, pp. 120-2, and Barnett Rubin, The Fragmentation of Afghanistan, Yale University Press, 2002, pp. 197-8. See also Rubin, Testimony Before the House Foreign Affairs Subcommittee on Europe and the Middle East and Asian and Pacific Affairs, Mar. 7, 1990.

[63] Jason Barnes, "The Desert Village that Feeds UK's Heroin Habit," *The Observer* (UK), Dec. 12, 1999.

[64] The Bonn Agreement, Dec. 5, 2001.

[65] Afghan Religious Scholars Urge End To Opium Economy, *Associated Press*, Aug. 3, 2004.

[66] Transitional Islamic State of Afghanistan, National Drug Control Strategy, May 18, 2003. Available at [http://www.cnd.gov.af/ndcs.html].

[67] Islamic Republic of Afghanistan, The 1384 (2005) Counter Narcotics Implementation Plan, Feb. 16, 2005. Available at [http://www.cnd.gov.af/imp_plan.htm].

[68] Statement of James E. Stahlman, Assistant Operations Officer, U.S. Central Command, Committee on House Government Reform Subcommittee on Criminal Justice, Drug Policy, and Human Resources, May 10, 2005.

[69] *Agence France Presse*, "Afghanistan Launches Poppy Eradication Force," Feb. 2, 2005.

[70] David Shelby, "United States to Help Afghanistan Attack Narcotics Industry," *Washington File*, U.S. Department of State, Nov. 17, 2004.

[71] Ibid.

[72] "Afghan Religious Scholars Urge End To Opium Economy," *Associated Press*, Aug. 3, 2004.

[73] Interior Ministry spokesman Lutfullah Mashal. *Agence France Presse*, "Afghan Drugs Kingpin Seized by US was Untouchable in Afghanistan: Experts," Apr. 27, 2005.

[74] Author interview with U.S. officials, Kabul, Afghanistan, Jan. 2005 and Washington, D.C., May 2005.

[75] Sources: Author interviews with USAID officials, Kabul, Afghanistan, January 2005; and USAID Alternative Livelihoods Conference, Washington, D.C., May 2005.

[76] USAID has established a "Good Performer's Fund" to reward districts that end cultivation with high visibility infrastructure development projects.

[77] USAID, Alternative Livelihoods Update: Issue 3, Apr. 1-15, 2005; author consultation with USAID Afghanistan Desk Office, Jan. 2006.

[78] Author consultation with USAID Afghanistan Desk Office, Jan. 2006.

[79] DEA Administrator Karen P. Tandy, House Committee on Government Reform Subcommittee on Criminal Justice, Drug Policy and Human Resources, Feb. 26, 2004.

[80] Ibid.

[81] Statement of Michael Braun, Chief of Operations - Drug Enforcement Agency, Before the House Committee on International Relations, Mar. 17, 2005.

[82] Defense Department response to CRS inquiry, Nov. 12, 2004.

[83] Testimony of Thomas W. O'Connell, Assistant Secretary of Defense for Special Operations and Low-intensity Conflict Before House International Relations Committee, Feb. 12, 2004; and Defense Department response to CRS inquiry, Nov. 12, 2004.

[84] Statement of Lennard J. Wolfson, Assistant Deputy Director for Supply Reduction, Office of National Drug Control Policy, Committee on House Government Reform Subcommittee on Criminal Justice, Drug Policy, and Human Resources, May 10, 2005.

[85] Philip Webster, "4,000 Troops to be Sent to Troubled Afghan Province," *The Times* (London), Jan. 25, 2006.

[86] Author conversation with DEA official, Washington, D.C., May 2005.

[87] National Drug Control Strategy, Transitional Islamic State of Afghanistan, May 18, 2003.

[88] "Poppy cultivation is likely to continue until responsible governmental authority is established throughout the country and until rural poverty levels can be reduced via provision of alternative livelihoods and increased rural incomes... Drug processing and trafficking can be expected to continue until security is established and drug law enforcement capabilities can be increased. " State Department, INCSR, Mar. 2005.

[89] See Syed Saleem Shahzad, "U.S. Turns to Drug Baron to Rally Support," *Asia Times*, Dec. 4, 2001; Charles Clover and Peronet Despeignes, "Murder Undermines Karzai Government," *Financial Times*, July 8, 2002; Susan B. Glasser, "U.S. Backing Helps Warlord Solidify Power," *Washington Post*, Feb. 18, 2002; Ron Moreau and Sami Yousafzai, with Donatella Lorch, "Flowers of Destruction," *Newsweek*, July 14, 2003; Andrew North, "Warlord Tells Police Chief to Go," *BBC News*, July 12, 2004; Steven Graham, "Group: Warlords to Hinder Afghan Election," *Associated Press*, Sept. 28,

2004; and Anne Barnard and Farah Stockman, "U.S. Weighs Role in Heroin War in Afghanistan," *Boston Globe*, Oct. 20, 2004.

[90] Rubin, "Road to Ruin: Afghanistan's Booming Opium Industry," Oct. 7, 2004.

[91] Testimony of Mary-Beth Long, Deputy Assistant Secretary of Defense for Counternarcotics before the House Committee on International Relations, Mar. 17, 2005.

[92] "U.S. CENTCOM views narcotrafficking as a significant obstacle to the political and economic reconstruction of Afghanistan... Local terrorist and criminal leaders have a vested interest in using the profits from narcotics to oppose the central government and undermine the security and stability of Afghanistan." Major Gen. John Sattler, USMC, Dir. of Operations-US CENTCOM before the House Committee on Government Reform Subcommittee on Criminal Justice, Drug Policy, and Human Resources, Apr. 21, 2004.

[93] S.Rept. 109-69.

[94] Afghanistan's National Drug Control Strategy expects that farmers with a "legacy of debt" will find that their "situation will be exacerbated by eradication efforts." A September 2004 British government report argues that "if not targeted properly, eradication can have the reverse effect and encourage farmers to cultivate more poppy to pay off increased debts." Response of the Secretary of State for Foreign and Commonwealth Affairs (UK) to the Seventh Report from the House of Commons Foreign Affairs Committee, Sep. 2004.

[95] Office of the Spokesperson to the President — Transitional Islamic State of Afghanistan, "About the Commitment by the Government of Afghanistan to the Fight Against Narcotics and Concerns About the Aerial Spraying of Poppy Fields."

[96] See David Brunnstrom, "Afghans Committed to Drug War But Against Spraying," *Reuters*, Nov. 19, 2004; and Stephen Graham, "Afghan Government Concerned at Spraying of Opium Crops by Mystery Aircraft," *Associated Press*, Nov. 30, 2004.

[97] Carlotta Gall, "Afghan Poppy Farmers Say Mystery Spraying Killed Crops," *New York Times*, Dec. 5, 2004, and *Reuters*, "U.S. Says Drug Lords May Have Sprayed Afghan Opium," Dec. 2, 2004.

[98] See Nicholas Rufford, "Secret Bio-weapon Can Wipe Out Afghan Heroin," *Sunday Times* (London), May 26, 2002; Antony Barnett, "UK in Secret Biological War on Drugs," *Observer* (London), Sept. 17, 2000; Juanita Darling, "Fungi May Be the Newest Recruits in War on Drugs Colombia," *Los Angeles Times*, Aug. 30, 2000.

[99] According to a USDA official, "The Department of Agriculture, as an agency, is opposed to the idea [of using mycoherbicides in Afghanistan]: The science is far from complete; There are real environmental and possible human health negative implications; There are very real image problems... the use of any agent like this would be portrayed as biological warfare." USDA response to CRS inquiry, Oct. 19, 2004.

In: Asian Economic and Political Development
Editor: Felix Chin

ISBN: 978-1-61122-470-2
© 2011 Nova Science Publishers, Inc.

# CAPABILITY BUILDING FOR INNOVATIONS, PUBLIC POLICY AND ECONOMIC GROWTH IN ASIA: LESSONS FOR SCIENCE AND TECHNOLOGY POLICY

## *Lakhwinder Singh*[*]

Department of Economics, Punjabi University,
Patiala 147002, India

## ABSTRACT

Transformation of East Asian countries from imitation to reaching the frontier areas of innovations in a short span of time is a question that has been explored in this paper. Asian continent has emerged as the hub of innovative activities in the fast pace of globalization. Within Asian continent, there are wide differentials in the stage of economic development and transformation as well as in the national innovation systems. Two distinct patterns of economic transformation and systems of innovations which have evolved over time are-one, based on building strong industrial sector as an engine of innovations and growth; two, the engine of growth is the service sector and innovation system is heavily dependent on foreign capital and technology. Public innovation policies played active role in the process of evolving distinct national innovation systems of Asian type. This paper, while drawing lessons from public innovation policy of the successful innovators of East Asian countries, brings out the need for public innovation policies to develop industrial sector rather than prematurely move towards service sector oriented economic growth.

**Keywords**: Technology policy, technological indicators, national innovation system, structural transformation, innovation institutions, economic growth, Asia.

## 1. INTRODUCTION

Innovations spur growth and economic transformation is widely acclaimed in economic growth literature. Innovations entails organizational as well as changes in the rules of the game. Thus, transition in the national innovation system is the fundamental determinant of long-run economic growth and development. This is being reflected through the changes, which are occurring in the economic structure of an economy as well as in the structure of the

---

[*] E-mail address:lkhw2002@yahoo.com;lakhwindersingh07@gmail.com.

innovation system. Since the national economies are growing in the interdependent world, therefore national innovation system is continuously being influenced by the changes occurring in other parts of the world. Asian continent has distinctly achieved high rates of economic growth and has emerged as the growth pole of the global economy. It has also emerged as the hub of innovative activities in the fast pace of globalization. Within Asian continent, there are wide differentials in the stage of economic development and transformation as well as in the national innovation systems. Two distinct patterns of economic transformation and systems of innovations which has evolved over time are-one, based on building strong industrial sector as an engine of innovations and growth; two, the engine of growth is the service sector and innovation system is heavily dependent on foreign capital. Recently, while recognizing the innovative capacity of some of the Asian countries, foreign R&D has devastated the boundaries of the Asian innovation system. Domestic agents of production have realized that there lies a dire need for the support of the state when innovations are being done on the frontiers of knowledge. Situational assessment surveys have also supported the view that Asian countries are fast approaching towards the frontiers of knowledge and innovations. Asian countries, themselves are competing to fast approach towards frontiers of knowledge and innovations so that newer areas of commercial activities can be explored and exploited in the global market. Transformation of East Asian countries from imitation to reaching the frontier areas of innovations in a short span of time is a question, which begs for an explanation. This paper attempts to provide some plausible answers and is divided into five sections. Apart from introductory section one, the transformation of the production structure and the factors that have determined it are analyzed in section two. Innovation systems across Asian countries and indicators of innovations based on input-output measures as well as situational assessment surveys have been presented in section three. Fourth section contains the discussion related to innovation policies and institutional arrangements, which caused the success in some cases and lack of it in others. Fifth section investigates the role of international agencies to enact rules of the game in an open innovation system and the national governments in terms of enacting innovative interventions in the fast globalizing world economy. Policy implications for other developing countries that emerge from the innovations and fast development experience of the successful East Asian countries are presented in the concluding section.

## 2. STRUCTURAL TRANSFORMATION IN ASIA

The evolutionary economics has recognized the role of technology and institutions in the process of long run economic growth. The interaction between economic and non-economic factors stressed by the theories of evolutionary economic growth generates dynamism in the economic system that brings in continuous economic transformation. The factors that drive economic growth (technologies and institutions) and structural transformation in one era to the other itself go on changing. The process of economic growth thus brings in economic transformation and non steady state economic growth. Technology has emerged as a distinct and key factor that determines changes in the long run economic growth and structure of the economy. It needs to be noted here that the innovations are of two types that is radical and incremental. Radical innovations open up new opportunities and push the frontiers of knowledge, which dramatically alter the existing economic structure. Incremental innovations not only improve the practices of the existing technologies but are potent factor of diffusion of the radical innovation that engineer structural change in the economic system. However, imitation tends to erode differences in technological competencies across economic activities and over time that reduces differentials and gaps in economic activities. Therefore, radical and incremental innovations are a source of structural transformation and divergence in economic growth and imitation acts as an agent of reducing productivity gaps and initiates the process of convergence. Both the processes of innovations are continuously remains in action and the combination of the two that actually determine the economic transformation and convergence in the economic system (Fagerberg and Verspagen, 2001).

Fast rate of economic growth and closing the productivity gaps have been the major feature of economic transformation of the East Asian countries during four decades of the twentieth century. This process of fast economic growth has not only increased per capita income but has made the East Asian economies as a hub of economic activities and widely acknowledged as the growth pole of the fast changing global economy. It is worth noting here that the East Asia has followed a distinct path of economic transformation for generating dynamism in their respective economic systems. The global economy as a whole has become service oriented (Table 1.). The service sector contributed 68 per cent of the total GDP of the global economy in the year 2004. Industrial sector contributed 28 per cent of the GDP and rest of the 4 per cent GDP contributed by agriculture sector in the year 2004. This clearly brings out the fact that transformation process has reduced the role of agriculture in global economy and now the engine of economic growth is the service sector. It is important to note here that the less developed countries have also become heavily dominated by service sector. This seems to be premature economic transformation and defying the standard pattern of economic growth, which have dramatically improved the per capita income as well as working condition in the advanced economies. The developing countries, which prematurely become service oriented economies remain unable to grow at a fast rate and could not able to raise per capita income and living conditions of the majority of the workforce. However, the East Asian economies have followed the standard pattern of economic growth and transformation and successfully reduced the importance of agriculture sector both in terms of income and work force. China, Indonesia, and Malaysia are three countries, which have been generating income from the industrial sector higher than the service sector. South Korea and Thailand are the two other countries, which have been generating more than forty per cent of the GDP from the industrial sector (Table 1). If we compare East Asian countries with South Asian countries as well as with the global economy, it is the South East Asian countries where the engine of growth is industrial sector rather than agriculture and service sectors. The transformation process, which followed the standard pattern, is considered as a superior because of the fact that it along with raising the productivity and standard of living also brings in institutional, organizational and cultural changes. These changes make society more capable, productive, innovative and peaceful.

The engine of successful structural transformation of East Asian countries has been regarded as industrialization. The process of fast industrialization and continuous changes in the industrial structure requires huge amount of investment in fixed capital that was provided by the high savings rates recorded in the East Asian countries (Table 2). East Asian countries have saved more than 30 per cent of the GDP and recently China recorded 42 per cent savings of GDP.

**Table 1. Sectoral distribution of GDP across Asian Countries: 1960, 1980, 1990, 2000 and 2004**

| Sector/ Country | Agriculture | | | | Industry | | | | Services | | | |
|---|---|---|---|---|---|---|---|---|---|---|---|---|
| | 1960 | 1980 | 1990 | 2004 | 1960 | 1980 | 1990 | 2004 | 1960 | 1980 | 1990 | 2004 |
| Bangladesh | 57 | 50 | 30 | 21 | 07 | 16 | 22 | 27 | 36 | 34 | 48 | 52 |
| Nepal | - | 62 | 52 | 40 | - | 12 | 16 | 23 | - | 26 | 32 | 37 |
| India | 50 | 38 | 31 | 21 | 20 | 26 | 28 | 27 | 30 | 36 | 41 | 52 |
| China | 47 | 30 | 27 | 13 | 33 | 49 | 42 | 46 | 20 | 21 | 31 | 41 |
| Pakistan | 46 | 30 | 26 | 22 | 16 | 25 | 25 | 25 | 38 | 46 | 49 | 53 |
| Sri Lanka | 32 | 28 | 26 | 18 | 20 | 30 | 26 | 27 | 48 | 43 | 48 | 55 |
| Indonesia | 54 | 24 | 19 | 15 | 14 | 42 | 39 | 44 | 32 | 34 | 42 | 41 |
| Philippines | 26 | 25 | 22 | 14 | 28 | 39 | 35 | 32 | 46 | 36 | 44 | 54 |
| Thailand | 40 | 23 | 13 | 10 | 19 | 29 | 37 | 44 | 41 | 48 | 50 | 46 |
| Malaysia | 36 | 22 | 15 | 10 | 18 | 38 | 42 | 50 | 46 | 40 | 43 | 40 |
| South Korea | 37 | 15 | 09 | 04 | 20 | 40 | 42 | 41 | 43 | 45 | 50 | 56 |
| Hong Kong | 04 | 01 | - | - | 39 | 32 | 25 | 11 | 57 | 67 | 74 | 89 |
| Singapore | 04 | 01 | - | 00 | 18 | - | 38 | 35 | 78 | 61 | - | 65 |
| World | - | 07 | 06 | 04 | - | 38 | 33 | 28 | - | 53 | 61 | 68 |

**Source**: World Bank (2006) World Development Indicators 2006, Washington, D.C.: The World Bank.

Rapid industrial growth and transformation requires continuous accumulation of the new capital assets and thus dependent heavily on increasing in investment in the capital assets. Capital formation as a share of GDP was remained very high during the fast pace of industrial development of the East Asian countries. In the recent period, some of the East Asian countries have shown a decline in the capital formation (Table 2). Saving and investment rates have remained quite low in the global economy as well as in the South Asian countries which can be regarded as an important factor of slow growth of the industrial sector in particular and the economy as a whole in general. The success of industrialization is highly constrained by the availability of right kind of skilled manpower. This was provided by the East Asian countries compared with the South Asian countries where the indicators of human capital lag behind. Adequate supply of skilled manpower has allowed East Asian countries to move up the industrial ladder from textile to simple assembly of machines and to high-tech industries. International trade has been regarded as a potent factor in the successful industrial transformation of the East Asian countries. Furthermore, it is the importance of capital goods and parts for assembly that has had stronger impact on productivity growth (Yusuf, 2003). Industrial productivity and rate of economic growth has been widely acclaimed as fundamentally dependent on the science and technological development. East Asian countries achieved higher value added per worker in the manufacturing (Table 2) while investing heavily in science and technology compared with the South Asian countries (Singh, 2006). FDI as a factor of faster economic growth has been very important in the economies of Malaysia, Thailand, Singapore, Indonesia and China. However, South Korea and Taiwan have been able to achieve high productivity growth based on domestic investment and more so in science and technology. Therefore, there are two distinct patterns of economic transformation in East Asia, one based heavily on FDI and other on domestic efforts. Productivity differentials show that productivity of industrial activities is very high in the later case (Table 2).

**Table 2. Savings, capital formation and productivity across Asian Countries**

| Country | Gross savings as a per cent of GDP 2004 | Capital formation as a per cent of GDP | | Labour productivity in manufacturing 1995-99 $ per year |
|---|---|---|---|---|
| | | 1990 | 2004 | |
| Bangladesh | 31 | 17 | 24 | 1711 |
| Nepal | 27 | 18 | 26 | - |
| India | 23 | 24 | 24 | 3118 |
| China | 42 | 35 | 39 | 2885 |
| Pakistan | 23 | 19 | 17 | - |
| Sri Lanka | 19 | 23 | 25 | 3405 |
| Indonesia | 24 | 31 | 23 | 5139 |
| Philippines | 37 | 24 | 17 | 10781 |
| Thailand | 31 | 41 | 27 | 19946 |
| Malaysia | 35 | 32 | 23 | 12661 |
| South Korea | 34 | 38 | 30 | 40916 |
| Hong Kong | 32 | 28 | 22 | 32611 |
| Singapore | 45* | 36 | 18 | 40674 |
| World | 20 | 23 | 21 | - |

**Source**: As in Table 1.

## 3. CAPABILITY BUILDING FOR INNOVATIONS IN ASIA

Knowledge, science and technology have become a key component of contemporary economic and social systems. Recent spurt in economic literature on evolutionary and endogenous growth theory has empathetically argued how knowledge has become a decisive factor in economic systems of production. Knowledge accumulation not only explains existing across country and inter as well as intra economic activity productivity gaps, but also predicts increase in productivity gaps if knowledge accumulation differentials persist and perpetuate. Thus knowledge generation and accumulation process have severe implications for the future status of the national economic system in the fast changing global economy. It is important to note here that the knowledge generation process in the national economic system has undergone a fundamental non-reversible structural change in the developed countries. It is the transition from fundamental research to applied one. This phenomenon has been described as a dual "crowding out". Firms are now increasingly engaged in applied research and do not finance fundamental research either in house or in the institutions of higher learning is one form of crowding out. The other form of crowding out is the near absence of fundamental research from the public laboratories and the university research (Soete, 2006). This kind of change in the knowledge generation process has occurred towards the last quarter of the twentieth century. Another great transition in the knowledge production that has also occurred is the emergence of Asia as a hub of research and development activities leaving behind Europe. North America continues to dominate in R&D and accounted for 37 per cent of the world's R&D expenditure in 2002. Asia has emerged as the second largest investor in innovative activities with 32 per cent share of global R&D. Europe's share of global R&D expenditure is just 27 per cent (UNESCO, 2004). The share of R&D expenditure of North America and Europe has declined at a rate about one per cent during the period 1997 to 2002.The R&D expenditure has been increasing in Asia at a 4 per cent per annum during the same period. This clearly shows that Asian countries have been able to strengthen the national innovation systems. This has occurred because of the fact that the fast growth of industrialization exhaust soon the opportunities of adaptation and thus force the economic agents of production to investment more in innovative activities to maintain the lead in productivity growth and competitive advantage over the immediate rivals. It needs to be noted here that there exist substantial differentials in innovative activities across Asian countries (Table 3).

The most important input indicator of innovation is research and development expenditure intensity. South Korea has remarkably achieved high R&D intensity, that is, 2.64 mean value for the period 1996-2003. This high R&D intensity is comparable with the United States of America but lower in comparison with the highest spender countries like Israel, Sweden and Japan with R&D intensities 4.93, 3.98 and 3.15 respectively. Taiwan and Singapore are the other two high R&D intensity achievers with 2.20 and 2.15 R&D-GDP ratios respectively. China is fast catching up with high R&D intensity countries of East Asia. China's R&D intensity for the period 1996-2003 was 1.31 (Table 3). China has recorded dramatic growth of R&D expenditure with doubling its global share from 4 per cent to 9 per cent during the period 1997 to 2002(UNESCO, 2004). Rest of the East Asian countries has been increasing their respective R&D intensities, however, expending less than one per cent of GDP. Among the South Asian countries, India has well developed national innovation system but slowly forging ahead in innovations yet spending less than one per cent of GDP (0.88 average of 1996-2003).

Human capital engaged in national innovation system is another important input indicator of innovations. This is the only active factor that makes use of the innovation infrastructure arrangements and feeds on innovations as well as generates new knowledge and improves upon the existing one. Therefore, quantity and quality of researchers engaged in various innovation activities does matter for the outcomes of innovations. The highest number of researchers, 6517 per million people, was employed by Taiwan in innovation activities followed by Singapore (4745 per million people) and South Korea (3187 per million people) during the period 1996-2003 (Table 3). Other important countries, which have engaged significant number of scientists and engineers in innovative activities, are China and Hong Kong (663 and 1564 per million researchers respectively). When we compare East Asian countries with South Asian countries in terms of number of researchers employed in innovation activities, South Asian countries lag much behind the East Asian countries (Table 3). This clearly shows the edge of East Asian countries in innovation infrastructure and capability to generate innovations.

Innovation capability index (ICI) has been developed by UNCTAD based on three kinds of broad measures such as innovation inputs, innovation outputs and human resource base for technology activity. This index is based on quantitative criteria to arrive at values for the countries and on the basis of values countries are reckoned in terms of global ranks among the 117 countries. Two Asian countries, that is, Taiwan and South Korea ranked, as high innovation capability with global ranking in 2001 was 15 and 19 respectively. China and other East Asian countries were recorded medium innovation capability ranks among the 117 countries (Table 3). It is important to note here that all the South Asian countries recorded values quite low and global ranking falls in the category of low innovation capability countries (UNCTAD, 2005). It needs to be noted here that China and India in terms of absolute level of R&D expenditure and researchers engaged in innovation activities are global powers but there reckoning is low because of their large population size. Situation assessment survey based on qualitative information with regard to assess the innovation capability also shows a similar picture and confirms the transition of the Asian countries on the technological ladders. Survey based three indices-scores and ranks- technological sophistication index, company spending R&D index and firm level technology absorption index have shown wide differentials across Asian countries. Taiwan and South Korea, according to three indices, are high innovation capability countries among the 80 countries under consideration. However, other East Asian countries ranked either medium or low innovation capability countries on the basis of three qualitative innovation capability indices developed by World Economic Forum (Table 3).

### Table 3. Input indicators of innovations across Asian countries

| Country | Researchers in R&D per million people 1996-2002 | Share of R&D expenditure in GDP (in per cent) 1996-2002 | UNCTAD innovation capability index 2001 | Technological Sophistication index | Company spending on R&D index | Firm level technology absorption index |
|---|---|---|---|---|---|---|
| Bangladesh | - | - | 0.121 (106) | 2.3 (77) | 2.4 (75) | 4.1 (71) |
| Nepal | 59 | 0.66 | - | - | - | - |
| India | 119 | 0.85 | 0.285 (83) | 3.8 (42) | 3.6 (32) | 5.5 (16) |
| China | 663 | 1.31 | 0.358 (74) | 3.9 (39) | 3.6 (34) | 4.7 (48) |
| Pakistan | 86 | 0.22 | 0.137 (100) | - | - | - |
| Sri Lanka | 181 | 0.18 | 0.317 (79) | 3.2 (58) | 3.4 (39) | 4.6 (57) |
| Indonesia | - | - | 0.261 (87) | 3.0 (63) | 3.3 (48) | 4.7 (49) |
| Philippines | - | - | 0.423 (64) | 3.2 (56) | 3.0 (55) | 4.4 (63) |
| Thailand | 286 | 0.24 | 0.488 (54) | 3.8 (41) | 3.3 (45) | 5.2 (31) |
| Malaysia | 299 | 0.69 | 0.467 (60) | 4.6 (23) | 4.1 (23) | 5.3 (25) |
| South Korea | 3187 | 2.64 | 0.839 (19) | 5.2 (17) | 4.8 (11) | 5.8 (10) |
| Hong Kong | 1564 | 0.60 | 0.563 (45) | 4.5 (25) | 3.4 (37) | 5.2 (32) |
| Singapore | 4745 | 2.15 | 0.748 (26) | 5.6 (9) | 4.6 (16) | 5.9 (9) |
| Taiwan | 6517 | 2.20 | 0.865 (15) | 5.3 (13) | 4.9 (10) | 6.0 (6) |

**Source**: World Bank (2006); UNCTAD (2005); and Cornelius, Porter and Schwab (2003).

Output measures of innovation presented in Table 4 shows dramatic differentials in innovations across Asian countries. South and South East Asian countries have emerged as significant contributors to global pool of knowledge. In absolute numbers, China, India and South Korea contributed to the global pool of knowledge through publishing research papers in scientific and engineering journals. Singapore and Hong Kong have also contributed significantly while publishing 2061 and 1817 research papers respectively in 2001 in scientific and engineering journals. Other South and East Asian countries lag far behind in terms of their contribution to global pool of knowledge. High-Tech exports as a share of manufacturing which is another output measure of innovation shows very high degree of science based manufactured commodities provided to the global economy by the South -East Asian countries. However, South Asian countries performed poorly on this count. Higher contribution of most of the East Asian countries in high tech exports seems to be based on the intra industry trade because of the presence of MNCs in these countries. On the contrary, high-tech exports originating from Taiwan and South Korea are based on the domestic companies, which had been nurtured by the national innovation system of the respective countries. Somewhat similar trends can be found in terms of patent applications filed by the residents of innovator countries in the US patent office. The number of patent applications has dramatically increased during the period 1991-1993 to 2001-2003 in most of the Asian countries (Table 4). Royalty payments made by the Asian countries indicates that Asian countries are still highly dependent in terms of technology from the developed countries. However, majority of the countries do receive payments in lieu of technology exports and licensing of technology. South Korea has dramatically bridged the gap between payments made and payments received. This clearly indicates that countries, which have developed national innovation systems, are able to reduce foreign dependence on technology.

**Table 4. Output indicators of Innovations across Asian countries**

| Country | Scientific and technical journal articles in numbers 2001 | High-Tech exports and its share in manufacturing 2003 | | Royalty and license fees in million dollars 2002 | | Patent applications by residence of inventor | |
|---|---|---|---|---|---|---|---|
| | | $millions | % | Receipts | Payments | 1991-1993 | 2001-2003 |
| Bangladesh | 177 | 3 | 0.00 | - | 5 | - | - |
| Nepal | 39 | 1 | 0.00 | - | - | - | - |
| India | 11076 | 2840 | 5.00 | 25 | 421 | 56 | 909 |
| China | 20978 | 161603 | 30.00 | 236 | 4497 | 130 | 849 |
| Pakistan | 282 | 150 | 1.00 | 10 | 95 | | |
| Sri Lanka | 76 | 60 | 1.00 | - | - | 10 | 64 |
| Indonesia | 207 | 5809 | 16.00 | 221 | 990 | 10 | 13 |
| Philippines | 158 | 13913 | 64.00 | 12 | 270 | 10 | 50 |
| Thailand | 727 | 18203 | 30.00 | 14 | 1584 | - | - |
| Malaysia | 494 | 52868 | 55.00 | 20 | 782 | 19 | 165 |
| South Korea | 11037 | 75742 | 33.00 | 1790 | 4450 | 1472 | 8356 |
| Hong Kong | 1817 | 80119 | 32.00 | 341 | 864 | 146 | 679 |
| Singapore | 2603 | 87742 | 59.00 | 224 | 5647 | 85 | 788 |
| Taiwan | - | - | - | - | - | 2598 | 12453 |

**Source**: World Bank (2006).

East Asian countries such as Malaysia, Indonesia and Philippines that are FDI dependent still have to depend more on foreign services of technology and hence higher royalty payments compared with receipts.

Asian countries have been continuously interacted in the international economy to bring in technology and practices, which are superior and beneficial for enhancing its domestic requirements. Domestic efforts to absorb technologies developed somewhere else have allowed Asian economies to put in place institutional arrangements for supporting economic agents of production to become internationally competitive while reducing foreign dependence on technology. This process can be characterized as technology import substitution. Technology import substitution process has enabled the national innovation system to develop competitive advantage for the firms producing goods and services in these typical areas. Therefore, the leading global players of knowledge activities have recognized the innovative capability of the Asian countries and revealed in a recent UNCTAD survey their preference to locate R&D centers in Asian countries. Foreign affiliate R&D centers have been growing at a fast pace in the Asian countries. China alone received 700 foreign affiliate R&D centers between 2002 and 2004. India and Singapore is now hosting more than hundred foreign affiliate R&D centers respectively. China, India and Singapore have a very high degree of incidence of establishing foreign affiliate R&D centers up to 2004. The situation assessment survey has also revealed that the leading TNCs will prefer to locate R&D centers in most of the Asian countries (Table 5). China and India have emerged undisputed sites for location of foreign R&D centers between 2005 and 2009 and were preferred by 61.8 per cent and 29.4 per cent respectively of the firms surveyed in 2004. Their respective global ranks are first and third. Other important Asian countries, which have been highly rated as preferred location for R&D centers by global knowledge players, are Singapore (rank 11), Taiwan (rank 12), Malaysia (rank 15), South Korea (rank 16) and Thailand rank (17) (Table 5). This is an ample proof of the well-developed innovative infrastructural facilities and conducing innovation institutional arrangements along with highly skilled innovative and cheap human capital.

**Table 5. Indicators of foreign firm innovation investment destinations**

| Country | Current foreign R&D location of TNCs 2004 (per cent) | Prospective R&D location of TNCs 2005-2009 |
|---|---|---|
| China | 35.3 (3) | 61.8 (1) |
| India | 25.0 (6) | 29.4 (3) |
| Singapore | 17.6 (9) | 4.4 (11) |
| Taiwan | 5.9 (23) | 4.4 (12) |
| Malaysia | - | 2.9 (15) |
| South Korea | 4.4 (26) | 2.9 (16) |
| Thailand | 4.4 (27) | 2.9 (17) |

**Source**: UNCTAD (2005).

## 4. Public Policy Support for Innovations across Asian Countries

Economic growth and competitive advantage of national economies in the post world war period remained highly dependent on public support policies (Stern, 2004). Economic agents of production have been nurtured through the support of right kind of economic incentives and institutional arrangements. Innovativeness of the economic agents of production in a national economy thus has remained also highly dependent on technology policy instruments and institutional arrangements (Yusuf, 2003). It has been widely acknowledged and recognized that the leading developed countries and industries, which are adding to the global pool of knowledge through novel innovations and maintaining competitive edge, are highly dependent on well enacted public support system in terms of instruments and institutions (Jaumotte and Pain, 2005; Ruttan, 2001). Public support-direct and indirect-for technology generation and diffusion has been justified on the ground that economic agents of production generally under invest in innovation related activities compared with socially desirable level (Arrow, 1962; Nelson, 1959). Why do firms generally under-invest because of the fact that knowledge has a quasi-public good characteristic? Therefore, knowledge is difficult to appropriate perfectly by the generators even if what so ever the institutional arrangements for appropriation of knowledge are made. If there exist a knowledge gap between the two economic agents of production, then follower have an advantage of receiving some amount of knowledge without paying for it has been characterized as spillover effect. Innovations are risky activities and involve huge amount of resources along with proven lower private returns than that of the public returns (Jones and Williams, 1998). Thus, private funding agencies and institutions are usually reluctant to finance such projects. This results into shortage of financial resources to individual agents, which are involved in innovative activities and is popularly called as financial market failures. Innovative activities usually employ highly skilled labour and in the absence of appropriate educational institutions, skilled labour shortages generally result. This is an accepted responsibility of the state to mitigate the skill shortages of the labor which will provide desired human capital to private economic agents engaged in innovative activities. Asymmetric information is the other source of justification for the public policy intervention in innovative economic activities and also direct and indirect support to those who are engaged in innovative activities.

In order to address the market failure, governments of the developed countries have been putting in place a whole host of direct and indirect measures to encourage economic agents to commit more resources for innovative activities. The governments of developed countries have now well designed set of five principal policies to alleviate particular forms of market failure leading to under-invest in innovation (see for detail Jaumotte and Pain, 2005). This response of the governments of the developed countries have not only eased perceived constraints on the incentive to private agents to innovate but have also allowed them to provide lead to push forward technology frontiers and remain competitive in the fast changing international economy.

East Asian countries have emerged as front-runners in industrial economic activities during the import substitution regimes and have accumulated vast experience of public policy making. Public policy making in Asian countries and elsewhere have not only addressed appropriately market failures but also fundamentally remained developmental in nature.

Economic transition has allowed these countries to accumulate technology development experience while putting in place desired instruments and institutional arrangements which have had helped innovations to take place. The national innovation system in each one of the Asian countries has evolved during the period of economic transformation to address the problem of backward technology, which recently has shown dividends. This process of moving from imitation to innovation has been covered in relatively at a short span of time compared with the developed countries. However, there exist wide differentials in stage of technology development and support of public technology policy across Asian countries. One commonality which emerged from the technology development policy in committing resources for R&D is the dramatic shift from public funding to private one (Yusuf, 2003).

**Table 6. Institutional support indicators of innovations across Asian countries**

| Country | Subsidies and tax credit for firm-level R&D | Quality of science and math education | University-industry research collaboration | Govt. procurement of advance technology products | Intellectual property protection |
|---|---|---|---|---|---|
| Bangladesh | 2.2 (69) | 3.3 (68) | 2.2 (77) | 2.5 (73) | 2.1 (77) |
| India | 4.3 (18) | 5.1 (17) | 3.4 (42) | 3.3 (55) | 3.4 (51) |
| China | 4.0 (21) | 4.4 (31) | 4.5 (16) | 4.7 (10) | 3.6 (45) |
| Sri Lanka | 3.1 (39) | 4.0 (44) | 2.9 (57) | 4.5 (13) | 4.0 (37) |
| Indonesia | 2.3 (67) | 3.6 (60) | 3.5 (40) | 3.7 (40) | 2.4 (72) |
| Philippines | 2.6 (61) | 3.6 (58) | 3.2 (49) | 3.0 (64) | 2.7 (64) |
| Thailand | 3.4 (30) | 4.0 (45) | 3.8 (29) | 3.8 (34) | 4.0 (38) |
| Malaysia | 4.7 (8) | 4.5 (28) | 3.8 (28) | 4.7 (7) | 4.4 (33) |
| South Korea | 4.6 (12) | 4.9 (22) | 4.3 (20) | 4.8 (6) | 4.5 (29) |
| Hong Kong | 2.0 (45) | 4.1 (43) | 3.6 (35) | 3.9 (29) | 5.2 (17) |
| Singapore | 5.4 (2) | 5.3 (10) | 5.0 (9) | 5.2 (1) | 5.7 (12) |
| Taiwan | 5.2 (3) | 5.2 (15) | 5.2 (7) | 5.1 (3) | 4.6 (27) |

**Note**: Figures in parentheses are global ranks according to scores based on Executive Opinion Survey, 2002.
**Source**: Cornelius, Porter and Schwab (2003).

Government support extended by Singapore and Taiwan to their respective firms doing R&D in terms of subsidies and tax concessions is ranked very high among the 80 countries for which data was collected by the World Economic Forum. Singapore and Taiwan recorded score points 5.4 and 5.2 out of seven points scores and ranked second and third respectively in the global reckoning (Table 6). Singapore government allowed firms double deduction on R&D expenses as tax incentive for R&D. The government has also enacted incentive schemes for companies such as innovation development scheme, funds for industrial clusters and promising local enterprise scheme. The tax system of Taiwan has also provided full deductibility for R&D expenses and also allowed accelerated depreciation. Malaysia and Korea were ranked $8^{th}$ and $12^{th}$ with score points 4.7 and 4.6 respectively so far as tax incentives and subsidies are concerned. Malaysia supported firms' R&D while providing nine different categories of tax incentives. The Korea government successfully supported private R&D by giving tax credits, allowed accelerated depreciation and lowering of import tariffs. Two emerging innovative countries-India and China- have been able to successfully support, in terms of providing subsidies and tax incentives, firm level R&D. Global ranks of Indian and Chinese subsidies and tax credit support at firm level were $18^{th}$ and $21^{st}$ with scores points 4.2 and 4.0 respectively (Table 6). Firm's perception of fiscal support of the government of Thailand is also quite satisfactory. However, the other South Asian and East Asian country countries have shown the availability of fiscal incentives for innovative activities but the firm perception and global ranking is quite low. This is understandable because of the fact that input and output indicators of these countries have also shown the early stage of development of their innovation systems.

The model of innovations emerged in the recent past in developed countries is the relationship between government, university and business enterprises. This is known in the literature of national innovation system as triple helix era. The university has emerged as a knowledge enterprise where government and business enterprises invest in research and draw on the commercially viable new knowledge generated by the university. This linkage is now considered essential for speedy delivery and uses of knowledge by business enterprises so that pace and competitive edge can be maintained in the dynamic global economy. It needs to be noticed here that Taiwan, Singapore and China have emulated the model of innovations triple helix era. This is clear from the high global ranking recorded by the business enterprises obtained on the basis of score points as per the perceptions of the business enterprises (Table 6). South Korea has also scored quite high on this count but still regarded as relatively having weak linkage between public research institutions and business enterprises (Yusuf, 2003). University-industry linkage was very weak in most of the Asian countries. It is almost at the stage of inception. This is where governments of these countries have to take measures such as extending financial support to educational institutions and public research institutions to graduate themselves from mere knowledge disseminator institutions to creators of knowledge. It is important to note here that supply and quality of researchers required for R&D was regarded very highly for countries such as Singapore, Taiwan and India (Table 6). Other countries of Asian need substantive efforts in this respect to fulfill the requirements of the firms to ensure supply and quality of the skilled manpower. Government support in terms of procurement of advance technology products has been rated high and secured global ranks first, third, sixth, seven and tenth by Singapore, Taiwan, Korea, Malaysia and China respectively (Table 6). However, South Asian country ranks on this count are very low except Sri Lanka compared with East Asian countries. Technology development experience of East Asian countries has shown that capability building and strengthening national innovation system under the lax intellectual property regime were quite helpful. It needs to be noted here that the stage of development and intellectual property protection is positively correlated. However, protection of intellectual property at early stage of national innovation system inhibits innovative activities. Therefore, lower global ranking in intellectual property protection recorded by the business perception survey is understandable (Table 6). On the whole, East Asian countries have emerged among the front-runners in terms of technology policy support to business enterprises a reason of successful development of national innovation system especially of Taiwan, Korea and Singapore. South Asian countries and other developing countries needs to learn a lesson or two from innovative and dynamic public technology policy support extended by the East Asian countries in terms of instruments and institutions for making business enterprises innovative.

# 5. OPEN NATIONAL INNOVATION SYSTEM AND POLICY AGENDA FOR NATIONAL AND INTERNATIONAL PUBLIC AGENCIES

National innovation systems have been evolved in the developed countries without external intervention and political pressures. Competitive edge of developed economies and of industries has been achieved with substantive public support both direct and indirect. This does not mean that developed countries have not learned from the experience of each other's during the evolution and development of national innovation system. Firms chosen to invest in other developed countries as well as formulated joint ventures to draw on the best practices of others are an ample proof of learning from each other's. Therefore, the national innovation systems have remained quite open and learning took place mainly under the framework of national technology policy.

On other hand, East Asian economies surged ahead in transformation process and succeeded in industrialising their economies as well as building innovation capabilities during the last quarter of the twentieth century. National innovation system is still at its stage of infancy. South Asian countries are striving to put in place the national innovation system, which allows its firms to be productive and competitive. It is important to note here that there are wide differentials in productivity and per capita income across countries. This reflects the knowledge gaps and application of knowledge gaps for productive economic activities. However, openness in trade based on rules and regulations framed by global governance institutions have allowed in securing monopoly rights to firms that have gained competitive edge from their respective national innovation systems. The intellectual property rights enacted and implemented by World Trade Organisation has been increasingly being questioned both by the academic economists and governments as well as some global institutions. An interesting contribution in this regard is by the World Development Report of the World Bank 1998/1999. This report clearly identified the role of the government in developing countries to develop the capabilities to generate knowledge at home along with providing help to domestic agents of production to take advantage of the large global stock of knowledge. It is significant to note here that the United Nations Development Prorgramme (UNDP) has gone much ahead in terms of identifying the knowledge gaps existing between developed and developing countries and articulated the arguments against the strict intellectual property rights regime enacted and implemented by the World Trade Organization (WTO). Furthermore, the UNDP has not only suggested innovative and fundamental role of the governments of the developing countries in generating capabilities that matter for knowledge development but also identified knowledge as a global public good and role of international community in reducing the knowledge gaps (UNDP, 2001; and Stiglitz, 1999).

Apart from making suitable public innovation policies to strengthen national innovation systems, the government of developing countries should also strive hard to seek cooperation among themselves as well as of the international institutions and agencies to negotiate in the WTO framework. Specifically, the negotiation should be with regard to MNCs operation in their markets, for doing similar innovative investment as has been done in the home countries. It should also assess losses of domestic firms and seek compensation for using it to create innovative capabilities to strengthen innovative infrastructure at home. The two-step strategy suggested above will go a long way to make capable domestic agents of production to catch up spillover effect created by the international capital and fill the knowledge gap for sustained economic growth.

## CONCLUSION

The analysis of structural transformation and national innovation system of Asian countries show that there are wide differentials in the pattern of structural transformation and technology development. Some of the East Asian countries have emerged another pole of innovations and technology development. East Asian experience of technology development has numerous lessons for the developing countries in general and South Asian countries in particular in a fast globalizing world economy. First and foremost lesson, which should be learnt from East Asian experience to succeed in the global economy, is to reinvent the role of state to strengthen the national innovation institutional system. The developing countries are engaged in economic reforms to reduce the role of the state and provide larger space to market forces, which essentially make the state scarce in economic activities. This strategy of making the state scarce in developing countries suffers from the draw back of substitutability of the state and the market and reduces the competitiveness of the domestic agents of production in the international economy. It is important to note here that intervention of the state in a fast globalizing world economy is more difficult but at the same time is very crucial and strategic. Therefore, reinventing the role of government policy in crafting the national innovation institutional arrangements for building and strengthening competitive advantage is direly needed. The East Asian economies have grown in an environment of import substitution and lax intellectual property regime which now is not available to the developing economies. Intellectual property regime enacted and imposed by the WTO has been restricting developing economies to put in place the national innovation system which has proven adverse effect on the global innovations and more particularly least developed countries. Multinational corporations invade developing country markets without contributing towards generation of domestic innovation capabilities. The role of international institutions is to evolve policies which should decrease the knowledge gap through imposing conditions on multinational corporations to contribute in an equal measure the percentage of sales revenue expenditure on R&D in the host country as is being done in the home country. Reduction of fiscal deficit under the reform programme has easy options for the governments of the developing countries to cut down expenditure on institutions, which are the backbone of economic development such as education, health and infrastructure. Further curtailing support to the R&D institutions- public and private-has a capacity to weaken the institutions, which from a long-term perspective matter a lot for economic growth and welfare.

# REFERENCES

Arrow, K.J. (1962), "Economic Welfare and the Allocation of Resources of Invention" in R. Nelson (ed.) *The Rate and Direction of Inventive Activity: Economic and Social Factors,* Princeton: Princeton University Press.

Cornelius, P.K. (ed.) (2003) The Global Competitiveness Report 2002-2003, *World Economic Forum*, New York: Oxford University Press.

Fagerberg, J. and Verspagen, B. (2001) "Technology-Gaps, Innovation-Diffusion and Transformation: An Evolutionary Interpretation", Eindhoven Centre for Innovation Studies, Eindhoven: Eindhoven University of Technology.

Jaumotte, F. and Pain, N. (2005) "An Overview of Public Policies to Support Innovations" *Economic Department Working Papers* No. 456, Organisation for Economic Co-operation and Development (OECD).

Jones, C.I. and J.C. Williams (1998), "Measuring the Social Return to R&D", *Quarterly Journal of Economics*, vol.113, pp. 1119-1135

Nelson, R.R. (1959), "The Simple Economics of Basic Scientific Research", Journal of Political Economy, vol.67, pp. 297-306

Ruttan, V.W. (2001) *Technology, Growth, and Development: An Induced Innovation Perspective*, New York: Oxford University Press.

Singh, Lakhwinder (2006) "Innovations, High-Tech Trade and Industrial Development: Theory, Evidence and Policy", *UNU-WIDER Research Paper* No. 2006/27, United Nations University-World Institute for Development Economics Research, Helsinki, Finland, 2006.

Soete, L. (2006) "A Knowledge Economy Paradigm and its Consequences" *Working Paper Series* No. WP 2006-001, UNU-MERIT.

Stern, N. (2004) "Keynote Address-Opportunities for India in a Changing World", in Francois Bourguignon and Boris Pleskovic (eds.) *Accelerating Development, Annual World Bank Conference on Development Economics*, New York: Oxford University Press.

Stiglitz, J. E. (1999) "Knowledge As a Global Public Good", in Inge Kaul, Isabelle Grunberg and Marc A. Stern (eds.) Global Public Goods: *International Cooperation in the 21st Century*, New York: Oxford University Press.

UNCTAD (2005) *World Investment Report 2005: Transnational Corporations and the Internationalization of R&D,* New York: United Nations.

UNDP (2001) *Making New Technologies Work for Human Development: Human Development Report* 2001, New York: Oxford University Press.

UNESCO (2004) *UIS Bulletin on Science and Technology Statistics*, Issue No.1, April 2004, UNESCO Institute of Statistics.

World Bank (1998/1999) *World Development Report*, Oxford: Oxford University Press.

Yusuf, S. (2003) *Innovative East Asia: The Future of Growth*, Washington, D.C.: The World Bank.

World Bank (2006) *World Development Indicators* 2006, Washington, D.C.: The World Bank.

# INDEX

# C

## E

**G**

# M

# O

## S

## T

## X

## Y